CALIFORNIA LEGAL ETHICS

Seventh Edition

■ ■ ■

By

Richard C. Wydick

Professor of Law, Emeritus
University of California, Davis

Rex R. Perschbacher

Daniel J. Dykstra Chair in Law
University of California, Davis

Debra Lyn Bassett

Justice Marshall F. McComb Professor of Law
Southwestern Law School

This book is a California edition of
Schwartz, Wydick, Perschbacher & Bassett,
Problems in Legal Ethics, Ninth Edition

AMERICAN CASEBOOK SERIES®

WEST®

A Thomson Reuters business

Mat #40877239

610 Opperman Drive
St. Paul, MN 55123
1–800–313–9378

Printed in the United States of America

ISBN: 978–0–314–92708–8

PREFACE

The book is intended for use in California law school courses that teach the fundamentals of legal ethics. The book is to be used in conjunction with the current edition of West's *Professional Responsibility Standards, Rules, and Statutes* (John S. Dzienkowski, ed.). Either the full or the abridged edition of that book will suffice.

This Seventh Edition includes the following features:

• *The Problem Method:* Each chapter begins with a set of problems for discussion in the classroom. Some of the problems are drawn from decided cases, ethics opinions, and the writings of scholars in the field. Others are drawn from our own experience in teaching and law practice and from discussions we have had with judges and practicing lawyers. We have attempted to provide realistic problems—the kind that arise with disturbing frequency in the daily practice of law.

• *Background Readings:* For each major topic, we have included background reading material that illustrates the variety of sources to which a lawyer or judge can turn when seeking answers to ethics questions. The materials include ethics rules, judicial opinions, ethics committee opinions, and excerpts from articles and books written by judges, lawyers, and law teachers.

• *Supplemental Readings:* In each chapter, we have suggested supplemental readings from *The Law of Lawyering* by Geoffrey Hazard and William Hodes, and from the American Law Institute's *Restatement (Third) of the Law Governing Lawyers* (2000).

• *Descriptive Text:* Some chapters include text in which we attempt to pack a lot of information into a few pages. Examples are Chapter Two, which includes a description of the organized bar and its functions; Chapter Four, which includes a history of lawyer advertising and solicitation; and Chapter Six, which includes a summary of the law of legal malpractice.

• *Multiple Choice Questions:* At the end of each chapter, except Chapters One and Fourteen, we have included some multiple choice questions. The Appendix at the back of the book gives our proposed answers and the reasoning behind them. Some of the questions review material that is covered in the chapter, and others cover points that are not otherwise mentioned in the book.

We hope you enjoy the book.

RICHARD C. WYDICK
REX R. PERSCHBACHER
DEBRA LYN BASSETT

Summary of Contents

CHAPTER 3. BEGINNING AND ENDING THE LAWYER–CLIENT RELATIONSHIP

CHAPTER 4. ADVERTISING AND SOLICITATION

CHAPTER 5. ATTORNEY FEES AND FIDUCIARY DUTIES

TABLE OF CONTENTS

CHAPTER 5. ATTORNEY FEES AND FIDUCIARY DUTIES

Page

CHAPTER 6. COMPETENCE, DILIGENCE, AND UNAUTHORIZED PRACTICE

CHAPTER 7. CONFIDENTIAL INFORMATION

CHAPTER 10. BIAS IN (AND OUT OF) THE COURTROOM

CHAPTER 11. CONFLICTS OF INTEREST—LAWYERS, CLIENTS, AND THIRD PARTIES

CHAPTER 12. CONFLICTS OF INTEREST—CONFLICTS BETWEEN TWO CLIENTS

CHAPTER 13. LAWYERS IN LAW FIRMS AND SPECIALIZED PRACTICE AREAS

Page

CHAPTER 14. JUDICIAL CONDUCT

APPENDIX: ANSWERS TO MULTIPLE CHOICE QUESTIONS

TABLE OF CASES

The principal cases are in bold type. Cases cited or discussed in the text are in roman type. References are to pages. Cases cited in principal cases and within other quoted materials are not included.

Table of References to ABA Model Rules

MODEL RULES OF PROFESSIONAL CONDUCT

MODEL RULES OF PROFESSIONAL CONDUCT

TABLE OF REFERENCES TO CALIFORNIA RULES OF PROFESSIONAL CONDUCT

CALIFORNIA RULES OF PROFESSIONAL CONDUCT

CALIFORNIA LEGAL ETHICS

Seventh Edition

Chapter One

Introduction to Legal Ethics

■ ■ ■

What This Chapter Covers

I. **How to Use This Book**
II. **Short Form Citations**
III. **Purposes of This Book**
IV. **Self-Regulation?**
   A. Lawyer Codes
   B. Governmental Interventions
   C. Other Developments and Complications

Reading Assignment

Wydick, Perschbacher, & Bassett, Chapter 1.

ABA Model Rules: Rule 4.4(b).

Discussion Problems

1. You represent client Claremont, who is the plaintiff in a civil action against five corporate defendants, each of which has its own lawyer. After extensive discovery, the case is almost ready for trial. Your secretary has just handed you a six page document that arrived on your fax machine a few minutes ago. The cover page states that the document was sent by one of the defense lawyers and that the intended recipients were the other four defense lawyers. Nothing on the cover page indicates that you were intended to receive the document; apparently the sender mistakenly speed-dialed your fax number along with those of the four defense lawyers. The "subject" line on the cover page states: "Confidential Memo to Defense Counsel re Settlement Negotiations in *Claremont*." The cover page is a standard law office form with the following boilerplate notice printed at the bottom: "This is a confidential communication protected by the attorney-client privilege, the work product doctrine, or both." You are aware that some law firms routinely use cover sheets with that boilerplate for all fax messages, whether or not they are confidential. Puzzled, you flip to the first page of the memo. The opening paragraph says: "I have

discussed with my client the idea of initiating settlement negotiations in the *Claremont* case. This memo states my client's position on settlement and outlines the negotiating tactics I think we should use with plaintiff's counsel." At that point you stop reading. What should you do now?

2. For many years you have served as legal counsel to the members of a family in a variety of matters. When the mother and father died, their son Samuel and daughter Dena each inherited about $750,000. Samuel is unmarried but has an 11 year-old child, Clara, who lives in his home under his care. You now represent Samuel in business, investment, and estate planning matters. From things Samuel has told you in confidence, and from things you have observed about him, you have concluded that he has developed a serious drug addiction problem that makes him unfit to take care of himself, his estate, and Clara. Now Dena has come to you and has asked you to petition the court to appoint a conservator for Samuel. You know from your prior dealings with Samuel that he will adamantly oppose this idea. What should you do?

3. Three years ago, lawyer Leon represented client Curtis in a worker's compensation matter. Pursuant to a settlement agreement, the compensation insurance company has since been sending Leon compensation checks once a month. In accordance with an agreement between Leon and Curtis, Leon deducts 10% from each check as his legal fee, and remits the remainder to Curtis. A week ago, during a routine review of the file, Leon discovered that the insurance company made a mistake in computing the amount of the monthly checks; it has been sending almost twice the amount that Curtis is entitled to receive under the settlement agreement. When Leon informed Curtis of this fact, Curtis said: "Well, I knew something must be wrong, but with inflation and all, I can barely make ends meet as it is. Don't rock the boat." What should Leon do?

HOW TO USE THIS BOOK

Each chapter of this book starts with a reading assignment. The reading assignments consist of some pages in this book, and some portions of a paperback supplement called *Professional Responsibility Statutes, Rules, and Standards on the Legal Profession* (Thomson–West). You will need a copy of the supplement to use in conjunction with this book.

The subsequent chapters also suggest some supplemental reading in other books that should be available in your local law library:

- GEOFFREY HAZARD & WILLIAM HODES, THE LAW OF LAWYERING (3d ed. 2001);
- THE RESTATEMENT (THIRD) OF THE LAW GOVERNING LAWYERS (2000), prepared by the American Law Institute.

After you finish the assigned reading, work through the Discussion Problems posed at the beginning of the chapter. Make notes of your answers and your reasoning to use later in class, when you discuss the problems with your classmates and professor.

Finally, work the Multiple Choice Questions at the end of each chapter (except this one and Chapter 14). Some of these questions review material that is found elsewhere in the chapter. Other questions cover material that is not otherwise mentioned in the chapter, but you should be able to answer them from the assigned readings. In the Appendix at the end of this book, you will find proposed answers to the Multiple Choice questions.

SHORT FORM CITATIONS

The following table explains the short form citations used in this book:

ABA Code	American Bar Association Model Code of Professional Responsibility.
DR	Disciplinary Rule, a part of the ABA Code.
EC	Ethical Consideration, a part of the ABA Code.
ABA Model Rules	American Bar Association Model Rules of Professional Conduct.
CJC	American Bar Association Code of Judicial Conduct.
CRPC	California Rules of Professional Conduct.
Cal.Bus. & Prof.Code	California Business and Professions Code.
Hazard & Hodes	The Law of Lawyering (3d ed. 2001).
Restatement	Restatement (Third) of the Law Governing Lawyers (2000).

PURPOSES OF THIS BOOK

This book will introduce you to the rules of ethics that apply to lawyers and judges in the United States. Every state has ethics rules that apply to lawyers, and a lawyer who does not follow them can be censured, or suspended from law practice, or disbarred. Likewise, every state has rules that govern the conduct of judges, and a judge who does not follow them can be censured, or suspended, or removed from the bench. Further, in most states, you cannot be admitted to practice law until you pass a bar examination that covers the ethics rules that apply to lawyers and judges.

Thus, this book has two purposes. First, we hope it will help you learn most of what you need to know about legal ethics to be admitted to law practice. Second, and far more important, we hope it will start you on a career-long process of studying, critically examining, and applying the legal ethics principles that you will study here.

SELF-REGULATION?

It is commonly said that the legal profession in the United States is self-regulated. However, as commentators have explained, this assertion is demonstrably untrue. The fragmented sources of provisions governing lawyers are the subjects of the following excerpts.

THE MYTH OF SELF-REGULATION

Fred C. Zacharias
93 Minn. L. Rev. 1147 (2009).

Law in the United States is a heavily regulated industry. Lawyers are licensed in each state. They are governed by professional rules, usually adopted and enforced by state supreme courts. The courts regulate lawyers separately as well, through supervisory decisions in the course of litigation and by implementing common law civil liability rules that govern legal practice. These include malpractice, breach of fiduciary duty, and other causes of action. Administrative agencies—particularly federal agencies—also establish and implement rules governing lawyers who practice before them. Federal and state legislatures play a further role in regulating the bar, providing statutory regulations and criminal penalties that apply to lawyers.

Nevertheless, courts, commentators, and legal ethics regulators continue to conceptualize law as a "self-regulated profession." A Westlaw search reveals more than five hundred law review articles that refer to the concept in the last ten years alone. The preamble to the recently revised ABA Model Rules of Professional Conduct maintains an emphasis on the importance of self-regulation, presenting the Model Rules themselves as a form of self-regulation despite the fact that the Rules are intended to be adopted as enforceable law by state supreme courts. The Preamble states:

> The legal profession is largely self-governing. Although other professions also have been granted powers of self-government, the legal profession is unique in this respect because of the close relationship between the profession and the processes of government and law enforcement. * * *
>
> To the extent that lawyers meet the obligations of their professional calling, the occasion for government regulation is obviated. Self-regulation also helps maintain the legal profession's independence from government domination. * * *
>
> The legal profession's relative autonomy carries with it special responsibilities of self-government. The profession has a responsibility to assure that its regulations are conceived in the public interest and not in furtherance of parochial or self-interested concerns of the bar. Every lawyer is responsible for observance of the Rules of Professional Conduct. A lawyer should also aid in securing their observance by other lawyers. Neglect of these responsibilities compromises the independence of the profession. * * *

LEGAL ETHICS FALLS APART

John Leubsdorf[1]
57 Buff. L. Rev. 959 (2009).

In recent decades, the law governing lawyers has begun to fragment. Nowadays, a lawyer's duties often cannot be found in a single body of rules, such as the ABA Model Rules of Professional Conduct, but are likely to vary with the lawyer's specialty, the tribunal or agency before which the lawyer practices, the state or states in which the lawyer is acting, and other factors. The sources of those duties may well include not just the traditional duo of courts and bar associations but also state and federal legislators, administrators, and others. Ironically, this centrifugal movement has coincided with the promulgation of the Restatement of the Law Governing Lawyers (2001), a work grounded on the assumption that lawyers are subject to a single, integrated body of law, albeit also a work that has drawn attention to the fact that much of that law is not to be found in lawyer codes such as the Model Rules.

Although the products of this fragmentation are varied and sometimes inconsistent, five trends do stand out. First, the innovations have tended on the whole to restrain the freedom of lawyers to pursue their clients' interests at the expense of others. No doubt they reflect the view—common outside the profession and among academics—that lawyers are too adversarial. Often, the interests to be protected are those of the government itself, and the innovation can be seen as restricting the independence of the bar. Sometimes they are those of opposing parties or the public. In either case, the lawyer increasingly becomes not just an advocate and advisor but a gatekeeper as well, so that not just the details of legal representation but its rationale and function are changing. And even when the new regulations appear to leave intact the substance of previous rules balancing the interests of clients and those of nonclients, they often impose more stringent penalties that will sway lawyers to pay more attention to the latter.

Second, the innovations tend to enact requirements that are relatively particularized in their content and in their addressees compared to the generalities addressed to all lawyers that prevail in the lawyer codes. As the functions of lawyers have multiplied, as their numbers have increased, and as faith in their high mindedness has declined, lawmakers have turned to narrower and more specific provisions. These provisions in turn foster specialization by making it harder for lawyers to venture into new fields of practice.

Third, despite being narrow, the new requirements have often included nonlawyers as well as lawyers within their scope. The regulators may not even mention lawyers specifically, and may not have considered how lawyers might differ from others doing the same sort of thing. Likewise,

1. Reprinted with the permission of John Leubsdorf and the Buffalo Law Review.

they may not have addressed existing regulation by the bench and bar—though in other instances, it has been the real or perceived inadequacy of that regulation that opened the way for new interventions. That lawyers, like everyone else, are forbidden to break their contracts or engage in fraud is nothing new; but they are now subject to a web of additional and particularized requirements. Ultimately, we might often find it more convenient to think of some practitioners as tax or bankruptcy professionals or the like rather than as lawyers.

Fourth, more and more regulators have sought to regulate the bar. If once the American Bar Association's codes dominated the field, now courts have become increasingly unwilling to defer to them, and legislators and administrators have become increasingly unwilling to defer to either bar associations or courts. We are witnessing the decline of the ideal of professional self-regulation at the same time that the ideal has been almost entirely demolished in England.

Fifth, the new regulators—whether legislative, administrative, or judicial—tend to be federal ones. Although state supreme courts continue to promulgate professional rules and state legislatures occasionally seek to regulate lawyers, the more important and striking initiatives during recent decades have come from the federal government. In this respect, innovation has been centripetal rather than centrifugal. Considering the growth of multijurisdictional practice and the tendency toward federalization of many bodies of law, one can expect this trend to continue. We seem to be moving from a system of rules that are uniform for all lawyers but vary from state to state to one of nationwide rules that vary by specialty.

The fragmentation of the law of the legal profession has begun to bring about a number of more general consequences. It complicates the lives of lawyers, and increases the need for them to obtain advice about their own obligations, as well as the need for law firms to provide internal mechanisms to promote compliance. It means that, more than in the past, changes in the law governing lawyers will result from a political process involving trade offs among various interested groups inside and outside the profession, worked out in a variety of judicial, administrative, and legislative bodies, and often including competition among those bodies.

A further consequence of all these trends is hence to accelerate the trend for professional responsibility to be seen less as a field of personal morals or professional customs and more as one of hard law, often rather technical law. The traditional approach embodied in the lawyer codes bridged or obscured that distinction. The term "legal ethics" could be read as a moral one or as referring to social standards embodying the customs of the profession. The norms recognized by the lawyer codes could be seen as crystallizations of moral obligations such as honesty and fidelity as they apply to agents in an adversary system, or as standards protecting the legal rights of clients and nonclients and the proper operation of the laws. And lawyers could easily persuade themselves that if they followed the professional rules they were acting ethically in every sense. But to the extent that the rules come to be seen just as law, imposed by many lawmakers who are lobbied by many interested groups, and varying from specialty to specialty, thoughtful lawyers will be pressed to recognize their own personal responsibility for choosing how to act within the legal world those rules create. Indeed, there will be room within the profession for differing views about how lawyers should act, which will in turn promote further fragmentation.

* * *

I. State Court Regulation and Its Challengers

During the nineteenth and most of the twentieth centuries, the great bulk of the rules governing lawyers in England and the United States were promulgated by the bench. The bench in turn tended to defer to the customs and values of the profession. Judges were former practicing lawyers, and often continued to be active in professional activities. They might take a broader view of the public interest than their practicing colleagues, but their starting point was usually the outlook and customs they had known as practitioners. Between them, the bench and the profession developed rules and principles applicable to all practitioners. Gradually, previous reliance on the common background and shared values of most practitioners was replaced by the system of self-regulation by bench and bar that is now yielding in turn to diverse governmental regulation supplemented by market forces.

This was the pattern in England, with the obvious qualification that barristers and solicitors were subject to differing regimes. Early legislation recognized the power of the courts to discipline misbehaving barristers and solicitors (or their precursors), and the courts also recognized causes of action against misbehaving solicitors. Barristers later set up their own disciplinary systems in the Circuit messes and the Inns of Court, the latter involving the participation of judges among the Benchers of the Inns. For solicitors, the path to self regulation was longer and harder, probably because of their lower status. The Law Society's precursor was founded only in 1739, and the Society acquired disciplinary power only in the early twentieth century. By the end of the twentieth century, both solicitors and barristers had promulgated codes of conduct; previously, practitioners had to rely on precedent, treatises and professional customs. Meanwhile, during the last twenty years, government ministers and legislators have roared onto the English scene, reforming legal services has become a significant political issue, and the role of the profession and the courts in regulating lawyers has declined.

In the United States, state supreme courts were likewise the prime regulators, typically acting in interplay with the bar. For a long time, access to the profession and professional conduct were only lightly regulated. Yet by the end of the nineteenth century there was an extensive common law of lawyering, and professional literature on the ethics of lawyering had begun to emerge. An organized bar only began to develop late in that century, and the Canons of Ethics that the American Bar Association approved in 1908 were not binding in most jurisdictions. Moreover, the development of university law schools hindered the organized bar from controlling its own recruitment and training through the apprenticeship systems common in other nations. Not until the ABA's Model Code of Professional Responsibility was issued in 1969 did most state supreme courts turn the bar's rules into law by adopting them as rules of court. And many of those rules were themselves based on state court decisions. By promulgating professional rules, and by seeking to invigorate their traditionally feeble disciplinary systems, these courts confirmed their primacy, while the participation of the organized bar in these processes reinforced its own authority.

Although the dominant role of the state courts was sometimes threatened by state legislatures, starting in the late nineteenth century courts developed the doctrine of "inherent power" to fend off many such intrusions. Under that doctrine, the state supreme court not only regulated the practice of law but also excluded legislative regulation. Courts continue to invoke their power to strike down even innocuous or beneficial statutes. Nevertheless, some statutes affecting the practice of law have survived, either because courts in some states do not recognize the inherent powers doctrine in its full strength or because the statutes were enacted and accepted before that doctrine arose. For example, legislatures have sometimes succeeded in preventing or limiting the professional monopoly by allowing nonlawyers to represent even litigants without restriction or more recently by allowing certain kinds of nonlitigative practice by nonlawyers. Sometimes competitors have overcome the profession in pitched battles, as when Arizona real estate brokers secured an amendment to the state constitution to override a decision denying them the right to draft sales contracts.

The principles of lawyering recognized by the state courts were for the most part uniform for all lawyers. The distinction between barristers and solicitors soon faded away in the United States, and was not replaced by any other recognized split. There were a few exceptions, aside from the obvious one that some rules varied from state to state. For example, the Model Code laid down special provisions for prosecutors and other government lawyers, lawyers who were also government officials, and former judges, presumably based on the special characteristics of those functions. In addition, some formally general rules pressed harder on low status lawyers than on the elite. Nevertheless, until recent decades it was broadly true that all the lawyers in each state were subject to the same rules.

Uniformity does not equal perfection: the first half of the twentieth century was not a golden age of lawyer regulation. Professional rules were riddled by gaps and skewed by professional self interest. Enforcement was feeble at best. Indeed, not the least consequence of the proliferation of regulators to be described here has been the awakening shock they administered to professional rulemakers and disciplinary systems.

State supreme court domination began to erode in the late 1960s and 1970s as the federal government began to influence lawyer rules, and as the size of the bar dramatically increased. The Supreme Court relied on the First Amendment to strike down state barriers to group legal services, solicitation of public interest cases, and lawyer advertising. It held unconstitutional certain restrictions on admission to state bars. It invoked the antitrust laws to limit the powers of bar associations to impose minimum fees and other anticompetitive practices, an enterprise in which the Justice Department and Federal Trade Commission joined. It applied Title VII's prohibition of employment discrimination to law firm partnership decisions, which in the long run could not help but affect the conditions in which law firm lawyers practice. Others likewise began to apply employment legislation to law firms and house counsel, rejecting the claim that lawyers are different. And federal courts began to take a more prominent role than state courts in shaping the common law of lawyering, for example when they formulated rules disqualifying lawyers suing former clients in matters substantially related to the former representation, rules that were later codified by the American Bar Association.

During the same period, Congress preempted state regulation of employee group legal services plans and instituted the Legal Services Corporation, the activities of whose lawyers it promptly began to supervise. Federal legislators did not have to fear the inherent powers doctrine, which has not been considered by the federal courts to bar legislation. However, even some state legislatures became increasingly active. California legislation of the late 1970s imposed nonlawyer members on the State Bar's Board of Governors, limited medical malpractice contingent fees, and required lawyers to submit to fee arbitration. State legislatures also followed Congress by imposing on former government lawyers rules more stringent than those of the bar. And perhaps an academic may be forgiven for viewing the proliferation of professional responsibility scholarship that resulted from making that subject compulsory as the arrival of another regulatory force, albeit one with only persuasive power and often divided against itself. The way was open for a new era in which many regulators strove to regulate segments of the bar or professional practices.

During the last twenty-five years, more governmental regulators have appeared on the scene while old competitors of the courts have expanded their activities. New enactments, often limited by field of practice, have implemented a grab bag of policies centering around the government's own interests, the protection of nonclients from lawyers believed to be too adversarial, and sometimes the protection of clients from self-interested lawyers. * * *

II. Protecting the Government by Regulating Lawyers

Protection of the government's own interests is a striking feature of recent governmental interventions. That had scarcely been a goal of regulation by the bar and bench, though the ethics codes do contain some provisions that in practice bear primarily on the criminal defense bar.

Where the bar's main focus has usually been on the lawyer-client relationship and the adversary system, new regulations often make lawyers gatekeepers charged to protect public and governmental interests.

* * *

[A.] Reining in the Criminal Defense and Legal Services Bars

Confronting the government in court is at the core of the bar's concept of itself, even though most contemporary lawyers never or rarely do it. Here too Congress has been active, often in conjunction with the Department of Justice, sometimes under the banner of wars on crime or terrorism, and sometimes in response to asserted abusive lawyering. The results have impacted the professional obligations of criminal defense and legal services lawyers.

Because it ultimately did not prevail, the Justice Department's effort to exempt its own lawyers, in part, from the rules applying to other lawyers deserves only passing mention. The Thornburgh Memorandum of 1989 and its successor, the Reno rules of 1994, sought to limit the application to federal lawyers of the rule forbidding a lawyer to have direct contact with a party represented by counsel except with counsel's permission. Although there were genuine questions as to how that rule does or should apply to prosecutors, the attempt to resolve those issues by the Attorney General's fiat aroused controversy and resistance. Ultimately, Congress decreed that federal lawyers should be subject to the same rules as other lawyers in the states where they engaged in their duties. Thus the Attorney General's regulatory initiative was snuffed out by a Congressional initiative, inserted in an appropriations bill by a Representative with a personal grudge, and creating its own problems. But other governmental interventions have been more effective.

1. Forfeiting attorney fees. During recent decades, Congress has given United States Attorneys the ability to prevent private defense counsel from being paid in many cases by expanding the scope of statutes providing for the forfeiture of defendants' assets. Such statutes have long existed, and two 1970 statutes provided for forfeiture in drug and criminal enterprise cases. But it was the Comprehensive Forfeiture Act of 1984 that put U.S. Attorneys into the fee forfeiture business. They have remained in it ever since, despite some modest legislative cutbacks responding to extreme examples of forfeiture. Some state prosecutors have joined the game, either by participating in federal forfeiture proceedings or by using state forfeiture statutes.

Several features of the federal legislation make it a formidable weapon against privately retained counsel. Congress broadly defined the assets subject to forfeiture, so that they include essentially all the assets with which a professional criminal could hire a lawyer. The prosecutor need not wait until the defendant is convicted to obtain the property, but may seek preliminary injunctive relief freezing the assets claimed to be forfeited, including those that have already been paid to third parties. Lawyers are not immune; indeed, the court has no discretion to exempt assets on the ground that they are needed to secure counsel. The lawyer will then be paid only if the assets are held not subject to forfeiture or the lawyer proves that when paid she was reasonably without cause to believe that the property was subject to forfeiture. The Supreme Court has indicated that a lawyer's ability to demonstrate such ignorance "will, as a practical matter, never arise."

The forfeiture statute, in short, makes it possible for U.S. Attorneys to de-fund private counsel in a large class of cases, a power some of them have recently sought to expand. The Court nevertheless upheld attorney fee forfeiture against Constitutional challenges, on the ground that a defendant has no Constitutional right to pay a lawyer with unlawfully acquired assets. That is a plausible argument, though the four dissenters also had a case. The fact remains that, however constitutional they may be, forfeiture statutes regulate the bar by creating an obstacle to payment of private criminal defense counsel.

Forfeiture statutes also give rise to a new conflict of interest for defense counsel. The prosecutor's ability to block defense counsel's fees, where it exists, pushes counsel to defer to the prosecutor's wishes, and thus alters the rules under which defense counsel operate. The prosecutor, after all, represents an opposing party; and the Justice Department considers that whether to seek attorney fee forfeiture is a matter of prosecutorial discretion, albeit one calling for uniform and fair application and for due regard to the possible impact on communications between lawyer and client. Technically, the Justice Department does not pay defense counsel's fee, so the professional rule governing third party payment does not apply. Yet functionally an arrangement in which a third party can prevent payment poses the same danger as one in which a third party provides payment, to wit, that the lawyer will yield to the third party's interests even when they conflict with those of the client. The client's informed consent is required for third party payment, but the client has no way to deny consent to attorney fee forfeiture except by renouncing private counsel and seeking appointed counsel (assuming he can show he has no assets not subject to forfeiture). In effect, then, the new law of forfeiture subjects some criminal defendants to attorney conflicts of interest from which the law of lawyering has sought to guard clients. * * *

So far as fee forfeiture is concerned, the new regime instituted by the 1984 statute not only gives prosecutors discretion to interfere with opposing counsel's fee arrangements but also institutes a fee arrangement previously banned: a contingent fee for defending a criminal case. Once a court freezes the funds on which defense counsel depends for payment, counsel is likely to be paid only if the client is acquitted. The official view, which is open to question, is that such contingent arrangements give defense counsel an undesirable incentive to defend a client by improper means. Ironically, this rationale is just the opposite of the rationale for limiting prosecutorial influence over what defense counsel is paid. One might argue that these two features of fee forfeiture cancel each other out: counsel's fear of losing payment should his client be convicted will counteract his fear of defending so zealously as to provoke the prosecutor to attack the funds from which he will be paid. But things will not work out so neatly. The contingent fee incentive arises only once the prosecutor seeks forfeiture, while the incentive to avoid a prosecutorial forfeiture attempt operates before the attempt occurs. And once forfeiture is sought, the lawyer can preserve his fee not only by prevailing at trial but through a plea bargain that gives the prosecutor the conviction she wants but frees the funds needed to pay defense counsel. In short, fee forfeiture has influenced the law governing lawyers in at least two ways: giving the prosecution power over defense counsel's pay and instituting a sort of contingent fee.

When Congress expanded forfeiture, it did not focus on how this would affect the regulation of lawyers. Its main concern was with depriving participants in organized crime of any resulting assets. Although some in Congress were aware that the Comprehensive Forfeiture Act of 1984 might be applied to funds used to pay lawyers, they did not discuss whether this was desirable, much less how it would change professional rules. The Supreme Court was aware of the impact on such rules, dismissing them in a footnote when it upheld attorney fee forfeiture against Constitutional challenges. But when Congress later passed the Civil Asset Forfeiture Reform Act it again did not explicitly advert to attorney fee forfeitures or their impact on lawyering. Considering that fee forfeitures are just an aspect of forfeitures in general, which are just an aspect of crime legislation, which is just one of many matters before Congress, that is not surprising. But we should also not be surprised if inadvertent regulation turns out to be imperfect.

2. Limiting confidentiality. Recent government initiatives have limited the confidentiality of communications between lawyers and clients. These initiatives date back to the Reagan era's proliferation of grand jury subpoenas to criminal defense lawyers. They do not represent a coordinated campaign, but could better be described as piecemeal nibbles serving various governmental interests. Some of them affect lawyers in civil matters, but their main impact is on criminal defense counsel.

(a) As part of the War on Terror, Attorney General Ashcroft authorized monitoring of communications between prisoners and their lawyers. Monitoring requires a finding of reasonable suspicion that the communications might be used to facilitate terrorism; the prisoner and lawyer must be given advance notice; privileged communications are to be discarded; and information from the monitoring may not be disclosed to prosecutors or others unless a judge approves or acts of violence or terrorism are imminent. These safeguards, however, have not always been honored. The notice requirement is a two edged sword, since it permits the argument that the defendant has waived the attorney-client privilege for monitored conversations.

(b) The Secretary of Defense has also become a regulator of lawyers. Although his rules governing defense counsel in military commission trials have recently lost some of their original stringency, they still require civilian counsel to disclose "information relating to the representation of my client to the extent that I reasonably believe necessary to prevent the commission of a future criminal act that I believe is likely to result in death or substantial bodily harm, or significant impairment of national security." Most states do not require lawyers to disclose even confidential information identifying an imminent threat to human life, and none treats a danger to national security as a ground for disclosure. An extra twist is that, while defense counsel may be obligated to disclose certain client confidences to the government, they also participate in certain hearings from which their clients are excluded, and apparently may not tell their clients without approval about classified materials discussed at those hearings.

(c) By inducing corporations to waive their attorney-client privilege in order to avoid indictment, prosecutors found another way to restrict the confidentiality of communications between clients and lawyers. In this case, the government's goal is to punish and deter corporate crime, or at least to promote well publicized prosecutions of corporate employees, in response to Enron and other corporate scandals. The "Thompson Memorandum" of 2003 instructed federal prosecutors to consider a corporation's willingness to waive its privilege in deciding whether to indict it, on the theory that willingness eases the government's task and demonstrates the corporation's wish to reform itself. The same theory supported Deferred Prosecution Agreements in which the Justice Department agreed not to prosecute corporations that agree to waive their privilege and cooperate in other ways. Responding to widespread criticism, the more recent "McNulty Memorandum" and "Filip Policy" moderated the Thompson Memorandum, though it remains to be seen whether they have put the genie back in its bottle. Meanwhile, several other federal agencies have adopted similar policies. The federal Sentencing Guidelines have long listed "disclosure of all pertinent information known by the organization" as a prerequisite for sentence reduction based on cooperation. * * *

Whatever the justification for the government's approach to prosecuting corporate crime, it clearly restricts an employee's ability to speak to corporate counsel with practical assurance that what she says will remain private. As a result, counsel must consider issues of professional responsibility ranging from what warning to give an interviewed employee to whether counsel should now be considered subject to all the Constitutional and professional obligations of a government lawyer. These impacts on lawyers and their clients confronting the federal government contrast strikingly with Congress' recent enactment of Federal Rule of Evidence 502, which among other effects encourages disclosures to the government by limiting the scope of the resulting waiver of privilege.

(d) The Deficit Reduction Act of 1984 requires those engaged in a trade or business, including lawyers, to report to the Treasury the amount and payor of all cash payments of more than ten thousand dollars. The lawyers unsuccessfully challenging it have typically been engaged in criminal defense, presumably because their clients are more likely to pay in cash and disclosure of their identities is more likely to incriminate them and expose them and their lawyers to forfeiture. This legislation has some similarity to * * * 2004 tax shelter legislation * * *, which requires advisors—including lawyers—in certain transactions to report them to the Internal Revenue Service and to maintain lists of participants for government inspection.

Technically, it might be said that these statutes do not change the law of lawyering. As courts have pointed out when upholding and enforcing them, the attorney-client privilege does not usually protect the identity of clients or their financial transactions with lawyers. In exceptional cases in which the privilege applies, courts have found ways to exempt lawyers from disclosing the client's name. Turning from privilege to the lawyer's duty of confidentiality, fees and client identity do constitute confidential information that a lawyer may not reveal unless an exception applies, but compliance with a valid law is one of the exceptions. Beyond technicality, it can be argued that a client who is only able to pay in cash is probably paying with the proceeds of crime. Likewise, if the promoter of a tax shelter is required to disclose information about a tax shelter to the IRS, why not the lawyer who helped the promoter set up the shelter?

Nevertheless, it makes a difference when lawyers must routinely report the identity and fees of certain clients or face substantial penalties. Sometimes lawyers will report to avoid trouble even when their clients might have had a valid reason not to. Like placing a government surveillance camera at the entrance of a lawyer's office, such requirements, even if justified, change the expectations of clients and reduce the confidentiality that lawyers can offer them.

3. Controlling legal services lawyers. Since its creation in 1974, the Legal Services Corporation has helped many people who could not otherwise afford lawyers, but has evoked fierce opposition. As a result, it has been grossly underfunded and subjected to numerous Congressional restrictions. Underfunding is the more serious problem, but regulation by restriction is what will be considered here.

Forbidding Legal Services Corporation lawyers to accept many kinds of cases and clients might not look like professional regulation, but it is. True, it may be a valid Constitutional argument that Congress may decide which services to subsidize and may require its grantees to use grants only to provide those services. But the result is to exclude much of the very limited pool of lawyers available to represent the poor from certain kinds of practice, which are to that extent unavailable to poor clients. The situation is comparable, albeit less sweeping, to legislation excluding treatments of certain diseases from Medicare and Medicaid. Congress extended the impact of its prohibitions by providing that they extend to all of a legal services organization's activities, not just those federally funded.

Many states have likewise enacted similar restrictions for activities funded by their Interest on Lawyer Trust Account (IOLTA) plans, which are the main source of funding for legal services in civil matters outside the Legal Services Corporation. So, poor people may be able to obtain legal assistance in certain legal matters only from lawyers in private practice willing to live up to their obligation to help those who cannot afford to pay. It is also possible that, had Congress not created the Legal Services Corporation and saddled it with restrictions, a less restrictive system might have come into existence. If that is so, which is far from certain, Congress is not just declining to fund certain services, but has blocked others from offering them.

The restrictions in question are significant ones. Prisoners and most illegal aliens may receive no services at all, even though they have long been considered especially in need of help. Others may not receive services in matters of abortion, desegregation, redistricting, certain evictions of people with drug records from public housing, or assisted suicide. Note that the first three of these categories concern Constitutional rights. If a state's ethics rules were to impose such restrictions on part of the bar, it would be considered a radical innovation.

Another class of Congressional restrictions is based, not on the client or the nature of the case, but on the services a Legal Services Corporation lawyer may provide; therefore it regulates how lawyers may practice law, forbidding certain otherwise lawful means of representing clients. The Supreme Court struck down one such restriction, reasoning that to allow legal services lawyers to represent clients seeking welfare rights while prohibiting them from trying to change or challenge existing law in the process was an infringement of free speech. However, prohibitions on class actions, legislative representation, and participation in agency rulemaking remain on the books. So does a ban on accepting cases resulting from in-person solicitation, even though such solicitation is lawful when not conducted for pecuniary gain.

* * *

V. Regulation Beyond the State and Federal Government

The centrifugal forces pulling at legal ethics are not limited to * * * governmental bodies. * * * The profession itself has increasingly become the site of competing opinions and groups; clients and insurers seek to shape professional practices and a lawyer admitted in one state must reckon, more and more, with lawyers and rules from other jurisdictions.

* * *

B. Clients and Others

There have always been clients who have their own ideas about how their lawyers should behave, but corporate clients have now begun to assert themselves more systematically and collectively as a force molding lawyer behavior. House counsel from different corporations have developed and shared techniques for reducing the cost of litigation, including shopping for lawyers, alternative fee arrangements, litigation planning and budgeting, and advance approval requirements for research projects, depositions, or the assignment of new lawyers to the case. * * *

Far more controversial has been the imposition of cost control techniques by liability insurers. The ethical problem here is that in many states only the insured and not the insurer is the client of a lawyer defending a case against the insured for which the insurer is liable under the insurance policy, while in other states both insurer and insured are clients. Under the first view, and perhaps the second as well, the insurer's payment for the lawyer does not entitle it to interfere "with the lawyer's independence of professional judgment." Detailed control over what the lawyer does, or at least what the lawyer gets paid to do, may well violate this prohibition. Furthermore, insurers spend more than fifteen billion dollars a year on defense counsel, which gives them a strong interest in minimizing lawyer fees and the insurance defense bar a strong interest in resisting.

Efforts of insurers to reshape defense practices have therefore led to disputes about whether insurers may assign house counsel to defend cases, whether they may require outside counsel to accept a standard flat fee, and whether they may require advance insurer approval for measures taken by outside counsel. Controversy reached the American Law Institute, where insurance company lawyers lobbied with some success for relaxation of the rules. Whatever one may think of the process or the result, they show that pressure groups from outside the bar can influence the profession's own formulations of its rules. No doubt the influence of insurers on what defense counsel actually do has been even greater than precedents and Restatements indicate. Lawyers who depend on insurance company referrals will think twice before they reject insurance company initiatives.

Another group of insurers, legal malpractice insurers, has likewise begun to regulate law firm practices, largely in response to the multiplication of large malpractice damage awards. Malpractice insurers advise their insureds how to prevent malpractice claims. They also require measures such as written retainers, conflict checking procedures, and calendaring systems. And they exercise more subtle control by excluding some activities from coverage or charging higher rates to lawyers who engage in them. In some of these activities, it is ultimately malpractice law itself that does the regulating, with insurers acting as messengers to make sure that lawyers hear and heed the voice of the law. But a messenger is also an interpreter, and insurers can give malpractice law a broader and deeper impact than it might otherwise have.

* * *

[M]ultistate and multinational lawyers must navigate among different sets of rules. The divergence and increasing complexity of state ethics rules has given rise to books seeking to state the professional rules of a single state. Sometimes the rules are not just different but incompatible: a lawyer working on a transaction in New Jersey and New York might find herself required to disclose her client's fraud in the first state and forbidden to do so in the second. And in transnational practice, a lawyer might have to deal with a foreign colleague in a nation in which certain communications between counsel may not be disclosed to the client, or in which disclosures to corporate house counsel are not protected by an evidentiary privilege, or in which lawyers may not interview potential witnesses. Such situations are increasingly prevalent. United States law firms export more than four billion dollars of services yearly. * * *

Although this proliferation of standards and jurisdictions might suggest that interstate and transnational lawyers are doomed to perplexity, the reality is different. States rarely discipline their own lawyers for conduct occurring elsewhere, or discipline another state's lawyer (except for sanctioning litigation misconduct) for conduct within the state. The obstacles include lack of investigative personnel, lack of interest, and perhaps the very multiplication of rules and disciplinary authorities we have been discussing. In any event, interstate and transnational lawyers are confronted less by over-regulation than by a regulatory vacuum.

Conclusion

The regulations we have surveyed embrace almost every kind of legal practice: banking, bankruptcy, class actions, corporate and securities law, criminal defense, debt collection, insurance defense, legal services, tax, and transnational. Some might be dismissed as window dressing, but their cumulative impact for many lawyers is enormous. They cover almost every subject considered by traditional rules and codes: advertising and solicitation, advice to clients, confidences and privilege, conflicts of interest, decision-making authority, duties to nonclients, fees, honesty, and malpractice.

Although each innovation has its own history, a number of more general factors seem to be at work. Some of these can best be appreciated from the viewpoint of the regulators. Because almost every other part of the economy is now subject to external regulation, and because the work of lawyers is entwined with the rest of the economy, lawyers cannot expect to escape outside regulation. As the number and functions of lawyers increase, lawyers have become too important to be left to the exclusive control of the bench and bar. * * *

BEGINNING CONSIDERATIONS

RICO v. MITSUBISHI MOTORS CORPORATION

Supreme Court of California, 2007.
42 Cal.4th 807, 171 P.3d 1092, 68 Cal.Rptr.3d 758.

CORRIGAN, J.

Here we consider what action is required of an attorney who receives privileged documents through inadvertence and whether the remedy of disqualification is appropriate. We conclude that, under the authority of State Comp. Ins. Fund v. WPS, Inc. (1999) 70 Cal.App.4th 644, 82 Cal.Rptr.2d 799 (State Fund), an attorney in these circumstances may not read a document any more closely than is necessary to ascertain that it is privileged. Once it becomes apparent that the content is privileged, counsel must immediately notify opposing counsel and try to resolve the situation. We affirm the disqualification order under the circumstances presented here.

FACTUAL BACKGROUND

Two Mitsubishi corporations (collectively Mitsubishi or defendants), and the California Department of Transportation (Caltrans), were sued by various plaintiffs after a Mitsubishi Montero rolled over while being driven on a freeway. Subsequently, Mitsubishi representatives met with their lawyers, James Yukevich and Alexander Calfo, and two designated defense experts to discuss their litigation strategy and vulnerabilities. Mitsubishi's case manager, Jerome Rowley, also attended the meeting. Rowley and Yukevich had worked together over a few years. Yukevich asked Rowley to take notes at the meeting and indicated specific areas to be summarized. The trial court later found that Rowley, who had typed the notes on Yukevich's computer, had acted as Yukevich's paralegal. At the end of the six-hour session, Rowley returned the computer and never saw a printed version of the notes. Yukevich printed only one copy of the notes, which he later edited and annotated. Yukevich never intentionally showed the notes to anyone, and the court determined that the sole purpose of the document was to help Yukevich defend the case.

The notes are written in a dialogue style and summarize conversations among Yukevich, Calfo, and the experts. They are dated, but not labeled as "confidential" or "work product." The printed copy of these compiled and annotated notes is the document at issue here.

Less than two weeks after the strategy session, Yukevich deposed plaintiffs' expert witness, Anthony Sances, at the offices of plaintiffs' counsel, Raymond Johnson. Yukevich, court reporter Karen Kay, and Caltrans counsel Darin Flagg were told that Johnson and Sances would be late for the deposition. After waiting in the conference room for some time, Yukevich went to the restroom, leaving his briefcase, computer, and case file in the room. The printed document from the strategy session was in the case file. While Yukevich was away, Johnson and Sances arrived. Johnson asked Kay and Flagg to leave the conference room. Kay and Flagg's departure left only the plaintiffs' representatives and counsel in the conference room. Yukevich waited approximately 5 minutes, then knocked and asked to retrieve his briefcase, computer, and file. After a brief delay, he was allowed to do so.

Somehow, Johnson acquired Yukevich's notes. Johnson maintained that they were accidentally given to him by the court reporter. Yukevich insisted that they were taken from his file while only Johnson and plaintiffs' team were in the conference room. As a result, Mitsubishi moved to disqualify plaintiffs' attorneys and experts. The trial court ordered an evidentiary hearing to determine how Johnson obtained the document.

The court reporter was deposed and denied any specific recollection of the Sances deposition. She could not testify what she had done with the deposition exhibits that night and could only relate her general practice. She said she generally collects exhibits and puts them in a plastic covering. She did not remember ever having given exhibits to an attorney. She also testified that she had never seen the document in question. If documents other than exhibits remain on a conference table, she leaves them there. The trial court found that the Sances deposition took place over approximately eight hours. It was a document-intense session and documents were placed on the conference table.

Another member of plaintiffs' legal team submitted a declaration supporting Johnson's assertion that he received the document from the reporter. The court ultimately concluded that the defense had failed to establish that Johnson had taken the notes from Yukevich's file. It thus ruled that Johnson came into the document's possession through inadvertence.

The court found the 12–page document was dated, but not otherwise labeled. It contained notations by Yukevich. Johnson admitted that he knew within a minute or two that the document related to the defendants' case. He knew that Yukevich did not intend to produce it and that it would be a "powerful impeachment document." Nevertheless, Johnson made a copy of the document. He scrutinized and made his own notes on it. He gave copies to his co-counsel and his experts, all of whom studied the document. Johnson specifically discussed the contents of the document with each of his experts.

A week after he acquired Yukevich's notes, Johnson used them during the deposition of defense expert Geoffrey Germane. The notes purportedly indicate that the defense experts made statements at the strategy session that were inconsistent with their deposition testimony. Johnson used the document while questioning Germane, asking about Germane's participation in the strategy session.

Defense Counsel Calfo defended the Germane deposition. Yukevich did not attend. Calfo had never seen the document and was not given a copy during the deposition. When he asked about the document's source, Johnson vaguely replied that, "It was put in Dr. Sances' file." Calfo repeatedly objected to the "whole line of inquiry with respect to an unknown document." He specifically said that, "I don't even know where this exhibit came from."

Only after the deposition did Johnson give a copy of the document to Calfo, who contacted Yukevich. When Yukevich realized that Johnson had his only copy of the strategy session notes and had used it at the deposition, he and Calfo wrote to Johnson demanding the return of all duplicates. The letter was faxed the day after Germane's deposition. The next day, defendants moved to disqualify plaintiffs' legal team and their experts on the ground that they had become privy to and had used Yukevich's work product. As a result, they complained, Johnson's unethical use of the notes and his revelation of them to co-counsel and their experts irremediably prejudiced defendants.

The trial court concluded that the notes were absolutely privileged by the work product rule. The court also held that Johnson had acted unethically by examining the document more closely than was necessary to determine that its contents were confidential, by failing to notify Yukevich that he had a copy of the document, and by surreptitiously using it to gain maximum adversarial value from it. The court determined that Johnson's violation of the work product rule had prejudiced the defense and "the bell cannot be unrung by use of in limine orders." Accordingly, the court ordered plaintiffs' attorneys and experts disqualified.

Plaintiffs appealed the disqualification order. The Court of Appeal affirmed.

DISCUSSION

Attorney Work Product

Plaintiffs contend that the Court of Appeal erred by holding that the entire document was protected as attorney work product. We reject that contention.

The Legislature has protected attorney work product under California Code of Civil Procedure section 2018.030, which provides, "(a) A writing that reflects an attorney's impressions, conclusions, opinions, or legal research or theories is not discoverable under any circumstances. [¶] (b) The work product of an attorney, other than a writing described in subdivision (a), is not discoverable unless the court determines that denial of discovery will unfairly prejudice the party seeking discovery in preparing that party's claim or defense or will result in an injustice."

The Legislature has declared that it is state policy to "[p]reserve the rights of attorneys to prepare cases for trial with that degree of privacy necessary to encourage them to prepare their cases thoroughly and to investigate not only the favorable but the unfavorable aspects of those cases." (§ 2018.020, subd. (a).) In addition, the Legislature declared its intent to "[p]revent attorneys from taking undue advantage of their adversary's industry and efforts." (Code Civ. Proc., § 2018.020, subd. (b).)

Thus, the codified work product doctrine absolutely protects from discovery writings that contain an "attorney's impressions, conclusions, opinions, or legal research or theories." (§ 2018.030, subd. (a); see Wellpoint Health Networks, Inc. v. Superior Court (1997) 59 Cal.App.4th 110, 120, 68 Cal.Rptr.2d 844.) The protection extends to an attorney's written notes about a witness's statements. (See Rodriguez v. McDonnell Douglas Corp. (1978) 87 Cal.App.3d 626, 649, 151 Cal.Rptr. 399 (*Rodriguez*); see also Dowden v. Superior Court (1999) 73 Cal.App.4th 126, 135, 86 Cal. Rptr.2d 180.) "[A]ny such notes or recorded statements taken by defendants' counsel would be protected by the absolute work product privilege because they would reveal counsel's 'impressions, conclusions, opinions, or legal research or theories' within the meaning of [the work product doctrine]." (Nacht & Lewis Architects, Inc. v. Superior Court (1996) 47 Cal.App.4th 214, 217, 54 Cal.Rptr.2d 575.) When a witness's statement and the attorney's impressions are inextricably intertwined, the work product doctrine provides that absolute protection is afforded to all of the attorney's notes. (*Rodriguez*, *supra*, 87 Cal.App.3d at p. 648, 151 Cal.Rptr. 399.)

Plaintiffs urge that the document is not work product because it reflects the statements of declared experts. They are incorrect. The document is not a transcript of the August 28, 2002 strategy session, nor is it a verbatim record of the experts' own statements. It contains Rowley's summaries of points from the strategy session, made at Yukevich's direction. Yukevich also edited the document in order to add his own thoughts and comments, further inextricably intertwining his personal impressions with the summary. (See *Rodriguez*, *supra*, 87 Cal.App.3d at pp. 647–648, 151 Cal.Rptr. 399.) In this regard, the trial court found: "As to the content of the document, although it doesn't contain overt statements setting forth the lawyer's conclusions, its very existence is owed to the lawyer's thought process. The document reflects not only the strategy, but also the attorney's opinion as to the important issues in the case. Directions were provided by Mr. Yukevich as to the key pieces of information to be recorded, and Mr. Yukevich also added his own input as to the important details, by inserting other words in the notes. The attorney's impressions of the case were the filter through which all the discussions at the conference were passed through on the way to the page." The court concluded, "[T]his court determines that the attorney's directions to record only portions of the conference specific to the attorney's concerns in the litigation are sufficient to support the finding that the notes are covered by the absolute work product [doctrine], as the choices in statements to record show the thought process and are too intertwined with the document."

Although the notes were written in dialogue format and contain information attributed to Mitsubishi's experts, the document does not qualify as an *expert's* report, writing, declaration, or testimony. The notes reflect the *paralegal's* summary along with *counsel's* thoughts and impressions about the case. The document was absolutely protected work product because it contained the ideas of Yukevich and his legal team about the case. (§ 2018.030, subd. (a).)

Ethical Duty Owned Upon Receipt of Attorney Work Product

Because the document is work product we consider what ethical duty Johnson owed once he received it. Plaintiffs rely on Aerojet–General Corp. v. Transport Indemnity Insurance (1993) 18 Cal.App.4th 996, 22 Cal. Rptr.2d 862 (*Aerojet*), to argue that because the document was inadvertently received, Johnson was duty bound to use the nonprivileged portions of it to his clients' advantage. This argument fails. *Aerojet* is distinguishable because there are no "unprivileged portions" of the document.

A review of *Aerojet*, *supra*, 18 Cal.App.4th 996, 22 Cal.Rptr.2d 862, demonstrates that it does not assist plaintiffs. Aerojet's insurance brokers had sent a package of materials to Aerojet's risk manager. The risk manager sent them on to Aerojet's attorney, DeVries. Among these documents was a memo from an attorney at an opposing law firm. It was never ascertained how opposing counsel's memo found its way into the package of documents. The memo revealed the existence of a witness whom DeVries ultimately deposed. When opposing counsel learned that DeVries had received the memo and thus discovered the witness, counsel sought sanctions. The trial court imposed monetary sanctions under section 128.5, subdivision (a). (*Aerojet*, at pp. 1001–1002, 22 Cal.Rptr.2d 862.) The Court of Appeal reversed the sanctions order.

The *Aerojet* court first noted that DeVries was free of any wrongdoing in his initial receipt of the document. The court also observed that the existence and identification of the witness was not privileged. "Nor can 'the identity and location of persons having knowledge of relevant facts' be concealed under the attorney work product rule.... [Citations.]" (*Aerojet*, *supra*, 18 Cal.App.4th at p. 1004, 22 Cal.Rptr.2d 862.) Defendants claimed no prejudice to their case as a result of the witness's disclosure. Indeed, they prevailed at trial. (*Ibid.*) Because counsel was blameless in his acquisition of the document *and because* the information complained of was not privileged, DeVries was free to use it. (*Id.* at p. 1005, 22 Cal.Rptr.2d 862.) Plaintiffs' reliance on *Aerojet* founders on the facts that distinguish it. Here, Yukevich's notes were absolutely protected by the work product rule. Thus, Johnson's reliance on *Aerojet* is unavailing, particularly in light of the clear standard set out in *State Fund*, *supra*, 70 Cal.App.4th 644, 82 Cal.Rptr.2d 799.

In *State Fund*, *supra*, 70 Cal.App.4th 644, 82 Cal.Rptr.2d 799, the plaintiff sent defendant's attorney (Telanoff) three boxes of documents that were identical to the documents provided during discovery. Inadvertently, plaintiff also sent 273 pages of forms entitled, "Civil Litigation Claims Summary," marked as "ATTORNEY–CLIENT COMMUNICATION/ATTORNEY WORK PRODUCT," and with the warning, "DO NOT CIRCULATE OR DUPLICATE." (*Id.* at p. 648, 82 Cal.Rptr.2d 799.) In addition, "[t]he word 'CONFIDENTIAL' [was] repeatedly printed around the perimeter of the first page of the form." (*Ibid.*) When counsel discovered the mistake and demanded return of the documents, Telanoff refused. The trial court, relying on American Bar Association (ABA) Formal Ethics Opinion No. 92–368 (Nov. 10, 1992), imposed monetary sanctions.

The Court of Appeal framed the issue as follows: "[W]hat is a lawyer to do when he or she receives, through the inadvertence of opposing counsel, documents plainly subject to the attorney-client privilege?" (*State Fund*, *supra*, 70 Cal.App.4th at p. 651, 82 Cal.Rptr.2d 799.) After determining that the documents were privileged and that inadvertent disclosure did not waive the privilege, the court discussed an attorney's obligation. The Court of Appeal disagreed that the ABA opinion should regulate Telanoff's conduct. The court noted that the ABA Model Rules on which the opinion was based "do not establish ethical standards in California, as they have not been adopted in California and have no legal force of their own. [Citations.]" (*Id.* at pp. 655–656, 82 Cal.Rptr.2d 799.) Likewise, the court held that an "ABA formal opinion does not establish an obligatory standard of conduct imposed on California lawyers." (*Id.* at p. 656, 82 Cal.Rptr.2d 799.) Thus, under the circumstances, "Telanoff should not have been sanctioned for engaging in conduct which has been condemned by an ABA formal opinion, but which has not been condemned by any decision, statute or Rule of Professional Conduct applicable in this state." (*Ibid.*)

The *State Fund* court went on to articulate the standard to be applied prospectively: "When a lawyer who receives materials that obviously appear to be subject to an attorney-client privilege or otherwise clearly appear to be confidential and privileged and where it is reasonably apparent that the materials were provided or made available through inadvertence, the lawyer receiving such materials should refrain from examining the materials any more than is essential to ascertain if the materials are privileged, and shall immediately notify the sender that he or she possesses material that appears to be privileged. The parties may then proceed to resolve the situation by agreement or may resort to the court for guidance with the benefit of protective orders and other judicial intervention as may be justified." (*State Fund*, *supra*, 70 Cal.App.4th at pp. 656–657, 82 Cal.Rptr.2d 799.) To ensure that its decision was clear in setting forth the applicable standard in these cases, the court explicitly stated that it "declared the standard governing the conduct of California lawyers" in such instances. (*Id.* at p. 657, 82 Cal.Rptr.2d 799.)

The existing *State Fund* rule is a fair and reasonable approach. The rule supports the work product doctrine (§ 2018.030), and is consistent with the state's policy to "[p]reserve the rights of attorneys to prepare cases for trial with that degree of privacy necessary to encourage them to prepare their cases thoroughly and to investigate not only the favorable but the unfavorable aspects of those cases" and to "[p]revent attorneys from taking undue advantage of their adversary's industry and efforts." (§ 2018.020, subds. (a), (b).)

The *State Fund* rule also addresses the practical problem of inadvertent disclosure in the context of today's reality that document production may involve massive numbers of documents. A contrary holding could severely disrupt the discovery process. As amicus curiae The Product Liability Advisory Council, Inc. argues, "Even apart from the inadvertent disclosure problem, the party responding to a request for mass production must engage in a laborious, time consuming process. If the document producer is confronted with the additional prospect that any privileged documents inadvertently produced will become fair game for the opposition, the minute screening and re-screening that inevitably would follow not only would add enormously to that burden but would slow the pace of discovery to a degree sharply at odds with the general goal of expediting litigation."

Finally, we note that "[a]n attorney has an obligation not only to protect his client's interests but also to respect the legitimate interests of fellow members of the bar, the judiciary, and the administration of justice." (Kirsch v. Duryea (1978) 21 Cal.3d 303, 309, 146 Cal.Rptr. 218, 578 P.2d 935.) The *State Fund* rule holds attorneys to a reasonable standard of professional conduct when confidential or privileged materials are inadvertently disclosed.

Here, it is true that Yukevich's notes were not so clearly flagged as confidential as were the forms in *State Fund*, *supra*, 70 Cal.App.4th 644, 82 Cal.Rptr.2d 799. But, as the Court of Appeal observed, "[T]he absence of prominent notations of confidentiality does not make them any less privileged." The *State Fund* rule is an objective standard. In applying the rule, courts must consider whether reasonably competent counsel, knowing the circumstances of the litigation, would have concluded the materials were privileged, how much review was reasonably necessary to draw that conclusion, and when counsel's examination should have ended. (*Id.* at pp. 656–657, 82 Cal.Rptr.2d 799.)

The standard was properly and easily applied here. Johnson admitted that after a minute or two of review he realized the notes related to the case and the Yukevich did not intend to reveal them. Johnson's own admissions and subsequent conduct clearly demonstrate that he violated the *State Fund* rule. We note, however, that such admissions are not required for the application of the objective standard in evaluating an attorney's conduct.

Disqualification of Counsel and Experts

The court properly applied the *State Fund* rule and determined that Johnson violated it. The next question is whether disqualification was the proper remedy. We review the court's disqualification order for abuse of discretion. (People ex rel. Dept. of Corporations v. Spee–Dee Oil Change

Systems, Inc. (1999) 20 Cal.4th 1135, 1143, 86 Cal.Rptr.2d 816, 980 P.2d 371.)

The *State Fund* court held that "[m]ere exposure" to an adversary's confidences is insufficient, standing alone, to warrant an attorney's disqualification. (*State Fund, supra*, 70 Cal.App.4th at p. 657, 82 Cal.Rptr.2d 799.) The court counseled against a draconian rule that "[could] nullify a party's right to representation by chosen counsel any time inadvertence or devious design put an adversary's confidences in an attorney's mailbox." (*Ibid.*) However, the court did not "rule out the possibility that in an appropriate case, disqualification might be justified if an attorney inadvertently receives confidential materials and fails to conduct himself or herself in the manner specified above, assuming other factors compel disqualification." (*Ibid.*)

After reviewing the document, Johnson made copies and disseminated them to plaintiffs' experts and other attorneys. In affirming the disqualification order, the Court of Appeal stated, "The trial court settled on disqualification as the proper remedy because of the unmitigable damage caused by Johnson's dissemination and use of the document." Thus, "the record shows that Johnson not only failed to conduct himself as required under *State Fund*, [*supra*, 70 Cal.App.4th 644, 82 Cal.Rptr.2d 799,] but also acted unethically in making full use of the confidential document." The Court of Appeal properly concluded that such use of the document undermined the defense experts' opinions and placed defendants at a great disadvantage. Without disqualification of plaintiffs' counsel and their experts, the damage caused by Johnson's use and dissemination of the notes was irreversible. Under the circumstances presented in this case, the trial court did not abuse its discretion by ordering disqualification for violation of the *State Fund* rule.

Plaintiffs attempt to justify Johnson's use of the document by accusing the defense experts of giving false testimony during their depositions. Plaintiffs allege that the statements attributed to the experts in the document contradicted their deposition statements and that the experts lied about the technical evidence involved in the case. As an initial matter, we are not persuaded that any of the defense experts ever actually adopted as their own the statements attributed to them. The document is not a verbatim transcript of the strategy session, but Rowley's summary of points that Yukevich directed him to note. Yukevich then edited the document, adding his own thoughts and comments. As the trial court observed, the document was an interpretation and summary of what others thought the experts were saying.

Moreover, we agree with the Court of Appeal that, "when a writing is protected under the absolute attorney work product privilege, courts do not invade upon the attorney's thought processes by evaluating the content of the writing. Once [it is apparent] that the writing contains an attorney's impressions, conclusions, opinions, legal research or theories, the reading stops and the contents of the document for all practical purposes are off limits. In the same way, once the court determines that the writing is absolutely privileged, the inquiry ends. Courts do not make exceptions based on the content of the writing." Thus, "regardless of its potential impeachment value, Yukevich's personal notes should never have been subject to opposing counsel's scrutiny and use."

We also reject plaintiffs' argument that the crime or fraud exception should apply to privileged work product in this civil proceeding. Under the work product doctrine "[a] writing that reflects an attorney's impressions, conclusions, opinions, or legal research or theories *is not discoverable under any circumstances*." (§ 2018.030, subd. (a), italics added.) With respect to such a writing, the Legislature intended that the crime or fraud exception only apply "in any official investigation by a law enforcement agency or proceeding or action brought by a public prosecutor . . . if the services of the lawyer were sought or obtained to enable or aid anyone to commit . . . a crime or fraud." (§ 2018.050) By its own terms, the crime or fraud exception does not apply here.

Disposition

We affirm the Court of Appeal's judgment.

Chapter Two

Sources and Application of Legal Ethics Rules

■ ■ ■

What This Chapter Covers

I. The Organization of the Bar
  A. Admission to Practice in the Courts of a State
    1. Residency Requirements
    2. Character Requirements
    3. Admission to Practice in California
  B. Admission to Practice in the Courts of Other States
  C. Admission to Practice in the Federal Courts
  D. Membership in Bar Associations
    1. State Bar Associations
    2. American Bar Association
    3. City, County, and Special Interest Bar Associations

II. Sources of Legal Ethics Rules
  A. State Codes of Conduct, Statutes, and Court Rules
  B. American Bar Association Model Code of Professional Responsibility
  C. American Bar Association Model Rules of Professional Conduct
  D. American Bar Association Code of Judicial Conduct
  E. Ethics Opinions and Ethics Hot Lines

III. Lawyer Disciplinary Proceedings
  A. Conduct Subject to Discipline
  B. How Discipline Is Imposed
  C. Types of Discipline
  D. Discipline by Federal Courts

Reading Assignment

Wydick, Perschbacher, & Bassett, Chapter 2.

ABA Model Rules:

Preamble, Scope and Terminology;

Rules 5.5 and 8.1 through 8.5.

CRPC 1–100 through 1–300.

Cal. Bus. & Prof. Code §§ 6067–6068, 6076–6077, 6100–6117, 6125–6126.

Cal. Code Civ. Pro. § 1282.4.

Cal. S.Ct. Rules on Multijurisdictional Practice, Rules 9.40, 9.45–9.48.

Supplemental Reading

Hazard & Hodes:

Discussion of ABA Model Rules 5.5 and 8.1 through 8.5.

Cal. Family Code § 8800 (conflicts of interest in adoption proceedings).

Restatement (Third) of the Law Governing Lawyers §§ 1, 5 (2000).

Discussion Problems

1. Under the laws of California, what requirements will you have to meet to be admitted to practice? [*See* Cal. Bus. & Prof. Code §§ 6060 & 6062.]

2. In the *Kwasnik* case, *infra:*

   a. Trace the character investigation procedure that was followed. How were the facts determined? Who should bear the burden to show an applicant's good (or lack of good) character?

   b. Do you think that the decision in the *Kwasnik* case was correct given the circumstances?

   c. Should some conduct forever bar an applicant from becoming a lawyer? What about murder? child molestation? major securities or bank fraud? tax evasion? dozens of arrests at pro- or anti-abortion demonstrations? drunken driving convictions?

   d. If an applicant should be allowed to show rehabilitation, how long should the rehabilitation period be and who should decide? Can numerical standards be set?

3. To practice in California, will you have to become a member of:

   a. The State Bar of California?

   b. The city or county bar association in the area where you open your office?

   c. The American Bar Association?

4. Suppose that you have recently been admitted to practice before the California Supreme Court.

   a. Client Arnold asks you to represent him in a lawsuit pending in the United States District Court for the Northern District of California. Under what circumstances may you represent him?

   b. Client Betty asks you to represent her in an appeal pending in the United States Court of Appeals for the Ninth Circuit. Under what circumstances may you represent her?

c. Client Carlos asks you to represent him in an appeal that is pending in the United States Supreme Court. Under what circumstances may you represent him?

d. Client Deborah, an economics professor who lives and teaches at a California university, asks you to represent her in a dispute over consulting fees for work she did for a business in Colorado. You regularly represent and advise Deborah regarding her consulting work in California. The dispute in Colorado appears headed for arbitration or other alternative dispute resolution proceedings in Colorado. Under what circumstances may you represent her? [*See* ABA Model Rule 5.5(c).]

e. Client Edgar asks you to defend him in an automobile negligence case pending in Arizona, right across the river from your office in California. Under what circumstances may you represent him?

f. Your law partner, attorney Thomas, suggests opening a branch office of the firm in Nevada. Thomas is admitted to practice in both California and Nevada, but you and the other lawyers in the firm are admitted only in California. Under what circumstances may the firm open the branch office? [*See* ABA Model Rule 7.5(b).]

5. Lawyer Lawrence has come to you for legal advice. He has told you in confidence that he and a group of his friends formed a real estate investment venture. They entrusted him with a large sum of money to invest for them, but he diverted part of it for his own use. They have not yet discovered what he did, and he has asked you for legal guidance.

a. If Lawrence was acting in the real estate transaction in his personal capacity, not as a lawyer, is he subject to discipline by the state bar for what he did?

b. Do you have an ethical obligation to report him to the state bar?

6. In the *Mountain* case and the *Drociak* case, *infra*:

a. How do you suppose the state bar first became aware of the misconduct?

b. Trace the procedure followed in each case. How were the facts determined? Who decided what discipline to impose?

c. Do you think the discipline imposed on lawyer Mountain was appropriate in the circumstances?

d. Do you think the discipline imposed on lawyer Drociak was appropriate in the circumstances?

THE ORGANIZATION OF THE BAR

In the United States, admission to the bar and lawyer discipline have traditionally been matters of state concern. Lawyers are not admitted to practice in the United States, they are admitted to practice in a particular state or states. Separate rules govern admission to the various federal courts. Only recently has the states' near absolute control over their bars been challenged. However, the increased nationalization of commerce has broken down the model of local lawyer serving local client. Today, there are major law firms with offices in many cities and states throughout the United States and the world. This increased practice across state lines and the increasing mobility of our population, including lawyers, has generated challenges to the states' residency requirements for membership in the bar. The consumer movement has also led to constitutional and antitrust challenges to the state bars' restrictions on lawyer advertising and fee regulation. These developments are discussed in this chapter and Chapter Four. Responding in part to these changes, the American Bar Association, in August 2002, amended its principal rule dealing with unauthorized and multijurisdictional practice of law, ABA Model Rule 5.5. In California, the California Supreme Court adopted rules allowing in-house counsel and public interest lawyers not yet admitted to practice in California to practice on a limited basis without obtaining full admission to the bar. In addition, the rules allow out-of-state lawyers to practice in California under very limited circumstances. Although this chapter focuses on admission to the bar, sources of ethics rules and lawyer discipline in general, in practice a lawyer will inquire into the admission, ethics, and discipline rules of the particular state(s) involved.

Admission to Practice in the Courts of a State

In most states, admission to practice law is gained by graduating from law school, passing the state's bar examination, and demonstrating that you possess good moral character.

1. Residency Requirements

In the past, many states imposed residency requirements, but, since 1985, the Supreme Court has repeatedly struck down such requirements. In the first case, *Supreme Court of New Hampshire v. Piper,* 470 U.S. 274, 105 S.Ct. 1272, 84 L.Ed.2d 205 (1985), the Court held that the New Hampshire Supreme Court's refusal to swear in a Vermont resident who had passed the state's bar examination violated the Constitution's privileges and immunities clause. The Court established a narrow exception if a state can demonstrate "substantial" reasons for discriminating against nonresidents and can show that the difference in treatment bears a close relation to those reasons. Using similar reasoning, in *Frazier v. Heebe,* 482 U.S. 641, 107 S.Ct. 2607, 96 L.Ed.2d 557 (1987), the Court invoked its supervisory power to invalidate a residency requirement imposed by the United States District Court for the Eastern District of Louisiana.

Later, in *Supreme Court of Virginia v. Friedman,* 487 U.S. 59, 108 S.Ct. 2260, 101 L.Ed.2d 56 (1988), the Court struck down a Virginia rule that let permanent Virginia residents licensed out-of-state waive into the Virginia bar, but required non-Virginia residents to take the state bar examination. According to the Court, Virginia's rule violated the privileges and immunities clause because it burdened the right to practice law by discriminating among otherwise equally qualified applicants.

Finally, in *Barnard v. Thorstenn,* 489 U.S. 546, 109 S.Ct. 1294, 103 L.Ed.2d 559 (1989), the Court confronted perhaps its best chance to find "substantial" reasons to discriminate against nonresidents in bar admissions when it took up two New York and New Jersey lawyers' challenges to the Virgin Islands bar's one-year residency requirement. The Virgin Islands bar offered five justifications for its residency requirement: (1) the Virgin Islands' geographic isolation and communications difficulties would make it difficult for nonresidents to attend court proceedings on short notice; (2) delays in accommodating nonresident lawyers' schedules would increase the courts' caseloads; (3) delays in publication and lack of access to local statutory and case law would adversely affect nonresident lawyers' competence; (4) the bar does not have adequate resources to supervise a nationwide bar membership; and (5) nonresident bar members would be unable to take on a fair share of indigent criminal defense work.

The Supreme Court, in an opinion by Justice Kennedy, found none of the reasons substantial enough to justify excluding nonresidents from the Virgin Islands bar. Requiring nonresident lawyers to associate local counsel would satisfy the Virgin Islands' first two concerns, a solution the Court had also suggested in *Piper.* The Court rejected congested dockets and the difficulty in maintaining knowledge of local law as any justification for the exclusion of nonresidents from the bar. Dues paid by the nonresidents should supply the resources needed to meet the additional administrative burdens of supervising them. Only the fifth justification raised any serious concern. In *Piper,* the Court had recognized that nonresident lawyers could be required to share the burden of representing indigent criminal defendants as a condition of bar membership. In *Barnard,* the Court decided that requiring nonresident lawyers to meet this burden *personally* "is too heavy a burden on the privileges of nonresidents and bears no substantial relation to the [Virgin Islands'] objective." Justices Rehnquist, White and O'Connor dissented. They believed that "the unique circumstances of legal practice in the Virgin Islands * * * could justify upholding this simple residency requirement" under *Piper.*

The eventual impact of the residency-restriction cases may be ironic. In the past, some states allowed resident lawyers admitted in another state to "waive" into the bar without taking their own bar examination. Although this was often based on reciprocity (see below), it gave an advantage to lawyers who already resided in the state when they sought admission. Because the Supreme Court's decisions now require equality in treatment between in-state and out-of-state applicants to the bar, residence-based waivers are no longer allowed. These states must either allow any nonresident admission upon waiver on the same basis as residents, or abolish the waiver privilege. Illinois, for example, abolished the privilege rather than allowing waivers to non-residents (although the reciprocity privilege was later restored). The bottom line may be increased barriers to admission, rather than a relaxation of barriers for lawyers already in practice who wish to change or expand their geographical practices.

2. Character Requirements

All states require that an applicant for admission to the bar possess "good moral character," although enforcement of this requirement is uneven and sporadic. The California State Bar has a large paid staff devoted to screening bar applicants. The elements of good moral character remain vague, but there is general agreement that they include honesty, respect for the law and respect for the rights of others. Applicants are most likely to get into difficulty for dishonesty on the bar application, recent criminal conduct, and fraud or other financial misdeeds. From time-to-time the bar has also sought to bar applicants on ideological, political, and moral grounds. In *Konigsberg v. State Bar,* 353 U.S. 252, 77 S.Ct. 722, 1 L.Ed.2d 810 (1957), the Supreme Court rejected mere membership in the Communist Party as proof that an applicant lacked good moral character. More difficult are cases involving past criminal conduct or other misdeeds with an intervening passage of time or evidence of rehabilitation. Consider the following case.

KWASNIK v. STATE BAR OF CALIFORNIA

Supreme Court of California, 1990.
50 Cal.3d 1061, 269 Cal.Rptr. 749, 791 P.2d 319.

BY THE COURT:

Petitioner Richard E. Kwasnik seeks review of the refusal of the State Bar to certify him to this court for admission to the bar on the ground that he lacks the requisite good moral character. (Bus. & Prof.Code, § 6066; Cal.Rules of Court, rule 952(c); Rules Regulating Admission to Practice Law, rule I, § 11.) For the reasons set forth below, we conclude petitioner should be admitted to the bar.

FACTS

Petitioner graduated from Brooklyn Law School in June 1966. He was admitted to the practice of law in New York in 1967.

In November 1970 petitioner was involved in an automobile accident that resulted in the death of Steven Smilanich, a husband and father of three children. Although a grand jury investigated the accident, no criminal charges were filed. Petitioner pleaded guilty to "driving while impaired," a traffic infraction, and was fined $50.

The decedent's widow (hereafter Smilanich) and decedent's three minor children filed a wrongful death action against petitioner in a New York court, which resulted in a judgment against him in the amount of $232,234.16 in July 1974. Petitioner's automobile insurance carrier paid the policy limit of $10,000 to Smilanich. In 1975 Smilanich filed attachment proceedings against petitioner to enforce the judgment by garnishing his wages; he previously had made no payments on the judgment. Once he received a notice of levy, petitioner began making payments of approximately $42 every two weeks. Between 1975 and January 1980, petitioner paid $4,649. He has paid nothing since January 1980.

In November 1980, after Smilanich's attorney rejected a settlement offer of $15,000, petitioner filed a petition for bankruptcy in the United States Bankruptcy Court for the Southern District of Florida. * * * The only debt scheduled for discharge in the bankruptcy petition was the Smilanich judgment; petitioner listed none of his other then-existing debts. The Smilanich judgment was discharged by the bankruptcy court in March 1981.

A. Florida Bar Proceedings

[In 1980, the Florida State Bar found Kwasnik failed to meet their standards of conduct and fitness and refused to admit him. He sought reevaluation in 1986. The Florida bar again found he failed to meet their moral character requirements. However, the Florida Supreme Court rejected the bar's recommendation and held he had demonstrated sufficient rehabilitation to qualify for admission. In 1988 Kwasnik was admitted to practice in Florida.]

B. California Bar Proceedings

In July 1987 petitioner passed the Attorney's Examination of the California Bar Examination. His certification to practice was delayed, however, pending a moral character investigation. In June 1988 a formal hearing was held before a three-member hearing panel of the State Bar Court. Prior to the hearing petitioner entered a stipulation of facts with the State Bar. The hearing panel found that he had sustained his burden of proof that he is of good moral character and recommended that he be admitted to the California Bar.

Pursuant to a request for reconsideration, the hearing panel again recommended that he be admitted to the practice of law and issued a finding of facts that closely tracked the stipulation between the parties. First, it concluded that petitioner's description on his California Bar application of the disposition of the Smilanich suit as a "verdict for defendant" was not an intentional misstatement made to deceive. Second, it found that he accepted full responsibility for the three acts considered by the Florida Bar. Third, it concluded that the discharge of the Smilanich judgment in bankruptcy discharged both the legal and moral obligations of petitioner. Finally, it noted that except for the Smilanich matter petitioner's record is unblemished; that his conduct, as evidenced by the testimonial letters he submitted, established he is of a good moral character; and that he has an excellent reputation in the community for honesty, reliability, fairness and integrity. The hearing panel concluded that if he were admitted to the practice of law petitioner would be able to meet the professional and fiduciary duties of his practice.

The Review Department of the State Bar Court (hereafter the review department), however, made its own findings and disagreed with the hearing panel's conclusions. First, the review department detailed certain circumstances attendant on petitioner's bankruptcy: (1) between 1975 and 1979, when Kwasnik made payments only pursuant to garnishment proceedings, he earned an annual salary of between $15,000 and $32,000, totaling at least $100,000, while living rent-free at his mother's home and putting his wife through five years of college; and (2) petitioner misled Smilanich's attorney in 1980 by expressing an intention to take a one-year leave of absence when he had already accepted a new job in Florida.

Second, the review department cited a report issued by the Florida Bar after a formal rehabilitation hearing held in November 1986 on petitioner's application for reevaluation. The Florida Bar found that petitioner had taken no steps to fulfill his moral obligation to Smilanich since 1980. It noted that he had neither contacted the survivors nor made any further payment to them, despite the fact that he and his wife earned a combined income of $90,000 and owned $225,000 of equity in a home valued at $250,000. In addition, the review department noted that the Florida Bar found petitioner to be less than candid at the rehabilitation hearing, especially when asked why his New York home was in his wife's name.

Finally, the review department concluded that petitioner had demonstrated a lack of good moral character by failing to accept "any responsibility whatsoever for the Smilanich family which was victimized by his drunken driving." It found he ignored the rights of the Smilanich family under the wrongful death judgment until after garnishment proceedings were instituted, and then paid only the minimum in order to avoid the wage garnishment. Accordingly, in March 1989 the review department, by a vote of 11 to 4, found that petitioner did not possess the requisite good moral character and recommended that he not be admitted to the practice of law in California. The four members voting for petitioner's admission noted that the finding of lack of good moral character was based entirely on his failure to honor a moral obligation to pay a wrongful death judgment discharged in bankruptcy. They concluded petitioner should be admitted because he had successfully established his good moral character by his practice of law in sister jurisdictions and the attestations of judges and lawyers.

DISCUSSION

This court may admit to the practice of law any applicant whose qualifications have been certified to it by the Committee of Bar Examiners (hereafter the Committee). (Bus. & Prof.Code, § 6064.) To qualify, an applicant must, among other things, be of "good moral character." (Id., § 6060, subd. (b).)

"Good moral character" has traditionally been defined in California as the "absence of proven conduct or acts which have been historically considered as manifestations of 'moral turpitude.' " (*Hallinan v. Commit-*

tee of Bar Examiners (1966) 65 Cal.2d 447, 452, 55 Cal.Rptr. 228, 421 P.2d 76 (hereafter *Hallinan*).) Good moral character also is defined statutorily to include "qualities of honesty, fairness, candor, trustworthiness, observance of fiduciary responsibility, [observance] of the laws of the state and the nation and respect for the rights of others and for the judicial process." (Rule X, § 101(a)) * * *.

Because the commission of an act constituting "moral turpitude" is a statutory ground for disbarment (Bus. & Prof.Code, § 6106) and is perhaps the most frequent subject of inquiry in disciplinary proceedings, "insofar as the scope of inquiry is concerned, the distinction between admission and disciplinary proceedings is today more apparent than real." (*Hallinan,* supra, 65 Cal.2d at p. 452, 55 Cal.Rptr. 228, 421 P.2d 76.) The common issue is whether the applicant for admission or the attorney sought to be disciplined "is a fit and proper person to be permitted to practice law, and that usually turns upon whether he has committed or is likely to continue to commit acts of moral turpitude." (Id. at p. 453, 55 Cal.Rptr. 228, 421 P.2d 76.) * * *

The burden is on the applicant to prove good moral character. (*Hallinan,* supra, 65 Cal.2d at p. 451, 55 Cal.Rptr. 228, 421 P.2d 76.) If he is successful, the Committee must rebut that showing with evidence of bad character. Any applicant who is denied certification may seek review of the Committee's action in this court. (Bus. & Prof.Code, § 6066; Cal.Rules of Court, rule 952(c); Rules Regulating Admission to Practice Law, rule I, § 11.) In that review we give great weight to the Committee's findings, but they are not conclusive. We examine the evidence and make our own determination as to its sufficiency, resolving reasonable doubt in favor of the applicant. (*Hallinan,* supra, 65 Cal.2d at pp. 450–451, 55 Cal.Rptr. 228, 421 P.2d 76.)

Petitioner contends he has established his rehabilitation and good moral character. We agree. Petitioner introduced fifteen letters attesting to his character: seven from judges before whom he had appeared, seven from attorneys with whom he had practiced, and one from a pastor with whom he had worked on an interfaith council. The letters praise petitioner's personal and professional integrity and his reputation both as a competent trial attorney and as a member of the community.

Traditionally we have accorded significant weight to testimonials submitted by attorneys and judges regarding an applicant's moral fitness, on the assumption that such persons possess a keen sense of responsibility for the integrity of the legal profession. This is especially true when, as here, the references are aware of the circumstances that prompted the inquiry into the applicant's moral character.

In addition, the hearing panel and the review department both recognized that except for the events surrounding the wrongful death action, petitioner has an "unblemished record"; this is true not only of certain litigation in which petitioner was a party, in which his conduct did "not reflect badly on his moral character," but also of a 20–year period as a practicing member of the New York Bar, during which time he was never the subject of a disciplinary proceeding. Whether or not all petitioner's activities for which his superiors at the New York Legal Aid Society lauded him were simply part of his responsibilities, e.g., training and advising younger attorneys, there is extensive evidence that he acted diligently in that capacity. In addition, petitioner served competently in a fiduciary role as trustee of a $400,000 trust established by the City of New York for petitioner's paraplegic cousin; the Associate General Counsel of New York City who was in charge of that trust also submitted a letter on petitioner's behalf. Finally, as noted above, the Florida Supreme Court determined on the same evidence that petitioner was of good moral character and admitted him to the Florida Bar.

Business and Professions Code section 6106 states that an act of moral turpitude, dishonesty, or corruption constitutes a cause for disbarment or suspension of an attorney, regardless of whether the act is committed in his capacity as an attorney. Because the misconduct in this case is not in any way related to petitioner's practice of law, however, we should accord it less weight than we would professional misconduct in evaluating his moral fitness for admission to the bar. * * *

[Kwasnik and the State Bar disagreed over whether the State Bar refused to certify him *solely* because he obtained a bankruptcy discharge of the Smilanich judgment. The court reasoned that if the State Bar's denial was based on a claim that Kwasnik owed a moral obligation to the Smilanich family, it would violate the Bankruptcy Act § 525(a) [governmental unit may not deny a license to a person "solely because" he has not paid a debt that was discharged under the Bankruptcy Act] and the Constitution's supremacy clause by frustrating the purposes of Congress in enacting the Bankruptcy Act. The court found the evidence unrelated to the discharge was diminished by the passage of time and by the absence of similar, more recent misconduct, and thus did not reflect on his moral fitness to practice law. The court distinguished two other cases involving bankruptcy discharges in part because the debt Kwasnik discharged was unrelated to his practice of law, and was not a debt owed as a result of professional misconduct.]

DISPOSITION

* * * Accordingly, we order petitioner admitted to the California Bar. This holding is consistent with our charge to protect the public and its confidence in the legal profession rather than to impose punishment. (*Gary v. State Bar* (1988) 44 Cal.3d 820, 827, 244 Cal.Rptr. 482, 749 P.2d 1336.) The State Bar has presented no evidence that petitioner is now a danger to the public in the practice of law or that he does not merit public confidence.

It is ordered that the Committee of Bar Examiners certify petitioner Richard E. Kwasnik to this court as a person qualified to be admitted to practice law.

[JUSTICE KENNARD'S and JUSTICE ARABIAN'S concurring opinions and CHIEF JUSTICE LUCAS' dissenting opinion are omitted.]

ADMISSION TO PRACTICE IN CALIFORNIA

The Committee of Bar Examiners, which is part of the State Bar of California, has the power to examine all applicants for admission to practice law in the State of California. [Rules Regulating Admission to Practice Law in California, Rule I § 2.] To be certified for admission, an applicant must be at least 18 years old, of good moral character, and a graduate of an accredited law school or a graduate of an unaccredited law school who passed the first year law students' examination. The applicant must also pass the General Bar Examination (or the Attorneys' Bar Examination if the applicant is admitted to practice in another state) and must pass the multi-state professional responsibility examination. [*Id.*, Rules II–X.]

Once the applicant has fulfilled these requirements, the Examining Committee certifies the applicant to the Supreme Court for admission to the bar. If admitted, the applicant then takes an oath and becomes a member of the State Bar of California. [Cal.Bus. & Prof.Code §§ 6064, 6067.] An applicant who has been refused admission has the right to have his or her case reviewed by the California Supreme Court. [Cal.Bus. & Prof.Code § 6066.]

A member of the State Bar of California may be classified "active" or "inactive." [Cal.Bus. & Prof.Code § 6066.] A member is presumed an active member unless the member requests, or is involuntarily placed, on inactive status. [Cal.Bus. & Prof.Code § 6004.] Inactive members are not entitled to practice law. [Cal.Bus. & Prof.Code § 6006.] A member may be placed on involuntary inactive status for a number of reasons, including after a hearing where it was determined that the member is unable to practice law competently or without substantial threat of harm to his or her clients, or if there is a reasonable probability that the State Bar will prevail on the merits of an underlying disciplinary matter. [Cal.Bus. & Prof.Code § 6007.]

ADMISSION TO PRACTICE IN OTHER STATES AND THE FEDERAL COURTS

An attorney who has been admitted in one state and who wants to represent a particular client in a court of another state may also petition that court to appear *pro hac vice*, i.e., "for this turn only." There is no right to appear *pro hac vice* [*see Leis v. Flynt*, 439 U.S. 438, 99 S.Ct. 698, 58 L.Ed.2d 717 (1979)], and each case requires a separate petition. In some jurisdictions, the attorney must enlist a local attorney as co-counsel. This requirement is to assure compliance with local procedure and provide accountability to the court, although some argue that it is really an economic device to protect the local bar. In addition to *pro hac vice* admission, most states allow some limited practice activities by lawyers admitted in another state, including limited admission for in-house counsel, for members of the military, for provision of pro bono services, and even for law faculty members. ABA Model Rule 5.5 permits lawyers admitted in another state, and not disbarred or suspended from practice there, to provide several categories of limited or temporary legal services in a state in which they are not admitted to practice. California has adopted liberalized limited practice rules as well. [*See* Cal. S.Ct. Rules on Multijurisdictional Practice, Rules 9.64–9.67.]

A majority of the states, but not California, have reciprocity arrangements that allow an attorney who has practiced in one state for a set number of years to gain full admission to practice in another state simply by filing a petition. But these arrangements are of no help to a lawyer from a state that does not reciprocate. Thus, if State A does not have an admission by petition procedure, but requires all attorneys from other states to take a bar examination, then even states that do permit admission by petition will require attorneys from State A to take a bar exam, though it may be a shorter one than is required of non-attorney applicants.

An attorney who wants to practice in a federal court must be separately admitted to the bar of that court, because each federal court maintains its own separate bar. Typically, admission is granted upon motion by an attorney who is already a member of that court's bar and who can affirm that the applicant is a person of good moral character. Admission to a federal district court typically requires that the applicant be admitted in the state in which the federal court sits. Admission to a federal court of appeals requires that the applicant be admitted in the courts of any state. Admission to the United States Supreme Court requires that the applicant have practiced before the courts of a state for at least three years.

SHELLER v. SUPERIOR COURT

California Court of Appeal, 2008.
158 Cal.App.4th 1697, 71 Cal.Rptr.3d 207.

CROSKEY, ACTING P.J.

A Texas attorney appearing *pro hac vice* for plaintiffs in a class action sent a communication to prospective class members which contained at least one misrepresentation. The trial court issued an order to show cause why the attorney's *pro hac vice* status should not be revoked. After a hearing, the trial court declined to revoke the attorney's *pro hac vice* status, and instead ordered the attorney to reimburse the defendant for substantial attorney's fees, as a condition for retaining his *pro hac vice* status. The trial court also formally reprimanded the Texas attorney. The attorney appeals. We conclude the trial court lacked authority to impose attorney's fees as a sanction and also lacked authority to issue the formal reprimand. We therefore reverse the trial court's order. However, we also conclude that the trial court has the authority to revoke an attorney's *pro hac vice* status in certain circumstances, and therefore remand for further proceedings.

Factual and Procedural Background

The challenged order arises in the context of a class action against Farmers New World Life Insurance Company and Farmers Group, Inc. (collectively "Farmers"). The action alleges Farmers committed unfair business practices in connection with Farmers's Universal Life and Flexible Premium Universal Life insurance policies. Specifically, the action alleges that the insurance policies were set up so that Farmers would collect premiums from policyholders that were insufficient to keep the policies in force—resulting in either an untimely lapse of the policies or a substantial increase in premiums. The initial complaint was filed on November 5, 2003. The named plaintiff, Pauline Fairbanks, was not only a Farmers insured, but also a Farmers *agent*. At the time the complaint was filed, Fairbanks was represented by Attorney Scott A. Marks, who is a California attorney.

At the same time, Attorney David L. Sheller, who is admitted to practice in Texas, was pursuing a similar class action against Farmers in Texas. On February 2, 2004, Attorney Sheller filed an application to appear *pro hac vice* as lead counsel on behalf of Fairbanks in the instant action. The application was granted.

From as early as November 1, 2004, the trial court suggested that Fairbanks might not be an ideal class representative for the insureds, as she had also been a Farmers agent. In June 2005, Attorney Sheller, but not Attorney Marks, sent a written communication to some 350 Farmers policyholders, seeking additional class representatives. The letter was in the form of a flyer, boldly captioned, "Attention Farmers Insurance Group Policy Holders!!!" The flyer began, "A potential class action lawsuit has been filed against [Farmers] in the State Court of Los Angeles County. We are concerned Farmers may have given you misleading information about this lawsuit. Our intention is to help policyholders and give them accurate information." The flyer went on to state, "If you have purchased such a policy, we may be able to help you. We are looking for other people who have purchased such Farmers policies. If you have, you may be accepted as a 'class representative.' If accepted, you are paid for your time in an amount set by the judge."

Upon learning of this flyer, Farmers filed an ex parte motion for a temporary restraining order preventing plaintiffs' counsel from sending further pre-certification communications to potential members of the class, or, in the alternative, to prevent any such communications without prior court approval. Farmers's motion was based not only on the June 2005 flyer, but also on two other communications which allegedly contained factual misrepresentations about the insurance policies at issue: a September 2003 letter and a telephone survey of 500 Farmers policyholders Attorney Sheller had commissioned. Farmers supported its motion with an expert declaration to the effect that both the September 2003 letter and the June 2005 flyer violated the California Rules of Professional Conduct. As to the statement in the June 2005 flyer indicating that

Farmers "may have given [policyholders] misleading information about this lawsuit," Farmers submitted a declaration that it had never made a general mailing to its policyholders, much less a misleading one.

A hearing on Farmers's ex parte motion was held on July 28, 2005. Attorney Sheller was present. At the hearing, the trial court expressed concern that "there seems to be some hucksterism going on here by plaintiffs." While the trial court believed that the September 23, 2003 letter did not comply with the Rules of Professional Conduct, the court was most concerned by the June 2005 flyer. Specifically, the court found the statement, "If accepted, you are paid for your time in an amount set by the judge" to be both inappropriate and simply untrue. Not only are class representatives not always entitled to recover, they may in fact be liable for court costs if the defendant prevails. Attorney Sheller responded, "As far as the [issue] of whether or not the class rep[resentative] is going to be paid or not, our contract specifically states that if we lose, they can be liable for costs of court. And without divulging any attorney communications, it is my standard practice to tell people that they can lose." The court responded that Attorney Sheller "just admitted a bait and switch to me," in that Attorney Sheller initially represented to prospective class members that they would be "paid for [their] time," but when the class members signed Attorney Sheller's agreement, they were then told that they could be responsible for costs in the event of a loss. The court believed the misrepresentation to be intentional. Attorney Sheller stated that he had no intention to mislead, and added, "I think now it will be changed. It won't happen again." The trial court restrained plaintiffs' counsel from any further pre-certification communications with potential class members without court pre-approval. Finding the June 2005 flyer particularly violative of the ethical rules, the trial court, on its own motion, set an order to show cause why Attorney Sheller's *pro hac vice* status should not be revoked.

There followed substantial discovery and briefing. Farmers submitted a supplemental declaration from its expert, confirming her opinion that the June 2005 flyer constituted an ethics violation. Farmers also submitted the declaration of a Texas ethics expert, who concluded the flyer violated Texas rules as well.

In response to the order to show cause, plaintiff argued that the 2005 flyer was accurate "with one minor exception." Plaintiff stated her counsel now realized the statement indicating class representatives would be paid for their time was "oversimplified and incorrect." According to plaintiff's response, "[Attorney] Sheller concedes that this was in error and that he is responsible for this mistake, and he wishes to correct it immediately by a further letter to the potential class, upon the [c]ourt's approval." Plaintiff explained that the "mistake arose because several lay people looked at the notice in an effort to make it simpler and easier to understand for the average person. [Attorney] Sheller was involved with the review and should have looked at it again and given it more thought before it went out the door to 350 people. However, in the usual press of time and because he did not give extra thought to a letter before it was sent out, [Attorney] Sheller made a human mistake." As to the representation in the flyer that Farmers may have given misleading information about the lawsuit, plaintiff stated, "This sentence was placed in the letter because [Attorney] Sheller has twelve (12) years of experience in life insurance sales fraud cases. It has been [Attorney] Sheller's experience that when people learn of an alleged problem with their policy, by whatever means, most of the time they contact their agent or the home office. Many times when they call their agent or the home office, they are given inaccurate or misleading information that there is not really a problem at all. [Attorney] Sheller has experienced this in this case with policyholders who received the notice in question. This happens so frequently in these cases that it is [Attorney] Sheller's opinion that this is a general business practice in the life insurance industry."

A draft "Corrective Notice and Apology" was attached, which repeated the bulk of the text of the flyer, including the sentence, "If accepted, you are paid for your time in an amount set by the judge." However, the next paragraph, written in bold type, states, "The sentence 'If accepted, you are paid for your time in an amount set by the Judge' is inaccurate. The Court finds that sentence is an ethical violation by Plaintiff's counsel, David L. Sheller. In actuality, you might not be paid at all and could be personally liable for court costs, if the Plaintiff loses." The draft corrective notice did not restate Attorney Sheller's concern that "Farmers may have given you misleading information about this lawsuit," nor did it retract that statement as ethically improper or otherwise inaccurate.

Attorney Sheller submitted the declaration of his own ethics expert opining that there is "nothing materially misleading" about the original flyer. As to the assertion in the flyer that class representatives would be paid for their time, Attorney Sheller's expert noted that Attorney Sheller conceded "that he neglected to specifically state that the judge might not award any amount." The expert concluded this was, "at worst a de minimis omission" as "it cannot be misleading or in any way improper not to have told a client what is obvious to every plaintiff, if you are not the prevailing party, you won't recover a monetary settlement." The expert then made the fairly remarkable assertion that "[Attorney] Sheller also has pointed out that he contractually obligated himself to bear any costs that might be imposed against the class representative, so that there simply was never an issue regarding the class representative's potential exposure to monetary costs." In fact, Attorney Sheller had not pointed this out at all. The only evidence before this court on this issue was Attorney Sheller's representation at the July 28, 2005 hearing that his "contract specifically states that if we lose, they can be liable for costs of court."

A hearing was held on the order to show cause on December 2, 2005. The trial court noted that its main concern was the representation in the flyer that class representatives would be paid for their time "[i]f accepted," while, in fact, class representatives could receive nothing and, according to Attorney Sheller's retainer agreement, actually be responsible for costs. Attorney Sheller argued that there was no ethical violation in the flyer, because there is no requirement that an attorney advertisement include a statement that if the client loses, there will be no recovery. Farmers argued that the error was not one of mere omission, but an affirmative statement that class representatives *would* be paid for their time.

Later in the hearing, Attorney Marks argued, for the first time, that there had been no "bait and switch" because Attorney Sheller had, in fact, obligated himself to pay all costs in the event of a loss. Attorney Marks gave the court a document, which was unauthenticated and had not been previously disclosed to Farmers. The document was a one-sentence letter, purportedly written in July 2004, from Attorney Sheller to Fairbanks, reading simply, "In the unlikely event we lose the case and there are costs that are incurred to you, I will pay them completely." When it was pointed out that this letter was in complete opposition to what had been represented at the July 2005 hearing, Attorney Marks responded that Attorney Sheller had been upset at the July 2005 hearing, and that while he had told the court what his *retainer* provided, he should have informed the court that he had promised to indemnify Fairbanks for costs, and would do the same with future class representatives. The court then questioned whether it was ethical for an attorney to agree to indemnify his client for costs that might be imposed against the client; the ethics experts for both parties were in attendance and, predictably, had opposing views on the issue.

The trial court indicated its intention to sanction Attorney Sheller in some manner, and asked the parties for input on any possible lesser sanction to the revocation of Attorney Sheller's *pro hac vice* status. Attorney Sheller's expert had suggested, in her declaration, that "a reprimand would be the maximum penalty to be appropriately imposed in this matter." Attorney Sheller argued that the prohibition on further precertification contact with the class without court approval would be sufficient. Farmers, which had incurred over $140,000 in fees on this issue, argued that, if Attorney Sheller's *pro hac vice* status was not revoked, he should at least be ordered to compensate Farmers for its attorney's fees.

The trial court allowed one final round of briefing. Attorney Sheller admitted that the flyer was "not well written" and apologized "for his mistakes" in drafting it. The court questioned whether it was ethical for an attorney to agree to indemnify his client for costs that might be imposed against the client; the ethics experts for both parties were in attendance and had opposing views on the issues. Attorney Sheller argued that, when he had written that if accepted, class representatives would be "paid for [their] time in an amount set by the judge," he simply meant that an impartial judicial officer would decide "how much justice, if any[,] an injured person will receive." He argued that his flyer caused no harm, and that any complaints about the flyer were "stylistic in nature." Attorney Sheller argued that he is a passionate advocate, who must be zealous in order to survive as a sole practitioner opposing a firm. He suggested that "[d]iscipline should only be administered when it is demonstrated that the attorney is representing his own interests as opposed to the clients' [interests]." As such, he argued that issuing a new flyer remedying the first flyer would be an appropriate remedy. At no point did Attorney Sheller ever suggest that the trial court lacked the authority to revoke his *pro hac vice* status, issue a reprimand, or sanction him monetarily.

On February 27, 2006, the trial court issued its order discharging the order to show cause. The court stated that the June 2005 flyer "reads like a crass commercial as opposed to a professional advertisement." The court concluded that the flyer "contained at least one statement that was not true," specifically, the representation that class representatives would be paid for their time. The court also found unethical Attorney Sheller's July 28, 2005 misrepresentation in open court that his retainer agreement specifically states that plaintiffs can be liable for costs in the event the case is lost, given that Attorney Sheller had, in actuality, agreed to reimburse Fairbanks for any costs incurred in this action. The court did not accept Attorney Sheller's claim of overzealousness as an excuse, and specifically concluded that, with respect to the June 2005 flyer, Attorney Sheller had been more concerned with attracting additional clients than with representing Fairbanks's interests. While the trial court believed that Attorney Sheller's conduct would justify the revocation of his *pro hac vice* status, the court in its discretion declined to do so. Instead, the court imposed on Attorney Sheller the responsibility to pay two-thirds of Farmers's attorney's fees, $95,009, as a condition of retaining his *pro hac vice* status. Additionally, the trial court formally reprimanded Attorney Sheller for his conduct. Attorney Sheller filed a timely notice of appeal.

Issues on Appeal

We first address whether Attorney Sheller can raise any challenge to the court's legal authority to order him to pay attorney's fees to Farmers, and formally reprimand him, in light of Attorney Sheller's failure to raise these arguments before the trial court. Exercising our discretion to reach these purely legal issues, we conclude that no authority existed for the trial court's order, and that it therefore must be reversed. We also consider whether a trial court has the inherent authority to revoke an attorney's *pro hac vice* status. We conclude that such authority exists, allowing a trial court to revoke an attorney's *pro hac vice* status in, at the least, any circumstance in which it could disqualify a California attorney from a particular case. We therefore remand for the trial court to determine whether to exercise its discretion to revoke Attorney Sheller's *pro hac vice* status.

Discussion

1. Scope of the Appeal

On appeal, Attorney Sheller challenges the trial court's authority to order him to pay Farmers's attorney's fees, to formally reprimand him, and—although the order was not made—to revoke his *pro hac vice* status. Farmers responds that these contentions are forfeited, as Attorney Sheller never challenged the trial court's authority to make any such orders. The application of the forfeiture rule is not automatic; appellate courts have discretion to excuse such forfeiture. (*In re* S.B. (2004) 32 Cal.4th 1287, 13 Cal.Rptr.3d 786, 90 P.3d 746.) Parties have been permitted to raise new issues on appeal where the issue is purely a question of law on undisputed facts. (Frink v. Prod (1982) 31 Cal.3d 166, 170, 181 Cal.Rptr. 893, 643 P.2d 476.) This is an appropriate case for the exercise of such discretion. We are here concerned with the purely legal issue of the scope of a trial court's authority to sanction a foreign attorney appearing *pro hac vice*. It would be a miscarriage of justice to allow a sanction imposed without legal authority to remain in effect simply because the attorney failed to challenge it.

Farmers also contends that the order formally reprimanding Attorney Sheller is not an appealable order. Indeed, it appears that the order is not. (See Code Civ. Proc., § 904.1.) We exercise our discretion, however, to treat the notice of appeal as a petition for writ of mandate, and address the issue.

2. Inherent Power of the Trial Courts

In order to properly discuss the issues raised by this appeal, we must first address the inherent powers of a trial court. All courts possess inherent supervisory or administrative powers to enable them to carry out their duties. (Bauguess v. Paine (1978) 22 Cal.3d 626, 635–636, 150 Cal.Rptr. 461, 586 P.2d 942.) Code of Civil Procedure section 128 reflects these powers, but is not their source. That section provides, in pertinent part, that each court has the power "[t]o control in furtherance of justice, the conduct of its ministerial officers, and of all other persons in any manner connected with a judicial proceeding before it, in every matter pertaining thereto." (Code Civ. Proc., § 128, subd. (a)(5).)

Prior to the enactment of the State Bar Act, attorney discipline was administered by the courts under their inherent judicial power. (1 Witkin, Cal. Procedure (4th ed. 1996) Attorneys, § 616, p. 727.) As originally enacted, the State Bar Act did not attempt to curtail or limit the previously existing judicial power to impose discipline. (See Bus. & Prof. Code, fmr. § 6087 [nothing in the State Bar Act "shall be construed as limiting or altering the powers of the courts of this state to disbar or discipline members of the bar"].) However, in 1951, the State Bar Act was amended to exclude superior courts and appellate courts from exercising such jurisdiction, leaving the Supreme Court as the sole judicial entity with jurisdiction over attorney discipline. (Bus. & Prof. Code, §§ 6087, 6100; Jacobs v. State Bar (1977) 20 Cal.3d 191, 196, 141 Cal.Rptr. 812,

570 P.2d 1230.) Thus, in California, the inherent judicial power of the superior court does *not* extend to attorney disciplinary actions. That power is exclusively held by the Supreme Court and the State Bar, acting as its administrative arm. (Jacobs v. State Bar, *supra*, 20 Cal.3d at p. 198, 141 Cal.Rptr. 812, 570 P.2d 1230.)

Trial courts in California are not, however, powerless to sanction attorneys for improper conduct or to control the proceedings before them to prevent injustice. Thus, trial courts may conduct contempt proceedings, dismiss sham actions, admonish counsel in open court, strike sham pleadings, and report misconduct to the State Bar. (1 Witkin, Cal. Procedure (4th ed. 1996), Attorneys, § 620, p. 731.) In an appropriate case, the trial court may exercise its inherent power to control the conduct of its ministerial officers to disqualify an attorney in an action before it. (In re Complex Asbestos Litigation (1991) 232 Cal.App.3d 572, 585, 283 Cal. Rptr. 732.) Issues of disqualification often arise when an attorney has a conflict of interest, such as when the attorney has been exposed to confidential information of a former client who is in an adverse position in current litigation. (Id. at pp. 586–587, 283 Cal.Rptr. 732; Roush v. Seagate Technology, LLC (2007) 150 Cal.App.4th 210, 219, 58 Cal.Rptr.3d 275.) "A motion to disqualify counsel brings the client's right to the attorney of his or her choice into conflict with the need to maintain ethical standards of professional responsibility." (Knight v. Ferguson (2007) 149 Cal.App.4th 1207, 1212, 57 Cal.Rptr.3d 823.) "Disqualification motions implicate several important interests, among them are the clients' right to counsel of their choice, the attorney's interest in representing a client, the financial burden of replacing a disqualified attorney, and tactical abuse that may underlie the motion. [Citation.] The 'paramount' concern in determining whether counsel should be disqualified is 'the preservation of public trust in the scrupulous administration of justice and the integrity of the bar.' [Citations.] It must be remembered, however, that disqualification is a drastic course of action that should not be taken simply out of hypersensitivity to ethical nuances or the appearance of impropriety." (Roush v. Seagate Technology, LLC, supra, 150 Cal.App.4th at pp. 218–219, 58 Cal.Rptr.3d 275.) "The purpose of disqualification is not to punish a transgression of professional ethics. [Citation.] Disqualification is only justified where the misconduct will have a 'continuing effect' on judicial proceedings." (Baugh v. Garl (2006) 137 Cal.App.4th 737, 744, 40 Cal. Rptr.3d 539.)

The question has arisen as to whether the inherent power of a trial court includes the power to sanction attorneys for bad faith conduct by requiring the payment of attorney's fees. The United States Supreme Court has held that the inherent power of federal district courts encompasses this power. (Chambers v. NASCO, Inc. (1991) 501 U.S. 32, 44–45, 111 S.Ct. 2123, 115 L.Ed.2d 27.) In *Chambers*, the United States Supreme Court began with the premise that a federal court has the inherent power "to control admission to its bar and to discipline attorneys who appear before it." (*Id.* at p. 43, 111 S.Ct. 2123.) A court's inherent powers must be exercised with restraint and discretion, and "[a] primary aspect of that discretion is the ability to fashion an appropriate sanction for conduct which abuses the judicial process." (*Id.* at pp. 44–45, 111 S.Ct. 2123.) The Supreme Court reasoned that, since a district court contains the inherent power to dismiss an action within its discretion, the lesser sanction of the imposition of attorney's fees is also within its inherent power. (*Id.* at p. 45, 111 S.Ct. 2123.)

The California Supreme Court has reached the opposite result. (Bauguess v. Paine, supra, 22 Cal.3d at p. 637, 150 Cal.Rptr. 461, 586 P.2d 942.) The California Supreme Court concluded that "[i]t would be both unnecessary and unwise to permit trial courts to use fee awards as sanctions apart from those situations authorized by statute." (*Ibid.*) The California Supreme Court acknowledged that a trial court has the power of contempt to sanction disruptive or disrespectful attorneys, and that procedural safeguards have been enacted to govern contempt proceedings. Without such procedural safeguards in place, "serious due process problems would result were trial courts to use their inherent power, in lieu of the contempt power, to punish misconduct by awarding attorney's fees to an opposing party or counsel." (*Id.* at p. 638, 150 Cal.Rptr. 461, 586 P.2d 942.) Concluding that the use of the courts' inherent power to punish misconduct by awarding attorney's fees "may imperil the independence of the bar and thereby undermine the adversary system," the California Supreme Court concluded that the power to impose such sanctions must be created by the Legislature with appropriate safeguards. (*Id.* at pp. 638–639, 150 Cal.Rptr. 461, 586 P.2d 942.) The reasoning of *Bauguess* has been extended to "any sanction occasioned by attorney conduct." (Yarnell & Associates v. Superior Court (1980) 106 Cal.App.3d 918, 923, 165 Cal.Rptr. 421 [concerned with monetary sanctions].)

3. Admission Pro Hac Vice

Most, if not all, States allow an out-of-state attorney to appear *pro hac vice*. (Leis v. Flynt, *supra*, 439 U.S. at pp. 441–442, 99 S.Ct. 698.) However, it is not a right granted by the Constitution. (*Id.* at p. 442, 99 S.Ct. 698.)

California Rules of Court, Rule 9.40, governs the admission of attorneys *pro hac vice* in California. An attorney who is a member in good standing of the bar of another state who has been retained to appear in a particular cause pending before a court of this state may, "in the discretion of such court" be permitted to appear as counsel *pro hac vice*. (Cal. Rules of Court, rule 9.40(a).) No person is eligible to appear *pro hac vice* if the person is a California resident, regularly employed in California, or regularly engaged in substantial business in California. (*Ibid.*) Repeated appearances *pro hac vice* constitute cause to deny an application. (Cal. Rules of Court, rule 9.40(b).) An attorney seeking to appear *pro hac vice* must file an application indicating the courts to which the applicant has been admitted, and that the applicant is a member in good standing in those courts. An applicant must indicate that he or she "is not currently suspended or disbarred in any court," but there is no requirement for including any history of discipline imposed. (Cal. Rules of Court, rule 9.40(d).)

While there does not appear to be a statement of the scope of a court's discretion in ruling on an application to appear *pro hac vice* in a civil case, our Supreme Court has concluded that, when a criminal defendant seeks to be represented by an attorney appearing *pro hac vice*, the court's exercise of discretion should be limited by the individual's right to defend himself in whatever manner he desires. (Magee v. Superior Court (1973) 8 Cal.3d 949, 952, 106 Cal.Rptr. 647, 506 P.2d 1023.) The defendant's choice of counsel should be interfered with only to avoid significant prejudice to the defendant himself or "a disruption of the orderly processes of justice unreasonable under the circumstances of the particular case." (*Ibid.*)

While in some jurisdictions the State Bar has no power to discipline attorneys appearing *pro hac vice* (e.g., State Industries, Inc. v. Jernigan (Fla.App.2000) 751 So.2d 680, 682), an attorney appearing *pro hac vice* in California is "subject to the disciplinary jurisdiction of the State Bar with respect to any of his or her acts occurring in the course of such appearance." (Cal. Rules of Court, rule 9.40(f); see also Birbrower, Montalbano, Condon & Frank v. Superior Court (1998) 17 Cal.4th 119, 130, 70 Cal.Rptr.2d 304, 949 P.2d 1; Cal. Rules of Prof. Conduct, rule 1–100(D)(2).) Additionally, once permitted to appear *pro hac vice*, a foreign attorney in California "is subject to the jurisdiction of the courts of this state with respect to the law of this state governing the conduct of attorneys to the same extent as a member of the State Bar of California." (Cal. Rules of Court, rule 9.40(f).)

4. Revocation of Pro Hac Vice Status

No case in California has yet addressed whether a trial court has the authority to revoke an attorney's *pro hac vice* status. Numerous other courts, however, have considered the issue, and determined that trial courts possess that authority. (See Attorneys: Revocation of State Court Pro Hac Vice Admission, 64 A.L.R.4th 1217.) The parties have not cited to, and independent research has not disclosed, an opinion from any jurisdiction concluding that trial courts lacked the authority to revoke an attorney's *pro hac vice* status.

However, the legal basis for the authority to revoke an attorney's *pro hac vice* status has varied. Some jurisdictions expressly include the authority to revoke *pro hac vice* status in their statutes or rules allowing *pro hac vice* appearances. (See Del. Super. Ct. Rules of Civ. Proc., rule 90.1 ["The court may revoke a *pro hac vice* admission sua sponte or upon the motion of a party, if it determines, after a hearing or other meaningful opportunity to respond, the continued admission *pro hac vice* to be inappropriate or inadvisable"]; N.C. Gen. Stat. § 84–4.2 ["Permission granted (to appear *pro hac vice*) may be summarily revoked by the General Court of Justice or any agency . . . on its own motion and in its discretion"]; Wis. Supr. Ct. Rules, rule 10.03(4) ["Permission to the nonresident lawyer (to appear *pro hac vice*) may be withdrawn by the judge granting it if the lawyer by his or her conduct manifests incompetency to represent a client in a Wisconsin court or by his or her unwillingness to abide by the rules of professional conduct for attorneys and the rules of decorum of the court"].) Federal courts have concluded the authority to revoke an attorney's *pro hac vice* status is included within the inherent power of a federal court "to control admission to its bar and to discipline attorneys who appear before it." (Lasar v. Ford Motor Company (9th Cir. 2005) 399 F.3d 1101, 1118; In re Complaint of PMD Enterprises, Inc. (D.N.J. 2002) 215 F.Supp.2d 519, 530.) Finally, some courts have found the power to revoke an attorney's *pro hac vice* status within a trial court's inherent power to regulate practice before it and protect the integrity of its proceedings. (See, e.g., Walls v. City of Toledo (2006) 166 Ohio App.3d 349, 850 N.E.2d 789, 792; Bank of Hawaii v. Kunimoto (1999) 91 Hawai'i 372, 984 P.2d 1198, 1213.)

Moreover, jurisdictions differ on the conduct of the *pro hac vice* attorney that will be sufficient to justify revocation of *pro hac vice* status. In some jurisdictions, the trial court may revoke an out-of-state attorney's *pro hac vice* status for any conduct which "adversely impacts the administration of justice." (E.g., State Industries, Inc. v. Jernigan, *supra*, 751 So.2d at p. 682 [this is a broad standard that would permit revocation of *pro hac vice* status for conduct that would be permissible by a local attorney]; Williams & Connolly, LLP v. People for the Ethical Treatment of Animals, Inc. (2007) 273 Va. 498, 643 S.E.2d 136, 148 [conduct justifying sanctions under statute is a sufficient basis to revoke *pro hac vice* status under this standard].) In some jurisdictions, violation of an established disciplinary standard justifies revocation of *pro hac vice* status. (E.g., In re Complaint of PMD Enterprises, Inc., *supra*, 215 F.Supp.2d at p. 531.) Other jurisdictions require bad faith of the *pro hac vice* attorney before such status can be revoked. (Baldwin Hardware Corp. v. Franksu Enterprise Corp. (Fed. Cir. 1996) 78 F.3d 550, 562 [trial court's order prohibited counsel from appearing *pro hac vice* before it in the future].) Still other jurisdictions grant trial courts a very broad discretion, which permits revocation of *pro hac vice* status for reasons which do no amount to misconduct. (E.g., Brown v. Wood (1974) 257 Ark. 252, 516 S.W.2d 98, 99–101 [not an abuse of discretion to revoke an attorney's pro hac vice status for concerns that the *pro hac vice* attorney's extensive practice would adversely affect the trial court's ability to move its docket along].) In Ohio, the courts have not yet determined the outer limits of the trial courts' authority to revoke *pro hac vice* status, but have concluded that, at the least, conduct which would support disqualification of a local attorney is sufficient to justify revocation of a *pro hac vice* attorney's status. (Royal Indemnity Co. v. J.C. Penney Co. (1986) 27 Ohio St. 3d 31, 501 N.E.2d 617, 622.) In Washington, *pro hac vice* status can be revoked for conduct that constitutes contempt, adversely affects the conduct of the litigation, or violates the code of professional responsibility. (Hallmann v. Sturm Ruger & Co., supra, 639 P.2d at p. 808.)

In this admittedly non-uniform state of the law, we now consider whether California trial courts have the authority to revoke an attorney's *pro hac vice* status. We consider the three legal bases that have been found by other jurisdictions to support such authority: (1) express provision in statute or rule; (2) implied in court's authority to control admission to its bar and discipline attorneys who appear before it; and (3) implied in court's inherent power to regulate practice before it and protect the integrity of its proceedings. California has no express provision granting trial courts the right to revoke an attorney's *pro hac vice* status. Unlike federal courts, California trial courts do not possess the power to control admission to the bar and discipline attorneys. But California trial courts do possess the inherent power to regulate practice before them and protect the integrity of their proceedings. In determining whether this power encompasses the authority to revoke an attorney's *pro hac vice* status, we look at the language of the governing court rule. An attorney appearing *pro hac vice* "is subject to the jurisdiction of the courts of this state with respect to the law of this state governing the conduct of attorneys to the same extent as a member of the State Bar of California." (Cal. Rules of Court, rule 9.40(f).) Given that a California trial court's inherent power includes the authority to disqualify a California attorney, and that revocation of an out-of-state attorney's *pro hac vice* status is, in effect, a disqualification of the out-of-state attorney, we conclude that a California trial court's inherent powers include the authority to revoke an attorney's *pro hac vice* status when that attorney has engaged in conduct that would be sufficient to disqualify a California attorney. While it may be that a California trial court has the authority to revoke an attorney's *pro hac vice* status under other circumstances as well, we need not reach the issue of the precise limits of a trial court's authority in this appeal.

5. The Trial Court's Order

In this case, the trial court ordered Attorney Sheller to pay Farmers's attorney's fees. The order had no statutory basis, and the trial court could not have imposed a similar order on a California attorney. Similarly, the trial court formally reprimanded Attorney Sheller. Again, this is not a sanction that the trial court would have had jurisdiction to impose on a California attorney. Farmers suggests that, even though these sanctions could not have been imposed on a California attorney, the sanctions can be upheld in this case as *lesser* sanctions to the permissible sanction of revocation of Attorney Sheller's *pro hac vice* status. The conclusion does not follow. Indeed, it has already been established that although a trial court has the inherent power to disqualify a California attorney, it does not have the power to impose the apparently lesser sanctions of attorney's fees and a formal reprimand. There is simply no reason to conclude that, even though a trial court has the inherent power to revoke an out-of-state attorney's *pro hac vice* status, it somehow has the power to impose every conceivably lesser sanction on that attorney—especially when the trial court does not possess the jurisdiction to impose those sanctions on a California attorney. An attorney appearing *pro hac vice* submits to the "jurisdiction of the courts of this state with respect to the law of this state governing the conduct of attorneys to the same extent as a member of the State Bar of California." (Cal. Rules of Court, rule 9.40(f).) The attorney appearing *pro hac vice* does not submit to the disciplinary jurisdiction of the California courts to a *greater* extent than California attorneys. The trial court's order was error.

However, on remand, the court can also consider whether Attorney Sheller's *pro hac vice* status should be revoked. Moreover, the trial court can consider imposition of any other sanction procedurally available and justified by the facts. Specifically, but not exclusively, the court can consider whether Attorney Sheller should be reported to the State Bar for the initiation of disciplinary proceedings. (Cf. In the Matter of Fletcher (Ind. 1998) 694 N.E.2d 1143 [Indiana Supreme Court disciplines an Illinois attorney for misconduct when appearing *pro hac vice*; attorney is prohibited from appearing *pro hac vice* in Indiana for a term of two years].)

On appeal, Attorney Sheller argues that, at most, he committed a "marginal infraction," rendering the imposition of any sanctions an abuse of discretion. Here, we disagree. While we conclude that the trial court lacked jurisdiction to impose the sanctions ordered, this should in no way be interpreted as our approval of Attorney Sheller's conduct in this matter. Attorney Sheller mailed an advertising flyer to 350 of Farmers's policyholders, seeking additional class representatives and informing them, "If accepted, you are paid for your time in an amount set by the judge." This statement is completely false; it indicates to the policyholders that they would be paid "for [their] time," in other words, that they would be paid *regardless* of the outcome of the action. We also share the trial court's concern that Attorney Sheller's explanations for his conduct were contradictory and his purported justifications were wholly inadequate. While Attorney Sheller's status as a *pro hac vice* attorney does not permit the trial court to sanction him in a manner that a California attorney could not be sanctioned, we express no opinion as to whether Attorney Sheller's conduct is worthy of the sanction of revocation of his *pro hac vice* status or any other permissible sanction.

Disposition

The order requiring Attorney Sheller to pay Farmers's attorney's fees is reversed. The petition for writ of mandate with respect to the order reprimanding Attorney Sheller is granted, and the trial court is directed to vacate the order. The case is remanded for further proceedings consistent with the views expressed in this opinion. The parties are to bear their own costs on appeal.

LAWYER ASSOCIATIONS

Lawyers organize themselves into formal groups, not only because of tradition and natural inclination, but also because there is official encouragement to do so. The Preamble to the ABA Model Rules suggests the goals sought by lawyer associations: to improve the law, legal education, the administration of justice, and the quality of services rendered by the legal profession; to promote law reform; to increase the availability of adequate legal assistance to those who cannot afford it; and to help preserve the independence of the legal profession by assuring that self-regulation is conducted in the public interest.

In the United States, lawyers have organized themselves into different kinds of groups according to geography (*e.g.*, the Ohio State Bar Association), age (*e.g.*, the Barristers Club of San Francisco, for lawyers under age 36), ancestry (*e.g.*, the Asian Bar Association), gender (*e.g.*, the National Association of Women Lawyers), and areas of legal interest (*e.g.*, the American Trial Lawyers Association).

1. Nationwide Organizations

There are dozens of nationwide organizations of lawyers. For example, the National Bar Association was organized in 1925 in response to discrimination against African–American lawyers by other nationwide lawyer groups. Many of the present activities of the National Bar Association concern civil rights issues. The National Conference of Black Lawyers was formed in 1969 and is active in a variety of legal and political fields.

Another example is the National Lawyers Guild, formed in 1936 to work for social reform. In 1950, the House Un–American Activities Committee called it "the foremost legal bulwark of the Communist Party,"[a] but that charge withered later in the decade.[b] Its present activities involve labor and immigration law, race relations, women's rights, disarmament, and prisoner rights.

A final example is the American Law Institute, formed in 1923. Its members are judges and lawyers from across the country, and its most well-known project is the Restatements of the Law, including the Restatement (Third) of the Law Governing Lawyers.

2. The American Bar Association

The largest of the nationwide bar organizations is the American Bar Association. Described by one scholar as scarcely more than a minor social group when it was organized in 1878, it now has a membership of roughly 400,000, including 38,000 student members—about one-third of the lawyers in the country. The ABA holds itself out as the national voice of the legal profession.

---

a. H.R.Rep. No. 3123, 81st Cong., 2d Sess. (1950).

b. 1959 Atty.Gen.Ann.Rep. 259.

The ABA functions through an elaborate structure consisting of its officers, the House of Delegates, the Board of Governors, and the Assembly. The House of Delegates is the designated source of control, policy formulation, and administration. Designed to be representative of the legal profession, it is made up of representatives or delegates from each state, from state and other bar associations, and from other organizations of the legal profession, such as the American Law Institute. The Board of Governors is empowered to perform, between meetings of the House of Delegates, the functions that the House itself might perform. The Assembly is composed of all members who register at the annual meeting. Members may present resolutions, and if adopted by the Assembly, the resolutions are sent to the House of Delegates for approval, disapproval, or amendment.

Much of the ABA's work is accomplished through subgroups. The largest of these are called sections; they are devoted to distinct areas of practice or professional interest such as natural resources law, public utility law, antitrust law, general practice, and tort and insurance practice. The sections have committees which focus on specific areas of interest. For example, the Section of International Law has more than 50 committees, including a committee on the law of the sea and a committee on international communications. Presently, there are more than 1,400 sectional committees.

One section of the ABA is the Law Student Division. Its goals include developing awareness of and participation in organized bar activities, furthering academic excellence, and promoting professional responsibility. The Law Student Division publishes its own journal, the Student Lawyer. Students who attend ABA-accredited law schools are eligible for membership, and presently some 38,000 law students belong to the Division.

In addition to the sections, there are approximately 70 smaller groups termed commissions, task forces, or committees. For example, the ABA Model Rules of Professional Conduct are the product of the Commission on Evaluation of Professional Standards.

ABA publications include the monthly American Bar Association Journal, which is distributed regularly to all members. Additionally, each section publishes a periodical which relates to its particular field of law and is sent automatically to each section member.

Another ABA function is to accredit law schools. The ABA sets both quantitative and qualitative standards for accreditation. For example, it requires all students in accredited law schools to receive instruction in legal ethics, and that may well be why you are reading this book.

3. State Bar Associations

Each state has a statewide bar association, organized like the American Bar Association, although not so elaborately structured nor involved in so many activities. Typical functions of a state bar association include helping the state's highest court run the lawyer discipline system, conducting continuing legal education programs for the members, establishing and interpreting legal ethics rules, setting statewide certification standards for legal specialists, lobbying and conducting other political activities regarding issues that affect the legal profession, helping make legal services available to people who cannot pay, and setting standards for lawyer referral services, legal aid offices, and the like.

A significant distinction between the national organizations and many state bar associations is compulsory membership. Membership in all of the national organizations is voluntary. By contrast, many states require that all lawyers practicing in the state belong to the state bar association. The lawyer's license to practice law is membership in the state bar, which must be renewed annually by payment of dues. This form of compulsory membership is usually described as a *mandatory* or *integrated* bar.

Proponents of the mandatory bar claim that it can be more effective in fulfilling its professional responsibilities because it speaks and acts with one voice. Moreover, this effectiveness is enhanced by the predictable income from dues, which facilitates planning and budgeting. Opponents claim coerced membership is undemocratic, particularly when the organization acts or speaks out on some political, social or other matter outside the traditional scope of the legal profession. In a voluntary organization, the dissenter can always resign, but in an integrated bar exercising this option means leaving law practice. Critics also assert that mandatory bars beget their own ever-growing and increasingly expensive bureaucracies.

Critics of compulsory bar membership have had little success in making changes from within the bar associations. They have fared only slightly better in court challenges. In *Lathrop v. Donohue,* 367 U.S. 820, 81 S.Ct. 1826, 6 L.Ed.2d 1191 (1961), the Supreme Court (without a majority opinion) upheld the Wisconsin Supreme Court's ruling that compulsory bar membership does not violate either the right of free association or free speech. However, *Lathrop* left unanswered the question whether an integrated bar may use the mandatory dues of its members to support political or ideological positions and activities with which its members may disagree. That question was answered about thirty years later in *Keller v. State Bar of California*, 496 U.S. 1, 110 S.Ct. 2228, 110 L.Ed.2d 1 (1990). There the Court held that an integrated bar *must not* use its members' mandatory dues to fund "activities of an ideological nature" that are not germane to "regulating the legal profession and improving the quality of legal services."

Having lost the *Keller* case, for the next 10 years the State Bar of California permitted its members to deduct a ratable portion of their annual dues if they did not wish to support the State Bar's lobbying and other political activities on matters that do not relate to the legal profession or the quality of legal services. *See also Morrow v. State Bar of California*, 188 F.3d 1174 (9th Cir.1999), *cert. denied,* 528 U.S. 1156, 120 S.Ct. 1162, 145 L.Ed.2d 1073 (2000) (members cannot get an injunction against State Bar's political activities that are not germane to regulation of the legal profession). Finally, in 2002, the California State Bar split off the Conference of Delegates of California Bar Associations as a separate entity with separate dues. Members of the Conference of Delegates will debate and approve proposals to change California law, regardless of their relationship to the legal profession.

4. Local Bar Associations

Bar associations organized on a local level, such as county or city, are voluntary in membership. Some are organized along subject or special interest lines such as trial practice. These organizations provide continuing professional education, act as a public voice on legal issues, serve as a medium for new lawyers to become acquainted with other practitioners, and function as social groups. Some local bar associations such as The Association of the Bar of the City of New York may be as powerful as statewide bar associations.

SOURCES OF GUIDANCE ON LEGAL ETHICS

1. State Rules, Statutes, and Rules of Court

Each state has a set of ethics rules that govern the lawyers in that state. In addition, some states have special statutes that govern the conduct of lawyers, and most courts have local rules that apply to all lawyers who appear before them. Thus, a lawyer who is beginning practice in a jurisdiction must consult several sources—the state ethics rules, the state statutes, and the local rules of court—to find out what is expected of him or her in that jurisdiction.

2. ABA Model Code of Professional Responsibility

In 1969, the American Bar Association promulgated the ABA Model Code of Professional Responsibility (the "ABA Code") as a model for the various states to follow in adopting their own sets of legal ethics rules. It was widely accepted, and within a few years almost all of the states had adopted ethics rules patterned closely on the ABA Code.

3. ABA Model Rules of Professional Conduct

In 1977, the ABA began work on the ABA Model Rules of Professional Conduct (the "ABA Model Rules"). The ABA Model Rules were designed to replace the ABA Code—that is, to become a new model for the states to follow. After extensive debate and a long process of compromise and amendment, a final version of the ABA Model Rules was adopted by the ABA House of Delegates in 1983.

The ABA Model Rules did not receive the quick, warm reception that the states had given the ABA Code fourteen years earlier. The debate over the ABA Model Rules served to focus attention on several key issues—particularly the confidentiality of client information—on which there was no clear consensus among the members of the legal profession. Roughly 40 states and other jurisdictions have adopted new legal ethics rules patterned on the ABA Model Rules, but most of those have altered some of the important rules, such as those concerning confidentiality. A few other states have revised their legal ethics rules, drawing partly on the ABA Model Rules for guidance. Finally, a few states have retained their old rules patterned on the ABA Code.

Beginning in 1997, an ABA task force called the Ethics 2000 Commission undertook a full reexamination of the ABA Model Rules, and proposed dozens of changes. Many of the proposed changes were designed to repair drafting defects and to resolve ambiguities in the Model Rules. However, the Commission also proposed a fair number of important substantive changes, including significant changes to the confidentiality and conflict of interest rules. These changes provoked heated disagreement within the legal profession. The Commission's changes were debated by the House of Delegates during 2001–2002, and, although many minor changes were adopted, most of the most far reaching changes were rejected. With the consideration and adoption of the substance of the recommendations of the ABA Commission on Multijurisdictional Practice in August 2002, and additional revisions to the ABA Model Rules in 2003, the ABA has issued a revised version of the ABA Model Rules, and it is now up to the states and other jurisdictions that follow the Model Rules to consider whether to adopt the ABA's changes.

4. California Rules of Professional Conduct

California lawyers are governed by two documents. The first is the State Bar Act, a set of statutes promulgated by the California legislature and codified as part of the California Business and Professions Code. The second is the California Rules of Professional Conduct, a set of legal ethics rules promulgated by the State Bar of California and adopted by the California Supreme Court. These legal ethics rules are currently undergoing revision; you can follow the revision process at http://www.calbar.ca.gov/state/calbar/calbar_generic.jsp?cid=10145&n=96067.

5. ABA Model Code of Judicial Conduct

The American Bar Association has promulgated the ABA Model Code of Judicial Conduct (the "CJC") as a model for the various states to follow in adopting their own sets of rules for judges. The present version of the CJC was adopted by the ABA in 2007. It replaces earlier versions, which were adopted in 1972 and 1990. We anticipate that within the next few years most states will revise their judge rules to conform in whole or in part to the 2007 CJC.

6. Advisory Opinions of Ethics Committees

The ABA and many state and local bar associations have ethics committees—groups of lawyers who meet to consider, debate, and write opinions about questions of legal ethics. Some ethics committees publish their opinions, and these published opinions offer useful guidance on how the ethics rules apply to particular fact situations. They are not binding on any court or disciplinary body, but they are often cited as authority. You can find the ABA's formal opinions and many states' opinions on Westlaw. A convenient print source of ethics opinions is the ABA/BNA Lawyers' Manual on Professional Conduct, a looseleaf service published jointly by the American Bar Association and the Bureau of National Affairs, Inc. Ethics opinions are also available on websites maintained by various state bar associations. California, for example, provides links to the full text of ethics opinions issued by the State Bar of California Committee on Professional Responsibility and Conduct, at www.calbar.ca.gov/state/calbar/calbar_generic.jsp?cid=10133&id=1129.

7. Ethics Hot Lines

Some state and local bar associations provide quick ethics research service by telephone. For example, an attorney who has an ethics question can call the California State Bar Ethics Hotline at (800) 238–4427 (toll-free inside California) or (415) 538–2150 (outside California). The hotline staff will refer the caller to the relevant cases, opinions, and other authorities, but the staff does not give advice. Similarly, the ABA operates ETHICSearch, an ethics research service that refers a caller to the relevant authorities, but does not dispense advice. The ABA charges a fee—currently $45 per hour for ABA members, and $60 per hour for non-members after an initial free consultation. You can call ETHICSearch at (800) 285–2221 (option 8); write to ETHICSearch, Center for Professional Responsibility, American Bar Association, 321 North Clark Street, Chicago, IL 60610; fax ETHICSearch at (312) 988–5491; or complete an online form at www.abanet.org/cpr/ethicsearch/form/html. When using a telephone service, a careful lawyer will keep a written record that includes the question, the response, and the identity of the person who responded.

DISCIPLINE

"Discipline" refers to the penalties imposed by a disciplining agency on an attorney who has breached a rule or statute for which discipline can be imposed. Three types of discipline are common: disbarment, suspension and reprimand (either public or private).

The mildest form of discipline is the reprimand, which is mild in the sense that such discipline does not limit the attorney's right to practice law. A private reprimand is an unpublished, private communication in writing from the agency to the attorney. A public reprimand is published—usually in publications aimed only at attorneys, but sometimes in the public press as well. It names the attorney and describes the improper conduct, thus serving both an educational and a warning function.

Suspension is a more stringent level of punishment because the attorney is prohibited from practicing law for the term of the suspension, which can range from several months to several years. Moreover, suspension may include the requirement that the attorney take and pass a legal ethics bar examination before being readmitted to active practice. Sometimes the suspension is stayed and the attorney is placed on conditional probation. For example, an attorney recovering from addiction to alcohol or other drugs may be permitted to continue practicing law but required to undergo psychiatric or other specialized supportive or rehabilitative help and to make progress reports on that help to the disciplining agency.

The most serious type of discipline is disbarment. Although disbarment typically means permanent removal from the practice of law, in some states a disbarred attorney may subsequently petition for readmission. Sometimes the petitioning attorney must retake the regular bar examination and an ethics examination to be readmitted.

California has a similar system, with the mildest disciplinary sanctions referred to as private and public reproval. The names of disciplined lawyers are published monthly in the *California Bar Journal*, a newspaper-like publication sent to all California lawyers every month.

Violation of the disciplinary rules and some statutes constitutes grounds for imposition of discipline. Moreover, an attorney can be disciplined for committing a crime that reflects adversely on his or her honesty, trustworthiness, or fitness as an attorney. [ABA Model Rule 8.4.] The crime need not be committed in one's role as an attorney, but can be totally unrelated to the practice of law. Further, an attorney can be disciplined for conduct that involves dishonesty, fraud, deceit, or misrepresentation, or that prejudices the administration of justice, or for stating an ability to improperly influence a government agency or official, or for helping a judge violate the law or the rules of judicial ethics. [*Id.*] Finally, discipline can be imposed for specific statutory violations—for example, statutes that prohibit ambulance chasing, having improper sexual relations with clients, or advocating the violent overthrow of the government. [*See, e.g.,* Cal. Bus. & Prof. Code §§ 6106.1, 6106.9, and 6151–52.]

Each state has procedural rules for attorney discipline cases. The typical procedure operates something like the following. First, an investigator looks into conduct that has been brought to the attention of the disciplinary agency. The investigator then reports to a disciplinary board the results of the investigation and recommendations for disposition of the matter. The board reviews the recommendations and then, as appropriate, dismisses the matter, requests additional investigation or issues a private or public reprimand upon consent of the attorney. Additionally, the board may file a formal complaint with the state supreme court, seeking specific action such as reprimand, suspension, disbarment or other sanctions. The supreme court then appoints a referee to conduct hearings and make findings and recommendations, which can be either for dismissal or imposition of discipline. Both the board and the attorney may appeal the referee's report, typically to the state supreme court, which makes a final disposition of the case.

How are disciplinary matters brought to the attention of the disciplinary agency? Usually the matter is reported by an unhappy client, an adversary party or attorney, or a judge. Another source is attorneys who hear about the misconduct from a non-privileged source. In most jurisdictions, such an attorney is required to report the misconduct to the disciplinary agency if the misconduct raises a substantial question about the other attorney's honesty, trustworthiness, or fitness to practice. [*See generally* ABA Model Rule 8.3(a).]

Most disciplinary agencies keep careful records of all complaints about lawyers. A case history on a lawyer's professional life is thus established. Each incident—even those where no discipline or only mild discipline is imposed—may have increasing impact on subsequent charges by contributing to an overall pattern.

In addition, most states have reciprocal discipline statutes, which require lawyers who are disciplined in another jurisdiction to report that disciplinary incident to all other jurisdictions to which they are admitted to practice law—which can result in additional impositions of discipline by those other jurisdictions. (*See* Cal. Bus. & Prof. Code § 6049.1 (a certified copy of the final order of disciplinary proceedings elsewhere, showing that a California lawyer has committed professional misconduct in another jurisdiction, is conclusive evidence that the lawyer is culpable of professional misconduct in California; "elsewhere" can include other states, separate courts, and also federal agencies).)

IN RE MOUNTAIN

Supreme Court of Kansas, 1986.
239 Kan. 412, 721 P.2d 264.

A formal complaint was filed against R. Keith Mountain, attorney respondent, by Arno Windscheffel, disciplinary administrator * * * alleging respondent violated the Lawyers Code of Professional Responsibility. Respondent answered denying he had violated his legal or ethical duty. A hearing before a disciplinary panel was held * * *. Respondent appeared in person and by his attorney * * *.

The panel made its final hearing report containing * * * findings of fact and conclusions of law * * *.

* * *

[A portion of the hearing panel's findings of facts can be paraphrased as follows. Mr. and Mrs. M, who wished to adopt a baby, contacted lawyer Mountain through a county health worker. The health worker told the M's about an expectant mother named A.S. who wanted to put her baby up for adoption. Mountain agreed to represent the M's for $500, of which $250 was paid in advance. Mountain then contacted A.S. and her grandmother.

[Mountain told the M's that A.S. and the grandmother needed $300 in financial help. The M's sent Mountain the money, and Mountain sent it on to A.S. Mountain then convinced A.S. and the grandmother that he was representing them, although they were on welfare and paid him no fee.

The grandmother decided that the M's were not wealthy enough to adopt the child. Mountain then suggested other couples who would be willing to adopt the child and told the grandmother that she would receive $5,000 under a new arrangement with a different adopting couple.

[Shortly thereafter, Mountain sent the grandmother $500 in "prenatal expenses." The record did not disclose whether the $500 was advanced by Mountain or by someone else. Then Mountain called the M's, told them that the fetus indicated some abnormalities, that members of A.S.'s family were attempting to prevent the adoption, that the adoption would probably be "messy," and that the M's should abandon the adoption. Saddened, the M's agreed not to go on with the adoption. Meanwhile, Mountain had already made arrangements with another couple to adopt the baby, and the second couple paid Mountain a total of $17,000. Mountain did not disclose these facts to the M's. About two weeks later, the M's telephoned Mountain and asked questions about the adoption and medical tests. Mountain became adamant and told the M's that the adoption was off.

[The gynecologist who treated A.S. said that the medical tests on the fetus were normal, that Mountain had never called him to find out the results of the medical tests, and that he had never told Mountain about any abnormalities of the fetus.

[In due course, A.S. gave birth to a normal baby girl. Mountain arranged to have the baby adopted by the second couple. Mountain claimed that part of the $17,000 paid to him by the second couple was for a fee earned earlier in a different matter. Mountain paid about $750 for postbirth care of the baby and paid the grandmother $5,000; there was no showing about what happened to the rest of the $17,000.

[After the M's hired a new attorney, G, to look into the matter on their behalf, Mountain sent the M's $250 as a refund of the fee advance they had given him. He did not refund the $300 which the M's had advanced to him for financial support of A.S. When attorney G asked Mountain about the adoption, Mountain at first said that he had represented the M's but that A.S. had ultimately given the baby to a second couple and that Mountain had not handled the adoption by the second couple. Later, Mountain changed his story and claimed that he represented only A.S. and the grandmother throughout the entire matter.

[The hearing panel reached conclusions of law, a portion of which can be paraphrased as follows:

[1. Mountain represented the M's and at the same time represented the second couple in violation of the conflict of interest rules.

[2. Mountain made a false statement to the M's when he told them that the fetus was abnormal when in fact he had not conferred with the gynecologist.

[3. Mountain failed to carry out his agreement to represent the M's in the matter.

[4. Mountain made false statements to attorney G about Mountain's role in the matter.

[5. Mountain served as a procurer of a baby for adoption, which is morally repugnant and in violation of DR 1–102(A)(5) and (6).

[6. Mountain collected a clearly excessive fee from the second couple.]

Respondent took exceptions to the panel's final hearing report and took this appeal. Respondent neither filed a brief nor appeared for oral argument though personally notified.

We have examined the record and find substantial competent evidence to support the findings of fact of the hearing panel. The facts support the panel's conclusions of law * * *. We conclude the panel's recommendation that respondent be disbarred is appropriate.

IT IS THEREFORE ORDERED that R. Keith Mountain be and he is hereby disbarred from the practice of law in the State of Kansas and the Clerk of the Appellate Courts is directed to strike his name from the rolls of attorneys authorized to practice law in the State of Kansas. * * *

DROCIAK v. STATE BAR OF CALIFORNIA

Supreme Court of California, 1991.
52 Cal.3d 1085, 278 Cal.Rptr. 86, 804 P.2d 711.

The Court:

The Review Department of the State Bar Court recommends petitioner Joseph L. Drociak be suspended from the practice of law for one year, stayed, and that he be placed on probation for two years under certain conditions, including 30 days' actual suspension. Petitioner concedes he violated Business and Professions Code, section 6106 (commission of an act involving moral turpitude), section 6068, subdivision (d)(failing to employ "such means only as are consistent with truth"), and Rules of Professional Conduct, former rule 7–105(1)(same)(presently rule 5–200(B) under new Rules of Professional Conduct that became effective May 27, 1989)(all future section and rule references are to these respective sources unless otherwise indicated). The sole issue in the present proceeding is whether the recommended discipline is excessive. We adopt the recommendation of the review department.

I. Facts and procedure

The hearing panel found the following facts: Petitioner was admitted to practice law in 1964 and has no record of discipline. He has a solo practice of criminal and personal injury cases and employs support staff of six secretaries, paralegals and investigators.

In March 1985, petitioner was retained by Jane House to represent her in a personal injury action against Greyhound Bus Lines, Inc. (Greyhound). As was his custom with many of his clients, petitioner had House sign a number of undated, blank verification forms. In March 1986, petitioner filed a complaint on House's behalf. When Greyhound sought discovery through interrogatories and a request for documents, petitioner wrote to House, requesting she visit his office to prepare answers to the discovery requests. Between May and August 1986, he wrote four such letters to House but received no reply. He told counsel for Greyhound, Temple Harvey, that he had "temporarily lost contact" with House.

After receiving a number of extensions for discovery and still failing to contact House, petitioner consulted House's file and answered the interrogatories himself, attaching one of House's presigned verifications. Later he served responses to the request for documents, again attaching one of House's presigned verifications.

Trial in House v. Greyhound was set for November 1986. When petitioner failed to appear, the matter was dismissed.

[In late 1986 or early 1987, petitioner first learned that House had been dead since October 1985.]

* * *

The hearing panel concluded petitioner violated sections 6106 and 6068, subdivision (d), and former rule 7–105(1). Section 6106 provides, "The commission of any act involving moral turpitude, dishonesty or corruption * * * constitutes a cause for disbarment or suspension." Section 6068, subdivision (d), requires an attorney "To employ, for the purpose of maintaining the causes confided to him or her such means only as are consistent with truth, and never to seek to mislead the judge or any judicial officer by an artifice or false statement of fact or law." Former rule 7–105(1) tracks section 6068, subdivision (d), and likewise requires an attorney to "employ, for the purpose of maintaining the causes confided to him such means only as are consistent with truth * * *."

The panel found the following facts in aggravation: Petitioner's admission that he had other clients sign blank verifications demonstrated a "pattern of misconduct"; his acts disclosed dishonesty and concealment; his use of presigned verifications posed a threat to the administration of justice (in that unverified information in discovery responses might be inaccurate, and the opposing party might rely on that information in agreeing to an "undeserved" settlement); and petitioner "demonstrated no remorse for his actions."

The hearing panel found these facts in mitigation: In 25 years of practice, petitioner has no record of prior discipline; he believed his acts were in the best interests of his clients, many of whom move without leaving a forwarding address and are thus difficult to locate; there was no financial harm to House * * *; and petitioner was cooperative with the State Bar, and was "candid and open in his acknowledgment of his wrongful acts." (The last finding appears inconsistent with the final finding in aggravation.)

The hearing panel recommended the above-described discipline. The review department adopted the panel's findings and recommendation on a nine-to-four vote (three of the dissenters felt the discipline excessive; the fourth believed it too lenient and would have imposed ninety days' actual suspension).

II. Challenge to various findings

[Petitioner challenged certain ancillary "findings" made by the hearing panel and adopted by the review department as unsupported by the record. He claimed the findings cast him in a "false light" and led the review department to affirm the hearing panel's "excessive" recommendation of 30 days' actual suspension. The court agreed, adding, "we fail to understand why the review department adopted the findings in toto, without making appropriate modifications. For example, the hearing panel (a single referee who identified himself in the panel decision as 'an insurance defense attorney') twice characterized petitioner's law practice as a 'mill operation' and four times alluded to 'findings'—unsupported in the record, and certainly inflammatory—that petitioner allowed members of his staff to 'forge' clients' names to verifications."] * * *

III. Discipline

It is well established that we exercise our independent judgment in determining whether the recommended discipline is appropriate, excessive, or inadequate. In exercising our authority we traditionally accord great weight to the review department's determination.

Petitioner insists this deference is inappropriate here in light of the unsupported "findings" described above (pt. II, *ante*) that may have improperly "colored" the review department's recommendation in this case. Even granting less than usual deference, however, we still conclude the review department's recommendation is appropriate.

* * *

The findings set out above are supported by the record and amply establish petitioner's misconduct.

* * *

The Standards for Attorney Sanctions for Professional Misconduct (Rules Proc. of State Bar; hereafter standards) make violation of section 6106 punishable by disbarment or actual suspension. (Std. 2.3.) The same provision applies to a violation of former rule 7–105(1). Likewise, standard 2.6(a) makes a violation of section 6068, subdivision (d), punishable by disbarment or suspension. We employ the standards as guidelines to determine the discipline necessary and appropriate to protect the public.

Petitioner insists that various factors in mitigation—his lengthy record without discipline, the asserted hardship on his office staff if he is compelled to cease practice even for a short period, his recent changes in office practices, the absence of harm to his client, and most important, his avowed intent to assist his client by his misconduct—make a 30–day actual suspension inappropriate.

We disagree. Discipline is imposed in order to protect the public by deterring future misconduct by attorneys. The impact of otherwise appropriate discipline on an attorney or his office staff is irrelevant to this purpose, and should not be considered by this court. Moreover, we have repeatedly rejected petitioner's assertion that his conduct is less culpable because he was motivated primarily by a desire to protect a client. (*Codiga v. State Bar* (1978) 20 Cal.3d 788, 793, 144 Cal.Rptr. 404, 575 P.2d 1186 [''deceit by an attorney is reprehensible misconduct whether or not harm results and without regard to any motive or personal gain''].) Petitioner's prior ''clean'' record is commendable, but it does not render the recommended 30–day actual suspension inappropriate.

Petitioner concedes there is no case involving the ''particular misconduct'' at issue here, but cites a number of cases in which attorneys received either less discipline than that recommended here for assertedly similar misrepresentations, or the same discipline in the face of more egregious violations. The State Bar also cites a number of assertedly similar cases, many with distinguishable aggravating facts, in which attorneys received the same (or greater) discipline recommended here. Exercising our independent judgment, on the facts of this case we are satisfied that the recommended discipline, including a 30–day actual suspension, is necessary and appropriate to protect the public and to deter future misconduct.

IV. Disposition

Petitioner is suspended from law practice for one year, which term will be stayed during two years of supervised probation. Conditions of this probationary period include: (i) 30 days' actual suspension and (ii) compliance with the terms set out in the review department's decision, including the requirements that he complete a course on law office management, and that he develop a law office management plan. In addition, petitioner shall take and pass the Professional Responsibility Examination within one year of the effective date of this order. This order is effective on finality of this decision in this court (see Cal.Rules of Court, rule 953(a)).

MULTIPLE CHOICE QUESTIONS

The multiple choice questions at the end of each of the following chapters of this book use some key words and phrases that are defined below. The definitions are the ones used on the Multistate Professional Responsibility Examination in 2009, but the MPRE definitions sometimes change. To find the current MPRE definitions, look in the MPRE Information Booklet, published yearly by the National Conference of Bar Examiners.

• *Subject to discipline* asks whether the conduct described in the question would subject the lawyer to discipline under the provisions of the ABA Model Rules of Professional Conduct. In the case of a judge, the test question also asks whether the judge would be subject to discipline under the ABA Model Code of Judicial Conduct.

• *May* or *proper* asks whether the conduct referred to or described in the question is professionally appropriate in that it:

a. would not subject the lawyer or judge to discipline; and

b. is not inconsistent with the Preamble, Comments, or text of the ABA Model Rules of Professional Conduct or the ABA Model Code of Judicial Conduct; and

c. is not inconsistent with generally accepted principles of the law of lawyering.

• *Subject to litigation sanctions* asks whether the conduct described in the question would subject the lawyer or the lawyer's law firm to sanctions by a tribunal such as contempt, fine, fee forfeiture, disqualification, or other sanction.

• *Subject to disqualification* asks whether the conduct described in the question would subject the lawyer or the lawyer's law firm to disqualification as counsel in a civil or criminal matter.

• *Subject to civil liability* asks whether the conduct described in the question would subject the lawyer or the lawyer's law firm to civil liability, such as claims arising from malpractice, misrepresentation, and breach of fiduciary duty.

• *Subject to criminal liability* asks whether the conduct described in the question would subject the lawyer to criminal liability for participation in, or aiding and abetting criminal acts, such as prosecution for insurance and tax fraud, destruction of evidence, or obstruction of justice.

1. Attorney Alford is admitted to practice before the highest court of State A, but not in State B. Client Clara lives in State A, but she runs a business in State B. She asks Alford to defend her in a lawsuit pending in a trial court of State B. The suit involves the proper interpretation of a State B business tax statute. Would it be *proper* for Alford to represent Clara?

A. Yes, if the State B court admits him *pro hac vice*, that is, for the sole purpose of litigating this case.

B. Yes, because State B cannot constitutionally discriminate against non-resident attorneys.

C. No, because Clara's business is conducted in State B, and he is not admitted to practice in State B.

D. No, because the suit involves the interpretation of a State B statute, and he is not admitted to practice in State B.

2. Lawyer Linda is admitted to practice in State A, but not in State B. Her cousin asks her to write a letter recommending him for admission to practice law in State B. Linda knows that her cousin is educationally well-qualified to be a lawyer, but she regards him as thoroughly dishonest. *May* Linda write a letter stating that her cousin is fit to practice law?

A. No, because Linda is not a member of the bar of State B.

B. No, because Linda would be making a false statement of a material fact.

C. Yes, because her belief about her cousin's lack of honesty is merely her own opinion.

D. Yes, because the bar of State B will decide for itself whether her cousin is a person of good moral character.

3. Law graduate Samuel has passed State C's bar examination. For which of the following reasons could State C constitutionally refuse to admit Samuel to practice?

I. Samuel plans to live in neighboring State D and to commute to work at a law office in State C.

II. Samuel is an active member of the Founding Fathers Party, a small but vocal political organization that advocates radical realignment of the respective powers of the state and federal governments.

III. Samuel is not a citizen of the United States.

IV. Two years ago, Samuel was convicted of federal tax fraud.

A. None of the above.

B. All of the above.

C. II, III, and IV only.

D. IV only.

4. One of lawyer Leon's clients gave him a "Little Yellow Box," an electronic device that enables one to make free long distance telephone calls from a pay phone. Leon used it occasionally to call his mother in Des Moines. Use of such a device is a misdemeanor under the applicable state law. Leon was arrested for using the device. At his trial, he denied ever having it in his possession. The judge did not believe him, found him guilty, and fined him $1,000. That same week, Leon's law partner, Leona, went backpacking in the mountains. She was arrested by a Forest Ranger for violating a state statute that makes it a misdemeanor to pick mushrooms in a state forest during certain months. Leona did not know about the statute. Leona pleaded guilty to the charge, and the judge fined her $1,000.

A. Both Leon and Leona are *subject to discipline*.

B. Neither Leon nor Leona is *subject to discipline*.

C. Leon is *subject to discipline*, but Leona is not.

D. Leona is *subject to discipline*, but Leon is not.

5. When law student Sabrina was 17–years–old, a juvenile court in State A convicted her of shoplifting a $2,500 fur coat. She served eight months in a juvenile correction facility and thereafter was under the supervision of a parole officer for one year. After her parole, she completed high school, college, and law school, and she led a totally law-abiding life. When Sabrina applied for admission to practice law in State B, she was required to fill out a questionnaire. One question asked her to disclose "all

convictions, including juvenile convictions." In answering that question she put "not applicable," on the theory that her juvenile offense in State A was irrelevant to her present moral character. The bar of State B did not learn about her State A conviction until six months after she had been admitted to practice in State B. Is Sabrina *subject to discipline*?

A. Yes, because she withheld a material fact when she answered the questionnaire.

B. Yes, because a person who has committed a crime involving dishonesty or false statement is disqualified from practicing law.

C. No, because her prior juvenile conviction was not relevant to her moral character at the time of her application to the bar.

D. No, because State B's questionnaire is an unconstitutional invasion of privacy.

6. Attorney Arner is a member of the bar of State C. While on vacation in State D, Arner was stopped by a police officer for driving a rental car 95 mph in a 65 mph speed zone. Arner offered the police officer five crisp $100 bills, saying: "Do you think we can make this little problem go away?" Thereupon he was arrested for attempted bribery of a police officer, a felony. He was ultimately convicted of that offense in State D and was fined $10,000. Is Arner *subject to discipline* in State C?

A. No, because his conduct took place beyond the jurisdiction of State C.

B. Yes, because his conduct involves dishonesty and suggests that he is unfit to practice law.

C. No, because his conduct was not connected with the practice of law.

D. Yes, because commission of any criminal act is grounds for professional discipline.

7. Client Cathcart hired lawyer Lindell to prepare an estate plan. In connection with that work, Cathcart told Lindell in strict confidence about a criminal fraud perpetrated by Cathcart's former lawyer, Foreman. Lindell urged Cathcart to report Foreman's conduct to the state bar. For unstated reasons, Cathcart refused to do so and refused to allow Lindell to do so. What is the *proper* course of conduct for Lindell in this situation:

A. To keep the information in confidence, as Cathcart has instructed.

B. To speak with Foreman in confidence, to inform him what Cathcart said, and to urge Foreman to rectify his fraud.

C. To report the information to the state bar, despite Cathcart's instruction not to do so.

D. To write an anonymous letter to the state bar, relating the facts disclosed by Cathcart.

Answers to the multiple choice questions will be found in the Appendix at the back of the book.

Chapter Three

Beginning and Ending the Lawyer-Client Relationship

■ ■ ■

What This Chapter Covers

I. Beginning the Lawyer-Client Relationship
- A. Duty to Take Some Kinds of Cases
  - 1. General Rule: Lawyers Are Not Public Utilities
  - 2. Exceptions to the General Rule
  - 3. *Pro Bono Publico* Service
- B. Duty to Reject Some Kinds of Cases

II. Ending the Lawyer-Client Relationship
- A. General Rule: Duty to Follow Through
- B. Mandatory Withdrawal
  - 1. Fired!
  - 2. Client Not in Good Faith
  - 3. Violation of Disciplinary Rule
  - 4. Lawyer's Mental or Physical Incapacity
- C. Permissive Withdrawal
- D. "Do I Still Get Paid?"

III. Frivolous Claims

Reading Assignment

Wydick, Perschbacher, & Bassett, Chapter 3.

ABA Model Rules: Rules 1.16, 1.18, 3.1, and 6.1 through 6.2.

CRPC 2–400, 3–200, 3–700, 4–100(A)(2) and (B)(4).

Cal. Bus. & Prof. Code § 6068(c), (d), (g) and (h).

Cal. Code Civ. Proc. §§ 128.5 and 128.7.

Supplemental Reading

Hazard & Hodes:

Discussion of ABA Model Rules 1.16, 3.1, and 6.1 through 6.2 [A discussion of lawyers' duties to prospective clients, covered by ABA Model Rule 1.18, is found at § 2.3.]

Restatement (Third) of the Law Governing Lawyers §§ 14, 15, 16, 17, 19, 31–33, 37, 39, and 40 (2000).

Discussion Problems

1. When attorney Sheila was admitted to law practice a few years ago, she took the Attorney's Oath in which she promised "never to reject, for any consideration personal to [her]self, the cause of the defenseless or the oppressed." Sheila's grandparents narrowly escaped from Austria in 1939 to avoid the Holocaust. Although her law practice is primarily business-oriented, she has served in several cases as a vigorous and skillful advocate of individual civil liberties. The American Nazi Party has asked her to represent one of its members who was arrested for participating in an allegedly illegal street rally in her city. The Party has ample funds to pay a lawyer, but the other skilled trial lawyers in the city have refused to get involved in the case. Sheila believes that the city's refusal to issue a rally permit was a violation of the First Amendment, and she believes that she could present an effective defense. But she is repelled by the defendant and his political beliefs. Further, she knows that her reputation and her law practice will suffer because several of her business clients are among the prominent citizens who actively opposed the Nazi rally.

   a. Does Sheila have an ethical obligation to take the case?

   b. Suppose the defendant were indigent, that the Party could not fund his defense, and that the Public Defender could not represent him because of a conflict of interest. If the court appointed Sheila to defend him, may she refuse?

2. Suppose you have recently become a partner in a small law firm that has a broad, general practice. You are attending a partnership meeting where the item under discussion is a memorandum signed by all three of the newly-hired associates. They have asked the firm to establish a policy that permits and encourages every lawyer in the firm to devote the equivalent of 100 billable hours per year to representing indigent clients. (The lawyers in the firm average about 1,800 billable hours per year.) The state pays a modest fee to court-appointed counsel in criminal cases, but there is no compensation scheme for civil matters, and the state's legal services program has been sharply cut due to lack of public funding. One of your partners has argued that to adopt the proposed policy, the firm will either have to cut its present overhead, or cut the present pay of the staff and the lawyers, or raise its fees to paying clients by about 5%. The discussion has come to a close. How will you vote on the proposal, and why?

3. From what you have learned thus far, give five illustrations in which a lawyer would be subject to discipline for accepting or continuing employment in a matter.

4. Judicial opinions sometimes state: "A client has a right to discharge a lawyer at any time, with or without cause, subject to liability for payment for the lawyer's services." Is there any situation in which the first part of that statement is not true?

5. Last August, California lawyer Simon agreed to represent plaintiff Noreen in a personal injury suit pending in California. Their fee agreement provided that Simon would receive 20% of the net recovered by settlement, or 30% of the net recovered after trial, or 40% of the net recovered after trial and appeal. The percentages were to be computed after deducting litigation expenses. The agreement further provided that in no event would Simon's fee be less than $5,000 nor more than $10,000. After Simon spent about 100 hours on the case, Noreen fired him for no apparent reason. She repaid $1,000 for litigation expenses he had advanced on her behalf, but she refused to pay him any fee. Later, she hired another lawyer who promptly settled the suit for $13,000, without incurring any additional litigation expenses. Assume that the reasonable value of Simon's 100 hours' work is $6,000. What are Simon's rights, if any, against Noreen?

6. Compare the *Holmes* case, *infra*, with the *Kriegsman* case, *infra*. Do you disagree with the result in either case? Why was the attorney allowed to withdraw in *Holmes*, but not in *Kriegsman*?

BEGINNING THE LAWYER–CLIENT RELATIONSHIP

A. PROSPECTIVE CLIENTS AND UNSOLICITED COMMUNICATIONS

Note that the ABA Model Rules contain, at Rule 1.18, a provision concerning a lawyer's duties to prospective clients, such as individuals who come to the lawyer's office to discuss a legal situation but who have not yet retained the lawyer. Does Model Rule 1.18 provide a clear answer for situations where a prospective client has sent the lawyer an unsolicited e-mail message directly (having obtained the lawyer's e-mail address from the law firm's website) or has used a feature from the firm website to make a legal inquiry? The Association of the Bar of the City of New York has issued an ethics opinion stating that when an individual submits an unsolicited e-mail message to a law firm under circumstances where the firm did not have a meaningful opportunity to avoid its receipt, the firm was not precluded from representing a client who was adverse to the individual in the same or a substantially related matter. See Ass'n of the Bar of the City of New York, Formal Op. 2001–1, available at http://www.nycbar.org/Publications/reports. The San Diego County Bar Association similarly held that such a communication was not confidential and the attorney could continue to represent an existing client adverse to the individual in the same matter. Moreover, the San Diego County Bar opinion authorized the lawyer to use, in ensuing litigation, the individual's admission made in the unsolicited communication. See San Diego County Bar Ass'n, Ethics Op. 2006–1, available at http://www.sdcba.org/ethics/ethicsopinion06–1.htm.

B. DUTY TO TAKE SOME KINDS OF CASES

1. General Rule: Lawyers Are Not Public Utilities

The general rule is that lawyers are not public utilities. [*See* RESTATEMENT (THIRD) OF THE LAW GOVERNING LAWYERS § 14, comment b (2000).] A public utility has a duty to serve anybody who wants service and can pay for it. A lawyer need not serve just anyone who walks into the office with the money in hand. Subject to the important exceptions stated below, a lawyer may reject work for any reason that suits her.

2. Exceptions to the General Rule

THE ATTORNEY'S OATH

When you are admitted to law practice, you will take an oath, as required by state law. In some states, the oath is in brief form—a promise to uphold the constitution and laws of the state and the United States, and to perform the duties of an attorney to the best of your ability. California's longer form provides in part:

It is the duty of an attorney:

a. To support the Constitution and laws of the United States and of this State.

b. To maintain the respect due to the courts of justice and judicial officers.

c. To counsel or maintain such actions, proceedings, or defenses only as appear to him or her legal or just, except the defense of a person charged with a public offense.

d. To employ, for the purpose of maintaining the causes confided to him or her such means only as are consistent with truth, and never to seek to mislead the judge or any judicial officer by an artifice or false statement of fact or law.

e. 1. To maintain inviolate the confidence, and at every peril to himself or herself to preserve the secrets, of his or her client.

2. Notwithstanding paragraph (1), an attorney may, but is not required to, reveal confidential information relating to the representation of a client to the extent that the attorney reasonably believes the disclosure is necessary to prevent a criminal act that the attorney reasonably believes is likely to result in death of, or substantial bodily harm to, an individual.

> f. To advance no fact prejudicial to the honor or reputation of a party or witness, unless required by the justice of the cause with which he or she is charged.
>
> g. Not to encourage either the commencement or the continuance of an action or proceeding from any motive corrupt of passion or interest.
>
> h. *Never to reject, for any consideration personal to himself or herself, the cause of the defenseless or the oppressed.* [Emphasis added]

[Cal. Bus. & Prof. Code § 6068.]

In addition, in California, lawyers may not unlawfully discriminate on the basis of race, national origin, sex, sexual orientation, religion, age, or disability in accepting or terminating the representation of a client. [*See* CRPC 2–400.]

WHO SHOULD PAY WHEN THE CLIENT CANNOT?

Reread ABA Model Rules 6.1 and 6.2. ABA Model Rule 6.1 is a watered-down version of an earlier draft that said:

> A lawyer *shall* [emphasis added] render unpaid public interest legal service. A lawyer may discharge this responsibility by service in activities for improving the law, the legal system, or the legal profession, or by providing professional services to persons of limited means or to public service groups or organizations. A lawyer shall make an annual report concerning such service to appropriate regulatory authority.

When the draft was released, it generated considerable heat in the practicing bar. Here is a typical comment:

> True, many people can't afford a lawyer. But that is a problem of society as a whole. It ought to be solved by a general tax to support free legal services, not by a confiscatory levy on lawyers only. Should I have to bear more than my share of society's collective problem just because of the profession I am in?

What do you think of this line of argument? Would you support an ethics rule that requires all lawyers to perform a set amount of service *pro bono publico* each year?

In 1993, the ABA's House of Delegates voted narrowly to amend Rule 6.1 to emphasize the expectation that lawyers contribute a fixed number of hours per year to pro bono activities—with 50 hours as the default number—and that "a substantial majority of the (50) hours" be devoted to serving the poor either in person or through organizations. The Rule also calls upon lawyers to make voluntary financial contributions to organizations serving the poor. More recently, the ABA Ethics 2000 Commission debated at length whether to recommend changing Rule 6.1

to make the pro bono obligation mandatory. The Commission ultimately decided not to recommend that change, but to report that the present voluntary system is not working and that the ABA should redouble its effort to encourage voluntary pro bono service. The Rule was strengthened, at least in its aspirational sense, by adding a new first sentence: "Every lawyer has a professional responsibility to provide legal services to those unable to pay."

California has no legal ethics rule concerning pro bono service, but the Board of Governors of the State Bar of California periodically exhorts California lawyers to devote at least 50 hours per year to pro bono work for indigent clients.

If lawyers are merely urged to do pro bono work, will they do it? A February 2009 study by the ABA Standing Committee on Pro Bono and Public Service found that 73 percent of the respondents reported providing pro bono legal services in the preceding year; the average attorney in this study provided 41 hours of pro bono service. Only one-quarter of the survey respondents reported providing 50 or more hours of pro bono service. [ABA Standing Comm. on Pro Bono & Public Service, *Supporting Justice II: A Report on the Pro Bono Work of America's Lawyers* (Feb. 2009), available at www.abaprobono.org/report2.pdf.]

In criminal matters, public funds are generally available to provide modest compensation to private lawyers who represent indigent criminal defendants. But public funds are generally not available to compensate private lawyers who represent indigent persons in civil matters. May a court nevertheless order a private lawyer to provide free legal service to an indigent civil litigant? What do you think of the answer provided by the court in *Bothwell v. Republic Tobacco Co.,* below?

BOTHWELL v. REPUBLIC TOBACCO CO.

United States District Court, District of Nebraska, 1995.
912 F.Supp. 1221.

MEMORANDUM AND ORDER

PIESTER, UNITED STATES MAGISTRATE JUDGE.

Before me for consideration is a motion, submitted by plaintiff's appointed counsel, Paula Metcalf, seeking reconsideration and vacation of my order appointing her to represent plaintiff in this case. For the reasons set forth below, I shall grant the motion and vacate my order of appointment.

BACKGROUND

In March 1994 plaintiff Earl Bothwell, who at the time was incarcerated at the Hastings Correctional Center, submitted to this court a request to proceed in forma pauperis, a civil complaint, and a motion for appointment of counsel. I provisionally granted plaintiff's request to proceed in forma pauperis, pending receipt of trust account statements from his correctional institution. I then ordered that plaintiff's complaint be filed.

[Bothwell alleged he switched from smoking factory-manufactured cigarettes to his own rolled cigarettes when federal warning labels appeared on cigarette packages in 1969, mistakenly believing they were safer because loose tobacco came without warning labels. In 1986 Bothwell became aware that he suffered from emphysema, asthma, heart disease, and "bronchial and other respiratory diseases." He later learned that the loose tobacco products he had been using "were stronger that [sic] [factory-produced] cigarettes and were twice as harmful and deadly."

[Eventually the magistrate judge required defendants to respond to Bothwell's strict liability and breach of implied warranty of fitness claims and granted his request for appointment of counsel.]

Following a series of motions to withdraw and appointments of substitute counsel, I appointed Paula Metcalf as plaintiff's counsel.

* * *

DISCUSSION

In her brief in support of her motion to reconsider and vacate [the order appointing her as Bothwell's counsel], Metcalf contends that my order appointing her as counsel is "contrary to law and clearly erroneous" because "a federal court has no statutory or inherent authority to force an attorney to take an ordinary civil case for no compensation."

STATUTORY AUTHORITY

Insofar as concerns statutory authority, Metcalf is correct. Plaintiff in this case is proceeding in forma pauperis pursuant to 28 U.S.C. § 1915(d). In Mallard v. United States District Court, 490 U.S. 296, 109 S.Ct. 1814, 104 L.Ed.2d 318 (1989), the United States Supreme Court held, in a 5–4 decision, that section 1915(d)[3] does not authorize a federal court to require an unwilling attorney to represent an indigent litigant in a civil case. Id. at 300–08, 109 S.Ct. at 1817–22. In so holding, the Court focused on the language of section 1915(d), which provides that a court may "request" an attorney to accept a court appointment. Id. at 300–07, 109 S.Ct. at 1817–21. The Court examined other statutes and reasoned that, when Congress wanted to require compulsory service, it knew how to do so explicitly. The Court concluded that by using the term "request," Congress was demonstrating its desire not to require such service of attorneys who are appointed to represent indigent litigants. Id. However, the Court in Mallard left open the question of whether federal courts possess the inherent power to require an unwilling attorney to accept an appointment. Id. at 310, 109 S.Ct. at 1823.

3. Section 1915(d) provides as follows: The court may request an attorney to represent any [person claiming in forma pauperis status] unable to employ counsel and may dismiss the case if the allegation of poverty is untrue, or if satisfied that the action is frivolous or malicious. 28 U.S.C. § 1915(d).

INHERENT AUTHORITY

After conducting an extensive review of authority and commentary addressing this issue, I am convinced that a federal district court does possess the inherent power to compel an unwilling attorney to accept a civil appointment. The origin and scope of that power are discussed below.

[The court here reviewed three categories of inherent powers identified in the Third Circuit opinion, Eash v. Riggins Trucking Inc., 757 F.2d 557 (3d Cir.1985) (en banc).]

* * *

Specifically, then, this court's inherent power to compel representation of the indigent exists for two primary purposes: (1) to ensure a "fair and just" adjudicative process in individual cases; and (2) to maintain the integrity and viability of the judiciary and of the entire civil justice system. These two purposes mirror the dual functions that lawyers serve in the civil justice system. First, they act as advocates in individual cases working to peacefully resolve civil disputes between citizens. Second, by their ready availability to act in that capacity, they preserve the credibility of the courts as a legitimate arm of the civil justice system. The following discussion explores the court's inherent authority to conscript unwilling counsel to achieve each of the foregoing purposes.

(1) "Fair and Just" Process in Individual Cases

As noted above, in seeking to bring about the fair and just resolution of a case, a court may exercise its inherent power to appoint individuals to act as "instruments" of the court. While it is established that a plaintiff has no constitutional right to counsel in a civil case, counsel nevertheless may be necessary in a particular civil proceeding to ensure fairness and justice in the proceeding and to bring about a fair and just outcome.

The American legal system is adversarial in nature. * * * Attorneys, because they are trained in the advocacy skills of cross examination and argument, are a necessary component in a properly functioning adversarial system. Thus, the notion that the adversarial system is an effective method for ferreting out the truth presumes that both sides have relatively equal access to adequate legal assistance from those trained in the art of advocacy.

Where one side is without adequate legal representation, the adversarial system may not be effective. * * *

If the lack of legal representation is the free choice of the unrepresented party or if it results from factors unrelated to the indigency of the plaintiff, our system is not offended. Where, however, one party is unable to obtain legal representation because of indigency, the resulting disparity of advocacy skills clearly offends the principle of "equality before the law" underlying our system. Further, a substantial disparity in access to legal representation caused by the indigency of one of the parties threatens the adversarial system's ability to produce a just and fair result.[2]

Access to legal representation in this country is gained primarily through the private market. For the most part, the market is an effective mechanism for providing legal services to those who need them. However, the market sometimes fails to provide counsel regardless of the merits of the claims at issue. Where the person whose claims have been rejected by the private market is indigent, he or she may seek representation through a legal aid organization. However, the ability of such organizations to meet the needs of the indigent has taken a serious hit over the past fifteen years in the form of reduced funding to the Legal Services Corporation ("LSC"), the federal entity responsible for funding state and local legal aid offices. In 1981, the LSC had almost reached its stated goal of providing two legal services lawyers for every 10,000 poor persons. In 1982, the LSC budget was slashed from $321 million to $241 million. Those funding cuts resulted in a drastic reduction in the number of legal services attorneys, as well as the closing of many legal aid offices nationwide. The effect of those cuts is still felt today; to attain the 1981 ratio of lawyers to poor people, it is estimated that the current Legal Services Corporation budget would have to be nearly doubled. Rather than increasing that budget, however, the current Congress is considering further cuts in legal services funding. Also being considered are greater restrictions on the types of practice which legal aid organizations can provide to the indigent. Compounding the problem of legal access for the poor is the growing apathy of the private bar to the plight of many indigent litigants. The inevitable net result of these factors is that the poor, indeed most of the so-called "middle class," have less realistic access to advocacy services from lawyers.

The foregoing discussion establishes that: 1) courts possess the inherent power to bring to their assistance those "instruments" necessary to ensure a "fair and just" adjudicative process in individual cases; 2) in many, if not most, cases, due to the adversarial nature of our system, lawyers are a necessary component in ensuring such a "fair and just" process; 3) to a significant degree, neither the private marketplace nor public or charitable efforts provide indigent litigants with adequate access to legal assistance; and 4) to that extent, such failure threatens the reliability of the results of the adversarial process. On these bases, I conclude that, when indigency is the principal reason for disparate access to the civil justice system in an individual case, a federal court does possess the inherent authority to bring about a fair and just adjudicative process by conscripting an unwilling lawyer to represent the indigent party. A further basis for the existence of such authority is set forth below.

* * *

2. Some might argue that this same reasoning applies in all cases where there is a disparity in the financial status of the parties because the party with greater wealth can hire a more qualified advocate. However, I do not subscribe to the view that a more expensive attorney is necessarily a better advocate.

LAWYERS AS OFFICERS OF THE COURT

The extent to which attorneys are linked to the judiciary, as "officers of the court" or otherwise, has been the topic of much commentary over the past fifteen years.

One of the most oft-cited federal cases for the proposition that attorneys are "officers of the court" is United States v. Dillon, 346 F.2d 633, 636–37 (9th Cir.1965), cert. denied, 382 U.S. 978, 86 S.Ct. 550, 15 L.Ed.2d 469 (1966). In an appendix to its opinion in Dillon, the Court of Appeals for the Ninth Circuit traced the history of the officer-of-the-court doctrine to English common law. The court noted that English "serjeants-at-law" were required " 'from a very early period * * * to plead for a poor man.' " Id. at 636 (quoting Holdsworth's History of English Law, vol. 2, p. 491 (3d ed., 1923)). The court further noted that, "in colonial America, there was, in addition to the common law, a more extensive statutory recognition of the obligation to represent indigents upon court order." Id. at 637. The court in Dillon concluded that "the obligation of the legal profession to serve indigents on court order is an ancient and established tradition, and that appointed counsel have generally been compensated, if at all, only by statutory fees * * * usually payable only in limited types of cases." Id. at 635.

The accuracy of the historical justifications for the officer-of-the-court doctrine extolled by the Ninth Circuit in Dillon has been questioned recently by courts and commentators. These critics of the Dillon analysis contest the use of English tradition to support the doctrine. Under the ancient English legal system there were two classes of lawyers: attorneys or serjeants-at-law and barristers. Serjeants-at-law were considered an elite class of lawyers who enjoyed the privileges of the judiciary, including various immunities. Judicial appointments were made exclusively from their ranks. Serjeants-at-law took an oath to serve the King's people and uphold justice and were required to accept court appointments to represent the poor. Critics of Dillon concede that a serjeant-at-law truly was an officer of the court; they contend, however, that "[h]e has no counterpart in American practice." Critics claim that modern American lawyers more closely resemble English barristers, who were not considered officers of the court.

The critics also challenge the Dillon court's reliance on colonial tradition, contending that there is no clear history in the American colonies of compelled representation in the civil context. These critics conclude that the officer-of-the-court doctrine may not properly be asserted as a justification for compelled representation of indigents.

The critics' challenges to the validity of the officer-of-the-court doctrine, while forceful, are flawed in several respects. First, the claim that there is no direct counterpart to the serjeants-at-law in the American legal system actually serves to underscore the void in needed representation of indigent litigants. Because there is no special class of attorneys in the American system whose primary task is to provide such representation in civil cases, and, as discussed above, the realistic opportunities available to the poor to participate in the civil justice system are, at best, extremely limited, there simply is, at present, no other source than the private bar capable of providing representation to indigents.

Second, even assuming that the historical foundation for the officer-of-the-court doctrine is not as solid as once thought, the fact remains that court-compelled appointments for indigents have been made for centuries. In fact, one legal historian has traced the requirement of indigent representation back to the ecclesiastical courts of the thirteenth century.

Third, quite apart from any role the officer-of-the-court doctrine may have played in England or the colonies, that doctrine has become and is part of the fabric of American jurisprudence.

Finally, critics of the officer-of-the-court doctrine have failed to recognize the role that the availability of lawyers has played and continues to play in maintaining the integrity of the civil justice system. Because the ready availability of lawyers is necessary to ensuring the perception, and indeed the reality, of fairness, their accessibility as officers of the court is necessary not only to the preservation of the justice system itself but to the ordered liberty of our society. For all of the foregoing reasons, I conclude that it is inappropriate to discard the officer-of-the-court doctrine as a justification for compelled representation of the indigent.

MONOPOLY OF LAWYERS

A further justification which has been advanced for the view that attorneys are obligated to comply with court-ordered appointments is the monopoly theory. Under that theory, attorneys must provide legal services to indigents without compensation by virtue of the exclusive privilege they have been granted to practice law. Regulation of attorney licensing limits the number of individuals who may practice law. As a result, those relatively few individuals who are licensed benefit financially, thereby compensating them for any financial losses incurred by representing indigents. Also, because meaningful access to the courts can be had only through these licensed attorneys, they are required to represent those who are unable to afford representation.

The monopoly theory has not escaped criticism. It has been challenged as an inaccurate portrayal of the American legal system. Specifically, critics have argued that no monopoly actually exists because every individual is free to represent themselves in court or, alternatively, to pursue a legal career. However, even if theoretically each potential litigant in the population at large had the intellectual capacity to become a lawyer, it is quite improbable that either their opponents or the courts in which they are embattled would stay the pursuit of claims while they did so. As discussed supra, meaningful access to the courts often requires representation by someone previously trained, if not experienced, in the practice of law. Thus, while the monopoly may not prevent a party from gaining access to the courts, it very well may prevent the administration of equal justice. Additionally, as one commentator has noted, "a litigant's freedom to pursue a legal career is 'sheer illusion'" due to the rigid training program and the prohibitive costs involved in obtaining a legal education.

It has been further argued by critics of the monopoly theory that, given the large number of attorneys in practice and competitive nature of the legal profession, no true monopoly exists. However, it is undeniable that licensed attorneys do benefit financially from the prohibition against the unauthorized practice of law.

Finally, critics claim that other groups enjoying monopolies as a result of state licensing, such as doctors, nurses, teachers, insurance agents, brokers, and pharmacists, do not bear an obligation to provide free services to the poor. While that is true, it misses the point. The practice of law—that is, the representation of others before the civil courts—is not simply a private enterprise. It is, in addition, a contribution to society's ability to manage its domestic affairs, a necessary condition of any civilized culture. Attorneys have a unique relationship to government not shared by other licensed groups. This relationship, which has been described as "symbiotic," places attorneys in "an intermediary position between the court and the public" where they are "inextricably linked to the public sector despite [their] dual position as a private businessperson."

By virtue of this special relationship between the bench and the bar, courts are dependent upon attorneys to aid in carrying out the administration of justice. While other professions also contribute to private gain and to the betterment of society's standards of living, no other group holds the exclusive key to meaningful participation in a branch of government and the protection of rights. This monumental difference between attorneys and other licensed groups justifies imposition of different conditions on the practice of the profession.

ETHICAL OBLIGATION OF LAWYERS

An additional justification for the court's exercise of inherent power to compel representation is the ethical obligation of attorneys to provide representation to indigent litigants. This obligation arises from the law's ideals of professionalism and commitment to public service. In addition, the local rules of this court require availability for such service. NELR 83.4(f) provides:

> All members of the bar of this court are subject to be appointed to represent indigent litigants. This is an ethical obligation of attorneys in fulfillment of the underlying precepts of Canon 2 of the Code of Professional Responsibility.

NELR 83.4(f).

The "underlying precepts of Canon 2" require, inter alia, that a lawyer appointed to represent an indigent litigant "not seek to be excused" from that obligation "except for compelling reasons." Code of Professional Responsibility, EC 2–29. Rather, the attorney is to "find time to participate in serving the disadvantaged" and render "free legal services to those unable to pay reasonable fees." Id. at EC 2–25; see also Model Rule of Professional Conduct 6.1 ("a lawyer should aspire to render * * * legal services without fee or expectation of fee to [ ] persons of limited means"). While these obligations are not expressed in mandatory terms, they clearly indicate that service to the indigent is an essential characteristic of any ethical attorney. Two aspects deserve further attention.

First, these moral and ethical obligations to provide legal services to the poor do not exist merely to prompt the practicing lawyer to be a "good" person, respected in the profession. Rather, they are a recognition of the critical role of the lawyer in ensuring the fair and just adjudication of disputes, and the need for such advocacy in ensuring the existence of the system.

Second, these obligations are not self-executing. Platitudes are nice, of course, but if these aspirational "goals" are to be achieved and to have any meaning in fact, there must be some mechanism for gaining compliance. It makes little sense to give only lip service to these ideals while the legitimacy of the court system is being challenged by other means of resolving private disputes. If our society is to have a legitimate civil justice system, the courts must be empowered to take necessary measures to create and maintain it. In a more genteel and public-spirited time, the mere suggestion by a court that a private attorney should provide free representation might be met with acceptance of the duty as a necessary means to ensure fairness and the justice system itself; perhaps that history contributes to the lack of mandatory requirements today. In any event, I view the attorney's ethical obligation to render services to the poor as the "flip side" of the court's inherent authority to provide "instruments" to ensure fairness and justice, and to maintain the relevance of the court system in resolving civil disputes. Both serve the same end: the preservation of a civil means to resolve private disputes.

A "NEW" MODEL?

As one commentator has recognized, the foregoing justifications can be combined into a cogent model justifying the exercise of inherent power to compel representation of the indigent. * * *

Our governmental system is built partially upon the concept of citizens being able to redress their grievances and resolve their civil disputes in courts. A judiciary committed to observing notions of fairness, justice, and equality before the law is of paramount importance in maintaining public confidence in that system. Lawyers are essential in maintaining the system because the only realistic way the populace at large can obtain "equal justice" is through the advocacy of those trained in the law. If public confidence in the system wanes, in time, people will find, and indeed already have found, other, less civil, methods of resolving their differences. Thus, attorneys occupy a unique role in preserving the ordered liberty included in the concept of "domestic tranquility." They are therefore vital to preserving the viability of the third branch of government.

In accordance with the foregoing discussion, I conclude that, despite authority suggesting otherwise, this court possesses the inherent power to compel representation of an indigent litigant. I further conclude that there are ample historical and theoretical justifications for the existence of that power.

However, the inquiry does not end there. A question remains as to whether that power should be exercised in this particular case.

NECESSITY OF EXERCISING AUTHORITY

In deciding whether to exercise the authority to compel representation I first note that a court must exercise its inherent powers "with restraint and discretion." The common thread running through inherent powers jurisprudence is the concept of necessity. * * * Thus, while this court possesses the inherent power to compel representation of an indigent plaintiff, the power should be exercised only where reasonably necessary for the administration of justice. In other words, the appointment of counsel must be necessary to bring about a fair and just adjudicative process.

In * * * determining whether counsel should be appointed for an indigent plaintiff, the court should consider such factors as (1) the factual complexity of the case, (2) the ability of the plaintiff to investigate the facts, (3) the existence of conflicting testimony, (4) the plaintiff's ability to present his claims and (5) the complexity of the legal issues. An additional factor * * * is the plaintiff's ability to obtain counsel on his own. A plaintiff, before seeking appointment of counsel by the court, must diligently seek out private representation. Plaintiff alleges that he "tried several times * * * to get an attorney [ ] in the Des Moines, Iowa area" to represent him. Notwithstanding plaintiff's apparent diligence, he has failed to obtain private counsel.

For reasons set forth more fully below, I conclude that plaintiff's failure to obtain private counsel was not the result of his indigency but rather a result of the "marketability," or lack thereof, of his claims. This "marketability" analysis, which I believe to be a proper additional consideration in determining whether to appoint counsel, involves an examination of the nature and circumstances of a particular case to determine whether the litigant's failure to obtain counsel is attributable to indigence, or instead to any of a number of other factors activated in the marketplace but unrelated to indigence. It requires some analysis of the market, the case, and the litigant, rather than a face-value acceptance of the market's exclusion of the litigant's claims as a true indicator of the claims' merit. Thus, the "marketability" analysis involves several steps.

The first step in the "marketability" analysis is to ask whether, realistically, there is a "market" of lawyers who practice in the legal area of the plaintiff's claims. Many indigent litigants, particularly prisoners, raise civil rights claims pursuant to 42 U.S.C. § 1983. There are relatively few private attorneys who practice in the area of civil rights. Also, there are few, if any, lawyers willing to assume cases on a contingent-fee basis where the indigent plaintiff primarily seeks forms of relief other than monetary damages, such as injunctive or declaratory relief. As a result, in many cases, there simply is no true "market" to look to when determining whether an indigent plaintiff should be appointed counsel. In such cases, there should be no further inquiry into the "marketability" of a plaintiff's claims. Rather, the appointment of counsel should rest on those other factors commonly used in determining whether to appoint counsel.

In cases where such a "market" of lawyers is found to exist, a second question must be addressed: Does the plaintiff have adequate access to that market? This inquiry is necessary for two major reasons. First, many indigent litigants are physically unable to access private counsel regardless of the merits of their claims. This is especially true where the litigant is incarcerated. The practical ability of prisoners and other institutionalized persons to communicate with private counsel is severely restricted. Second, there may be communication barriers of language or language skills; barriers of physical, emotional, or mental disabilities; or educational or cultural barriers that block understanding between attorney and client. The point is that the existence of lawyers "out there" in the private market does not establish their accessibility to a particular plaintiff. Where a "market" of attorneys exists but a party does not have adequate, realistic access to it, no further "marketability" inquiry is necessary because such inquiry could not yield a reliable conclusion regarding the involvement of indigence as a factor in the litigant's failure to obtain counsel.

If there is a market and the litigant had realistic access to it, the third step in the "marketability" analysis must be performed. That step requires an examination of the typical fee arrangements used in the particular area of the law implicated by the indigent plaintiff's complaint. Specifically, if contingent-fee or other low-cost financing arrangements are generally available in the area of law and would be feasible for the plaintiff, further examination is proper.

* * *

Once it is determined that an accessible market exists, that the plaintiff has the ability to access that market, and that feasible fee arrangements are available, the final and most important step in the analysis must be performed. The court must determine whether the market's rejection of the party's claims was the result of indigency, for, as noted above, indigency is the touchstone which authorizes the court to exercise the inherent power to correct unequal access to advocacy services. There are many factors to consider when a lawyer is approached about taking a person's claims into litigation. These factors might include, but would not be limited to, the merits of the claims; the existence of precedent to support the claims; the costs of investigating the claims, handling the discovery needed to prepare the case for trial, and trying the case; the relationship of those costs to the amount of a likely recovery, discounted by the probability of recovery; the lawyer's time available to pursue the claims and the impact upon his/her other practice obligations, as well as upon those of partners or associates; the likeability of the litigant; the popularity of the claims; and the potential settlement value of the claims. So long as the market's rejection of the claims was based on the interplay of these and other such factors, and not on the indigency of the plaintiff, the notions of equal justice discussed above are not offended and compelling an attorney to represent that plaintiff is not necessary to the achievement of a fair and just adjudicative process.

Applying the foregoing "marketability" analysis to this case, I first conclude that there was an adequate "market" of lawyers practicing in the general area of plaintiff's claims. Plaintiff raises product liability claims, as opposed to civil rights claims under 42 U.S.C. § 1983. As such, a greater number of private attorneys were available to represent him than would be for a typical indigent litigant.

* * *

I further conclude that plaintiff had ready access to that "market" of lawyers. Plaintiff is not incarcerated nor has he alleged any other substantial barriers which might have prevented him from communicating with private attorneys. He thus had the unfettered ability to communicate with private attorneys in his immediate locale and elsewhere. Additionally, many of the attorneys who work in products liability and personal injury claims do so on a contingent fee basis. Under a contingent fee arrangement, there typically is no requirement that the plaintiff advance costs, although the plaintiff would remain liable for them ultimately. Thus, despite plaintiff's indigency, there were feasible fee arrangements available to plaintiff.

The foregoing factors indicate that, unlike most cases initiated by indigent litigants, there was a "market" of private attorneys for plaintiff's claims and that, unlike most indigent litigants, plaintiff had open access to that market and has, in fact, accessed that market, albeit unsuccessfully. It thus is proper to determine whether that market's rejection of plaintiff's claims was the result of his indigency.

I conclude that it was not. The mere existence of indigency as a condition of the plaintiff did not prevent him from suggesting to lawyers that they consider his claims. Rather, he has had the same opportunity as middle- or upper-class plaintiffs to subject his claims to the scrutiny of tort attorneys. That this "market" of attorneys has thus far rejected his claims is the result of factors unrelated to his indigency. Primary among these factors is undoubtedly the enormous cost of litigating claims against tobacco companies.

* * *

Plaintiff asserts that most of the attorneys he contacted requested payment of a retainer which he was unable to afford. However, due to the enormous costs involved in this type of litigation and the unlikelihood of settlement, the amount of money required for an adequate retainer would likely be so great that even a middle-class or upper-middle-class citizen would be unable to afford it. As such, the rejection of plaintiff's claims was not based on his indigency, but rather on marketability factors such as the expenses involved and the unlikelihood of settlement.

Because it is the lack of marketability of his claims, as opposed to his indigency, which has prevented plaintiff from obtaining counsel, the notions of equal justice discussed above have not been offended. As such, it is not reasonably necessary to the administration of justice for this court to compel Metcalf to represent plaintiff. Accordingly, I shall not exercise this court's inherent authority to do so.[22]

* * *

OUTLOOK FOR THE FUTURE

Because the court did not finally appoint Metcalf to represent Bothwell, Judge Piester declined to address Metcalf's objections to the appointment based on the Fifth and Thirteenth Amendments. Although Metcalf's claim of involuntary servitude seems far-fetched, a California appellate court, in *Cunningham v. Superior Court of Ventura County,* 177 Cal. App.3d 336, 222 Cal.Rptr. 854 (2d Dist., 1986), concluded that an attorney ordered to represent an indigent defendant in a paternity action without compensation was denied equal protection of the law. *Cunningham* is flawed as a constitutional equal protection case. In *Madden v. Township of Delran*, 126 N.J. 591, 601 A.2d 211 (1992), the New Jersey Supreme Court decided these same constitutional claims against a lawyer who was assigned by the court to represent an indigent criminal defendant without pay. Nevertheless, *Cunningham* and *Madden* both express the courts' reluctance to find lawyers duty-bound to represent indigent clients without compensation.

The Supreme Court has never directly considered the constitutionality of mandatory pro bono duties. The closest it came was in the 1989 case, *Mallard v. U.S. Dist. Court for Southern Dist. of Iowa,* 490 U.S. 296, 109 S.Ct. 1814, 104 L.Ed.2d 318 (1989) (cited in *Bothwell*), with inconclusive results. Mallard was an Iowa lawyer specializing in bankruptcy and securities law. The Iowa bar operates a Volunteer Lawyers Project (VLP), under which lawyers are randomly selected for assignment to parties appearing *in forma pauperis* in federal court under 28 U.S.C.A. § 1915(d). In June 1987, VLP asked Mallard to represent three prison inmates in a § 1983 civil rights action against prison officials. Mallard filed a motion to withdraw with the district court, claiming that he was not a litigator and that accepting the case would violate his ethical obligation to provide competent representation. He also asserted that the mandatory appoint-

22. Because I decline to exercise the court's inherent authority, I need not address Metcalf's contention that the exercise of that authority in this case would contravene the Fifth and Thirteenth Amendments of the Constitution. However, the majority of courts which have addressed those issues have found no constitutional violations.

ment exceeded the court's authority under § 1915(d) which provides, "The court may request an attorney to represent" an indigent litigant. The district court denied Mallard's motion, and the Supreme Court reversed in a 5–4 decision.

The Court held that § 1915(d) "does not authorize coercive appointments of counsel," but limited its decision to the specific language of § 1915(d). If Congress had intended assignments to be mandatory, it would have used "appoint" or "assign" or other mandatory language instead of "request." Accordingly, the Court left open the possibility that a court may have inherent power to require a lawyer to represent any indigent party without compensation. The majority cautioned:

> We do not mean to question, let alone denigrate, lawyers' ethical obligation to assist those who are too poor to afford counsel, or to suggest that requests made pursuant to § 1915(d) may be lightly declined because they give rise to no ethical claim. On the contrary, in a time when the need for legal services among the poor is growing and public funding for such services has not kept pace, lawyers' ethical obligations to volunteer their time and skills *pro bono publico* is manifest.

[490 U.S. at 310, 109 S.Ct. at 1822–23.] Justice Kennedy, concurring, added:

> Our decision today speaks to the interpretation of a statute, to the requirements of the law, and not to the professional responsibility of the lawyer. Lawyers, like all those who practice a profession, have obligations to the State. Lawyers also have obligations by virtue of their special status as officers of the court. Accepting a court's request to represent the indigent is one of those traditional obligations.

[490 U.S. at 310–11, 109 S.Ct. at 1823.] The four dissenters criticized the majority's narrow and technical approach to the statute. In addition, they argued Mallard had joined the Iowa bar knowing of the implicit obligation to participate in the VLP. They concluded a more accurate interpretation of the word "request," would be "respectfully command."

RUSKIN v. RODGERS

Appellate Court of Illinois, 1979.
79 Ill.App.3d 941, 35 Ill.Dec. 557, 399 N.E.2d 623.

[Plaintiff sued defendant for specific performance of a written agreement for purchase of an apartment building and its conversion into condominiums. Plaintiff prevailed at trial. On appeal, defendant charged numerous errors, including the following.]

Defendant contends he was deprived of a fair trial because of denial by the trial court of defendant's motions for continuance and substitution of attorneys. * * * [D]efendant requested a continuance * * * two days before the previously set trial date.

In matters of this kind, the trial court possesses broad discretion in allowing or denying a motion for continuance. Denial of such a motion will not be disturbed on appeal unless there has been a manifest abuse of discretion or a palpable injustice. * * * Furthermore, because of the potential inconvenience to the parties, witnesses, and the court, especially grave reasons for granting a continuance must be given once a case has reached the trial stage.

In the case before us, the trial court denied a motion two days before trial. We cannot say the trial court manifestly abused its discretion or that its action resulted in a palpable injustice. The record does not reflect any lack of preparation by any of the able counsel in the trial court.

Defendant further contends the trial court erred in denying the motion for substitution of attorneys during the course of trial. Defendant contends that an individual has an absolute right to replace his attorney at any time with or without cause.

* * *

In the case before us, defendant attempted to discharge his attorney during the course of the trial. The attorney was at that time cross-examining the first witness. To allow defendant to substitute attorneys at this point would have been extremely disruptive to the trial and would have resulted in a significant and prejudicial delay. This is particularly true where, as here, the impetus behind the discharge of the attorney appeared to be predicated upon emotional whim rather than upon any apparent sound reason.

The [two] cases cited by defendant in support of the proposition that a client has an absolute right to discharge his attorney at all times are readily distinguishable. * * * Neither case goes to the issue of substitution of attorneys during the course of a trial. We find no error in this regard.

ROSENBERG v. LEVIN

Supreme Court of Florida, 1982.
409 So.2d 1016.

The issue to be decided concerns the proper basis for compensating an attorney discharged without cause by his client after he has performed substantial legal services under a valid contract of employment. * * *

We hold that a lawyer discharged without cause is entitled to the reasonable value of his services on the basis of quantum meruit, but recovery is limited to the maximum fee set in the contract entered into for those services. We have concluded that without this limitation, the client would be penalized for the discharge and the lawyer would receive more than he bargained for in his initial contract. * * *

The facts of this case reflect the following. Levin hired Rosenberg and Pomerantz to perform legal services pursuant to a letter agreement which provided for a $10,000 fixed fee, plus a contingent fee equal to fifty percent of all amounts recovered in excess of $600,000. Levin later discharged Rosenberg and Pomerantz without cause before the legal controversy was resolved and subsequently settled the matter for a net recovery of $500,000. Rosenberg and Pomerantz sued for fees based on a "quantum meruit" evaluation of their services. After lengthy testimony, the trial judge concluded that quantum meruit was indeed the appropriate basis for compensation and awarded Rosenberg and Pomerantz $55,000. The district court also agreed that quantum meruit was the appropriate basis for recovery but lowered the amount awarded to $10,000, stating that recovery could in no event exceed the amount which the attorneys would have received under their contract if not prematurely discharged.

The issue submitted to us for resolution is whether the terms of an attorney employment contract limit the attorney's quantum meruit recovery to the fee set out in the contract. This issue requires, however, that we answer the broader underlying question of whether in Florida quantum meruit is an appropriate basis for compensation of attorneys discharged by their clients without cause where there is a specific employment contract. The Florida cases which have previously addressed this issue have resulted in confusion and conflicting views.

* * *

There are two conflicting interests involved in the determination of the issue presented in this type of attorney-client dispute. The first is the need of the client to have confidence in the integrity and ability of his attorney and, therefore, the need for the client to have the ability to discharge his attorney when he loses that necessary confidence in the attorney. The second is the attorney's right to adequate compensation for work performed. To address these conflicting interests, we must consider three distinct rules.

CONTRACT RULE

The traditional contract rule adopted by a number of jurisdictions holds that an attorney discharged without cause may recover damages for breach of contract under traditional contract principles. The measure of damages is usually the full contract price, although some courts deduct a fair allowance for services and expenses not expended by the discharged attorney in performing the balance of the contract. Some jurisdictions following the contract rule also permit an alternative recovery based on quantum meruit so that an attorney can elect between recovery based on the contract or the reasonable value of the performed services.

Support for the traditional contract theory is based on: (1) the full contract price is arguably the most rational measure of damages since it reflects the value that the parties placed on the services; (2) charging the full fee prevents the client from profiting from his own breach of contract; and (3) the contract rule is said to avoid the difficult problem of setting a value on an attorney's partially completed legal work.

QUANTUM MERUIT RULE

To avoid restricting a client's freedom to discharge his attorney, a number of jurisdictions in recent years have held that an attorney discharged without cause can recover only the reasonable value of services rendered prior to discharge. This rule was first announced in *Martin v. Camp*, 219 N.Y. 170, 114 N.E. 46 (1916), where the New York Court of Appeals held that a discharged attorney could not sue his client for damages for breach of contract unless the attorney had completed performance of the contract. The New York court established quantum meruit recovery for the attorney on the theory that the client does not breach the contract by discharging the attorney. Rather, the court reasoned, there is an implied condition in every attorney-client contract that the client may discharge the attorney at any time with or without cause. With this right as part of the contract, traditional contract principles are applied to allow quantum meruit recovery on the basis of services performed to date. Under the New York rule, the attorney's cause of action accrues immediately upon his discharge by the client, under the reasoning that it is unfair to make the attorney's right to compensation dependent on the performance of a successor over whom he has no control.

The California Supreme Court, in *Fracasse v. Brent*, 6 Cal.3d 784, 494 P.2d 9, 100 Cal.Rptr. 385 (1972), also adopted a quantum meruit rule. That court carefully analyzed those factors which distinguish the attorney-client relationship from other employment situations and concluded that a discharged attorney should be limited to a quantum meruit recovery in order to strike a proper balance between the client's right to discharge his attorney without undue restriction and the attorney's right to fair compensation for work performed. The *Fracasse* court sought both to provide clients greater freedom in substituting counsel and to promote confidence in the legal profession while protecting society's interest in the attorney-client relationship.

Contrary to the New York rule, however, the California court also held that an attorney's cause of action for quantum meruit does not accrue until the happening of the contingency, that is, the client's recovery. If no recovery is forthcoming, the attorney is denied compensation. The California court offered two reasons in support of its position. First, the result obtained and the amount involved, two important factors in determining the reasonableness of a fee, cannot be ascertained until the occurrence of the contingency. Second, the client may be of limited means and it would be unduly burdensome to force him to pay a fee if there was no recovery. The court stated that: "[S]ince the attorney agreed initially to take his chances on recovering any fee whatever, we believe that the fact that the success of the litigation is no longer under his control is insufficient to justify imposing a new and more onerous burden on the client." *Id.* at 792, 494 P.2d at 14, 100 Cal.Rptr. at 390.

QUANTUM MERUIT RULE LIMITED BY THE CONTRACT PRICE

The third rule is an extension of the second that limits quantum meruit recovery to the maximum fee set in the contract. This limitation is believed necessary to provide client freedom to substitute attorneys without economic penalty. Without such a limitation, a client's right to discharge an attorney may be illusory and the client may in effect be penalized for exercising a right.

The Tennessee Court of Appeals, in *Chambliss, Bahner & Crawford v. Luther*, 531 S.W.2d 108 (Tenn.Ct.App.1975), expressed the need for limitation on quantum meruit recovery, stating: "It would seem to us that the better rule is that because a client has the unqualified right to discharge his attorney, fees in such cases should be limited to the value of the services rendered or the contract price, whichever is less." 531 S.W.2d at 113. In rejecting the argument that quantum meruit should be the basis for the recovery even though it exceeds the contract fee, that court said:

> To adopt the rule advanced by Plaintiff would, in our view, encourage attorneys less keenly aware of their professional responsibilities than Attorney Chambliss * * * to induce clients to lose confidence in them in cases where the reasonable value of their services has exceeded the original fee and thereby, upon being discharged, reap a greater benefit than that for which they had bargained.

531 S.W.2d at 113. Other authorities also support this position.

CONCLUSION

We have carefully considered all the matters presented, both on the original argument on the merits and on rehearing. It is our opinion that it is in the best interest of clients and the legal profession as a whole that we adopt the modified quantum meruit rule which limits recovery to the maximum amount of the contract fee in all premature discharge cases involving both fixed and contingency employment contracts. The attorney-client relationship is one of special trust and confidence. The client must rely entirely on the good faith efforts of the attorney in representing his interests. This reliance requires that the client have complete confidence in the integrity and ability of the attorney and that absolute fairness and candor characterize all dealings between them. These considerations dictate that clients be given greater freedom to change legal representatives than might be tolerated in other employment relationships. We approve the philosophy that there is an overriding need to allow clients freedom to substitute attorneys without economic penalty as a means of accomplishing the broad objective of fostering public confidence in the legal profession. Failure to limit quantum meruit recovery defeats the policy against penalizing the client for exercising his right to discharge. However, attorneys should not be penalized either and should have the opportunity to recover for services performed.

Accordingly, we hold that an attorney employed under a valid contract who is discharged without cause before the contingency has occurred or before the client's matters have concluded can recover only the reasonable value of his services rendered prior to discharge, limited by the maximum contract fee. We reject both the traditional contract rule and the quantum meruit rule that allow recovery in excess of the maximum contract price because both have a chilling effect on the client's power to discharge an attorney. Under the contract rule in a contingent fee situation, both the discharged attorney and the second attorney may receive a substantial percentage of the client's final recovery. Under the unlimited quantum meruit rule, it is possible, as the instant case illustrates, for the attorney to receive a fee greater than he bargained for under the terms of his contract. Both these results are unacceptable to us.

We further follow the California view that in contingency fee cases, the cause of action for quantum meruit arises only upon the successful occurrence of the contingency. If the client fails in his recovery, the discharged attorney will similarly fail and recover nothing. We recognize that deferring the commencement of a cause of action until the occurrence of the contingency is a view not uniformly accepted. Deferral, however, supports our goal to preserve the client's freedom to discharge, and any resulting harm to the attorney is minimal because the attorney would not have benefitted earlier until the contingency's occurrence. There should, of course, be a presumption of regularity and competence in the performance of the services by a successor attorney.

In computing the reasonable value of the discharged attorney's services, the trial court can consider the totality of the circumstances surrounding the professional relationship between the attorney and client. Factors such as time, the recovery sought, the skill demanded, the results obtained, and the attorney-client contract itself will necessarily be relevant considerations.

We conclude that this approach creates the best balance between the desirable right of the client to discharge his attorney and the right of an attorney to reasonable compensation for his services. * * *

HOLMES v. Y.J.A. REALTY CORP.

Supreme Court of New York, Appellate Division, 1987.
128 A.D.2d 482, 513 N.Y.S.2d 415.

[Attorney Donald J. Goldman appealed from the denial of his motion to be relieved as counsel for the defendants.] Plaintiff brought this action to recover damages for personal injuries allegedly sustained when she slipped and fell on a defective step at an apartment building owned by defendants. Since defendants maintained no liability insurance coverage, they independently retained Goldman to undertake their defense. Defendant Y.J.A. Realty Corp. ("Y.J.A.") is the landlord of the premises * * * [and] defendant Yori Abrahams is the sole shareholder, officer and director of the corporation.

It appears that a written retainer agreement was executed by Abrahams on behalf of himself and Y.J.A. when Goldman was hired by them. This retainer agreement provided that Goldman's legal fees would be billed periodically at the rate of $125 per hour for law office activity and $400 per day for each court appearance. The record contains Goldman's detailed itemized bill * * * for his legal services showing a balance due from these clients of $2,275.30 after crediting a payment on account of $3,500. Goldman averred that although a demand for payment of this bill had been made by him upon defendants for a period of over five months prior to his application to be relieved, defendants not only refused to make any payment (despite their financial ability to do so), but also that defendant Abrahams had verbally berated and abused him by accusations of disloyalty and conflict of interest. * * *

* * *

[O]nce representation of a client in litigation has commenced, counsel's right to withdraw is not absolute. Here, however, that is the beginning and not the end of the inquiry. DR 2–110(C)(1)(d) of the Code of Professional Responsibility states that an attorney's withdrawal from employment is permissible where a client "renders it unreasonably difficult for the lawyer to carry out his employment effectively." DR 2–110(C)(1)(f) provides for like relief where a client "deliberately disregards an agreement or obligation to the lawyer as to expenses and fees." Where a client repudiates a reasonable fee arrangement there is no obligation on the part of counsel to finance the litigation or render gratuitous services. * * * This application was supported by a detailed statement of legal services rendered which is an appropriate consideration on an application of this kind. * * * We note further that although the litigation has been pending for three years, no note of issue has yet been filed. Thus defendants will have ample time to retain new counsel if they be so advised. Nor will plaintiff be visibly prejudiced by any delay in trial attributable to this withdrawal. * * * [The motion to withdraw is granted.]

KRIEGSMAN v. KRIEGSMAN

Superior Court of New Jersey, Appellate Division, 1977.
150 N.J.Super. 474, 375 A.2d 1253.

Appellants Messrs. Rose, Poley, Bromley and Landers (hereinafter "the Rose firm") appeal from an order of the Chancery Division denying their application to be relieved as attorneys for plaintiff Mary–Ann Kriegsman in this matrimonial action.

On December 22, 1975, plaintiff, who had been previously represented by other counsel, retained the Rose firm to represent her in a divorce action against her husband, defendant Bernard Kriegsman. The Rose firm requested and received consent to substitution of attorneys from plaintiff's former attorney. Plaintiff then paid an initial retainer of $1,000, plus $60 in court costs, with the understanding that she would be responsible for additional fees and expenses as litigation progressed. In March 1976 plaintiff paid the Rose firm another $1,000, plus $44 which was to be applied against costs.

During the 3½ months that the Rose firm represented plaintiff prior to its motion the firm had made numerous court appearances and had engaged in extensive office work in plaintiff's behalf. The unusual amount of work required was necessitated in part by the fact that defendant appeared *pro se*, was completely uncooperative and had refused to comply with some of the orders entered by the court. As of April 5, 1976 the Rose firm alleged that it had spent 110 hours on plaintiff's case, billed at $7,354.50, and had incurred disbursements of approximately $242. Since, by then, plaintiff was on welfare and since she apparently did not have sufficient funds to pay the additional fees incurred, the Rose firm contended that they were entitled to be relieved from further representation. Plaintiff opposed the application before the court, pointing out

> First of all, this case, I think, has accumulated a file this thick. I think at this point, for another attorney to step in, it would be very difficult to acquaint himself with every motion that has been brought up before this court. I feel that Mr. Koserowski [an associate in the Rose firm] has been with me, representing me, for four months, and when this case finally does go to trial, hopefully soon, he has all this knowledge at his fingertips. Whereas another attorney would have to, I don't know how they can, wade through all of this, and really become acquainted with it. That's the first thing. Secondly, when I first went to this law firm, I spoke to Mr. Rose, and he knew exactly my circumstances. He knew that there were very few assets in the marriage. He knew that I would have to borrow money from relatives to pay the thousand dollar retainer fee that they asked for. They knew that my husband was going to represent himself, which would be a difficult situation. They also knew that he had done certain bizarre things, such as sending letters to people, and doing strange things; so, therefore, we might expect a difficult case from him. Yet, they consented to take my case. Of course, I don't think any attorney can guess, when he consents to represent somebody, what might occur. I imagine some cases go to trial immediately things get resolved, and my case is probably the other extreme, where everything possible has happened. I think it's unfortunate, and I think they've done a very fine job of representing me. I feel they should continue.

Judge Cariddi in the Chancery Division agreed with plaintiff and denied the application of the Rose firm, but set the case down for trial within the month. The Rose firm appealed.

* * *

When a firm accepts a retainer to conduct a legal proceeding, it impliedly agrees to prosecute the matter to a conclusion. The firm is not at liberty to abandon the case without justifiable or reasonable cause, or the consent of its client. We are firmly convinced that the Rose firm did not have cause to abandon plaintiff's case, and that the trial judge properly exercised his discretion when he denied the firm's application and scheduled an early trial date. It was to plaintiff's and the firm's advantage that the matter be heard and disposed of as expeditiously as possible. With trial imminent, it would be extremely difficult for plaintiff to obtain other representation, and therefore she clearly would be prejudiced by the Rose firm's withdrawal.

* * *

Since the Rose firm undertook to represent plaintiff and demanded and was paid a retainer of $2,000, they should continue to represent plaintiff through the completion of trial. The firm should not be relieved at this stage of the litigation merely because plaintiff is unable to pay to them all of the fees they have demanded. *See Drinker, Legal Ethics*, 140, n. 4 (1953). We are not unmindful of the fact that the Rose firm has performed substantial legal services for plaintiff and clearly is entitled to reasonable compensation therefor. Nevertheless, an attorney has certain obligations and duties to a client once representation is undertaken. These obligations do not evaporate because the case becomes more complicated or the work more arduous or the retainer not as profitable as first contemplated or imagined. Attorneys must never lose sight of the fact that "the profession is a branch of the administration of justice and not a mere money-getting trade." Canons of Professional Ethics, No. 12. As Canon 44 of the Canons of Professional Ethics so appropriately states: "The lawyer should not throw up the unfinished task to the detriment of his client except for reasons of honor or self-respect." Adherence to these strictures in no way violates the constitutional rights of the members of the firm.

Affirmed.

FRIVOLOUS CLAIMS

ABA Model Rule 3.1 prohibits an attorney from taking a frivolous legal position—that is, a position that, under the facts, has no basis in existing law and that cannot be supported by a good faith argument for extending, modifying, or reversing the existing law. Under ABA Model Rule 1.16, an attorney must refuse employment (or must withdraw from employment) if the employment would require the attorney to violate a disciplinary rule or other law. Similarly, California Business and Professions Code § 6068 and CRPC 3–200(A) and (B) require California lawyers to "counsel or maintain such actions, proceedings, or defenses only as appear to him or her legal or just," and not to take legal positions that are in bad faith or that have no sound legal basis.

Aside from professional discipline, what might happen to an attorney who pursues a frivolous claim on behalf of a client? One possibility is a suit against the attorney and client by the adversary for malicious prosecution. That tort requires the adversary to prove four elements: (1) the initiation or continuation of the underlying action; (2) lack of probable cause; (3) malice; and (4) favorable termination of the underlying action. [*See* Restatement (Second) of Torts, §§ 674–681B (1977).] In testing probable cause, courts that follow the modern view use an objective standard—would a reasonable attorney have pursued the claim? But some courts still use a subjective standard—did this attorney know that the claim was frivolous? The malice element can be established by proof of actual ill will or proof that the claim was commenced or pursued for an improper purpose; it can also be inferred from the lack of probable cause.

Another possibility is the imposition of sanctions in the underlying action against the offending attorney, or the client, or both. In recent years Rule 11 of the Federal Rules of Civil Procedure has become a popular device for imposing sanctions in civil actions in the federal courts. [*See generally* Schwarzer, *Rule 11 Revisited,* 101 Harv.L.Rev. 1013 (1988).] Rule 11 requires every pleading and other court paper to be personally signed by an attorney (or by a litigant representing him or herself). In "presenting" such a paper to the court (by signing, filing, submitting or advocating), the attorney or party certifies to the best of his or her "knowledge, information, and belief, formed after a [reasonable inquiry]": (1) the paper is not being presented for any improper purpose, such as harassment or to run up an opponent's expenses; (2) that the claims, defenses and other legal contentions are warranted by existing law or by a nonfrivolous argument for a change or reversal in existing law or the establishment of new law; (3) that the factual allegations have evidentiary support or are likely to have support after further investigation or discovery; and (4) that factual denials are likewise warranted by the evidence or identified as reasonably based on lack of information or belief. From 1983 through 1993 sanctions for a violation of Rule 11 were mandatory, but now they are once again discretionary. The sanctions must be no more than necessary for deterrence, and they should not usually result in shifting attorney fee expenses between the parties. Rule 11 contains additional safeguards against surprise sanction requests and a 21–day period to withdraw a paper challenged as violating the Rule.

But Rule 11 is not the only sanctioning authority available to the courts. For example, 28 U.S.C.A. § 1927 (2000) states that an attorney or other person who "so multiplies the proceedings in any case unreasonably and vexatiously" may be ordered personally to pay the "excess costs, expenses, and attorney fees" reasonably incurred by the victim. Frivolous federal court appeals can be sanctioned under Federal Rule of Appellate Procedure 38 and 28 U.S.C.A. § 1912 (2000). Even broader power to sanction lawyers for taking frivolous legal positions can be found in the "inherent power" doctrine. In *Chambers v. NASCO, Inc.,* 501 U.S. 32, 111 S.Ct. 2123, 115 L.Ed.2d 27 (1991), the Supreme Court ruled that federal courts have the inherent power to sanction bad faith conduct by lawyers and parties whether the conduct at issue is covered by one of the other sanctioning provisions or not. [*See generally* Gregory P. Joseph, *Rule 11 is Only the Beginning,* A.B.A.J., May 1, 1988, at 62–65.] Similar sanction provisions are available under state law rules or statutes. [*See, e.g.,* Cal.Code Civ.Proc. §§ 128.5 (court may order party or party's attorney to pay another party's reasonable expenses, including attorney's fees, incurred "as a result of bad-faith actions or tactics that are frivolous or solely intended to cause unnecessary delay") and 128.7 (the substantial equivalent of the amended Federal Rule 11).]

MULTIPLE CHOICE QUESTIONS

Answer these questions using the definitions found at the end of Chapter Two.

1. For many years, lawyer Snyder has represented a professional football team, the Raptors, in business law matters. On the team's behalf, Snyder has filed a breach of contract case against the City Board of Commissioners concerning the stadium that the city leases to the Raptors. Snyder is counsel of record in the suit, and he has conducted all of the discovery for the Raptors. The trial date is fast approaching, and the Raptors' owners have retained a famous trial lawyer, Marvin Slick, to serve as Snyder's co-counsel and to do the actual trial work. Although Snyder envies Slick's win-loss record, he regards Slick as little more than a highly-educated con artist with whom he cannot possibly work. Which of the following *may* Snyder do?

A. Immediately seek the court's permission to withdraw from the case.

B. Promptly instruct the team owners to terminate their arrangement with Slick.

C. Ask the team owners to consent to his withdrawal, if he believes that is in their best interests.

D. Advise Slick to withdraw, if Snyder believes that is in the best interests of the team owners.

2. Attorney Arbuckle is admitted to practice in State A. The State A Rules of Court require court permission before an attorney can withdraw from a pending case. The courts of State A have statutory authority to impose litigation sanctions on lawyers who violate the Rules of Court. State A does not recognize attorney retaining liens on client's funds, property, or litigation files (that is, an attorney cannot keep these items to secure payment of his or her fee). Arbuckle agreed to defend Clauzoff in a civil action for theft of the plaintiff's trade secrets. Clauzoff agreed to pay Arbuckle $100 per hour, and he gave Arbuckle a $10,000 advance for litigation expenses. Three times, the plaintiff scheduled the taking of Clauzoff's deposition, and all three times Clauzoff failed to show up. Further, despite repeated promises, Clauzoff failed to send Arbuckle some documents that Arbuckle needed in order to draft responses to the plaintiff's interrogatories. After Arbuckle put in 40 hours on the case, he billed Clauzoff $4,000, but Clauzoff refused to pay the fee bill. Finally, Arbuckle decided to have nothing further to do with the case; when plaintiff's counsel telephoned, Arbuckle told her that he had resigned as the lawyer for Clauzoff. Clauzoff asked Arbuckle to hand over the litigation files and to refund the unspent part of the $10,000 expense advance, but Arbuckle refused both requests. Which of the following statements are correct?

I. Arbuckle is *subject to litigation sanctions* for stepping out of the case without the court's consent.

II. Arbuckle is *subject to discipline* for withdrawing from the case without adequate grounds.

III. Arbuckle is *subject to discipline* for refusing to hand over the litigation files to Clauzoff.

IV. Arbuckle is *subject to discipline* for refusing to refund the unspent part of the expense advance.

A. All of the above.

B. I and IV only.

C. II, III, and IV only.

D. I, III, and IV only.

3. Jason P. Worthington III is among the wealthiest men in New York society. When his son was arrested for selling illegal drugs to his prep school classmates, Worthington sought the legal services of the prestigious old firm of Bradbury & Crosswell. The Bradbury firm practices almost nothing but securities and banking law. For which of the following reasons *may* the Bradbury firm decline employment in the case?

I. That Worthington is not among the firm's regular clients.

II. That the firm is not experienced in criminal litigation.

III. That Worthington can obtain better service at lower fees from lawyers with more experience in criminal litigation.

IV. That the firm does not want to take time away from its regular work for a matter such as this one.

A. All of the above.

B. None of the above.

C. III only.

D. II only.

4. When attorney Hodges graduated from law school three years ago, she opened a solo practice in a small rural community close to the state's major prison. Her primary interests are family law and real estate law. Her practice is growing very slowly, despite her long work hours. She is barely able to make financial ends meet. The presiding judge of the local State District Court has asked her to serve as court-appointed counsel in a civil action that was originally filed *in propria persona* by an indigent inmate of the prison. From the roughly drawn complaint, the presiding judge believes there may be some merit in the inmate's allegations of brutality by some of the guards and gross neglect on the part of the warden. State law allows attorney fees to be awarded to a plaintiff in a civil action of this type, but only if the plaintiff is victorious. Attorney Hodges realizes that she will not be paid for her work if she loses the case, and she is very concerned about the financial loss she may suffer if she

takes time away from her regular practice. Further, she is worried about harming her reputation because the warden and many prison employees form the nucleus of her community. Which of the following statements are correct?

I. She *may* decline to serve on the ground that her practice is primarily in the fields of real estate and family law.

II. She *may* decline to serve if she believes in good faith that she cannot reasonably take the financial risk involved.

III. She *may* decline to serve if she believes in good faith that to serve would seriously injure her reputation in the community.

IV. She *may* decline to serve if she believes in good faith that some of her present clients will be offended if she takes the case.

A. All of the above.

B. None of the above.

C. II only.

D. I, II, and IV only.

5. Lawyer Yeager has been retained by the officers of Amalgamated Finishers and Patternworkers Union, Local 453, to draft a new set of bylaws for the local. Yeager strongly disagrees with one of the provisions the officers want included in the new bylaws. The provision would deny members of the local the right to vote on some issues that involve the expenditure of union funds. Although Yeager believes that the provision is lawful and consistent with the national union charter, she believes it would be unwise and inconsistent with the best interests of the members of the local. If the union can obtain other counsel without serious loss, *may* Yeager withdraw from the matter?

A. Yes, but only if she obtains the consent of her client.

B. Yes, because her client is asking her to do something that is against her best judgment.

C. No, because she is obliged to carry out the lawful objectives of her client.

D. No, unless her client has breached the agreement under which she agreed to perform the work.

6. For a century or more, the commercial fishing industry in Northport has been dominated by two feuding clans, the VonRutz family and the McCabe family. The McCabes hired lawyer Lang to sue the VonRutzes in federal court for predatory pricing in violation of the federal antitrust laws. The complaint alleges that the VonRutzes have been selling their fish below cost with the intent of driving the McCabes out of business, which would give the VonRutzes monopoly power in the Northport area. The information that was available to Lang when he drafted the complaint supported the "below cost" allegation. During pretrial discovery, however, it became obvious that the Von Rutzes never sold their fish below their

"average total cost." Under the applicable law, that means that they could not possibly have been engaged in predatory pricing, and no good faith argument can be made for changing that law. Nevertheless, the McCabes instructed Lang to move for summary judgment, explaining: "The Von-Rutzes caused misery for our fathers and our grandfathers and our great grandfathers. Winning isn't important—we just want to remind those rotten VonRutzes that it's expensive to mess with the McCabes." If Lang follows his clients' instruction to move for summary judgment:

A. Lang will not be *subject to discipline* because he is obliged to follow his clients' instructions on matters that affect the clients' substantial legal rights.

B. Lang will be *subject to litigation sanctions* because discovery has revealed that his clients' claim is frivolous.

C. Lang will be *subject to civil liability* for malicious prosecution, no matter what the ultimate outcome of the predatory pricing case.

D. Lang will be not be *subject to discipline* because he did not know until pretrial discovery that his clients' claim was frivolous.

Answers to the multiple choice questions appear in the Appendix at the back of the book.

CHAPTER FOUR

ADVERTISING AND SOLICITATION

■ ■ ■

What This Chapter Covers

I. **Historical Summary**
II. **The *Bates* case**
III. **Historical Summary, Continued**
IV. **The *Went For It* case**

Reading Assignment

Wydick, Perschbacher, & Bassett, Chapter 4.

ABA Model Rules 7.1 through 7.5.

CRPC 1–320(B)-(C); 1–400; California Standards for Attorney Communications (printed after CRPC 1–400).

Skim Cal.Bus. & Prof. Code §§ 6150–54; 6157–6159.2.

Supplemental Reading

Hazard & Hodes:

Discussion of ABA Model Rules 7.1 through 7.5.

Discussion Problems

1. Suppose you have just opened your law practice in a town where you do not know many people. In which of the following ways may you seek to build your clientele?

a. May you join a social club for the sole purpose of meeting new people and luring them as clients?

b. May you call on other lawyers at their offices and let them know that you are willing to take on work that they are too busy to handle?

c. May you volunteer to give a seminar on estate planning for the local chapter of Young Businesswomen of America, hoping to get legal business from some of those who attend?

d. May you list your name with the local court as a person who is willing to take court-appointed cases? May you contribute to the re-election campaign fund of a local judge, hoping to secure good court appointments from the judge?

e. May you list your name with the lawyer referral service run by the local bar association? How does such a lawyer referral service operate?

f. May you place advertisements for your services? In what media? What restrictions are there on the content of your advertising?

g. May you publish a brochure that describes your law practice, states the kinds of matters you handle, and provides a schedule of the fees you charge for a variety of routine legal services? May you put the same information on a website? May you use www.winbig.com as your site address?

h. May you advertise yourself as a "Super Lawyer" or "Best Lawyer" when you have been included in a "Super Lawyers" poll for a magazine advertising supplement or in "Best Lawyers in America"?

2. Suppose that the Surgeon General has recently determined that prolonged exposure to a chemical known as DNXP causes a type of blood disease in humans. DNXP is used in the manufacture of certain types of plastics, and many plastics workers have contracted the disease. Lawyer Lovette practices personal injury and workers' compensation law in a town that has four plastics factories. She would like to represent afflicted plastics workers who wish to bring legal proceedings against their employers and the manufacturers of DNXP.

a. May she put an ad in the local newspaper, informing plastics workers of their legal rights respecting exposure to DNXP and inviting interested persons to contact her?

b. The town business directory provides a separate directory listing of all plastics workers, giving their names, postal addresses, e-mail addresses, and telephone numbers. May Lovette send an informative letter via the postal service to each plastics worker, inviting the worker to contact her for further information? Is your answer the same if Lovette uses e-mail rather than the postal service?

c. May Lovette hire a team of telephone callers who will use the business directory to phone each plastics worker, give a brief description of the DNXP problem, and invite the worker to contact Lovette for more information?

d. May Lovette stand on the public sidewalk outside the gates of one of the plastics factories at quitting time and pass out handbills that state her willingness to represent workers in DNXP cases? May she initiate conversations with workers on that subject? May she initiate such communications in a real-time Internet chatroom?

3. On your way down the courthouse hall after a hearing, you saw a tired-looking woman holding a crying infant. She was obviously confused and needed help. When you spoke to her, she handed you a paper and asked in halting English where she was supposed to go. The paper was a summons to appear that morning in an unlawful detainer action filed by her landlord. When you responded to her in her native language, her face broke into a wide smile. You briefly explained to her the nature of an unlawful detainer hearing, and you asked if she had a lawyer. When she said no, you offered to represent her at the hearing for a modest fee. Was your offer proper? Would it be proper if you had offered to represent her for free?[a]

HISTORICAL SUMMARY

A. ADVERTISING

Back in the 1800s, lawyers in the United States sometimes advertised their services in newspapers. But when the American Bar Association adopted its original Canons of Professional Ethics in 1908, Canon 27 said:

> The most worthy and effective advertisement possible, even for a young lawyer, is the establishment of a well-merited reputation for professional capacity and fidelity to trust. This cannot be forced, but must be the outcome of character and conduct. * * * [S]olicitation of business by circulars or advertisements, or by personal communications, or interviews not warranted by personal relations, is unprofessional. * * * Indirect advertisement for business by furnishing or inspiring newspaper comments concerning causes in which the lawyer has been or is engaged * * * the importance of the lawyer's positions, and all other like self-laudation, defy the traditions and lower the tone of our high calling, and are intolerable.

In short, lawyers were to be passive receivers of legal business, not active seekers of it. A person who needed a lawyer could simply ask a friend or neighbor to recommend a good one, and in that fashion the trade of honest, competent lawyers would grow and prosper.

Over the years, Canon 27 was amended and re-amended to draw ever-finer distinctions about the precise ways in which lawyers could ethically hold themselves out to the public. A lawyer could have a "shingle," a small, dignified sign to mark the office door. A lawyer could be identified in a "reputable law list," a directory readily available to other lawyers (but not to ordinary citizens) that provided biographic information. A lawyer could make "customary use" of "simple professional cards," and

a. Our thanks to Professor Monroe Freedman of the Hofstra University School of Law for inspiring this hypothetical question. He discusses the hypothetical in Monroe Freedman & Abbe Smith, *Understanding Lawyers' Ethics* 357 (3d ed. 2004). *See also* Deborah L. Rhode, *Solicitation*, 36 J. Legal Educ. 317 (1986).

could put limited kinds of information on a "letterhead," the formal stationery used in the office. Patent lawyers, trademark lawyers, and proctors in admiralty could so designate themselves in public communications, but ordinary lawyers could not tell the public what kinds of law they practiced.

As the complexity of the rules grew, so did the ingenuity of the lawyers who sought to evade them. The resulting tension created considerable work for those members of the profession who wrote ethics opinions and imposed discipline on the miscreants. When discipline was imposed, it was customarily coupled with a thorough denunciation. Thus, in censuring one Leon A. Berezniak, Esq., the Supreme Court of Illinois wrote:

> The advertisements of respondent are very obnoxious and disgusting, not only because they are gotten up after the manner of quack doctors and itinerant vendors of patent medicines and other cure-alls, but because of the fact that they contain statements that cast reflections upon the common honesty, proficiency, and decency of the profession generally of which he insists he is a distinguished member.[b]

Thus, in the period between 1910 and 1975, the bar and the courts created a remarkable body of law and lore, of which the following is but a small sample:

- A New York attorney was censured for (among other things) sending typewritten letters to businessmen with whom he had no prior relationship, inviting them to use him for their collection claims and other legal work.[c]
- A California attorney was censured for (among other things) putting signs on his house to advertise reduced fees for his services as lawyer, notary public, and tax consultant.[d]
- A Nebraska attorney was suspended for putting a classified advertisement in the local newspapers, offering to do divorces for "$15 and costs."[e]
- It was deemed unethical for an attorney-physician to state on his letterhead that he was both a lawyer and a doctor, and it was likewise unethical for him to send out formal announcements that he had opened an office for the practice of both professions.[f]
- It was deemed unethical for an attorney to have his name listed in boldface type in the telephone book.[g]

---

b. *People ex rel. Chicago Bar Association v. Berezniak*, 292 Ill. 305, 127 N.E. 36 (1920).

c. *In re Gray*, 184 App.Div. 822, 172 N.Y.S. 648 (1918).

d. *Libarian v. State Bar*, 21 Cal.2d 862, 136 P.2d 321 (1943) (large signs); 25 Cal.2d 314, 153 P.2d 739 (1944) (small signs).

e. *State ex rel. Hunter v. Crocker*, 132 Neb. 214, 271 N.W. 444 (1937).

f. ABA Formal Op. 183 (1938).

g. ABA Formal Op. 284 (1951).

- An Arizona attorney was censured for (among other things) advertising by means of matchbooks printed with his name and profession.[h]
- It was deemed unethical for an attorney to send Christmas cards that mentioned his profession (except cards that merely pictured the scales of justice or a lawyer dressed as Santa Claus), and it was deemed unethical to send any sort of Christmas card to a present client, or to another lawyer, with whom the sender had no close personal or social relationship.[i]
- It was said that an attorney (hypothetically named Doe) could ethically erect a building and call it the "Doe Building," but not the "Doe Law Building" (nor even plain "Law Building," unless it were to be inhabited by numerous other lawyers).[j]
- It was said that an attorney could ethically allow his name to be put on a sign in the lobby of an office building, if the sign were used as a building directory, albeit a sign with a light.[k] However, a New York attorney was censured for using a neonlit sign in his office window.[l]
- A California attorney, who was called the "King of Torts," was suspended for allowing his name to be used in advertising an expensive Scotch whisky, where the court inferred that his intent was to promote his law practice as well as the whisky.[m]

B. SOLICITATION

Client-getting activity that involves personal contact (face-to-face contact, live telephone contact, or—under the ABA Model Rules—real-time electronic contact) which is initiated by a lawyer (or the lawyer's agent) and a specific potential client is called "solicitation," to distinguish it from "advertising," which is general communication with the public at large. In the most blatant form of solicitation, "ambulance-chasing," the lawyer hires agents to urge injured people to employ the lawyer to represent them.[n]

Canon 28 of the 1908 ABA Canons of Professional Ethics was specifically directed at solicitation. It warned lawyers not to stir up litigation, nor to volunteer advice to a stranger to bring a lawsuit, nor to seek out injured persons or defects in land titles in the hope of gaining employment, nor to pay prison guards or hospital attendants for referring potential clients, nor to hire runners or agents to do any such dirty work.

---

h. *In re Maltby*, 68 Ariz. 153, 202 P.2d 902 (1949).

i. ABA Formal Op. 309 (1963).

j. ABA Informal Op. 441 (1961).

k. ABA Informal Op. 800 (1964).

l. *In re Duffy*, 19 A.D.2d 177, 242 N.Y.S.2d 665 (1963).

m. *Belli v. State Bar of California*, 10 Cal.3d 824, 112 Cal.Rptr. 527, 519 P.2d 575 (1974).

n. *See* Annot., "*Disbarment—Ambulance Chasing*," 67 A.L.R.2d 859 (1959).

Solicitation has traditionally been punished more harshly than advertising,[o] and for better reason. The bar and courts are concerned with the effect of solicitation on those solicited—especially unsophisticated lay people, when under stress and unable to exercise careful, informed judgment about the hiring of a lawyer.

C. THE FORCES OF CHANGE—ANTITRUST AND THE FIRST AMENDMENT

The ABA Model Code of Professional Responsibility was promulgated in 1969; it was the predecessor to the ABA Model Rules. The ABA Code came complete with bans on advertising and solicitation. But simultaneously, it spoke of a lawyer's ethical obligation to help lay people recognize legal problems and to assure that legal service was available to all who needed it. Soon the bar began to feel the tension between these two positions.

In the early 1970s, distinguished members of the bar began to argue that lay people could not select a lawyer intelligently unless they were given more information than the ABA Code allowed. On another front, antitrust experts began to ponder the anti-competitive effects of the lawyer advertising ban. Ordinary commercial competitors could not lawfully agree to refrain from advertising.[p] Was the mantle of professionalism enough to protect lawyers from the Sherman Antitrust Act? The United States Justice Department thought not, and in 1976 it sued the American Bar Association as a conspiracy in restraint of trade.[q]

D. THE *BATES* CASE

In the following pages, you will read *Bates v. State Bar of Arizona,* 433 U.S. 350, 97 S.Ct. 2691, 53 L.Ed.2d 810 (1977), which concerned two Arizona lawyers who violated Arizona's ban on lawyer advertising. The U.S. Supreme Court ruled that the advertising ban was immune from attack under the Sherman Antitrust Act because the ban had been promulgated by an arm of the state government, the Arizona Supreme Court. However, *Bates* holds that the First Amendment commercial speech doctrine protects attorney advertising that is truthful and not misleading. Ironically, the Court based its First Amendment conclusion on arguments that carry the strong flavor of antitrust: free competition among lawyers raises quality and reduces prices, and competition works best when consumers are well informed about their choices.

---

o. *Compare id. with* Annot., "*Attorney Advertising—Discipline*," 39 A.L.R.2d 1055 (1955).

p. *United States v. Gasoline Retailers Association, Inc.*, 285 F.2d 688 (7th Cir.1961) (agreement among gas stations not to post prices on curb signs held illegal per se).

q. *United States v. American Bar Association*, Civil No. 76–1182 (D.D.C.1976). The suit was dismissed after the Supreme Court decision in *Bates v. State Bar of Arizona*, 433 U.S. 350, 97 S.Ct. 2691, 53 L.Ed.2d 810 (1977). *See* Trade Reg. Rptr., 1970–79 U.S. Antitrust Cases 53, 658 (1980).

BATES v. STATE BAR OF ARIZONA

Supreme Court of the United States, 1977.
433 U.S. 350, 97 S.Ct. 2691, 53 L.Ed.2d 810.

[In 1974, Arizona lawyers Bates and O'Steen opened a "legal clinic" to provide low cost service to people of moderate means. They did only "routine" legal work, and they made heavy use of paralegal assistants, standard legal forms, and modern office equipment. In 1976, they sought to increase their volume by running the newspaper ad that you see on the next page. When the State Bar of Arizona tried to discipline them, they appealed to the United States Supreme Court, claiming violations of the Sherman Act and the First Amendment free speech clause (as applied to the states through the Fourteenth Amendment). The Court rejected the Sherman Act argument because Arizona's advertising rules had been duly approved by the Arizona Supreme Court—the Sherman Act does not reach a restraint of trade that is conceived and supervised by a state government. But the Court held that lawyers' "commercial speech" is entitled to some protection under the First Amendment. As you will see from the following portions of the majority opinion, the Court's First Amendment analysis is, ironically, heavily seasoned with antitrust.]

The issue presently before us is a narrow one. First, we need not address the peculiar problems associated with advertising claims relating to the *quality* of legal services. Such claims probably are not susceptible of precise measurement or verification and, under some circumstances, might well be deceptive or misleading to the public, or even false. Appellee does not suggest, nor do we perceive, that appellants' advertisement contained claims, extravagant or otherwise, as to the quality of services. Accordingly, we leave that issue for another day. Second, we also need not resolve the problems associated with in-person solicitation of clients—at the hospital room or the accident site, or in any other situation that breeds undue influence—by attorneys or their agents or "runners." Activity of that kind might well pose dangers of overreaching and misrepresentation not encountered in newspaper announcement advertising. Hence, this issue also is not before us. Third, we note that appellee's criticism of advertising by attorneys does not apply with much force to some of the basic factual content of advertising: information as to the attorney's name, address, and telephone number, office hours, and the like. The American Bar Association itself has a provision in its current Code of Professional Responsibility that would allow the disclosure of such information, and more in the classified section of the telephone directory. DR 2–102(A)(6) (1976). We recognize, however, that an advertising diet limited to such spartan fare would provide scant nourishment.

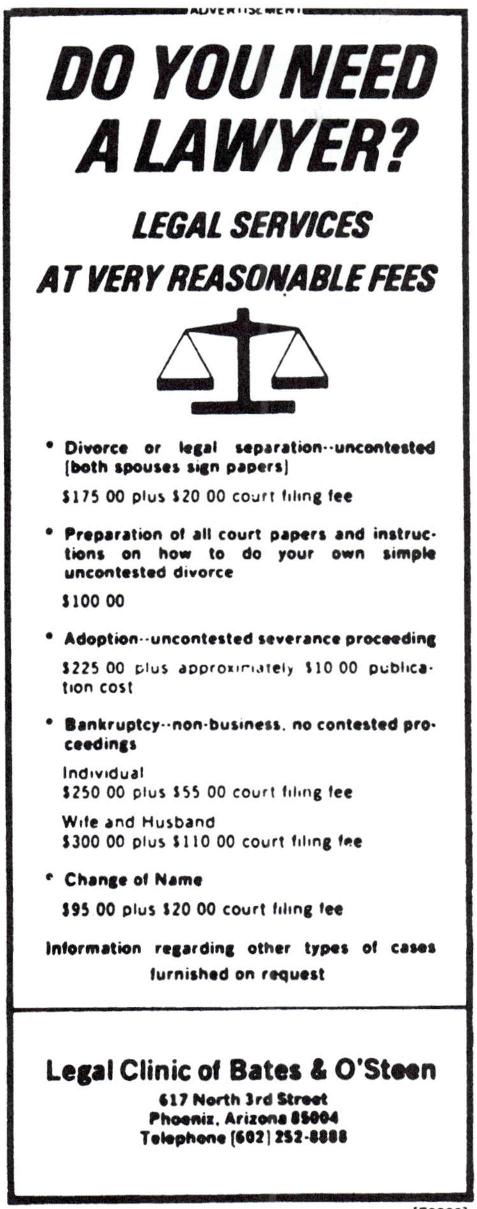

[E2922]

The heart of the dispute before us today is whether lawyers also may constitutionally advertise the *prices* at which certain routine services will be performed. Numerous justifications are proffered for the restriction of such price advertising. We consider each in turn:

1. *The Adverse Effect on Professionalism.* Appellee places particular emphasis on the adverse effects that it feels price advertising will have on

the legal profession. The key to professionalism, it is argued, is the sense of pride that involvement in the discipline generates. It is claimed that price advertising will bring about commercialization, which will undermine the attorney's sense of dignity and self-worth. The hustle of the marketplace will adversely affect the profession's service orientation, and irreparably damage the delicate balance between the lawyer's need to earn and his obligation selflessly to serve. Advertising is also said to erode the client's trust in his attorney: Once the client perceives that the lawyer is motivated by profit, his confidence that the attorney is acting out of a commitment to the client's welfare is jeopardized. And advertising is said to tarnish the dignified public image of the profession.

We recognize, of course, and commend the spirit of public service with which the profession of law is practiced and to which it is dedicated. The present Members of this Court, licensed attorneys all, could not feel otherwise. And we would have reason to pause if we felt that our decision today would undercut that spirit. But we find the postulated connection between advertising and the erosion of true professionalism to be severely strained. At its core, the argument presumes that attorneys must conceal from themselves and from their clients the real-life fact that lawyers earn their livelihood at the bar. We suspect that few attorneys engage in such self-deception. And rare is the client, moreover, even one of the [sic] modest means, who enlists the aid of an attorney with the expectation that his services will be rendered free of charge. *See* B. Christensen, Lawyers for People of Moderate Means 152–153 (1970). In fact, the American Bar Association advises that an attorney should reach "a clear agreement with his client as to the basis of the fee charges to be made," and that this is to be done "[a]s soon as feasible after a lawyer has been employed." Code of Professional Responsibility EC 2–19 (1976). If the commercial basis of the relationship is to be promptly disclosed on ethical grounds, once the client is in the office, it seems inconsistent to condemn the candid revelation of the same information before he arrives at that office.

Moreover, the assertion that advertising will diminish the attorney's reputation in the community is open to question. Bankers and engineers advertise, and yet these professions are not regarded as undignified. In fact, it has been suggested that the failure of lawyers to advertise creates public disillusionment with the profession. The absence of advertising may be seen to reflect the profession's failure to reach out and serve the community: Studies reveal that many persons do not obtain counsel even when they perceive a need because of the feared price of services or because of an inability to locate a competent attorney. Indeed, cynicism with regard to the profession may be created by the fact that it long has publicly eschewed advertising, while condoning the actions of the attorney who structures his social or civic associations so as to provide contacts with potential clients.

It appears that the ban on advertising originated as a rule of etiquette and not as a rule of ethics. Early lawyers in Great Britain viewed the law as a form of public service, rather than as a means of earning a living, and they looked down on "trade" as unseemly. *See* H. Drinker, Legal Ethics, 5, 210–211 (1953). Eventually, the attitude toward advertising fostered by this view evolved into an aspect of the ethics of the profession. *Id.*, at 211. But habit and tradition are not in themselves an adequate answer to a constitutional challenge. In this day, we do not belittle the person who earns his living by the strength of his arm or the force of his mind. Since the belief that lawyers are somehow "above" trade has become an anachronism, the historical foundation for the advertising restraint has crumbled.

2. *The Inherently Misleading Nature of Attorney Advertising.* It is argued that advertising of legal services inevitably will be misleading (a) because such services are so individualized with regard to content and quality as to prevent informed comparison on the basis of an advertisement, (b) because the consumer of legal services is unable to determine in advance just what services he needs, and (c) because advertising by attorneys will highlight irrelevant factors and fail to show the relevant factor of skill.

We are not persuaded that restrained professional advertising by lawyers inevitably will be misleading. Although many services performed by attorneys are indeed unique, it is doubtful that any attorney would or could advertise fixed prices for services of that type. The only services that lend themselves to advertising are the routine ones: the uncontested divorce, the simple adoption, the uncontested personal bankruptcy, the change of name, and the like—the very services advertised by appellants. Although the precise service demanded in each task may vary slightly, and although legal services are not fungible, these facts do not make advertising misleading so long as the attorney does the necessary work at the advertised price. The argument that legal services are so unique that fixed rates cannot meaningfully be established is refuted by the record in this case: The appellee, State Bar itself sponsors a Legal Services Program in which the participating attorneys agree to perform services like those advertised by the appellants at standardized rates. App. 459–478. Indeed, until the decision of this Court in *Goldfarb v. Virginia State Bar*, 421 U.S. 773, 95 S.Ct. 2004, 44 L.Ed.2d 572 (1975), the Maricopa County Bar Association apparently had a schedule of suggested minimum fees for standard legal tasks. We thus find of little force the assertion that advertising is misleading because of an inherent lack of standardization in legal services.

The second component of the argument—that advertising ignores the diagnostic role—fares little better. It is unlikely that many people go to an attorney merely to ascertain if they have a clean bill of legal health. Rather, attorneys are likely to be employed to perform specific tasks. Although the client may not know the detail involved in performing the task, he no doubt is able to identify the service he desires at the level of generality to which advertising lends itself.

The third component is not without merit: Advertising does not provide a complete foundation on which to select an attorney. But it seems peculiar to deny the consumer, on the ground that the information is incomplete, at least some of the relevant information needed to reach an informed decision. The alternative—the prohibition of advertising—serves only to restrict the information that flows to consumers. Moreover, the argument assumes that the public is not sophisticated enough to realize the limitations of advertising, and that the public is better kept in ignorance than trusted with correct but incomplete information. We suspect the argument rests on an underestimation of the public. In any event, we view as dubious any justification that is based on the benefits of public ignorance. *See Virginia Pharmacy Board v. Virginia Consumer Council*, 425 U.S., at 769–770, 96 S.Ct., at 1829–1830. Although, of course, the bar retains the power to correct omissions that have the effect of presenting an inaccurate picture, the preferred remedy is more disclosure, rather than less. If the naiveté of the public will cause advertising by attorneys to be misleading, then it is the bar's role to assure that the populace is sufficiently informed as to enable it to place advertising in its proper perspective.

3. *The Adverse Effect on the Administration of Justice.* Advertising is said to have the undesirable effect of stirring up litigation. The judicial machinery is designed to serve those who feel sufficiently aggrieved to bring forward their claims. Advertising, it is argued, serves to encourage the assertion of legal rights in the courts, thereby undesirably unsettling societal repose. There is even a suggestion of barratry. *See, e.g.*, Comment, A Critical Analysis of Rules Against Solicitation by Lawyers, 25 U.Chi. L.Rev. 674, 675–676 (1958).

But advertising by attorneys is not an unmitigated source of harm to the administration of justice. It may offer great benefits. Although advertising might increase the use of the judicial machinery, we cannot accept the notion that it is always better for a person to suffer a wrong silently than to redress it by legal action. As the bar acknowledges, "the middle 70% of our population is not being reached or served adequately by the legal profession." ABA, Revised Handbook on Prepaid Legal Services 2 (1972). Among the reasons for this underutilization is fear of the cost, and an inability to locate a suitable lawyer. Advertising can help to solve this acknowledged problem: Advertising is the traditional mechanism in a free-market economy for a supplier to inform a potential purchaser of the availability and terms of exchange. The disciplinary rule at issue likely has served to burden access to legal services, particularly for the not-quite-poor and the unknowledgeable. A rule allowing restrained advertising would be in accord with the bar's obligation to "facilitate the process of intelligent selection of lawyers, and to assist in making legal services fully available." ABA Code of Professional Responsibility EC 2–1 (1976).

4. *The Undesirable Economic Effects of Advertising.* It is claimed that advertising will increase the overhead costs of the profession, and that these costs then will be passed along to consumers in the form of

increased fees. Moreover, it is claimed that the additional cost of practice will create a substantial entry barrier, deterring or preventing young attorneys from penetrating the market and entrenching the position of the bar's established members.

These two arguments seem dubious at best. Neither distinguishes lawyers from others, *see Virginia Pharmacy Board v. Virginia Consumer Council*, 425 U.S., at 768, 96 S.Ct., at 1828, and neither appears relevant to the First Amendment. The ban on advertising serves to increase the difficulty of discovering the lowest cost seller of acceptable ability. As a result, to this extent attorneys are isolated from competition, and the incentive to price competitively is reduced. Although it is true that the effect of advertising on the price of services has not been demonstrated, there is revealing evidence with regard to products; where consumers have the benefit of price advertising, retail prices often are dramatically lower than they would be without advertising. It is entirely possible that advertising will serve to reduce, not advance, the cost of legal services to the consumer.

The entry-barrier argument is equally unpersuasive. In the absence of advertising, an attorney must rely on his contacts with the community to generate a flow of business. In view of the time necessary to develop such contacts, the ban in fact serves to perpetuate the market position of established attorneys. Consideration of entry-barrier problems would urge that advertising be allowed so as to aid the new competitor in penetrating the market.

5. *The Adverse Effect of Advertising on the Quality of Service.* It is argued that the attorney may advertise a given "package" of service at a set price, and will be inclined to provide, by indiscriminate use, the standard package regardless of whether it fits the client's needs.

Restraints on advertising, however, are an ineffective way of deterring shoddy work. An attorney who is inclined to cut quality will do so regardless of the rule on advertising. And the advertisement of a standardized fee does not necessarily mean that the services offered are undesirably standardized. Indeed, the assertion that an attorney who advertises a standard fee will cut quality is substantially undermined by the fixed-fee schedule of appellee's own prepaid Legal Services Program. Even if advertising leads to the creation of "legal clinics" like that of appellants'—clinics that emphasize standardized procedures for routine problems—it is possible that such clinics will improve service by reducing the likelihood of error.

6. *The Difficulties of Enforcement.* Finally, it is argued that the wholesale restriction is justified by the problems of enforcement if any other course is taken. Because the public lacks sophistication in legal matters, it may be particularly susceptible to misleading or deceptive advertising by lawyers. After-the-fact action by the consumer lured by such advertising may not provide a realistic restraint because of the inability of the layman to assess whether the service he has received meets

professional standards. Thus, the vigilance of a regulatory agency will be required. But because of the numerous purveyors of services, the overseeing of advertising will be burdensome.

It is at least somewhat incongruous for the opponents of advertising to extol the virtues and altruism of the legal profession at one point, and, at another, to assert that its members will seize the opportunity to mislead and distort. We suspect that, with advertising, most lawyers will behave as they always have: They will abide by their solemn oaths to uphold the integrity and honor of their profession and of the legal system. For every attorney who overreaches through advertising, there will be thousands of others who will be candid and honest and straightforward. And, of course, it will be in the latter's interest, as in other cases of misconduct at the bar, to assist in weeding out those few who abuse their trust.

In sum, we are not persuaded that any of the proffered justifications rise to the level of an acceptable reason for the suppression of all advertising by attorneys.

[The Court held that the First Amendment "overbreadth" doctrine did not apply in the context of lawyer advertising, but it ruled that the advertisement in question was not so obviously misleading as to be subject to regulation.]

In holding that advertising by attorneys may not be subjected to blanket suppression, and that the advertisement at issue is protected, we, of course, do not hold that advertising by attorneys may not be regulated in any way. We mention some of the clearly permissible limitations on advertising not foreclosed by our holding.

Advertising that is false, deceptive, or misleading of course is subject to restraint. *See Virginia Pharmacy Board v. Virginia Citizens Consumer Council*, 425 U.S., at 771–772, and n. 24, 96 S.Ct., at 1830–1831. Since the advertiser knows his product and has a commercial interest in its dissemination, we have little worry that regulation to assure truthfulness will discourage protected speech. And any concern that strict requirements for truthfulness will undesirably inhibit spontaneity seems inapplicable because commercial speech generally is calculated. Indeed, the public and private benefits from commercial speech derive from confidence in its accuracy and reliability. Thus, the leeway for untruthful or misleading expression that has been allowed in other contexts has little force in the commercial arena. Compare *Gertz v. Robert Welch, Inc.*, 418 U.S. 323, 339–341, 94 S.Ct. 2997, 3006–3007, 41 L.Ed.2d 789 (1974), and *Cantwell v. Connecticut*, 310 U.S., at 310, 60 S.Ct., at 906, with *NLRB v. Gissel Packing Co.*, 395 U.S., at 618, 89 S.Ct., at 1942. In fact, because the public lacks sophistication concerning legal services, misstatements that might be overlooked or deemed unimportant in other advertising may be found quite inappropriate in legal advertising. For example, advertising claims as to the quality of services—a matter we do not address today—are not susceptible of measurement or verification; accordingly, such claims may be so likely to be misleading as to warrant restriction. Similar objections might justify restraints on in-person solicitation. We do not foreclose the possibility that some limited supplementation, by way of warning or disclaimer or the like, might be required of even an advertisement of the kind ruled upon today so as to assure that the consumer is not misled. In sum, we recognize that many of the problems in defining the boundary between deceptive and nondeceptive advertising remain to be resolved, and we expect that the bar will have a special role to play in assuring that advertising by attorneys flows both freely and cleanly.

As with other varieties of speech, it follows as well that there may be reasonable restrictions on the time, place, and manner of advertising. *See Virginia Pharmacy Board v. Virginia Consumer Council*, 425 U.S., at 771, 96 S.Ct. at 1830. Advertising concerning transactions that are themselves illegal obviously may be suppressed. *See Pittsburgh Press Co. v. Human Relations Comm'n*, 413 U.S. 376, 388, 93 S.Ct. 2553, 37 L.Ed.2d 669 (1973). And the special problems of advertising on the electronic broadcast media will warrant special consideration.

The constitutional issue in this case is only whether the State may prevent the publication in a newspaper of appellants' truthful advertisement concerning the availability and terms of routine legal services. We rule simply that the flow of such information may not be restrained, and we therefore hold the present application of the disciplinary rule against appellants to be violative of the First Amendment.

The judgment of the Supreme Court of Arizona is therefore affirmed in part and reversed in part.

HISTORICAL SUMMARY, CONTINUED

A. THE *OHRALIK* AND *PRIMUS* CASES—SOLICITATION

The year after *Bates,* the Supreme Court decided a pair of cases that sketched the line between permissible and impermissible solicitation by lawyers.

In *Ohralik v. Ohio State Bar Association,* 436 U.S. 447, 98 S.Ct. 1912, 56 L.Ed.2d 444 (1978), the Court approved indefinite suspension from law practice for an old-fashioned ambulance chaser. Lawyer Ohralik learned about an auto accident in which two 18–year–old girls had been injured. He was casually acquainted with one of them and called her parents, who said she was in traction at the hospital. After visiting her parents at their home, he visited the girl in the hospital, offered to represent her, and asked her to sign a fee agreement. She said she would have to discuss it with her parents. With a tape recorder concealed under his raincoat, he returned to her parents' home where he volunteered some advice about how much they could recover under the uninsured motorist clause of their auto insurance policy. The parents told him that their daughter had telephoned and had agreed to let him represent her. He returned to the hospital two days later and had the girl sign a one-third contingent fee agreement.

Ohralik paid an uninvited visit to the second girl at her home, again carrying his concealed tape recorder. He told her about representing the first girl and about recovering money under the uninsured motorist clause. He asked if she wanted to file a claim, and she replied that she did not really understand what was going on. He then offered to represent her for a one-third contingent fee, to which she responded, "O.K." The next day, the second girl's mother told Ohralik that she and her daughter did not want to sue anyone or have him represent them, and that if they did decide to sue they would go to their own lawyer. Ohralik insisted that the girl had entered into a binding agreement; he refused to withdraw and ultimately tried to get the girl to pay him $2,466.66, representing one-third of his estimate of the worth of her claim.

The first girl also fired Ohralik and hired another lawyer to settle her claim. Ohralik sued her for breach of the contingent fee agreement, and he recovered $4,166.66, one-third of what she had received. After both girls complained to the state bar, Ohralik was suspended indefinitely from law practice.

The U.S. Supreme Court affirmed the disciplinary order, rejecting Ohralik's claim that the First Amendment protected his conduct. Unlike the advertisements approved in *Bates,* the Court said, in-person solicitation of fee-paying legal business poses significant dangers for the lay person who gets solicited. The lay person can be subjected to a high pressure sales pitch that demands immediate response and gives no time for comparison and reflection. Further, in-person solicitation gives no opportunity for counter-information by the organized bar, or others who might offer calmer advice.

Ohralik conceded that the state had a compelling interest in preventing fraud, undue influence, intimidation, overreaching, and other forms of vexatious conduct; however, he argued that the state could not discipline him without proving that his particular acts produced one of those evils. In short, Ohralik argued that the state must prove actual harm.

The Court rejected his argument, holding that a state may adopt prophylactic rules that forbid in-person solicitation of fee-generating legal business under circumstances that are likely to produce fraud, undue influence, or similar evils. Further, such a rule could be applied against Ohralik because he approached the girls when they were especially vulnerable, he urged his services upon them, he used a concealed tape recorder, he described his fee arrangement in a slick and tantalizing manner, and he refused to withdraw when asked to do so. All of this created a clear potential for overreaching, sufficient to justify the discipline imposed. [*Compare Ohralik with Edenfield v. Fane,* 507 U.S. 761, 113 S.Ct. 1792, 123 L.Ed.2d 543 (1993), which struck down a prophylactic rule against in-person solicitation by accountants. The Court said that accountants, unlike lawyers, are not trained in the art of persuasion, and accountants' clients are less likely to be duped than lawyers' clients. Do you agree?]

The second of the two solicitation cases, *In re Primus,* 436 U.S. 412, 98 S.Ct. 1893, 56 L.Ed.2d 417 (1978), offers a sharp contrast to the ambulance-chasing in *Ohralik.* Edna Smith Primus, a private practitioner in South Carolina, was a member and officer in the local chapter of the American Civil Liberties Union. At the request of another organization, she met with some women who allegedly had been sterilized, or threatened with sterilization, as a condition of receiving Medicaid benefits. She informed the women of their legal rights and suggested the possibility of a lawsuit. Later, the ACLU informed Primus that it would supply free legal counsel to the women who had been sterilized by one Dr. Clovis Pierce. Primus wrote a letter to one of the women to inform her of the ACLU offer. South Carolina publicly reprimanded Primus for solicitation.

In overturning the South Carolina reprimand, the U.S. Supreme Court distinguished Primus's conduct from Ohralik's conduct, saying that Primus had not been guilty of "in-person solicitation for pecuniary gain," but had simply conveyed an offer of free legal help by a recognized civil rights group. Further, the motive was partly political. Civil rights cases such as *NAACP v. Button,* 371 U.S. 415, 83 S.Ct. 328, 9 L.Ed.2d 405 (1963), establish that the First Amendment protects collective activity undertaken to gain meaningful access to courts and that the government can regulate such activity only with narrow specificity. The ACLU was seeking to use the sterilization litigation as a vehicle for political expression and association, as well as a means of communicating useful information to the public. That kind of speech is more precious than the commercial speech in *Ohralik.* Accordingly, the states may not regulate it without showing *actual* abuse; a showing of potential abuse is not enough. Since there was no evidence that Primus had overreached, or misrepresented, or invaded anyone's privacy, the discipline imposed on her was unconstitutional.

Could you draft a manageable disciplinary rule that embodies the Supreme Court's distinctions between Ohralik's conduct and Primus's conduct? How did the drafters of ABA Model Rule 7.3 deal with the problem?

B. THE ADOPTION OF THE ABA MODEL RULES

A few weeks after the *Bates* case was decided, the ABA amended the ABA Code to loosen the advertising ban a little, but not much. The amended ABA Code provisions purported to limit the types of information lawyers could advertise, and they retained many antique rules about law office signs, letterheads, professional cards, and the like.

In 1983, the ABA House of Delegates adopted the ABA Model Rules, which were designed to replace the ABA Code as a model for state ethics rules. The ABA Model Rules contained liberal provisions on advertising and solicitation that were drafted to comply with *In re R.M.J.*, 455 U.S. 191, 102 S.Ct. 929, 71 L.Ed.2d 64 (1982). In that case a unanimous Court ruled that under the commercial speech doctrine a state may flatly prohibit lawyer advertising that is false or misleading, and that a state may regulate advertising that is *not* misleading if the state can demonstrate that the regulation directly serves a substantial state interest, and that the regulation is no more extensive than is necessary to serve that interest. In the years since 1983, the advertising and solicitation provisions of the ABA Model Rules have been amended several times, to keep up with the Supreme Court's decisions in the area. For thoughts on the future direction of advertising regulation, see Fred C. Zacharias, *What Direction Should Legal Advertising Regulation Take?*, 2005 The Prof. Lawyer 45.

C. THE CALIFORNIA RULES ON ADVERTISING AND SOLICITATION

Like the ABA Model Rules, CRPC 1–400 was drafted to comply with the United States Supreme Court commercial speech decisions, and it has been amended several times to keep current with those decisions. One unique feature of California's approach is the California Standards for Attorney Communications (printed after CRPC 1–400). The standards create a set of rebuttable presumptions that certain kinds of advertising statements are misleading. The presumptions shift the burden of proof to the attorney in a disciplinary proceeding. Suppose, for example, that the state bar seeks to discipline an attorney for advertising that includes a guarantee or prediction about the outcome of a legal matter. The attorney would carry the burden of proving by a preponderance of the evidence that the guarantee or prediction was *not* misleading.

The California legislature has also gotten into the act by passing some attorney advertising statutes, Cal.Bus. & Prof.Code §§ 6157–6158.3. In some respects, the statutes are more restrictive than CRPC 1–400. You can decide for yourself whether the statutes are a valuable addition to the law in this field.

D. THE *PEEL* CASE—CLAIMS OF SPECIALIZATION

Unlike the medical profession, the organized bar has been slow to recognize specialization. As originally drafted, ABA Model Rule 7.4 allowed a lawyer to tell the public that she practices in a certain field, or that she restricts her practice to a certain field. However, the original rule prohibited a lawyer from stating or implying that she is a "specialist" in a field, subject to three exceptions:

- A lawyer admitted to practice in the U.S. Patent and Trademark Office could call herself a "patent attorney," or something similar;

- A lawyer engaged in admiralty practice could call herself a "proctor in admiralty," or something similar; and
- A lawyer could call herself a "certified specialist" in a field of law if she had been certified by the bar of her state.

Peel v. Attorney Registration & Disciplinary Com'n, 496 U.S. 91, 110 S.Ct. 2281, 110 L.Ed.2d 83 (1990), involved a lawyer who had been certified as a specialist in trial advocacy, not by the bar of his state, but rather by the National Board of Trial Advocacy, a private organization that uses high, rigorously-enforced standards for certifying trial advocates. *Peel* establishes that a lawyer who is certified under those circumstances may call himself a certified specialist, provided that he identifies the organization that certified him and takes related steps to avoid misleading the public. ABA Model Rule 7.4 was subsequently amended to accord with the *Peel* decision. The comments to ABA Model Rule 7.4 clarify that an attorney may state that she is a "specialist," that she practices a "specialty," or that she "specializes in" particular areas. However, a lawyer may state that he or she is "certified" as a specialist in a particular field only when the certifying organization—which must be clearly identified in the communication—has been accredited by the American Bar Association or been approved by an appropriate state authority.

E. THE *ZAUDERER, SHAPERO,* AND *WENT FOR IT* CASES—THE SHADOWLAND BETWEEN ADVERTISING AND SOLICITATION

Zauderer v. Office of Disciplinary Counsel of the Supreme Court of Ohio, 471 U.S. 626, 105 S.Ct. 2265, 85 L.Ed.2d 652 (1985), involved a lawyer who placed a newspaper ad that was aimed at a narrow audience—users of the Dalkon Shield, an intrauterine contraceptive device that allegedly injured many women. A divided Court held that Zauderer could not be disciplined simply for placing an ad that concerned a specific legal problem and that was designed to lure a narrow group of potential clients. (He could, however, be disciplined for a misleading statement in the ad.) Justice O'Connor (joined by Chief Justice Burger and Justice Rehnquist) dissented in part, arguing that the states should be free to prohibit lawyers from using ads that contain "free samples" of legal advice. Ordinary merchants can offer free samples of their wares, Justice O'Connor argued, but free samples of legal advice are too likely to mislead laypersons, who often lack the knowledge and experience to judge the sample before they buy.

If narrowly targeted newspaper ads are permissible, then what about solicitation letters mailed to potential clients whom the lawyer knows to be facing a specific, present legal problem? The Court answered that question in *Shapero v. Kentucky Bar Ass'n,* 486 U.S. 466, 108 S.Ct. 1916, 100 L.Ed.2d 475 (1988). Lawyer Shapero wanted to mail solicitation letters (which were assumed to be truthful and not misleading) to people he knew were facing foreclosure on their homes for failure to pay their debts. A slim majority of the Supreme Court held in Shapero's favor. The majority said the solicitation letters were more analogous to the targeted newspaper ads in *Zauderer* than they were to the in-person solicitation in *Ohralik*. In-person solicitation creates a grave risk that the lawyer will invade the client's privacy, overreach, or use undue influence. That risk is far less with a letter, which the recipient can set aside for later study, ignore, or simply throw in the trash. Moreover, in-person solicitation cannot be policed because it happens in private and there is usually no certain proof of who said what, but solicitation letters can be policed by requiring copies to be sent to the regulatory agency. Thus, a state cannot ban solicitation letters outright, but it *can* impose *reasonable regulations* on their use.

In a vigorous dissent, Justice O'Connor (joined by Chief Justice Rehnquist and Justice Scalia) called for a reconsideration of the *Bates* case, which you read above. According to Justice O'Connor, *Bates* accepted a simplistic economics argument that attorney advertising would increase competition, raise quality, and lower price. That would be true in markets for ordinary goods, and it might even be true in the short run in the market for legal services. But in the long run, Justice O'Connor argued, allowing attorneys to hawk their wares will eventually destroy the professionalism that limits the "unique power" attorneys wield in our political system. If Justice O'Connor had it her way, states would have "considerable latitude" to ban advertising that is even "potentially" misleading and to ban even truthful advertising that undermines the substantial governmental interest in promoting high ethical standards in the legal profession.

As you will see below, Justice O'Connor did have it her way, at least partly, in *Florida Bar v. Went for It, Inc.*, 515 U.S. 618, 115 S.Ct. 2371, 132 L.Ed.2d 541 (1995). Writing for herself and four colleagues, she upheld a Florida rule that prohibits lawyers from mailing solicitation letters to victims and their families for 30 days following an accident.

FLORIDA BAR v. WENT FOR IT, INC.

Supreme Court of the United States, 1995.
515 U.S. 618, 115 S.Ct. 2371, 132 L.Ed.2d 541.

O'CONNOR, J. delivered the opinion of the Court, in which REHNQUIST, C.J., and SCALIA, THOMAS, and BREYER, JJ., joined.

Rules of the Florida Bar prohibit personal injury lawyers from sending targeted direct-mail solicitations to victims and their relatives for 30 days following an accident or disaster. This case asks us to consider whether such rules violate the First and Fourteenth Amendments of the Constitution. We hold that in the circumstances presented here, they do not.

* * *

[After a two year study of the effects of lawyer advertising on the public, the Florida Bar adopted Rule 4–7.4(B)(1), which] provides that "[a] lawyer shall not send, or knowingly permit to be sent, ... a written communication to a prospective client for the purpose of obtaining professional employment if: (A) the written communication concerns an action for personal injury or wrongful death or otherwise relates to an accident or disaster involving the person to whom the communication is addressed or a relative of that person, unless the accident or disaster occurred more than 30 days prior to the mailing of the communication." * * *

* * *

[A Florida lawyer and his wholly-owned lawyer referral service challenged the rule. Relying on *Bates* and its progeny, the district court and the court of appeals held the rule unconstitutional. After reviewing the history of the commercial speech doctrine, Justice O'Connor wrote:]

Nearly two decades of cases have built upon the foundation laid by *Bates*. It is now well established that lawyer advertising is commercial speech and, as such, is accorded a measure of First Amendment protection. See, *e.g., Shapero v. Kentucky Bar Assn.,* 486 U.S. 466, 472, 108 S.Ct. 1916, 1921, 100 L.Ed.2d 475 (1988); *Zauderer v. Office of Disciplinary Counsel of Supreme Court of Ohio,* 471 U.S. 626, 637, 105 S.Ct. 2265, 2274, 85 L.Ed.2d 652 (1985); *In re R.M.J.,* 455 U.S. 191, 199, 102 S.Ct. 929, 935, 71 L.Ed.2d 64 (1982). Such First Amendment protection, of course, is not absolute. We have always been careful to distinguish commercial speech from speech at the First Amendment's core. " '[C]ommercial speech [enjoys] a limited measure of protection, commensurate with its subordinate position in the scale of First Amendment values,' and is subject to 'modes of regulation that might be impermissible in the realm of noncommercial expression.' " *Board of Trustees of State University of N.Y. v. Fox,* 492 U.S. 469, 477, 109 S.Ct. 3028, 3033, 106 L.Ed.2d 388 (1989), quoting *Ohralik v. Ohio State Bar Assn.,* 436 U.S. 447, 456, 98 S.Ct. 1912, 56 L.Ed.2d 444 (1978). We have observed that " '[t]o require a parity of constitutional protection for commercial and noncommercial speech alike could invite dilution, simply by a leveling process, of the force of the Amendment's guarantee with respect to the latter kind of speech.' " 492 U.S., at 481, 109 S.Ct., at 3035, quoting *Ohralik, supra,* 436 U.S., at 456, 98 S.Ct., at 1918.

Mindful of these concerns, we engage in "intermediate" scrutiny of restrictions on commercial speech, analyzing them under the framework set forth in *Central Hudson Gas & Electric Corp. v. Public Service Comm'n of N.Y.,* 447 U.S. 557, 100 S.Ct. 2343, 65 L.Ed.2d 341 (1980). Under *Central Hudson,* the government may freely regulate commercial speech that concerns unlawful activity or is misleading. Commercial speech that falls into neither of those categories, like the advertising at issue here, may be regulated if the government satisfies a test consisting of three related prongs: first, the government must assert a substantial interest in support of its regulation; second, the government must demonstrate that the restriction on commercial speech directly and materially advances that interest; and third, the regulation must be " 'narrowly drawn' ". * * *

* * *

The Florida Bar asserts that it has a substantial interest in protecting the privacy and tranquility of personal injury victims and their loved ones against intrusive, unsolicited contact by lawyers. * * * This interest obviously factors into the Bar's paramount (and repeatedly professed) objective of curbing activities that "negatively affec[t] the administration of justice." * * * Because direct mail solicitations in the wake of accidents are perceived by the public as intrusive, the Bar argues, the reputation of the legal profession in the eyes of Floridians has suffered commensurately. * * * The regulation, then, is an effort to protect the flagging reputations of Florida lawyers by preventing them from engaging in conduct that, the Bar maintains, " 'is universally regarded as deplorable and beneath common decency because of its intrusion upon the special vulnerability and private grief of victims or their families.' "

We have little trouble crediting the Bar's interest as substantial. On various occasions we have accepted the proposition that "States have a compelling interest in the practice of professions within their boundaries, and . . . as part of their power to protect the public health, safety, and other valid interests they have broad power to establish standards for licensing practitioners and regulating the practice of professions." *Goldfarb v. Virginia State Bar,* 421 U.S. 773, 792, 95 S.Ct. 2004, 2016, 44 L.Ed.2d 572 (1975); see also *Ohralik, supra,* 436 U.S., at 460, 98 S.Ct., at 1920–1921; *Cohen v. Hurley,* 366 U.S. 117, 124, 81 S.Ct. 954, 958–959, 6 L.Ed.2d 156 (1961). Our precedents also leave no room for doubt that "the protection of potential clients' privacy is a substantial state interest." See *Edenfield v. Fane,* 507 U.S. 761, 769, 113 S.Ct. 1792, 1799, 123 L.Ed.2d 543 (1993). In other contexts, we have consistently recognized that "[t]he State's interest in protecting the well-being, tranquility, and privacy of the home is certainly of the highest order in a free and civilized society." *Carey v. Brown,* 447 U.S. 455, 471, 100 S.Ct. 2286, 2295–2296, 65 L.Ed.2d 263 (1980). Indeed, we have noted that "a special benefit of the privacy all citizens enjoy within their own walls, which the State may legislate to protect, is an ability to avoid intrusions." *Frisby v. Schultz,* 487 U.S. 474, 484–485, 108 S.Ct. 2495, 2502–2503, 101 L.Ed.2d 420 (1988).

Under *Central Hudson*'s second prong, the State must demonstrate that the challenged regulation "advances the Government's interest 'in a direct and material way.' " * * *

* * *

[The State cannot rely on speculation or conjecture; it must demonstrate that the harms it recites are real, and that the regulation will in fact alleviate them to a material degree.]

The Florida Bar submitted a 106–page summary of its 2–year study of lawyer advertising and solicitation to the District Court. That summary contains data—both statistical and anecdotal—supporting the Bar's contentions that the Florida public views direct-mail solicitations in the immediate wake of accidents as an intrusion on privacy that reflects poorly upon the profession. As of June 1989, lawyers mailed 700,000 direct solicitations in Florida annually, 40% of which were aimed at accident victims or their survivors. * * * A survey of Florida adults commissioned by the Bar indicated that Floridians "have negative feelings about those attorneys who use direct mail advertising." * * * Fifty-four percent of the general population surveyed said that contacting persons concerning accidents or similar events is a violation of privacy. * * * A random sampling of persons who received direct-mail advertising from lawyers in 1987 revealed that 45% believed that direct-mail solicitation is "designed to take advantage of gullible or unstable people"; 34% found such tactics "annoying or irritating"; 26% found it "an invasion of your privacy"; and 24% reported that it "made you angry." * * * Significantly, 27% of direct-mail recipients reported that their regard for the legal profession and for the judicial process as a whole was "lower" as a result of receiving the direct mail. * * *

The anecdotal record mustered by the Bar is noteworthy for its breadth and detail. With titles like "Scavenger Lawyers" (The Miami Herald, Sept. 29, 1987) and "Solicitors Out of Bounds" (St. Petersburg Times, Oct. 26, 1987), newspaper editorial pages in Florida have burgeoned with criticism of Florida lawyers who send targeted direct mail to victims shortly after accidents. The study summary also includes page upon page of excerpts from complaints of direct-mail recipients. For example, a Florida citizen described how he was " 'appalled and angered by the brazen attempt' " of a law firm to solicit him by letter shortly after he was injured and his fiancee was killed in an auto accident. * * * Another found it " 'despicable and inexcusable' " that a Pensacola lawyer wrote to his mother three days after his father's funeral. * * * Another described how she was " 'astounded' " and then " 'very angry' " when she received a solicitation following a minor accident. * * * Still another described as " 'beyond comprehension' " a letter his nephew's family received the day of the nephew's funeral. * * * One citizen wrote, " 'I consider the unsolicited contact from you after my child's accident to be of the rankest form of ambulance chasing and in incredibly poor taste.... I cannot begin to express with my limited vocabulary the utter contempt in which I hold you and your kind.' " * * * [W]e conclude that the Bar has satisfied the second prong of the *Central Hudson* test. * * *

[T]he Court of Appeals determined that this case was governed squarely by *Shapero v. Kentucky Bar Assn.,* 486 U.S. 466, 108 S.Ct. 1916, 100 L.Ed.2d 475 (1988). Making no mention of the Bar's study, the court concluded that " 'a targeted letter [does not] invade the recipient's privacy any more than does a substantively identical letter mailed at large. The invasion, if any, occurs when the lawyer discovers the recipient's legal affairs, not when he confronts the recipient with the discovery.' " In many cases, the Court of Appeals explained, "this invasion of privacy will involve no more than reading the newspaper."

While some of *Shapero*'s language might be read to support the Court of Appeals' interpretation, *Shapero* differs in several fundamental respects from the case before us. First and foremost, *Shapero*'s treatment of privacy was casual. * * * [T]he State in *Shapero* did not seek to justify its regulation as a measure undertaken to prevent lawyers' invasions of privacy interests. * * * Rather, the State focused exclusively on the special dangers of overreaching inhering in targeted solicitations. * * * Second, in contrast to this case, *Shapero* dealt with a broad ban on *all* direct-mail solicitations, whatever the time frame and whoever the recipient. Finally, the State in *Shapero* assembled no evidence attempting to demonstrate any actual harm caused by targeted direct mail. The Court rejected the State's effort to justify a prophylactic ban on the basis of blanket, untested assertions of undue influence and overreaching. 486 U.S., at 475, 108 S.Ct., at 1922–1923. Because the State did not make a privacy-based argument at all, its empirical showing on that issue was similarly infirm.

* * *

[In the present case,] the harm targeted by the Florida Bar cannot be eliminated by a brief journey to the trash can. The purpose of the 30–day targeted direct-mail ban is to forestall the outrage and irritation with the state-licensed legal profession that the practice of direct solicitation only days after accidents has engendered. The Bar is concerned not with citizens' "offense" in the abstract, but with the demonstrable detrimental effects that such "offense" has on the profession it regulates. * * * Moreover, the harm posited by the Bar is as much a function of simple receipt of targeted solicitations within days of accidents as it is a function of the letters' contents. Throwing the letter away shortly after opening it may minimize the latter intrusion, but it does little to combat the former. * * *

Passing to *Central Hudson*'s third prong, we examine the relationship between the Florida Bar's interests and the means chosen to serve them. See *Board of Trustees of State University of N.Y. v. Fox,* 492 U.S., at 480, 109 S.Ct., at 3034–3035. With respect to this prong, the differences between commercial speech and noncommercial speech are manifest. In *Fox,* we made clear that the "least restrictive means" test has no role in the commercial speech context. "What our decisions require, instead, is a 'fit' between the legislature's ends and the means chosen to accomplish those ends, a fit that is not necessarily perfect, but reasonable; that represents not necessarily the single best disposition but one whose scope is 'in proportion to the interest served,' that employs not necessarily the least restrictive means but . . . a means narrowly tailored to achieve the desired objective." *Ibid.* (citations omitted). Of course, we do not equate this test with the less rigorous obstacles of rational basis review; in

Cincinnati v. Discovery Network, Inc., 507 U.S. 410, 417, n. 13, 113 S.Ct. 1505, 1510 n. 13, 123 L.Ed.2d 99 (1993), for example, we observed that the existence of "numerous and obvious less-burdensome alternatives to the restriction on commercial speech . . . is certainly a relevant consideration in determining whether the 'fit' between ends and means is reasonable."

* * *

[Our view of this case might differ] if the Bar's rule were not limited to a brief period and if there were not many other ways for injured Floridians to learn about the availability of legal representation during that time. Our lawyer advertising cases have afforded lawyers a great deal of leeway to devise innovative ways to attract new business. Florida permits lawyers to advertise on prime-time television and radio as well as in newspapers and other media. They may rent space on billboards. They may send untargeted letters to the general population, or to discrete segments thereof. There are, of course, pages upon pages devoted to lawyers in the Yellow Pages of Florida telephone directories. * * *

[T]he record contains considerable empirical survey information suggesting that Floridians have little difficulty finding lawyers when they need one. * * * Finding no basis to question the commonsense conclusion that the many alternative channels for communicating necessary information about attorneys are sufficient, we see no defect in Florida's regulation.

Speech by professionals obviously has many dimensions. There are circumstances in which we will accord speech by attorneys on public issues and matters of legal representation the strongest protection our Constitution has to offer. See, *e.g., Gentile v. State Bar of Nevada,* 501 U.S. 1030, 111 S.Ct. 2720, 115 L.Ed.2d 888 (1991); *In re Primus,* 436 U.S. 412, 98 S.Ct. 1893, 56 L.Ed.2d 417 (1978). This case, however, concerns pure commercial advertising, for which we have always reserved a lesser degree of protection under the First Amendment. Particularly because the standards and conduct of state-licensed lawyers have traditionally been subject to extensive regulation by the States, it is all the more appropriate that we limit our scrutiny of state regulations to a level commensurate with the " 'subordinate position' " of commercial speech in the scale of First Amendment values. *Fox,* 492 U.S., at 477, 109 S.Ct., at 3033, quoting *Ohralik,* 436 U.S., at 456, 98 S.Ct., at 1918–1919.

We believe that the Florida Bar's 30–day restriction on targeted direct-mail solicitation of accident victims and their relatives withstands scrutiny under the three-part *Central Hudson* test that we have devised for this context. The Bar has substantial interest both in protecting injured Floridians from invasive conduct by lawyers and in preventing the erosion of confidence in the profession that such repeated invasions have engendered. The Bar's proffered study, unrebutted by respondents below, provides evidence indicating that the harms it targets are far from illusory. The palliative devised by the Bar to address these harms is narrow both in scope and in duration. The Constitution, in our view, requires nothing more.

The judgment of the Court of Appeals, accordingly, is *reversed.*

[We have omitted the dissenting opinion of Justice Kennedy, joined by Justices Stevens, Souter, and Ginsburg.]

MULTIPLE CHOICE QUESTIONS

Answer these questions using the definitions found at the end of Chapter Two.

1. Mark Norris is a newscaster for the local television station. Every weeknight, following the evening news, he presents a ten-minute segment entitled "This Funny Town." It is patterned on an old-fashioned newspaper gossip column. Most of it concerns the private lives and peccadilloes of the prominent and would-be prominent citizens of the community. Judges and lawyers are among Mr. Norris's favorite subjects. He and attorney Philos have arrived at a tacit arrangement. Whenever Philos hears a piece of juicy gossip about a local judge or lawyer, he passes it along to Norris. In return, Norris frequently recommends Philos's legal services in his broadcasts. For example, Norris calls Philos "a fearless courtroom ace," or he states opinions such as: "if you want to win your case, hire Philos." Is Philos *subject to discipline?*

A. Yes, because Philos is providing something of value to Norris for recommending his services.

B. Yes, because a lawyer can be disciplined for demeaning other members of the legal profession.

C. No, unless he gives false or privileged information to Norris.

D. No, because Philos's conduct is a protected form of speech under the First and Fourteenth Amendments.

2. Three years ago, attorneys Hooten and Snod formed a law partnership called Hooten & Snod. A year later, Hooten died, and Snod continued practicing under the former firm name. Then Snod hired a salaried associate, attorney Tremble, and, the firm name was changed to Hooten, Snod & Tremble. The following year, Snod left law practice to become a commissioner on the Federal Trade Commission. Tremble took over the practice and continued to use the same name. Later, because he had more space in the office than he needed, he entered into a space-sharing agreement with attorney Gangler. The sign on the door now reads Tremble & Gangler, Attorneys at Law. Which of the following are correct?

I. After Hooten died, it was *proper* for Snod to continue using the firm name Hooten & Snod.

II. When Snod hired Tremble, it was *proper* to change the firm name to Hooten, Snod & Tremble.

III. After Snod joined the FTC, it was *proper* for Tremble to continue using Snod as part of the firm name.

IV. The present sign on the door is *proper*.

A. All of the above.

B. I, II, and III only.

C. I and II only.

D. I only.

3. Attorney Anton advertised on the local television station. His advertisement stated in relevant part: "The most I will charge you for any type of legal work is $100 per hour, and if your problem is not complicated, the hourly fee will be even lower." Which of the following propositions are correct?

I. Anton *may* advertise on the local television station so long as his advertisement is not false or misleading.

II. If Anton charges $125 per hour for complicated legal work, he will be *subject to discipline* for using a misleading advertisement.

III. If Anton's advertisement fails to state that some other lawyers in the community charge substantially lower fees, he will be *subject to discipline*.

A. Only II is correct.

B. Only I and III are correct.

C. Only I and II are correct.

D. Only II and III are correct.

4. Lawyer Del Campos practices in a town in which 25% of the people are Mexican–American and another 20% have recently immigrated to the United States from Mexico. The bar of his state does not certify specialists in any field of law nor does it approve private organizations that certify legal specialists. However, Del Campos has been certified as a specialist in immigration law by the American Association of Immigration Attorneys, a private organization accredited by the ABA. Del Campos wants to put an advertisement in the classified section of the local telephone book. Which of the following items of information *may* he include in his advertisement?

I. That he "serves clients who are members of the Continental Prepaid Legal Service Plan."

II. That he "speaks Spanish."

III. That he has been "certified as an immigration specialist by the American Association of Immigration Attorneys."

IV. That he can "arrange credit for fee payments."

A. All of the above.

B. None of the above.

C. I, II, and IV only.

D. I and III only.

5. Attorney Salmon published a brochure entitled, "What to Do When You Are Injured." It contains accurate, helpful information on obtaining medical treatment, recording details of the event, notifying insurance companies, not making harmful statements, and the like. The cover of the brochure identifies Salmon as a "Personal Injury Attorney" and gives his office address and telephone number. One afternoon, Salmon was standing in a crowd of people that saw a pregnant woman knocked down in a pedestrian crosswalk by a speeding car. A few days later, Salmon mailed the woman a copy of his brochure, together with a letter stating that he had witnessed the accident and was willing to represent her for a reasonable fee should she wish to sue the car driver. The outside envelope stated that the envelope contained "Advertising Material." The bar in Salmon's state does not have a 30–day waiting period of the kind involved in *Went For It, Inc.,* above.

A. Salmon is *subject to discipline,* both for sending the woman the brochure and for sending her the letter.

B. Salmon is *subject to discipline* for sending the woman the letter, but not for sending her the brochure.

C. Salmon is *subject to discipline* for offering his legal services, for a fee, to a person who was not a relative, client, or former client.

D. Salmon's conduct was *proper.*

6. Attorney Gresler offered a free half-day seminar for nurses, hospital attendants, and emergency medical personnel on personal injury law as it relates to accident victims. During the seminar, he told the group about the importance of preserving items of physical evidence, keeping accurate records of medical treatment, accurately recording statements made by the victim and others about the accident, and the like. At the close of the seminar, he passed out packets of his professional cards and invited the members of the group to give them to accident victims. Was Gresler's conduct *proper*?

A. Yes, because a lawyer has an ethical obligation to help non-lawyers recognize legal problems and handle those problems correctly.

B. Yes, because his conduct is protected by the Free Speech clause of the First and Fourteenth Amendments.

C. No, because he invited members of the group to hand out his professional cards to accident victims.

D. No, because he dispensed legal advice to people with whom he had no prior professional relationship.

7. After graduating from law school, three young women formed their own new firm dedicated to the law of women's rights in the workplace. They established an attractive site on the Internet. Their website includes very specific biographical information about each of

them, including information about their families, their hobbies, and all the academic and athletic honors they received in college and law school. The site also includes detailed, thoroughly researched position papers they have written on current legal issues in their field of law practice. The position papers are written so they can be understood by a lay audience. The website includes an e-mail link that allows site visitors to ask legal questions of the three lawyers. The question form requires the questioner to supply enough information about him or herself to permit the lawyers to do a conflict of interest check before responding to the question. The questioner supplies a credit card number, and the lawyers charge a small fee for e-mailing an answer to the question. The lawyers do not answer questions from site visitors who live outside the state in which the lawyers have their office. If a question is too difficult to answer competently by e-mail, the lawyers invite the questioner to come to their office for a free initial consultation. Is the conduct of the three lawyers *proper?*

A. No, because their website includes personal information about the three lawyers that is not relevant to the potential client's selection of a lawyer.

B. No, because the e-mail feature permits the three lawyers to dispense legal advice to people they have never met and with whom they have never established a lawyer-client relationship.

C. Yes, but only if the fee for e-mailing an answer to a question is not unreasonably high.

D. Yes, but only if the position papers are on non-controversial legal issues that do not require a specialized knowledge of women's employment law.

8. The firm of Wilkens & Crosse has existed for many years in Chicago. Now it wishes to open an office in Los Angeles. The Los Angeles office will be established as a separate partnership. Some of the proposed Los Angeles partners are admitted to practice only in California, and they will not become partners in the Chicago firm. Some of the Chicago partners are admitted to practice in both Illinois and California; they will retain their partnership in the Chicago firm, and they will also become partners in the Los Angeles firm. The letterheads of both firms will accurately identify which lawyers are admitted to practice in which jurisdictions. The two firms will regularly refer work back and forth, and each firm will be available to the other firm and its clients for consultation and advice. Further, on some occasions, partners and associates will be transferred from one firm to the other. Each firm will advertise itself as an "affiliate" of the other firm. Is the arrangement *proper*?

A. Yes, provided that the nature of the "affiliate" relationship is explained.

B. Yes, because "affiliate" is a broad term that can cover many kinds of relationships.

C. No, because a partner of a firm in one state is not permitted to be a partner of a firm in a different state.

D. No, because the arrangement contemplates the referral of work from one firm to the other in violation of the solicitation rule.

Answers to the multiple choice questions will be found in the Appendix at the back of the book.

CHAPTER FIVE

ATTORNEY FEES AND FIDUCIARY DUTIES

■ ■ ■

What This Chapter Covers

I. Attorney Fees
- A. Setting Fees
  1. Excessive Fees
  2. Factors in Fee Setting
  3. Contingent Fees
- B. Lending Money to Clients
- C. Splitting Fees With Other Lawyers

II. Fiduciary Duties
- A. Commingling
- B. Safeguarding Property
- C. Notifying Clients, Keeping Records, and Paying Promptly

Reading Assignment

Wydick, Perschbacher & Bassett, Chapter 5.

ABA Model Rules 1.5, 1.8(e) and 1.15.

CRPC 2–200, 4–100, 4–200, and 4–210.

Cal.Bus. & Prof. Code §§ 6146–6149.5, 6210–6212.

Supplemental Reading

Hazard & Hodes:

Discussion of ABA Model Rules 1.5, 1.8(e), and 1.15.

Restatement (Third) of the Law Governing Lawyers §§ 34–47 (2000).

Discussion Problems

1. After graduating from law school three years ago, Dolores became a solo practitioner in a medium-sized city. She has a general civil and criminal practice, and she puts in about 60 hours a week at the office. That yields her a weekly average of 40 billable hours. She takes a two-week vacation in the summer and another two weeks spread throughout

the rest of the year. She and some other solo practitioners occupy a nicely furnished suite of offices under a lease-service arrangement. The leasing company provides them a good law library and also provides receptionist, secretary, delivery, and photocopy services. The lease-service fee plus Dolores's other overhead expenses total about $7,000 per month.

House painter Leonard wants Dolores to represent him in a dispute with an unhappy customer over a $6,000 unpaid painting bill. Dolores offered to handle the matter for an hourly fee, but Leonard wants a flat fee set in advance. Dolores has not handled precisely this kind of case before, and she knows that she will have to do about two hours of basic legal research that would be unnecessary for a more experienced lawyer. She estimates that, in addition to the two hours of basic research, it will take her about 10 billable hours to complete the matter. Assume that the average lawyer in the community would charge Leonard about $1,500.

a. What do you think would be a fair fee for Dolores to charge Leonard? How did you arrive at that figure?

b. Suppose that Dolores quotes Leonard a flat fee of $1,750 and that they make an oral agreement to that effect. Is Dolores subject to discipline?

c. Suppose Leonard wants a contingent fee rather than a flat fee. Dolores agrees to take the case for 35% of whatever amount she recovers for Leonard. Under what, if any, circumstances would that be proper?

d. Suppose that Leonard paints portraits rather than houses, and that the amount in controversy is $60,000 rather than $6,000. How, if at all, would that change your estimate of a fair fee?

2. The law firm of Pursleigh, Siege, Rose–Murray & Tine limits its practice to business law. Much of the firm's work comes from two large clients—Universal Telecom (a worldwide supplier of modern communications equipment and services) and ShopRite, Inc. (a nationwide chain of retail discount stores). Tara Gunn was fresh out of law school when she joined the firm as an associate. Due to the low cost of living in the region, Tara's starting salary was the equivalent of new associates' salaries in New York and other major cities. During her first year at the firm, Tara picked up the following pieces of information about the firm's billing and promotion policies. What is your reaction to each piece of information?

a. During Tara's first month at the firm, she wondered how the firm charges clients, so she asked her supervising partner, who said: "The partner in charge of the matter does the billing. At the end of each billing period, for each lawyer who worked on the matter, the billing partner totals the number of hours worked and multiplies the hours by the billing rate for that lawyer. The more skill and experience the lawyer has, the higher the billing rate. Sometimes the billing partner makes an adjustment to reflect a variety of factors, such as the inexperience of the lawyer, the difficulty of the task, the result achieved, the amount at stake, and so forth. The adjustment can go either up or down, and our clients know that. Sometimes, a client complains about a bill—especially ShopRite, which has a tiny-minded auditor who pecks over every bill looking for nits. When we get a complaint, we sit down with the client and work it out. Does that answer your question?"

b. Associate Albert joined the firm about six months before Tara. One day at lunch, he told Tara: "I spent over 30 hours last week researching a patent licensing issue for Universal Telecom. I felt *so* stupid because I didn't take the IP licensing course in school—when I finally found the right nest of cases, it turned out to be a simple issue with a clear answer. I stayed late at the office three nights in a row to get it done, but I didn't dare log more than 10 hours total, because my boss would think I'm a dolt."

c. When Tara was recruited for the firm, she was told that the firm wants its lawyers to have plenty of time for their families, for the community, and for their own interests and pursuits. Tara was told that the "billable hour target" for associates is 1,800 hours per year. She was also told that associates receive year-end bonuses and raises commensurate with their performance and growth during the year, as determined by the firm's Budget Committee. After she started work, Tara learned from various sources that in recent years associates who log around 1,800 billable hours receive only a token bonus and raise, and that the big money goes to those who log from 2,000 to 2,400 billable hours. Tara also learned that associates in the 1,800 hour range seldom make partner.

d. Associate Allison told Tara that she and other experienced associates have learned "survival skills," such as never logging less than 8 billable hours per day or 40 billable hours per week. Short phone calls help, she said, because the firm's minimum charge for a phone call is 6 minutes (.1 hour), so one can log a half-hour by making five two-minute phone calls. Further, Allison said, she and other associates log "think and worry time." She explained: "When you are working hard on a client's problem, you don't stop thinking about it when you go down the hall to use the restroom, or when you are munching a sandwich at the lunch counter, or when you are cleaning up the baby's room at home, or when you lie awake at night worrying about the questions for tomorrow's deposition. All of that time can be logged if you keep track of it and label it something like 'review and analysis of . . .' or 'preparation for deposition of. . . .' "

e. Tara asked associate Arnold to share his "survival skills" with her. He responded: "The key is to be systematic. First, learn to record your time whenever you switch tasks during the day. When you are working on client A's task, and client B sends you an e-mail that needs a prompt answer, make sure that interruption gets recorded immediately. If you leave the time logging until the end of the day, you will forget half of the interruptions and distractions that consumed your time, and you will wonder how it could have taken you so long to do client A's task. Second, learn to avoid re-inventing the wheel. Most of my work is employment discrimination and sexual harassment cases for ShopRite and Universal Telecom. I've concluded that sexual harassment cases come in five basic patterns. Once I figured out the patterns, I developed five sets of standard forms and checklists. They are on my computer, and when a new case comes along, my secretary and I can churn out the pleadings, the interrogatories, the pretrial motions, and so forth in a third of the time it used to take. I know how long it used to take, and that's how much time I log for the task. By being systematic, I have been able to bill around 2,300 hours in each of the last two years. My supervising partner is delighted, the client is well served, and I'm headed for partnership."

3. Dringle bought a sailboat and a motorboat from Seaboard Marine Supply Company on credit, and he failed to make timely payments on either boat. Seaboard hired attorney Welch to collect the two debts. Welch sent a series of appropriate demand letters to Dringle. Finally, Dringle left a check, a message, and a set of keys at Welch's office. The message said: "Here is a check for the $7,500 I owe Seaboard on the sailboat. I have no way to pay for the motorboat, so here are the keys to it; you will find it tied to the dock at the City Marina." At the time, Welch was in trial and working 16 hours a day, so she put the message, the check, and the keys in an envelope, labeled it "Seaboard Marine," and put the envelope in her office safe. Her trial ended two weeks later, and that very day she deposited the check in her client trust account and notified Seaboard about the keys and the location of the motorboat. Did Welch handle the matter properly?

4. Attorney Arner agreed to represent client Corman in a suit against defendant Drews. Arner's written fee agreement with Corman provided that Arner would receive $75 per hour for his work, and that the fee "may be deducted from the proceeds of said litigation before payment thereof to" Corman. Corman won a judgment for $50,000, and Drews sent Arner a check in that amount, made payable to Corman. Arner consulted his time records and concluded that he had spent 153.3 hours on the case, for a total fee of $11,500. Arner endorsed the check with Corman's name and presented it at the bank where he maintained his client trust account. He had $38,500 deposited in the client trust account, and he took the other $11,500 in the form of a bank cashier's check, made payable to him personally. That same day, he wrote to Corman as follows:

> Drews' check came in today. I have expended 153.3 hours on the matter, for a total fee of $11,500. Accordingly, I am holding $38,500 for your account, and I will send you a check in that sum promptly upon receiving word from you that the fee computation is correct and in accordance with our agreement.

Did Arner handle the matter properly?

ROBERT L. WHEELER, INC. v. SCOTT

Supreme Court of Oklahoma, 1989.
777 P.2d 394.

KAUGER, JUSTICE.

The dispositive question is whether, after summary judgment was entered against Robert L. Scott (appellant/client) in a mortgage foreclosure proceeding, and after the trial court subsequently reduced the fee charged by Scott's attorney from $140,116.87 to $125,723.00, the fee was still excessive. After a careful examination of the standards enunciated in [prior cases,] we find that it was.

FACTS

* * * Robert L. Scott (client/appellant), a geologist and a geophysicist, hired Robert L. Wheeler (appellee/lawyer) to represent him after he was unable to pay a business loan. During the next ten months, Wheeler represented Scott in the collection and lien foreclosure action filed against Scott by the mortgagee, United Oklahoma Bank. In the first five months of Wheeler's representation, Scott was billed for legal services in the amount of $54,275.37 representing 524.5 hours and averaging 108.5 hours per month which he paid. During the next five months, Scott was billed $85,841.50 for legal services representing 753.4 hours, averaging 150.6 hours per month which he did not pay.

* * * [The bank then] moved for summary judgment. Two days before the hearing on the bank's motion, the lawyer told his client that if the attorney fees were not paid, he would withdraw from the case. Scott did not pay, and Wheeler did not withdraw. Instead, a first year associate was sent to oppose the bank's motion for summary judgment. The bank's motion was granted, and the attorney withdrew from the case * * *. Thereafter, Scott retained new counsel, and the case was settled.

* * * [Wheeler then] filed an action to collect unpaid attorney fees. Scott answered, asserting that the fees were excessive for the following reasons:

1) The case was never tried. Summary judgment was entered against him.

2) The client was billed a total of 1295.9 hours. However, a first year associate, who had failed to pass the bar at the first sitting, and who had been admitted to the bar for only five months before beginning work on the case, billed 853.5 hours at $110.00 an hour.

3) The firm representing the bank charged the bank $75,534.10 for 850 hours. These hours were for three attorneys with an average of ten to twenty years of experience, who normally bill at $150.00 an hour. However, because the lawyers are on retainer with the bank, they reduced their normal hourly rate in this case.

4) The bank's motion for summary judgment alleged that although a large amount of money and property was involved, the foreclosure was a simple case complicated by unfounded and legally unsound assertions by Scott's counsel. The bank's lawyer repeated these assertions at the hearing on attorney fees, and he also testified that his first year associates were billed at $85.00 an hour.

5) As prevailing party, the opposing attorney received $75,534.10 in attorney fees.

After hearing the evidence, the trial court reduced the hourly rate of the first year associate from $110.00 to $80.00, and the total attorney's fee from $140,116.87 to $125,723.00. Scott appealed. The Court of Appeals affirmed * * *. We granted certiorari * * * to address the question of the reasonableness of the attorney fee.

* * *

A proper resolution of this case requires a thorough examination and balancing of the * * * [twelve factors we discuss below:] * * *

1. *Time and labor required*

The most visible and the most readily explainable portion of a bill for attorney fees is the time and labor expended by an attorney in performing services for a client. However, it is not the only relevant factor, and it must be considered in conjunction with the other enumerated criteria. Fees cannot be awarded on the basis of time alone—the use of time as the sole standard is of dubious value. Were fees to be calculated based only on the time spent on a case, worthy use of time would cease to be a virtue, a premium would be placed on inexperience, inefficiency, and inability, and expeditious disposition of litigation would go unrewarded.

Time spent in acquiring a basic law school education in the area of law concerned cannot be regarded as one of the determinative factors of a reasonable attorney fee. Attorneys are presumed to have acquired a working knowledge of fundamental legal principles as well as the ability to examine and apply the law. This does not mean that an attorney, within the limitations ordinarily necessary for a competent and skillful lawyer, should not be compensated for the time spent in necessary research. It does mean that if a lawyer takes on a case in an area in which he or she is totally unfamiliar or inexperienced, the client should not have to pay for every minute of the lawyer's preparation. Here, for example, a comparison of the time charged for preparation of the case by each of the law firms reflects that it is unlikely that billing 1295.9 billable hours, 853.5 of which were by a first year lawyer, was proper when the prevailing law firm staffed by seasoned counsel charged for 850 hours. In short, a reasonable attorney's fee in a given case does not necessarily result from simple multiplication of the hours spent times a fixed hourly rate.

2. *Novelty or difficulty of issues*

The attorney for the prevailing party testified at the hearing, and he stated in his motion for summary judgment, that this was a simple case. He also noted that although a large sum of money was involved, the case had been unduly complicated by opposing counsel's unfounded and legally unsound assertions. One of the basic considerations in establishing the reasonable value of legal services is the type, extent, and difficulty of the services rendered. Substance must control over form. The intricacy and difficulty of the questions involved, and not necessarily the amount of manual legal work exhibited by the number of papers in the file of the case, must control.

3. *The skill requisite to perform*

Another factor, which must be considered with the novelty or difficulty of the issues, is whether the services are routine, or whether exceptional skill or effort is required. Wheeler testified that he relied on his oil and gas expertise in designing his strategy. However, this expertise apparently did not come into play before summary judgment was entered because the attorney did not determine the value of the oil producing properties until after it was rendered. (The declining value of the properties was the reason given by the bank for settling the cause for less than the amount entered in its favor on summary judgment.)

4. *Loss of opportunity for other employment*

The fact that the employment for which compensation is sought deprived the attorney of the opportunity to secure other employment is another element of some significance in determining a reasonable fee. The court must consider not only the loss of other employment because of the time taken by the matter at hand, but also the fact that there may be involved in the matter certain elements which might cause the attorney to lose future business because of an association with the case. The attorney testified that this case neither required that he refuse to represent a potential client, nor did he introduce any evidence that his association with this case deprived him of future business.

5. *The customary fee*

Generally, courts consider the amounts customarily charged or allowed for similar services in the same locality. Only two witnesses were presented, and their testimony was conflicting. The expert called by Scott testified that the amount the prevailing party received, $75,500.00, was reasonable compensation. The expert witness, who testified on behalf of Wheeler, stated that $140,000.00 was a reasonable fee.

6. *Whether the fee is fixed or contingent*

Although the court initially looks to the hourly rate for comparable representation where compensation is guaranteed, it must adjust the basic hourly rate where compensation is contingent by assessing the likelihood of success at the outset of the representation. Although contingent fee contracts are subject to restrictions, especially if the client is a minor, such agreements have generally been enforced unless the contract is unreasonable. The contingent fee system allows persons who could not otherwise afford to assert their claims to have their day in Court. In this case, a contingent fee is not involved. The parties agreed that the fee would be based on an hourly rate.

7. *Time limitations imposed by the client or circumstances*

This element is pertinent if an attorney must adjust the firm's other work load to accommodate the particular pressing needs of a client. Generally, additional fees have been allowed when the client failed timely to notify the attorney of such problems. There was no evidence implying any unusual time restrictions.

8. *The amount involved and the results obtained*

In establishing reasonable attorney fees, the court may properly consider the amount involved in litigation. This case involved over ten million dollars. However, this cannot be the sole component to be weighed. If the amount implicated, even though large in denomination, neither increases measurably the work nor enlarges the principles of law, it cannot be the deciding factor in setting a very high fee.

Closely related to the element of the amount or value of the property at issue, is the solution achieved by the attorney. While the court should consider all the guidelines, it must also contemplate the benefit to the client as a result of the services. The attorney testified that his client needed what he provided—time for opportunity to accomplish settlement—either to extend the client's loan or to make arrangements to fit his cash flow and current financial condition. (We note that after the attorney withdrew, the client and the bank settled.)

9. *Experience, reputation, and ability of the attorney*

The attorney's standing in the profession for learning, ability, skill, and integrity is recognized as a proper matter for consideration in assessing the value of the services provided and can be a basis for a higher award. The reverse is also true: inexperience, apparent lack of ability, or poor performance may reduce the award. Here, it appears from the time sheets and the appearances in court, that the primary attorney was the first year associate. The testimony by the expert witnesses indicated that the first year associate had not established a reputation in the legal community sufficient to command a higher fee.

10. *The undesirability of the case*

Apparently, this was an ordinary case to foreclose a lien which the client had little chance of winning, and that the client's best solution was the settlement obtained after the attorney withdrew from the case.

11. *Casual or regular employment*

The nature and length of the professional relationship between the client and the attorney is also subject to review. Clients who do not routinely employ the attorney should not expect the lower legal fees normally negotiated with clients who regularly hire or retain counsel. Scott was not a regular client.

12. Awards in similar cases

There was no evidence presented concerning awards in similar cases, other than the amount received by the prevailing party.

CONCLUSION

The proper determination of reasonable attorney fees requires a balancing and thorough consideration of the * * * [twelve factors we have discussed.] Apparently, the trial court gave too much weight to the time spent on the case and failed to consider adequately the other applicable standards. Setting attorney fees would be a simple matter if numbers could be inserted mechanically into a universally valid formula. Unfortunately, this is not the case. Here, it is obvious that much of the time expended was unnecessary by any reasonable standard. Under our detailed analysis of the guidelines—particularly the excessive time spent, the relative simplicity of the issues (except where they were needlessly multiplied and complicated by counsel), the very average lawyering skill required, the nonpreclusion of other employment, the entry of summary judgment, the customary fee, the absence of restrictive time limitations, and the inexperience of the lawyer who did the bulk of the work—we find that the fee allowed by the trial court is excessive. [Reversed and remanded with directions.]

ABA FORMAL OPINION 93-379

American Bar Association Committee on Ethics and Professional Responsibility, 1993*

Consistent with the Model Rules of Professional Conduct, a lawyer must disclose to a client the basis on which the client is to be billed for both professional time and any other charges. Absent a contrary understanding, any invoice for professional services should fairly reflect the basis on which the client's charges have been determined. In matters where the client has agreed to have the fee determined with reference to the time expended by the lawyer, a lawyer may not bill more time than she actually spends on a matter, except to the extent that she rounds up to minimum time periods (such as one-quarter or one-tenth of an hour). A lawyer may not charge a client for overhead expenses generally associated with properly maintaining, staffing and equipping an office; however, the lawyer may recoup expenses reasonably incurred in connection with the client's matter for services performed in-house, such as photocopying, long distance telephone calls, computer research, special deliveries, secretarial overtime, and other similar services, so long as the charge reasonably reflects the lawyer's actual cost for the services rendered. A lawyer may not charge a client more than her disbursements for services provided by third parties like court reporters, travel agents or expert witnesses, except to the extent that the lawyer incurs costs additional to the direct cost of the third-party services.

The legal profession has dedicated a substantial amount of time and energy to developing elaborate sets of ethical guidelines for the benefit of its clients. Similarly, the profession has spent extraordinary resources on interpreting, teaching and enforcing these ethics rules. Yet, ironically, lawyers are not generally regarded by the public as particularly ethical. One major contributing factor to the discouraging public opinion of the legal profession appears to be the billing practices of some of its members.

It is a common perception that pressure on lawyers to bill a minimum number of hours and on law firms to maintain or improve profits may have led some lawyers to engage in problematic billing practices. These include charges to more than one client for the same work or the same hours, surcharges on services contracted with outside vendors, and charges beyond reasonable costs for in-house services like photocopying and computer searches. Moreover, the bases on which these charges are to be assessed often are not disclosed in advance or are disguised in cryptic invoices so that the client does not fully understand exactly what costs are being charged to him.

The Model Rules of Professional Conduct provide important principles applicable to the billing of clients, principles which, if followed, would ameliorate many of the problems noted above. The Committee has decided to address several practices that are the subject of frequent inquiry, with the goal of helping the profession adhere to its ethical obligations to its clients despite economic pressures.

The first set of practices involves billing more than one client for the same hours spent. In one illustrative situation, a lawyer finds it possible to schedule court appearances for three clients on the same day. He spends a total of four hours at the courthouse, the amount of time he would have spent on behalf of each client had it not been for the fortuitous circumstance that all three cases were scheduled on the same day. May he bill each of the three clients, who otherwise understand that they will be billed on the basis of time spent, for the four hours he spent on them collectively? In another scenario, a lawyer is flying cross-country to attend a deposition on behalf of one client, expending travel time she would ordinarily bill to that client. If she decides not to watch the movie or read her novel, but to work instead on drafting a motion for another client, may she charge both clients, each of whom agreed to hourly billing, for the time during which she was traveling on behalf of one and drafting a document on behalf of the other? A third situation involves research on a particular topic for one client that later turns out to be relevant to an inquiry from a second client. May the firm bill the second client, who agreed to be charged on the basis of time spent on his case, the same amount for the recycled work product that it charged the first client?

The second set of practices involves billing for expenses and disbursements, and is exemplified by the situation in which a firm contracts for the expert witness services of an economist at an hourly rate of $200. May the firm bill the client for the expert's time at the rate of $250 per hour? Similarly, may the firm add a surcharge to the cost of computer-assisted research if the per-minute total charged by the computer company does not include the cost of purchasing the computers or staffing their operation?

The questions presented to the Committee require us to determine what constitutes reasonable billing procedures; that is, what are the services and costs for which a lawyer may legitimately charge, both generally and with regard to the specific scenarios? This inquiry requires an elucidation of the Rule of Professional Conduct 1.5 and the Model Code of Professional Responsibility DR 2–106.

Disclosure of the Bases of the Amounts to Be Charged

At the outset of the representation the lawyer should make disclosure of the basis for the fee and any other charges to the client. This is a two-fold duty, including not only an explanation at the beginning of engagement of the basis on which fees and other charges will be billed, but also a sufficient explanation in the statement so that the client may reasonably be expected to understand what fees and other charges the client is actually being billed.

Authority for the obligation to make disclosure at the beginning of a representation is found in the interplay among a number of rules. Rule 1.5(b) provides that

> When the lawyer has not regularly represented the client, the basis or rate of the fee shall be communicated to the client, preferably in writing, before or within a reasonable time after commencing the representation.

The Comment to Rule 1.5 gives guidance on how to execute the duty to communicate the basis of the fee:

> In a new client-lawyer relationship . . . an understanding as to the fee should be promptly established. It is not necessary to recite all the factors that underlie the basis of the fee, but only those that are directly involved in its computation. It is sufficient, for example, to state that the basic rate is an hourly charge or a fixed amount or an estimated amount, or to identify the factors that may be taken into account in finally fixing the fee. When developments occur during the representation that render an earlier estimate substantially inaccurate, a revised estimate should be provided to the client. A written statement concerning the fee reduces the possibility of misunderstanding. Furnishing the client with a simple memorandum or a copy

> of the lawyer's customary fee schedule is sufficient if the basis or rate of the fee is set forth.

> This obligation is reinforced by reference to Model Rule 1.4(b) which provides that

> A lawyer shall explain a matter to the extent reasonably necessary to permit the client to make informed decisions regarding the representation.

While the Comment to this Rule suggests its obvious applicability to negotiations or litigation with adverse parties, its important principle should be equally applicable to the lawyer's obligation to explain the basis on which the lawyer expects to be compensated, so the client can make one of the more important decisions "regarding the representation."

An obligation of disclosure is also supported by Model Rule 7.1, which addresses communications concerning a lawyer's services, including the basis on which fees would be charged. The rule provides:

> A lawyer shall not make a false or misleading communication about the lawyer or the lawyer's services. A communication is false or misleading if it:
>
> (a) contains a material misrepresentation of fact or law, or omits a fact necessary to make the statement considered as a whole not materially misleading.

It is clear under Model Rule 7.1 that in offering to perform services for prospective clients it is critical that lawyers avoid making any statements about fees that are not complete. If it is true that a lawyer when advertising for new clients must disclose, for example, that costs are the responsibility of the client, *Zauderer v. Office of Disciplinary Counsel,* 471 U.S. 626 (1985), it necessarily follows that in entering into an actual client relationship a lawyer must make fair disclosure of the basis on which fees will be assessed.

A corollary of the obligation to disclose the basis for future billing is a duty to render statements to the client that adequately apprise the client as to how that basis for billing has been applied. In an engagement in which the client has agreed to compensate the lawyer on the basis of time expended at regular hourly rates, a bill setting out no more than a total dollar figure for unidentified professional services will often be insufficient to tell the client what he or she needs to know in order to understand how the amount was determined. By the same token, billing other charges without breaking the charges down by type would not provide the client with the information the client needs to understand the basis for the charges.

Initial disclosure of the basis for the fee arrangement fosters communication that will promote the attorney-client relationship. The relationship will be similarly benefitted if the statement for services explicitly reflects the basis for the charges so that the client understands how the fee bill was determined.

Professional Obligations Regarding the Reasonableness of Fees

Implicit in the Model Rules and their antecedents is the notion that the attorney-client relationship is not necessarily one of equals, that it is built on trust, and that the client is encouraged to be dependent on the lawyer, who is dealing with matters of great moment to the client. The client should only be charged a reasonable fee for the legal services performed. Rule 1.5 explicitly addresses the reasonableness of legal fees. The rule deals not only with the determination of a reasonable hourly rate, but also with total cost to the client. The Comment to the rule states, for example, that "[a] lawyer should not exploit a fee arrangement based primarily on hourly charges by using wasteful procedures." The goal should be solely to compensate the lawyer fully for time reasonably expended, an approach that if followed will not take advantage of the client.

Ethical Consideration 2–17 of the Model Code of Professional Responsibility provides a framework for balancing the interests between the lawyer and client in determining the reasonableness of a fee arrangement:

> The determination of a proper fee requires consideration of the interests of both client and lawyer. A lawyer should not charge more than a reasonable fee, for excessive cost of legal service would deter laymen from utilizing the legal system in protection of their rights. Furthermore, an excessive charge abuses the professional relationship between lawyer and client. On the other hand, adequate compensation is necessary in order to enable the lawyer to serve his client effectively and to preserve the integrity and independence of the profession.

The lawyer's conduct should be such as to promote the client's trust of the lawyer and of the legal profession. This means acting as the advocate for the client to the extent necessary to complete a project thoroughly. Only through careful attention to detail is the lawyer able to manage a client's case properly. An unreasonable limitation on the hours a lawyer may spend on a client should be avoided as a threat to the lawyer's ability to fulfill her obligation under Model Rule 1.1 to "provide competent representation to a client." "Competent representation requires the legal knowledge, skill, thoroughness and preparation necessary for the representation." Model Rule 1.1. Certainly either a willingness on the part of the lawyer, or a demand by the client, to circumscribe the lawyer's efforts, to compromise the lawyer's ability to be as thorough and as prepared as necessary, is not in the best interests of the client and may lead to a violation of Model Rule 1.1 if it means the lawyer is unable to provide competent representation. The Comment to Model Rule 1.2, while observing that "the scope of services provided by a lawyer may be limited by agreement," also notes that an agreement "concerning the scope of representation must accord with the Rules.... Thus, the client may not be asked to agree to representation so limited in scope as to violate Rule 1.1. . . ."[3]

On the other hand, the lawyer who has agreed to bill on the basis of hours expended does not fulfill her ethical duty if she bills the client for more time than she actually spent on the client's behalf.[4] In addressing the hypotheticals regarding (a) simultaneous appearance on behalf of three clients, (b) the airplane flight on behalf of one client while working on another client's matters and (c) recycled work product, it is helpful to consider these questions, not from the perspective of what a client could be forced to pay, but rather from the perspective of what the lawyer actually earned. A lawyer who spends four hours of time on behalf of three clients has not earned twelve billable hours. A lawyer who flies for six hours for one client, while working for five hours on behalf of another, has not earned eleven billable hours. A lawyer who is able to reuse old work product has not re-earned the hours previously billed and compensated when the work product was first generated. Rather than looking to profit from the fortuity of coincidental scheduling, the desire to get work done rather than watch a movie, or the luck of being asked the identical question twice, the lawyer who has agreed to bill solely on the basis of time spent is obliged to pass the benefits of these economies on to the client. The practice of billing several clients for the same time or work product, since it results in the earning of an unreasonable fee, therefore is contrary to the mandate of the Model Rules. Model Rule 1.5.

Moreover, continuous toil on or overstaffing a project for the purpose of churning out hours is also not properly considered "earning" one's fees. One job of a lawyer is to expedite the legal process. Model Rule 3.2. Just as a lawyer is expected to discharge a matter on summary judgment if possible rather than proceed to trial, so too is the lawyer expected to complete other projects for a client efficiently. A lawyer should take as much time as is reasonably required to complete a project, and should certainly never be motivated by anything other than the best interests of the client when determining how to staff or how much time to spend on any particular project.

It goes without saying that a lawyer who has undertaken to bill on an hourly basis is never justified in charging a client for hours not actually expended. If a lawyer has agreed to charge the client on this basis and it turns out that the lawyer is particularly efficient in accomplishing a given result, it nonetheless will not be permissible to charge the client for more hours than were actually expended on the matter. When that basis for billing the client has been agreed to, the economies associated with the result must inure to the benefit of the client, not give rise to an

3. Beyond the scope of this opinion is the question whether a lawyer, with full disclosure to a sophisticated client of the risks involved, can agree to undertake at the request of the client only ten hours of research, when the lawyer knows that the resulting work product does not fulfill the competent representation requirement of Model Rule 1.1.

4. Rule 1.5 clearly contemplates that there are bases for billing clients other than the time expended. This opinion, however, only addresses issues raised when it is understood that the client will be charged on the basis of time expended.

opportunity to bill a client phantom hours. This is not to say that the lawyer who agreed to hourly compensation is not free, with full disclosure, to suggest additional compensation because of a particularly efficient or outstanding result, or because the lawyer was able to reuse prior work product on the client's behalf. The point here is that fee enhancement cannot be accomplished simply by presenting the client with a statement reflecting more billable hours than were actually expended. On the other hand, if a matter turns out to be more difficult to accomplish than first anticipated and more hours are required than were originally estimated, the lawyer is fully entitled (though not required) to bill those hours unless the client agreement turned the original estimate into a cap on the fees to be charged.

Charges Other Than Professional Fees

In addition to charging clients fees for professional services, lawyers typically charge their clients for certain additional items which are often referred to variously as disbursements, out-of-pocket expenses or additional charges. Inquiries to the Committee demonstrate that the profession has encountered difficulties in conforming to the ethical standards in this area as well. The Rules provide no specific guidance on the issue of how much a lawyer may charge a client for costs incurred over and above her own fee. However, we believe that the reasonableness standard explicitly applicable to fees under Rule 1.5(a) should be applicable to these charges as well.

The Committee, in trying to sort out the issues related to these charges, has identified three different questions which must be addressed. First, which items are properly subject to additional charges? Second, to what extent, if at all, may clients be charged for more than actual out-of-pocket disbursements? Third, on what basis may clients be charged for the provision of in-house services? We shall address these one at a time.

A. General Overhead

When a client has engaged a lawyer to provide professional services for a fee (whether calculated on the basis of the number of hours expended, a flat fee, a contingent percentage of the amount recovered or otherwise) the client would be justifiably disturbed if the lawyer submitted a bill to the client which included, beyond the professional fee, additional charges for general office overhead. In the absence of disclosure to the client in advance of the engagement to the contrary, the client should reasonably expect that the lawyer's cost in maintaining a library, securing malpractice insurance, renting of office space, purchasing utilities and the like would be subsumed within the charges the lawyer is making for professional services.

B. Disbursements

At the beginning of the engagement lawyers typically tell their clients that they will be charged for disbursements. When that term is used, clients justifiably should expect that the lawyer will be passing on to the client those actual payments of funds made by the lawyer on the client's behalf. Thus, if the lawyer hires a court stenographer to transcribe a deposition, the client can reasonably expect to be billed as a disbursement the amount the lawyer pays to the court reporting service. Similarly, if the lawyer flies to Los Angeles for the client, the client can reasonably expect to be billed as a disbursement the amount of the airfare, taxicabs, meals and hotel room.

It is the view of the Committee that, in the absence of disclosure to the contrary, it would be improper if the lawyer assessed a surcharge on these disbursements over and above the amount actually incurred unless the lawyer herself incurred additional expenses beyond the actual cost of the disbursement item. In the same regard, if a lawyer receives a discounted rate from a third-party provider, it would be improper if she did not pass along the benefit of the discount to her client rather than charge the client the full rate and reserve the profit to herself. Clients quite properly could view these practices as an attempt to create additional undisclosed profit centers when the client had been told he would be billed for disbursements.

C. In–House Provision of Services

Perhaps the most difficult issue is the handling of charges to clients for the provision of in-house services. In this connection the Committee has in view charges for photocopying, computer research, on-site meals, deliveries and other similar items. Like professional fees, it seems clear that lawyers may pass on reasonable charges for these services. Thus, in the view of the Committee, the lawyer and the client may agree in advance that, for example, photocopying will be charged at $.15 per page, or messenger services will be provided at $5.00 per mile. However, the question arises what may be charged to the client, in the absence of a specific agreement to the contrary, when the client has simply been told that costs for these items will be charged to the client. We conclude that under those circumstances the lawyer is obliged to charge the client no more than the direct cost associated with the service (*i.e.,* the actual cost of making a copy on the photocopying machine) plus a reasonable allocation of overhead expenses directly associated with the provision of the service (*e.g.,* the salary of a photocopy machine operator).

It is not appropriate for the Committee, in addressing ethical standards, to opine on the various accounting issues as to how one calculates direct cost and what may or may not be included in allocated overhead. These are questions which properly should be reserved for our colleagues in the accounting profession. Rather, it is the responsibility of the Committee to explain the principles it draws from the mandate of Model Rule 1.5's injunction that fees be reasonable. Any reasonable calculation of direct costs as well as any reasonable allocation of related overhead should pass ethical muster. On the other hand, in the absence of an agreement to the contrary, it is impermissible for a lawyer to create an additional source of profit for the law firm beyond that which is contained in the provision of professional services themselves. The lawyer's stock in trade is the sale of legal services, not photocopy paper, tuna fish sandwiches, computer time or messenger services.

CONCLUSION

As the foregoing demonstrates, the subject of fees for professional services and other charges is one that is fraught with tension between the lawyer and the client. Nonetheless, if the principles outlined in this opinion are followed, the ethical resolution of these issues can be achieved. [*See generally* Lisa G. Lerman, *Blue–Chip Bilking: Regulation of Billing and Expense Fraud by Lawyers*, 12 Geo. J. Legal Ethics 205 (1999).]

THE BILLABLE HOURS TREADMILL

In mid–2002, the ABA Commission on Billable Hours issued a report[a] that urges the legal profession to stop using billable hours as the primary measure of a lawyer's worth and the primary determinant of a client's fee. Supreme Court Justice Stephen Breyer introduces the report by asking why so many lawyers ignore society's need for law reform work and for pro bono legal services. Here is his answer:

> The villain * * * is what some call the "treadmill"—the continuous push to increase billable hours. * * * How can a practitioner undertake pro bono work, engage in law reform efforts, even attend bar association meetings, if that lawyer also must produce 2100 or more billable hours each year, say sixty-five or seventy hours in the office each week. The answer is that most cannot, and for this, both the profession and the community suffer.
>
> The treadmill's pressure is partly financial: law firm salaries have grown exponentially; at the same time, younger lawyers must repay law school loans that may amount to $100,000 or more. But the pressure also reflects the increasing complexity and specialization of the law itself, along with growing demands by clients for a precise accounting of the services for which they pay.[b]

The worship of billable hours is a relatively new religion for lawyers. Before 1960 or so, many lawyers didn't even keep formal records of the amount of time they spent on various clients' legal matters. For routine legal matters (such as the drafting of a simple will), many lawyers simply billed their clients in accordance with "minimum fee schedules" published by state or local bar associations—a kind of price fixing that would be illegal per se if done in an ordinary business.

---

a. ABA Commission on Billable Hours Report, 2001–2002, <http://www.abanet.org/careercounsel/billable/toolkit/bhcomplete.pdf> (visited September 6, 2002). The views expressed in the report have not been approved by the ABA House of Delegates or the ABA Board of Governors, so they do not reflect official ABA policy.

b. *Id.* at vii.

For more complicated legal matters, lawyers in those days used the "multitude of factors" method that is reflected in today's ABA Model Rule 1.5(a). At the end of the legal matter, (or the end of the year, or quarter, or month), the billing lawyer would look over the client's file to review what had been done, by which lawyers, how long it took, how much was at stake, how difficult it was, and what results had been accomplished for the client. Then the billing lawyer would write up a "Statement for Services Rendered" containing a sketchy description of the various tasks that were completed during the billing period, followed by a dollar figure showing the amount the client owed for legal fees. (Simultaneously, the client would receive a separate bill itemizing the "Disbursements," meaning the amounts the lawyer had expended on the client's behalf for court filings, service of process, court reporters, long distance telephone charges, investigation expenses, out-of-town travel expenses, and the like.) In those days, clients generally trusted their lawyers. Fee disputes were uncommon, and clients rarely demanded a more detailed explanation of the legal fees they were asked to pay.

During the 1970s, four forces elevated the billable hour to its present exalted position. First, the United States Supreme Court held that the Sherman Antitrust Act prohibits bar associations from publishing "minimum fee schedules."[c] Second, the Court decided the *Bates* case,[d] which you read in the last chapter, holding that lawyers may advertise their wares and their prices, and opening a new era of competition in the legal profession. Third, lawyers started listening to self-styled experts in law office management, who were teaching that lawyers who keep meticulous time records make more profit than those who don't. Fourth, clients began to demand more detailed explanations of legal fees, especially corporate clients with legal departments that were told to keep watch over the work done and fees charged by outside counsel.

When a law firm uses billable hours to charge a client (or as the first step in charging a client), the firm must set a billing rate for each lawyer or each category of lawyers. For example, the billing rate for associates with one year of experience might be $X per hour, and the billing rate for partners with twenty years of experience might be $5X per hour. If billable hours were the *sole determinant* of a fee bill to a client, then computing the bill would be a simple exercise in multiplication and addition. The billing lawyer would multiply the number of hours each lawyer worked on the matter times that lawyer's billing rate, and the resulting sums would be added up to produce the total fee. Few firms would admit to using billable hours as the *sole determinant* of a bill to a client; most would say that they use billable hours as the *first step*, followed by a judgmental step in which the billing lawyer adjusts the fee, either up or down, by considering the *other factors* listed in ABA Model Rule 1.5(a).

---

c. *See* Goldfarb v. Virginia State Bar, 421 U.S. 773 (1975).

d. Bates v. State Bar of Arizona, 433 U.S. 350 (1977).

The ABA report finds that law firms increased their reliance on billable hours during the 1970s and 1980s.[e] The report continues:

> Under a [law firm] budget based on billable hours, the best way to increase revenue was either increase the * * * [billing rate for each lawyer] or increase the number of hours worked. During the 1970s and 1980s, the system based on both lawyer rates and billable hours worked. Firms set billable hour *goals* for their partners and associates. However, as competition among lawyers increased and the economy fluctuated, many lawyers could not increase their rates enough to cover increased expenses. As a result, the number of billable hours worked had to be increased. Firms began taking a harder line and billable-hour *goals* became billable-hour *commitments*. During the 1990s, those billable-hour commitments reached unreasonably high levels in many firms.[f]

In his preface to the billable hours report, the then-ABA President Robert Hirshon wrote:

> Today, unintended consequences of the billable hours model have permeated the profession. * * * [M]any young attorneys are leaving the profession due to a lack of balance in their lives. The unending drive for billable hours has had a negative effect not only on family and personal relationships, but on the public service role that lawyers traditionally have played in society. The elimination of discretionary time has taken a toll on pro bono work and our profession's ability to be involved in our communities. At the same time, professional development, workplace stimulation, mentoring and lawyer/client relationships have all suffered as a result of billable hour pressures.[g]

The billable hours model is seriously flawed, President Hirshon wrote:

> The billable hour is fundamentally about quantity over quality, repetition over creativity. With no gage for intangibles such as productivity, creativity, knowledge, or technical advancements, the billable hours model is a counter-intuitive measure of value. Alternatives that encourage efficiency and improve processes not only increase profits and provide earlier resolution of legal matters, but are less likely to garner ethical concerns.[h]

The ABA report examines the flaws in the billable hours model in greater detail. Here are some of the conclusions:

1) The billable hours model doesn't encourage the lawyer to prepare a project plan or case plan at the outset. The lawyer can simply start working and reporting hours. Lack of planning can produce inefficiency and raise the client's costs. In contrast, a billing arrangement that

---

e. *See* ABA report, *supra* note a, at 3.

f. *Id.* Emphasis added.

g. *Id.* at ix.

h. *Id.*

includes a flat fee or contingent fee component forces the lawyer to plan from the start.[i]

2) The billable hours model doesn't enable the client to predict how much the legal services will cost. How can the client make a sensible cost-benefit judgment if the client doesn't know the cost half of the equation? But, a lawyer might respond, legal matters are notoriously unpredictable—one cannot tell in advance how much time and effort a matter might take. The report concedes that *some* legal matters are unpredictable enough to warrant an hourly charge, but "too often hourly billing becomes a crutch for the lawyer who is not sufficiently knowledgeable * * * [or] productive, or is unwilling to share with the client the risk of the lawyer's own inefficiency."[j]

3) The billable hours model penalizes the efficient, productive lawyer and rewards the slow plodder who racks up many billable hours. True, that won't happen if the efficient, productive lawyer is assigned a higher billing rate, and is paid a proportionately higher wage, but the ABA report argues that too often the billing rate spread and wage spread are not large enough to reward efficiency and productivity. Moreover, the billable hours model discourages lawyers from taking advantage of "research on the shelf" (such as a set of interrogatories the firm used two years ago in a case just like this one), and taking advantage of technological change (such as drafting on a word processor rather than giving dictation to a legal secretary).[k]

4) The billable hours model may discourage communication between lawyer and client. For example, suppose a law firm that charges a minimum quarter-hour for every phone call. When the client becomes aware that a five-minute telephone inquiry to his lawyer costs him a minimum quarter-hour of the lawyer's time, the client may stop making inquiries, even legitimate ones. On the other hand, when the lawyer discovers that she can rack up a full hour of billable time by making four short phone calls, she may snow her clients under with routine reports, causing them to instruct her to accomplish more and communicate less.[l]

Neither the ABA report, nor any thoughtful lawyer, argues that law firms should stop all use of time as a measure of legal fees and lawyer productivity. "Time spent" has always been, and should continue to be, an important factor in setting fees and setting compensation to lawyers. The ABA report does, however, encourage law firms to continue experimenting with alternative methods of charging clients and paying lawyers. No alternative method is right for every firm in every case, but here are three of the alternative methods described in the ABA report:

1) *Fixed or Flat Fees.* A fixed or flat fee is a specified dollar figure the firm will charge the client for a specified piece of legal work. [Some firms

---

i. *Id.* at 5–6.

j. *Id.* at 6.

k. *Id.*

l. *See id.*

use the trendier label "task-based billing."] Fixed or flat fees are the most common alternative to hourly fees; they are especially popular with medium-sized law firms doing transaction work (rather than litigation).[m] One reason they are used less often in litigation is that they do not make the client consider litigation costs when making or responding to a settlement proposal.[n] However, in 2009, O'Melveny and Myers announced its intention to become "the leader in providing high-end legal services on a fixed fee basis," and both Mayer Brown and Reed Smith moved to institute fixed fees for transactional work.

2) *Contingent Fees.* As is discussed in the following section of this chapter, contingent fees have started to spread in the United States from their point of origin in the personal injury field. In a pure contingent fee arrangement, the lawyer's fee depends entirely on the outcome of the matter—if the client achieves the desired result, the lawyer gets a handsome reward, but if the client does not achieve that result, the lawyer gets nothing. The ABA report mentions that in Japan, lawyers traditionally charge a fairly low base fee to finance the case, followed by a final fee that depends on the outcome of the matter. This approach allows the Japanese lawyer to cover costs "and to focus not on the time spent, but on the results, which is where the clients focus."[o]

3) *Hybrid Billing Methods.* As the name suggests, hybrid alternatives combine the features of two or more other billing methods.[p] One fairly common hybrid is the flat fee plus an hourly rate for work in excess of a specified maximum. (For example, lawyer L might agree to do the first 500 hours of work for a $100,000 flat fee, plus $100 per hour for work in excess of the 500 hours.) Another hybrid is the hourly fee plus a contingent fee. (For example, lawyer L might agree to do all the necessary work for $100 per hour, plus 5% of whatever amount the client recovers in excess of one million dollars.)

The ABA report also considers how an individual lawyer or paralegal might be paid for working on matters that are not billed by the hour.[q] For example, suppose a firm is handling a matter for a fixed fee of $1,800,000. Suppose that the work will take three months to complete, and that the client will pay $600,000 at the end of each month. Suppose also that the matter will require half the time of one partner, the full time of two associates, and the full time of one paralegal. Each of the four people would be assigned a series of tasks and revenue targets. For example, the paralegal's first task might be to find, assemble, digest, and index all of the client's documents that are relevant to the matter, and the revenue target for that task might be $35,000. When the client pays the first $600,000 at the end of the first month, part of it would be set aside to help

m. *Id.* at 16.

n. *Id.*

o. *Id.* at 18.

p. *Id.* at 18.

q. *Id.* at 27–30.

cover the firm's overhead. The remainder would be available to pay the four people working on the matter, measured by how much each had accomplished. For example, if the paralegal completed all of the first task, he or she would receive all of the $35,000 target. The ABA report continues:

> There are many benefits to this approach. First, it accommodates a mix of fee arrangements and does not penalize people who are efficient on fixed fee projects (and who may generate equal revenue with less effort than someone billing on an hours basis.) Second, it de-emphasizes billable hours as the primary measure of performance. Third, it gets lawyers more invested in the management of the matter * * *. Because the measurement is related to fee collection rather than only hours (the "realization rate"), lawyers on the matter will be more involved in managing the matter effectively, such as reducing write-offs and billing and collecting on a timely basis. Fourth, it encourages people to think about pricing. If * * * [a person's] target is $500,000, * * * [the person] can get there in any number of ways and with various levels of effort. The mix is, to some degree, up to * * * [the person].[r]

The ABA report concludes with some suggestions for law firms that want to continue using the billable hours model, but that want to make it more efficient and less odious.[s] For example, suppose the firm's present policy is to require 2,000 billable hours per year from associates, and to give a bonus of $5,000 for each additional 100 billable hours. The firm purports to encourage associates to do more pro bono work, and it counts the first 50 pro bono hours toward the 2,000 billable hours requirement. If the firm is serious about wanting associates to do more pro bono work, it could count the first 100 pro bono hours toward the 2,000 requirement. Alternatively, the firm could establish a separate bonus for pro bono work. For example, after meeting the 2,000 billable hours requirement, a lawyer could earn one (but only one) bonus of $5,000 for 100 additional hours of ordinary work, plus a second $5,000 bonus for 100 additional hours of pro bono work.

Questions about the Billable Hours Treadmill

1) Do you think that increased use of alternative billing and compensation models would produce fees that are fairer to clients?

2) Do you think that increased use of alternative billing and compensation models would encourage lawyers to work more efficiently?

3) Do you think that increased use of alternative billing and compensation models would improve the quality of life for lawyers?

---

r. *Id.* at 29.

s. *See id.* at 43–55.

QUESTIONS AND ANSWERS ABOUT CONTINGENT FEES

1. *How does a contingent fee work, other than in plaintiff's personal injury cases?*

In the United States, contingent fees are quite common in personal injury cases, but that is not true in other common law jurisdictions, where fee-shifting (making the loser pay the winner's fees) and extensive legal aid programs are the norm. In the U.S., contingent fees have become increasingly common in other kinds of litigation (*e.g.* patent infringement), in non-litigation matters (*e.g.* a public stock offering where the lawyer's fee depends on the capital generated), and in various matters where the contingency is the amount saved, rather than the amount gained (*e.g.* a breach of contract case in which the defense lawyer's fee depends on the amount the defendant saves by winning).

2. *What's wrong with charging a contingent fee in a criminal case?*

ABA Model Rule 1.5 continues the traditional rule that a lawyer must not use a contingent fee when defending someone in a criminal case. The reasons for the rule have never been convincingly stated. Is it possible that the rule drafters think criminal defense lawyers might be tempted to manufacture or suppress evidence if they were working on contingency? Isn't the same temptation present in civil litigation? Note that the Restatement (Third) of the Law Governing Lawyers § 35(1)(a) (2000) prohibits contingent fees for prosecutors as well as criminal defense lawyers. In the United States (unlike many other common law nations), prosecutors are usually government employees working for a steady salary. On the rare occasions that the government hires a private lawyer to prosecute a case, the pay should not be contingent on winning a conviction because that might tempt the private prosecutor "to seek convictions more than justice." [*Id.*, comment f(ii).]

3. *What's wrong with charging a contingent fee in a domestic relations case?*

The question overstates the scope of the rule. ABA Model Rule 1.5(d)(1) prohibits a contingent fee in a domestic relations case only if the contingency is getting a divorce, or the amount of alimony, support, or a property settlement. The rule does *not* prohibit a contingent fee for legal work done to collect unpaid money due under an alimony or support decree or a property settlement. [ABA Model Rule 1.5, comment 6.]

4. *Can a contingent fee ever be unreasonably high?*

Like all attorney fees, the amount of a contingent fee must not be unreasonable. [*See* ABA Model Rule 1.5(a); ABA Formal Op. 94–389; Restatement (Third) of the Law Governing Lawyers § 35 (2000).] A contingent fee can be higher than an hourly fee or a fixed fee because the lawyer bears the risk of not being paid at all if the matter is lost. [Restatement, *supra,* § 35, comment c.] Further, reasonableness is measured at the time of making the contingent fee agreement, not at the time the fee becomes due. [ABA Formal Op. 94–389.] For example, suppose lawyer L agrees to represent plaintiff P who claims that defendant D

Corporation stole P's valuable trade secrets. At the outset, both P and L anticipate a long, difficult battle, and L agrees to do the legal work in exchange for one-third of whatever P wins. As it turns out, D Corporation doesn't want to fight, and the case settles quickly for a handsome sum. It is ethical for L to hold P to the contingent fee bargain, even though it gives L a fee that would be unreasonably high if measured on an hourly basis. If luck had run the other way, and the case had taken four times as much work as L and P expected, P could hold L to the bargain; what's fair for one is fair for the other. [*See* Restatement, *supra*, § 35, comment c.]

5. *Suppose the lawyer knows at the outset that the case is a sure winner—is a contingent fee proper?*

You have put your finger on one situation in which a court or disciplinary agency may well conclude that a contingent fee is unreasonably high. [Remember, however, that the "sure winner" is more likely to appear in academic discussions than in real life.] Let's suppose that P was injured when she was hit by D's car. P consulted lawyer L. The moment P told L about the accident, L could see that D was at fault and that P's injuries are serious enough to warrant a large damage award. Without explaining these points to P, L had her sign his standard contingent fee agreement, giving him one-third of whatever P wins by settlement, judgment, or appeal. After a few hours work, L convinced D's insurance company to make P a very generous settlement offer, which P accepted with pleasure. Must P pay L one-third of her settlement? A court or disciplinary agency might very well rule that L's fee is unreasonably high, because L didn't tell P how strong her case was before getting her to sign the contingent fee agreement. [Restatement, *supra,* § 35, comment c; ABA Formal Op. 94–389.]

6. *I've heard that contingent fees can be either "static" or "sliding," but I don't understand what that means.*

In the simplest kind of contingent fee agreement, the lawyer's percentage remains static—it does not change, no matter what happens in the case. For example, if the agreement provides that the lawyer will be paid 35% of the client's net recovery (that is, the recovery after deducting litigation expenses), then the lawyer will get 35% no matter whether the case settles within a week or ends ten years later after two trips to the United States Supreme Court. A more complicated contingent fee agreement puts the lawyer's percentage on a sliding scale. For example, the agreement might provide that lawyer gets 25% if the case ends before a trial date is set, or 35% if it ends between the setting of a trial date and entry of judgment by the trial court, or 45% if the case is set for briefing on appeal. ABA Formal Op. 94–389 approves this kind of sliding scale as a rough way of making the fee reflect the amount of work the lawyer does.

Another type of sliding scale makes the lawyer's percentage go up as the client's recovery goes up. For example, the agreement might give the lawyer 15% of the first $100,000, 20% of the next $100,000, and 25% of everything above that. This kind of sliding scale reflects the fact that the lawyer's skill and diligence are better measured by the last dollar of recovery than by the first dollar. That is, maybe any old lawyer could have obtained $100,000 for the client, but only a very skilled, diligent lawyer could have obtained over $200,000. ABA Formal Op. 94–389 also approves this kind of sliding scale.

Notice that the California legislature has imposed a *reverse* sliding scale in medical malpractice cases. Cal. Bus. & Prof. Code § 6146(a) sets a downward slope on the lawyer's share of the recovery—40% of the first $50,000, down to 33-1/3% of the next $50,000, down to 25% of the next $500,000, bottoming out at 15% of anything over $600,000.

LOANS TO CLIENTS

When you read ABA Model Rule 1.8(e) about loans to clients, note that the prohibition applies only in a litigation context, that is, where litigation is pending or contemplated. Note also that the prohibition has only one exception: the lawyer may lend the client money to cover court costs and litigation expenses. Early drafts of the Restatement of the Law Governing Lawyers § 36 (2) would have allowed a lawyer to lend a client money to cover a client's other expenses (food, shelter, medical care, basic business expenses and the like) during litigation, where financial hardship might otherwise force the client into an early settlement or dismissal. The lawyer could not offer or promise such a loan before being hired. The liberal loan provision was at first approved by the membership of the American Law Institute, but it was removed later in the process. Do you see any policy reasons for prohibiting lawyers from lending their clients enough money to get along during litigation? Are there any opposing policy reasons? Do you see any differences between ABA Model Rule 1.8(e) and CRPC 4–210?

WRITTEN FEE AGREEMENTS

Do you see any significant differences between the ABA Model Rules and the California law concerning written fee agreements? *Compare* ABA Model Rule 1.5(b) *with* Cal. Bus. & Prof. Code §§ 6147, 6147.5, and 6148.

ARBITRATION OF FEE DISPUTES

Cal. Bus. & Prof. Code §§ 6200–6206 provide for arbitration of fee disputes between California lawyers and their California clients. Arbitration is voluntary for the client, but mandatory for the lawyer if the client wants to arbitrate. Before suing a client to collect a fee, a California lawyer must notify the client of the right to arbitrate. The client then has 30 days to request arbitration. The parties may agree in writing to be bound by the arbitrator's decision; if they do not agree to be bound, either party is entitled to a court trial of the fee dispute after the arbitration. [*See also* ABA Formal Op. 02–425 (a fee agreement may properly include an agreement for binding arbitration of both fee and malpractice disputes, if the client has been advised of the advantages and disadvantages of arbitration and has given her informed consent).]

CLIENT TRUST ACCOUNTS

ABA Model Rule 1.15 requires attorneys to keep clients' money and property separate from their own, to maintain adequate records, to notify clients promptly when money or property is received on their behalf, and to deliver promptly any money or property that belongs to clients. [*See also* Restatement (Third) of the Law Governing Lawyers § 44 (2000).]

1. What is a Client Trust Account?

Attorneys frequently receive money either from clients or on behalf of clients. For example, an attorney who does collection work may receive money from the client's debtor. Or, the plaintiff's attorney in a personal injury case may receive settlement money from the defendant or the defendant's insurance company. Or, the defense attorney in such a case may receive money from the defendant to be used in paying off a judgment. Or, an attorney in a business transaction may receive money from the client for use on the client's behalf later in the transaction. In each of these examples, the money belongs to the client, and the attorney must put it into a client trust account. The client trust account must be separate from the attorney's personal account and the law office account, and the attorney must never commingle personal or law office funds with the client's funds in the trust account. [The attorney may, however, put enough of her personal funds or office funds into the client trust account to pay the bank's service charges on that account.]

When a lawyer receives a large sum to be held for a long period, the lawyer should make a specific agreement with the client about how the sum is to be handled. Absent a specific agreement, the lawyer should put the sum into a separate, interest-bearing trust account at a bank. The interest, of course, belongs to the client, not to the lawyer. The lawyer should use a separate, interest-bearing trust account if the interest to be earned will exceed the cost of keeping a separate account. [*See id., comment* d; *Carroll v. State Bar*, 166 Cal.App.3d 1193, 213 Cal. Rptr. 305 (1985).]

Typically, however, a lawyer receives relatively small sums, to be held for relatively short periods, on behalf of many different clients. The lawyer traditionally lumps these sums together in a single trust account in a bank. Usually this account is a checking account, not a savings account, because a checking account makes transactions easier and provides a simple, clean record of what went where. Prior to the 1980s, banks did not pay interest on checking accounts, and in those days, the banks were blessed with free use of money that lawyers across the nation were holding for their clients. Further, even when banks began offering interest-bearing checking accounts, most lawyers did not take advantage of them because it was too costly to prorate the interest among clients. In the 1980s, state bars discovered a way to end this gratuitous subsidy of the banking industry. State bars started permitting or requiring lawyers to use special interest-bearing accounts (called IOLTA, "Interest on Lawyer Trust Accounts") for small sums that are to be held for relatively brief periods. The bank sends the interest on these IOLTA accounts directly to a foundation that uses the money to fund legal service programs for under-represented people. [*See, e.g.*, Cal.Bus. & Prof.Code §§ 6210–6212.] In 1999, IOLTA programs generated $139 million nationwide. [*See* Caitlin Liu, *Court Ruling Threatens a Major Funding Source for Legal Aid*, L.A. Times, Jan. 22, 2001 at B3.]

IOLTA funds have helped lawyers to pursue causes that some conservative organizations perceive as undesirable—causes such as gay rights, immigration law clinics, domestic violence clinics, and the like. One conservative group, the Washington Legal Foundation, convinced the U.S. Supreme Court to rule that the interest on an IOLTA account is the "private property" of the clients whose funds are put in the account. [*Phillips v. Washington Legal Foundation,* 524 U.S. 156, 118 S.Ct. 1925, 141 L.Ed.2d 174 (1998).] In that case, the Court did not decide whether the IOLTA program resulted in a Fifth Amendment "taking" for which "just compensation" was due. The Court subsequently held that although the clients' interest was taken for a public use, there was no violation of the Just Compensation Clause because the clients suffered no net loss. [*Brown v. Legal Foundation of Washington*, 538 U.S. 216, 123 S.Ct. 1406, 155 L.Ed.2d 376 (2003).]

2. *What Goes Into the Client Trust Account?*

Suppose that you have agreed to represent a client in some litigation. The two of you have signed a letter agreement in which you have agreed to do the work for a specified hourly fee. At the close of your initial two-hour interview with the client, she hands you $1,000, consisting of the following sums: $100 is to pay your fee for the initial interview. $400 is an advance for expenses that you will incur as the case proceeds—court filing fees, the sheriff's fee for serving the complaint, deposition travel, and the like. The remaining $500 is an advance to cover your fee for work that you will do on the case within the next few weeks. How much, if any, of the $1,000 must go into your client trust account?

FEE FOR COMPLETED WORK

Obviously the $100 payment for the initial interview does not go into your client trust account. That payment covers work you have already done—it belongs to you, and you would be guilty of commingling if you put it into your client trust account.

EXPENSE ADVANCE

What about the $400 that the client has advanced for expenses? The expense advance is regarded as "client's property" under ABA Model Rule

1.15, so you must deposit it in the client trust account. The reason is obvious; if you put the expense advance it in your own account or your office account, you might spend it and have nothing left to pay the client's expenses when they arise. Moreover, if you withdraw or get fired before the advance has been consumed, you must refund the remainder to the client. [*See* ABA Model Rule 1.16(d).]

ADVANCE ON ATTORNEY FEES

What about the $500 advance on attorney fees? ABA Model Rule 1.15(c) specifies that legal fees paid in advance must be put into the client trust account, "to be withdrawn by the lawyer only as fees are earned."

Somewhere in your legal training, you have probably read or heard the term "retainer." Beware of that term, because lawyers use it in different senses, and they seldom explain what they mean. Sometimes lawyers use "retainer" to describe the contract by which a client hires a lawyer. For instance, "It is proper for a *retainer* agreement to include a clause that requires arbitration of fee and malpractice disputes." [*See* ABA Formal Op. 02–425.]

Other times, "retainer" means a fee that the client pays the attorney simply to be available should the client need legal assistance during a specified period or with respect to a specified matter. The Restatement (Third) of Law Governing Lawyers § 34, comment e, uses the phrase "engagement retainer fee" when it means that kind of fee. [*See also* CRPC 3–700(D)(2) (defining "true retainer fee" as one "paid solely for the purpose of ensuring the availability of the [attorney] for the matter").] The attorney earns that kind of fee by agreeing to be available, not by performing services. Indeed, from the client's point of view, one benefit of such a fee is to make a particular attorney *unavailable* to a potential adversary in the event of litigation. That kind of fee belongs to the lawyer when it is paid, and it should *not* be put into the client trust account. [*See* Wisconsin State Bar Formal Opinion E–86–9 (1986).] That kind of fee must be reasonable in amount; if it is excessive, the attorney is subject to discipline. When and if the client actually needs legal services, the attorney will provide them for an additional hourly fee that is often lower than the attorney's ordinary rate.

Attorneys also use the term "retainer" to mean a lump sum paid by a client at the outset of a matter. Sometimes the fee agreement states that the "retainer" is to cover a specified amount of work, and that if more work is needed the client will pay for it at a specified rate. A retainer of that sort belongs to the attorney when it is paid, and it therefore does not go into the client trust account. [*See, e.g.,* Texas State Bar Op. 431 (1986).]

Finally, attorneys sometimes use the term "retainer" to mean an advance payment of fees for work that the lawyer will perform in the future. If the attorney withdraws or is fired before completing the work, the attorney must refund the unearned portion of the advance. [*See* ABA

Model Rule 1.16(d).] The attorney must put the advance into the client trust account. [ABA Model Rule 1.15(c).] At reasonable intervals, the attorney should provide the client an accounting of the work done and the amount that the attorney proposes to deduct from the advance. If the client does not dispute the amount, the attorney may then withdraw it from the client trust account and put it to his or her own use.

The obvious moral of this discussion is to be clear when you draft your fee agreement with your client. If some primordial urge drives you to use the term "retainer," at least explain what you mean in terms that both you and the client will understand.

3. *What Records Must the Attorney Keep?*

ABA Model Rule 1.15(a) requires an attorney to keep "complete records" of all clients' money and property that comes into the attorney's possession. For clients' money, the attorney should keep a ledger sheet for each client, a journal for each bank account, all bank statements and cancelled checks, and a monthly reconciliation of the ledger sheets, journals, and bank documents. For clients' property other than money, the attorney should keep a journal that shows that the property is, for whom it is held, when it was received, and when and to whom it was handed over. The records should be kept for the number of years specified by local rule (usually about five years).

4. *What is a "Client Security Fund"?*

All 50 states have established "client security funds," a source of money that can be used to reimburse the hapless clients of dishonest lawyers. In some states, all lawyers are required to make a small annual contribution to the fund; in other states, the contributions are voluntary.

Client security funds are generally not large enough to provide full reimbursement to all claimants, but they can provide at least partial reimbursement to many victims. For example, in 2001, California's client security fund paid out $4.4 million to 609 victims. Every practicing California lawyer pays $35 per year into the fund. [*See* Kristina Horton Flaherty, *Client Security Fund Comes to the Rescue,* CAL. BAR J., Aug. 2002, at 1.]

MULTIPLE CHOICE QUESTIONS

Answer these questions using the definitions found at the end of Chapter Two.

1. Criminal defense lawyer Lenox agreed to represent defendant Denmon at Denmon's trial for arson. Lenox and Denmon orally agreed on the following attorney fee arrangement. If Denmon were acquitted, the fee would be $25,000. If Denmon were convicted of any lesser included offense, the fee would be $5,000. If Denmon were convicted of arson, the fee would be $500. Lenox further agreed to advance all litigation expenses,

subject to Denmon's promise to repay Lenox whatever the outcome of the case. Which of the following statements are correct?

I. Lenox is *subject to discipline* for not putting the fee agreement in writing.

II. It was *proper* for Lenox to agree to advance the litigation expenses.

III. Lenox is *subject to discipline* for charging a contingent fee in a criminal case.

IV. It was *proper* for Lenox to require Denmon to repay the advanced litigation expenses whatever the outcome of the case.

A. Only I, II, and IV are correct.

B. Only I and III are correct.

C. Only II and IV are correct.

D. All of the statements are correct.

2. Attorney Kimberly represented client Marsha in a divorce proceeding in a non-community property jurisdiction that has a no-fault divorce law. Marsha was married for 25 years, and during the marriage her husband became a very wealthy business executive. The two children of the marriage grew up and left home. Marsha had a savings account of her own, but she was not wealthy, and she had no marketable job skills. Kimberly convinced Marsha to sign a contingent fee agreement, in which Kimberly's fee would be 25% of whatever property settlement Marsha would get in the divorce decree. The divorce court awarded Marsha a $10 million dollar property settlement. Marsha refused to pay Kimberly the $2.5 million fee due under the fee agreement, saying that it was unreasonably high. After trying without success to settle the fee dispute amicably, Kimberly sued Marsha to collect the fee. *May* the court award Kimberly less than $2.5 million?

A. No, because Kimberly took the risk of not being paid anything when she took the case on contingency, and she is entitled to be compensated for that risk.

B. Yes, because Kimberly acted improperly in using a contingent fee agreement in a divorce case, where the amount of the fee was controlled by the amount of the property settlement.

C. No, because a contingent fee agreement is permissible in a domestic relations case, except where the contingency is the granting of a divorce.

D. Yes, because it is unethical for a lawyer to sue her own client to collect a fee.

3. Lawyer Leland is admitted to practice only in Kentucky. He regularly represents Holiday Hotels, Inc., a Kentucky corporation with its principal offices in Lexington. Holiday was sued for trademark infringement in Oregon, and Holiday asked Leland to oversee the case and to

select appropriate Oregon counsel to do the trial work. With Holiday's approval, Leland selected Oregon attorney Alvarez, and Alvarez paid Leland $1,000 for the referral. Leland oversaw all of the work in the case, and he conducted all of the discovery that took place in Kentucky. Alvarez conducted all of the discovery that took place in Oregon, and he prepared the case for trial and served as trial counsel. At the conclusion of the case, Leland and Alvarez submitted separate bills to Holiday for their respective services. Which of the following statements is correct?

A. It was *proper* for Leland and Alvarez to bill Holiday separately, assuming that each bill was reasonable in amount.

B. It was *proper* for Alvarez to pay Leland $1,000 for the referral, since the two lawyers shared the work and responsibility for the case.

C. Leland and Alvarez are *subject to discipline* for failing to submit a single bill to Holiday, because the two lawyers shared the work and responsibility for the case.

D. The arrangement was *proper,* unless the total fee Holiday paid was higher than it would have been absent the $1,000 referral fee.

4. After Carlson was injured in a car wreck, he was treated in the hospital for twelve days by physician Patino; she billed him $7,500 for her medical services. The wreck put Carlson out of work, and he had no way to pay Patino's bill. He hired attorney Aragon to sue the person who caused the wreck; in a written fee agreement, Aragon promised to do the work for a contingent fee. Aragon decided that Patino would make a good expert witness in the case. Aragon and Carlson agreed that Aragon would lend Carlson $7,500 to pay Patino's medical bill and that Aragon would advance the money needed to pay Patino at $100 per hour for the time she spent preparing to testify and testifying as an expert witness. Carlson agreed to pay back Aragon at the conclusion of the case. Which one of the following statements is correct?

A. Aragon is *subject to discipline* for taking the case on a contingent fee.

B. Aragon is *subject to discipline* for agreeing to lend Carlson the $7,500.

C. Aragon is *subject to discipline* for participating in an agreement to pay a witness for giving testimony.

D. Aragon is *subject to discipline* for agreeing to advance the money needed to pay Patino's expert witness fee.

5. Attorney Arnstein agreed to represent client Clemens in a products liability suit against Draxco, Inc. Clemens refused to discuss Arnstein's fee at the outset of the case; rather, Clemens insisted on a provision in the retainer agreement that Arnstein would do the work "for a reasonable fee, to be deducted from the proceeds" of the case. After a

long period of discovery, Arnstein arranged a very favorable settlement between Clemens and Draxco. Draxco paid the $175,000 settlement by a check made payable to Arnstein. Arnstein immediately deposited the check in his client trust account and invited Clemens to come by the office to settle their affairs. When Clemens arrived, Arnstein gave him a bill for $25,000. He computed that amount by multiplying the number of hours he spent on the case (350) times his normal hourly rate ($65), and adding an extra $2,250 because of the generousness of the settlement he had achieved for Clemens. When Clemens looked at the bill, he turned scarlet and began to shout that the fee was outrageously high. Arnstein explained the basis of his charge, and he offered to arbitrate the matter through the local bar association, but Clemens refused. When Clemens demanded immediate payment of the entire $175,000, Arnstein gave him a check, drawn on his client trust account, in the amount of $150,000. Arnstein kept the other $25,000 in his client trust account, pending ultimate resolution of the fee dispute. Which one of the following statements is correct?

A. Arnstein's handling of the matter was *proper*.

B. Arnstein is *subject to discipline* for charging Clemens more than his normal hourly rate.

C. Arnstein is *subject to discipline* for depositing the entire proceeds of Draxco's check in his client trust account.

D. Arnstein is *subject to discipline* for keeping the $25,000 in his client trust account pending resolution of the fee dispute.

6. Client Fujitomi entrusted lawyer Lee with $10,000, to be used six weeks later to close a business transaction. Lee immediately deposited it in her client trust account; at the time, it was the only money in that account. Later that same day, the local bar association called Lee and asked her to rush out to the Municipal Court to take over the defense of an indigent drunkard, Watkins, who was being tried for violating an obscure municipal statute. Because of chaos in the Public Defender's Office, Watkins was being tried without benefit of counsel. By the time Lee arrived, the judge had already found Watkins guilty and sentenced him to pay a fine of $350 or spend 30 days in jail. Under a peculiar local rule of court, the only way to keep Watkins from going to jail was to pay the fine immediately and to request a trial *de novo* in the Superior Court. Therefore, Lee paid the fine with a check drawn on her client trust account, and Watkins promised to repay her within one week. Which one of the following statements is correct?

A. Lee's handling of the Watkins matter was *proper*.

B. Lee would have been *subject to litigation sanction* if she had allowed Watkins to go to jail.

C. If Lee had paid Watkins' fine out of her personal bank account, that would have been *proper*.

D. Lee would be *subject to discipline* for handling the matter in any manner other than she did.

7. Attorney Ayers represents client Canfield as plaintiff in a suit to compel specific performance of a contract. Canfield contracted to purchase Thunderbolt, a thoroughbred race horse, from defendant Dennis in exchange for $1,500,000 worth of corporate bonds owned by Canfield. Canfield transferred the bonds to Dennis, but Dennis refused to deliver Thunderbolt. Two months before the scheduled trial date, Canfield gave Ayers the following instructions: "I am leaving tomorrow on a six-week sailing trip through the South Pacific, and you will not be able to reach me by any means. If Dennis makes any reasonable settlement offer before I return, please accept it, but try to get the horse if you can." A week later, Dennis's lawyer called Ayers and said: "Dennis wants to capitulate. He will either return the bonds, or he will turn over Thunderbolt. He insists on an immediate response, so call me back this afternoon." Ayers believes in good faith that Thunderbolt is a tired nag, worth far less than $1,500,000. Further, Ayers discovers that it will cost nearly $1,000 to keep Thunderbolt in a safe, bonded stable until Canfield's return. What is the *proper* course of action?

A. Get the bonds and put them in a safe deposit box until Canfield returns.

B. Tell Dennis's lawyer that he cannot respond until Canfield returns.

C. Get Thunderbolt and house him in the safe, bonded stable at Canfield's expense until Canfield returns.

D. Get Thunderbolt and turn him out to pasture on Ayers' farm until Canfield returns.

Answers to the multiple choice questions will be found in the Appendix at the end of the book.

CHAPTER SIX

COMPETENCE, DILIGENCE, AND UNAUTHORIZED PRACTICE

■ ■ ■

What This Chapter Covers

I. Professional Discipline for Lack of Competence or Diligence
- A. Taking on Cases You Are Not Competent to Handle
- B. Neglecting Cases You Have Taken On
- C. Contracting Away Liability for Malpractice
- D. Limiting the Scope of the Representation

II. Liability for Malpractice
- A. Relationship Between Professional Discipline and Liability for Malpractice
- B. What Constitutes Legal Malpractice
- C. Avoiding Liability for Malpractice

III. Unauthorized Practice and Other Relations with Non–Lawyers
- A. Assisting Unauthorized Practice
- B. Splitting Fees with Non-lawyers
- C. Non-lawyers in Law Firms
- D. Multi–Jurisdictional and Multi–Disciplinary Practice

Reading Assignment

Wydick, Perschbacher, & Bassett, Chapter 6.

ABA Model Rules:

Preamble: A Lawyer's Responsibilities, notes 4 and 7 [printed at the beginning of the ABA Model Rules];

Rules 1.1 through 1.4, 1.8(h), 1.18, and 5.3 through 5.5.

CRPC 1–200, 1–300 through 1–320, 3–110, 3–400, 3–500 and 3–510.

Cal.Bus. & Prof.Code §§ 6105, 6125–6126.

Cal.S.Ct. Rules on Multijurisdictional Practice, Rules 9.45–9.48.

Supplemental Reading

Hazard & Hodes:

Discussion of ABA Model Rules 1.1 through 1.4, 1.8(h), and 5.3 through 5.5(b).

Restatement (Third) of the Law Governing Lawyers §§ 3–4, 10–12, and 48–58 (2000).

Discussion Problems

1. Lawyer Layton graduated at the top of her class from a famous law school that provides a "national" legal education, and she now practices probate law in Arizona, the only jurisdiction in which she is licensed to practice. Purely for her own enjoyment, Layton regularly uses her home computer to communicate about legal topics with strangers on the Internet. A few months ago, Layton responded to a request for legal advice made by one Cushing, a woman from Rhode Island. Cushing's request was directed to any lawyer willing to answer, not specifically to Layton. Cushing's request described a blatant act of malpractice committed by the Rhode Island lawyer who represented her in her Rhode Island divorce case. The malpractice had occurred 35 months earlier; Cushing realized at the time that her divorce lawyer had made a grave mistake, but she had never done anything about it. Cushing's Internet message asked whether she had a valid claim against her divorce lawyer for malpractice. Layton, relying on her national education at the famous law school, and without doing a scrap of legal research, sent a message to Cushing via the Internet, expressing her opinion that the divorce lawyer's conduct was indeed actionable malpractice, and advising Cushing that it was not too late to sue because the statute of limitations for legal malpractice is four years. If Layton had spent a few minutes in the law library or on WESTLAW, she would have discovered that the Rhode Island statute of limitations is three years, not four. Cushing, lulled into inaction by Layton's advice, did not get around to suing the divorce lawyer until two months later, at which point she discovered that the three year statute of limitations had run.

a. Is Layton guilty of practicing law in Rhode Island without a license?

b. Is Layton subject to discipline for incompetence?

c. Is Layton liable to Cushing for legal malpractice?

2. Client Cameron hired the firm of Alarcon & Brown to represent her as plaintiff in a products liability action. Cameron gave the firm a $5,000 advance on attorney fees. The firm's management committee assigned the case to associate attorney Anson. Before doing any significant amount of work on the case, Anson left the firm for personal reasons. The management committee then reassigned the case to associate Benson. Due to his heavy work load, Benson did not get around to filing the complaint for 10 months. Eventually the case came to trial before Judge Jergins as trier of fact. Judge Jergins took the case under submission for 18 months,

despite a state statute that requires judges to decide cases within 90 days. During that 18 months, Benson did nothing to speed Judge Jergins along, believing that to do so might annoy him to Cameron's detriment. Ultimately Judge Jergins entered judgment in Cameron's favor, but Cameron was angry that justice had been so long delayed. Does Cameron have a valid claim for legal malpractice? Is this an appropriate case for professional discipline? If so, who should be disciplined?

3. While attempting to board a commercial airliner, Chandler was personally injured and publicly humiliated by an employee of the airline company. She hired attorney Adams to sue the company. Adams neglected the matter, and Chandler eventually complained to the state bar. When Adams received a letter of inquiry from the state bar, he checked Chandler's file and discovered that he had let the statute of limitations on Chandler's claim run. Adams met with Chandler, told her honestly what happened, and offered to pay her $6,500 out of his own pocket. That amount was $2,000 more than the medical costs she had incurred as a result of the personal injury. Chandler accepted this offer and signed a form prepared by Adams that released him "from all further responsibility and liability in the aforementioned matter." Adams gave Chandler his personal check for $6,500; the back of the check stated: "Endorsement acknowledges full payment and release of all claims." Adams duly reported the settlement to the state bar. Did Adams handle the matter properly?

4. Crampton lost the use of his right leg when a nurse gave him improper medication at the hospital. Crampton consulted attorney Arlene; she told Crampton that she had never handled a medical malpractice claim before, but that she would do her best on Crampton's behalf. Ultimately Crampton's case went to trial and was lost. Then Crampton sued Arlene for legal malpractice, claiming these defects in Arlene's performance:

a. Arlene failed to consult with any expert on hospital operations; an expert could have testified that the number of nurses at the hospital was insufficient to give proper care to all the patients.

b. Arlene used only one expert medical witness at the trial, and the jury might have been more impressed had several experts testified.

c. Arlene failed to find out whether there were any eyewitnesses around (aides or other nurses) when Crampton received the improper medication.

d. Arlene failed to discover a State Department of Health regulation setting the proper staff/patient ratio in hospitals.

Is Arlene guilty of malpractice for taking on the case in the first place? Do any of the four defects constitute good grounds for a legal malpractice claim?

5. Lawyer Levitt got a phone call this afternoon from lawyer Huffington, house counsel for Infoscope, Inc., a large software company that

Levitt had previously represented in several matters. Huffington told Levitt that a consumer had sued Infoscope in Levitt's jurisdiction for violating the Nelson–Sturgis Act, a federal consumer protection law. Huffington explained that Infoscope had been sued in a half dozen similar cases in other jurisdictions, and that Infoscope had won every case on summary judgment. Huffington said: "Our lawyers in the prior cases have already researched every possible legal question, and I will send you a complete set of the legal memos they prepared for us. Further, we have already been through extensive discovery, and I will send you all the documents, deposition transcripts, and other materials collected in the earlier cases." Then Huffington made Levitt a proposal, as follows: "Our Board of Directors is tired of high legal bills, and the Board has allocated $125,000 to dispose of this case. That's to cover legal fees, litigation expenses, and settlement or judgment—everything. I'm offering you the case on that basis. It should be a good money-maker for you. You'll start by sending the plaintiff a set of interrogatories, and I can supply you with the set we used successfully in the two most recent cases. You will also need to take the plaintiff's deposition, but I can give you a complete outline of all the points to cover. Finally, you'll need to move for summary judgment, but I'll supply you with the motion papers and briefs from the prior cases. Whatever part of the $125,000 is left over will be your legal fee." May Levitt represent Infoscope on the terms Huffington has proposed?

6. Attorneys Ames, Bell, and Chen are the three shareholders in a law firm that is organized as a professional corporation. The hardest working person in the firm is Daley, a non-lawyer. Her title is "Office Manager," and her duties include keeping the financial and billing records, supervising the office staff, and managing the client file system. When she has time, she also helps the lawyers with research and prepares drafts of routine legal documents.

a. Daley's brother and sister want to buy a small piece of real estate as an investment, and they want to keep the legal costs as low as possible. Over the years, Daley has picked up enough knowledge of real estate law to know exactly what to do. Would it be proper for Daley to do the basic legal work, provided that Chen looks over the work to make sure that it is accurate and complete?

b. One of Daley's friends selected Ames, Bell, & Chen to represent him in a major matter, thanks largely to his friendship with Daley. May the firm pay Daley a bonus equal to 10% of the fees earned in this matter?

c. The firm proposes to set up a retirement program that will be funded in part by fees earned by the lawyers. Would it be proper to include Daley as a participant in the retirement program?

d. The state's professional corporation statute requires corporate officers to be shareholders. Bell is officially named as the corporate treasurer, but in fact Daley does all the financial work. May the attorneys sell Daley a token number of shares and name her as the corporate treasurer?

LEGAL MALPRACTICE

A. THE RELATIONSHIP BETWEEN LEGAL MALPRACTICE AND DISCIPLINE BY THE BAR

As used here, the term "legal malpractice" refers to the attorney's civil liability to a client or other injured person for professional misconduct or negligence. Malpractice actions differ from disciplinary actions. First, the forum for a malpractice action is a civil court, not a disciplinary hearing. Second, in a malpractice action the attorney's adversary is an injured person, not a disciplinary authority. Third, the purpose of a malpractice action is to obtain compensation for the injured person, not necessarily to punish the attorney nor to protect the public. [*See generally* Manuel R. Ramos, *Legal Malpractice: The Profession's Dirty Little Secret,* 47 Vand.L.Rev. 1657 (1994).]

If an attorney violates a statute that governs the legal profession or a rule of legal ethics, does that automatically mean that the attorney has also committed legal malpractice? What answer do you find in paragraph 20 of the Preamble/Scope section at the beginning of the ABA Model Rules? The Restatement (Third) of the Law Governing Lawyers § 52(2) (2000) gives a more precise answer: in a negligence action, the trier of fact may consider the defendant lawyer's breach of such a statute or rule as an aid to understanding and applying the standard of care, provided that the statute or rule was designed to protect people in plaintiff's position. Section 52, comment f, explains that such a statute or rule tends to show how lawyers do act and how they ought to act. A statute or rule can also protect a lawyer from liability. For example, if the client claims that the lawyer abandoned her for no good reason, the lawyer may be able to show that the client insisted that the lawyer do something illegal or unethical, thus requiring the lawyer to withdraw. [*See* ABA Model Rule 1.16(a)(1); CRPC 3–700(B).]

B. THEORIES OF LEGAL MALPRACTICE LIABILITY

Several legal theories are available to the plaintiff in a legal malpractice case, and the choice of theory can be important because of differences in the measure of damages and the applicable statutes of limitations. Malpractice plaintiffs often plead an assortment of theories, hoping that at least one of them will work.

One possible theory is intentional tort. For instance, an attorney can be sued for misuse of funds, or abuse of process, or misrepresentation. A second possible theory is breach of fiduciary duty. An attorney's fiduciary duties to a client include keeping the client's confidences, safeguarding the client's money and property, avoiding conflicts of interest, being honest with the client, adequately informing the client, and following the client's instructions. [*See* RESTATEMENT (THIRD) OF THE LAW GOVERNING LAWYERS § 49, comment b (2000).]

A third possible theory is breach of contract. One source of contractual duties is the express agreement (either written or oral) by which the client hires the attorney to perform legal services. Even if there is no express agreement, a court may imply a promise by the attorney to use ordinary skill and care to protect the client's interests.

The fourth and most common theory is unintentional tort—ordinary negligence. Here the plaintiff must prove the familiar elements of a negligence case: a duty of care, a breach of that duty, actual cause, proximate cause, and damages. These elements are discussed in the following paragraphs.

1) To Whom Does an Attorney Owe a Duty of Care?

Obviously, an attorney owes a duty of care to a client. [*See* RESTATEMENT (THIRD) OF THE LAW GOVERNING LAWYERS § 50 (2000).] A person can become a client without formal fanfare and without paying a fee to the attorney. The Restatement § 14(1)(b) explains that a person can become a client simply by asking the attorney for legal help, if the attorney does not decline to give the help, and if the attorney knows or should know that the person will reasonably rely on the attorney to give the help. [*See, e.g., DeVaux v. American Home Assur. Co.*, 387 Mass. 814, 444 N.E.2d 355 (1983).]

Does an attorney owe a duty of care to a non-client? The answer is "yes" in four situations:

- *Prospective client.* An attorney owes a duty of care to a *prospective* client. [*See* ABA Model Rule 1.18; Restatement, *supra*, §§ 15 and 51.] For example, suppose prospective client PC reveals important confidential information to attorney A, to enable A to check for conflicts of interest before agreeing to represent PC. If A negligently reveals PC's confidential information to an outsider, A has breached his duty of care to PC.
- *Invited reliance.* An attorney owes a duty of care to a non-client if the attorney *invites* the non-client to rely on work the attorney does for a client, and if the non-client does rely. [*See* Restatement, *supra*, § 51(2).] The same is true if the client does the inviting and the attorney does not object. [*Id.*] For example, suppose that client C agrees to sell a ship to buyer B. B asks C to supply a lawyer's opinion letter that the ship is not encumbered by liens. Lawyer L agrees with C to do the research and write the letter, realizing that B will rely on her work. If L's research is negligent, L has breached her duty of care to B. In some jurisdictions, the general tort law

curtails this duty of care to a non-client if the non-client's relationship to the transaction is too remote. [*See id.* § 51(2)(b) and comment e.]

- *Non-client is intended to benefit.* An attorney owes a duty of care to a non-client if the attorney knows that one of the client's primary reasons for getting the legal service is to benefit the non-client. For example, suppose client C hires attorney A to draft a will leaving C's entire estate to T. If A drafts the will negligently and the estate passes to C's heirs instead of T, A has breached her duty of care to T. [*See, e.g., Lucas v. Hamm*, 56 Cal.2d 583, 15 Cal.Rptr. 821, 364 P.2d 685 (1961), *cert. denied*, 368 U.S. 987, 82 S.Ct. 603, 7 L.Ed.2d 525 (1962); *see also Perez v. Stern*, discussed in 26 Law. Man. Prof. Conduct 64 (2/3/10).] The Restatement limits this type of duty of care to situations in which the lawyer's duty to the non-client will enhance, not impair, the lawyer's duty to the client. [*See* Restatement, *supra*, § 51(3)(b) and (c).]
- *Breach of fiduciary duty by client.* Suppose X creates a trust for the benefit of B. The trust instrument names T as trustee and names lawyer L to serve as counsel to the trustee. L's client is T, in T's capacity as trustee, not in T's personal capacity. T has fiduciary duties to B, and L is in a unique position to know whether T is performing those duties faithfully. According to the Restatement § 51(4), L owes a duty of care to B, but only if the following three conditions are satisfied: (1) L knows that he must act to prevent or rectify a breach of fiduciary duties by T that is criminal, or fraudulent, or that L helped T commit; (2) B is not reasonably able to protect himself; and (3) the duty of care to B will not significantly impair L's ability to perform his duties to T.

2) What is the Standard of Care?

What is the appropriate standard of care? If the attorney defendant is a general practitioner, then the standard of care is the skill and knowledge ordinarily possessed by attorneys under similar circumstances. [R. Mallen & J. Smith, *Legal Malpractice* § 19.2 (5th ed. 2000); *see also* Restatement, *supra*, § 52(1) ("competence and diligence normally exercised by lawyers in similar circumstances").] If an attorney purports to be a specialist, or acts in a specialized area of the law, then the attorney must exercise the skill and knowledge possessed by attorneys who practice that specialty. [*See* Mallen & Smith, *supra,* § 19.4; Restatement, *supra*, § 52, comment d.] The relevant geographic area for defining the standard of care is the jurisdiction (normally a state) in which the lawyer rendered the questioned legal services. [*See* Restatement, *supra,* § 52, comment b.] Lawyers in rural areas are held to the same standard of skill and knowledge as lawyers in more urban areas. [Mallen & Smith, *supra*, § 19.5.] That sword cuts both ways, however. Knowledge of local conditions, customs, court rules, prejudices, practices, and personalities may be vital to the outcome of a matter, so an attorney from an urban area who fails to check local rules, practices, or customs may find himself committing malpractice. [*See id.*]

3) Breach of the Duty of Care

The standard wisdom teaches that lawyers are not liable for "mere errors in judgment." Thus, in *Hodges v. Carter*, 239 N.C. 517, 80 S.E.2d 144 (1954), it was said:

> An attorney who acts in good faith and in an honest belief that his advice and acts are well-founded and in the best interest of his client is not answerable for a mere error of judgment or for a mistake in a point of law which has not been settled by the court of last resort in his state and on which reasonable doubt may be entertained by well-informed lawyers.

But note carefully the last three words of that quotation. The judgment must be a *well-informed* judgment, not one made in ignorance. A lawyer is expected to know the settled principles of law; if she does not know them, she is expected to look them up, using the standard research techniques used by ordinarily prudent attorneys. If the answers are there to be found, and if she does not find them, she has breached the duty of care. [*See Smith v. Lewis*, 13 Cal.3d 349, 118 Cal.Rptr. 621, 530 P.2d 589 (1975).] If a principle of law is unsettled and open to debate, the attorney is expected to do reasonable research and to "make an informed decision as to a course of conduct based upon an intelligent assessment of the problem." [*Id.; see generally* Mallen & Smith, *supra*, §§ 18.4–18.7.]

In the trial of a case, an attorney is often called upon to make tactical decisions, such as what questions to ask a witness on cross-examination. The attorney will not be second-guessed in a later malpractice case, so long as the tactical decision was based on a well-informed judgment. An attorney can, however, be held liable for failing to conduct a reasonable fact investigation, or failing to find and interview key witnesses, or failing to consult with appropriate experts, or failing to discover pertinent statutes, regulations, and the like. [*See Woodruff v. Tomlin*, 616 F.2d 924 (6th Cir.1980).]

4) Actual Cause

As in ordinary negligence litigation, a malpractice plaintiff must prove actual cause—which usually means proof that the injury would not have happened *but for* the defendant's negligent act. [*See* Mallen & Smith, *supra*, § 8.5; *see also* Restatement, *supra*, § 53, comment b.] For example, suppose malpractice plaintiff P alleges that lawyer L represented her at the trial of a contract case, and that her damage recovery was sharply reduced because L failed to do adequate legal research and to present appropriate evidence on the damage issue. In the malpractice case, P must prove by a preponderance of the evidence that she would have gotten a larger damage recovery in the underlying contract case *but for* L's negligence. In this way, a malpractice trial sometimes becomes a "trial within a trial.'' [Restatement, *supra,* § 53, comment b.] At the malpractice trial, P will present the damages evidence that she claims L ought to have presented, and L will play the role and carry the burdens of the contract defendant. The trier of fact in the malpractice case will have to decide what damage recovery would have been awarded in the contract case if L had done the necessary research and presented the necessary evidence.

Sometimes the *but for* analysis is inadequate to determine actual cause. Where that is true, a court can use the *substantial factor* analysis. That is, where several acts unite to cause an injury—and any one of them alone would have been sufficient to cause it—the malpractice plaintiff can prevail by showing that the defendant lawyer's negligence was a *substantial factor* in causing the injury.

5) Proximate Cause

Again as in ordinary negligence litigation, a malpractice plaintiff must prove, not just actual cause, but proximate cause—that it is fair to hold defendant liable for unexpected injuries or for expected injuries that happen in unexpected ways. [*See* Mallen & Smith, *supra,* § 8.5; *see also* Restatement, *supra,* § 53 (using ''legal cause'' as the equivalent of ''proximate cause'').] For example, suppose that H (age 75) marries W (age 25). Each has children from a prior marriage. H wants his estate to pass to W's children, not to his own who are already well provided for. Attorney A negligently drafts H's will in a way that will accomplish that result only if W outlives H. Then W is killed in a car crash, and H dies a few months later without having changed his will. W's children sue attorney A for malpractice, and A argues lack of proximate cause. Since a reasonably prudent attorney should have foreseen that H might outlive W, and might not change his will after W's death, a court would probably conclude that proximate cause has been established.

6) Damages

Legal malpractice plaintiffs usually seek monetary balm for their injuries, and they must therefore plead and prove damages. Direct damages are those for the immediate, natural, and anticipated consequences of the wrong, for example, the value of the plot of land that the plaintiff lost because of the defendant's negligent title search. A malpractice plaintiff can also collect consequential damages, meaning damages for loss that flows indirectly but foreseeably from the defendant's negligence. [*See* Mallen & Smith, *supra,* § 20.1.] For instance, suppose that client C hires attorney A to defend him in a suit for alleged theft of trade secrets belonging to C's former employer. Due to A's negligence, C lost the case and had to pay a large judgment to the former employer. Further, the loss so injured C's professional reputation that no one would hire him. If the injury to C's reputation was foreseeable, A will be liable to C, not only for the amount of the judgment, but also for C's loss of earnings. [*Id.* § 20.12.]

C. DEFENSES TO LEGAL MALPRACTICE CLAIMS

One solid defense to a legal malpractice claim is that the attorney reasonably believed that the action was required by a law or a legal ethics rule. [Restatement, *supra*, § 54(1) and comment h.] For example, suppose that the applicable legal ethics rule requires a lawyer in a civil case to try to withdraw if her client insists on giving perjurious testimony. [*See* ABA Model Rule 1.16(a)(1); CRPC 3–700(B)(2).] The legal ethics rule would be a complete defense in a malpractice action for client abandonment brought against a lawyer who withdrew because her client insisted on committing perjury.

In jurisdictions that recognize comparative or contributory negligence in negligence cases generally, those doctrines will apply to the same extent in a legal malpractice case based on negligence. [Restatement, *supra*, § 54, comment d.] Further, a client cannot base a legal malpractice case on something that the client, after receiving proper advice, instructed the lawyer to do or not do. [*Id.*, comment h.] For example, suppose the lawyer carefully explains to her client why she needs to interview all the witnesses who might know about the matter at hand. If the client specifically instructs the lawyer not to interview witness X, the client cannot later claim that the lawyer was negligent in not interviewing X.

Assumption of the risk and failure to mitigate damages can be partial defenses in a legal malpractice case, to the extent that the local law recognizes them in ordinary cases. However, the nature of the attorney-client relationship can lessen the usefulness of those doctrines. [*Id.*, comment e.] Similarly, the nature of the attorney-client relationship may lessen the usefulness of the *in pari delicto* doctrine (which bars a plaintiff from recovering when the plaintiff and defendant cooperated in an illegal venture and are equally culpable). [*Id.*, comment f.]

Statutes of limitations apply in legal malpractice claims in the ordinary manner, subject to three special principles:

- First, the statute of limitations ordinarily does not run on a client's malpractice claim while the lawyer continues to represent the client in the matter at hand or a substantially related matter. [*Id.*, comment g.]
- Second, even though the statute of limitations in an ordinary case would start to run when the harm occurs, the statute of limitations in a legal malpractice case does not start to run until the lawyer discloses the supposed malpractice to the client, or the facts that the client knows—or reasonably should know—clearly indicate that the malpractice occurred. [*Id.*]
- Third, the statute of limitations does not start to run until the alleged malpractice significantly injures the plaintiff. For example, suppose lawyer L drafts and supervises the signing of a land sale contract in which client C agrees to buy Red Ranch from seller S. C

and S sign the contract without witnesses, and state law makes a land sale contract voidable if it is signed without witnesses. Client C is not injured until S refuses to sell the ranch—up to then, C has not been injured by L's malpractice. [*Id.*]

D. VICARIOUS LIABILITY

A law firm is civilly liable for injuries caused by an employee or principal of the firm who was acting in the ordinary course of the firm's business, or with actual or apparent authority. [*See* Restatement, *supra*, § 58(1).] Thus the firm is liable if client C is injured because Partner A's secretary negligently failed to pass along a vital telephone message. Likewise the firm is liable if one of its partners, associates, or contract lawyers commits an act of legal malpractice.

If a law firm is organized as a partnership without limited liability, the general law of partnership makes each partner liable jointly and severally with the firm. Thus, if partner A's secretary negligently fails to pass along a vital telephone message, thus causing grave injury to client C, partner B (who had nothing to do with the matter) may end up having to sell her home to pay the malpractice damages. [*Id.* § 58(2).] This seemingly harsh result flows from the general law of respondeat superior. Vicarious liability helps maintain the quality of legal services, by making both the firm and its principals stand behind the work of every lawyer and employee in the firm. [*Id.*, comment b.] Further, many law firms are thinly capitalized, so vicarious liability helps assure that claims against the firm will be paid. [*Id.*]

On the other hand, the public has come to accept the idea that businesses have only limited liability for their wrongs. Moreover, it strains credulity to believe that a partner in a modern law firm can monitor and manage the behavior of everyone else in the firm. [*See id.*] Thus, legislatures have created new kinds of entities—professional corporations, limited-liability general partnerships, and limited-liability companies. Under the new legislation, a law firm generally remains vicariously liable for injuries caused by an employee or principal who was acting in the ordinary course of the firm's business, or with actual or apparent authority. However, the principals of the firm are generally not personally liable for negligence or misconduct in which they did not participate personally or as supervisors. [*Id.*, comment c.] Some states require the principals of limited liability firms to carry adequate legal malpractice insurance and to meet other requirements.

E. MALPRACTICE INSURANCE

In August 2004, the ABA House of Delegates adopted the "Model Court Rule on Insurance Disclosure" (a model court rule, not an ethics rule), which requires private practitioners—but not government lawyers or in-house lawyers—to report annually whether they carry malpractice insurance. This information would then be made available to the public so that prospective clients can make informed decisions about whether to retain a particular lawyer. Lawyers failing to comply with the rule would be subject to suspension from the practice of law until they comply; supplying false information would subject the lawyer to "appropriate disciplinary action." The model court rule does not require lawyers to disclose policy limits, but only whether they maintain professional liability insurance. In California, lawyers who do not carry malpractice insurance (about 20 percent of California's active attorneys) must, under most circumstances, disclose this to their clients. [Cal. Rules of Prof. Conduct, rule 3–410 (not applicable to governmental lawyers or in-house counsel).] Although the ABA Model Rules do not require lawyers to carry malpractice insurance, approximately half of the states now require lawyers to disclose whether they carry malpractice insurance. Prudent lawyers regard adequate malpractice coverage as an essential, albeit expensive, part of law practice. Americans tend to be quick in looking to courts to resolve conflicts. Further, a client who has been injured by a lawyer's ineptitude often prefers to sue for malpractice, rather than start disciplinary proceedings, which are typically slow and which provide no recompense to the injured client. Money may seem better than blood, and unhappy clients can be tempted by malpractice verdicts that occasionally reach the multimillion dollar mark.

In comparison shopping for malpractice insurance, be aware that policies differ dramatically in their features. [*See generally* Ronald E. Mallen, The Law Office Guide to Purchasing Legal Malpractice Insurance (2001 ed.); H. Robert Fiebach, *Shopping for Malpractice Insurance,* A.B.A.J., March 1993 at 98; R. Minto & M. Morton, *The Anatomy of Legal Malpractice Insurance: A Comparative View,* 64 N.D.L.Rev. 547 (1988); F. Goldfein, *Legal Malpractice Insurance,* 61 Temple L.Rev. 1285 (1988).] For example:

- In past years, some insurers offered "occurrence" policies, which covered the lawyer for acts or omissions made during the policy term, regardless of when the claim was asserted. At present, a lawyer can obtain only a "claims made" policy, which covers the lawyer for unforeseen claims made during the policy period, no matter when the act or omission occurred. If the lawyer has changed jobs or changed insurance companies, she may need supplemental "prior acts" coverage, to prevent gaps in her insurance coverage.

- Liability policies generally require the insurer to defend the lawyer against covered claims. Most policies give the insurer the right to select defense counsel, but others allow the insured lawyer to participate in the selection. Further, policies differ respecting the decision to settle a case. Most require the consent of the insured lawyer, but some policies provide that if the lawyer refuses to settle, the insured's liability is limited to the amount for which the claim could have been settled. Other policies provide that if the insurer and the insured disagree on whether to settle, a peer review panel will make the final decision.

• The limits of liability can make an important difference in the cost of insurance. The higher the policy limits, the higher the premium. A policy with limits of $500,000/$1 million usually means that the insurer will pay no more than $500,000 for all claims arising out of a single act (regardless of the number of claimants), and will pay no more than $1 million for all claims during the policy term. Policies differ in how they treat the expenses of defending claims. Typically, defense costs are included in the policy limits, which means that the lawyer should buy policy limits high enough to cover both potential liability and defense costs.

• The size of the deductible can also make an important difference in the cost of a policy. A lawyer who self-insures for the first $100,000 of liability will obviously pay a lower premium than one whose policy has a deductible of only $10,000. Further, most policies provide for a per claim deductible, but a few specify an aggregate deductible during the policy term.

• Policies differ as respects the persons who are covered. The cost of a policy depends partly on whether it covers only the present lawyers and non-lawyers in the firm, or whether it also covers predecessor firms, persons formerly with the firm, and lawyers who are "of counsel" to the firm. Further, some policies do not cover employees of the firm unless an additional premium is paid.

• Policies vary in the kinds of acts and omissions they cover. All of them cover the conduct of the insured when rendering professional legal services to others, but some also cover conduct as a fiduciary (for example, as a trustee or executor), some cover judicially imposed sanctions (under Fed.R.Civ.P. 11, for example), and some cover practice-related personal injury such as false arrest, libel, and malicious prosecution.

• All policies contain exclusions, and the number and breadth of exclusions will affect the cost of the insurance. Typical exclusions are for claims of dishonest, fraudulent, or criminal conduct, claims arising from incidental legal service provided to a business owned by the insured, claims arising out of the insured's conduct as an officer or director of a business, claims of sexual harassment or illegal discrimination, and claims that the insured knew or should have known about at the time he or she bought the policy.

When shopping for insurance, remember that (as with other products and services) you generally get about what you pay for. A bargain premium is no bargain if you get less coverage than you expect and need. Information in insurance company brochures and statements by sales representatives are helpful, but in the end there is no substitute for carefully studying the insurance policy itself.

THE ETHICS OF SECOND-RATE LEGAL SERVICE

Is it ethical for a lawyer to supply second-rate legal service to a client who does not want to pay for first-rate service? At what point do client-imposed limits on the budget, the means, and the scope of a representation prevent the lawyer from doing a competent, diligent job?

The ethics committee of the Association of the Bar of the City of New York explored those two issues in an report entitled *The Evolving Lawyer–Client Relationship and its Effect on the Lawyer's Professional Obligations* [51 The Record 441 (1996).] The committee began by observing that the nature of law practice has changed dramatically over the past two decades. In prior years, clients tended to defer to their lawyers, usually letting the lawyers select the means for resolving a matter, and usually letting the lawyers decide how much time and money the matter required. [*See id.* at 441–45.] All that has changed, the committee said. Competition has increased in the legal profession. Clients, both the rich and the poor, have become sensitive to the cost of legal services. Advances in technology have removed communications barriers between client and attorney, thus allowing the client to keep close track of what the lawyer is doing. Institutional clients are demanding more control over details that were traditionally left to the lawyer's judgment, such as which lawyers in a firm will work on a case, when and how much discovery should be conducted, and what tactics the lawyers should pursue at what stages of the case. [*Id.*] As a consequence,

> [r]ather than retain an attorney to handle a matter as he or she deems appropriate, many clients today demand involvement not only in defining the objectives of a representation but also in selecting the means to achieve the objectives. The relationship increasingly is being defined by lawyer and client alike as a joint venture. [*Id.* at 441.]

The ABA Model Rules and the CRPC require a lawyer to represent a client competently and to act promptly and diligently in serving a client. [ABA Model Rules 1.1 and 1.3; CRPC 3–110.] Comment 1 to ABA Model Rule 1.3 explains that a lawyer must

> act with commitment and dedication to the interests of the client and with zeal in advocacy upon the client's behalf. A lawyer is not bound, however, to press for every advantage that might be realized for a client. For example, a lawyer may have authority to exercise professional discretion in determining the means by which a matter should be pursued. See Rule 1.2. The lawyer's duty to act with reasonable diligence does not require the use of offensive tactics or preclude the treating of all persons involved in the legal process with courtesy and respect.

The Comment speaks of representing the client with zeal, but the zeal must stay within the bounds of the law. [*See* paragraph 9 of the Preamble to the ABA Model Rules.] If the client wants the lawyer to act dishonestly, or to commit fraud, or to do something prejudicial to the administration of justice, the lawyer must refuse. [ABA Model Rule 8.4(b)-(d).] Likewise, if the client wants the lawyer to do something that violates the rules of legal ethics, the lawyer must refuse. [ABA Model Rule 8.4(a); CRPC 3–700 (B)(2); *see* The Record, *supra*, at 450–51.] Therefore, when the client wants the lawyer's service, but insists on a budget too low to let the lawyer provide the service competently and diligently, some authorities require the lawyer to decline the representation, or to withdraw if the representation has already begun. [*See* ABA Model Rule 1.16(a)(1); Alabama State Bar Ethics Op. RO–98–02 (1998) (lawyer retained by insurance company to defend insured must not accede to insurance company's litigation management guidelines that require, among other things, advance company approval for legal research longer than three hours); Indiana Legal Ethics Comm. Op. 3 (1998) (similar insurance company guidelines imposing financial disincentives that may undermine quality of legal service).]

The Restatement of the Law Governing Lawyers offers a more subtle approach to the problem of second-rate legal service. The Restatement permits a lawyer and client to agree to limit a duty that the lawyer would otherwise owe to the client, provided that the limit is *reasonable* in the circumstances and that the client is *adequately informed* and *consents* to the limit. [RESTATEMENT (THIRD) OF THE LAW GOVERNING LAWYERS § 19(1) (2000). This general provision does not apply where the Restatement states a more specific rule, as with waiver of conflicts of interest.]

Unlike ABA Model Rule 1.2, which authorizes limitations upon the scope of the representation, § 19(1) of the Restatement applies specifically to agreements "to limit a *duty* that a lawyer would otherwise owe to the client." One of the illustrations following Restatement § 19 hypothesizes a corporation that wants to impose a tight budget on the lawyer who will defend it in a law suit. The lawyer explains to the corporation's house counsel that the budget will not allow for much discovery, which will reduce the chances of winning. If the corporation *consents* after being properly *informed* about the consequences, and if the limitation on the lawyer's duty is *reasonable* in the circumstances, the corporation will have waived its right to more thorough representation. One consequence of that waiver is that the corporation cannot later claim that the lawyer committed malpractice by failing to do more discovery. The commentary to § 19(1) argues that a *reasonable* agreement to limit the lawyer's duty would *not* violate the general rule that prohibits a lawyer from trying to escape malpractice liability by prospective contract with the client. [*Compare* Restatement, *supra,* § 19, comment a, *with* Restatement § 54(2); *see also* M. Sue Talia, *The Ethics of Unbundling*, Cal. Lawyer, Jan. 2006, at 37.]

How do you think the principle expressed in Restatement § 19(1) should apply when an insurance company hires a lawyer to defend its insured, specifying that the lawyer must follow a strict budget and must have each significant action approved in advance by a non-lawyer "litigation manager" employed by the insurance company?

MULTI-JURISDICTIONAL AND MULTI-DISCIPLINARY PRACTICE

A. MULTI-JURISDICTIONAL PRACTICE

The unauthorized practice of law, as prohibited by ABA Model Rule 5.5, encompasses both non-lawyers and lawyers licensed in other states. [*See* ABA Model Rule 5.5(a) (prohibiting lawyer from practicing law in a jurisdiction "in violation of the regulation of the legal profession in that jurisdiction, or assist another in doing so.").] Although *pro hac vice* ("for this turn only") provisions authorize courts or administrative agencies to permit an out-of-state attorney to represent a client in a particular matter pending before the tribunal, a growing number of practitioners and commentators have called for a loosening of unauthorized practice restrictions in light of the globalization of modern legal practice. [*See, e.g., Symposium: Ethics and the Multijurisdictional Practice of Law*, 36 S.Tex. L.Rev. 657–1105 (1995).] The Final Report of the ABA Commission on Multi-Jurisdictional Practice (MJP) recommended a number of revisions to ABA Model Rule 5.5 to the ABA House of Delegates, which voted, at its August 2002 meeting, to approve the proposed changes in substantially the same form as recommended.

In calling for the adoption of this provision, the MJP Committee noted unanimous testimony that "cross-border legal practice" was common, on the increase, inevitable, and necessary due to the "explosion of technology and the increasing complexity of legal practice." In brief, amended Rule 5.5 allows a lawyer licensed and in good standing in one jurisdiction to practice, temporarily, in another jurisdiction when the lawyer (1) works in association with a lawyer licensed in the host state; (2) represents clients in, or is participating in, an arbitration, mediation, or other alternative dispute resolution proceeding; (3) performs non-litigation work that arises out of, or is reasonably related to, the lawyer's home-state practice; or (4) provides litigation-related services in a state where the lawyer expects to be admitted.

California allows out-of-state lawyers to practice law in California under limited circumstances. The applicable California rules govern in-house counsel, legal services attorneys, litigation attorneys who are in California in anticipation of litigation or in connection with litigation elsewhere, and non-litigation attorneys temporarily in California. [*See* Cal. S.Ct. Rules on Multijurisdictional Practice, Rules 9.45–9.48; *see also* Birbrower, Montalbano, Condon & Frank, P.C. v. Superior Court, 17 Cal.4th 119, 949 P.2d 1, 70 Cal.Rptr.2d 304 (1998).]

B. MULTI-DISCIPLINARY PRACTICE

Multi-disciplinary practice (MDP) is also related to the unauthorized practice of law. The notion of multi-disciplinary practice flows from the desire of lawyers and law firms to provide "one-stop shopping," and therefore to permit firms to provide both legal and nonlegal professional services. For example, the authorization of MDPs might permit lawyers, accountants, engineers, and economists to create—and work within—a common organization. MDPs involve both association and fee sharing between lawyers and members of other professions. Currently, ABA Model Rule 5.4 prohibits the creation of MDPs on both counts. Rule 5.4(a) prohibits lawyers from sharing fees with non-lawyers, and Rule 5.4(b) prohibits the creation of a partnership between a lawyer and a non-lawyer if the partnership will engage in the practice of law. [*See also* CRPC 1–310, 1–320.]

Probably for as long as there have been lawyers, lawyers have occasionally offered other non-legal services to their clients. In fact, ABA Model Rule 2.1 encourages lawyers when giving advice to clients to "refer not only to law but to other considerations such as moral, economic, social and political factors, that may be relevant to the client's situation." Clients often expect business advice, real estate advice, and even marital advice from their lawyers. A flat refusal to respond to such requests may well cost the lawyer the client. Less nobly, lawyers have occasionally, perhaps often, operated non-law businesses either as a part of their firm or as a related entity. For example, a lawyer practicing real estate may well operate a title business as well. A well-connected Washington, D.C. megafirm may offer its clients lobbying services in addition to legal work. According to the comment to ABA Model Rule 5.7, ancillary law-related services include "title insurance, financial planning, accounting, trust services, real estate counseling, legislative lobbying, economic analysis, social work, psychological counseling, tax preparation, and patent, medical or environmental consulting."

Such "ancillary" operations pose several dangers. Clients may be confused over whether they are a client of the firm or of the ancillary business; non-lawyers may influence the law practice in ways inconsistent with the lawyers' professional obligations; the non-law business and law practice may raise serious conflict of interest problems. Perhaps operating an ancillary business makes it painfully clear that the law practice is a business as well. Whatever the reasons, until recently the bar's ethical rules either ignored the issue of ancillary businesses or flatly prohibited their operation in connection with a law practice. Beginning in the late 1980s, competing interests within the ABA began to develop conflicting rule proposals on ancillary businesses. One group offered a highly restrictive proposal that would confine ancillary business activities within the law firm incidental to the provision of legal services and limit such services to clients of the law firm. Another group favored a rule that (a) generally permitted ancillary business activities both within the law firm and through related entities if the firm disclosed the relationship to the law firm; and (b) generally treated a client-customer as a client of the law firm unless the client-customer was fully informed to the contrary; and (c) provided safeguards that client-customers would be treated in accordance with the lawyers' professional obligations. In August 1991, the ABA adopted the restrictive alternative as Model Rule 5.7. In less than a year, it was repealed. No state had adopted the Rule. After a two year hiatus, the ABA, in 1994, adopted the current Rule 5.7. The current rule does little more than remind lawyers that they are subject to the rules of professional responsibility when providing "law-related services" unless the client understands that they are not legal services and do not enjoy the protection of the lawyer-client relationship. [*See also* ABA Formal Opinion 94–388 (1994).] Can you find a better way through these competing interests?

If anything, the ABA's attempts to deal with multi-disciplinary practice issues has been even more controversial. In 1998, the ABA set up its Commission on Multidisciplinary Practice to study efforts by non-lawyer professional service firms, such as accounting firms, to provide legal services to the public. The Commission issued a final report in 1999, recommending a relaxation of the prohibitions, found primarily in Model Rule 5.4, on splitting fees with a non-lawyer, allowing non-lawyer investment in law firms, and permitting lawyers to practice law within accounting firms and other non-lawyer controlled businesses. That August, the ABA's House of Delegates refused to take up the Commission's recommendations, and returned the Report to the Commission for further study. The Commission returned to the House of Delegates in August 2000 with a modified proposal to allow multi-disciplinary practice as long as the lawyers involved have "control and authority" to insure lawyer independence in rendering legal services. The ABA overwhelmingly rejected the recommendation and any attempt to amend Model Rule 5.4.

According to the ABA's report, a MDP is "a partnership, professional corporation, or other association or entity that includes lawyers and nonlawyers and has one, but not all, of its purposes the delivery of legal services to a client(s) other than the MDP itself or that holds itself out to the public as providing nonlegal, as well as legal, services." [ABA, Commission on Multidisciplinary Practice, Report (1999).] A more helpful definition may be that given by the New York State Bar Association in its Report of Special Committee on Multidisciplinary Practice and the Legal Profession (1999) that gives three categories of multidisciplinary practices: "1. entities (other than traditional law firms) that hire lawyers to practice law; 2. law firms that hire individuals other than lawyers to perform professional functions for clients within the firm other than the practice of law; and 3. entities (other than traditional law firms) that provide a variety of professional services and blur the distinctions among those professions by hiring and directing a variety of professionals in the delivery of such services." However defined, the current debate grows out of the efforts of the major accounting firms (the "Big Five" firms) to hire lawyers and offer a variety of law-related services to their clients in the United States, including tax advising, estate planning, and litigation support and dispute resolution, a phenomenon that has been underway in Europe in a more advanced form for some time. Although rejected by the ABA and only grudgingly tolerated by the New York Bar Association's Report, which recommended an ethics rule that would allow lawyers to "enter into strategic alliances and other contractual relationships with non-lawyers" but not allow non-lawyer ownership or investment in law firms, the growth of MDP shows no sign of abating. Scholarly debate over MDP is also escalating. For a fuller review of these issues, see *The Future of the Profession: A Symposium on Multidisciplinary Practice*, 84 Minn. L.Rev. 1083–1654 (2000).

MULTIPLE CHOICE QUESTIONS

Answer these questions using the definitions found at the end of Chapter Two.

1. On June 1st, client Catlin hired attorney Acevedo to sue defendant Degan for securities fraud. Catlin and Acevedo realized that the complaint would have to be filed by September 15th to be within the statute of limitations. Acevedo was very busy with other matters. Starting in mid-August, Catlin telephoned Acevedo every few days to see what progress Acevedo was making. Acevedo repeatedly assured Catlin that he was assembling the facts and preparing preliminary drafts of the complaint, but in truth Acevedo was doing nothing on the case. On September 10th, Catlin learned from Acevedo's secretary that Acevedo had still not started to work on the case. At that point, Catlin fired Acevedo and hired a different lawyer who was able to get the complaint on file by September 15th. Although Acevedo did not charge Catlin any fee, Catlin reported the matter to the state bar. Which of the following is most nearly correct?

   A. If Acevedo would have been able to complete the necessary work by September 15th, his conduct was *proper*.

   B. Since Catlin suffered no damage due to Acevedo's delay, Acevedo's conduct was *proper*.

   C. Even though Catlin suffered no damage due to Acevedo's delay, Acevedo is *subject to civil liability* for malpractice.

   D. Acevedo is *subject to discipline* for neglecting Catlin's case and for lying to Catlin about the status of the matter.

2. Lawyer Lloyd was an associate attorney employed by the law firm of Ames & Baker. The firm is an ordinary partnership, not a limited liability entity. Client Cress hired Ames to sue one of his competitors for false advertising. Ames assigned Lloyd to do the necessary research and draft the complaint. Lloyd confined her research to state law. Any reasonably competent general practitioner would have discovered a more favorable body of parallel federal law under Section 43(a) of the Lanham Act.

Ames eventually brought the case to trial on state law theories only, and Cress lost. Had the case been tried under the Lanham Act, Cress would have won a large judgment. Which of the following propositions are correct?

I. Lloyd is *subject to civil liability* for malpractice.

II. If Lloyd is *subject to civil liability* for malpractice, then so is Ames.

III. If Lloyd and Ames are *subject to civil liability* for malpractice, then so is Baker.

IV. None of the three lawyers is *subject to civil liability* for malpractice.

A. Only IV is correct.

B. Only I is correct.

C. Only I, II, and III are correct.

D. Only I and II are correct.

3. The Community Association for the Homeless (CAH) is a non-profit charitable corporation that provides food and temporary shelter for homeless persons. CAH subsists on charitable donations and volunteer labor provided by members of the community. CAH owns a large old home in the downtown area, but it has virtually no other assets. Seeking to assist CAH in a time of financial need, Corliss Cheng decided to lend CAH $500,000, interest-free, for two years. Lawyer Landsman offered his services without a fee to represent CAH in the transaction and to prepare the necessary loan papers. Cheng was not represented by a lawyer in the transaction. Landsman prepared a suitable promissory note. The officers of CAH duly executed the note and presented it to Cheng in return for the $500,000. A year later, CAH was overcome by financial disaster; the corporation was dissolved, and its creditors took over its few remaining assets. Cheng received only $2,000. Any reasonably competent general practitioner would have advised Cheng to secure the interest-free loan by obtaining a deed of trust on CAH's large old home. Cheng sued Landsman for legal malpractice. Which of the following is most nearly correct?

A. Landsman is *subject to civil liability* for malpractice in the suit brought by Cheng.

B. Landsman is not *subject to civil liability* for malpractice because he did the legal work as a volunteer, not for a fee.

C. Landsman is not *subject to civil liability* for malpractice because he did not purport to represent Cheng in the transaction.

D. Landsman is not *subject to civil liability* for malpractice because the injury to Cheng was not foreseeable.

4. Attorney Applegate represented client Cortez as plaintiff in an employment discrimination action against Delta Corporation. After considerable pretrial discovery, Applegate and Cortez concluded that Delta had

indeed unlawfully discriminated against Cortez but that they probably would be unable to convince a jury of that fact. They decided not to pour any more money into pretrial discovery and to trust to good luck when the case came to trial. Before the case was set for trial, Delta moved for summary judgment. Delta's motion was granted, and the case was dismissed. Then Delta sued Applegate for legal malpractice, alleging that he was negligent in advising Cortez to maintain the suit against Delta and that Delta had been injured to the extent of its litigation costs and attorney fees. In Delta's action against Applegate, which of the following is most nearly correct?

A. Applegate is not *subject to civil liability* for malpractice, even if he lacked a good faith belief that Cortez would win at trial.

B. Applegate is *subject to civil liability* for malpractice if he lacked a good faith belief that Cortez would win at trial.

C. Applegate is not *subject to civil liability* for malpractice because his conduct was not the actual cause of Delta's injury.

D. Applegate is *subject to civil liability* for malpractice if he was negligent in advising Cortez to oppose Delta's motion for summary judgment.

5. For many years attorney Abrams has done all of the routine business law work for Carmondy Corporation. Now Carmondy has asked him to represent it in negotiating a contract to supply electronic components to the U.S. Navy. Abrams knows nothing about government contract law except that it is a highly specialized field governed by a mass of technical regulations. Which of the following would be *proper* for Abrams to do?

I. To decline to represent Carmondy, and to charge Carmondy a nominal fee for finding Carmondy a lawyer who specializes in government contract law.

II. To agree to represent Carmondy, provided that Carmondy will consent to the association of a lawyer who specializes in government contract law.

III. To agree to represent Carmondy, and then to subcontract the substantive legal work to a lawyer who specializes in government contract law.

IV. To agree to represent Carmondy, intending to master the field of government contract law with reasonable speed and efficiency.

A. All of the above.

B. None of the above.

C. II or III only.

D. I, II, or IV only.

6. Attorney Aoki and client Cramer entered into a written agreement in which Aoki agreed to represent Cramer in a real estate venture in

return for a specified hourly fee. The agreement provided that any malpractice or fee dispute would be arbitrated by a neutral arbitrator selected by mutual agreement. Eventually Aoki and Cramer did get into a dispute. Cramer refused to pay Aoki's quarterly bill, and Aoki refused to do any more work until Cramer paid. Cramer also threatened to sue Aoki for malpractice, claiming that he had lost money because of her negligent advice. Which of the following propositions are correct?

I. Aoki is *subject to discipline* for trying to avoid a lawsuit for malpractice by including the arbitration provision in her contract with Cramer.

II. Aoki is *subject to discipline* for refusing to do further work until Cramer paid her bill.

III. It would be *proper* for Aoki to insist that Cramer abide by the arbitration provision in their contract.

IV. If Aoki wants to settle her dispute with Cramer outside of the arbitration agreement, she *must* advise Cramer to obtain independent representation for that purpose.

A. I, II, and IV only.

B. III and IV only.

C. II and III only.

D. I and IV only.

7. Solo practitioner Pearce hired non-lawyer Nelson to serve as her secretary and all-purpose assistant. Pearce put Nelson in charge of her client trust account and her office account and instructed her about how the accounts were to be handled. Several months later, Pearce learned that Nelson had a criminal record, including two prior convictions for embezzlement from a former employer. Since Nelson appeared to be handling the accounts properly, Pearce decided to leave well enough alone. After several more months, Pearce noticed that $1,500 was missing from the office account. Nelson explained that she had borrowed the money to pay her mother's funeral expenses and that she would repay it out of her next paycheck. Nelson did repay the money, and Pearce decided to let Nelson continue to manage the accounts. Then, a year later, Nelson disappeared along with $30,000 from Pearce's client trust account. The clients whose money was taken sued Pearce for negligence and breach of fiduciary duties. Which of the following propositions are correct?

I. Pearce is *subject to discipline* for allowing a non-lawyer to handle her client trust account.

II. If Pearce did not adequately supervise Nelson's handling of the client trust account, then Pearce is *subject to discipline*.

III. Pearce is *subject to civil liability* for malpractice to the injured clients if she was negligent in allowing Nelson to handle the client trust account.

IV. If Pearce had a subjective, good faith belief that Nelson was trustworthy, then Pearce is not *subject to civil liability* for malpractice to the injured clients.

A. II and III only.

B. I, II, and III only.

C. IV only.

D. II and IV only.

8. Supervising lawyer Liggett assigned paralegal Prentice to search through the massive business files of Liggett's client to find documents responsive to a federal court order for production of documents. After several months' work, Prentice ended up with 170 large cartons full of documents that were responsive to the court order. Most of the documents were harmless, but a few were quite damaging to the legal position taken by Liggett's client. Instead of arranging the documents in the same logical order in which she found them in the client's files, Prentice intentionally jumbled the order of the documents. Her purpose was to make it exceedingly difficult, if not impossible, for the adversary to find the damaging documents and to understand their significance. Before the documents were produced for the adversary, Prentice told Liggett what she had done. Liggett responded: "Good—that ought to slow the bastards down. In the future, however, don't do anything like that without checking with me first; we might get in trouble otherwise." Which of the following statements are correct?

I. Since document production requires the skill and judgment of a lawyer, Liggett is *subject to discipline* for delegating the task to Prentice, even if he had adequately supervised her work.

II. Liggett's conduct was *proper* since he admonished Prentice and instructed her not to engage in similar conduct in the future.

III. Assuming that all responsive documents were produced, Liggett's conduct was *proper,* since the adversary has no right to insist that the documents be arranged in any particular order.

IV. Even if all responsive documents were produced, Liggett is *subject to discipline* because he failed to take steps to mitigate the consequences of Prentice's misconduct.

A. II only.

B. I and IV only.

C. IV only.

D. II and III only.

Answers to the multiple choice questions will be found in the Appendix at the back of the book.

CHAPTER SEVEN

CONFIDENTIAL INFORMATION

■ ■ ■

What This Chapter Covers

I. Comparison of the Ethical Duty and the Attorney-Client Privilege
- A. Compulsion vs. Gossip
- B. Sources of Information
- C. Revelation vs. Use of Information

II. Exceptions to the Ethical Duty
- A. Client Consent or Implied Authority
- B. Prevent Future Harm/Mitigate or Rectify Financial Injury
- C. Self–Defense
- D. Court Order or Other Law

III. California's Position on Exceptions to Confidentiality

Reading Assignment

Wydick, Perschbacher, & Bassett, Chapter 7.

ABA Model Rules:

Rules 1.2(d) and cmt. 10, 1.6, 1.8(b), 1.9(b), 3.3, 3.4(a), and 4.1.

CRPC 3–100, 5–200.

Cal. Bus. & Prof. Code §§ 6068(d), (e), 6128(a).

Cal. Evid. Code §§ 950–962.

Supplemental Reading

Hazard & Hodes:

Discussion of ABA Model Rules 1.6, 1.8(b), 1.9(b), 3.3, 3.4(a), and 4.1.

Restatement (Third) of the Law Governing Lawyers §§ 59–86 (2000).

Discussion Problems

1. In your law school course in evidence law, you studied (or will study) the attorney-client privilege. Briefly stated, the attorney-client

privilege gives the client a legal right to prevent a witness from revealing confidential communications between the client and his or her attorney, or between their respective agents. The holder of the privilege is the client; the attorney can invoke the privilege on behalf of the client, but not on the attorney's own behalf. The privilege applies whenever a governmental body can use the twin powers of subpoena and contempt to compel the giving of information. How does the attorney-client privilege differ from the attorney's ethical duty to preserve the client's confidential information? Consider the following situations:

a. While standing around at a P.T.A. potluck supper, lawyer L gossips with a friend about the reasons that L's client V wants to divorce her husband. Does the attorney-client privilege apply at P.T.A. potluck suppers? Does the ethical duty?

b. Lawyer L is defending client X in a drunk driving case. Through her own investigation, L learns from a loquacious bartender that X stops in for several double martinis every night after work. Does the attorney-client privilege protect that information? If not, is L free to reveal it to whomever she wishes?

c. Client Y tells lawyer L in confidence that he wants to purchase Blackacre to build a new shopping center. Acting as an undisclosed principal, lawyer L instructs her agent to buy Blackacre, hoping to turn a quick profit on resale to Y. Has L violated the attorney-client privilege? Has she violated the ethical duty?

d. Suppose instead that lawyer L buys Greenacre, which adjoins Blackacre, knowing that it will triple in value when Y builds the shopping center on Blackacre. Has L violated the ethical duty?

e. Client Z told lawyer L in confidence: "Yesterday I intentionally burned down my barn because I need the fire insurance money. I want you to represent me in collecting on my insurance policy." L declined to represent Z, who then hired lawyer M to pursue the insurance claim. (Having learned his lesson, Z did not tell M about intentionally burning the barn.) The insurance company refused to pay, asserting that Z burned the barn to get the insurance money. At the trial of Z's insurance claim, the insurance company lawyer called L to the witness stand and asked: "What did Z tell you about burning the barn?"

(1) Should the court sustain Z's claim of attorney-client privilege?

(2) When Z left L's office, should L have warned the insurance company that Z was planning to file a fraudulent claim?

2. Dorman is in jail, awaiting trial for the first-degree murder of a young girl. Attorney Anthony is appointed by the court to defend Dorman. Dorman tells Anthony in confidence that he killed not only that girl, but also two other young girls. Dorman tells Anthony where he hid the other two bodies. Anthony goes to the hiding place and discovers that Dorman

has told him the truth. Nobody else knows that the other two girls are dead; their parents and the police are searching for them as runaway children. What should Anthony do?

3. On the afternoon of August 11th last year, a woman walked into your law office, stated her name, and said in confidence: "I'm the driver the police are looking for in that fatal hit and run accident last week." You agreed to represent her, and you advised her about the wisdom of surrendering to the police, but she rejected your advice. The police have never discovered the identity of the hit and run driver. Just prior to the expiration of the statute of limitations, the parents of the hit and run victim filed a wrongful death action against a Jane Doe defendant. Acting on a hunch, the parents' lawyer has subpoenaed you as a deposition witness and has asked you for the names of all persons who consulted you on the afternoon of August 11th. What should you do?

4. Your law practice includes some criminal defense work. A few minutes ago, one of your steady clients stormed into your office, waiving a pistol and announcing that he just killed his probation officer. You have urged him to allow you to surrender him to the authorities, but he has refused, stating that they will catch him sooner or later and that he wants to enjoy his last bit of freedom. He has laid the pistol on your desk, and he is about to walk out. What should you do about the pistol?

5. Your client, Enos Furman, is in the business of leasing expensive equipment to farmers. First, he arranges long term equipment leases with the farmers. Then he borrows money from banks to purchase the equipment; he uses the long term leases as security for the bank loans. You have acted as Furman's lawyer in ten of these lease-loan transactions over the past two years. Today he revealed to you, in strict confidence, that some of the leases he used in those transactions were fake—he forged them and thus tricked the banks into lending him money which he has long since spent. He has solemnly promised you that he will never do that again, and he has asked you to serve as his lawyer in a series of new lease-loan transactions. What are your ethical obligations in this situation?

WASHINGTON v. OLWELL

Supreme Court of the State of Washington, 1964.
64 Wash.2d 828, 394 P.2d 681.

May an attorney refuse to produce, at a coroner's inquest, material evidence of a crime by asserting the attorney-client privilege or by claiming the privilege against self-incrimination on behalf of his client? These are the issues raised in this appeal.

September 18, 1962, a coroner's inquest was held for the purpose of investigating the circumstances surrounding the death of John W. Warren. Several days prior to the date of the inquest, appellant was served with a subpoena duces tecum, which said, in part:

"* * * bring with you all knives in your possession and under your control relating to Henry LeRoy Gray, Gloria Pugh or John W. Warren."

Thereafter, at the coroner's inquest the following exchange took place between a deputy prosecutor and appellant:

"* * *

"Q. Now, Mr. Olwell, did you comply with that? [Subpoena]

"A. I do not have any knives in my possession that belong to Gloria Pugh, or to John W. Warren, and I did not comply with it as to the question of whether or not I have a knife belonging to Henry LeRoy Gray.

"Q. Now, I would ask you, do you have a knife in your possession or under your control relating to or belonging to Henry LeRoy Gray?

"A. I decline to answer that because of the confidential relationship of attorney and client; and to answer the question would be a violation of my oath as an attorney.

"* * *

"Q. And for the record, Mr. Olwell, in the event you do have in your possession a knife or knives that would be called for under the subpoena duces tecum, I take it your answer would be that you received these at the time you were acting as the attorney for Mr. Gray, is that correct?

"A. That is correct."

Further, on examination by the coroner, the following occurred:

"Mr. Sowers: * * * As the Coroner of King County I order you to do so [answer] under the provisions of the law set forth in the legislature under R.C.W. 36.24.050.

"Mr. Olwell: I decline to surrender any of my client's possessions, if any, because of the confidential relationship of attorney and client because under the law I cannot give evidence which under the law cannot be compelled from my client himself."

The events preceding the issuance of the subpoena and the coroner's inquest (as shown by the record as supplemented by some undisputed statements in the parties' briefs) are substantially as follows: Henry LeRoy Gray and John W. Warren engaged in a fight on September 7, 1962, which resulted in Warren's being mortally injured by knife wounds. On or about September 8, 1962, Gray was taken into custody by the Seattle Police Department and placed in jail. During his incarceration, Gray admitted the stabbing of Warren and was willing to co-operate and to aid in the investigation of the homicide. According to a detective of the police department, Gray was not sure what became of the knife he had used in the fight with Warren.

September 10, 1962, David H. Olwell, appellant, was retained as attorney for Gray, who was still confined in jail. Mr. Olwell conferred with his client and then, between the time of that conference and the issuance of the subpoena duces tecum, he came into possession of certain evidence (a knife). It is not clear whether appellant came into possession of this knife through his own investigation while acting as attorney for Gray or whether possession of it was obtained as the result of some communication made by Gray to Olwell during the existence of their attorney and client relationship. This factor is important in determining whether the evidence could be considered as a privileged communication (which is discussed below.)

Therefore, at the time of the inquest, appellant was in possession of a knife that, at that time, was considered as a possible murder weapon.[1] Thereafter the coroner issued the subpoena duces tecum previously quoted.

Appellant appeared at the coroner's inquest and the exchange between appellant, the deputy prosecutor, and the coroner took place as described above. At that time, appellant refused to comply with the subpoena duces tecum and raised the issues presented in this appeal. Thereafter, appellant was cited to appear in the Superior Court of King County, where he was found to be in contempt because of his actions at the coroner's inquest on September 18, 1962. Appellant was given 10 days within which to purge himself of contempt, and, upon his failure to do so, an order was entered adjudging him to be in contempt and directing that he serve two days in the county jail. From that order finding him in contempt, Mr. Olwell appeals.

* * *

To be protected as a privileged communication, information or objects acquired by an attorney must have been communicated or delivered to him by the client, and not merely obtained by the attorney while acting in that capacity for the client. Dupree v. Better Way, Inc., 86 So.2d 425 (Fla.1956). See, also, 97 C.J.S. Witnesses § 283. This means that the securing of the knife in this case must have been the direct result of information given to Mr. Olwell by his client at the time they conferred in order to come within the attorney-client privilege. Although there is no evidence relating thereto, we think it reasonable to infer from the record that appellant did, in fact, obtain the evidence as the result of information received from his client during their conference. Therefore, for the purposes of this opinion and the questions to be answered, we assume that the evidence in appellant's possession was obtained through a confidential communication from his client. If the knife were obtained from a third person with whom there was no attorney-client relationship, the commu-

1. It is stated in respondent's brief that, on April 25, 1963, Henry LeRoy Gray was tried and convicted of murder and is now serving a life sentence for the crime. Furthermore, a knife other than the one involved in this proceeding was subsequently discovered to be the weapon used by Gray in the fight.

nication would not be privileged, and the third person could be questioned concerning the transaction.[3]

Further, communications concerning an alleged crime or fraud, which are made by a client to the attorney after the crime or the fraudulent transaction has been completed, are within the attorney-client privilege, as long as the relationship of attorney and client has been established. Therefore, we find nothing significant in the fact that the communication was made after and concerned the events of a homicide.

In the present case we do not have a situation that readily lends itself to the application of one of the general rules applicable to the attorney-client privilege. Here, we enter a balancing process which requires us to weigh that privilege (which is based on statute and common law), and, as discussed later herein, the privilege against self-incrimination (which is constitutional), against the public's interest in the criminal investigation process. Generally speaking, the public interest at times must yield to protect the individual. Also, we must not lose sight of the policy behind the attorney-client privilege, which is to afford the client freedom from fear of compulsory disclosure after consulting his legal adviser.

* * *

On the basis of the attorney-client privilege, the subpoena duces tecum issued by the coroner is defective on its face because it requires the attorney to give testimony concerning information received by him from his client in the course of their conferences. The subpoena names the client and requires his attorney to produce, in an open hearing, physical evidence allegedly received from the client. This is tantamount to requiring the attorney to testify against the client without the latter's consent. RCW 36.24.080 makes testifying in a coroner's inquest similar to testifying in a superior court, and, therefore, the attorney-client privilege should be equally applicable to witnesses at a coroner's inquest. We, therefore, hold that appellant's refusal to testify at the inquest for the first reason stated by him was not contemptuous.

We do not, however, by so holding, mean to imply that evidence can be permanently withheld by the attorney under the claim of the attorney-client privilege. Here, we must consider the balancing process between the attorney-client privilege and the public interest in criminal investigation. We are in agreement that the attorney-client privilege is applicable to the knife held by appellant, but do not agree that the privilege warrants the attorney, as an officer of the court, from withholding it after being properly requested to produce the same. The attorney should not be a depository for criminal evidence (such as a knife, other weapons, stolen property, etc.), which in itself has little, if any, material value for the purposes of aiding counsel in the preparation of the defense of his client's case. Such evidence given the attorney during legal consultation for information purposes and used by the attorney in preparing the defense of

3. The state suggests that the knife was obtained from Gray's ex-wife, but it failed to offer any proof of this alleged fact to show that a privileged communication did not, in fact, exist.

his client's case, whether or not the case ever goes to trial, could clearly be withheld for a reasonable period of time. It follows that the attorney, after a reasonable period, should, as an officer of the court, on his own motion turn the same over to the prosecution.

We think the attorney-client privilege should and can be preserved even though the attorney surrenders the evidence he has in his possession. The prosecution, upon receipt of such evidence from an attorney, where charge against the attorney's client is contemplated (presently or in the future), should be well aware of the existence of the attorney-client privilege. Therefore, the state, when attempting to introduce such evidence at the trial, should take extreme precautions to make certain that the source of the evidence is not disclosed in the presence of the jury and prejudicial error is not committed. By thus allowing the prosecution to recover such evidence, the public interest is served, and by refusing the prosecution an opportunity to disclose the source of the evidence, the client's privilege is preserved and a balance is reached between these conflicting interests. The burden of introducing such evidence at a trial would continue to be upon the prosecution. [The court then explains that the client's Fifth Amendment privilege against self-incrimination could not serve as a shield for the attorney.]

As was previously stated, the attorney should not be a depository for the suppression of such criminal evidence. If the attorney is given such evidence by his client, he should not be able to assert the privilege against self-incrimination which is personal to the client and must be claimed by the client alone. The attorney can aid in its preservation by informing the client of his right to claim the privilege against self-incrimination.

Because the subpoena duces tecum in this case is invalid, since it required the attorney to testify without the client's consent regarding matters arising out of the attorney-client relationship, the order of the trial court finding appellant to be in contempt and punishing him therefor is hereby reversed with directions to dismiss this proceeding.

PEOPLE v. MEREDITH

Supreme Court of California, 1981.
29 Cal.3d 682, 175 Cal.Rptr. 612, 631 P.2d 46.

Defendants Frank Earl Scott and Michael Meredith appeal from convictions for the first degree murder and first degree robbery of David Wade. Meredith's conviction rests on eyewitness testimony that he shot and killed Wade. Scott's conviction, however, depends on the theory that Scott conspired with Meredith and a third defendant, Jacqueline Otis, to bring about the killing and robbery. To support the theory of conspiracy the prosecution sought to show the place where the victim's wallet was found, and, in the course of the case this piece of evidence became crucial. The admissibility of that evidence comprises the principal issue on this appeal.

At trial the prosecution called Steven Frick, who testified that he observed the victim's partially burnt wallet in a trash can behind Scott's residence. Scott's trial counsel then adduced that Frick served as a defense investigator. Scott himself had told his former counsel that he had taken the victim's wallet, divided the money with Meredith, attempted to burn the wallet, and finally put it in the trash can. At counsel's request, Frick then retrieved the wallet from the trash can. Counsel examined the wallet and then turned it over to the police.

The defense acknowledges that the wallet itself was properly admitted into evidence. The prosecution in turn acknowledges that the attorney-client privilege protected the conversations between Scott, his former counsel, and counsel's investigator. Indeed the prosecution did not attempt to introduce those conversations at trial. The issue before us, consequently, focuses upon a narrow point: whether under the circumstances of this case Frick's observation of the *location* of the wallet, the product of a privileged communication, finds protection under the attorney-client privilege.

This issue, one of first impression in California, presents the court with competing policy considerations. On the one hand, to deny protection to observations arising from confidential communications might chill free and open communication between attorney and client and might also inhibit counsel's investigation of his client's case. On the other hand, we cannot extend the attorney-client privilege so far that it renders evidence immune from discovery and admission merely because the defense seizes it first.

Balancing these considerations, we conclude that an observation by defense counsel or his investigator, which is the product of a privileged communication, may not be admitted unless the defense by altering or removing physical evidence has precluded the prosecution from making that same observation. In the present case the defense investigator, by removing the wallet, frustrated any possibility that the police might later discover it in the trash can. The conduct of the defense thus precluded the prosecution from ascertaining the crucial fact of the location of the wallet. Under these circumstances, the prosecution was entitled to present evidence to show the location of the wallet in the trash can; the trial court did not err in admitting the investigator's testimony.

* * *

We first summarize the evidence other than that relating to the discovery and location of the victim's wallet. * * *

On the night of April 3, 1976, Wade (the victim) and Jacqueline Otis, a friend of the defendants, entered a club known as Rich Jimmy's. Defendant Scott remained outside by a shoeshine stand. A few minutes later codefendant Meredith arrived outside the club. He told Scott he planned to rob Wade, and asked Scott to go into the club, find Jacqueline Otis, and ask her to get Wade to go out to Wade's car parked outside the club.

In the meantime, Wade and Otis had left the club and walked to a liquor store to get some beer. Returning from the store, they left the beer in a bag by Wade's car and reentered the club. Scott then entered the club also and, according to the testimony of Laurie Ann Sam (a friend of Scott's who was already in the club), Scott asked Otis to get Wade to go back out to his car so Meredith could "knock him in the head."

When Wade and Otis did go out to the car, Meredith attacked Wade from behind. After a brief struggle, two shots were fired; Wade fell, and Meredith, witnessed by Scott and Sam, ran from the scene.

Scott went over to the body and, assuming Wade was dead, picked up the bag containing the beer and hid it behind a fence. Scott later returned, retrieved the bag, and took it home where Otis and Meredith joined him.[2]

We now recount the evidence relating to Wade's wallet, basing our account primarily on the testimony of James Schenk, Scott's first appointed attorney. Schenk visited Scott in jail more than a month after the crime occurred and solicited information about the murder, stressing that he had to be fully acquainted with the facts to avoid being "sandbagged" by the prosecution during the trial. In response, Scott gave Schenk the same information that he had related earlier to the police. In addition, however, Scott told Schenk something Scott had not revealed to the police: that he has seen a wallet, as well as the paper bag, on the ground near Wade. Scott said that he picked up the wallet, put it in the paper bag, and placed both behind a parking lot fence. He also said that he later retrieved the bag, took it home, found $100 in the wallet and divided it with Meredith, and then tried to burn the wallet in his kitchen sink. He took the partially burned wallet, Scott told Schenk, placed it in a plastic bag, and threw it in a burn barrel behind his house.

Schenk, without further consulting Scott, retained Investigator Stephen Frick and sent Frick to find the wallet. Frick found it in the location described by Scott and brought it to Schenk. After examining the wallet and determining that it contained credit cards with Wade's name, Schenk turned the wallet and its contents over to Detective Payne, investigating officer in the case. Schenk told Payne only that, to the best of his knowledge, the wallet had belonged to Wade.

The prosecution subpoenaed Attorney Schenk and Investigator Frick to testify at the preliminary hearing. When questioned at that hearing, Schenk said that he received the wallet from Frick but refused to answer further questions on the ground that he learned about the wallet through a privileged communication. Eventually, however, the magistrate threatened Schenk with contempt if he did not respond "yes" or "no" when asked whether his contact with his client led to disclosure of the wallet's location. Schenk then replied "yes," and revealed on further questioning

2. Meredith offered an alibi defense. He testified that he spent the evening at the Kit-Kat Club and another club across the street, and was never in the vicinity of Rich Jimmy's. Two witnesses partially corroborated his alibi.

that this contact was the sole source of his information as to the wallet's location.

At the preliminary hearing Frick, the investigator who found the wallet, was then questioned by the district attorney. Over objections by counsel, Frick testified that he found the wallet in a garbage can behind Scott's residence.

Prior to trial, a third attorney, Hamilton Hintz, was appointed for Scott. Hintz unsuccessfully sought an *in limine* ruling that the wallet of the murder victim was inadmissible and that the attorney-client privilege precluded the admission of testimony concerning the wallet by Schenk or Frick.

At trial Frick, called by the prosecution, identified the wallet and testified that he found it in a garbage can behind Scott's residence. On cross-examination by Hintz, Scott's counsel, Frick further testified that he was an investigator hired by Scott's first attorney, Schenk, and that he had searched the garbage can at Schenk's request. Hintz later called Schenk as a witness: Schenk testified that he told Frick to search for the wallet immediately after Schenk finished talking to Scott. Schenk also stated that Frick brought him the wallet on the following day; after examining its contents Schenk delivered the wallet to the police. Scott then took the stand and testified to the information about the wallet that he had disclosed to Schenk.

The jury found both Scott and Meredith guilty of first degree murder and first degree robbery. It further found that Meredith, but not Scott, was armed with a deadly weapon. Both defendants appeal from their convictions.

Defendant Scott concedes, and we agree, that the wallet itself was admissible in evidence. Scott maintains, however, that Evidence Code section 954 bars the testimony of the investigator concerning the location of the wallet. We consider, first, whether the California attorney-client privilege codified in that section extends to observations which are the product of privileged communications. We then discuss whether that privileged status is lost when defense conduct may have frustrated prosecution discovery.

Section 954 provides, "[T]he client * * * has a privilege to refuse to disclose, and to prevent another from disclosing, a confidential communication between client and lawyer * * *." Under that section one who seeks to assert the privilege must establish that a confidential communication occurred during the course of the attorney-client relationship.

Scott's statements to Schenk regarding the location of the wallet clearly fulfilled the statutory requirements. Moreover, the privilege did not dissolve when Schenk disclosed the substance of that communication to his investigator, Frick. Under Evidence Code section 912, subdivision (d), a disclosure which is "reasonably necessary" to accomplish the purpose for which the attorney has been consulted does not constitute a waiver of the privilege. If Frick was to perform the investigative services for which Schenk had retained him, it was "reasonably necessary," that Schenk transmit to Frick the information regarding the wallet.[3] Thus, Schenk's disclosure to Frick did not waive the statutory privilege.

The statutes codifying the attorney-client privilege do not, however, indicate whether that privilege protects facts viewed and observed as a direct result of confidential communication. To resolve that issue, we turn first to the policies which underlie the attorney-client privilege, and then to the cases which apply those policies to observations arising from a protected communication.

The fundamental purpose of the attorney-client privilege is, of course, to encourage full and open communication between client and attorney. "Adequate legal representation in the ascertainment and enforcement of rights or the prosecution or defense of litigation compels a full disclosure of the facts by the client to his attorney * * *. Given the privilege, a client may make such a disclosure without fear that his attorney may be forced to reveal the information confided to him." (*City & County of S.F. v. Superior Court, supra*, 37 Cal.2d at p. 235, 231 P.2d 26. *See also People v. Canfield* (1974) 12 Cal.3d 699, 705, 117 Cal.Rptr. 81, 527 P.2d 633; *People v. Atkinson* (1870) 40 Cal. 284, 285.)

In the criminal context, as we have recently observed, these policies assume particular significance: " 'As a practical matter, if the client knows that damaging information could more readily be obtained from the attorney following disclosure than from himself in the absence of disclosure, the client would be reluctant to confide in his lawyer and it would be difficult to obtain fully informed legal advice.' * * * Thus, if an accused is to derive the full benefits of his right to counsel, he must have the assurance of confidentiality and privacy of communication with his attorney." (*Barber v. Municipal Court* (1979) 24 Cal.3d 742, 751, 157 Cal.Rptr. 658, 598 P.2d 818, citing *Fisher v. United States* (1976) 425 U.S. 391, 403, 96 S.Ct. 1569, 1577, 48 L.Ed.2d 39.)

Judicial decisions have recognized that the implementation of these important policies may require that the privilege extend not only to the initial communication between client and attorney but also to any information which the attorney or his investigator may subsequently acquire as a direct result of that communication. In a venerable decision involving facts analogous to those in the instant case, the Supreme Court of West

3. Although prior cases do not consider whether section 912, subdivision (d) applies to an attorney's investigator, the language of that subdivision covers the circumstances of the instant case. An investigator is as "reasonably necessary" as a physician or psychiatrist (*People v. Lines* (1975) 13 Cal.3d 500, 119 Cal.Rptr. 225, 531 P.2d 793), or a legal secretary, paralegal or receptionist. (*See Anderson v. State* (Fla.App.1974) 297 So.2d 871; *City & County of S.F. v. Superior Court* (1951) 37 Cal.2d 227, 231 P.2d 26). Because the investigator, then, is a person encompassed by the privilege, he stands in the same position as the attorney for purposes of the analysis and operation of the privilege; the investigator cannot then disclose that which the attorney could not have disclosed. (*City & County of S.F. v. Superior Court, supra*, 37 Cal.2d at p. 236, 231 P.2d 26, *see also* Evid.Code, § 952 and Law Revision Com. comment thereto.) Thus, the discussion in this opinion of the conduct of defense counsel, and of counsel's right to invoke the attorney-client privilege to avoid testifying, applies also to a defense investigator.

Virginia held that the trial court erred in admitting an attorney's testimony as to the location of a pistol which he had discovered as the result of a privileged communication from his client. That the attorney had observed the pistol, the court pointed out, did not nullify the privilege: "All that the said attorney knew about this pistol, or where it was to be found, he knew only from the communications which had been made to him by his client confidentially and professionally, as counsel in this case. And it ought therefore, to have been entirely excluded from the jury. It may be, that in this particular case this evidence tended to the promotion of right and justice, but as was well said in *Pearce v. Pearce*, 11 Jar. 52, in page 55, and 2 De Gex & Smale 25–27: 'Truth like all other good things may be loved unwisely, may be pursued too keenly, may cost too much.' " (*State of West Virginia v. Douglass* (1882) 20 W.Va. 770, 783.)

This unbearable cost, the *Douglass* court concluded, could not be entirely avoided by attempting to admit testimony regarding observations or discoveries made as the result of a privileged communication, while excluding the communication itself. Such a procedure, *Douglass* held, "was practically as mischievous in all its tendencies and consequences, as if it has required [the attorney] to state everything, which his client had confidentially told him about this pistol. It would be a slight safeguard indeed, to confidential communications made to counsel, if he was thus compelled substantially, to give them to a jury, although he was required not to state them in the words of his client." (*Id.*, at p. 783.)

More recent decisions reach similar conclusions. In *State v. Olwell* (1964) 64 Wash.2d 828, 394 P.2d 681, the court reviewed contempt charges against an attorney who refused to produce a knife he obtained from his client. The court first observed that "[t]o be protected as a privileged communication * * * the securing of the knife * * * must have been *the direct result of information* given to Mr. Olwell by his client." The court concluded that defense counsel, after examining the physical evidence, should deliver it to the prosecution, but should not reveal the source of the evidence; "[b]y thus allowing the prosecution to recover such evidence, the public interest is served, and by refusing the prosecution an opportunity to disclose the source of the evidence, the client's privilege is preserved and a balance reached between these conflicting interests." (P. 685.)[4] (See also *Anderson v. State* (D.C.App.Fla.1974) 297 So.2d 871.)

4. The parties discuss an earlier Washington case. *State v. Sullivan* (1962) 60 Wash.2d 214, 373 P.2d 474. Defendant in that case revealed the location of the victim's body to his counsel, who informed the sheriff. At trial the prosecution called defense counsel to testify to the location. The appellate court reversed the conviction, apparently on the ground that it was unnecessarily prejudicial to call defense counsel as a prosecution witness when sheriff's deputies and other witnesses who had seen the body were available.

The *Sullivan* court stated a general rule which supports the result we reach here—that attorney-client communications remain privileged "regardless of the manner in which it is sought to put the communications in evidence, whether by direct examination, cross-examination, or *indirectly as by bringing of facts brought to knowledge solely by reason of a confidential communication.*" (P. 476, quoting 58 Am. Jur., Witnesses, § 466.) (Emphasis by the *Sullivan* court.) The decision expressly left open, however, whether defense counsel could be called to prove the location of the body if other witnesses were unavailable.

Finally, we note the decisions of the New York courts in *People v. Belge* (Sup.Ct.1975) 83 Misc.2d 186, 372 N.Y.S.2d 798, affirmed in *People v. Belge* (App.Div.1975) 50 A.D.2d 1088, 376 N.Y.S.2d 771. Defendant, charged with one murder, revealed to counsel that he had committed three others. Counsel, following defendant's directions, located one of the bodies. Counsel did not reveal the location of the body until trial, 10 months later, when he exposed the other murders to support an insanity defense.

Counsel was then indicted for violating two sections of the New York Public Health Law for failing to report the existence of the body to proper authorities in order that they could give it a decent burial. The trial court dismissed the indictment; the appellate division affirmed, holding that the attorney-client privilege shielded counsel from prosecution for actions which would otherwise violate the Public Health Law.[5]

The foregoing decisions demonstrate that the attorney-client privilege is not strictly limited to communications, but extends to protect observations made as a consequence of protected communications. We turn therefore to the question whether that privilege encompasses a case in which the defense, by removing or altering evidence, interferes with the prosecution's opportunity to discover that evidence.[7]

In some of the cases extending the privilege to observations arising from protected communications the defense counsel had obtained the evidence from his client or in some other fashion removed it from its original location (*State v. Olwell, supra*, 394 P.2d 681; *Anderson v. State, supra*, 297 So.2d 871); in others the attorney did not remove or alter the evidence (*People v. Belge, supra*, 372 N.Y.S.2d 798; *State v. Sullivan, supra*, 373 P.2d 474). None of the decisions, however, confronts directly the question whether such removal or alteration should affect the defendant's right to assert the attorney-client privilege as a bar to testimony concerning the original location or condition of the evidence.

When defense counsel alters or removes physical evidence, he necessarily deprives the prosecution of the opportunity to observe that evidence

5. In each of the cases discussed in text, a crucial element in the court's analysis is that the attorney's observations were the direct product of information communicated to him by his client. Two decisions, *People v. Lee* (1970) 3 Cal.App.3d 514, 83 Cal.Rptr. 715 and *Morrell v. State* (Alaska 1978) 575 P.2d 1200, held that an attorney must not only turn over evidence given him by *third parties*, but also testify as to the source of that evidence. Both decisions emphasized that the attorney-client privilege was inapplicable because the third party was not acting as an agent of the attorney or the client.

7. We agree with the parties' suggestion that an attorney in Schenk's position often may best fulfill conflicting obligations to preserve the confidentiality of client confidences, investigate his case, and act as an officer of the court if he does not remove evidence located as the result of a privileged communication. We must recognize, however, that in some cases an examination of evidence may reveal information critical to the defense of a client accused of crime. If the usefulness of the evidence cannot be gauged without taking possession of it, as, for example, when a ballistics or fingerprint test is required, the attorney may properly take it for a reasonable time before turning it over to the prosecution. (*Olwell, supra*, 394 P.2d pp. 684–685.) Similarly, in the present case the defense counsel could not be certain the burnt wallet belonged in fact to the victim: in taking the wallet to examine it for identification, he violated no ethical duty to his client or to the prosecution. (*See generally Legal Ethics and the Destruction of Evidence* (1979) 88 Yale L.J. 1665.)

in its original condition or location. As the Amicus Appellate Committee of the California District Attorneys Association points out, to bar admission of testimony concerning the original condition and location of the evidence in such a case permits the defense in effect to "destroy" critical information; it is as if, he explains, the wallet in this case bore a tag bearing the words "located in the trash can by Scott's residence," and the defense, by taking the wallet, destroyed this tag. To extend the attorney-client privilege to a case in which the defense removed evidence might encourage defense counsel to race the police to seize critical evidence. (See *In re Ryder* (E.D.Va.1967) 263 F.Supp. 360, 369; Comment, *The Right of a Criminal Defense Attorney to Withhold Physical Evidence Received From His Client* (1970) 38 U.Chi.L.Rev. 211, 227–228.)

We therefore conclude that courts must craft an exception to the protection extended by the attorney-client privilege in cases in which counsel has removed or altered evidence. Indeed, at oral argument defense counsel acknowledged that such an exception might be necessary in a case in which the police would have inevitably discovered the evidence in its original location if counsel had not removed it. Counsel argued, however, that the attorney-client privilege should protect observations of evidence, despite subsequent defense removal, unless the prosecution could prove that the police probably would have eventually discovered the evidence in the original site.

We have seriously considered counsel's proposal, but have concluded that a test based upon the probability of eventual discovery is unworkably speculative. Evidence turns up not only because the police deliberately search for it, but also because it comes to the attention of policemen or bystanders engaged in other business. In the present case, for example, the wallet might have been found by the trash collector. Moreover, once physical evidence (the wallet) is turned over to the police, they will obviously stop looking for it; to ask where, how long, and how carefully they would have looked is obviously to compel speculation as to theoretical future conduct of the police.

We therefore conclude that whenever defense counsel removes or alters evidence, the statutory privilege does not bar revelation of the original location or condition of the evidence in question.[8] We thus view the defense decision to remove evidence as a tactical choice. If defense counsel leaves the evidence where he discovers it, his observations derived

8. In offering the evidence, the prosecution should present the information in a manner which avoids revealing the content of attorney-client communications or the original source of the information. In the present case, for example, the prosecutor simply asked Frick where he found the wallet; he did not identify Frick as a defense investigator or trace the discovery of the wallet to an attorney-client communication. In other circumstances, when it is not possible to elicit such testimony without identifying the witness as the defendant's attorney or investigator, the defendant may be willing to enter a stipulation which will simply inform the jury as to the relevant location or condition of the evidence in question. When such a stipulation is proffered, the prosecution should not be permitted to reject the stipulation in the hope that by requiring defense counsel personally to testify to such facts, the jury might infer that counsel learned those facts from defendant. (Cf. *People v. Hall* (1980) 28 Cal.3d 143, 152, 167 Cal.Rptr. 844, 616 P.2d 826.)

from privileged communications are insulated from revelation. If, however, counsel chooses to remove evidence to examine or test it, the original location and condition of that evidence loses the protection of the privilege. Applying this analysis to the present case, we hold that the trial court did not err in admitting the investigator's testimony concerning the location of the wallet.

EXCEPTIONS TO THE ETHICAL DUTY OF CONFIDENTIALITY

A. CLIENT CONSENT OR IMPLIED AUTHORITY

Re-read ABA Model Rule 1.6(a). You will see that it allows a lawyer to reveal a client's confidential information if the client has given informed consent, or if the nature of the representation impliedly authorizes the lawyer to reveal the confidential information. For example, suppose a client hires you to prepare and file an environmental impact report for the client's proposed construction project. To do that, you will have to tell the government and the public many of the confidential details of the proposed project, and your client realizes that fact. You have *implied authority* to reveal those details in the report. [*See* ABA Model Rule 1.6(a) and comment 5.]

B. PREVENT FUTURE HARM/MITIGATE OR RECTIFY FINANCIAL INJURY

Re-read ABA Model Rule 1.6(b)(1)-(3) and Comments 6–8. Suppose that a client goes to his lawyer and, in confidence, asks for some legal advice in conjunction with his plan to commit two future crimes: (1) a fraud that will bilk innocent people of their life savings, and (2) a brutal murder, to cover up the fraud. Suppose that after the client states his evil plan, the lawyer tries to talk him out of it. The client flies into a rage, vows to carry out the plan, and storms out of the lawyer's office. The lawyer is convinced that the client will really do it. May the lawyer warn the appropriate authorities and the intended victims in an effort to foil the client's plan? This situation is governed, not by the attorney-client privilege, but by the lawyer's ethical duty of confidentiality.

ABA Model Rule 1.6(b) has a curious history. The old ABA Model Code (the precursor of the ABA Model Rules) allowed the lawyer to voluntarily reveal the client's confidentially stated intent to commit *any* kind of future crime, together with information needed to prevent the crime from being committed. [*See* ABA Model Code of Professional Responsibility DR 4–101(C)(3).] The Model Code paid no attention to the kinds of harm the future crime might cause.

In the early 1980s, the ABA Model Rules drafting committee proposed a rule that would allow the lawyer to reveal the client's confidential information under more limited circumstances: (1) to prevent the client from committing a crime that would cause imminent death or substantial bodily injury; (2) to prevent the client from committing a crime or fraud that would cause substantial financial injury; and (3) to rectify the consequences of a client's crime or fraud in furtherance of which the lawyer's services had been used. When the committee's draft came before the ABA House of Delegates for approval, the delegates threw out the second and third categories, leaving only the first: that a lawyer could only reveal a client's confidential information to prevent the client from committing a future crime that would cause imminent death or substantial bodily injury.

Only a small minority of the 50 states accepted the House of Delegates' bob-tailed version of the rule. Instead, most states allowed the lawyer to reveal future crimes that would cause imminent death, substantial bodily injury, or substantial financial injury. The ABA Ethics 2000 Commission tried to resolve the division of authority, but the House of Delegates again rejected a confidentiality exception designed to prevent serious financial injury, as distinct from serious bodily injury or death. The ABA Ethics 2000 Commission was victorious, however, on a related point, modifying the death or substantial bodily injury exception in ABA Model Rule 1.6(b)(1) to apply even if: (1) no crime is involved; and (2) even if the death or bodily injury is not "imminent" but is merely "reasonably certain," and (3) even if the death or bodily injury is caused by someone or something other than the lawyer's client. [*Accord* RESTATEMENT (THIRD) OF THE LAW GOVERNING LAWYERS § 66 (2000).]

Finally, in 2003, the ABA House of Delegates amended ABA Model Rule 1.6 to add two exceptions to the duty of confidentiality. The amended rule permits a lawyer to disclose confidential information to prevent a client from committing a crime or fraud that would cause substantial financial injury, as well as to prevent, mitigate, or rectify substantial financial injury due to a client's crime or fraud, when the client is using or has used the lawyer's services in the matter. [*See also* Comment to ABA Model Rule 4.1 (noting that under some circumstances it may be necessary for the lawyer both to withdraw from the representation and "to disaffirm an opinion, document, affirmation or the like" to avoid assisting the client's crime or fraud).]

C. SELF-DEFENSE

Now re-read ABA Model Rule 1.6(b) and the Comments that accompany it. Subsection (b)(5) allows a lawyer to reveal a client's confidential information in "self-defense," for example: to defend against a claim of legal malpractice or ineffective assistance of counsel; to defend against a civil or criminal charge that the lawyer was involved in the client's wrongdoing; and to obtain relief against a client who has breached a fee agreement or the like. [*Accord* RESTATEMENT (THIRD) OF THE LAW GOVERNING LAWYERS §§ 64 and 65 (2000).]

ABA Model Rule 1.6(b)(4) allows a lawyer to reveal a client's confidential information in order to get legal advice about complying with the rules of legal ethics. For example, a lawyer might call the state bar association ethics hotline or an outside legal ethics expert and pose an ethics question that is based on the client's confidential information.

D. COURT ORDER OR OTHER LAW

ABA Model Rule 1.6(b)(6) allows a lawyer to disclose a client's confidential information where that is necessary to comply with a court order or with some other law. Read Comments 10 and 11 to that Rule. Can you think of a law that trumps Rule 1.6 and requires a lawyer to reveal a client's confidential information? Does the law of attorney-client privilege ever do that? Under what circumstances?

CALIFORNIA'S POSITION ON EXCEPTIONS TO CONFIDENTIALITY

California's ethical duty of confidentiality has an even more interesting history than ABA Model Rule 1.6. California is now working on new rules that would be similar to the ABA Model Rules, but meanwhile it still uses a combination of the California Rules of Professional Conduct and the State Bar Act, found in the California Business and Professions Code. Historically, California had no separate rule addressing a lawyer's ethical duty of confidentiality, so that the only confidentiality provision was that found in section 6068(e) of the Business and Professions Code—a single sentence of the Attorney's Oath stating that "[i]t is the duty of an attorney ... [t]o maintain inviolate the confidence, and at every peril to himself or herself to preserve the secrets, of his or her client." The gender-neutral pronouns are a modern addition, but otherwise the sentence is a ceremonial relic of the 19th century, cribbed from David Dudley Field's civil procedure code, which in turn had taken it from an old oath used in Switzerland. [*See* Charles W. Wolfram, *The U.S. Law of Client Confidentiality: Framework for an International Perspective*, 15 Fordham Int'l L.J. 529, 534 (1991–92).] The broad language of this provision, the lack of any stated exceptions, and the very limited number of judicially-created exceptions, rendered California's duty of confidentiality the most stringent in the country. For years, efforts to create exceptions to the duty of confidentiality that would parallel exceptions in the ABA Model Rules were rebuffed. In 2004, California finally adopted a separate confidentiality rule, but declined to adopt all of the exceptions found in ABA Model Rule 1.6. California's rule contains only one exception—when necessary "to prevent a criminal act that the [lawyer] reasonably believes is likely to result in death of, or substantial bodily harm to, an individual." [CRPC 3–100; *see also* Cal. Bus. & Prof. Code § 6068(e)(2).] Moreover, California's rule expressly requires that, if possible, the lawyer first try to dissuade the client from committing the crime, or to persuade the client to prevent the threatened death or substantial bodily harm. Note that the exception applies only to future crimes; the rule contains no provision that would authorize rectifying a past crime. Note also that California's rule contains no exception for fraud or financial harm.

As is true of ABA Model Rule 1.6, California's rule contains no affirmative obligation to reveal confidential information; both rules are permissive rather than mandatory. Accordingly, lurking in the background is another unanswered question, one that touches lawyers' pocketbooks. If a lawyer has discretion to disclose a client's confidentially expressed intent to commit a crime that will cause death or substantial bodily injury, and if the lawyer decides not to disclose, and if the client does commit the crime, might the lawyer be civilly liable for failure to warn the intended victim? Remember that California is the birthplace of *Tarasoff v. University of California Board of Regents*, 17 Cal.3d 425, 551 P.2d 334 (1976), in which a psychotherapist failed to warn a young woman that a patient was planning to kill her. The California Supreme Court ruled that when a therapist determines (or should determine) that a patient "presents a serious danger of violence to another, he incurs an obligation to use reasonable care to protect the intended victim against such danger." [*Id.*, 551 P.2d at 340.] A 2004 California Court of Appeal decision extended the "duty to warn" to situations where the psychologist learned that the client had threatened to kill the victim from a third party, instead of directly from the patient. [*See Ewing v. Goldstein*, 120 Cal.App.4th 807, 15 Cal.Rptr.3d 864 (2004).] Could the *Tarasoff* principle be extended to cover lawyers as well as psychotherapists?

MULTIPLE CHOICE QUESTIONS

Answer these questions using the definitions found at the end of Chapter Two.

1. In which of the following situations would the information received by the attorney be covered by *both* the attorney-client privilege and the ethical duty to preserve the client's confidential information?

I. Lawyer L is defending client C in a tax fraud case. With C's consent, L hires a tax accountant to examine C's records, to talk with C, and to prepare some worksheets for L to use in defending the case. The accountant turns the worksheets over to L.

II. L is representing C in a boundary line dispute with C's neighbor. When combing through the county land records, L discovers that C's grantor apparently had no legal title to the land he purported to grant to C.

III. L is defending C in a first degree murder case. In the course of her investigation, L talks to a taxi driver who tells L that he remembers that on the night in question C rode in his taxi to an address near the scene of the murder.

IV. L represents C in an action for breach of an oral contract. When preparing the case for trial, L stumbles across an old newspaper clipping, reporting C's conviction of a felony in a distant state 15 years ago.

A. All of the above.

B. I, III, and IV only.

C. I only.

D. III only.

2. Client Christenson asked attorney Alder to prepare some legal papers in connection with Christenson's dissolution of marriage proceeding. In the course of conversation, Alder learned that Christenson intended to develop some beachfront property into condominiums. State law requires the filing of certain environmental impact statements with the State Commissioner of Real Estate and Development as a prerequisite to any development efforts, including advertising and zoning variances. Later Alder learned that Christenson was proceeding with the project and had not yet filed the required statements. Which of the following items are correct?

I. Alder *must* contact the State Commissioner of Real Estate and Development and reveal Christenson's intentions.

II. Alder *may* contact the State Commissioner of Real Estate and Development and reveal Christenson's intentions.

III. Alder *may* contact Christenson and urge him to take appropriate steps to rectify his wrong.

IV. It would be *proper* for Alder not to tell any outsider about his communications with Christenson.

A. I, III, and IV only.

B. II, III, and IV only.

C. III and IV only.

D. IV only.

3. Lawyer Lorenz represents client Cramer in a complex business case. The defendant has demanded production of a mass of Cramer's records that contain vital, confidential business information. The defendant has agreed to a protective order that prohibits it from misusing the information, and it has agreed to accept xerographic copies in lieu of the original records. Lorenz's office does not have a copying machine big enough to do the job efficiently. In these circumstances:

A. Lorenz *must* do the copying job herself on her small, slow office machine.

B. Lorenz *must* tell Cramer to make the copies himself, using his own facilities.

C. Lorenz *may* select a trustworthy copying firm to do the work, provided that she makes sure the firm's employees preserve the confidentiality of the records.

D. Lorenz *may* select a trustworthy copying firm to do the work, provided that she is personally present to supervise the work.

4. Attorney Aquino defended Dempsey in a criminal assault case. Before trial, Dempsey told Aquino in confidence that he beat up the victim without provocation. Due to Aquino's hard work, coupled with a stroke of luck, the jury found Dempsey not guilty. Then Dempsey refused to pay Aquino's fee. Aquino wrote to Dempsey as follows: "The jury found you not guilty, but your victim can still sue you for civil damages. If you do not pay my fee, and if I have to sue you to collect it, I will have to reveal the whole truth in open court, to explain why the amount of my fee is reasonable. Think this over carefully. I hope to receive your check by return mail." Which of the following is most nearly correct?

A. Even though heavy-handed, Aquino's letter was *proper* because he was simply explaining to Dempsey the consequences of refusing to pay the fee.

B. If Aquino sues Dempsey to collect the fee, Aquino will be *subject to discipline* because a lawyer is prohibited from using a civil suit to collect a fee.

C. Aquino's letter was *proper* because a lawyer is required to settle fee disputes amicably if possible.

D. If Aquino sues Dempsey to collect the fee, Aquino *may* reveal Dempsey's confidential communications, but only to the extent necessary to establish his claim against Dempsey.

5. Client Colbert has retained lawyer Lamb to represent her in divorce proceedings instituted by Colbert's husband. Colbert has moved out of the family home and is living in a distant town; she no longer sees her husband or their children. Colbert tells Lamb in confidence that, before the separation, she had been physically abusing the children. A state statute requires physicians and psychotherapists to report to the police all suspected cases of child abuse. The statute makes no mention of attorneys. Which of the following is most nearly correct?

A. If Lamb reports the child abuse to the police, he will be *subject to discipline*.

B. Lamb *may* report the child abuse to the police if he believes that the interests of justice will be served by doing so.

C. Lamb *must* report the child abuse to the police, because the state policy favors the protection of children.

D. Lamb *must* report the child abuse to the police, because child abuse is a crime that may result in death or serious bodily injury.

6. Eight years ago, attorney Arnott represented client Coleman in connection with a murder investigation. Coleman repeatedly assured Arnott that he was innocent. The investigation proved futile, and Coleman was never formally charged with any crime. At present Arnott is representing client Curtis in a child custody dispute between Curtis and her ex-husband. In that connection, Curtis tells Arnott in confidence about a murder committed eight years earlier by one Coleman, a friend of her ex-

husband. The details revealed by Curtis make it clear that Arnott's former client, Coleman, did commit the murder. Curtis insists that Arnott not tell anyone about the murder for fear that Coleman or some of her ex-husband's other friends may retaliate against her or her children. This jurisdiction has no statute of limitations on murder. Which of the following is most nearly correct?

A. Arnott *may* reveal the information to the prosecutor without Curtis's consent, because this jurisdiction has no statute of limitations on murder.

B. Arnott *must* reveal the information to the prosecutor because Coleman's evasion of the law is a continuing crime.

C. Arnott *must* keep the information in confidence unless Curtis changes her mind and consents to have it revealed.

D. Arnott *may* reveal the information to the prosecutor without the consent of either Curtis or Coleman, provided that he asks the prosecutor not to disclose the source of the information.

7. Lawyer Ling represented clients Clark and Craddock who were the sole partners in a business joint venture. In that connection, Clark and Craddock met frequently with Ling to discuss confidential matters relating to the business. One day Clark came alone to Ling's office. Before Ling could stop him, Clark disclosed that he had usurped a business opportunity that properly belonged to the joint venture. Ling informed Clark that she could not advise him on that topic. Further, Ling promptly withdrew as counsel to Clark and Craddock. Ultimately Craddock sued Clark for the usurpation. Craddock's lawyer subpoenaed Ling to testify at a deposition about the statements Clark made to Ling. At the deposition, Clark's lawyer asserted the attorney-client privilege on Clark's behalf. Ultimately the court ordered Ling to disclose what Clark said. Which of the following is most nearly correct?

A. It was *proper* for Ling to withdraw as counsel to Clark and Craddock. Further, Ling *must* disclose what Clark said.

B. It was *proper* for Ling to withdraw as counsel to Clark and Craddock. However, Ling will be *subject to discipline* if she discloses what Clark said.

C. Ling is *subject to discipline* for withdrawing as counsel to Clark and Craddock. Further, Ling will be *subject to discipline* if she discloses what Clark said.

D. Even if Ling believes that the court order is correct, she *must* refuse to disclose what Clark said.

Answers to the multiple choice questions will be found in the Appendix at the end of the book.

Chapter Eight

Candor in Litigation

■ ■ ■

What This Chapter Covers

I. The Attorney's Duty of Candor in Litigation
   A. Candor About the Law
   B. Candor About the Facts
   C. The Trilemma: Trust, Confidentiality, and Candor
   D. Falsity in Civil Matters

Reading Assignment

Wydick, Perschbacher & Bassett, Chapter 8.

ABA Model Rules 1.6, 3.3, 4.1, and 8.4(c).

CRPC 5–200, 5–220.

Cal.Bus. & Prof. Code §§ 6068(c), (d), (g), 6106, 6128(a).

Supplemental Reading

Hazard & Hodes:

Discussion of ABA Model Rules 1.6, 3.3, 4.1, and 8.4(c).

Rules 1.6, 3.3, and 4.1.

Restatement (Third) of Law Governing Lawyers §§ 111, 116–120 (2000).

Discussion Problems

1. Suppose you represent the defendant in a diversity of citizenship case that is in trial in the United States District Court for the Southern District of New York. The applicable law is that of the State of New York. One disputed legal issue is vital—in a malpractice action, what is the appropriate standard of care for a doctor of veterinary medicine who holds herself out as a specialist in ruminant epidemiology? The plaintiff's lawyer has failed to cite a very recent appellate decision that would support the plaintiff's position. So far as you know, the trial judge is unaware of the decision, but you know about it because it was reported in the current

issue of U.S. Law Week. In which of the following situations would you have an ethical duty to call the decision to the trial judge's attention?

a. Suppose it were a New York Court of Appeals decision in a veterinary malpractice case?

b. Suppose it were an Arizona Supreme Court decision in a veterinary malpractice case?

c. Suppose it were a New York Court of Appeals decision in a legal malpractice case involving a lawyer who held himself out as an expert in Robinson–Patman price discrimination litigation?

Are there any tactical reasons to go beyond what the ethics rules require?

2. Suppose you represent the defendant at the trial of a negligence case. The plaintiff has engaged in extensive discovery, but she has not found out about eyewitness X, an impartial third party who saw the accident clearly. X's testimony would establish that your client was at fault. At the trial, plaintiff's case in chief is insufficient to get the case to the jury, but the defect could be cured by X's testimony. Plaintiff is about to close her case in chief. When she does, it will be time for you to move for a directed verdict. You know that X lives nearby and is available as a witness. What will you do?

3. Suppose that you are counsel for the patentee of a U.S. patented prosthetic arm that enables an amputee to function almost perfectly. Your client is the defendant in a federal declaratory judgment action brought by a competitor to have the patent declared invalid under 35 U.S.C. § 102(b). That statute makes a patent invalid if the invention was in public use or on sale in the U.S. more than one year prior to the date of the U.S. patent application. The patent application was dated April 15, 2005. The plaintiff took your client's deposition and questioned him as follows:

Q: What date was the patented prosthetic arm first sold in the U.S.?

A: August 21, 2004.

Q: How do you know that so quickly and certainly?

A: Because when you guys sued, I checked the date on the hang-tag on the sample prosthesis in our sample vault. That date tells when the item was first sold anywhere in the world. We put a dated hang-tag on a sample of everything we invent, and we store the sample in the sample vault, so we will have an accurate record.

Q: How do we know that you put the right date on it?

A: Because we put it on there with pen and ink, and we are not slimeballs like some people I can think of.

After a few more questions, the deposition was adjourned for the lunch hour. During lunch, you admonished your client not to call the other side slimeballs. He responded:

They *are* slimeballs, and you have to fight slime with slime. Originally that hang-tag said 3/21/04, but I doctored it by turning the 3 into an 8, to make it say August 21, 2004. Pretty slick, no?

What must you do now?

4. Suppose that you are the in-house counsel for a drug company that has been sued in a state court products liability case. You have hired outside attorney Adney to defend the company. Technically speaking, you have the ultimate responsibility for all litigation matters, but you try never to second-guess the judgments of outside counsel. In the case at hand, the plaintiff alleges that he got bleeding stomach ulcers from taking Luxair, a drug made and sold by the company as a remedy for male pattern baldness. The active ingredient in Luxair is a chemical known as phlogestin. Plaintiff alleges that the company knew all along that Luxair creates a grave risk of stomach ulcers in males past age 40. Plaintiff demanded production of a host of documents, including "all documents relating to Luxair and the risk of stomach ulcers." When attorney Adney's paralegals searched the company files, they found no documents that mention both Luxair and stomach ulcers. However, in the company files pertaining to a different drug product that also contains phlogestin, the paralegals found a "smoking gun," namely a packet of research reports. The reports show that when defendant put Luxair on the market, it knew beyond doubt that phlogestin significantly increases the risk of stomach ulcers in males past age 40. Adney plans not to produce the research reports because they were not in the files pertaining to Luxair and they do not mention Luxair. Do you agree with Adney's plan?

5. Suppose that you are the defense lawyer for Decker who is charged with first degree murder. He has told you that he is innocent and that he was miles away from the scene of the crime, playing cards with three friends. You have interviewed the three friends, and they confirm his story. You plan to use Decker and the three friends as defense witnesses at Decker's jury trial.

a. Suppose that ten weeks before the trial, your investigator hands you information that clearly shows, beyond any fleeting whiff of doubt, that Decker and his friends are lying and that Decker did commit the murder. When you confront Decker, he says: "You are my lawyer, not my jury. I want to testify and to have my friends testify for me. Let the jury decide whether I am guilty." What should you do?

b. Suppose the same facts, except that you get the information and confront Decker ten minutes before you are to begin presenting the defense case-in-chief. What should you do?

c. Suppose that you do not get the information until ten minutes after you have presented the testimony of Decker and his friends. When you confront Decker, he says: "Your information is correct; I murdered that guy. But I think the jury believed me and my friends. Leave well enough alone." What should you do?

d. Suppose that you do not get the information until ten weeks after the jury has acquitted Decker. When you confront Decker, he says: "Your information is correct; I murdered that guy. But obviously the jury believed me and my friends. Leave well enough alone." What should you do?

e. Suppose that the information you receive from your investigator leaves some small room for doubt. When you confront Decker, he reaffirms his story about the card game. Does that change your answers to questions a through d?

THE TRILEMMA: TRUST, CONFIDENTIALITY, AND CANDOR

If a dilemma is a beast with two horns, then perhaps a trilemma has three. [*See* MONROE FREEDMAN & ABBE SMITH, UNDERSTANDING LAWYER'S ETHICS 159–195 (3d ed. 2004); Monroe Freedman, *Getting Honest About Client Perjury*, 21 Geo. J. Legal Ethics 133 (2008); Monroe Freedman, *Perjury: The Lawyer's Trilemma,* 1 Litigation 26 (Winter 1975).] We lawyers may occasionally face such a beast when representing a defendant in a criminal case:

Horn One: We are told to seek the client's trust and to find out everything the client knows about the case.

Horn Two: We are told to preserve our client's confidential information (except in very limited situations).

Horn Three: We are told to act with candor, to refrain from presenting evidence we know is false, and (in some situations) to reveal our client's frauds.

a. The Old ABA Model Code Position

At the outset, consider the duty expressed in the predecessor to the ABA Model Rules—ABA Model Code of Professional Responsibility DR 7–102(B)(1) says:

> A lawyer who receives information clearly establishing that * * * [h]is client has, in the course of the representation, perpetrated a fraud upon a person or tribunal shall promptly call upon his client to rectify the same, and if his client refuses or is unable to do so, he shall reveal the fraud to the affected person or tribunal, except when the information is protected as a privileged communication.

The "except" clause at the end was added by the ABA House of Delegates in a 1974 amendment to the ABA Code. Shortly thereafter, ABA Formal Opinion 341 (1975) interpreted the term "privileged communication" to include not only material that is protected by the attorney-client privilege, but also all other material that is protected by the ethical duty of confidentiality. That interpretation makes the "except" clause virtually swallow the rule. Do you see why? Eighteen states added the 1974 amendment to their own versions of the ABA Code, but the remainder did not.

b. The Narrative Testimony Position

Next, consider the advice formerly offered to criminal defense lawyers in Standard 4–7.7 of the ABA Standards for the Defense Function. When the ABA House of Delegates approved the other Standards for the Defense Function in 1979, it reserved judgment on 4–7.7, thus leaving the matter open for resolution by the drafters of the ABA Model Rules. [The drafters eventually rejected Standard 4–7.7, and it was disapproved by the ABA ethics committee in 1987.] Standard 4–7.7 reads as follows:

> *Standard 4–7.7 Testimony by the Defendant*
>
> (a) If the defendant has admitted to defense counsel facts which establish guilt and counsel's independent investigation established that the admissions are true but the defendant insists on the right to trial, counsel must strongly discourage the defendant against taking the witness stand to testify perjuriously.
>
> (b) If, in advance of trial, the defendant insists that he or she will take the stand to testify perjuriously, the lawyer may withdraw from the case, if that is feasible, seeking leave to the court if necessary, but the court should not be advised of the lawyer's reason for seeking to do so.
>
> (c) If withdrawal from the case is not feasible or is not permitted by the court, or if the situation arises immediately preceding trial or during the trial and the defendant insists upon testifying perjuriously in his or her own behalf, it is unprofessional conduct for the lawyer to lend aid to the perjury or use the perjured testimony. Before the defendant takes the stand in these circumstances, the lawyer should make a record of the fact that the defendant is taking the stand against the advice of counsel in some appropriate manner without revealing the fact to the court. The lawyer may identify the witness as the defendant and may ask appropriate questions of the defendant when it is believed that the defendant's answers will not be perjurious. As to matters for which it is believed the defendant will offer perjurious testimony, the lawyer should seek to avoid direct examination of the defendant in the conventional manner; instead, the lawyer should ask the defendant if he or she wishes to make any additional statement concerning the case to the trier or triers of the facts. A lawyer may not later argue the defendant's known false version of facts to the jury as worthy of belief, and may not recite or rely upon the false testimony in his or her closing argument.

c. Monroe Freedman's Position

Next, consider the view expressed by Professor Monroe Freedman in books and articles spanning over 40 years. The most recent is Monroe

Freedman, *Getting Honest About Client Perjury*, 21 Geo. J. Legal Ethics 133 (2008); *see also* MONROE H. FREEDMAN & ABBE SMITH, UNDERSTANDING LAWYER'S ETHICS (3d ed. 2004)[a], hereafter cited as "Freedman 2004," and the earliest and most famous is Monroe H. Freedman, *Professional Responsibility of the Criminal Defense Lawyer: The Three Hardest Questions*, 64 MICH. L. REV. 1469 (1966). Professor Freedman states the question thus: "Is it ever proper for a criminal defense lawyer to present testimony that she knows is perjurious?" The answer, he says, is "yes," and he goes on to explain why.

He begins by discussing and rejecting the other possible responses when a criminal defense lawyer discovers that her client is bent on committing perjury. One possible response is for the lawyer to withdraw. That is no solution, Freedman explains, because the client will get a new lawyer. The client now knows that when he tells a lawyer the truth, the lawyer withdraws, so the client will keep the new lawyer in the dark. The client will then testify falsely, just as he would have before, only this time the new lawyer (having been kept in the dark) has no chance to try to convince him not to do so. [Freedman 2004 at 164–65.] Moreover, withdrawal will usually require the judge's consent, and when the case is close to trial or in trial, the judge will want a very good excuse from the lawyer. The lawyer must then either be vague ("I have an ethics problem, Your Honor") or must be forthright and tell the judge that the client insists on committing perjury. Either way, the judge will know, or strongly sense, that the client insists on lying. If the client is convicted, in most instances the judge will set the sentence, and the possibility for grave prejudice to the client is obvious. [*Id.*]

A second possible response to the trilemma is the one recommended in ABA Standard for the Defense Function 4–7.7, quoted above—that is, let the defendant tell the false parts of his story in narrative fashion, without questioning by the defense lawyer. The defense lawyer cannot then rely on the false parts of the story in closing argument to the jury. That's no solution either, Professor Freedman argues, because:

> [t]he judge is certain to understand what is going on, and it is generally agreed that the jury usually will as well. Even if the jury does not realize the significance of the unusual manner in which the defendant is testifying, the jury is sure to catch on when the defense lawyer in closing argument makes no reference to the defendant's exculpatory testimony. [*Id.* at 166.]

A third possible response to the trilemma is "intentional ignorance." That is, the lawyer lets the client know early in the lawyer-client relationship that she does not really want to know what happened. Professor Freedman has no patience for lawyers who use that approach:

> Apart from the practical problems of requiring clients to do their own lawyering, we might question whether intentional ignorance is a moral resolution of the lawyer's ethical problem. Certainly, lawyers

> who practice intentional ignorance have the comfort of saying that they have never knowingly presented a client's perjury. On the other hand, by remaining ignorant, these same lawyers have disabled themselves from being in a position to dissuade their clients from committing the perjury. Lawyers can remain aloof from client perjury, but that does not prevent perjury from happening. Indeed, there is good reason to believe that there would be more perjury, not less, if lawyers did not know about it and were not in a position to discourage it. [*Id.* at 160.]

Professor Freedman also considers and rejects a variant of "intentional ignorance." Early in the lawyer-client relationship, a lawyer who uses the variant would ask the client what the prosecutor, or a hypothetical liar, is likely to *say* happened on the occasion in question. By that ruse, the defense lawyer can learn the worst case scenario without having to ask the defendant what really happened. [*See id.* at 193.] The lawyer can then—consciously or subconsciously—guide the defendant toward the least damaging version of the facts. [*See id.* at 205–11; *see also* Richard C. Wydick, *The Ethics of Witness Coaching*, 17 CARDOZO L. REV. 1 (1995).]

What does Professor Freedman think is the proper response to the trilemma? He recommends using the traditional model of the lawyer-client relationship. [Freedman 2004 at 169–70.] At the outset of the relationship, the lawyer should impress on the client the importance of telling the lawyer truthfully everything that happened. The lawyer should also promise the client to keep what the client says in confidence. If the client insists on testifying and is bent on committing perjury, the lawyer should attempt in every way possible to convince the client not to do it. A client who is impervious to legal and moral arguments against perjury may be convinced by a more practical argument—if the jury convicts him, and the judge thinks he lied on the witness stand, the judge is likely to impose an extra-harsh sentence on him. [*Id.* at 170.]

Professor Freedman then drops the other shoe:

> In the relatively small number of cases in which the client who has contemplated perjury rejects the lawyer's advice and decides to proceed to trial, to take the stand, and to give false testimony, the lawyer should go forward in the ordinary way. That is, the lawyer should examine the client in a normal professional manner and should argue the client's testimony to the jury in summation to the extent sound tactics justify doing so. [*Id.*]

Can Professor Freedman's conclusion be squared with one's personal standards of morality? He concedes that he is not completely comfortable with it. [*Id.* at 171.] A lawyer may be convinced that she would never lie to protect herself, even from a long prison term. Nevertheless, contemplating the possibility ought to give her compassion for a client who feels compelled to lie. [*Id.*] Freedman continues:

> Beyond that, we cannot find—in terms of personal morality—a more acceptable course. We find deep moral significance in the dignity

of the individual and in the way that dignity is respected in the American constitutional adversary system.... A lawyer is in no position in the first interview with a client to make an informed judgment as to whether a client is guilty or innocent, what defenses he might have, or what his degree of culpability might be. The lawyer must act, therefore, upon a presumption of innocence. The lawyer cannot serve the client as he deserves to be served if she does not know everything there is to know about the client's case. Accordingly, the lawyer must urge him to tell her everything, and the lawyer must pledge confidentiality. Having given that pledge, we would be morally bound to keep it. [*Id.*]

d. The ABA Model Rules Position

The committee that drafted the ABA Model Rules rejected the position of the old ABA Model Code, the narrative testimony position, and Professor Freedman's position. In 1983, the ABA House of Delegates adopted Model Rule 3.3, which was revised in 2002. [*See also* Restatement (Third) of the Law Governing Lawyers § 120 (2000).] Read Rule 3.3 carefully, especially Comments 5 through 15, and answer the following questions about it:

- What should a lawyer do when she first discovers that her criminal defendant wants to commit perjury?
- What about the withdrawal option?
- What must the lawyer do if her other efforts have failed?
- Does her duty have an ending point? What is it?

In *Nix v. Whiteside,* 475 U.S. 157, 106 S.Ct. 988, 89 L.Ed.2d 123 (1986), Chief Justice Burger (writing for himself and four others) traveled well out of his way to put a judicial stamp of approval on the procedure envisioned in ABA Model Rule 3.3. Defendant Whiteside was charged with murdering a marijuana dealer. Attorney Robinson was appointed to represent him. At first, Whiteside told Robinson that he stabbed the victim just as the victim was "pulling a pistol from underneath the pillow on the bed." [*Id.* at 160.] Whiteside said he had not actually seen a gun, but he was convinced that the victim had one. No gun was found at the scene. Robinson advised Whiteside that the existence of an actual gun was not critical to a claim of self-defense, and that a *reasonable belief* that there was a gun would suffice.

About a week before trial, Whiteside told Robinson for the first time that he had seen something "metallic" in the victim's hand. [*Id.* at 161.] When Robinson inquired further, Whiteside said: "In Howard Cook's case there was a gun. If I don't say I saw a gun, I'm dead." Robinson again explained that a reasonable belief would suffice, but Whiteside insisted on testifying that he had seen "something metallic." [*Id.*] At that point, Robinson told Whiteside that if Whiteside testified to that story, it would be Robinson's duty "to advise the Court of what he was doing," and Robinson said he would also "probably be allowed to impeach that particular testimony." [*Id.*] Robinson also indicated that he would try to withdraw if Whiteside insisted on testifying falsely.

Thus warned, Whiteside did not testify about having seen something metallic. Instead, he testified that he "knew" the victim had a gun, and he believed that the victim was reaching for it. On cross-examination, he admitted that he did not actually see a gun in the victim's hand. He was found guilty of second degree murder and sentenced to 40 years in prison. After exhausting his appeals, he claimed on federal habeas corpus that Robinson's refusal to let him testify as he wished was a denial of the effective assistance of counsel guaranteed by the Sixth Amendment.

The narrow issue presented to the Supreme Court was whether Whiteside was deprived of his right to effective counsel when his counsel told him that if he testified to a story the counsel believed was false, the counsel would try to withdraw and (failing that) would tell the judge that the story was false. The Court held that Whiteside was not deprived of the effective assistance of counsel—Robinson's conduct fell within the wide range of acceptable responses to proposed client perjury.

The Chief Justice explained that an ineffective assistance claim requires (a) serious error by the lawyer, and (b) prejudice to the defendant. Robinson did not make a serious error. A criminal defense attorney must be loyal to the client, but only within the bounds of lawful conduct. The attorney must not assist the client in presenting false evidence. True, a criminal defendant does have a constitutional right to testify in his own defense. [*See Rock v. Arkansas,* 483 U.S. 44, 49–53, 107 S.Ct. 2704, 97 L.Ed.2d 37 (1987).] But, Burger said, if he testifies falsely, he must bear the consequences. Part of the consequences may be withdrawal of counsel or revelation of the perjury by counsel. Moreover, Whiteside was not prejudiced. He ended up testifying truthfully at the trial. Perhaps he was deprived of counsel's help in presenting perjury, but the Constitution does not guarantee the right to have counsel's help in presenting perjury.

In a terse concurring opinion, Justice Brennan pointed out that much of the Chief Justice's opinion was unnecessary to the decision in the case:

> [L]et there be no mistake: the Court's essay regarding what constitutes the correct response to a criminal client's suggestion that he will perjure himself is pure discourse without the force of law. * * * Lawyers, judges, bar associations, students, and others should understand that the problem has not now been "decided." [*Id.* at 177.]

[The Restatement (Third) of the Law Governing Lawyers § 120 (2000) follows *Nix v. Whiteside* and ABA Model Rule 3.3. *See also* ABA Formal Opinion 87–353 (1987), in which the ABA ethics committee spells out the implications of *Nix* and Model Rule 3.3.]

Notice that ABA Model Rule 3.3(a)(3) forbids a lawyer from knowingly offering evidence that the lawyer "knows" is false. Model Rule 1.0(f) defines "knows" to mean having "actual knowledge of the fact in question," but it goes on to say that "a person's knowledge may be inferred from the circumstances." Does the "knows" standard require a lawyer to keep her client off the witness stand if she has a strong suspicion that his testimony will be false? Or if his story is not corroborated by other evidence in the case? Or if his story contradicts other evidence in the case? In *United States v. Midgett,* 342 F.3d 321 (4th Cir. 2003), a criminal defense lawyer refused to put his client on the stand because he believed that the client would testify falsely. The trial judge ordered the defendant either to accede to the lawyer's demand not to testify or to proceed without a lawyer. The defendant unwillingly gave up his right to testify, and he was convicted. The Fourth Circuit reversed the conviction, saying that the defense counsel's duty to his client didn't depend on whether he personally believed his client's story, nor on the amount of proof supporting or contradicting the story. Does the "knows" standard bring ABA Model Rule 3.3(a)(3) around to Professor Freedman's view of the client perjury problem? [*See* Monroe Freedman, *Getting Honest about Client Perjury,* 21 Geo. J. Legal Ethics 133, 142–48 (2008); *see also* 25 ABA/BNA Law. Man. Prof. Conduct 424 (2009); 25 ABA/BNA Law. Man. Prof. Conduct 174 (2009).]

California and the District of Columbia depart from the rest of the nation concerning the duties of a criminal defense lawyer whose client insists on taking the witness stand to commit perjury. [*See* D.C. Rule 3.3(b); California Commission for the Revision of the Rules of Professional Conduct, Proposed Rule 3.3(a)(3) (April 2009 draft).] The California case law is reflected in *People v. Johnson*, below.

PEOPLE v. JOHNSON

California Court of Appeal, Fourth District, 1998.
62 Cal.App.4th 608, 72 Cal.Rptr.2d 805 (1998),
cert. denied, 525 U.S. 914, 119 S.Ct. 262, 142 L.Ed.2d 215 (1998).[b]

KREMER, PRESIDING JUSTICE.

Anthony L. Johnson was convicted of numerous violent sexual offenses, kidnappings and robberies. He was sentenced to 5 consecutive life terms plus 440 years. On appeal, he contends he was denied his right to testify in his own defense * * * We conclude the court erred in denying Johnson his constitutional right to testify but find the error harmless beyond a reasonable doubt.

* * *

At trial, after the prosecution had completed its case-in-chief, defense counsel requested and was granted an in camera hearing. Johnson was present during the in-chambers conference. Defense counsel told the court he had "an ethical conflict" with Johnson about Johnson's desire to take the stand and testify. Defense counsel explained, "I cannot disclose to the court privileged communications relating to that, but I'm in a position

b. For ease in reading, we have omitted the court's footnotes, most of its citations, and most of the single and double quotation marks around material that the court quoted.

where I am not willing to call Mr. Johnson as a witness despite his desire to testify." In response to the court's question, Johnson indicated defense counsel had accurately described the situation and defense counsel indicated he would "[n]ot voluntarily" call Johnson as a witness. The court, misunderstanding the situation, told Johnson that his attorney had decided it was not in Johnson's "best interest to testify" and confirmed Johnson wanted to testify. The following exchange then occurred:

> "[DEFENSE COUNSEL]: Judge, this is not a trial tactic issue. This is an ethical conflict. If it were just a trial tactic, you know, in other words, a decision of what's the best choice, I always defer to the client's wishes in circumstances like this.
>
> "THE COURT: What exactly are you trying to tell me . . . that you won't examine him if he takes the stand?
>
> "[DEFENSE COUNSEL]: I think under the—based upon the information I have, I would be ethically barred from calling him as a witness under the law as I have come to know it and very specifically researched it regarding this particular issue.
>
> "THE COURT: Okay. It's always very difficult for a trial judge based on my experience at least to sit in on these. It is like having both your hands tied behind your back because you have to make a decision. If your call based on what you know is that you have an ethical problem that will compel you not to call him and that that's over his objection, then I'll note it for the record. He will not be called—
>
> "[DEFENSE COUNSEL]: That's fine.
>
> "THE COURT:—Based on that. And we'll go forward. And you have in essence done everything you are required to do as an attorney by placing it on the record. And at this point in time I'm going to have to abide by it because you're the one that's making the call on the ethical issue.
>
> "[DEFENSE COUNSEL]: Yes. I just want to be clear that this isn't a judgment situation that falls in the realm of a trial tactic. It's more than that.
>
> "THE COURT: All right. I will note, then, that you believe that there are ethical reasons, strong ethical reasons, apparently, because otherwise we wouldn't be sitting in here right now,—
>
> "[DEFENSE COUNSEL]: Correct.
>
> "THE COURT:—That cause you to come to the conclusion that you cannot under any circumstances call the client. And I will note that. And I will note that it's over his objection, and that he desires to testify."

Johnson did not testify.

A. Development of the Right to Testify

Under the early common law, interested parties, including persons accused of committing a crime, were disqualified from presenting sworn testimony. * * * This disqualification of parties from presenting sworn testimony was clearly established by the end of the 16th century in civil cases on the basis the party's testimony was untrustworthy. Disqualification of criminal defendants seems to have come somewhat later. In the sixteenth century it was necessary for an accused to conduct his own defense, since he was neither allowed to call witnesses in his behalf nor permitted the assistance of counsel. The criminal trial of this period has been described as a long argument between the prisoner and the counsel for the Crown, in which they questioned each other and grappled with each other's arguments with the utmost eagerness and closeness of reasoning. In the process the defendant could offer by way of explanation material that would later be characterized as testimony. * * *

By the 17th century in England, a criminal defendant was allowed to call witnesses and by 1701 had the right to call witnesses to testify under oath but the defendant himself was still precluded from giving sworn testimony. * * * This rule deeming criminal defendants incompetent to give sworn testimony was adopted in this country.* * * By the mid–19th century, parties and interested witnesses in civil cases were allowed to give sworn testimony in England and in most states in this country. The elimination of the disqualification was based primarily on an argument that a witness's motive for lying should go to the weight, not the admissibility, of testimony.

Criminal defendants, however, were still deemed incompetent to testify. The two main arguments against permitting criminal defendants to testify were: (1) criminal defendants were so likely to commit perjury to avoid conviction that their testimony was inherently untrustworthy and (2) permitting criminal defendants to testify would erode the constitutional right to remain silent and the presumption of innocence because suspicion would fall on the defendant who failed to testify.

Maine was the first state to enact a statute providing that a criminal defendant was competent to testify. A Maine Supreme Court justice was a primary proponent of deeming criminal defendants competent to testify. He justified competency as a necessary protection for the innocent and believed that incompetency had served the guilty as a shield and thus disserved the public interest. Competency, he thought, would open the accused to cross-examination and permit an unfavorable inference if he declined to take the stand to exculpate himself. * * *

* * * Within 20 years most states, including California, had eliminated the prohibition against criminal defendants providing testimony. Finally, by 1960, all states except Georgia, had provided a criminal defendant was competent to testify in his own behalf. * * * Experience under the American competency statutes was to change the minds of many who had opposed them. It was seen that the shutting out of his sworn evidence

could be positively hurtful to the accused, and that innocence was in fact aided, not prejudiced, by the opportunity of the accused to testify under oath.

In 1960, the United States Supreme Court struck down the last remaining state statute (in Georgia) which provided a criminal defendant was incompetent to give sworn testimony. (Ferguson v. Georgia, 365 U.S. 570 (1961).) The court held Georgia's statute which permitted only unsworn testimony by a criminal defendant denied the defendant his right to assistance of counsel during every step of the proceedings. * * *

* * *

In 1987, the United States Supreme Court explicitly held a criminal defendant had a constitutional right to testify on his own behalf. (Rock v. Arkansas, 483 U.S. 44 (1987).) The Supreme Court stated the right to testify is one of the rights that are essential to due process of law in a fair adversary process, and was protected by the Fifth, Sixth, and Fourteenth Amendments of the United States Constitution.

* * *

The criminal defendant's constitutional right to testify is unlike other matters of trial strategy which are in the control of defense counsel. A criminal defendant has the right to take the stand even over the objections of his trial counsel. As our Supreme Court explained in People v. Robles (1970) 2 Cal.3d 205, 215, 85 Cal.Rptr. 166, 466 P.2d 710: "[T]he right to testify in one's own behalf is of such fundamental importance that a defendant who timely demands to take the stand contrary to the advice given by his counsel has the right to give an exposition of his defense before a jury.* * * The defendant's insistence upon testifying may in the final analysis be harmful to his case, but the right is of such importance that every defendant should have it in a criminal case." * * *

B. An Attorney's Obligation Not to Present Perjured Testimony

A problem arises, as in this case, where the defendant asserts his right to testify and his attorney knows or suspects the defendant will give perjured testimony. A conflict then arises between the defendant's constitutional right to testify (and his Sixth Amendment right to the assistance of counsel) and the attorney's ethical obligation not to present perjured testimony.

Attorneys have long been prohibited by the attorney rules of professional conduct from participating in the presentation of perjured testimony. (See Nix v. Whiteside (1986) 475 U.S. 157, 166.) The California Rules of Professional Conduct require an attorney to "employ * * * such means only as are consistent with truth" and prohibit him from seeking "to mislead the judge, judicial officer, or jury by an artifice or false statement of fact or law." (Cal. Rules of Prof. Conduct, rule 5–200.) * * * [*Accord* ABA Model Rule 3.3(a).]

C. Solutions to the Problem of a Client's Intended Perjury

There has been much scholarly discussion of what an attorney should do when faced with a client who intends to commit perjury. Solutions range from the attorney providing full cooperation to his client in presenting the testimony to the attorney refusing to permit his client to testify. Intermediate solutions include persuading the client to not testify falsely, disclosing the perjurious intent to the court, making a motion to withdraw, or allowing the defendant to testify in a "free narrative" fashion. We examine these various options.

1. Full Cooperation with Presenting Defendant's Testimony even when Defendant Intends to Commit Perjury

Professor [Monroe] Freedman argues an attorney should fully cooperate with putting on his client's testimony even when the client intends to commit perjury. (See Freedman, Professional Responsibility of the Criminal Defense Lawyer: The Three Hardest Questions (1966) 64 Mich. L.Rev. 1469; Freedman, Understanding Lawyers' Ethics (1990).* * *) Professor Freedman argues the importance of client confidentiality and, as well, the attorney's duty to provide effective representation by gathering all necessary information are more important than an attorney's duty to be candid with the court. Therefore, Professor Freedman argues defense counsel must sometimes permit his client to commit perjury and be prepared to argue the client's perjurious testimony to the jury.

No court has endorsed this view. Freedman's approach has also been much criticized by the legal commentators because it conflicts with legal ethics rules prohibiting an attorney from knowingly participating in presenting perjured testimony as well as rules requiring an attorney to disclose a client's intention to commit a crime.

2. Persuading the Client not to Commit Perjury

All the legal commentators agree that when faced with a client who indicates he will commit perjury, an attorney should first attempt to persuade the client to testify truthfully. The United States Supreme Court has held an attorney acted consistently with professional rules of ethics and did not deny the defendant the right to effective assistance of counsel by persuading the defendant not to commit perjury. (Nix v. Whiteside, supra, 475 U.S. 157, 169.) * * *

The persuasion solution, when it succeeds, is the ideal solution since it involves neither the presentation of perjured testimony nor disclosure of client confidences. Yet, it does not answer the question of what should be done when the client insists on testifying falsely despite his attorney's best efforts to dissuade him.

3. Withdrawal From Representation

The [ABA] Model Rules * * * provide [that] an attorney should make a motion to withdraw from representation when the representation will result in a violation of law or rules of professional conduct. (Model Rules, rule 1.16(a)(1).) * * * In the California case of People v. Brown (1988) 203

Cal.App.3d 1335, 1339–1340, footnote 1, the court * * * stated that if an attorney is unable to dissuade his client from committing perjury, the attorney must make a motion to withdraw so as to not give implied consent to the use of perjurious testimony. * * *

This approach, while it protects the attorney's interest in not presenting perjured testimony, does not solve the problem. The court may deny the motion to withdraw. * * * Even if the motion to withdraw is granted, the problem remains. * * * [Withdrawal] could trigger an endless cycle of defense continuances and motions to withdraw as the accused informs each new attorney of the intent to testify falsely. Or the accused may be less candid with his new attorney by keeping his perjurious intent to himself, thereby facilitating the presentation of false testimony. Lastly, there is the unfortunate possibility that the accused may find an unethical attorney who would knowingly present and argue the false testimony. Thus, defense counsel's withdrawal from the case would not really solve the problem created by the anticipated perjury but, in fact, could create even more problems.

4. Disclosure to the Court

Another alternative is that the attorney should disclose the perjury to the court. Initially, we note that some of the other proposed solutions involve some disclosure, i.e., implicit in solutions of making a motion to withdraw or having the defendant testify in a narrative manner is, at least, an implicit disclosure to the court that the attorney believes the defendant may commit perjury. Disclosure has been criticized because it compromises the attorney's ethical duty to keep client communications confidential and results in a significant conflict of interest between the attorney and his client if the attorney discloses to the court that the defendant has perjured himself. Additionally, until the defendant actually takes the stand and testifies falsely, there is always a chance the defendant will change his mind and testify truthfully. Finally, disclosure is only a partial solution. If the disclosure occurs before the defendant has taken the stand, the disclosure will require some additional action, i.e., a decision as to whether the defendant's statement is, in fact, false and a further decision whether the defendant will be permitted to testify and in what form and manner. Disclosure before the defendant testifies could result in a mini-trial on the perjury issue before the defendant has had the opportunity to take the stand and testify truthfully.

5. The Narrative Approach

Under the narrative approach, the attorney calls the defendant to the witness stand but does not engage in the usual question and answer exchange. Instead, the attorney permits the defendant to testify in a free narrative manner. In closing arguments, the attorney does not rely on any of the defendant's false testimony. In the early 1970's, the American Bar Association adopted the narrative approach in its * * * Standards Relating to the Defense Function. * * * [But] Standard 7.7 adopting the free narrative approach [was ultimately rejected by the adoption of ABA Model

Rule 3.3.] * * * The narrative approach has been criticized on the basis [that] the attorney participates in committing a fraud on the court.

6. Refusing to Permit the Defendant to Testify

The opposite extreme from Professor Freedman's solution of full cooperation by the attorney in presenting the defendant's testimony is a refusal to permit the defendant to testify at all. This solution is justified by the theory that an attorney has an ethical obligation not to participate in the presentation of perjured testimony and the defendant has no right to commit perjury. * * * Preclusion of the testimony as a solution has been criticized because it essentially substitutes defense counsel for the jury as the judge of witness credibility; it puts the determination of whether the defendant is telling the truth or a lie into the hands of defense counsel. * * * Further, under this approach, a determination is made that the defendant will commit perjury before he has even taken the witness stand. As we noted before, until the defendant is actually on the stand, there is always the possibility the defendant will change his mind and testify truthfully. Further, a determination of whether the defendant will commit perjury may result in a mini-trial, with the attorney essentially "testifying" against the defendant. Finally, this approach, while safeguarding the attorney's ethical obligations not to participate in presenting perjured testimony, results in a complete denial of the defendant's right to testify.

7. California Cases

[The court reviewed two earlier California decisions that favor parts of the narrative approach. They are *People v. Guzman*, 45 Cal.3d 915, 248 Cal.Rptr.467, 755 P.2d 917 (1988) and *People v. Gadson*, 19 Cal.App.4th 1700, 24 Cal.Rptr.2d 219 (1993).]

8. The Narrative Approach Represents the Best Accommodation of the Competing Interests

None of the approaches to a client's stated intention to commit perjury is perfect. Of the various approaches, we believe the narrative approach represents the best accommodation of the competing interests of the defendant's right to testify and the attorney's obligation not to participate in the presentation of perjured testimony since it allows the defendant to tell the jury, in his own words, his version of what occurred, a right which has been described as fundamental, and allows the attorney to play a passive role. In contrast, the two extremes—fully cooperating with the defendant's testimony and refusing to present the defendant's testimony—involve no accommodation of the conflicting interests; the first gives no consideration to the attorney's ethical obligations, the second gives none to the defendant's right to testify. The other intermediate solutions—persuasion, withdrawal and disclosure—often result in no solution, i.e., the defendant is not persuaded, the withdrawal leads to an endless chain of withdrawals and disclosure compromises client confidentiality and typically requires further action.

We disagree with those commentators who have found the narrative approach necessarily communicates to the jury that defense counsel believes the defendant is lying. * * * [T]he jury may surmise the defendant desired to testify unhampered by the traditional question and answer format. * * * Because the defendant in a criminal trial is not situated the same as other witnesses, it would not be illogical for a jury to assume that special rules apply to his testimony, including a right to testify in a narrative fashion. We do not believe the possibility of a negative inference the defendant is lying should preclude the use of the narrative approach since the alternative would be worse, i.e., the attorney's active participation in presenting the perjured testimony or exclusion of the defendant's testimony, neither of which strikes a balance between the competing interests involved.

The danger that the defendant may testify falsely is mitigated by the fact that the defendant is subject to impeachment and can be cross-examined just like any other witness. The jury is no less capable of assessing the defendant's credibility than it is of any other witness. As the Supreme Court stated in Rock v. Arkansas, supra, 483 U.S. 44, 52, "Like the truthfulness of other witnesses, the defendant's veracity, which was the concern behind the original common-law rule, can be tested adequately by cross-examination." Further, to preclude the defendant's testimony entirely based on a possibility that defendant may lie, deprives the jury of making that assessment and may deprive the jury of hearing other, nonperjurious evidence to which the defendant would have testified about had he been given the opportunity. In utilizing the narrative approach, the jury has the benefit of hearing the defendant's version.

The narrative approach also avoids having a pre-perjury hearing, a mini-trial on whether the defendant might commit perjury if called to the stand; a hearing which could result in the attorney testifying against the client and which would require the court to be able to see into the future and determine that an individual who has stated only an intention to testify falsely (at least as according to his attorney) will actually testify falsely once on the witness stand.

* * *

We conclude the narrative approach best accommodates the competing interests of the defendant's constitutional right to testify and the attorney's ethical obligations.

* * *

The Attorney General argues the court properly excluded Johnson's testimony and points to language in United States Supreme Court cases stating that while a defendant has a constitutional right to testify, the defendant has no right to commit perjury. (See Nix v. Whiteside, supra * * * and Harris v. New York (1971) 401 U.S. 222. * * *) Initially, we note neither of these cases involved a holding that a defendant was properly precluded from testifying because he might commit perjury; in both cases the defendant actually testified. In Nix v. Whiteside, the defendant testified truthfully. The Supreme Court held the defendant was not denied * * * effective assistance of counsel by counsel's conduct in persuading the defendant not to testify falsely, including counsel's threats to withdraw from the case and impeach the defendant if he testified falsely. Nothing in the Nix v. Whiteside case provides that a court must prohibit a defendant from testifying if his attorney states a belief or knowledge the defendant will testify falsely if called to the stand. * * *

Similarly, in Harris v. New York, the issue was not whether a defendant should be prohibited from testifying based upon his attorney's belief or knowledge the defendant might commit perjury. Harris involved the issue of whether a defendant who elected to testify could be impeached with prior inconsistent statements taken in violation of his Miranda rights. In the course of so holding, the Supreme Court stated: * * * "Every criminal defendant is privileged to testify in his own defense, or to refuse to do so. But that privilege cannot be construed to include the right to commit perjury. Having voluntarily taken the stand, petitioner was under an obligation to speak truthfully and accurately, and the prosecution here did no more than utilize the traditional truth-testing devices of the adversary process. Had inconsistent statements been made by the accused to some third person, it could hardly be contended that the conflict could not be laid before the jury by way of cross-examination and impeachment. The shield provided by Miranda cannot be perverted into a license to use perjury by way of a defense, free from the risk of confrontation with prior inconsistent utterances." (Harris v. New York, supra, 401 U.S. 222, 225–226.)

* * *

In sum, neither of these cases holds a trial court should (as did the trial court here) deny a defendant his constitutional right to testify based on the possibility or probability the defendant might commit perjury. Rather, the Supreme Court held that a defendant is not denied effective assistance of counsel when his counsel persuades him not to testify falsely and that once a defendant elects to testify, he is subject to cross-examination and impeachment, including with statements taken in violation of his Miranda rights.

We conclude the trial court erred in denying Johnson his constitutional right to testify. The trial court should have followed the narrative approach, which has been approved by the courts in California and which would have best accommodated the conflicting interests of Johnson and his defense counsel. [The Court of Appeal went on to hold that the trial court's error was harmless beyond a reasonable doubt, because the evidence against Johnson was overwhelming.]

MULTIPLE CHOICE QUESTIONS

Answer these questions using the definitions found at the end of Chapter Two.

1. State X and State Y each have state trademark registration statutes that are substantially similar in purpose and wording to the Lanham Act (the federal trademark registration statute). For many years, Daisy Dairy has used the mark "Daisy" on dairy products it sells in State X, and it has registered the mark under the State X statute. Recently Noxatox Chemical began using the "Daisy" mark on cockroach poison it sells in State X. Daisy Dairy sued Noxatox under State X law in a State X court for intentional infringement of the "Daisy" mark. The complaint asks for an injunction, for an award of the profits made by Noxatox, and for money damages. Noxatox moved for summary judgment on the grounds that dairy products and cockroach poison do not compete with each other, that no sensible consumer could be deceived by the use of the same mark on such widely different goods, and that Daisy Dairy could not possibly have suffered monetary injury. The trial judge who will hear the motion is not well versed in trademark law, and the lawyer for Daisy Dairy failed to discover several pertinent court decisions. Which of the following decisions *must* the lawyer for Noxatox call to the judge's attention?

I. A United States Supreme Court decision which holds that the Lanham Act authorizes an injunction to stop intentional infringement, even where the defendant's goods do not compete with the plaintiff's goods.

II. A decision of the United States Court of Appeals for the circuit that includes State X and State Y, holding that an injunction can be issued under the Lanham Act where the nature of the defendant's goods could cast a distasteful or odious image on the plaintiff's goods.

III. A decision of the Supreme Court of State Y which holds that the State Y registration statute authorizes an accounting of the defendant's profits in a case of intentional infringement, even where the plaintiff cannot prove monetary injury.

IV. A decision of the Supreme Court of State X which holds that in actions for intentional trespass to real property, State X trial judges have the power of courts of equity to fashion equitable remedies, even where the plaintiff cannot prove monetary injury.

A. All of the above.

B. None of the above.

C. I, II, and IV only.

D. I and IV only.

2. Lawyer Penny represents client Paul in a family law matter. When Paul and Donna were divorced, the court gave Paul custody of their

infant son and gave Donna "reasonable" visiting rights. Paul is a busy accountant and often stays late at his office. While Paul is working, the baby stays at a baby sitter's house. Donna has started making unannounced visits to the baby sitter's house on the evenings when Paul works late. Paul believes Donna may try to kidnap the baby and disappear. Paul asks Penny to apply immediately for a temporary restraining order that forbids Donna from going near the sitter's house. The court rules of this jurisdiction provide that a temporary restraining order can be granted in an *ex parte* proceeding, without giving the adversary any notice or chance to be heard. Penny plans to use this *ex parte* rule. Penny has an affidavit from the sitter stating that when Donna makes her surprise visits, the baby cries and refuses to eat or sleep for hours thereafter. Just as Penny is leaving her office to go to the judge's chambers, her investigator arrives with three additional pieces of information. First, when Paul works late, the sitter sometimes leaves a ten-year-old neighbor girl in charge of the baby while the sitter grocery shops and runs errands. Second, Donna's unannounced visits are motivated by her concern for the baby's safety. Third, when Paul works late, Donna could conveniently keep the baby at her house until Paul is through at the office. Which of the following is most nearly correct?

A. Penny *must* present the judge with only those facts that favor Paul's position.

B. Penny *must* present the judge with only those facts that favor Paul's position, but she *must* respond candidly if the judge specifically asks for information that is adverse to Paul's position.

C. Penny *must* present the judge with all the relevant facts, even those that are adverse to Paul's position.

D. Penny *must* call Paul and tell him that she is withdrawing the application for a temporary restraining order.

3. The law of State X requires child adoptions to be approved by the court. Further, it prohibits cohabiting couples from adopting a child unless they are validly married. Attorney Anderson represented clients Carla and Carl in an adoption proceeding. They assured her that they were validly married. Among the papers she presented to the court in connection with the adoption proceeding was copy of Carla's and Carl's Certificate of Marriage, duly certified by the custodian of public records. In due course, the court approved the adoption. A year later, Carla and Carl returned to Anderson's office. Carla explained to her as follows: "When we came to you about the adoption, there's something we didn't tell you, because we didn't want to get into lots of complications. Carl was married once before. His wife moved out, and he hasn't heard from her since. When he and I began dating, we fell in love so fast that there wasn't time for him to go through a divorce before we got married. We don't want to do anything that might risk losing our child, but this has been bothering us, and we thought we should come to you for advice." What is the *proper* course of action for Anderson to take?

A. Advise Carla and Carl about the legal effect of the prior marriage on their current status and on the adoption.

B. Decline to advise Carla and Carl, thus avoiding the assistance of a continuing fraud.

C. Advise Carla and Carl to reveal their fraud to the court that approved the adoption, and warn them that she will do so if they do not.

D. Bring the matter to the attention of the court that approved the adoption, and let the court decide what remedial action is appropriate in the circumstances.

4. Client Curtis hired lawyer Lomax to defend him in a civil antitrust action brought by Pucci, a former retail distributor of products that Curtis sold to Pucci. Pucci alleges that Curtis terminated him as a distributor because Pucci sold the products below a minimum retail price set by Curtis. Pucci further alleges that the termination resulted from a secret agreement between Curtis and other distributors that Curtis would terminate any distributor who sold below the minimum retail price. Assume that such an agreement, even if coerced, would violate the antitrust law. When Lomax was preparing Curtis for his deposition, Lomax asked Curtis why he terminated Pucci. Curtis answered: "Because Pucci was a price cutter. My other distributors pressured me to do it." At that point, Lomax said: "If you say that at your deposition, you will lose this case. Before you say more, let me tell you about the law that applies here. If you, using your own business judgment, terminated Pucci because he was not doing a good job, or because he was not displaying or advertising your products effectively, then the termination would be lawful. If, on the other hand, you let your other distributors talk you into terminating him because his prices were too low, the termination would probably be unlawful. Now go back to your office, refresh your memory of this event, and we will talk again tomorrow morning about your reasons for terminating Pucci." Was Lomax's conduct *proper*?

A. Yes, because a lawyer has a duty to represent a client with zeal, using all lawful means to achieve the client's objectives.

B. No, because it is improper for a lawyer to discuss the substance of a client's testimony with the client before the client testifies.

C. Yes, because a lawyer has a duty to advise a client fully about the law that applies to a matter.

D. No, because it is improper for a lawyer to invite a client to give false testimony.

5. Attorney Arossio was defending Doyle in a drunk driving case. The state's drunk driving statute specifies a fine up to $1,000 for a first offense. For a second offense, it specifies a fine up to $10,000, plus a mandatory jail sentence of 60 days up to one year. Doyle told Arossio in confidence that he had one prior conviction for drunk driving. Arossio consulted the public records and found that Doyle's prior conviction had

never been properly recorded. Doyle decided to plead guilty. The hearing transcript shows the following colloquy:

The Court: Your guilty plea will be accepted, Mr. Doyle. Ms. Prosecutor, are there priors in this case?

Prosecutor: No, your Honor. The People ask the maximum fine of $1,000.

The Court: Very well. Mr. Arossio, since your client is a first-timer, I'm inclined toward a fine of $750. Is that acceptable?

For which of the following responses would Arossio be *subject to discipline*?

I. Yes, thank you, your Honor.

II. My client will accept the court's judgment, your Honor.

III. Since my client's blood-alcohol level wasn't much above the mark, and since his record is clean, I would ask your Honor for a fine of not more than $500.

IV. There's been a mistake, your Honor. My client has a prior conviction that does not appear on the record.

A. None of the above.

B. III and IV only.

C. I, II, and III only.

D. IV only.

6. Over the past several months, you and lawyer Lauder have been representing your respective clients in a complicated contract negotiation. The proposed contract has been drafted, redrafted, and revised dozens of times during the negotiation. Finally, your respective clients have struck a bargain; their bargain includes a key provision that your client long resisted and ultimately accepted with great reluctance. The final version of the contract has been prepared by Lauder's secretary and has been signed by Lauder's client. Lauder has sent it to you for signature by your client. You have read it carefully, and you have discovered that the secretary left out the provision mentioned above. Which of the following *may* you do?

A. Without consulting your client, call Lauder and direct her attention to the missing provision.

B. Call your client, explain the situation, and do whatever your client directs.

C. Call your client, explain the situation, and advise him to sign the contract.

D. Call Lauder's client and ask whether he ultimately decided not to insist on the provision.

Answers to the multiple choice questions will be found in the Appendix at the end of the book.

CHAPTER NINE

FAIRNESS IN LITIGATION

■ ■ ■

What This Chapter Covers

Reading Assignment

Wydick, Perschbacher, & Bassett, Chapter 9.

ABA Model Rules:

Rules 3.1 through 3.9, 4.2 through 4.4, and 8.3(a).

ABA Model Code of Judicial Conduct:

Rules 2.6, 2.9, 2.10, and 3.13.

CRPC 2–100, 3–200, 3–210, 5–100, 5–200, 5–220, 5–300, 5–310 and 5–320.

Cal.Bus & Prof.Code §§ 6068(b), (c), (d), (f) and (g); 6103; 6128(a).

Supplemental Reading

Hazard & Hodes:

Discussion of ABA Model Rules 3.1 through 3.9 and 4.4.

Restatement (Third) of the Law Governing Lawyers §§ 97–103; 105–110; 115–119 (2000).

Discussion Problems

1. You represent twelve plaintiffs in an action against Monolith Consolidated Industries, Inc., for race discrimination in employment. The case will be tried before a jury. As is customary in your community, the names and addresses of the 150 citizens on the jury panel have been published in the local newspaper.

a. May you hire a private investigator to find out whatever he can about the attitudes of individual jury panel members toward race discrimination?

b. May you have your paralegal assistant search the public records in the County Records Office to find out which jury panel members own real property? To find out the political party affiliation of those jury panel members who are registered to vote?

c. In the jurisdiction where you plan to practice, do trial lawyers usually obtain information about jury panel members in advance of *voir dire*? How do they obtain it?

2. During the trial of the above case, you and one of the jurors find yourselves riding the elevator together on the way up to the courtroom one morning.

a. Suppose the juror turns to you and says: "Well, good morning, counselor! Do you have some red-hot testimony to keep us all awake today?" How should you respond?

b. Suppose the juror turns to you and says: "Well, good morning, counselor! What did you think of that lousy ball game on TV last night?" How should you respond?

3. During the noon recess in the above case, you are having lunch at a cafe near the courthouse. You observe a female juror sitting at a secluded table in the back, talking in hushed tones with a young man, a law student who works part-time as a paralegal for the firm that represents your adversary, Monolith Consolidated. What, if anything, should you do about that?

4. In the above case, the jury returned a verdict against your clients; judgment was entered accordingly, and the jury was dismissed.

a. On your way out of the courthouse, may you stop to chat with one of the jurors, to ask for her comments on the way you presented the evidence and on your closing argument?

b. The day after the trial ended, you learned that during jury deliberations the foreman asked the bailiff for a deposition transcript that had been used at the trial. Part of the transcript had been received in evidence, but the rest had not. Apparently, the bailiff delivered the entire transcript to the jury room. May you interview some of the jurors to find out whether this is true?

5. Prior to trial, and without consulting counsel for Monolith Consolidated, you contacted several former and current Monolith Consolidated employees to see if they had information that would support plaintiffs' claims. Was this proper?

6. One of your trial witnesses in the above case was Edgar Taylor, a former assembly line employee of Monolith Consolidated. At the trial, he testified about a conversation he had overheard between a union official and the head of Monolith Consolidated's personnel department. Shortly after he overheard that conversation, Monolith Consolidated laid him off. He had to move out of state to find a new job. When you asked him to be a witness at the trial, he refused, stating that he did not want to take the time away from his new job. To convince him to come, you promised him that your clients would pay:

- His travel, hotel, meal, and incidental expenses;
- His lost wages, due to time away from his job; and
- One hundred dollars per day, as compensation for his time and trouble in coming to testify.

a. Was that proper?

b. Was it proper to interview him without notifying Monolith Consolidated's counsel?

7. In preparing the above case for trial, you requested production of a large volume of Monolith Consolidated's employment records. After the usual preliminary skirmishing, adversary counsel finally agreed to produce them. As is common in such cases, you and adversary counsel orally agreed that Monolith Consolidated would copy the records (at your clients' expense), deliver the copies to you, and keep the originals available should you wish to examine them. The copies Monolith Consolidated delivered to you (nine large boxes full) were legible, but so light as to be extremely tedious to read. Later, after you had paid the copying bill, you learned (quite by accident) that adversary counsel had instructed the copying machine operator to "make the copies hard to read." What should you do in this situation?

8. At the final pretrial conference in the above case, the trial judge heard oral argument on the admissibility of several key items of evidence. The trial judge decided not to rule on the point until her law clerk could complete his own search of the authorities. Two days later, while reading the newest advance sheets, you found an evidence decision that directly supports the argument you were making. What is the proper way for you to call the new decision to the court's attention?

9. The trial of the above case has attracted considerable attention from the local news media. The trial judge has forbidden cameras and recorders inside the courtroom, but during every recess reporters swarm around the trial participants, asking questions. Late one afternoon, the trial judge calls the evening recess just after Monolith Consolidated has completed the direct examination of one of its key witnesses. You gravely doubt the credibility of this witness, and tomorrow morning you will have your chance to cross-examine. As you walk down the courthouse steps, news reporters surround you, asking for your comment on the witness's testimony and on your plans for tomorrow's cross-examination. Considering both ethics and tactics, how will you respond?

10. You are a young Assistant District Attorney. Your boss is Earl Lubeman, a wily politician who has been the elected District Attorney for the past 14 years. He has assigned you to prosecute Emmet Stubbs for arson. When the arresting officer interrogated Stubbs, in the presence of his lawyer, Stubbs told the following story:

> I did burn down that house, but it was an accident. I was drunk, and I went in there to get warm and have a smoke. The place caught fire, and I was lucky to get out alive. I'll tell you something else. Remember about five years ago, when Earl Lubeman convicted Randy Coots for burning down the Catholic Church? Coots has been sitting in the state pen ever since, but he didn't do it. I did. I took the golden chalice from the altar, wrapped it up in my sweatshirt, and hid it in the tractor shed of Meryl Dutton's farm.

The next day, your investigator came back from the Dutton farm with the sweatshirt and golden chalice in hand. At that point, you went to D.A. Lubeman and told him the story. You were dumbstruck when he responded: "Randy Coots may not have burned down the church, but he did a hundred other things as bad or worse. The world is better off with him in prison, so just forget what happened five years ago and see if you can reach a plea deal with Emmet Stubbs." What should you do about Randy Coots?

WITNESS COACHING

To what extent may a lawyer work with a witness before the witness testifies? Professor Wydick considers that question in *The Ethics of Witness Coaching*, 17 Cardozo L. Rev. 1 (1995).* He says that the "standard wisdom" about coaching witnesses is as follows:

> First, a lawyer may discuss the case with the witnesses before they testify. A lawyer in our common law adversary system has an ethical and legal duty to investigate the facts of the case, and the investigation typically requires the lawyer to talk with the witnesses—the people who know what happened on the occasion in question. More-

* ©1995. Reprinted with permission.

over, the adversary system benefits by allowing lawyers to prepare witnesses so that they can deliver their testimony efficiently, persuasively, comfortably, and in conformity with the rules of evidence.

Second, when a lawyer discusses the case with a witness, the lawyer must not try to bend the witness's story or put words in the witness's mouth. As an old New York disciplinary case puts it: "[The lawyer's] duty is to extract the facts from the witness, not to pour them into him; to learn what the witness does know, not to teach him what he ought to know."

Third, a lawyer can be disciplined by the bar for counseling or assisting a witness to testify falsely or for knowingly offering testimony that the lawyer knows is false.

According to Professor Wydick, when a lawyer interviews and prepares a witness, the lawyer typically does these things:

- discusses the witness's perception, recollection, and possible testimony about the events in question;
- reviews documents and other tangible items to refresh the witness's memory or to point out conflicts and inconsistencies with the witness's story;
- reveals other tangible or testimonial evidence to the witness to find out how it affects the witness's story;
- explains how the law applies to the events in question;
- reviews the factual context into which the witness's testimony will fit;
- discusses the role of the witness and effective courtroom demeanor;
- discusses probable lines of cross-examination that the witness should be prepared to meet;
- rehearses the witness's testimony, by role playing or other means.

From this, he elaborates 23 different "legitimate reasons for a lawyer's statement or question to a witness":

- to investigate the facts, that is, to find out about the events in question;
- to find out what the witness perceived and can testify to from personal knowledge;
- to determine how accurately the witness perceived the events and what conditions may have hindered or assisted his or her perception;
- to test the witness's memory about what he or she perceived;
- to discover how certain the witness is about what he or she remembers;
- to determine adverse or favorable conditions that may have affected the witness's memory;

- to refresh the witness's memory of things he or she once remembered but has since forgotten;
- to find out whether exposure to relevant documents, other items of tangible or testimonial evidence, or some non-evidentiary stimulus will help refresh the witness's memory;
- to test the witness's ability to communicate his or her recollections accurately;
- to find out what the witness means by words or expressions used in his or her story;
- to test the witness's truthfulness;
- to warn the witness that his or her credibility may be attacked and that some kinds of acts in his or her past may be exposed in open court;
- to ascertain whether the witness has a good or bad character as respects truthfulness;
- to find out whether the witness has previously been convicted of a crime that could be used to impeach his or her credibility;
- to uncover instances of non-criminal conduct that could be used to impeach the witness's credibility;
- to discover whether the witness's story has been influenced by bias or prejudice;
- to find out whether the witness's story has been influenced, properly or improperly, by the statements or conduct of some other person;
- to find out whether the witness has previously made statements that are either consistent or inconsistent with his or her present story;
- to test the witness's demeanor in response to various stimuli s/he may encounter when he or she testifies (for example, the witness's likely response to harsh questioning by a cross-examiner);
- to explain the role of a witness, the obligations imposed by the oath, and the formality of court proceedings;
- to inform the witness about the physical surroundings in which he or she will testify, the persons who will be present, and the logistical details of being a witness;
- to explain to the witness why he or she should listen to questions carefully, not guess, not volunteer information that has not been asked for, be alert to objections, and the like;
- to advise the witness about appropriate attire and physical appearance in court, distracting mannerisms, inappropriate language and demeanor, and the effective delivery of testimony.

These are all acceptable. Nevertheless, when a lawyer is left alone with a witness, the fallibility of human memory also allows lawyers to alter the witness's story and perhaps even the witness's memory itself. Professor Wydick divides "witness coaching" into three "grades":

Grade One witness coaching is where the lawyer knowingly and overtly induces a witness to testify to something the lawyer knows is false. "Overtly" is used to mean that the lawyer's conduct is "openly" or "on its face" an inducement to testify falsely. Grade One witness coaching obviously interferes with the court's truth-seeking function and corrodes the morals of both the witness and the lawyer. Sometimes it goes undetected by adversaries, judges, and disciplinary authorities, but when it is detected, it can and should be punished under the present lawyer disciplinary rules and perjury statutes.

Grade Two witness coaching is the same as Grade One, except that the lawyer acts *covertly*. Thus, Grade Two is where the lawyer knowingly but covertly induces a witness to testify to something the lawyer knows is false. "Covertly" is used to mean that the lawyer's inducement is masked. It is transmitted by implication. Grade Two witness coaching is no less harmful to the court's truth-seeking function than Grade One, nor less morally corrosive, nor less in breach of the lawyer disciplinary rules and perjury statutes, but it is less likely to be detected and successfully punished. Grade Two witness coaching falls within a range of conduct that cannot be effectively controlled by disciplinary rules or criminal laws; it must therefore be controlled by a lawyer's own informed conscience. To have an *informed* conscience about witness coaching, a lawyer needs to understand how messages get transmitted covertly between a speaker and a hearer. Professor Wydick then describes philosopher Paul Grice's "theory of conversational implicature" and suggests a method of analysis that incorporates Grice's theory.

Grade Three witness coaching is where the lawyer does not knowingly induce the witness to testify to something the lawyer knows is false, but the lawyer's conversation with the witness nevertheless alters the witness's story. Given the malleable nature of human memory, Grade Three witness coaching is very hard to avoid. It lacks the element of corruption that Grades One and Two have, but it does alter a witness's story and can thus interfere with the court's truth-seeking function. Therefore, when a lawyer's conversation with a witness serves a proper purpose, such as refreshing the witness's memory, the lawyer should nonetheless conduct the conversation in the manner that is least likely to produce inaccurate testimony.

Finally, Professor Wydick suggests methods for conducting a non-suggestive witness interview to minimize the dangers of improper witness suggestion, which include (1) using recall first, and then recognition; (2) using neutral questions; and (3) ordering questions based on the pattern the witness is likely to have used when originally storing the information.

LIND v. MEDEVAC, INC.

California Court of Appeal, First District, 1990.
219 Cal.App.3d 516, 268 Cal.Rptr. 359.

PETERSON, ASSOCIATE JUSTICE.

[Attorney B. Mark Fong, Jr. and his law firm appeal from the trial court's award of sanctions against them for contacting jury members after trial of a personal injury action.]

I. FACTUAL AND PROCEDURAL BACKGROUND

In July 1984, Edward P. Lind, by and through his conservator Wendell J. Lind, (plaintiff) filed a complaint for personal injuries. Named as defendants were Medevac, Inc.; its employees, Dana Young and Carol Ferguson; and others. Plaintiff was represented by attorney Marc C. Barulich of the firm of Barulich and Barulich. Defendants were represented by appellants B. Mark Fong, Jr. and his law firm, Robert A. Harlem, Inc. & Associates.

In January 1988, the matter was tried before a jury which rendered a judgment in favor of defendants. Plaintiff then moved for a new trial or in the alternative for judgment notwithstanding the verdict (JNOV). The motions were based, inter alia, upon allegations of jury misconduct. Defendants opposed the motion, noting that plaintiff had not submitted juror affidavits in support of the motion for new trial as required by Code of Civil Procedure section 658. In reply, plaintiff claimed that he had been prevented from obtaining juror affidavits by a letter defense counsel had sent to the jurors. The text of that letter is as follows:

"Dear [Juror]: [¶] This is to thank you again for your service as a juror. I know that my clients, Carol Ferguson and Dana Young[,] are glad at last to put the events of four years ago behind them. [¶] On occasion, following a jury trial, the losing side will hire an investigator to contact the trial jurors. The purpose of these investigators is to impeach the jury's verdict. The [investigator] will ask you about your deliberations in the jury room and will prepare a statement for your signature. This statement will then be presented to the judge to convince him to set aside the jury's verdict as improper. [¶] You are under no obligation to speak with these investigators and need not sign anything. You worked with your fellow jurors to reach a fair result. I would not want to see that result set aside because of sharp investigative tactics. [¶] Please contact me should anyone attempt to speak with you about your jury service. I would like to be present should you choose to speak with an investigator. [¶] Should you have any questions or wish to discuss the case, please do not hesitate to contact me. Again, thank you for your time and service. [¶] Very truly yours, [/S/] B. Mark Fong"

The court denied the motion for JNOV concluding the verdict was supported by substantial evidence. The motion for new trial was denied because it was not supported by any juror affidavits. However, the trial judge expressed disapproval of the letter appellants had sent to the jurors, and set a hearing for Fong and his law firm to show cause why they should not be sanctioned for "deliberately interfering" with plaintiff's right to obtain juror affidavits to support a motion for new trial.

* * * After hearing the arguments of counsel, the court imposed sanctions of $20,000 against appellants, holding the letter they sent violated the rules of professional conduct in that it was likely to adversely influence the jurors in their present and future jury service. This timely appeal followed.

II. DISCUSSION

Appellants challenge the court's imposition of sanctions on both substantive and procedural grounds. Substantively, they argue that the letter they sent was proper and did not violate the rules of professional conduct. Procedurally, appellants claim that the trial court lacked the authority to impose sanctions in the manner in which it did.

A. *The Letter*

At the time these proceedings were held, former rule 7–106 of the Rules of Professional Conduct (now rule 5–320) provided in part, "(D) After discharge of the jury from further consideration of a case with which the member of the State Bar was connected, the member of the State Bar shall not ask questions of or make comments to a member of that jury that are intended to harass or embarrass the juror or to influence the juror's actions in future jury service. [¶] (E) A member of the State Bar shall not conduct directly or indirectly an out of court investigation of either a venireman or a juror of a type likely to influence the state of mind of such venireman or juror in present or future jury service."

* * *

* * * The trial court properly rejected the argument that a juror's "present" jury service could not be affected *solely* because counsel's contact with the juror came after the jury was discharged. We affirm the trial court's implicit finding that the Rules of Professional Conduct concerning counsel's contact with jurors remain fully applicable in the period from jury discharge to expiration of the time for filing new trial motions in the case in which those jurors served.

The trial court did not commit error in finding the letter which appellants sent to the jurors in the present case violated rule 7–106. That finding was supported by substantial evidence. The letter asserts that a fellow member of the bar might employ "sharp investigative tactics" to "impeach" the jury's verdict and have it set aside as "improper." The lower court found this letter could easily adversely influence a juror in his "present" or "future" jury service. Taken as a whole, the letter advising a juror, inter alia, that the verdict of his jury could be "impeach[ed]" and set aside as "improper" certainly implies such juror may be falsely importuned to say or do something which might lead to that result, i.e., to the false conclusion the jury or some of its members undertook some wrongful or unlawful act in arriving at a verdict. This implication is clearly brought into focus by the letter's assertion that "sharp investigative tactics" may be used to accomplish this objective, thereby suggesting a subversive and false result is likely to be sought by losing counsel through his own actions or those of his post-trial investigator. It is common knowledge that it is increasingly difficult to obtain willing citizens to serve as members of a jury. Letters such as the one sent by appellants in the present case unprofessionally denigrate anticipated and unproven conduct of opponents, and will only exacerbate the reluctance of some persons to undertake jury service for fear their decisions will be falsely attacked and overturned by reason of unprofessional and improper conduct of counsel designed to achieve that result. They are likely, incidentally, to be perceived by jurors as converting the performance of their civic responsibility to serve as jurors into the center of a distasteful and acrimonious post-trial dispute between lawyers whose motives, they are told, are suspect and misleading.

The trial judge was justified in determining that the true purpose of the letter was to achieve the chilling result of preventing attempts by the losing side to communicate with jurors after their discharge, in a legitimate effort to determine if juror misconduct existed as grounds for a new trial, and to obtain permitted affidavits concerning any such misconduct.

Appellants urge it has been a "common experience" among trial lawyers that, after a trial has been completed, investigators acting on behalf of the losing party will privately approach jurors and use various plausible stories in order to "trick[ ]" the jurors into making statements which do not fairly reflect the nature of the jurors' deliberations. Thus, they claim they should not be sanctioned for warning jurors about potential abuses by investigators. We find this argument unpersuasive. Were we to adopt this rationale, we would do little more than approve unprofessional conduct of counsel on the ground like conduct of the other side was anticipated. We decline to sanction preemptive strikes of this nature. Attorneys who individually or through investigators employ such tactics may well be subject to discipline by the court, as well as appropriate authorities of the State Bar.

An attorney wishing to protect a verdict against such tactics can do so within the ethical mandates of the rules of professional conduct. For example, an attorney who wins a trial by jury should not be barred from writing jurors post verdict, thereby requesting that he be notified of any post-trial contact with the jurors by the adverse side; and that he be further allowed either to be present for any interviews granted the adverse side, or to discuss with the juror any telephonic or written communications received from the adverse side.

* * *

[The appellate court reversed and remanded the sanction award. The trial court had based its sanction on its inherent power to control proceedings under California Code of Civil Procedure § 128. However, under California case law, attorney fees could only be awarded under § 128.5, not § 128. Therefore, the case was remanded to the trial court to consider whether Fong and his firm had acted in bad faith or engaged in frivolous tactics to justify sanctions under § 128.5 (see Chapter 3, supra). The opinion added, "We also leave to the sound discretion of the trial court whether appellants' conduct was sufficiently serious to warrant review by the disciplinary authorities of the California State Bar."]

PUBLIC COMMENTS ABOUT PENDING LITIGATION

A. BACKGROUND

Although the idea of public and media access to trials is firmly rooted in American jurisprudence—indeed, the right to a public trial is part of the Sixth Amendment protection for the criminally accused—excessive publicity may also interfere with the equally important right to a fair trial. As a result, the interests of the media and the courts are sometimes at odds. Added to this mix is the danger that lawyers for the state, the accused, and the parties in civil actions may seek to argue their cases outside of court, using the media for the benefit of their clients or themselves. Historically, the First Amendment has required a showing of "actual prejudice or a substantial and imminent threat to fair trial" [*Nebraska Press Ass'n v. Stuart,* 427 U.S. 539, 96 S.Ct. 2791, 49 L.Ed.2d 683 (1976)] in order to restrict press coverage during a criminal trial, but has allowed trial courts to restrain lawyers' speech before and during trial on a significantly lower showing. [*See Sheppard v. Maxwell,* 384 U.S. 333, 362–63, 86 S.Ct. 1507, 1522–23, 16 L.Ed.2d 600 (1966).] Lawyers may also have ethical limitations on what they may say in advance of and during trial, although this must be balanced against their obligation to represent their clients zealously and effectively within the bounds of the law.

B. THE ABA ENTERS THE FRAY

The ABA's Canons of Professional Ethics (1908) "[g]enerally * * * condemned" newspaper publications by lawyers regarding pending or anticipated litigation because of the danger they would "interfere with a fair trial" and "otherwise prejudice the due administration of justice." When the ABA Code was promulgated in 1969, it relied upon recommendations of the Advisory Committee on Fair Trial and Free Press, created in 1964 on the recommendation of the Warren Commission's report on the assassination of President Kennedy. The Advisory Committee developed the ABA Standards Relating to Fair Trial and Free Press which covered the disclosure of information regarding criminal proceedings. The ABA used those standards in developing ABA Model Rule of Professional Responsibility 3.6. Meanwhile, the Supreme Court had identified the need for such a rule in *Sheppard v. Maxwell,* and, in 1966, the Judicial Conference of the United States authorized a special subcommittee to study whether further guidelines needed to be laid down to implement *Sheppard.* The result of that report was the "reasonable likelihood of prejudicing a fair trial" test used in the ABA 1969 Model Code. DR 7–107 of the Model Code used the laundry list of acceptable and prohibited statements similar to the Model Code's approach to advertising. [*See* Chapter 4, *supra.*] Ten years later, when the ABA amended its guidelines, the ABA changed the test from "reasonable likelihood" to "clear and present danger." [ABA Standard for Criminal Justice 8–1.1 (as amended in 1978) (2d ed. 1980, Supp.1986).] Today, the test under Standard 3–1.4 (for prosecutors) and Standard 4–1.4 (for defense counsel) is "a substantial likelihood of prejudicing a criminal proceeding."

The Model Rules of Professional Conduct, drafted in the early 1980s, did not grant as much protection to lawyers who made extrajudicial statements when fair trial rights were involved. Model Rule 3.6 adopted yet another test, the "substantial likelihood of material prejudice" test, and that was where the law stood at the time of the *Gentile* case.

C. THE *GENTILE* CASE

In *Gentile v. State Bar of Nevada,* 501 U.S. 1030, 111 S.Ct. 2720, 115 L.Ed.2d 888 (1991), the Supreme Court directly addressed whether state-imposed limitations on extrajudicial statements in criminal cases violated the right of free speech. Gentile, a Nevada lawyer, represented Sanders in a criminal trial. The defendant was charged with stealing drugs and money used in an undercover operation conducted by the Las Vegas police. The trial attracted a great deal of publicity. During a pre-trial press conference, Gentile made several inflammatory statements, accusing a detective of actually stealing the drugs and travelers' checks and framing Sanders. Six months later, a jury acquitted Sanders on all counts.

The State Bar of Nevada filed a complaint against Gentile for violating Nevada Supreme Court Rule 177 (almost identical to the then-current version of ABA Model Rule of Professional Conduct 3.6). The rule prohibited attorneys from making any "extrajudicial statement" that a reasonable person would expect to be spread among the public and to materially prejudice the proceedings. The disciplinary board found Gentile guilty of violating the bar rule. In a 5 to 4 decision, the Supreme Court reversed.

In an opinion by Justice Rehnquist, the Court stated that "[t]he regulation of attorneys' speech is limited." Advocating a "less demanding standard" for attorney's speech regarding their pending cases, the Court upheld the "substantial likelihood of materially prejudicing that proceeding" test. However, the Court struck down parts of the Nevada rule which specified that an attorney could make "general" statements about the defense without "elaboration." This standard would prove confusing to any attorney, since the language made it very unclear when one's statements were protected by the safe harbor provision of "general." Additionally, the Court pointed out that the general versus elaboration directions failed to even consider that a general statement could materially prejudice a case just as much as any elaboration on the defense. Consequently, the Court upheld the general test but struck down the more explicit language of the rule.

D. CURRENT RULES

In 1994, the ABA House of Delegates amended Model Rule 3.6 and 3.8 to reflect the *Gentile* decision. The amended rule 3.6 removed the portion of the rule which delineated what kind of comments would be held to be prejudicial to the comments section. The ABA also added a section in the rule allowing a lawyer to attempt to mitigate negative publicity not of the attorney's or client's creation notwithstanding paragraph (a)'s bar on extrajudicial statements. Notably, the ABA deleted a comment acknowledging that no rules could satisfy all the interests of a fair trial and those of free speech. The addition of subsection (g) to Rule 3.8 [now subsection (f)] imposed an additional responsibility on criminal prosecutors to "refrain from making extrajudicial comments that have a substantial likelihood of heightening public condemnation of the accused." [*See also* RESTATEMENT (THIRD) OF THE LAW GOVERNING LAWYERS § 109 (2000).] Prosecutors also must "exercise reasonable care to prevent investigators, law enforcement personnel, employees or other persons assisting or associated with the prosecutor in a criminal case from making an extrajudicial statement that the prosecutor would be prohibited from making under Rule 3.6 or this Rule." [*See* ABA Model Rule 3.8(f).]

MATTER OF VINCENTI

Supreme Court of New Jersey, 1983.
92 N.J. 591, 458 A.2d 1268.

Under some circumstances it might be difficult to determine precisely the point at which forceful, aggressive trial advocacy crosses the line into the forbidden territory of an ethical violation. But no matter where in the spectrum of courtroom behavior we would draw that line, no matter how indulgent our view of acceptable professional conduct might be, it is inconceivable that the instances of respondent's demeanor that we are called upon to review in these proceedings could ever be countenanced. The record lays bare a shameful display of atrocious deportment calling for substantial discipline.

I.

A panel of the local ethics committee (Committee) prepared a carefully documented report of 60 pages, unanimously adopted by the Committee as its presentment charging respondent with unethical conduct. With equally meticulous care the Disciplinary Review Board (DRB) embodied its determination, with which we are in accord, in a Decision and Recommendation. Our independent review of the entire record leads us to the same conclusion as was reached by the DRB, whose full opinion we here set forth and adopt as our own.

* * *

The respondent represented D.K., the defendant in a child abuse/neglect case involving the defendant's four children. * * * During this proceeding, respondent's in-court conduct, his out of court conduct towards lawyers, witnesses and bystanders in the courthouse, and his written communiques and applications relative to the D.K. proceeding reached a level of impropriety that mandated the filing of a 22 count ethics complaint.

* * *

It is sufficient to note examples of respondent's numerous improprieties here. He was frequently sarcastic, disrespectful and irrational, and accused the Court on numerous occasions of, *inter alia*, collusion with the prosecution, cronyism, racism, permitting the proceedings to have a "carnival nature", conducting a kangaroo court, prejudging the case, conducting a "cockamamie charade of witnesses" and barring defense counsel from effectively participating in the proceedings, conducting a sham hearing, acting outside the law, being caught up in his "own little dream world", and ex-parte communications with the prosecutor together with other equally outrageous, disrespectful and unsupported charges. These and other comments were made frequently throughout the proceedings and continued at length.

* * *

[In one instance] the respondent reviewed a witness's files while she was testifying and failed to return them thereafter. The Deputy Attorney General located the files on the counsel table and returned them to the witness, at the witness's request. The respondent, in open court, then accused the Deputy Attorney General of stealing the files, and accused her of being a "bald-faced liar", and "a thief, a liar and a cheat". He also filed an ethics complaint against the Deputy Attorney General for her actions.
* * *

[The] respondent further alleged that the trial judge had participated in extortion as well as cronyism, bias, prejudice, racism and religious bigotry during the trial, again without any basis in fact.

The respondent's improprieties continued. The respondent directed the following letter * * * to the trial judge, the text of which is set forth below:

> I wish to extend my sincerest good wishes for your speedy recovery from the obvious breakdown you suffered in chambers yesterday, Tuesday, December 11 * * *.

Hopefully, with some rest and relaxation from your most taxing schedule, you will be in a position to resume your judicial duties more appropriately than exhibited on the eleventh.

If, however, you feel somehow justified in pressing your demand for written recommendations, I must supply them, if for no other purpose than to demonstrate my client's continuing bona fides herein.

I must admit, with no small degree of trepidation, that we have no confidence in your rationality vis-a-vis this case. Your activities on the eleventh and throughout the trial clearly demonstrate an irrational predisposition to chastise Mr. D.K. and defense counsel. The cronyism I wrote of in our motion for new trial continues unabated.

You have simply closed your mind to our position and have retreated into a dream world not unlike the somnambulist in the early German classic story at the turn of the century.

How do we make any kind of recommendations to you while you sleep-walk through your judicial duties. How does one get through to you.

* * *

The statements made by respondent in that letter speak for themselves.

* * *

In addition to respondent's outrageous in-court conduct and equally outrageous written applications and communications, respondent, on numerous occasions, also engaged in reprehensible behavior towards witnesses, potential witnesses, opposing counsel, and other attorneys outside the courtroom but inside the Courthouse. A sampling of the improprieties follows:

1. On September 26 * * * outside the courtroom, respondent and Assistant Public Defender Eisert were discussing the issues of visitation. Argument ensued, during which, among other obscenities, respondent told Eisert to "go screw himself" * * *, and referred to Eisert as * * * "schmuckface", all in the presence of a number of individuals, some of whom were involved in the case.

2. On October 31 * * * Deputy Attorney General Rem and Eisert agreed to meet with respondent, at his request, for a settlement conference. The Lawyer's Lounge was selected. In addition to addressing insults at Rem, respondent referred to a female attorney, also in the lounge, as "Miss Wrinkles" [and] "Miss Bags" * * *.

3. Respondent on several occasions either unnecessarily subpoenaed individuals to testify or threatened those under subpoena by opposing counsel.

4. On December 6, 1979, in the Courthouse corridor, after attempting to intimidate a witness by directing her to answer everything he

asked, while his secretary wrote down her responses, respondent advised an attorney named Pearson who was standing with the witness but not involved in the proceeding to "just keep your god damn nose out of my business".

* * *

Respondent's performance did not conclude there. While Eisert, Pearson and Rem were conversing in the Courthouse, respondent approached, stating loudly that Rem should not be believed since "* * * she's a bald-faced liar". He then called Rem "fuckface", and while walking away again made the suggestion "* * * shove it up your ass". Within the next several minutes, respondent twice approached the group, each time pushing into Rem, causing her to lurch against a desk in the hallway.

* * *

We would hope, through this opinion, to serve some more salutary purpose than just the distasteful meting out of well-deserved public discipline to Mr. Vincenti. As pointed out earlier, * * * this ethics proceeding unveils conduct so bizarre, so outrageous, as not to bring us close to what in some other case might be the difficult problem of distinguishing between permissibly vigorous advocacy and an ethical transgression. Although we need not here attempt with exquisite precision to delineate the difference, it may nevertheless be useful to restate, in general terms, the obligation of New Jersey lawyers, that they may readily avoid entanglements of the sort that brings respondent before us.

Models abound. We adopt one formulated by Justice Frankfurter:

> Certainly since the time of Edward I, through all the vicissitudes of seven centuries of Anglo–American history, the legal profession has played a role all its own. The bar has not enjoyed prerogatives; it has been entrusted with anxious responsibilities. One does not have to inhale the self-adulatory bombast of after-dinner speeches to affirm that all the interests of man that are comprised under the constitutional guarantees given to "life, liberty and property" are in the professional keeping of lawyers. It is a fair characterization of the lawyer's responsibility in our society that he stands "as a shield," to quote Devlin, J., in defense of right and to ward off wrong. From a profession charged with such responsibilities there must be exacted those qualities of truth-speaking, of a high sense of honor, of granite discretion, of the strictest observance of fiduciary responsibility, that have, through the centuries, been compendiously described as "moral character." [*Schware v. Board of Bar Examiners*, 353 U.S. 232, 247, 77 S.Ct. 752, 760–761, 1 L.Ed.2d 796, 806 (1957) (Frankfurter, J., concurring).]

* * *

Respondent is suspended from the practice of law for one year and until the further order of the Court.

THE PROSECUTOR'S SPECIAL DUTIES

Prosecutors have the unique power to bring criminal prosecutions on behalf of the government. This power also entails a special duty to exercise the power in a responsible fashion. Comment 1 to ABA Model Rule 3.8 states, "A prosecutor has the responsibility of a minister of justice and not simply that of an advocate." Comment *h* to § 97 of the Restatement (Third) of the Law Governing Lawyers similarly notes, "Lawyers empowered by law to bring and press criminal charges have an authority that must be exercised with care to protect the rights of both the innocent and the guilty." But the prosecutor is also an advocate in the adversary system of criminal litigation. Thus the prosecutor is asked to assume a dual role as a partisan advocate and a quasi-judicial officer—a role difficult to achieve in practice.

The special ethical responsibilities of the prosecutor include restraint in prosecuting charges without probable cause; protecting the accused's right to counsel and other important pretrial rights; disclosing evidence that negates guilt or mitigates the offense or sentence; and exercising restraint in litigation tactics and out-of-court statements. [*See* ABA Model Rule 3.8.]

An important feature of the prosecutor's special duty is the obligation to tell the defense about any material that may favor the defense. The U.S. Supreme Court set out the constitutional minimum in *Brady v. Maryland*, 373 U.S. 83, 83 S.Ct. 1194, 10 L.Ed.2d 215 (1963), and explained it more fully in *United States v. Bagley*, 473 U.S. 667, 105 S.Ct. 3375, 87 L.Ed.2d 481 (1985). As explained in *Bagley*, the Due Process Clause of the Fifth and Fourteenth Amendments requires a prosecutor to disclose evidence that favors the defendant with respect to guilt on the merits, or impeachment of a prosecution witness, or punishment for the offense. Five Justices agreed that the duty to disclose applies when a failure to disclose "undermines confidence in the outcome of the trial" and thus deprives the defendant of a fair trial. This standard is met if there is a "reasonable probability" that, if the withheld material had been disclosed, "the result of the proceeding would have been different." In other words, to violate the Due Process Clause, the withheld material must have been a game-changer.

Now examine ABA Model Rule 3.8(d). Does the ethics rule set a more rigorous standard than the Due Process Clause sets? The answer given in ABA Formal Op. 09–454 (2009) is a resounding Yes. The ethics standard is more rigorous than the Due Process standard in four respects:

- The ethics standard requires the prosecutor to disclose anything "favorable to the defense," whether or not it would be likely to change the outcome and whether or not it would be independently admissible in evidence.
- The ethics standard requires the prosecutor to disclose anything that would favor the defense, even if the prosecutor thinks it is not

believable or not persuasive. However, the ethics standard applies only if the prosecutor "knows of" the material—it does not require the prosecutor to set out on a hunt for material that favors the defense.

- The prosecutor's disclosure must be "timely," that is, early enough for the defense to make the best use of it—in short, the sooner the better.
- The prosecutor must not ask the defendant to consent to non-disclosure of favorable material, for example as a condition of leniency in a plea bargain.

THE DUTIES OF THE CRIMINAL DEFENSE LAWYER

A lawyer who represents a client accused of a criminal offense also has duties that diverge from the general rules for litigating lawyers. Professor Wolfram comments that "[t]he effective limits on a defense lawyer's loyalty and zeal are quite unclear and can probably be captured only by a vague phrase such as 'advocacy in good faith.' " [WOLFRAM, MODERN LEGAL ETHICS 589 (1986).] Model Rule 3.1 contains a special exemption from the prohibition against making frivolous claims: "A lawyer for the defendant in a criminal proceeding, * * * may nevertheless so defend the proceeding as to require that every element of the case be established." Thus the criminal defense lawyer may require the prosecution to put on its proof even if there is no non-frivolous defense. Exceptions such as these are necessary to preserve the presumption that a criminal defendant is innocent until proven guilty. In fact, the American Bar Association in 1979 adopted a distinct set of standards for both criminal prosecutors and defense counsel. [*See* American Bar Association, ABA Standards for Criminal Justice, The Prosecution Function, The Defense Function (1992).]

WHY I DEFEND GUILTY CLIENTS

BARRY T. WINSTON[1]

Let me tell you a story. A true story. The court records are all there if anyone wants to check. It's three years ago. I'm sitting in my office, staring out the window, when I get a call from a lawyer I hardly know. Tax lawyer. Some kid is in trouble and would I be interested in helping him out? He's charged with manslaughter, a felony, and driving under the influence. I tell him sure, have the kid call me.

So the kid calls and makes an appointment to see me. He's a nice kid, fresh out of college, and he's come down here to spend some time with his

1. Copyright © 1986 by Harper's Magazine. All rights reserved. Reproduced from the December issue by special permission. Mr. Winston is a 1961 graduate of the University of North Carolina School of Law. He has represented people accused of crimes, in state and federal courts, for more than 40 years.

older sister, who's in med school. One day she tells him they're invited to a cookout with some friends of hers. She's going directly from class and he's going to take her car and meet her there. It's way out in the country, but he gets there before she does, introduces himself around, and pops a beer. She shows up after a while and he pops another beer. Then he eats a hamburger and drinks a third beer. At some point his sister says, "Well, it's about time to go," and they head for the car.

And the kid tells me, sitting there in my office, the next thing he remembers, he's waking up in a hospital room, hurting like hell, bandages and casts all over him, and somebody is telling him he's charged with manslaughter and DUI because he wrecked his sister's car, killed her in the process, and blew fourteen on the Breathalyzer. I ask him what the hell he means by "the next thing he remembers," and he looks me straight in the eye and says he can't remember anything from the time they leave the cookout until he wakes up in the hospital. He tells me the doctors say he has postretrograde amnesia. I say of course I believe him, but I'm worried about finding a judge who'll believe him.

I agree to represent him and send somebody for a copy of the wreck report. It says there are four witnesses: a couple in a car going the other way who passed the kid and his sister just before their car ran off the road, the guy whose front yard they landed in, and the trooper who investigated. I call the guy whose yard they ended up in. He isn't home. I leave word. Then I call the couple. The wife agrees to come in the next day with her husband. While I'm talking to her, the first guy calls. I call him back, introduce myself, tell him I'm representing the kid and need to talk to him about the accident. He hems and haws and I figure he's one of those people who think it's against the law to talk to defense lawyers. I say the D.A. will tell him it's O.K. to talk to me, but he doesn't have to. I give him the name and number of the D.A. and he says he'll call me back.

Then I go out and hunt up the trooper. He tells me the whole story. The kid and his sister are coming into town on Smith Level Road, after it turns from fifty-five to forty-five. The Thornes—the couple—are heading out of town. They say this sports car passes them, going the other way, right after that bad turn just south of the new subdivision. They say it's going like a striped-ass ape, at least sixty-five or seventy. Mrs. Thorne turns around to look and Mr. Thorne watches in the rearview mirror. They both see the same thing: halfway into the curve, the car runs off the road on the right, whips back onto the road, spins, runs off on the left, and disappears. They turn around in the first driveway they come to and start back, both terrified of what they're going to find. By this time, Trooper Johnson says, the guy whose front yard the car has ended up in has pulled the kid and his sister out of the wreck and started CPR on the girl. Turns out he's an emergency medical technician. Holloway, that's his name. Johnson tells me that Holloway says he's sitting in his front room, watching television, when he hears a hell of a crash in his yard. He runs outside and finds the car flipped over, and so he pulls the kid out from the driver's side, the girl from the other side. She dies in his arms.

And that, says Trooper Johnson, is that. The kid's blood/alcohol content was fourteen, he was going way too fast, and the girl is dead. He had to charge him. It's a shame, he seems a nice kid, it was his own sister and all, but what the hell can he do, right?

The next day the Thornes come in, and they confirm everything Johnson said. By now things are looking not so hot for my client, and I'm thinking it's about time to have a little chat with the D.A. But Holloway still hasn't called me back, so I call him. Not home. Leave word. No call. I wait a couple of days and call again. Finally I get him on the phone. He's very agitated, and won't talk to me except to say that he doesn't have to talk to me.

I know I better look for a deal, so I go to the D.A. He's very sympathetic. But. There's only so far you can get on sympathy. A young woman is dead, promising career cut short, all because somebody has too much to drink and drives. The kid has to pay. Not, the D.A. says, with jail time. But he's got to plead guilty to two misdemeanors: death by vehicle and driving under the influence. That means probation, a big fine. Several thousand dollars. Still, it's hard for me to criticize the D.A. After all, he's probably going to have the MADD mothers all over him because of reducing the felony to a misdemeanor.

On the day of the trial, I get to court a few minutes early. There are the Thornes and Trooper Johnson, and someone I assume is Holloway. Sure enough, when this guy sees me, he comes over and introduces himself and starts right in: "I just want you to know how serious all this drinking and driving really is," he says. "If those young people hadn't been drinking and driving that night, that poor young girl would be alive today." Now, I'm trying to hold my temper when I spot the D.A. I bolt across the room, grab him by the arm, and say, "We gotta talk. Why the hell have you got all those people here? That jerk Holloway. Surely to God you're not going to call him as a witness. This is a guilty plea! My client's parents are sitting out there. You don't need to put them through a dog-and-pony show."

The D.A. looks at me and says, "Man, I'm sorry, but in a case like this, I gotta put on witnesses. Weird Wally is on the bench. If I try to go without witnesses, he might throw me out."

The D.A. calls his first witness. Trooper Johnson identifies himself, tells about being called to the scene of the accident, and describes what he found when he got there and what everybody told him. After he finishes, the judge looks at me. "No questions," I say. Then the D.A. calls Holloway. He describes the noise, running out of the house, the upside down car in his yard, pulling my client out of the window on the left side of the car and then going around to the other side for the girl. When he gets to this part, he really hits his stride. He describes, in minute detail, the injuries he saw and what he did to try and save her life. And then he tells, breath by breath, how she died in his arms.

The D.A. says, "No further questions, your Honor." The judge looks at me. I shake my head, and he says to Holloway, "You may step down."

One of those awful silences hangs there, and nothing happens for a minute. Holloway doesn't move. Then he looks at me, and at the D.A., and then at the judge. He says, "Can I say something else, your Honor?"

All my bells are ringing at once, and my gut is screaming at me, Object! Object! I'm trying to decide in three-quarters of a second whether it'll be worse to listen to a lecture on the evils of drink from this jerk Holloway or piss off the judge by objecting. But all I say is, "No objections, your Honor." The judge smiles at me, then at Holloway, and says, "Very well, Mr. Holloway. What did you wish to say?"

It all comes out in a rush. "Well, you see, your Honor," Holloway says, "it was just like I told Trooper Johnson. It all happened so fast. I heard the noise, and I came running out, and it was night, and I was excited, and the next morning, when I had a chance to think about it, I figured out what had happened, but by then I'd already told Trooper Johnson and I didn't know what to do, but you see, the car, it was upside down, and I did pull that boy out of the lefthand window, but don't you see, the car was upside down, and if you turned it over on its wheels like it's suppose to be, the left-hand side is really on the right hand side, and your Honor, that boy wasn't driving that car at all. It was the girl that was driving, and when I had a chance to think about it the next morning, I realized that I'd told Trooper Johnson wrong, and I was scared and I didn't know what to do, and that's why"—and now he's looking right at me—"why I wouldn't talk to you."

Naturally, the defendant is allowed to withdraw his guilty plea. The charges are dismissed and the kid and his parents and I go into one of the back rooms in the courthouse and sit there looking at one another for a while. Finally we recover enough to mumble some Oh my Gods and Thank yous and You're welcomes. And that's why I can stand to represent somebody when I know he's guilty.

MULTIPLE CHOICE QUESTIONS

Answer these questions using the definitions found at the end of Chapter Two.

1. At the trial of a routine civil case in a United States District Court, defense lawyer Westerman presented the testimony of an insurance company investigator. On cross examination, plaintiff's lawyer established that on the day before the trial began, the investigator spent three hours in Westerman's office going over his testimony. On that occasion, Westerman showed the investigator some handwritten notes from the insurance company files, in an effort to refresh the investigator's recollection of some important dates. Plaintiff's counsel asked to have the notes brought to court the next morning; after hearing oral argument on the point, the judge ordered Westerman to bring them the next morning. Westerman

responded: "I'll bring them, judge, on the next cold day in Hell." The judge looked startled but chose to overlook the remark. Westerman intentionally failed to bring the notes to court the following day. Which of the following are correct?

I. Westerman is *subject to litigation sanctions* for discussing the investigator's testimony with him before the trial.

II. Westerman is *subject to litigation sanctions* for using the notes to refresh the investigator's memory of dates.

III. Westerman is *subject to litigation sanctions* for his rude remark to the judge.

IV. Westerman is *subject to litigation sanctions* for intentionally violating the Federal Rules of Evidence.

V. Westerman is *subject to litigation sanctions* for intentionally violating the judge's order.

A. All of the above.

B. II and V only.

C. I, II, III, and IV only.

D. III, IV, and V only.

2. Lawyer Lexington represents the plaintiffs in a civil action. His clients are three members of the congregation of All Souls' Divine Missionary Church, suing on behalf of themselves and others similarly situated. The defendants are All Souls' Divine Missionary Church, Inc., (a corporation) and Pastor Dorset, the spiritual leader of the church and president of the church corporation. Pastor Dorset and the church corporation are represented by separate defense lawyers. The complaint alleges that Pastor Dorset misappropriated large amounts of church money, and that the Board of Elders, acting as corporate directors, knew about it and failed to stop him. In the early discovery phase of the case, lawyer Lexington conducted a lengthy, private interview with the church bookkeeper, an employee of the church corporation; she brought the church books with her to the interview, and she and Lexington went over them in great detail. Lexington did this without the knowledge or consent of either defense lawyer. Which of the following is most nearly correct?

A. Lexington's conduct was *proper*, since the bookkeeper was not a party to the lawsuit.

B. Lexington's conduct was *proper*, since the bookkeeper was neither an officer nor a high-ranking employee of the church corporation.

C. Lexington is *subject to discipline*; he should have obtained the consent of both defense lawyers.

D. Lexington is *subject to discipline*; he should have obtained the consent of the church corporation's defense lawyer.

3. Deputy District Attorney Sanford has been assigned to prosecute defendant Rossi for arson. Shortly after the fire was extinguished, a three-person team of arson experts was sent by the City fire department to determine the cause of the fire. The team concluded that the fire was set by a professional arsonist, and the team's report so states. Shortly before trial, Sanford learned that Beaumont, the youngest and least experienced member of the team, had originally concluded that the fire resulted from an explosion in the furnace. Beaumont had tried to convince the other two team members that his original conclusion was correct, but they ultimately prevailed, and Beaumont signed the report without dissent. Sanford does not plan to offer the report in evidence at trial, and he does not plan to call any of the three team members as witnesses. Rather, he plans to use the testimony of two independent experts to establish that arson caused the fire. Which of the following is the *proper* thing for Sanford to do concerning the information about Beaumont?

A. Disclose it to Rossi's counsel, since it could be useful in Rossi's defense.

B. Instruct Beaumont not to mention his original conclusion to anyone.

C. Wait to see whether Rossi's counsel asks for the information in the regular course of criminal discovery.

D. Do nothing about it since he does not plan to offer the report or the testimony of the team members at the trial.

4. Attorney Paxton represents plaintiff Parker on a contingent fee basis in an action against Dougal Corp. for breach of an alleged employment contract between Dougal Corp. and Parker. Attorney Daniels represents Dougal Corp. in the matter. Dougal Corp. instructs Daniels to offer the plaintiff $35,000 to settle the case, and Daniels duly telephones Paxton and makes the offer of settlement. Paxton says he will take it up with Parker and get back to Daniels in due course. When Daniels hears nothing for two weeks, he calls Paxton back, but Paxton refuses to take Daniels' telephone call. Then Daniels writes Paxton a formal letter, re-making the settlement offer, requesting that Paxton consult Parker about it, and requesting a prompt response. Again, Daniels hears nothing from Paxton. Finally Daniels develops a strong suspicion that Paxton has not communicated the settlement offer to Parker. *May* Daniels send Parker a copy of his letter to Paxton?

A. No, because Daniels is not allowed to communicate directly with Parker.

B. Yes, if Daniels reasonably believes that Paxton has failed to communicate the settlement offer to Parker.

C. No, since Daniels cannot be sure that Paxton failed to communicate the settlement offer to Parker.

D. Yes, because the copy would simply advise Parker of Daniels' prior communication with Paxton.

5. Crebs had an automobile accident in his sports car, injuring his girlfriend, Victoria, who was riding in the front seat without her seatbelt fastened. Crebs consulted lawyer Limpett about his possible legal liability to Victoria. After making sure that Victoria had not already retained counsel, Limpett went to visit her, to find out how badly she was injured and to obtain her description of what happened the night of the accident. Victoria asked Limpett whether he thought she should make a claim against Crebs. Limpett gave her his honest opinion: litigation can be costly and time-consuming, and Crebs' liability was debatable. Further, he told her, since her medical expenses were fully covered by her own health insurance, she had little to gain by suing Crebs.

A. Limpett's conduct was *proper*, since Victoria was not represented by counsel when Limpett spoke with her.

B. Limpett's conduct was *proper*, because he gave Victoria his honest opinion about the matter.

C. Limpett's conduct was *proper*, provided that his visit with Victoria was an overture to a good faith settlement of the matter.

D. Limpett is *subject to discipline*, even if his ultimate objective was to reach a fair settlement of the matter.

Answers to the multiple choice questions will be found in the Appendix at the end of the book.

CHAPTER TEN

BIAS IN (AND OUT OF) THE COURTROOM

■ ■ ■

What This Chapter Covers

I. Types of Bias Lawyers Face
- A. Gender Bias
- B. Racial and Ethnic Bias
- C. Sexual Orientation Bias
- D. Other Forms of Bias, Including Sexual Harassment and Bias on the Basis of Disability, Age, or Religion

II. Settings for Bias
- A. Bias by Lawyers
- B. Bias by Judges
- C. Bias by Clients

III. How Can Bias Be Remedied?

Reading Assignment

Wydick, Perschbacher, & Bassett, Chapter 10.

Review ABA Model Rules:

Rules 1.8(j), 3.4, 3.5, 4.4, and 8.4.

CRPC 2–400 and 3–120.

ABA Model Code of Judicial Conduct

Canons 1–3; Rules 1.2, 2.2, 2.3, 2.11(A)(1), 2.12, 3.1, and 3.6.

Supplemental Reading

Hazard & Hodes:

Discussion of ABA Model Rules 1.8(j), 3.4, 3.5, 4.4, and 8.4.

Restatement (Third) of the Law Governing Lawyers §§ 5, 106–107 (2000).

Discussion Problems

1. Dan Mitchell is a partner in a mid-size law firm. He has assigned Beth Hammond, one of the firm's best associates, to a litigation matter for

his client, Modern Furnishings. Until now, Beth's work has involved research and drafting pleadings, but an important deposition is scheduled in three weeks. During a meeting between Dan and George Drake, the president of Modern Furnishings, George suggests that Beth might not be the "best choice" for taking the deposition. When pressed, George states that although Beth's work has been excellent, he would be "more comfortable" having a male associate conduct the deposition due to its importance to the litigation and the necessity for an "aggressive" approach. Does George's request reflect bias? What should Dan do? What should Beth do if she learns of George's concerns?

2. Ethan Baird, age seventy-three, was involved in an automobile accident injuring Cathy Stevens. Cathy sued Ethan to recover for her injuries; whether Ethan was negligent is disputed. While cross-examining Ethan, Cathy's attorney asked repeated questions concerning Ethan's age, his vision, and the length of time since his last driving test. At the conclusion of his cross-examination, Cathy's attorney commented, "The State needs to do a better job of keeping old coots off the highway." Does Cathy's attorney's questioning reflect bias? Is Cathy's attorney's questioning appropriate? What about her comment?

3. The deputy district attorney for the City of Brownstone was faced with the decision whether to indict a Mexican–American for an alleged assault. Responding to a colleague's question as to whether he intended to proceed with an indictment, the deputy said yes. The colleague noted the conflicting evidence in the case, and questioned whether the deputy had any hesitation. The deputy replied that "those people always have an alibi—they stick together." Does the deputy district attorney's reply reflect bias? Does it raise any ethical concerns?

4. Jennifer Holden is a twenty-eight year-old associate attorney at a large law firm. Jennifer works with Sam Baker, a partner in his mid-fifties. Clients regularly mistake Jennifer for a secretary, paralegal, or court reporter instead of a lawyer. Does this mistaken identity reflect bias? Why would this mistaken identity occur? What steps could be taken to avoid such misapprehensions in the future?

5. Judge Richard Jenkins recently was elected as a full-time state court trial judge.

a. Judge Jenkins belongs to a local private club that offers fine dining facilities and pleasant social opportunities. If the club's bylaws prohibit women and minorities from becoming members, must Judge Jenkins resign his club membership? What if the bylaws contain no such express prohibition, but the club has no women or minority members, and the club has refused all membership applications submitted by women and minorities?

b. In a criminal case being tried to a jury, the prosecutor is male; the defense attorney is a twenty-eight year-old woman. Judge Jenkins repeatedly has referred to defense counsel as "Missy," and his tone arguably contains more than a hint of condescension. Is Judge Jenkins subject to discipline?

c. The bailiff for Judge Jenkins' courtroom used a racial slur in referring to a Latino lawyer appearing before the judge. The attorney did not hear the comment. Judge Jenkins overheard the remark but elected to ignore it. Is Judge Jenkins subject to discipline?

d. During a meeting in Judge Jenkins' chambers at which only the lawyers and Judge Jenkins were present, the male prosecutor commented to the female defense attorney that he "wouldn't mind dating" her if he "were only twenty years younger." The prosecutor and Judge Jenkins both laughed. Is Judge Jenkins subject to discipline?

INTRODUCTION

With the increase of women and minorities in the bar has come increased attention to the presence of racial and gender bias as such bias affects the practice of law. It is not uncommon for allegations of gender and racial bias in the practice of law to be met with skepticism. After all, tremendous strides forward have been made since the days when open, direct discrimination against women and minorities was widely accepted. Recent studies, however, consistently reflect that such bias is merely less open and more subtle; it has not been eradicated. One 2005 study reported that more than 70% of women lawyers had experienced gender bias in the courtroom—indicating that bias and stereotypes persist in the practice of law. [*See* Tresa Baldas, *Gender Bias: Still a Problem*, 27 NAT'L L.J. 4 (Feb. 14, 2005).] Among other findings, an ABA report issued in February 2005 found that the percentage of minorities in the legal profession is notably lower than that of most other professions; in most cities, fewer than 3 percent of law firm partners are minorities; and minority attorneys experience difficulties in access to clients, business networks, mentoring, and training in law firms. [*See* Nancy McCarthy, *ABA Study Finds Minority Lawyers Have "Miles to Go" in the Profession*, CAL. BAR J. 1, 16 (Mar. 2005).] The federal courts, leading state courts, and bar associations have formed task forces and other groups to inquire into the presence of bias inside and out of court and what can be done to remedy it. Among the difficult questions raised is whether judges and lawyers have any special obligation to deal with what is a society-wide issue. These task force studies have resulted in regulations directed at eliminating bias in codes of judicial conduct and in states' ethical rules.

ASKING ABOUT GENDER IN COURTS

Judith Resnik
21 Signs 952 (1996)
http://womhist.alexanderstreet.com/vawa/doc17.htm

Women in the United States have long understood that their gender has affected, and sometimes defined, their interactions with legal institutions. In the 1960s and 1970s, as women's rights litigators fought for equality, they found some of the pain of discrimination in the very places to which they brought claims—the courts. * * *

"Gender bias in the courts" became the shorthand attached to the issue, and gender bias task forces became the primary method for gathering information specific to a particular court system about injuries suffered by women within the justice system. In contrast to women's rights litigation aimed at ensuring fair treatment in areas such as housing, education, or family law, task forces examined the justice system itself. They questioned whether courts provide equal treatment as promised to identifiable categories of individuals. As explained by a founding document of the gender bias task force movement, "As long as judges adhere to gender based myths, biases, and stereotypes, the intent of the laws can be compromised or subverted through the exercise of judicial discretion."

* * *

As of this writing, more than thirty jurisdictions have reports on gender, and more than ten on race and ethnicity. National conferences have been held on both topics, and in seven of the thirteen federal circuits, work has begun on projects considering gender and/or race and ethnicity. Hostility toward these projects has also emerged, as a few vocal federal judges have mounted a sustained attack. In the spring of 1995, at the request of Senator Charles E. Grassley, the General Accounting Office launched an investigation into federal funds spent on task forces. In September of 1995, Senators Grassley, Phil Gramm, and Orrin Hatch recommended on the congressional record that no federal funds be spent on such task forces. * * *

THE EFFECTS OF GENDER IN THE FEDERAL COURTS: THE FINAL REPORT OF THE NINTH CIRCUIT GENDER BIAS TASK FORCE

Pages 49–51, 56–57, 191–92, 194, 201 (July 1993).

> "Gender bias is alive and well. It has just gone underground. Instead of calling women 'girls,' they say things like 'You are not aggressive enough' or 'You need to be tougher.' It will take generations to eliminate it—if ever." (Margin comment, female attorney in a large private practice)

The research findings paint a complex picture of the ways in which gender does—and does not—affect professional interactions within the

Ninth Circuit. On the one hand, both the qualitative data from focus group interviews and the more quantitative data from the Task Force surveys indicate that women and men lawyers believe they themselves generally receive fair treatment from federal judges within the Ninth Circuit. Indeed, many women practitioners noted that the federal courts are relatively free of the problems of blatant sexism that they have experienced in some state court systems. Court employees, such as courtroom deputies and court interpreters, also report that their interactions with judges are generally free of gender bias.

Yet the data also suggest that gender adds an extra dimension to courtroom and law firm interactions, a dimension that is often discomforting and sometimes destructive to female counsel and perhaps to their clients. Women attorneys experience a variety of interactions that subtly and overtly undercut their own sense of professional worth. Some of these interactions take place in the courtroom during formal proceedings. But more occur "off the record," in the judge's chambers, or outside of the judge's hearing, in the corridors and law offices of the Ninth Circuit. Importantly, women single out their male colleagues and opponents as the source of much of the gender bias that affects interactions within the Circuit. Furthermore, in certain areas of practice, many attorneys report that women litigants receive different treatment from both judges and lawyers, even when women lawyers are not subject to such bias.

* * *

Not only are male attorneys not subjected to the same kinds of behavior that female attorneys report, they say they are unaware that it exists. Yet observations from third parties, the women judges within the Ninth Circuit, confirm the reports of gender-influenced interactions between male and female counsel.

Some within the legal profession suggest that differences in perceptions between men and women lawyers are a function of age; the view is that, as the "older generation" retires, these issues will recede in importance. However, the Task Force found sharp gender differences among younger attorneys as well as older attorneys in the Circuit. The differences in perception between women and men below the age of 40 mirrored that of women and men over the age of 40. This finding implies that an increase in sensitivity to the effects of gender on behavior will not automatically emerge with the passage of time.

* * *

Although female attorneys often related stories to us of inappropriate terms of address, they expressed particular concern about interactions in which women are demeaned or disparaged, subtly or overtly, before juries, clients and other counsel, by judges or opposing counsel. * * * Male judges were described as directing their comments and attention to male counsel and seemingly ignoring opposing female counsel; asking male counsel to speak before female counsel in situations where the woman attorney was in a position in which she as counsel would normally have been asked to speak first; and cutting off female counsel during argument more abruptly than male counsel. Many attorneys thought the judges involved in such incidents had no sense that their conduct was inappropriate.

* * *

A consistent finding is that gender remains relevant—in different ways, at different times, but frequently playing a role. * * * Although the judiciary aspires to a system of justice in which the gender of the participants is of no import, the results of this research document that in the current world, gender counts. Gender can have an effect on one as litigant, witness, lawyer, employee, or judge, both with regard to process and with regard to substantive outcome. * * * The second consistent finding, across general and specialized surveys of judges and lawyers, is that women and men who responded have significantly different views of the definition and prevalence of gender bias. * * * [M]en often responded that there was no problem, while women reported that gender not only counted, but also that gender bias caused injury.

* * *

Some believe that the passage of time is all that is needed to change attitudes towards women, but our data demonstrate that attitudes about gender bias do not depend upon the *age* of the respondent but rather upon the *gender* of the respondent. Men over and under fifty share the attitude that there is relatively little gender bias in the Circuit, while women over and under the age of fifty share the view that gender bias *is* a problem. Moreover, while some social science literature might have predicted that *role* would be the critical determinant of one's view—that is, that those who are judges would share views, and that those who are lawyers would share somewhat different views, our data demonstrate that *gender* is key across roles. Women judges and women lawyers report similar perceptions; men judges and men lawyers also have similar perceptions.

* * *

The judiciary has a critical role to play in setting norms both in and outside of the courtroom. The federal judiciary has, over the recent decades, increasingly taken on the responsibility of managing the pretrial process and structuring alternatives to adjudication, thereby moving beyond the courtroom to embrace a wider range of activities related to adjudication. Respondents to our questions repeatedly called for a comparable "managerial" mode in the area of gender bias.

Judges set the tone and establish the norms of proper behavior. Judges make key appointments, convene committees, and set the rules of the courtroom and chambers. Judges can lead by example and by using their authority and influence to ensure that the federal courts offer truly equal access to men and women judges, lawyers, employees, and litigants.

* * *

THE STUDY OF GENDER IN THE COURTS: KEEPING BIAS AT BAY

Lilia M. Cortina
27 Law & Social Inquiry 199 (2002).

Although volumes of data now document the reality of gender bias in the courts, resistance against efforts to correct bias has been formidable. Critics emphasize the lack of apparent "intention" behind much of the documented misbehavior, as if the absence of overt malice obviates the need for action. Somehow the issue of *impact* escapes these critics' attention. Expressing frustration with this misguided opposition, the Honorable Patricia Wald (former D.C. Circuit chief judge) noted in 1995:

> During the debate there was much talk of perceptions as opposed to reality: "What was in our heads" as opposed to "what was happening in the real world?" Women perceived they were treated differently; but we were told repeatedly the perception was of our own making. It didn't seem to matter that the women * * * reported actual incidents that happened to them or that they had personally observed. * * * Unless you could reach in and pull out the smoking discriminatory intent from the hearts and minds of the perpetrators, it was not worth bothering about.

* * *

WHAT'S GENDER GOT TO DO WITH IT? INCIVILITY IN THE FEDERAL COURTS

Lilia M. Cortina, Kimberly A. Lonsway, Vicki J. Magley, Leslie V. Freeman, Linda L. Collinsworth, Mary Hunter, and Louise F. Fitzgerald
27 Law & Social Inquiry 235 (2002).

* * * Our results portray a federal litigation environment where rudeness, disrespect, gender disparagement, and sexually inappropriate behaviors are alarmingly common. Specifically, almost two-thirds of attorneys have experienced general incivility, gendered incivility, and/or unwanted sexual attention while in litigation in the Eighth Circuit federal courts—with women encountering such mistreatment more frequently than men.

* * *

These results suggest that patterns of interaction in federal litigation replicate problematic gender relations from the larger society, including stereotypic, sexualized, and abusive treatment of women. Some of the interpersonal mistreatment that our participants describe fits the characteristics of "sex-role spillover," when expectations for women's behavior at home permeate the work realm. That is, some misbehavior involves treating women attorneys as mothers, wives, sexual partners, and daughters—roles in which some men are more accustomed to or comfortable seeing women. Women's narratives underscore this, describing experiences of such familiar or infantalizing terms of address as *sweetheart*, *dear*, and *Miss Girl Lawyer*. Sexualized jokes further suggest that conceptualizations of women as sex objects follow them into professional contexts, where such fantasies clearly do not belong.

* * *

WHAT JUDGES CAN LEARN FROM GENDER BIAS TASK FORCE STUDIES

Vicki C. Jackson
81 Judicature 15–18, 20–21, 38 (1997).*

As task force studies show, judges can be a powerful force for promoting equality of treatment for women and men in their courts. In 1963 a state court held in contempt an African–American female witness who refused to answer questions from a prosecutor because he called her by her first name. The U.S. Supreme Court summarily reversed her conviction, demonstrating its understanding of the degree to which differential treatment reflected patterns of racial subjugation condemned by the Constitution. Despite substantial progress toward racial justice and the acceptance of women on equal terms in the legal system in the last 30 years, court decisions and task force studies across the country show that biased treatment of women persists—even in the courts.

* * *

Most state court systems and more than half of the federal circuits have engaged in self-studies concerning the effects of gender, race, or other characteristics that can form the basis for invidious distinctions. Virtually all of the gender studies have found areas where gender inappropriately affects the treatment of participants in the courts' work.

* * *

The perception of gender bias in a judge is more harmful to the legal system than its appearance in other participants. The judge is the most powerful member of the legal system, holding the power of judgment. The judge is also the most potent symbol of the sought-for impartiality that parties must be able to count on in order to trust the justice system to do justice. Yet task force reports identify behavior—both in adjudication and

---

in nonadjudicatory interactions—that call into question the apparent neutrality of some judges.

Some of this behavior flows from unconsciously held stereotypes rather than from intentional invidious acts. An important part of task forces' work has been to pay close attention "to the existence of unconscious prejudice . . . [and thus] encourage those who work in the courts to listen to women's voices . . . [with the same] respect customarily accorded ideas advanced by men." For example, many task force surveys found that attorneys observed judges addressing female witnesses by their first names more often than male witnesses. Female attorneys, far more often than comparably aged male attorneys, report that judges assume they are not lawyers. Minority female attorneys in particular report this unconscious lack of respect, as well as overt questioning of their credentials by some judges. As Judge Patricia Wald of the D.C. Circuit has said, "No one infers conscious bias from [these data], but on the other hand, how can one discount the effect nonrecognition has on the woman lawyer (or the black lawyer) and the image that projects to everybody else in the courtroom? Honest mistake, of course; nonprejudicial error, I don't think so. It says to the misidentified player, you are not in friendly territory. This is not your game, yet."

* * *

It is also important that judges (who are still predominantly male) understand more fully the range of experiences that female as well as male litigants face. Society is pervasively organized around gender categories, and we can all harbor stereotypes of which we may be unconscious. The best of the task force reports help readers come to a better awareness of this possibility and thereby permit them to work harder towards objectivity and impartiality.

* * *

In addition to their impact on attorneys, judges are ordinarily the leaders of the employees of their courthouses. Many task force reports document how gender-biased conduct from employees such as court clerks, bailiffs, stenographers, and others can have a deleterious impact on participants' confidence in the fairness of the courts. Some jurisdictions found, for example, that some court clerks discouraged women from filing domestic violence complaints or misinformed them about the availability of pro se forms. By setting examples, and by adopting clear standards preventing gender-biased behavior by court officers and employees, judges can have a substantial impact on their behavior.

* * *

Apart from their influence on how attorneys and court employees behave, judges can influence one another's behavior. Through informal conversation, socializing, and observation, a diverse group of judges will become more aware of the life experiences and perspectives of others.

Sharing the perspectives that come from varied life experiences can be of value in courthouse chambers. Study after study finds a "gender gap" in the reported observations of female and male attorneys, and judges, about the levels of apparently biased behavior in their workplaces. Female and male judges also tend to differ, as groups, in their evaluation of the consequences of some forms of unequal treatment. Thus, for example, in the Ninth Circuit, 79 percent of the female judges, but only 44 percent of the male judges, thought that familiar forms of address to women may impact a case, and 41 percent of male judges but 67 percent of female judges thought comments on women's appearance may impact case outcomes. Some task force reports suggest that colleagues and attorneys may evaluate female judges more harshly than male judges; in one study more than half of the female attorneys said they had heard colleagues question female judges' competence to serve as judges. While the talents and attitudes of individual women and men cannot be determined by their gender, women (perhaps in part because of a greater likelihood of encountering biased behavior) may bring different perspectives and perceptions to the table than do men. Finally, women as judges are powerful role models, not only for women lawyers but for all participants. As we become accustomed to women exercising the power of judging, stereotypes about the relative competence and authority of women and men can be expected to diminish. The increasing numbers of women judges in most of the nation's court systems, then, itself has the potential to change societal stereotypes of what women do.

* * *

The task forces have been an important part of the legal profession's efforts to understand and overcome barriers to the full and equal participation and treatment of women. One of the advantages of task force research is that it permits fact gathering, identification of problems, and formulation of solutions in a nonadjudicatory context. The point is not to blame particular individuals but to explore practices that are perceived to, or may reflect, gender bias, to hold those practices up to the light for examination and discussion, and to improve awareness of and sensitivity to gender equality. Another benefit of the task force approach is in having studies in different jurisdictions, identifying what are and are not problem areas in particular court systems, while at the same time making information and innovation available across jurisdictions.

Understanding both the similarities, and the differences, in the experiences and circumstances of individual women and men is an important part of achieving justice. The task force's accumulation of data, statistical and narrative, adds to the background understandings that judges, lawyers, and others bring to their roles in the justice system. With more accurate understandings of what constitutes unconscious gender stereotyping, and through improved understanding of the at-times divergent realities of men and women, judges are in a better position to do individual justice. Better knowledge should be supplemented, where appropriate, by required changes in facilities, rules, and procedure. Egregiously biased conduct, whether by attorneys, court employees, or judges, should be subject to appropriate sanction. Educational programs to identify and challenge unconscious (or conscious) assumptions about how women and men should or do behave can be pursued. And where apparent bias based on gender infects an adjudicated result, courts of appeals must stand ready to reverse. Hopefully, these reports and the changes they recommend will eliminate or reduce the situations in which such bias affects parties in adjudication.

* * *

FINAL REPORT OF THE SPECIAL COMMITTEE ON RACE AND ETHNICITY TO THE D.C. CIRCUIT TASK FORCE ON GENDER, RACE, AND ETHNIC BIAS

Pages 4, 36–41 (Jan. 1995).

* * *

> When people perceive * * * bias in a legal system, whether they suffer from it or not, they lose respect for that system, as well as for the law. (Justice Sandra Day O'Connor, addressing the Ninth Circuit Judicial Conference on issues of gender bias.)
>
> I believe racial harmony comes from inattention rather than exacerbation. (I do not know whether I would have that opinion if I were not an aged white attorney.) (Margin comment, white male attorney, survey respondent.)
>
> Judges, probably like the rest of the country, don't want to put race on the table and openly discuss it. (African–American male attorney, focus group respondent.)
>
> There will always be inequities in our society. Trying to focus on our differences keeps us from focusing on the vast majority of our shared values and experiences. We are all Americans and race/ethnicity/gender should be downplayed rather than constantly focused [upon]. * * * [T]his questionnaire is offensive to those who believe that justice is blind. Quit wasting time and money on these efforts that only lead to more problems rather than finding any solutions. (Margin comment, white male attorney, survey respondent.)
>
> Most of us involved in the judicial process in this circuit are at least sophisticated enough to know to mask in our outward behavior any overt signs of racial discrimination. Problems persist in people's attitudes, perceptions, and assumptions about people of color that are manifested in more subtle ways * * * [such as] judges subconsciously presuming that lawyers of color aren't as good, smart, or prepared as

white lawyers. (Margin comment, African–American male attorney, survey respondent.)

* * *

The District of Columbia has more minorities practicing in major law firms than do most other metropolitan legal communities. At the same time, minorities hold on average no more than three percent of all partnerships in the area's larger firms, and six percent of all attorney positions in these firms. This held true among the respondents to the Committee's Attorney Survey: minority respondents in private practice were significantly less likely than were white respondents to be partners (41% compared to 62%, respectively).

* * *

Numbers alone give only part of the picture. Our research suggests that many minority attorneys have a very different experience as professionals than do white attorneys, and that the experiences of African–American, Hispanic, and Asian–American attorneys, the principal racial and ethnic minority groups practicing in D.C., also differ from one another in certain important respects. Attorneys in focus groups and in written comments on surveys remarked on the predominantly white makeup of the D.C. Circuit federal bench, bar, and the courthouse staff with whom they come into contact, and contrasted it with the local courts. As one said, in federal court, "The whole complexion of the city changes. You'd never believe that you're in a predominantly black city." A white survey respondent commented:

> "Part of the reason why I had too little experience to answer many of these questions is because, other than a pro se litigant, I have never been opposite minority counsel in a case, never been co-counsel with minority counsel on a case, and in the five years I have been associated with my firm, only one minority attorney has been hired. * * * I believe that this cannot be ignored in any survey of this kind." (Margin comment, white female attorney, private practice.)

Her remarks were echoed by an African–American respondent:

> "I have been practicing in this district and circuit for approximately 3.5 years. Prior to two weeks ago, I had never seen another African–American [in] either court as counsel or judge. * * * Seeing the [African–American] attorney made part of me do a small flip. I no longer felt as if I was the only one or that my presence was a fluke/freakish." (Margin comment, African–American female attorney, federal government.)

The demographics of the courthouse * * * "send very profound messages about what kind of a system of justice we have." Indeed, a number of attorneys participating in different focus groups suggested that the choice of forum makes a difference to clients; the[y] suggested that minority clients and individual parties perceived Superior Court as a fairer forum, while corporate clients perceived they had a better chance for a fair hearing in federal court. Attorneys, minority and non-minority, attributed this in part to the demographics of the court. A number of African–American attorneys commented in focus groups that they prefer practice in Superior Court, in part because they feel they get a better reception as minority professionals in the local courts, where there are more minorities among the staff, the bench, and the bar. Indeed, a majority of African–American attorneys, significantly more than white attorneys, reported that they had not been recognized as a lawyer by court personnel or other attorneys in the D.C. Circuit courts. Less than 20 percent of white attorneys reported the same experience, and less than 6 percent indicated that it had occurred more than two times. One African–American focus group participant reported that white lawyers in federal court have said to him: "[Y]ou're out of your league. You need to be across the street [in Superior Court]."

Hispanic and Asian–American attorneys did not indicate a preference for Superior Court practice, or suggest that local court was a "friendlier" forum for them as attorneys. To the contrary, several recounted incidents of differential (and unfavorable) treatment in both Superior Court and federal district court. Both Asian–American and Hispanic attorneys have been asked in D.C. federal court whether they spoke or read English. One Hispanic attorney was asked for his visa when he was filing a complaint in both federal district court and Superior Court. Hispanic and Asian–American attorneys commented that judges and staff frequently mispronounce their names, and that staff sometimes "giggle" when reading their names. The attorneys felt frustrated and embarrassed by such conduct. For these focus group participants, issues related to perceptions of language ability and citizenship appear to arise in both courts.

The professional experiences of African–American, Hispanic, and Asian–American attorneys, while different in certain aspects, nevertheless had several strong common factors. Principal among these were the need to overcome perceptions of incompetence, the difficulty of establishing oneself in the "mainstream" legal community, and a sense of exclusion from opportunities provided to serve or interact with the federal judiciary. As to the first factor, most participants in minority attorney focus groups agreed that minority attorneys constantly had to work to overcome a perception of incompetence. Minority attorneys found this to be true in a range of practice areas, notably commercial litigation and large, complex cases. This perception took a particular form with African–American attorneys, according to both men and women in different focus groups, who said their achievements were often discounted as the product of "affirmative action" rather than their own ability. Hispanic and Asian–American attorneys also reported confronting culturally-based stereotypes in the profession, and noted that perceptions of Asians as "hard-working" but "passive," and of Hispanics as "overly polite," contributed to a glass ceiling within the legal community.

The perception of minority attorneys as "incompetent" straddles all levels of the legal profession, according to survey respondents. Approximately one-third of respondents had heard at least one race-based remark about the competence of minorities to serve as judges, while less than one quarter had heard similar remarks about whites. One respondent reported that a partner in her law firm commented about an African–American judge: "Well, he's black, but he seems to be smart enough." Minority attorneys, unlike their non-minority counterparts, thus appear to encounter race as an issue that defines and affects their professional identity and career path.

Minorities uniformly lamented the lack of mentors in the legal profession. Some African–Americans who have advanced in the public and private sector are viewed as continuing to struggle to maintain their bona fides, and as having little time to mentor newer African–American attorneys. Many Hispanic and Asian–American attorneys participating in focus groups noted the lack of mentors. In addition to the relatively low numbers of Hispanics and Asian–Americans in the higher-level positions of the area legal community, a number of focus group participants commented that they are also "first-generation professionals," and have no relative or family friend to whom to turn for advice or mentoring.

The second two factors minority attorneys identified—establishing oneself in the "mainstream" legal community, and exclusion from service or interaction with the federal judiciary—are related, as we learned from interviews with judges and participants in focus groups. Minorities participating in focus groups discussed a general sense that a predominantly white "old boy network" still operates with particular force to affect opportunities in federal practice. Several attorneys commented on the separation between minority and white professionals, a factor that is seen to limit professional opportunities for minority attorneys. Informal social networks were seen as important means to learn about significant issues within the profession, to meet leaders of the bar and members of the judiciary and earn their trust and respect, and to ease professional dealings.

A number of minority attorneys described the federal and general D.C. legal community as comprised of separate social "spheres," "clubs," or "worlds." Comments from several African–American attorneys are illustrative:

> You have to realize that there is a minority and, for lack of a better word, majority bar, and * * * it's two separate worlds. And it makes a difference, because I think if you are involved with the white Bar you tend to get more credibility coming out of that environment. (African–American male, focus group participant.)
>
> When you sit down and break bread with somebody and you talk with somebody and see that they are not as stupid as you think, that changes perceptions. * * * If you never deal with us other than in the courtroom, and when you see us in the courtroom you have a

> perception that we are not your equal, how does it ever change? (African–American male, focus group participant.)
>
> When judges find out about you as a person, they treat you with more respect in the courtroom. (African–American male, focus group participant.)

In such an environment, the impact of even casual dealings between judges and lawyers, while subtle, may be profound. One African–American attorney described having been greeted by first name in a chance encounter with a federal judge: "[I] told some of my partners and other colleagues that maybe I've arrived now."

* * *

NEW JERSEY JUDICIARY, FINAL REPORT OF THE TASK FORCE ON SEXUAL ORIENTATION ISSUES: EXECUTIVE SUMMARY

Supreme Court of New Jersey (2001).
www.judiciary.state.nj.us/taskforce/summary.pdf

With the notable exception of marriage, gays and lesbians are afforded virtually all the legal rights, privileges, and protections to which all other New Jersey citizens are entitled. In this regard, the Executive, Legislative, and Judicial branches have clearly stated that as a matter of public policy this State will not tolerate differential treatment based on sexual orientation. This makes New Jersey one of eleven states to acknowledge gays and lesbians as targets of discrimination to be recognized along with other minorities. Nevertheless, despite legal protection, gays and lesbians are still affected by biased attitudes and behaviors.

In order to ascertain whether, and to what extent, sexual orientation bias exists in the New Jersey court system and/or among judiciary employees, the New Jersey Supreme Court formed the Task Force on Gay and Lesbian Issues. By forming the Task Force, the Court intended to signal "its strong commitment to the equal treatment of all individuals seeking justice in our court system."

* * *

Overall, the majority of survey respondents did not believe sexual orientation bias to be a problem in the court system or in the workplace for judicial employees. However, when the Task Force isolated responses by gays and lesbians a different perception was revealed. In question after question, gays and lesbians, in percentages far higher than heterosexuals, noted incidents of sexual orientation bias or indicated their belief that such bias affected the judicial process. The disparity of perception among gay/lesbian respondents and heterosexual respondents is not unexpected. Like any minority group, gays and lesbians are particularly aware of the kind of bias that personally affects them. Thus, although the actual number of gay/lesbian respondents was relatively low, the Task Force considers these findings significant because responses were consistent throughout the survey and were representative of the majority of the group most likely to be impacted by sexual orientation bias.

For example, gay/lesbian respondents were nearly seven times more likely than heterosexuals to report experiences or observations of bias against gay/lesbian litigants or witnesses. The most common type of bias reported was offensive remarks or gestures, again noted more frequently by gays and lesbians than heterosexuals. Respondents reported bias among all categories of participants in the judicial system.

Respondents were asked whether sexual orientation bias affected case outcomes. This area of inquiry went beyond reporting offensive remarks or gestures and focused on the substantive effect of bias. Ninety percent of those involved in the litigation process indicated that sexual orientation bias did not affect the outcome of a case that they observed or in which they participated, while 10% believed it did. However, gay/lesbian participants in litigation were more likely than heterosexuals (61% versus 6%) to believe bias affected outcomes. These findings were consistent in family, criminal, and civil litigation.

Focusing on the judicial workplace, approximately one-third of the court employees who responded reported observing or experiencing derogatory statements or inappropriate jokes about gays and lesbians. An even higher percentage of gay/lesbian court employees reported this type of bias. Most of these comments were attributed to co-workers, although judges and supervisors were also identified as the source of objectionable remarks. Again, gay/lesbian respondents were more likely than other court employees to report perceived discrimination in promotions/advancement.

In the area of professional appointments (e.g., guardian ad litem), most respondents had no experience. Among those familiar with this subject, 12% felt sexual orientation affected appointments. This number was substantially higher for gays and lesbians experienced with professional appointments, two-thirds of whom said they believed sexual orientation affected opportunities.

Offensive jokes or remarks were by far the most prevalent form of bias reported to the Task Force. The prevailing attitude among respondents was that jokes and comments were acceptable because offense was not intended. However, comments submitted with the survey reveal that, in fact, people were often offended by such joking.

The survey data revealed that the system for reporting of bias and/or discrimination was underutilized. Some of the reasons given were fear of reprisal and lack of effectiveness. Of those who did report bias, many were not satisfied with the results.

The Task Force has concluded that sexual orientation bias, whether actual or perceived, has the capacity to create a hostile work environment, affect case disposition, hinder professional opportunities, dissuade individuals from using the court system and undermine public confidence in judicial neutrality. Accordingly, in light of the Court's strong anti-discrimination policy, the Task Force recommends the following:

1. Distribute the full report to all judges, judiciary supervisors (team leaders), the president of the State Bar Association, each county bar association, statewide specialty bar associations and others the Court finds appropriate. Distribute the Executive Summary of this report to all judiciary employees along with a notice of how to obtain a copy of the full report. Make the full report available to the public through notice to the bar and other media;

2. The sexual orientation bias/discrimination component of education for judges and court employees should continue and be periodically reviewed for effectiveness. The education for judges and lawyers should continue to include a review of New Jersey law. Judges, lawyers, and court employees should be instructed that the Code of Judicial Conduct, the Rules of Professional Conduct, and the Code of Conduct for Judiciary Employees prohibit discrimination on the basis of sexual orientation. The Task Force further recommends that efforts be made to work with the Institute for Continuing Legal Education to incorporate education relating to sexual orientation bias into its program for new lawyers;

3. Employ all existing communications methods (e.g., the Judiciary's Infonet, Internet, newsletters, training, and posters) to publicize the mechanism for reporting bias/discrimination, and to ensure users of confidentiality of the reporting system; and

4. Appoint a working group which would oversee the implementation of these recommendations and assess the need for a follow-up study.

IN RE CHARGES OF UNPROFESSIONAL CONDUCT CONTAINED IN PANEL FILE 98–26

Supreme Court of Minnesota, 1999.
597 N.W.2d 563.

[The respondent in this disciplinary proceeding was a prosecutor. One of her cases involved an African–American male charged with the felony robbery of a Caucasian couple. Notes in the case file, written by the previous prosecutor, stated that the defendant's counsel believed race was a motivating factor in the indictment, and that defense counsel intended to have an African–American attorney join as co-counsel in the case. The respondent filed a motion seeking a court order which would prohibit "counsel for the defendant to have a person of color as co-counsel for the sole purpose of playing upon the emotions of the jury."]

After holding a hearing on charges of unprofessional conduct, a panel has three options: (1) "determine that there is not probable cause to believe that public discipline is warranted"; (2) determine that "public discipline is warranted [and] instruct the Director to file in this Court a petition for disciplinary action"; or (3) issue a private admonition to the attorney. Under the plain language of the rule, a panel may issue a private admonition only if the panel "concludes that the attorney engaged in conduct that was unprofessional but of an isolated and *non-serious* nature."

A complainant's right to petition this court for review of a panel's decision is governed by Rule 9(1). Upon review granted pursuant to such a petition, "if this Court finds that the Panel acted arbitrarily, capriciously, or unreasonably" in reaching its decision, we may "remand the matter back to the same or a different Panel, direct the filing of a petition for disciplinary action, or take any other action as the interest of justice may require." A decision is arbitrary and capricious if the decision maker relied on factors it is not permitted or intended to consider, "entirely failed to consider an important aspect of the problem, [or] offered an explanation for its decision that runs counter to the evidence before [the decision maker] or is so implausible that it could not be ascribed to a difference in view or the product of [the decision maker's] expertise. * * * Where there is room for two opinions on the matter, [a decision] is not 'arbitrary and capricious,' even though it may be believed that an erroneous conclusion has been reached." * * *

Even under this deferential standard of review, we cannot affirm the Panel's conclusion that respondent's race-based misconduct was non-serious. Racism, whether it takes the form of an individual's overt bigotry or an institution's subtle apathy, is, by its very nature, serious. In 1993, our own *Task Force on Racial Bias in the Judicial System* wrote that:

> In the specific case of African Americans, although the justice system is no longer made to enforce the ultimate social control of slavery or the complex codes of legal segregation that took its place, the justice system still finds itself being used as a powerful tool of the pervasive prejudice and the subtle, often elaborately camouflaged discrimination that still deeply scars our national life.

Minnesota Supreme Court Task Force on Racial Bias in the Judicial System, Final Report 5 (1993). When any individual engages in race-based misconduct it undermines the ideals of a society founded on the belief that all people are created equal. When the person who engages in this misconduct is an officer of the court, the misconduct is especially troubling. Left unchecked, such racially-based actions as we have here not only undermine confidence in our system of justice, but also erode the very foundation upon which justice is based.

Respondent's lack of malice and her apologies and remorse do not transform her misconduct from serious to non-serious. Regardless of her subsequent actions, respondent brought a motion that sought to prohibit an attorney from participating in a case based solely on the color of his skin. A counsel's race should never be used as a basis for calling for or placing any limits on that counsel's participation in any court proceedings. Respondent's motion could reasonably be interpreted as implying that an attorney of color would have no legitimate use on the case other than to arouse the passions of the jury. Moreover, respondent's motion came precariously close to infringing on the [defendant's] right to be represented by counsel of his choice. Such conduct, even if grounded in ignorance and poor judgment rather than malice, is unacceptable and inherently serious. Accordingly, we hold that it was arbitrary, capricious, and unreasonable for the Panel to conclude that respondent's race-based misconduct was non-serious. Because the rules empower panels to issue private admonitions only for non-serious violations, the private admonition issued by the Panel in this case cannot stand and, therefore, we reverse.

* * *

IN RE PLAZA HOTEL CORPORATION

United States Bankruptcy Court, E.D.Cal., 1990.
111 B.R. 882.

[In this case, the bankruptcy court granted a motion to disqualify the debtor's counsel for several reasons, including a conflict of interest and "unacceptable gender-biased behavior toward the trustees' female counsel."]

[O]f greater concern to the court is the gender bias that counsel has exhibited toward the women who represent the chapter 11 trustee and the United States Trustee in this court.

Counsel, in the course of this proceeding and in writing, referred to the woman who represents the United States Trustee as "office help" even though he knew that she was a lawyer. * * * He refused to respond to her written request for fuller disclosure of his apparent conflict of interest, which she had signed as designee of the United States Trustee.[3] He reasoned that he need not respond because "she decided that she knew more than the court" and that her job title was not sufficiently exalted.[4]

The condescending attitude towards the United States Trustee's lawyer that counsel evinced during the hearing gave gender-biased content and context to those remarks. They would not have been made but for the fact that the lawyer in question is female.

Gender-biased remarks are unworthy of counsel who appear in federal court, interfere with the orderly conduct of federal litigation in an atmosphere of equal justice, and are as sanctionable as the casting of racial or ethnic epithets and slurs among counsel. They merit, at a minimum, rebuke. In this instance, they are indicative of debtor's counsel's unwill-

3. A designee of the United States Trustee acts on behalf of the United States Trustee. 11 U.S.C. § 102(9).

4. A letter on the stationery of the United States Trustee that has a signature line that includes both the name of the United States Trustee and of the designee signing on behalf of the United States Trustee is an official communication from the United States Trustee.

ingness to assist the debtor in discharging its duties to cooperate with the chapter 11 trustee and the United States Trustee.

This court is greatly disappointed that a lawyer would think that it would brook such remarks and arguments sounding in gender bias. All counsel appearing in this court need to understand that such offensive remarks will be dealt with forcefully—he will be disqualified from representing the debtor.

* * *

IN RE VINCENTI

Supreme Court of New Jersey, 1998.
152 N.J. 253, 704 A.2d 927.

[The Supreme Court of New Jersey ordered the respondent disbarred, noting that "[a]t some point, a court is forced to conclude that it can no longer expose judges, lawyers, litigants, witnesses, and the public to the inexcusable conduct of a renegade attorney. We have passed that point. The only appropriate sanction for respondent's misconduct is disbarment." Respondent's behaviors included harassment and intimidation on the basis of sexual orientation.]

The Division of Youth and Family Services ("DYFS") filed a petition in Superior Court to terminate the parental rights of J.D., the natural mother of A.R.S. * * * James Valenti was appointed and served as law guardian for the child, A.R.S. * * *

[One of the witnesses called by DYFS] was a social worker. At the request of James Valenti, law guardian for A.R.S., the social worker conducted a bonding evaluation to address the issue of where A.R.S. should reside permanently. The social worker, too, was the victim of harassment and intimidation by respondent. At the ethics hearing, the social worker testified as follows about respondent's courtroom behavior:

> The thrust of his questions as I experienced them had less to do with the content than with an attempt to demean me, to ridicule me. I felt the nature of his cross-examination was highly personalized and had very little to do with the content or with trying to uncover the truth of the issues. For example, in the voir dire, he took a tremendous amount of time asking me what specific courses I had taken when I was in graduate school. At the time that I testified, I had—it had been fifteen years since I completed my doctorate and over twenty years since I completed my Masters degree. He wanted to know the specific names of the courses I had taken. I said I couldn't remember the specific names, but I could talk about the kinds of courses I took and how they were related to the work that I was doing. He ridiculed me for the fact that I could not remember the course name and went over that over and over again.

Respondent also made insinuations about the social worker's sexual orientation. He suggested that she inappropriately touched his client, J.D., during a bonding-evaluation session with J.D. and A.R.S. Respondent attached significance to the fact that the social worker used purple paper for taking notes in her office, despite her explanation that it was the easiest color for her eyes. Respondent even said that he would bring in an expert to talk about the meaning of using purple paper. Respondent also used sashaying and other body language to question her sexuality. As the social worker testified at the ethics hearing:

> The Court: Did he imply what meaning he read into this?
>
> The Witness: My view?
>
> The Court: Yeah.
>
> The Witness: Given his body language, given that it came on the heels of his suggesting that I had touched his client, that there was something about my sexual orientation that was revealed by the colors of the paper and the paper clip, as well. That's why I mentioned the body language, also, that on the heels of all of this and the context within which it was raised, certainly the implication was that there was something about my sexual orientation that he was alluding to.
>
> The Court: Is that what came across to you?
>
> The Witness: Yes absolutely, without question.

In addition, respondent took the social worker's notes from her during her testimony. He then toyed with her, refusing to return the notes. When she asked Judge Hanifan to instruct respondent to return the notes, respondent berated the judge for talking to the witness.

Unfortunately for the social worker, the conclusion of the *A.R.S.* trial did not signal the end of respondent's harassment toward her. About six months after the trial ended, she and Dr. Hagovsky, another witness who had testified in the *A.R.S.* matter, were invited to participate at a conference sponsored by the Association of Trial Lawyers of America. There was no connection between the trial and the conference. However, in a letter to Cary B. Cheifetz, the conference coordinator, respondent contended that the social worker and Hagovsky held "Nazi views" and suggested that it would be helpful if respondent attended the conference to denounce them. Although the letter could not be introduced into evidence because Cheifetz discarded it after receiving it, both Cheifetz and the social worker testified at the ethics hearing about the contents of the letter. While respondent complained that the letter was not produced, he did not deny having sent it.

* * *

IN RE KIRBY

Supreme Court of Minnesota, 1984.
354 N.W.2d 410.

This is a judicial discipline matter that comes before this court on the recommendation of the Board on Judicial Standards for removal of the

Honorable John J. Kirby, Judge of the Municipal Court, Ramsey County, for conduct prejudicial to the administration of justice which brings the judicial office into disrepute within the meaning of [Minnesota statutory and constitutional law as well as] Canons 1, 2A, 3A(3) and 3A(5) of the Code of Judicial Conduct. * * *

A 6–day hearing on the complaint against Judge Kirby was held before Referee/Judge [Bruce C.] Stone. * * * The findings and recommendations of Judge Stone were filed on January 31, 1984. Judge Stone found clear and convincing proof of seven instances of public intoxication and six instances of conducting judicial business with liquor on his breath, as well as a pattern of habitual tardiness with lack of concern for such conduct. For these acts of misconduct, Judge Stone recommended public reprimand of Judge Kirby and forfeiture of 2 months' salary.

With regard to the allegations of discourtesy to women lawyers, Judge Stone found clear and convincing evidence of two occasions on which Judge Kirby referred to two separate female attorneys as, in one instance, a "lawyerette" and in another instance, an "attorney generalette," but he found no showing that the comments were designed to injure. Aside from these two occasions, Judge Stone found that Judge Kirby "was courteous in his treatment of attorneys and litigants and conducted his courtroom with appropriate judicial demeanor." Judge Stone recommended that Judge Kirby's apology in open court for any offense caused by these comments, combined with the adverse publicity he has suffered for this conduct, constituted sufficient penalty and that any additional disciplinary action for these two incidents would be unduly harsh.

* * *

We first address the issue of Judge Kirby's discourtesy to female attorneys. Canon 3A(3) of the Code of Judicial Conduct states in pertinent part: "A judge should be patient, dignified, and courteous to litigants, jurors, witnesses, lawyers and others with whom he deals in his official capacity * * *."

In 1979 or 1980, in the office of the Clerk of Court, St. Paul, Minnesota, Judge Kirby referred to Mary Bjorklund, a prosecuting attorney, as "lawyerette" and asked her why she wasn't wearing a tie. While Judge Stone found there was no showing this comment was designed to injure, he also found that it was not made under circumstances that invited the good humored banter that sometimes exists among judges and lawyers and that Bjorklund was justifiably annoyed and disturbed.

On November 4, 1983, at a hearing in chambers, Judge Kirby referred to Penny Troolien, an attorney employed by the Minnesota Attorney General's office, as an "attorney generalette." Troolien, Judge Stone concluded, was also justifiably annoyed and disturbed. We agree with Judge Stone that such behavior is conduct prejudicial to the administration of justice that brings the judicial office into disrepute. But we cannot concur with Judge Stone's conclusion that no further punishment is warranted beyond the adverse publicity Judge Kirby suffered and the apology he made in open court. We do consider this conduct grounds for censure. Such appellations are offensive and tend to demean and to place the lawyer referred to on a less than equal footing with other lawyers. We are mindful of Plutarch's wise observation: "Tho' boys thro' stones at frogs in sport, the frogs do not die in sport, but in earnest." Male and female attorneys should be treated with equal respect and courtesy by the judges before whom they appear.

* * *

On the basis of his discourteous treatment of female attorneys, his public intoxication, his conducting of judicial business with alcohol on his breath and his habitual tardiness, we hereby publicly censure Judge John J. Kirby for conduct prejudicial to the administration of justice that brings the judicial office into disrepute.

* * *

STILL OFFICERS OF THE COURT: WHY THE FIRST AMENDMENT IS NO BAR TO CHALLENGING RACISM, SEXISM AND ETHNIC BIAS IN THE LEGAL PROFESSION

Andrew E. Taslitz & Sharon Styles-Anderson
9 Geo. J. Legal Ethics 781 (1996).[5]

A large and growing number of states and the District of Columbia have recently produced task force reports on racial, ethnic and gender bias in the administration of justice. These reports have consistently found evidence of a wide range of discriminatory conduct by lawyers directed toward witnesses, other lawyers and court personnel. Objectionable conduct ranges from glass ceilings facing female attorneys, to ethnic slurs intimidating or infuriating opposing attorneys and witnesses, to open jury appeals by lawyers asking for particular results based upon the race of the parties when race has no legitimate role to play in the legal issues facing the factfinder.

* * *

I. BACKGROUND

A. *Type of Concerns that Led to State Rules*

The state race, ethnic and gender bias task forces had varied origins. Some were judicial responses to minority coalitions or to citizens' panels conducting more general reviews of state court systems. At least one was a legislative project, and another was mandated by a state supreme court chief justice. All states held public hearings involving legal organizations, entities connected with state court systems and the larger public. The task forces often conducted empirical studies as well as attorney and judge surveys and consultations with academics, other experts and literature reviews. The task forces reached largely similar conclusions.

1. Gender

Florida adopted one of the broader rules, although it is not the broadest because it does not reach conduct outside the sphere of professional activity.[6] The legislative history of Florida's rule thus offers a fairly comprehensive list of the types of gender-based concerns, set forth below in outline form, that led to these rules. The list below includes quotations and illustrations from the Florida Supreme Court Gender Bias Study Commission's 1990 Report:

a. Treatment of Female Lawyers

(1) *Overtly Insulting Behavior*

Ex. "Debate got fairly heated, and the circuit judge said there was nothing worse than two women arguing. It gets better because then the bailiff commented, 'Meow.' "

(2) *Demeaning Sexual Innuendo*

Ex. "One of my co-counsel is my partner, who happens also to be my husband, and the judge came up to us and said, 'You know, with all this security here, I got to tell you, Mister, I sure would like to body search your wife.' "

(3) *Verbal Condescension to Gain a Tactical Advantage*

Ex. "In the middle of the argument, opposing counsel stands up and says 'Who is this girl? I mean, where is your card? Let me see your business card.' "

(4) *Non-Verbal Condescension or Rejection*

Ex. One woman attorney walked up to five chatting male attorneys, perhaps on the same case, and started talking to them only to have them turn their backs on her, continuing to talk to each other, while ignoring her completely.

(5) *Unequal Treatment*

Ex. "It has been my experience that male attorneys will interrupt me and raise their voices to drown me out during hearings and depositions with alarming frequency, requiring me to stop talking until they have finished and then inquire if I may be heard."

---

6. [Rule 4–8.4(d) of the Florida Rules of Professional Conduct (1994) provides:]

A lawyer shall not: * * * (d) engage in conduct in connection with the practice of law that is prejudicial to the administration of justice, including to knowingly, or through callous indifference, disparage, humiliate, or discriminate against litigants, jurors, witnesses, court personnel, or other lawyers on any basis, including, but not limited to, on account of race, ethnicity, gender, religion, national origin, disability, marital status, sexual orientation, age, socioeconomic status, employment, or physical characteristic.

(6) *Mistreatment Based on Allegedly Inappropriate Role Behavior*

Ex. Assertive advocacy by women is frowned upon, despite a mandate to do so to represent your client effectively. This puts the woman in a catch–22 situation. "If I'm not aggressive, then you say I'm too timid. If I'm aggressive, you say I'm a bitch."

(7) *Refusing to Recognize Female Authority*

Ex. 1. Acting surprised that a woman is actually an attorney.

Ex. 2. A judge asking a male lawyer, "Are you going to let *her* argue this motion?"

Ex. 3. Using first names of women but last names of men.

(8) *Ostracizing Women Who Complain Publicly About These Matters*

(9) *Employment-Related Issues*

> (1) Glass ceilings;
>
> (2) Disparate salaries and partnership shares;
>
> (3) Fewer opportunities to generate clients and fees.

(10) *Silencing*

Ex. Cutting off female attorneys and objecting to their questions and conduct but doing neither for male attorneys.

B. Treatment of Female Witnesses and Litigants

(1) Making women cry; pushing them until they do.

(2) According female witnesses' claims lesser credibility by virtue of their being female.

2. Race and Ethnicity

Concerns about racial and ethnic bias and discrimination often track those for gender. Examples include concerns about condescension, silencing and treating attorneys as less credible primarily because of their race. A concern that was greater for race than for gender, however, was overt slurs and insults.

Ex. 1. A Colorado case in which a deputy district attorney prosecuting two Hispanic males said to their defense counsel, "I don't believe either of those chili-eating bastards."

Ex. 2. One lawyer said to another, in the course of a stream of obscenities and invectives, "I see you are turning black again."

* * *

[H]ate speech, whether by lawyers or others, is a "psychic assault." Its impact is powerfully summarized by Mari Matsuda:

> As much as one may try to resist a piece of hate propaganda, the effect on one's self-esteem and sense of personal security is devastating. To be hated, despised, and alone is the ultimate fear of all human beings. However irrational racist speech may be, it hits right at the

emotional place where we feel the most pain. The aloneness comes not only from the hate message itself, but also from the government response of tolerance. When hundreds of police officers are called out to protect racist marchers, when the courts refuse redress for racial insult, and when racist attacks are officially dismissed as pranks, the victim becomes a stateless person. Target-group members must either identify with a community that promotes racist speech or admit that the community does not include them.[7] * * *

A consistent message in recent articles and reports is the necessity of avoiding bias as a general matter. Prejudice and bias are forms of disrespect, and undermine our legal system. [*See* Marsha S. Stern, *Courting Justice: Addressing Gender Bias in the Judicial System*, 1996 Ann. Surv. Am. L. 1.] Accordingly, lawyers and judges must also be aware of the potential for prejudice and bias more generally, including such area as bias on the basis of obesity or rural location. [*See* Debra Lyn Bassett, *Ruralism*, 88 Iowa L. Rev. 273 (2003); Adam Benforado, Jon Hanson & David Yosifon, *Broken Scales: Obesity and Justice in America*, 53 Emory L.J. 1645 (2004).]

MULTIPLE CHOICE QUESTIONS

Answer these questions using the definitions found at the end of Chapter Two.

1. Several associates from the mid-size law firm of Harrison & Malloy went out together for dinner at a local restaurant. During the course of the dinner, two members of the group confided that they were quite put off by the behavior of a male colleague, which they characterized as effeminate and as indicative of homosexuality.

A. The First Amendment protects the associates' comments.

B. Although the associates' comments reflect bias, under these circumstances the Model Rules contain no prohibition.

C. The associates' comments reflect bias and therefore the associates are subject to discipline.

D. The associates' comments do not reflect bias because they are entitled to their personal opinions.

2. Matthew Fontaine is confined to a wheelchair as the result of an automobile accident ten years ago. He practices law as a sole practitioner. Although Matthew generally handles non-litigation matters, he was per-

---

7. Mari J. Matsuda, *Public Response to Racist Speech: Considering the Victim's Story*, in WORDS THAT WOUND: CRITICAL RACE THEORY, ASSAULTIVE SPEECH, AND THE FIRST AMENDMENT 17, 25 (1993).

suaded to accept a litigation case to help "a friend of a friend." In the course of trial, Matthew asked to approach the bench in order to discuss a matter of some confidence. Due to the height of the bench, and Matthew's inability to stand, Matthew asked the judge to come around to the front of the bench in order to maintain the confidentiality of the discussion. The judge refused, and stated, "This is my court. If you people insist on practicing law, you have to deal with life's realities instead of asking for special favors."

A. The judge's response was appropriate.

B. The judge's response was inappropriate because he was required to accommodate Matthew's request.

C. The judge's response reflects bias and he is potentially subject to discipline.

D. The judge's response does not reflect bias but he should have sought some means of preserving confidentiality.

3. Charles Howard is a partner with a large international law firm. Charles finds one of his new clients, Tiffany Green, very attractive. Charles has been flirting with Tiffany and has asked her out to lunch and dinner on several occasions.

A. Charles's personal life is his business; a lawyer's personal life is not regulated by the Model Rules.

B. Charles has not yet violated the Model Rules, but his firm may prohibit its lawyers from dating clients.

C. The Model Rules prohibit lawyers from dating clients and therefore Charles is subject to discipline.

D. The Model Rules permit relationships between lawyers and clients so long as the relationship is consensual and no prejudice would result to the client.

4. Aaron Campbell is representing Bradley Whitehouse in a civil lawsuit in which Whitehouse allegedly wrongfully terminated the employment of Brenda Gale, who had been Whitehouse's housekeeper. Gale alleges she was fired after rebuffing Whitehouse's sexual advances. Whitehouse is a prominent, wealthy businessman. At trial, Campbell questioned Gale repeatedly about her sexual orientation, suggesting that Gale was a lesbian who filed the lawsuit as an opportunistic attempt to extort damages from Whitehouse. Campbell's line of questioning stemmed from his observation that Gale was 31, never married, and unattractive.

A. Campbell was required to provide a defense for his client, so he cannot be *subject to discipline*.

B. Although offensive, nothing in the ABA Model Rules prohibits such tactics.

C. Only the judge presiding over the trial has any obligation to address bias occurring in the courtroom.

D. Campbell is *subject to discipline.*

Answers to the multiple choice questions will be found in the Appendix at the end of the book.

CHAPTER ELEVEN

CONFLICTS OF INTEREST—LAWYERS, CLIENTS, AND THIRD PARTIES

■ ■ ■

What This Chapter Covers

Reading Assignment

Wydick, Perschbacher, & Bassett, Chapter 11.

ABA Model Rules:

Rules 1.2, 1.7, 1.8, 1.10, 1.13, 1.14, 1.18, 2.1, 3.7, and 5.4(c).

CRPC 1–600, 3–120, 3–300, 3–310, 3–320, 3–600, 4–210, 4–300, 4–400 and 5–210.

Cal.Bus. & Prof.Code § 6106.8.

Supplemental Reading

Hazard & Hodes:

Discussion of ABA Model Rules 1.2, 1.7, 1.8, 1.10, 1.13, 1.14, 2.1, 3.7, and 5.4(c).

Restatement (Third) of the Law Governing Lawyers §§ 15–16, 20–23, 26–27, 36; 43; 121–124, 125–127, 131, 134–135 (2000).

Discussion Problems

1. Attorney Wharton's law practice consists primarily of insurance defense work. Hamilton Casualty Co. has hired her to defend Silas Combs in a negligence case. The plaintiff in the case alleges that Combs' rice field was plowed negligently, so as to cause a large quantity of water to escape into plaintiff's adjoining tomato field. The water caused plaintiff's tomatoes to rot before harvest. Plaintiff's complaint demands $125,000 in damages. Combs' insurance policy with Hamilton Casualty has a top liability limit of $100,000. After extensive discovery, the case was set for trial. Six weeks before the trial date, plaintiff's lawyer called Wharton and offered to settle the case for $90,000. What are Wharton's ethical obligations in this situation?

2. Regulations adopted pursuant to the Sarbanes–Oxley Act can be found at 17 C.F.R. Part 205. These regulations impose a mandatory reporting duty to the client's chief legal officer or chief executive officer when a securities lawyer becomes aware of credible evidence that the client is materially violating a federal or state securities law. The CLO must investigate and report back to the securities lawyer. If the securities lawyer believes that the CLO did not achieve an appropriate response from the client, the securities lawyer must report the evidence to the board of directors, the audit committee of the board, or the outside directors. Moreover, the regulations define "securities lawyer" broadly. Not only do these regulations apply to lawyers who represent a securities issuer before the Securities and Exchange Commission, and lawyers who transact business with, or communicate with, the SEC. The regulations also apply to lawyers who give advice about a document that will be filed with the SEC, or who give advice about whether information must be filed with the SEC. For example, a company might ask the litigator who is defending it in a products liability case to write an opinion about the company's potential exposure in the case. If the litigator realizes that the opinion letter will go into the company's stock prospectus, the litigator has become a "securities lawyer." How do these provisions compare with ABA Model Rule 1.13? [*See generally* Fred C. Zacharias, *Coercing Clients: Can Lawyer Gatekeeper Rules Work?*, 47 B.C. L.Rev. 455 (2006).]

3. After attorney Sarah graduated from law school, she opened her own law office in a small seaside village. She longs for a cottage on the beach, but she has been unable to find one at the right price. Client Willis has retained her to help him find a way out of his financial distress. Among his few solid assets is a lovely cottage on a secluded end of the beach. Willis has been unable to pay the taxes on the cottage, and Sarah has advised him to put it up for public auction.

a. At the auction, may Sarah have her brother bid for her as undisclosed principal?

b. Suppose, instead, that Sarah simply agrees to buy the cottage directly from Willis, subject to the tax debt. Under what, if any, circumstances would that be proper?

c. Suppose, instead, that Sarah agrees to lend Willis enough money to pay off the back taxes on his cottage. Under what, if any, circumstances would that be proper?

4. Jefferson and Herchberger are involved in a boundary line suit concerning twelve acres of land that lies in a valley between their two farms. Lawyer Lennihan represents Herchberger in the suit.

a. May Lennihan purchase from Jefferson a 30% interest in that twelve acres?

b. May Lennihan purchase from Herchberger a 30% interest in that twelve acres?

c. May Lennihan agree with Herchberger to do the legal work in exchange for a 30% interest in that twelve acres if Herchberger wins the suit?

5. Client Curt hired attorney Annette to advise him during some difficult business negotiations with Danforth Corporation. The negotiations extended over many months; during that time, Annette developed a good working relationship with Curt and a thorough understanding of the factual and legal problems at hand. Only four people were present at the negotiating sessions: Curt, Annette, Danforth's vice-president, and Danforth's house counsel. Ultimately the negotiations failed, and Danforth sued Curt. A key contested issue at trial will be whether Curt made a certain statement during one of the negotiating sessions. Curt wants Annette to represent him at trial, but Danforth has moved to disqualify her on the ground that she may have to testify about Curt's making the alleged statement.

a. Should the court grant the motion to disqualify?

b. May Annette's law partner, Elmwood, serve as Curt's trial lawyer?

c. Does your answer to either question depend on whether Annette's testimony would be for Curt or against Curt?

6. For many years, attorney Alice has looked after the legal and financial affairs of her client Chadbourne, an aged widower. Chadbourne has asked Alice to prepare a new will for him, but he does not know whom to name as executor. He does not want an institutional executor, and he has no suitable friends or relatives.

a. May Alice suggest herself as executrix?

b. May Alice accept as thanks for all her kindness to Chadbourne over the years a modest picture frame she has admired when visiting Chadbourne's townhome?

c. May Alice accept Chadbourne's valuable townhome if given to her as a gift? What if it is left to her in Chadbourne's will?

7. The law firm of Shubert, DeWitt, & Howe specializes in family law matters. The firm has three partners and four associate lawyers.

a. Partner Rhonda Howe is representing client Curt Callen in a pending dissolution of marriage proceeding. Howe's own marriage was recently dissolved, so she is especially sympathetic to Callen's situation. On several occasions, she and Callen have discussed Callen's legal problems over long dinners. Howe now finds herself quite attracted to Callen as a person, and she believes the attraction is mutual. What advice would you give Howe in this situation?

b. Partner Shubert has been asked to represent client Cummings in a child custody dispute with Cummings' ex-husband. The ex-husband is represented by attorney Arnott, a partner in a different law firm. Arnott and Shubert are engaged to be married in the near future. Shubert believes that Cummings' matter could be handled adequately by the senior associate in Shubert's firm. What advice would you give Shubert in this situation?

ALLOCATING DECISION-MAKING BETWEEN LAWYER AND CLIENT

Under the traditional understanding of the lawyer-client relationship, the respective roles of lawyer and client are easy to state, but difficult to apply. The primary relationship is that of agent and principal, but the lawyer-agent's professional obligations require adjustment of the conventional agency relationship. Here is a statement of the more-or-less standard view from the California Supreme Court:

> The allocation of decision-making authority between client and attorney is a difficult problem. It involves practical, ethical and philosophical considerations. (See Burt, Conflict and Trust Between Attorney and Client (1981) *69 Georgetown L.J. 1015;* Note, Balancing Competing Discovery Interests in the Context of the Attorney–Client Relationship: A Trilemma (1983) *56 So.Cal.L.Rev. 1115*; Martyn, Informed Consent in the Practice of Law (1980) *48 Geo.Wash.L.Rev. 307;* Spiegel, Lawyering and Client Decisionmaking: Informed Consent and the Legal Profession (1979) *128 U.Pa.L.Rev. 41;* Spiegel, The New Model Rules of Professional Conduct: Lawyer–Client Decision Making and the Role of Rules in Structuring the Lawyer–Client Dialogue, 1980 *Am.Bar Found. Research J.* 1003; Lehman, The Pursuit of a Client's Interest (1979) *77 Mich.L.Rev. 1078.*) Clear guidance on the scope of an attorney's implied and apparent authority and the legal consequences of the allocation of that authority would benefit both attorneys and clients. Unfortunately, the majority fail to give any guidance.

> A reading of the cases and authorities reveals that when courts refer to "substantial rights," they mean important or "essential" rights, rights " 'affecting the merits of the cause' " or "serious steps" in the litigation. For example, the decision to settle or dismiss a cause of action affects a "substantial right," and an attorney must obtain the client's consent before taking either action. Similarly, because a "substantial right" is affected, an attorney has no independent authority to waive the right to appeal, to eliminate an essential defense, to dispose of a client's property, or to stipulate to a finding of negligence irrespective of the record.
>
> When no substantial right is implicated, an attorney must be free to act independently. It is essential to the efficient conduct of the client's case and the accomplishment of the client's ultimate goals that an attorney have the authority to make independent decisions in the day-to-day management of civil litigation. This authority "[allows] the lawyer-professional to apply his technical expertise[.]" (Spiegel, The New Model Rules of Professional Conduct: Lawyer–Client Decision Making and the Role of Rules in Structuring the Lawyer–Client Dialogue, supra, Am.Bar Found. Research J. at p. 1004.) It also protects the lawyer's professional reputation and preserves the lawyer's role as an officer of the court.
>
> The effective management of litigation requires independent decisions by the attorney regarding not only procedural matters but also certain substantive matters—for example, it may include the legal theories or arguments to be advanced. Routine and technical matters, including those ordinary matters which arise in the course of litigation, may be handled independently by the attorney as a necessary aspect of the professional management of the case. On the other hand, decisions which affect "substantial rights," whether they be denominated "procedural" or "substantive," must involve the client.
>
> Rather than define the standard as "substantial rights" versus "procedural matters," the inquiry should seek to differentiate between decisions affecting important, substantial rights and decisions on routine matters. This approach would provide the practitioner with more useful guidance.

Blanton v. Womancare, Inc., 38 Cal.3d 396, 409–10, 212 Cal.Rptr. 151, 159–60, 696 P.2d 645, 653–55 (1985) (Bird, C.J., concurring).

Self-consciously adopting a "middle view" between the traditional view that a client puts affairs in the lawyer's hands, who then does what the lawyer believes will best advance the client's interests and a client-centered view that treats the lawyer as servant of the client, the Restatement also endorses a view "that the client defines the goals of the representation and the lawyer implements them, but that each consults with the other." [*Introductory Note* to § 20, RESTATEMENT (THIRD) OF THE LAW GOVERNING LAWYERS (2000).] Under this view, except for certain matters reserved for the client or for the lawyer to decide, the allocation of authority between the lawyer and client is itself subject to consultation and agreement between lawyer and client.

Applying these rules becomes even more complicated when the identity of the client is elusive or when more than one representative claims to speak for the client. In this chapter we first take up the problem of conflicts between directions from the client and from others who may purport to speak for the client or represent the "true" interests of the client. We next take up the issue of determining just who is the client. Finally, the chapter deals with conflicts between the interests of the client and those of the client's own lawyer.

EMPLOYERS INSURANCE OF WAUSAU v. ALBERT D. SEENO CONSTRUCTION CO.

United States District Court, N.D.California, 1988.
692 F.Supp. 1150.

[Plaintiff, Employers Insurance of Wausau ("Wausau"), issued various insurance policies to defendant, Albert D. Seeno Construction Company ("Seeno"), a real estate developer, in connection with Seeno's construction of a large number of homes. Buyers of several hundred Seeno homes brought claims against Seeno for construction defects. After Seeno submitted the claims to Wausau, Wausau and Seeno disagreed over whether the claims were covered by Wausau's policies. Wausau reserved its rights to deny coverage, and Seeno exercised its rights to obtain independent *Cumis* counsel paid for by Wausau.[b] After further disagreements arose, Wausau brought this action, seeking a declaration it is not liable for the third-party claims. Wausau moved to disqualify Seeno's counsel, Archer; and Seeno cross-moved to disqualify Wausau's primary counsel, Robins.]

* * *

I. CROSS-MOTIONS TO DISQUALIFY UNDER CUMIS

Both parties bring motions to disqualify based on alleged breaches of the duties of counsel in the *Cumis* context, i.e., where the insured has exercised its right to select independent counsel paid for by the insurer because a conflict or potential conflict has arisen between the insurer and the insured. In brief, the insurer Wausau argues that the insured Seeno's choice of *Cumis* counsel, the Archer firm, has failed properly to represent Wausau's interests. Seeno, on the other hand, argues that the counsel chosen by Wausau, the Robins firm, has failed properly to represent Seeno's interests.

A. *Wausau's Motion to Disqualify the Archer Firm*

Plaintiff's first argument for disqualification of Seeno's counsel Archer is based on that firm's conceded double role as 1) *Cumis* counsel

b. *See, e.g., San Diego Navy Federal Credit Union v. Cumis Ins. Society, Inc.,* 162 Cal.App.3d 358, 208 Cal.Rptr. 494 (1984) (clearly establishing insured's right to select independent counsel paid for by insurer where an actual or potential conflict has arisen between insured and insurer); * * *.

opposing liability in the underlying home buyers' claims, and 2) counsel asserting coverage by Wausau.[c] Plaintiff argues that in its *Cumis* counsel role Archer is representing Wausau as well as Seeno, and that it is therefore an improper concurrent representation of adverse interests for Archer to represent Seeno in a coverage dispute such as the instant case, where Seeno's interests are directly adverse to Wausau.[d]

Plaintiff relies chiefly on cases stating that counsel retained by an insurer to defend an insured have both the insured and the insurer as clients. *E.g., Bogard v. Employers Casualty Co.,* 164 Cal.App.3d 602, 609, 210 Cal.Rptr. 578 (1985) ("The attorney hired by the insurance company to defend in an action against the insured owes fiduciary duties to two clients: the insurer and the insured." (citations omitted)). Wausau argues that the *Cumis* line of decisions has not changed the dual duties of liability defense counsel; it simply allows the insured rather than the insurer to select such counsel. *Cumis* counsel thus always represents both the insured and the insurer.

Wausau views *Cumis* counsel as properly concerned only with minimizing liability to third parties, and as necessarily completely *neutral* with respect to any coverage dispute between its two clients, the insured and the insurer. Accordingly, Wausau asserts that *Cumis* counsel is "independent" not of the insurer but rather in the sense that such counsel seeks to minimize liability in a neutral fashion, independent of any regard for the coverage position of either client. According to this argument, as *Cumis* counsel chosen by Seeno, Archer represents Wausau as well as the insured, and it is therefore a patent conflict for Archer also to represent Seeno's interests against Wausau in this coverage action.

* * *

In *Cumis,* the California Court of Appeal recognized that:

> In the usual tripartite relationship existing between insurer, insured and counsel, there is a single, common interest shared among them. Dual representation by counsel is beneficial since the shared goal of

---

c. For clarity, the Court shall use the term "liability" to refer to the potential liability of the insured or the insurer to a third party, and the term "coverage" to refer to the potential liability of the insurer to the insured, unless otherwise indicated.

d. The following are the most pertinent California Rules in this regard:

Rule 4–101. Accepting Employment Adverse to a Client

A member of the State Bar shall not accept employment adverse to a client or former client, without the informed and written consent of the client or former client, relating to a matter in reference to which he has obtained confidential information by reason of or in the course of his employment by such client or former client.

Rule 5–102. Avoiding the Representation of Adverse Interests

(A) A member of the State Bar shall not accept professional employment without first disclosing his relation, if any, with the adverse party, and his interest, if any, in the subject matter of the employment. A member of the State Bar who accepts employment under this rule shall first obtain the client's written consent to such employment.

(B) A member of the State Bar shall not represent conflicting interests, except with the written consent of all parties concerned.

[For current California versions, *see* CRPC 3–310—Eds.]

> minimizing or eliminating liability to a third party is the same. A different situation is presented, however, when some or all of the allegations in the [third-party] complaint do not fall within the scope of coverage under the policy. In such a case, the standard practice of an insurer is to defend under a reservation of rights where the insurer promises to defend but states it may not indemnify the insured if liability is found.

Id. at 364, 208 Cal.Rptr. 494.

In such situations, the court found, a conflict arises between the insurer and the insured, because it is in the insurer's interest for the third-party action to establish that any liability is outside the coverage of the policy, while it is in the insured's interest to show the opposite. After reviewing the ethical dilemma posed for counsel in this conflict situation, the *Cumis* court held that:

> [T]he [Model Code] Canons of Ethics impose upon lawyers hired by the insurer an obligation to explain to the insured and the insurer the full implications of joint representation in situations where the insurer has reserved its rights to deny coverage. If the insured does not give an informed consent to continued representation, counsel must cease to represent both. Moreover, * * * the insurer must pay the reasonable cost for hiring independent counsel by the insured. The insurer may not compel the insured to surrender control of the litigation.

162 Cal.App.3d at 375, 208 Cal.Rptr. 494 (citations omitted).

* * *

Plaintiff Wausau does not challenge *Cumis* itself and indeed concedes the right and has paid the considerable cost of defendant Seeno to be provided with *Cumis* counsel to defend many of the home buyers' claims. However, Wausau asserts that because the Archer firm is *Cumis* liability counsel, it is impermissible conflict for Archer to serve also as Seeno's coverage counsel. This argument thus requires that the Court determine whether *Cumis* counsel represent or owe duties to the insurer such that *Cumis* counsel cannot represent the insured in coverage disputes with the insurer.

The starting point for determining to whom *Cumis* counsel owe what duties is the seminal California case *Executive Aviation, Inc. v. National Ins. Underwriters,* 16 Cal.App.3d 799, 94 Cal.Rptr. 347 (1971). In finding that an insurer was obligated to pay for the fees of independent counsel selected by the insured, the court followed the "reasonable solution" proposed in *Prashker v. United States Guarantee Co.,* 1 N.Y.2d 584, 154 N.Y.S.2d 910, 136 N.E.2d 871 (1956), stating that:

> [W]here a conflict of interest has arisen between an insurer and its insured, the attorney to defend the insured in the tort suit should be selected by the insured and the reasonable value of the professional services rendered assumed by the insurer. If the insured and the

> insurer are represented by two different attorneys, each of whom is pledged to promote and protect the prime interests of his client, adequate representation is guaranteed and the deleterious effect of the conflict of interest imposed on an attorney who attempts the difficult task of representing both parties is averted.

Executive Aviation, 16 Cal.App.3d at 809, 94 Cal.Rptr. 347. Like the New York Court of Appeals in *Prashker,* the *Executive Aviation* court thus appears to have assumed that *Cumis* counsel would represent only the insured, and that the insurer would be entitled to counsel that would represent only the insurer.

Similarly, the *Cumis* court itself contemplated that being "the insureds' *independent* counsel" meant representing the insureds, and being independent of the insurer. *Cumis,* 162 Cal.App.3d at 375, 208 Cal.Rptr. 494 (emphasis added). Thus, the court quoted with approval statements such as:

> "Where a question exists as to whether an occurrence is within coverage, independent counsel *representing the insured's interests* is required. The insurer is contractually obligated to pay for *insured's independent counsel.*"

Id. at 374, 208 Cal.Rptr. 494 (quoting Dondanville, *Defense Counsel Beware: The Perils of Conflicts of Interest,* 26 Trial Law.Guide 408, 415 (1982)) (emphasis added). Nor does the *Cumis* court appear to have believed that it is ethically possible to continue joint representation without consent once conflict has arisen. To take another example quoted by the court: " 'once the insurer decides to assert a coverage defense, the same attorney may not represent both the insured and the insurer.' " *Id.* (quoting Committee on Professional Responsibility of the State Bar of Louisiana Opinion No. 342, 22 La.B.J. O–132 [within insert following page 46] (1974)). Indeed, it was precisely because "dual agency" representation is ethically impossible that the *Cumis* court required the insurer to pay for independent counsel for the insureds. *Id.* at 364–65 & n. 4, 374–75, 208 Cal.Rptr. 494. Since the attorney initially chosen by the insurer cannot ethically serve in both such capacities, the same logic requires the conclusion that the *Cumis* attorney for the insured may not either.

Other cases support the same conclusion.[e] For example, in *Bogard,* the court of appeal clearly recognized that *Cumis* counsel is hired to fulfill

---

e. Wausau's attempt to rely on *MGIC Indemnity Corp. v. Weisman,* 803 F.2d 500 (9th Cir.1986), is not compelling, although that case does contain the following broad language:

> When [counsel] took the defense of the suits against the [insureds], the [insureds] were their clients. But it is an untenable simplification to say that they had no duty to the [insurer] they knew would pay the legal fees of the [insureds]. A lawyer may have more than a single client in a lawsuit. A "client" is the person or entity on whose behalf a lawyer acts. [Counsel] were acting for the insurer as well as for the insured[s] * * *.
>
> * * * Anyone paying legal bills would want to know, and would be entitled to know, that the lawyers being paid were the very lawyers who started the suits they were now being compensated to defend. The alleged failure to disclose their activity would have been a breach of the fiduciary duty [counsel] owed [the insurer].

Id. at 504. * * *

the insurer's duty to provide "independent counsel to represent the *insured's* interests" in order to avoid "the impossible ethical dilemma with which the attorney representing both insured and insurer in such a [conflict] situation is faced." *Bogard,* 164 Cal.App.3d at 613, 210 Cal.Rptr. 578 (emphasis added); *see also id.* at 614, 210 Cal.Rptr. 578. Likewise in *United Pacific Ins. Co. v. Hall,* 199 Cal.App.3d 551, 245 Cal.Rptr. 99 (1988), the court had no doubt that "[t]he obligation of an insurer to provide independent *Cumis* counsel for an insured is premised on the ethical inability of an attorney to represent conflicting interests." *Id.* at 556, 245 Cal.Rptr. 99 (citation omitted). Nor has the Court discovered any case holding that *Cumis* counsel are somehow exempted from the ethical rules that make it impossible to represent conflicting interests without consent.

Case law thus leaves little doubt that *Cumis* counsel represent solely the insured, and accordingly that there is no ethical requirement that prevents *Cumis* counsel from representing the insured in coverage actions adverse to the insurer as well as in liability matters.[f]

* * *

At least one other factor indicates that Wausau's view of the role of *Cumis* counsel is unlikely to be accepted in California. The *Cumis* line of cases evolved out of express concern that counsel representing the insurer as well as the insured might prejudice the insured's coverage and liability positions by favoring the insurer's coverage position. *See, e.g., Cumis,* 162 Cal.App.3d at 364, 208 Cal.Rptr. 494 ("'The [insurance] Carrier is required to hire independent counsel because an attorney in actual trial would be tempted to develop the facts to help his real client, the Carrier Company, as opposed to the Insured, for whom he will never likely work again. * * * A lawyer who does not look out for the Carrier's best interest might soon find himself out of work.'" (quoting trial court opinion)). Given the nature of this problem and the courts' determination to allevi-

* * *

[I]t would certainly be "an untenable simplification," *MGIC,* 803 F.2d at 504, to read *MGIC* as holding that one who pays a lawyer's fee always becomes a client or that the lawyer automatically owes such a person duties of loyalty and candor. *See, e.g., Cumis,* 162 Cal.App.3d 358, 208 Cal.Rptr. 494; Model Code Ethical Canons ("EC") 5–1, 5–21 to 5–23; Model Code Disciplinary Rule ("DR") 5–107(A)–(B); Los Angeles Bar Association Ethics Committee Opinion No. 439 (February 24, 1986) [hereinafter Bar Opinion No. 439] at 5–6.

* * *

f. The Court also notes that an opinion of the Los Angeles Bar Association Ethics Committee on facts quite similar to those in this case has reached the same result, stating that:

> The clear implication of [*Cumis*] is that there is no attorney-client relationship between the insured's counsel and the insurer despite the fact that the insurer is paying for the independent counsel * * *.
>
> * * * Moreover *Cumis* holds that such an attorney[-]client relationship is impossible.

Bar Opinion No. 439 at 5–6. The committee therefore found it entirely proper for *Cumis* counsel representing the insured in a third-party action to represent the insured in the coverage case against the insurer as well. *See id.* at 6.

However, it should be obvious that this conclusion in no way suggests that the insurer is answerable for the cost of the insured's counsel's work in coverage actions; that expense of course must ordinarily be borne by the insured.

ate it, it seems highly unlikely that the *Cumis* line of decisions or the legislature's codification of it meant to allow the essential nature of the joint representation to remain the same, and merely to allow the insured rather than the insurer to make the initial selection of the counsel that would represent both of them. Rather, the Court believes that the *Cumis* decisions intended to eliminate the ethical dilemmas and temptations that arise along with conflict in joint representations, and that they accomplished this through mandating the insured's right to *Cumis* counsel that represent only the insured.

This is not to say, however, that *Cumis* counsel necessarily owe *no* duties to the insurer. The Court simply holds that any such duties do not as a matter of law create an attorney-client relationship between *Cumis* counsel and the insurer or otherwise make *Cumis* counsel vulnerable to disqualification at the instance of the insurer. The Court accordingly concludes that *Cumis* counsel do not as a matter of law have a relationship with the insurer that precludes such counsel from representing the insured in coverage disputes adverse to the insurer. Plaintiff has not shown that in law or fact the Archer firm has represented Wausau's interests, and it therefore cannot be concluded that Archer has breached the ethical strictures against representation of adverse interests. Plaintiff's first argument to disqualify the Archer firm is unavailing.

[The court also denied Seeno's motion to disqualify Wausau's counsel, finding Wausau's primary counsel did not represent Seeno either as a matter of law or as a matter of fact. Finally, the court denied Wausau's motion to disqualify Seeno's counsel based on the ground that a lawyer who had previously represented Wausau was now a partner in the Archer firm that represented Seeno. The court found grounds for the disqualification, but denied the motion because Wausau's counsel delayed in bringing it.]

ETHICS IN THE PRACTICE OF LAW

Geoffrey C. Hazard, Jr., 43–44, 46, 48–52.
(Yale University Press, 1978).*

The lawyer's professional responsibilities may not end with concern for his client, but clearly they start there. Confidential information is a secret if it relates to a client, valuable evidence if it relates to someone else. Conflict with the client must be avoided, conflict with everyone else is what a lawyer is retained to handle. How far a lawyer is prepared to go in partisan aggressiveness is the measure of what he will do, at the same time, for a client and to other people. Identifying the client is thus critical in the lawyer's orientation to "relevant others" and in their orientation to him.

In the traditional lore of the legal profession, identifying the client is not a problem. The client is the troubled fellow who walks into the office, papers in hand, wanting someone to help him in a legal matter. If all real world lawyer-client relationships began this way and involved nothing else, the question of client identity would always be answered before the relationship begins.

For the lawyer retained by an organization such as a corporation or government agency, identifying the client is much more complicated. Client identity is ambiguous, continuously problematic, and requires resolution by conscious choice. * * *

It is a problem that the Code of Responsibility simply evades. The Code says:

> A lawyer employed or retained by a corporation or similar entity owes his allegiance to the entity and not to a stockholder, director, officer, employee, representative, or other person connected with the entity.

The counterpart rule for government lawyers says it is the government that is the client. When the legal matter in question is between the organization and an outsider, these propositions are truisms—of course the client is the organization. When the legal matter poses a question within the corporation or the government, however, the "entity" referent provides no help. The unanswered question for the lawyer is: What individual should I treat as representing the organization so I can know whom to represent? Or, conversely: Whom should I decide to represent so I can know what individual to treat as the organization?

* * *

Corporate financial or legal crises * * * are directly the result of action or inaction by the corporation's officers and other employees working under their direction. Legal liability for the consequences begins with them, for the officers sometimes can be held personally liable to the corporation for getting it into trouble and may also be liable to outsiders, such as the government or creditors. If the derelictions are ones that the board of directors knew about, or should have known about if they had fulfilled their supervisory responsibility, the directors may be personally liable to the stockholders and to outsiders. The corporation itself is liable to third persons injured by the misconduct, such as victims of antitrust violations, but the existence and extent of its liability can depend on whether the conduct in question was "unauthorized," that is, violative of company policy. All these forms of potential liability increase if the conduct is persisted in and may take on an additional intentional quality if persisted in after counsel has appraised them to be wrongful. Furthermore, they may occasion not only damages liability but also criminal penalties and such sanctions as loss of license (for licensed industries) and delistment as an eligible contractor (for companies doing business with government agencies).

When a legal problem of this sort comes to the attention of the lawyer for the corporation, he has two issues to contend with. The first is how he should conduct himself apart from the question of client identity. * * *

Beyond this, the lawyer has to deal with the problem of identifying his client. The problem is difficult both morally and legally. The question has a moral aspect because the lawyer is faced with subordinating and perhaps seriously injuring the interest of a person who has trusted him in the past. * * * In the corporate setting, the individual can have been a business friend of long standing. When the heretofore client begins unburdening himself, he is only doing what the lawyer has encouraged him to do in the past. If the lawyer refuses to listen, he must appear to be violating a trusting relationship and to be abandoning a friendship. On the other hand, if the lawyer does listen, he can hear things that implicate not only the heretofore client but the organization that both of them are being paid to serve. And if the lawyer listens, he knows that the person before him supposes that the disclosure is confidential. If the lawyer is not certain that he can keep the disclosure confidential, his listening to it is the first step of what can turn out to be a betrayal of a confidence, and therefore a grave moral wrong.

In terms of the lawyer's legal obligations, the situation is equally complex. When the corporate officer begins talking, the lawyer must be mindful that a lawyer-client relationship is in the making. At this point, if the lawyer treats the corporate officer as the client, and if he learns things that may subject the officer to criminal or civil liability, the lawyer is bound by the rule of confidentiality not to disclose the matters to others, for example to the board of directors. But the lawyer's general retainer, if we may call it that, is to the corporation. The board will consider that it "is" the corporate client, and expect the lawyer eventually to advise the board what to do, including advice about the possibility of proceeding against the executive. The lawyer may find himself unable to do that without violating his professional duty to the executive. The board will then feel at least disappointed and very likely betrayed.

On the other hand, if the lawyer treats the executive as a nonclient, he must consider giving him some sort of "Miranda warning," that is, tell him that any disclosures he makes may have to be revealed to the board and perhaps to others. Giving a "Miranda warning" represents a decision by the lawyer that his client is the board of directors and not the officer. If such a warning is given, the lawyer will leave the executive in the lurch, perhaps requiring him to go elsewhere for legal advice and therewith drawing some kind of line between himself and the company he has been bound to serve.

* * *

The next stage of remove is the board of directors. Until it has received the bad news, the board most likely will have been highly supportive of—or perhaps dominated by—the officers whose conduct is immediately in question. The board may well be unreceptive to the lawyer's message unless it is solidly documented, but documentation may be lacking. If the lawyer does not disclose to the board what he knows, and the board "is" the corporation, then he is holding out on his client. If he does disclose, he may have betrayed what the executive thought was a confidence. Furthermore, when he takes the matter to the board he implicates the board members in the problem, because their responsibility and potential legal liability is affected by the extent of their knowledge. If they then take appropriate remedial action, their very action can alert potential adversaries of something afoot that may be the basis of legal action against the corporation. If they do not act, they may be regarded as having violated their duties to the stockholders and perhaps have become accomplices so far as concerns liability to outsiders. And so the lawyer may have to consider the stockholders as the "client."

* * *

PHILLIPS v. CARSON

Supreme Court of Kansas, 1987.
240 Kan. 462, 731 P.2d 820.

[Plaintiff Thelma Phillips sued attorney David Carson and his law firm for legal malpractice in connection with personal loans Carson obtained from Phillips. The lower court granted summary judgment against Carson. It also granted summary judgment in favor of Carson's law firm on the theory that Carson was not acting within the ordinary course of the firm's partnership business in connection with the personal loans he obtained from Phillips. The Supreme Court of Kansas affirmed the summary judgment against Carson and reversed the summary judgment in favor of the law firm.]

Mrs. Phillips and her husband, Robert L. Phillips, and Mr. and Mrs. Carson had been friends for several years prior to Mr. Phillips' death in 1978. Mrs. Phillips retained Carson and his law firm to handle the estate of her deceased husband. * * *

While the estate was pending, Mrs. Phillips paid fees totaling $80,000 to the firm. Carson told her that this fee was to take care of all of her legal business until the estate was closed. * * *

* * *

In August 1980, Carson told Mrs. Phillips that he was having financial problems, and Mrs. Phillips loaned him $200,000. Carson told her that she would be fully secured, and he gave her a note and a second mortgage on some Arizona property. These documents were properly executed and the mortgage was filed of record. In 1981, Phillips loaned Carson an additional $70,000. Because of his representations, she believed that this loan would get him over his current financial difficulties. She was concerned that he might harm himself, and she thought this loan would increase the chances that her first loan would be repaid. Later, Carson asked Mrs. Phillips to release her mortgage on the Arizona property so that he could refinance and sell that or another property. He offered her a mortgage on 90 acres he owned in Wyandotte County, and told Mrs. Phillips that this would put her in a better position. She relied upon

Carson's statement that she would be better secured and she trusted his advice as her attorney. On March 29, 1982, Mrs. Phillips released her mortgage on the Arizona property, and Carson gave her a new promissory note for $274,933.70, which included past due interest as principal. Carson also prepared and executed a mortgage on the Wyandotte County property to Mrs. Phillips, but he failed to file that mortgage with the Register of Deeds.

Carson at no time advised Mrs. Phillips to seek independent counsel regarding the loan transactions, and she did not discuss them with other partners of the Carson firm or with other counsel. In May 1982, Mrs. Phillips called Carson's office and learned that her mortgage had not been filed of record. She sought independent counsel, who secured the mortgage and filed it for record on July 23, 1982. Mrs. Phillips then demanded payment in full from Carson; it was not forthcoming. On September 10, 1982, Carson filed a Chapter 11 petition in the United States Bankruptcy Court. * * *

* * *

By her petition filed in this action, plaintiff claims that Carson, while acting as attorney for her and within the scope and course of the law partnership business and authority, and while acting in a fiduciary relationship towards her, negligently performed or failed to perform those legal duties entrusted to him to be performed on behalf of the plaintiff, listing some six allegedly negligent acts or omissions. These include negligently advising or failing to advise her of the legal nature, extent, and effect of the mortgage she was to receive, of the effect of her releasing the mortgage on the Arizona property, and of the extent of the superior liens on the Wyandotte County land; failing to timely draft the note and mortgage; failing to record the mortgage and perfect plaintiff's security interest; failing to fully advise her of the effect upon her of his financial consolidation; and filing his Chapter 11 petition which, under the circumstances, left her totally unsecured. She contends that a fiduciary relationship existed between Carson, the individual members of the firm, the partnership, and the plaintiff. She seeks actual damages of $274,933.70 plus accruing interest and costs.

* * *

[The Supreme Court rejected Carson's arguments that the summary judgment against him was improper. Though rarely granted in negligence cases, summary judgment is proper if there are no disputed issues of fact, and the Supreme Court agreed that there were none here.]

The Code of Professional Responsibility, by which attorneys in this state are governed, states:

"DR 5–104 *Limiting Business Relations with a Client.*"

(A) A lawyer shall not enter into a business transaction with a client if they have differing interests therein and if the client expects the lawyer to exercise his professional judgment therein for the protection of the client, unless the client has consented after full disclosure. 235 Kan. cxlvi.

A comment on this section of the Kansas Code of Professional Responsibility, pertinent here, is as follows:

> "It is not uncommon for attorneys to engage in business transactions with clients and other nonlawyers. Despite intentions to the contrary, members of the bar quite often use their legal knowledge or give advice on behalf of such joint efforts. In these situations courts are prone to find the existence of an attorney-client relationship upon the complaint of the lay party. The existence of retainer or fee charge is usually immaterial.
>
> * * *
>
> "An attorney who is confronted with the possibility of a joint business venture with a client is cautioned to consider the increased malpractice and ethical risks along with the financial considerations. In all such situations there should be a complete disclosure, and the client should be strongly urged to seek independent legal and other professional advice."

* * *

The trial court * * * found that Carson breached his professional duty to plaintiff by failing to advise her to secure outside independent legal and financial advice. * * * [That conclusion is] supported by the undisputed facts.

In *Ford v. Guarantee Abstract & Title Co.*, 220 Kan. 244, 553 P.2d 254 (1976), we summarized the duty of attorney to client * * *:

> "The relationship of an attorney to his client is fiduciary in character, binding the attorney to the highest degree of fidelity and good faith to his client on account of the trust and confidence imposed."
>
> "A fiduciary relation does not depend upon some technical relation created by, or defined in, law. It may exist under a variety of circumstances, and does exist in cases where there has been a special confidence reposed in one who, in equity and good conscience, is bound to act in good faith and with due regard to the interests of the one reposing the confidence."

Under the extensive factual record before us, we agree with the trial court that there existed an attorney and client relationship between Carson and Mrs. Phillips during the time that Carson secured loans from Mrs. Phillips, advised her or failed to advise her about them, and agreed to take care of preparing and filing all necessary documents in connection therewith. That relationship gave rise to the duty upon the attorney to properly, competently, and adequately counsel, advise, and represent the client. That duty was breached, not only in failing to file the final mortgage of record, but also in failing to advise Mrs. Phillips of the legal ramifications of the transaction, in failing to advise her of the legal consequences of the changes in security, in failing to recommend that she secure independent counsel, and in other ways pointed out by the trial court * * *. Finally, we agree with the trial court that Carson's extensive breaches of the Code of Professional Responsibility proximately caused injury to his client, and that she sustained substantial actual damages.

* * *

[The Supreme Court next considered the summary judgment granted in favor of Carson's law firm. The trial court ruled that Carson had clearly acted outside the scope of the partnership business in connection with the loans.]

The evidence here is clear that Carson and the partnership were representing Mrs. Phillips and were her attorneys for the primary purpose of probating the estate of her deceased husband. Additionally, the firm charged her a fee which was to cover not only the probate matter, but all other legal services she might require individually during the term of the probate. Additional legal services were provided for her * * * without additional charge.

Advising a client on the propriety of making loans, the legality and sufficiency of proposed security, the method of ascertaining the value of the security, the method of recording security documents and the like are all matters well within the scope of the general practice of law. Had Mrs. Phillips been considering a loan to a third person and had a member of the partnership advised her as Carson did (or as he failed to advise her), there would be little question of the firm's responsibility in the event that she sustained damages as a result of that action or omission. Similarly, the preparation of notes and mortgages, and the filing of mortgages for record, are matters well within the scope of the general practice of law handled daily by lawyers throughout this state.

* * *

Mrs. Phillips asserts that there is a factual question * * * regarding whether the transactions were apparently authorized by the partnership. She claims that it is the reasonable belief of the third party concerning the existence of apparent authority that is determinative. Certainly when a lawyer is consulting with a client on legal matters in the lawyer's office, the appearances to the client and the reasonable belief of the client are persuasive upon the issue. As the firm points out, however, the indication of authority must come from the principal. * * *

While in this case no partner in the firm told Phillips that Carson's actions were within his authority as a partner, no one told her that his actions were not within his authority as a member of the law firm. Two of the firm's employees, Doreen Benton and Judy Tranckino, did personal work for Mr. Carson, including preparation of the notes and mortgages herein. While Mrs. Phillips knew Mrs. Benton did personal work for Carson, no one told her that Benton's work on this project was not as a firm employee. The fact that Benton and Tranckino did personal work for Carson was known and not objected to by the other members of the law firm. Letters from Carson to Mrs. Phillips regarding this loan were on firm stationery and mailed in firm envelopes. Using firm supplies and personnel for personal business was apparently an acceptable practice within the firm. There was no firm policy prohibiting a partner from transacting business with a client, the only restriction regarding acceptance of a client being that a partner could not represent a client if doing so would cause a conflict with other clients of the firm. Whether Carson was apparently carrying on the usual business of the partnership, or whether his wrongful acts or omissions were in the usual course of business or with the authority of his partners * * * [are unresolved issues of material fact.]

The summary judgment entered by the trial court in favor of Thelma L. Phillips and against David W. Carson is affirmed. The summary judgment entered in behalf of the partnership * * * is reversed.

AAA PLUMBING POTTERY CORP. v. ST. PAUL INSURANCE CO. OF ILLINOIS

United States District Court, N.D. Illinois, 1995.
1995 WL 608548.

MEMORANDUM OPINION AND ORDER

PLUNKETT, DISTRICT JUDGE.

This matter is before us on defendant St. Paul Insurance Company of Illinois' ("St. Paul") motion for a protective order and to disqualify attorney Barry B. Gross ("Gross") from representing the plaintiffs, AAA Plumbing Pottery Corporation ("AAA") and its parent, Kokomo Sanitary Pottery Corporation ("Kokomo"), in this case. The plaintiffs have sued St. Paul for bad faith failure to settle a fraud action brought by Jerry D. Britton, which went to trial and resulted in a verdict against AAA in excess of $3,000,000. The current motion is based upon Gross' involvement in AAA's post-trial conduct and in settling the case following the verdict, all of which, St. Paul contends, make him a necessary witness whose testimony may be prejudicial to AAA. For the reasons set forth below, we grant the motion to disqualify Gross. In addition, St. Paul's request for a protective order is granted in part and denied in part.

BACKGROUND

I. The Workers Compensation Claims

[In two prior workers compensation actions brought by an AAA employee, Britton, AAA's insurance company, St. Paul, defended the actions on behalf of AAA. Around June 6, 1991, Britton's attorney proposed settling all of Britton's claims he might have against AAA for $200,000.] St. Paul rejected the demand, but, according to AAA, it never communicated the settlement offer to AAA.

St. Paul and AAA settled the workers compensation cases in November 1992 for $75,000.

II. The Britton Fraud Case

On June 7, 1991, Britton brought a civil action for fraud against AAA. Britton alleged that AAA had fraudulently induced him to return to work prematurely in June 1989 by misrepresenting that his doctor had approved his return to a specific job assignment, and that this conduct had led to his second back injury and permanent disability. Britton was again represented by Bohanan. [While St. Paul was named a defendant in this action, AAA, according to St. Paul, never filed an employer's liability claim under their insurance policy. AAA asserts that St. Paul rejected its demand for defense and coverage regarding the lawsuit.] In any event, AAA hired its own attorneys, the Alabama law firm of Henslee, Bradley & Robertson, P.C., to defend it in the Britton case.

On October 7, 1993, when the [Britton] trial was nearly over, AAA contacted William Gifford, a partner at Shefsky Froelich & Devine, Ltd. [a Chicago law firm] ("SF & D") asking for his advice regarding settlement of the case. After obtaining certain information regarding the lawsuit from AAA, Gifford consulted with Gross, a senior partner at SF & D, before advising AAA. Gross recommended that Gifford inquire about insurance coverage for the suit and that he advise AAA to follow the advice of its Alabama counsel with regard to settlement, as they were the most knowledgeable about the case. Gifford did so. Nonetheless, AAA refused to offer $100,000 to $125,000 to Britton, ignoring the advice of both SF & D and its Alabama attorneys, as well as the recommendation of the Alabama judge presiding over the trial. AAA instead offered only $50,000, which Britton rejected. The case went to the jury, which awarded Britton compensatory damages of $1,314,000 and punitive damages of $2,000,000.

III. After the Verdict

AAA filed a motion for judgment notwithstanding the verdict, or, alternatively, for a new trial or remittitur, which SF & D prepared, wholly or in part. [To support its claim that the punitive damage award was excessive, AAA claimed that the judgment was uninsured and paying it would put AAA out of business.]

After the verdict, SF & D also advised AAA to convey security interests, or mortgages, in virtually all of its fixed assets in favor of affiliated corporations, to protect those assets from attachment. AAA did so. Gifford's notes indicate that, apparently after the mortgages were recorded, two SF & D partners who worked on the security documents advised him that they could be considered fraudulent conveyances, but that Gross instructed him to go forward with them anyway. [The move left Britton unable to collect his judgment.]

[Britton's attorney] smelled a rat and promptly moved to set aside the mortgages as fraudulent conveyances. In addition, he pointed to the mortgages in his post-trial papers as one reason why the punitive damage award was proper. He also threatened to file another action against AAA on Britton's behalf, on the grounds that the mortgages were fraudulent conveyances and that AAA had allegedly failed to tender the Britton case to its insurers, leaving Britton unable to collect his judgment.

Although SF & D prepared the JNOV papers in the Britton case, it never obtained the Alabama court's permission to appear pro hac vice. Gifford explained at his deposition that AAA did not want the court and Britton to see that it was being represented by (and paying the fees of) a Chicago law firm at the same time it was claiming indigency regarding payment of the judgment, and his contemporaneous notes indicate that he was not to sit at counsel table or be introduced.

IV. The Britton Settlement

Before the post-trial motions were decided, AAA settled with Britton for $950,000, allegedly without St. Paul's knowledge. In return, Britton assigned his rights to the judgment, along with any claim he might have against St. Paul, to Kokomo [AAA's parent corporation].

[A provision in the settlement agreement specifically releasing two additional claims, including one based upon AAA's failure to tender the Britton case to St. Paul, was eventually deleted.] St. Paul suggests, based upon Gifford's deposition testimony, that Gross made the deletion. Its effect is that all of Britton's claims against AAA were lumped together under the terms of the settlement agreement, and there is no allocation among the claims, according to St. Paul. Moreover, AAA seeks in this action to hold St. Paul responsible for the full amount of the settlement agreement, despite the fact that these two claims clearly fall outside the provisions of the Policy.

As part of the settlement document, AAA and Kokomo executed a promissory note in favor of Britton, under which they agreed to pay him fifty percent of any recovery they obtain in this case, after payment of attorneys' fees.

V. This Lawsuit

In this case, AAA has sued St. Paul for bad faith in failing to communicate the June 6, 1991, settlement offer, alleging that it was denied any opportunity to independently settle Britton's claims against it (Count I). It also asserts a claim of negligence on the same facts (Count II). It further alleges that St. Paul breached the terms of the Policy because Britton's claim in the fraud case arose from his work-related injury in June 1989 (Count III). Kokomo asserts a claim on behalf of Britton for the $2,364,000 of the judgment which was not paid under the settlement agreement (Count IV).

St. Paul has filed a counterclaim, seeking a declaration that it did not engage in bad faith and has no obligation to indemnify AAA. It has also asserted as one of its affirmative defenses that the settlement of the

Britton case was made in bad faith, is collusive and fraudulent, unjustly enriched AAA and Kokomo, and violates public policy.

AAA and Kokomo are represented by SF & D. Gross is apparently the senior attorney responsible for this case, and he signed the complaint. Gifford is not participating in this action.

St. Paul has notified AAA and Kokomo of its intent to call Gross and Gifford as witnesses. Gifford has already been deposed, and at least some of SF & D's files relating to the Britton case have been produced. In bringing this motion, St. Paul originally sought to disqualify Gifford also, but, upon SF & D's representation that he is not participating in this case, it has withdrawn that request.

DISCUSSION

St. Paul contends that Gross' involvement in the Britton case makes him a necessary witness in this action. They argue that under Rule 3.7 of the Rules of Professional Conduct for the Northern District of Illinois, Gross must be disqualified from representing AAA in this case.

Rule 3.7 states, in pertinent part:

> (b) If a lawyer knows or reasonably should know that the lawyer may be called as a witness other than on behalf of the client, the lawyer may act as an advocate in a trial or evidentiary proceeding unless the lawyer knows or reasonably should know that the lawyer's testimony is or may be prejudicial to the client.

The court has the discretion to determine whether an attorney acting as an advocate may appear as a witness without withdrawing from the case. United States v. Morris, 714 F.2d 669, 671 (7th Cir.1983). In addition, the court may decide whether to permit an attorney to be called as a witness, and may forbid it "where evidence is easily available from other sources and absent 'extraordinary circumstances' or 'compelling reasons.'" United States v. Dack, 747 F.2d 1172, 1176 n. 5 (1984) (quoting United States v. Johnston, 690 F.2d 638, 644 (7th Cir.1982)).

St. Paul raises fifteen different factual issues on which it would ostensibly require Gross' testimony. We find most to be without merit or not to be "facts" at all. However, there are two related issues which give us pause. It is undisputed that Gross had a hand in drafting the settlement agreement, although there is substantial dispute between the parties as to how large his role was. Gross' timesheets for the early part of 1994 indicate that he made a number of entries for reviewing and revising the settlement document. The frequency of these entries indicate that his involvement was not merely that of a senior partner who does a quick review before a document is finalized. While others may have negotiated basic terms, such as the amount of money, it appears that Gross had a hand in structuring of the agreement. St. Paul has called the legitimacy of that settlement into question through its affirmative defenses. In the same vein, through discovery, St. Paul has obtained a draft of the settlement agreement in which Britton's release of his fraudulent conveyance and failure to tender claims against AAA was specifically mentioned. That provision was crossed out by hand on the draft, and the word "general" was written in the margin. The handwriting may be that of Gross. The claims based upon the fraudulent conveyances and the failure to tender are clearly beyond the scope of the Policy, yet AAA has sued St. Paul for the entire amount of the settlement. The fact that the release in the settlement agreement was intended to include those claims, the deletion of the specific mention of them, and the overall structure of the settlement agreement are issues upon which Gross' testimony is important. While others participated in negotiating and drafting that agreement, it is unlikely that they can testify as to Gross' precise role; he is the best source of that information. Moreover, they certainly could not testify as to Gross' reasoning and judgments; he is the only source of that information.[8]

Our inquiry does not stop there, for we must also determine whether Gross' testimony may be prejudicial to AAA. St. Paul obviously intends to use Gross' testimony to prove its affirmative defense that the settlement agreement was entered into in bad faith. Since the opposing party intends to use Gross' testimony to help prove its affirmative defense, Gross' testimony may well be prejudicial to AAA. There is sufficient likelihood of this that his disqualification is appropriate.

St. Paul has also made a brief argument that SF & D should be disqualified. It argues that under Rule 1.7(b), SF & D's representation of AAA and Kokomo would be materially limited by the firm's own interests. All of its arguments, however, go to Gross' conduct, or AAA's request in its complaint for the attorneys' fees it incurred in defending and settling the Britton case. SF & D can be disqualified only under Rule 1.10, which addresses imputed disqualifications. Under Rule 1.10(a), a firm may be disqualified only where one of its attorneys has an actual conflict of interest under Rules 1.7, 1.8(c), or 1.9. St. Paul has not established that Gross has a conflict of interest and cannot represent AAA under Rule 1.7(b); it has only established that Gross is a necessary witness and cannot appear as an advocate at the trial or in an evidentiary hearing in this case under Rule 3.7. However, we note that this situation may change if the plaintiffs attempt to rebut St. Paul's affirmative defense that the settlement agreement was made in bad faith by using an advice of counsel defense. If that should occur, a conflict of interest may exist, and we would reexamine the issue. At this time, however, SF & D is not disqualified from representing the plaintiffs in this suit.

Finally, St. Paul has asked for a protective order barring Gross from participating in the depositions in this case. Its arguments are unpersuasive, except to the extent that a videotape of a deposition may be replayed at trial in place of the witness' trial testimony. Under that circumstance,

8. Our analysis regarding Gross' role in the settlement agreement does not mean that St. Paul must limit its examination of him to that issue. It means simply that St. Paul has sufficiently demonstrated that his testimony is necessary on this issue to sustain its burden of showing that disqualification is appropriate.

Gross may not participate in the deposition or appear on the videotape. Otherwise, he is free to participate in any depositions taken in this action.

CONCLUSION

For the foregoing reasons, we grant defendant St. Paul Insurance Company of Illinois' motion to disqualify Barry B. Gross from representing the plaintiffs in this case. St. Paul's request for a protective order is granted in part and denied in part as set forth above.

MULTIPLE CHOICE QUESTIONS

Answer these questions using the definitions found at the end of Chapter Two.

1. Inventor Ivan and marketing genius Gene want to form a new corporation to market Ivan's amazing new design for motion picture projectors. They want to hire attorney Arnold to help them to do the necessary legal work and to help them find venture capital. Because they have almost no hard cash at present, they have asked Arnold to do this work for them in exchange for 4% of the capital stock of the new corporation. The remaining 96% will be divided equally between Ivan and Gene and their respective families. *May* Arnold agree to their proposal?

A. No, because a lawyer must not acquire a personal interest in the subject of the representation.

B. No, because a lawyer must not enter into a business transaction with clients.

C. Yes, but only if the 4% would not make the fee unreasonably high, and the transaction would be fair to the clients, and the terms are fully disclosed to the clients in an understandable writing, and the clients are advised in writing of the desirability of seeking outside counsel and given a chance to consult such outside counsel, and the clients consent in writing.

D. Yes, but only if Ivan and Gene give their informed consent and Arnold promises that he will never vote his stock or otherwise attempt to influence the governance of the corporation.

2. Lawyer Lenschell has recently opened his new law office. Timothy came to Lenschell's office and introduced himself as the "boyfriend" of Tina, a young woman who was just arrested on a prostitution charge. Timothy retained Lenschell to represent Tina and paid him an appropriate fee in advance. Timothy, who seemed to know a great deal about the law pertaining to prostitution despite being a layperson, explained to Lenschell that in prostitution cases in this district, a guilty plea usually results in a $500 fine, but no jail sentence. But if the defendant pleads not guilty, goes to trial, and is found guilty, the judge usually imposes a jail sentence. Timothy further explained that Tina did not want to go to jail, that he would pay her fine for her, and that Lenschell should therefore advise her to plead guilty. Lenschell met Tina for the first time at the

courthouse, shortly before her case was to be called on the criminal calendar for entry of her plea. In their hurried conference, Tina told Lenschell that Timothy was her pimp, not her "boyfriend." Further, she said that she wanted to escape from Timothy and from her life as a prostitute, and that she wanted to plead not guilty, thus risking a jail sentence, rather than become further indebted to Timothy. What is the *proper* course of conduct for Lenschell to follow in this situation?

A. To adhere to the instructions given by Timothy, and to advise Tina to plead guilty.

B. To give Tina whatever legal assistance she needs in entering her plea of not guilty.

C. To withdraw from the matter promptly, without advising Tina one way or the other on what plea to enter.

D. To telephone Timothy and ask for further instructions in light of Tina's unwillingness to plead guilty.

3. Lawyer Lattimer is on the in-house legal staff of Centennial Corporation, a major manufacturer of steel shipping containers. She regularly provides legal advice to Vice–President Markler, the executive in charge of sales and marketing. In the course of a routine preventive law project, Lattimer discovered that Markler had participated in a series of telephone conferences with his counterparts at the company's two main competitors. Further, she discovered that each such conference was promptly followed by an increase in the prices charged by the three companies. When Lattimer took this up with Markler, she first reminded him that she was not his personal lawyer, but rather the corporation's lawyer. Then she said: "If you have been discussing prices with our competitors, we may be in deep trouble. Your telephone conferences may violate the Sherman Antitrust Act, and that could mean civil and criminal liability, both for you and for the corporation. And, as you know, the corporation has a rule against rescuing executives who get in antitrust trouble." Markler responded as follows: "Ms. Lattimer, I know you're a good lawyer, but you don't know much about the real world. You can't run a business these days if you try to trample on your competition. Now don't worry yourself about my telephone conferences, because I'm sure you have better things to do with your time." If Markler remains uncooperative, which of the following expresses the *proper* course for Lattimer to take?

A. Draft a careful, complete memorandum about the matter for her own files, and maintain her conversation with Markler in strict confidence.

B. Describe the relevant facts in a carefully drafted letter to the Antitrust Division of the United States Department of Justice, and request an advisory opinion on the legality of the described conduct.

C. Describe the entire matter to Markler's immediate corporate superior, the Executive Vice President, and advise him to put a stop to Markler's telephone conferences.

D. Describe the relevant facts in a memorandum to the corporate Board of Directors, and advise the Board that she will resign unless something is done to stop Markler.

4. Attorney Tillis is a partner in the 138 person firm of Dahlberg & Sneed. The Citizens' Alliance for Coastal Preservation has asked Tillis to represent the Alliance in a public interest law suit against Vista del Oro, Inc., a real estate developer. Vista del Oro owns several thousand acres of beautiful coastline, about an hour's drive from the largest city in the state. It is building vacation homes to sell to the public. When the project is complete, the entire area will be fenced off to prevent access by non-owners. The Alliance seeks to force Vista del Oro to provide access paths across the property, so that members of the public can get from the state highway to the public beaches. Attorney Prentice is also a partner in Dahlberg & Sneed. He is a member of the Board of Directors of Vista del Oro, and he owns seven of the vacation home sites as a personal investment. No Dahlberg & Sneed lawyer has ever represented Vista del Oro, and none will do so in the present case. After careful consideration, Tillis has concluded that his representation of the Alliance would not be adversely affected by Prentice's interest. Which of the following conditions must be met if Tillis is to avoid being *subject to discipline* for representing the Alliance?

I. The Alliance consents after full disclosure.

II. Vista del Oro consents after full disclosure.

III. Prentice resigns as a director of Vista del Oro.

IV. Prentice sells his seven home sites.

A. All of the above.

B. III only.

C. I and II only.

D. I only.

5. In a private treble damage case arising under the federal price discrimination law (the Robinson–Patman Act), the defendant wants to prove that it had a good faith belief that its pricing system was lawful. As evidence of its good faith, the defendant wants to prove that, five years ago, the Federal Trade Commission carefully reviewed the defendant's pricing system and decided not to institute proceedings against the defendant. The proof of this is a letter from the FTC to defendant's lawyer, Smithers. At the treble damage trial, the defendant will need Smithers' testimony to authenticate the letter—Smithers will simply testify that he received the letter from the FTC. The defendant wants Smithers and his law partner, Hillner, to serve as its trial counsel in the treble damage case. Which of the following is correct?

A. Neither Smithers nor Hillner *may* serve.

B. Both Smithers and Hillner *may* serve.

C. Only Hillner *may* serve.

D. Smithers and Hillner *may* serve, but only if the plaintiff consents.

6. Client Parsons has asked lawyer Ekimoto to represent her, and nine other representatives of a plaintiff class, in an employment discrimination class action against Consolidated Telephone and Telegraph Corporation. The size of the plaintiff class and the size of the potential recovery are hard to estimate, but the case would conceivably produce a total recovery of nearly 15 million dollars. Lawyer Ekimoto and her two brothers are the beneficiaries of a trust fund established by their late parents. Among the trust assets are 1,000 shares of Consolidated common stock. Consolidated has 30 million shares of common stock outstanding. If Ekimoto reasonably believes that her interest in Consolidated will not affect her representation of the plaintiffs, *may* she serve as plaintiffs' counsel?

A. Yes, since the interest of a trust beneficiary is not regarded as disqualifying.

B. Yes, if she obtains the consent of the class representatives after full disclosure of her interest.

C. No, since even a small adverse financial interest creates an appearance of impropriety.

D. No, since there are other counsel available who could serve the plaintiff class without any potential conflict.

7. Biochemist Belloni invented a gene splicing process for making snake antitoxins. The invention was a major breakthrough because Belloni's antitoxins were far cheaper and more reliable than the natural variety produced from the venom of live snakes. She obtained a U.S. Patent on her process. Shortly thereafter, she was sued in a declaratory judgment action brought by United Laboratories, Inc. United sought a declaration that her U.S. Patent was invalid. Belloni asked lawyer Lothrup to represent her in the case. Lothrup agreed to do so on the following terms: (1) Belloni would pay Lothrup for the necessary legal work at Lothrup's regular hourly rate; (2) Lothrup would advance the litigation expenses, subject to repayment by Belloni no matter what the outcome of the case; and (3) at the outset, Belloni would assign to Lothrup a 10% ownership interest in the U.S. Patent.

A. The arrangement is *proper,* assuming that the total Lothrup earns from it is reasonable.

B. Lothrup is *subject to discipline* because the arrangement requires Belloni to pay back the advanced litigation expenses even if she loses the declaratory judgment case.

C. Lothrup is *subject to discipline* because the arrangement provides for an advance of litigation expenses by the lawyer in a civil case.

D. Lothrup is *subject to discipline* because the arrangement gives her a personal financial interest in the U.S. Patent which is the subject of the declaratory judgment case.

8. A statute of State X requires prison inmates to be provided "sanitary living conditions, suitable education and recreation facilities, and competent medical treatment." The statute authorizes inmates who are deprived of these benefits to sue the State Commissioner of Prisons for equitable relief. The statute also permits (but does not require) the courts to order State X to pay the attorney fees of successful inmate plaintiffs. At the request of the local bar association, private attorney Andrate agreed to represent a group of indigent inmates who were allegedly being deprived of proper medical attention at a State X prison. After extensive discovery proceedings, the State Commissioner of Prisons offered to settle the case by entering into a consent decree that would give the inmates all the equitable relief they could ever hope to receive, provided that Andrate would not request an award of attorney fees. Which of the following would be the *proper* thing for Andrate to do with respect to the settlement offer?

A. Explain it to his clients and let them decide whether to accept it or reject it.

B. Reject it on behalf of his clients because it does not provide for an award of attorney fees.

C. Accept it on behalf of his clients, even though it does not provide for an award of attorney fees.

D. Reject it on behalf of his clients because to do otherwise would discourage private attorneys from representing indigent inmates in future cases.

Answers to the multiple choice questions will be found in the Appendix at the end of the book.

CHAPTER TWELVE

CONFLICTS OF INTEREST—CONFLICTS BETWEEN TWO CLIENTS

■ ■ ■

What This Chapter Covers

I. Conflicts Between the Interests of Two Clients
- A. Directly Adverse Representation in the Same Matter
- B. Opposing Present Client in an Unrelated Matter
- C. Multiple Clients in the Same Matter
- D. Former Client's Confidential Information
- E. Opposing Former Client in a Substantially Related Matter
- F. Former Judges and Government Employees

Reading Assignment

Wydick, Perschbacher, & Bassett, Chapter 12.

ABA Model Rules:

Rules 1.7, 1.8(b), (g), and (i), 1.9 through 1.12, 1.18, and 6.3.

CRPC 1–120 and 3–310.

Cal.Bus. & Prof.Code § 6068(e).

Supplemental Reading

Hazard & Hodes:

Discussion of ABA Model Rules 1.7, 1.8(b), (g), and (i), 1.9 through 1.12, and 6.3.

Restatement (Third) of the Law Governing Lawyers §§ 15; 121–124, 128–130; 132–133 (2000).

Discussion Problems

1. The County Association of Real Estate Dealers (CARED) is a trade association composed of all the licensed real estate brokers and dealers in the county. Over the years, CARED has provided its members with standard forms of legal documents for use in routine real estate

transactions. Last year, the state passed a new statute that requires all legal documents affecting consumers to be expressed in "clear, simple English." Any document that does not comply is void. CARED hired attorney Adler to draft a new standard form apartment lease to comply with the new state statute. Adler did so, and CARED distributed the new form to its members. Dearbourne Realty & Investment Company (a CARED member) used the new form to lease one of its own apartment units to one Leon Beckner. Now Beckner seeks to have attorney Adler represent him in a law suit against Dearbourne to have the lease declared void. One of Beckner's several arguments is that two key paragraphs of the lease are totally incomprehensible to the average person. Adler has re-examined the two paragraphs and is inclined to agree that Beckner is very likely correct. May Adler represent Beckner in the lawsuit?

2. Aaron, Bropovski, and Carter were riding in a car driven by Duffy. The car was hit, head-on, by a truck driven by Emerson. Aaron, Bropovski, Carter, and Duffy have asked you to represent them in a suit against Emerson and his employer, United Fat and Tallow, Inc. Under what circumstances may you represent the four plaintiffs in this case?

3. You are one of only five lawyers in the little town of Sand Springs. You represent Sand Springs Hardware Company in a civil suit against Virgil McQuillan to collect $338 on an overdue charge account. Last week, McQuillan and one of his friends got drunk and were arrested trying to climb into the back window of a saloon after closing hours. They were charged with burglary, a felony. Neither man has funds to pay a lawyer.

a. McQuillan's friend is being represented by the County Public Defender, but she has declined to represent McQuillan too, on the ground that to do so would pose a conflict of interest. Is her position sound?

b. The court has asked you to defend McQuillan in the felony case. How should you respond to the court's request?

4. Two years ago, you represented Mr. W in setting up a close corporation for his business and for certain personal investments. That work has long since been completed, and you have not represented Mr. W since then. Now Mrs. W has asked you to represent her in divorce proceedings against Mr. W. The two of them are in sharp disagreement over the division of property, child support obligations, and alimony. Assume that this jurisdiction does not have community property. Under what, if any, circumstances may you represent Mrs. W?

5. From 1991 through 1999, lawyer Lageson was an attorney with the Argos & Bakeson firm. Argos & Bakeson's practice was primarily insurance defense work. While at Argos & Bakeson, Lageson worked on numerous matters for the Wazoo Insurance Company. In 1999, Lageson left Argos & Bakeson for the Cumis firm where he also did insurance defense work, including matters in which Wazoo insureds needed separate counsel because Wazoo reserved its rights to contest coverage of the claim. [*See Beckwith Machinery Co. v. Travelers Indem. Co., supra.*] Cumis

represents Duke Development, a real estate developer being sued by buyers of several hundred Duke-built homes for alleged construction defects. Duke has various insurance policies with Wazoo that it contends cover the defect claims. Wazoo disputes coverage and has sued Duke for a declaration it is not liable for the buyers' claims. Argos & Bakeson represents Wazoo and Cumis represents Duke in the declaratory relief action. Wazoo has moved to disqualify Cumis from the representation based on Lageson's former association with Argos & Bakeson.

a. Should Lageson personally be disqualified from representing Duke in *Wazoo Insurance Company v. Duke Development*?

b. If Lageson is personally disqualified, should the entire Cumis firm also be disqualified?

c. Are there any steps the Cumis firm could have taken to avoid its imputed disqualification?

d. Even if sufficient screening procedures can protect a private firm from disqualification, can you see why the former client who is the firm's adversary still might feel uneasy?

6. Until ten months ago, attorney Barneo was an Administrative Law Judge for the State Consumer Protection Commission. The Commission's Enforcement Division brought proceedings against Mandel Toy Company to stop Mandel from selling some allegedly dangerous toy rifles. The Commission attorney moved for a preliminary cease and desist order. Barneo was assigned to hear the motion. She declined to issue the order, stating on the record that "the evidence of dangerousness looks exceedingly thin at this time." Several months later, Barneo resigned her position and entered the private practice of law. Ultimately, after a full hearing before a different Administrative Law Judge, Mandel was ordered to take the toy rifles off the market. That order is now before the Appellate Division of the Commission, and Mandel has asked Barneo to argue the appeal on its behalf. May she do so?

STATE FARM MUTUAL AUTOMOBILE INSURANCE COMPANY v. K.A.W.

Supreme Court of Florida, 1991.
575 So.2d 630.

GRIMES, JUSTICE.

* * *

David Wilkerson was driving a rental car in which his wife and infant daughter were passengers when it was struck by another car. The Wilkersons retained the law firm of Sheldon J. Schlesinger, P.A. (Schlesinger firm) and filed suit against the driver and owner of the other vehicle and others for injuries suffered by the three of them in the accident. The action included a count against petitioner State Farm Mutual Automobile Insurance Company (State Farm), the Wilkersons' insurer, for uninsured motorist coverage. The Wilkersons also filed a separate malpractice action against various health care providers for alleged negligent treatment of their daughter after the accident. The Schlesinger firm represented the Wilkersons in the malpractice action.

After the personal injury action had proceeded for approximately one year, the Wilkersons added new defendants, including petitioners Interstate Fire and Casualty Company and Continental Casualty Company, which had issued uninsured motorist insurance to Wilkerson's employer. The following year, the Wilkersons' attorneys determined that David Wilkerson's negligence may have contributed to the automobile accident. Thereupon, Mr. Wilkerson discharged the Schlesinger firm as his counsel in the personal injury action and retained a former member of the Schlesinger firm as new counsel. Shortly thereafter, Mrs. Wilkerson and her daughter filed a second amended complaint in that action, adding David Wilkerson as a defendant. The Schlesinger firm continued to represent Mrs. Wilkerson and the daughter in that action, and Mr. Wilkerson consented to be sued up to the limits of his insurance coverage. The firm also continued to represent all three Wilkersons in the medical malpractice action.

Asserting their exposure as liability insurers of Mr. Wilkerson, each of the petitioners filed motions seeking the disqualification of the Schlesinger firm in the personal injury action. Petitioners objected to the potential for the Schlesinger firm to use confidential information gained during the course of the prior representation of Mr. Wilkerson in this action against him. In opposition to the motion, David Wilkerson filed an affidavit stating that he did not consider anything he discussed with Sheldon Schlesinger privileged because he had disclosed everything in his deposition and he did not feel that Mr. Schlesinger's representation of his wife and daughter disadvantaged him in any way. Mrs. Wilkerson also submitted an affidavit in which she stated that she and her daughter would be prejudiced if the Schlesinger firm were required to withdraw.

The trial court refused to disqualify the Schlesinger firm, finding that the petitioners lacked standing to request disqualification in the face of Mr. Wilkerson's consent to the firm's representation of his wife and child. In addition, the court found that the petitioners failed to show clearly and convincingly that they would be prejudiced or that the continued representation would interfere with the fair and impartial administration of justice. The Fourth District Court of Appeal denied the insurers' petitions for writ of certiorari, finding no proof of substantial prejudice or circumstances calling into question the fair and efficient administration of justice.

While not addressed by the majority opinion below, we shall first discuss the question of the petitioners' standing. The Wilkersons contend that an attorney may not be disqualified where the former client has consented to the representation.

* * * The rule urged by the Wilkersons is based on the premise that rules governing attorney conduct are intended for the protection of the client, who may either explicitly or implicitly waive that protection. On the other hand, the petitioners argue that they have standing because as insurance companies they will be liable for the payment of any judgment against David Wilkerson in this action.

* * *

The ethical principle at issue is an attorney's duty to maintain the confidences of his client. That principle is embodied in two rules of professional conduct. Rule Regulating The Florida Bar 4–1.6(a) provides that "[a] lawyer shall not reveal information relating to representation of a client * * * unless the client consents after disclosure to the client." The duty of confidentiality continues after termination of the attorney-client relationship. *See* Comment to rule 4–1.6.

Rule Regulating The Florida Bar 4–1.9 provides:

A lawyer who has formerly represented a client in a matter shall not thereafter:

> (a) Represent another person in the same or a substantially related matter in which that person's interests are materially adverse to the interests of the former client unless the former client consents after consultation; or
>
> (b) Use information relating to the representation to the disadvantage of the former client except as rule 4–1.6 would permit with respect to a client or when the information has become generally known.[1]

The purpose of the requirement that an attorney maintain client confidences is two-fold. It advances the interests of the client by encouraging a free flow of information and the development of trust essential to an attorney-client relationship. *Developments in the Law: Conflicts of Interest in the Legal Profession,* 94 Harv.L.Rev. 1244, 1316 (1981). However, it also serves a second purpose fundamental to a fair adversary system. Our legal system cannot function fairly or effectively if an attorney has an

---

1. Rule Regulating The Florida Bar 4–1.7 is also pertinent here. That rule provides:

(a) A lawyer shall not represent a client if the representation of that client will be directly adverse to the interests of another client, unless:

> (1) The lawyer reasonably believes the representation will not adversely affect the lawyer's responsibilities to and relationship with the other client; and
>
> (2) Each client consents after consultation.

Mr. Wilkerson is, in effect, both a former client of the Schlesinger firm for purposes of rule 4B1.9 (in the personal injury action) and a current client for purposes of rule 4–1.7 (in the medical malpractice action). The duty of confidentiality is present regardless of whether Mr. Wilkerson is viewed as the firm's former or current client.

[The Florida Rules are identical to ABA Model Rules 1.6, 1.7 and 1.9 as they existed before amendment in 1989—Eds.]

informational advantage in the form of confidences gained during a former representation of his client's current opponent. *Id.* at 1315–16; * * *.

The question then is whether the insurers may "stand in the shoes" of their insured for purposes of seeking disqualification of the Schlesinger firm on grounds of conflict of interest. Comments to the Rules of Professional Conduct indicate that under certain circumstances someone other than the client may request disqualification. Thus, where a conflict "is such as clearly to call in question the fair or efficient administration of justice, opposing counsel may properly raise the question." Comment to Rule Regulating The Florida Bar 4–1.7. * * *

We find that the facts of this case call into question the fair administration of justice. Mr. Wilkerson is not exposed to any personal liability because he may be sued only up to the amount of any available insurance coverage. * * * This is, in reality, not an action between Mr. Wilkerson and his child, but an action by the mother and child against the parent's insurance carriers. Mr. Wilkerson is in a position adverse to his daughter in theory only. He reasonably hopes to enhance his daughter's chance of recovery. The petitioners, on the other hand, will be acting in Mr. Wilkerson's defense, attempting to persuade the fact finder that he was not negligent in the automobile accident in order that they may avoid liability. Because of this situation, Wilkerson's consent to the firm's representation of his wife and daughter does not end the inquiry. Information disclosed by Mr. Wilkerson to his attorneys during the course of the attorney-client relationship could be used to prove that Mr. Wilkerson was negligent. This is adverse to the petitioners who are obligated to act in his defense. The unfairness of the situation results from the fact that Mrs. Wilkerson and her daughter have a potential informational advantage over those who must defend Mr. Wilkerson which was gained as a result of her law firm's former representation of Mr. Wilkerson in this action. It defies logic to suggest that the petitioners do not have a legitimate interest in seeking to prevent the opposing parties from using confidential information obtained from their insured through a prior attorney-client relationship. We conclude that the petitioners have standing to request the law firm's disqualification.

We next address the issue of the appropriate standard to apply to determine whether the Schlesinger firm should be disqualified. In conflict-of-interest cases such as this arising under the former Code of Professional Responsibility, one seeking to disqualify opposing counsel was required to show that (1) an attorney-client relationship existed, thereby giving rise to an irrefutable presumption that confidences were disclosed during the relationship, and (2) the matter in which the law firm subsequently represented the interest adverse to the former client was the same or substantially related to the matter in which it represented the former client. This standard was based on the Code of Professional Responsibility, Canon 4, which provided that an attorney should preserve the confidences and secrets of a client.

* * * The Rules of Professional Conduct requiring confidentiality serve the same purposes as the confidentiality requirements of the Code of Professional Responsibility. Similarly, the need for the irrefutable presumption continues to exist, just as under the former code. The presumption acknowledges the difficulty of proving that confidential information useful to the attorney's current client was given to the attorney. It also protects the client by not requiring disclosure of confidences previously given to the attorney. *See Government of India v. Cook Indus., Inc.,* 422 F.Supp. 1057, 1060 (S.D.N.Y.1976) (if two actions are substantially related, court will not require proof that attorney had access to confidential information, nor give weight to attorney's assertion that he had no access to and did not possess confidential information), *aff'd,* 569 F.2d 737 (2d Cir.1978).

Accordingly, we disagree with the court below that actual proof of prejudice is a prerequisite to disqualification under these circumstances. The Schlesinger firm represented Mr. Wilkerson in the personal injury action for more than two years, and the existence of this relationship raised the irrefutable presumption that confidences were disclosed. Moreover, the firm continues to represent Mr. Wilkerson in the medical malpractice action. Under Florida law, Mr. Wilkerson could be found liable in the instant case not only for those injuries which were sustained by his daughter in the automobile accident but also for any injuries she received as a result of any subsequent medical malpractice. Thus, even now Mr. Wilkerson may be disclosing confidences to the Schlesinger firm as his counsel in the medical malpractice action which could be used against him by the Schlesinger firm in the instant case.

In reaching our decision, we do not imply any misconduct on the part of the Schlesinger firm. In this respect, we find the statement in *Rotante v. Lawrence Hospital,* 46 A.D.2d 199, 200, 361 N.Y.S.2d 372, 373 (1974), apropos:

> While these facts neither indicate nor imply any departure from professional conduct or breach of any ethical canon, we cannot escape the conclusion that this is a situation rife with the possibility of discredit to the bar and the administration of justice. Obviously Mr. Turkewitz cannot erase from his mind the confidences he received from his former client or the plan of defense he envisaged. Though we do not dispute his good faith or the good faith of the firm representing plaintiff, both the possibility of conflict of interest and the appearance of it are too strong to ignore.

We quash the decision below and direct that the Schlesinger firm be disqualified from further representation of Mrs. Wilkerson and her minor child in this action.

It is so ordered.

ROSENFELD CONSTRUCTION COMPANY, INC. v. SUPERIOR COURT

California Court of Appeal, Fifth District, 1991.
235 Cal.App.3d 566, 286 Cal.Rptr. 609.

VARTABEDIAN, ASSOCIATE JUSTICE.

This is a petition for writ of mandate following respondent court's denial of the motion of petitioner, Rosenfeld Construction Company, Inc., to disqualify the law firm of Wild, Carter, Tipton & Oliver (hereafter Wild) in its representation of real parties in interest, Paul Sivas and Jeanet Sivas. * * *

PROCEDURAL AND FACTUAL BACKGROUND

Petitioner brought a motion for disqualification of opposing counsel, the Wild firm, on the basis it had formerly represented petitioner in a related matter.

The memorandum in support of the motion recited that in 1982, John Rosenfeld, petitioner's president, consulted Wild for advice and representation in a dispute with Mr. and Mrs. George Lawson regarding the Lawsons' failure to pay petitioner for constructing a home; * * *.

* * *

Wild acknowledged it represented petitioner for nearly four years in "relatively few matters," including the Lawson controversy.

The Lawsons had contended that the construction of their home was defective in the following respects: cabinetry, flooring, doors, water penetration into rooms and foundation, roof penetrations, moldings, painting, tile work and the grading of the property on which the house was constructed.

On November 18, 1988, real parties initiated a lawsuit against petitioner, alleging that it breached its contract with them by failing to construct their residence in conformity with the construction contract and industry standards, in particular in the following areas: cabinetry, flooring, doors, water penetration, painting, and grading of the lot on which the house was constructed.

At the time the lawsuit was commenced, real parties were represented by the law firm of Dowling, Magarian, Phillips & Aaron (hereafter Dowling). On January 8 or 9, 1991, as a consequence of attorney Steven E. Paganetti's change of employment from the Dowling firm to Wild, the Wild firm was substituted as counsel for real parties.

Petitioner's attorney, D. Tyler Tharpe, received the notice of substitution of attorneys on January 14, 1991. Tharpe had been present at the deposition of John Rosenfeld nearly a year earlier, at which time Rosenfeld had mentioned that petitioner was once represented by Wild. On

February 1, 1991, Tharpe reviewed the deposition testimony, which reminded him of petitioner's prior representation by Wild.

On February 4, 1991, the next business day, Tharpe called the matter to John Rosenfeld's attention; on that same day, Rosenfeld instructed Tharpe to contact Wild, demanding that it immediately withdraw as counsel for real parties. Tharpe did so. Wild declined.

Before respondent court, petitioner argued that the appropriate test to apply to determine if disqualification was necessary was the substantial relationship standard. Claiming that the subject matters of the two lawsuits were substantially related, petitioner asked the court to disqualify Wild from the representation of real parties in the instant matter.

Rosenfeld's declaration in support of the motion to disqualify contained his statement that he spent "dozens of hours" with Robert H. Oliver, Trevor C. Clegg, William H. Leifer, and Victor D. Ryerson of the Wild firm concerning the Lawson dispute. Rosenfeld declared:

> "[O]ver the course of those many years (1) I surrendered to WCT & O [Wild] all of the business' work files relating to the Lawson project, (2) I explained in detail to each of the above-mentioned attorneys at WCT & O my company's manner of operation, methods of construction and provision of warranty work, and (3) I disclosed to the same attorneys my strategies as they relate to handling customer complaints and the attorneys shared their strategies with me."

In his supplemental declaration, Rosenfeld further declared:

> "3. * * * Every attorney who assisted in representing ROSENFELD in the Lawson controversy met with me at one time or another, some more than others, and I shared confidential information with them about the nature of the complaints and the manner of ROSENFELD's construction as it related to the complaints. During the course of the prior representation, I shared my strategies with the WCT & O attorneys and they shared their strategies with me related to proving ROSENFELD's case against the Lawsons and defeating the Lawsons' claims against ROSENFELD.
>
> "4. There is no question in my mind that the attorneys at WCT & O, owing to their extended representation of ROSENFELD, each had access to and actually accessed information which is confidential in nature and which is substantially related to the present action."

Four attorneys from Wild submitted declarations in opposition to the motion. Robert Oliver declared that his firm represented Rosenfeld personally or the petitioner corporation "in relatively few matters through approximately 1985." He acknowledged that Wild represented petitioner in the controversy with the Lawsons and that the case ultimately involved litigation and arbitration, * * *. Oliver further declared that Paganetti had not discussed the "substance of the Rosenfeld Construction Company, Inc./Lawson case" with him. Oliver went on:

The file containing the *Rosenfeld Construction vs. Lawson* case has been closed for several years and stored in a location removed from our law offices. Only upon receiving correspondence alleging conflicts of interest was the file brought to this office so that declarations could be prepared by various partners in this firm.

William H. Leifer submitted a declaration in which he admitted he had reviewed the office file entitled Rosenfeld Construction Company, Inc. v. Lawson et al. Leifer noted:

Even after reviewing the file and reviewing the documents that I could find in the file, I still have no recollection of ever having talked to John Rosenfeld in person. * * * I have not in any fashion discussed with Mr. Paganetti any of the issues having to do with the Lawson matter and could not because I have no actual knowledge of the underlying facts giving rise to that case and I was not involved in any of the merits of the case except on a very limited basis as to the fact that it concerned a residence.

Trevor Clegg acknowledged that in 1983 he prepared and filed a complaint seeking foreclosure of petitioner's mechanic's lien on the Lawsons' residence and damages for breach of contract Clegg went on to note:

4. * * * In the course of preparing the complaint, I did conduct discussions with Mr. John Rosenfeld, * * * To the best of my recollection, those discussions were neither lengthy nor detailed. They did touch on the Lawsons' complaints, but with the exception noted below, I do not recall any extended or detailed discussion of those complaints. * * *

5. The one complaint that Mr. Rosenfeld and I discussed in some detail involved land subsidence or slippage around and under the Lawson residence. Mr. Rosenfeld maintained that the entire problem was the Lawsons' fault. * * *

6. The only materials in our file that we received from Rosenfeld Construction consisted of rather unenlightening communications to and from the Lawsons and the Contractors License Board; a few scribbled notes by Mr. Rosenfeld; and a chronology of events prepared by Mr. Rosenfeld.

Paganetti declared that he never had any conversations with any of his fellow attorneys at Wild concerning the Lawson matter, nor had he seen any written documents relating to the Lawson matter. * * *

The minute order of the court's ruling reads in its entirety, "Motion to disqualify is denied. No present counsel at 'Wild, Carter, Tipton & Oliver' have sufficient knowledge of prior 'Rosenfeld' representation to disqualify the firm from representing the Sivas. The court finds no actual or potential present conflict."

* * *

DISCUSSION

* * *

Rule 3–310 of the State Bar Rules of Professional Conduct provides for the avoidance of representation of adverse interests.[2] It has long been recognized that knowledge obtained by one member of a firm of lawyers is imputed to all the other members. "The imputed knowledge theory holds that knowledge by any member of a law firm is knowledge by all of the attorneys in the firm, partners as well as associates." (*Chadwick v. Superior Court* [1980] 106 Cal.App.3d 108, 116, 164 Cal.Rptr. 864.)

In 1953, the United States District Court for the Southern District of New York decided *T.C. Theatre Corp. v. Warner Bros. Pictures* (S.D.N.Y. 1953) 113 F.Supp. 265, in which the court held "[a] lawyer's duty of absolute loyalty to his client's interest does not end with his retainer. He is enjoined for all time, except as he may be released by law, from disclosing matters revealed to him by reason of the confidential relationship. Related to this principle is the rule that where any substantial relationship can be shown between the subject matter of a former representation and that of a subsequent adverse representation, the latter will be prohibited." (*Id.* at p. 268.) Further, "the former client need show no more than that the matter embraced within the pending suit wherein his former attorney appears on behalf of his adversary are substantially related to the matters or cause of action wherein the attorney previously represented him, the former client. The court will assume that during the course of the former representation confidences were disclosed to the attorney bearing on the subject matter of the representation. It will not inquire into their nature and extent. Only in this manner can the lawyer's duty of absolute fidelity be enforced and the spirit of the rule relating to privileged communications be maintained." (*Id.* at pp. 268–269.)

The court went on to note that to require a client to show the nature of the confidential information "would tear aside the protective cloak drawn about the lawyer-client relationship. For the court to probe further and sift the confidences in fact revealed would require the disclosure of the matters intended to be protected by the rule * * *. No client should ever be concerned with the possible use against him in future litigation of what he may have revealed to his attorney." (*T.C. Theatre Corp. v. Warner Bros. Pictures, supra,* 113 F.Supp. at p. 269.)

---

2. Rule 3–310 of the State Bar Rules of Professional Conduct (23 West's Ann.Cal.Codes, Civil and Crim.Rules, 1991 supp. pamph., p. 551) provides in pertinent part:

"(A) If a member has or had a relationship with another party interested in the representation, or has an interest in its subject matter, the member shall not accept or continue such representation without all affected clients' informed written consent.

"________

"(D) A member shall not accept employment adverse to a client or former client where, by reason of the representation of the client or former client, the member has obtained confidential information material to the employment except with the informed written consent of the client or former client."

In 1983, a California court first used the substantial relationship standard in *Global Van Lines, Inc. v. Superior Court* (1983) 144 Cal. App.3d 483, 192 Cal.Rptr. 609. That court held:

> When a substantial relationship has been shown to exist between the former representation and the current representation, and when it appears by virtue of the nature of the former representation or the relationship of the attorney to his former client confidential information material to the current dispute would normally have been imparted to the attorney or to subordinates for whose legal work he was responsible, the attorney's knowledge of confidential information is presumed. [Citation.]
>
> "This is the rule by necessity, for it is not within the power of the former client to prove what is in the mind of the attorney. Nor should the attorney have to 'engage in a subtle evaluation of the extent to which he acquired relevant information in the first representation and of the actual use of that knowledge and information in the subsequent representation.' [Citations.]" (*Global Van Lines, supra,* 144 Cal.App.3d at p. 489, 192 Cal.Rptr. 609.)

* * *

Subsequently, our court decided *River West, Inc. v. Nickel* (1987) 188 Cal.App.3d 1297, 234 Cal.Rptr. 33, in which we reversed the trial court's order disqualifying counsel for a conflict of interest. In *River West,* the prior representation occurred more than 27 years earlier and the moving party had notice of the conflict over 3 years before he made the motion to disqualify. We determined that due to the long wait in bringing the motion to disqualify, an exception to the substantial relationship test could be found.

* * *

While an exception was found on the particular facts, our court in *River West* left no doubt that the substantial relationship test is the proper standard. "Therefore, in the usual case when the substantial relationship of the matters is established, the inquiry ends and the disqualification should be ordered. If it were otherwise, a weighing process would be inevitable. The rights of the former client would be lined up against those of the new client, perhaps to the detriment of both. The purpose of the substantial relationship test is to avoid such an inquiry." (*River West, Inc. v. Nickel, supra,* 188 Cal.App.3d at p. 1304, 234 Cal.Rptr. 33.)

"Disqualification of an attorney from representing a former client does not require proof of actual possession of confidential information."

While the substantial relationship test is central to the determination of attorney disqualification, the standard itself has not received much critical scrutiny. Yet both parts of the test, "substantial" and "relationship," are susceptible to a variety of meanings and interpretations.

The recent case of *H.F. Ahmanson & Co. v. Salomon Brothers, Inc.* (1991) 229 Cal.App.3d 1445, 280 Cal.Rptr. 614 recognized the need for greater specificity in dealing with the standard. "The word 'substantial,' like other nonquantifiable denominators of measurement, is subject to a variety of interpretations. Use of the word 'relationship' implies a connection, but offers no guidance as to *what* is being connected: subject matters, facts, or issues." (*Id.* at p. 1453, 280 Cal.Rptr. 614.) The *Ahmanson* court looked to *Silver Chrysler Plymouth, Inc. v. Chrysler Mot. Corp.* (2d Cir.1975) 518 F.2d 751, 757, for an analysis of the substantial relationship test found in Judge Adams's concurring opinion. Judge Adams suggested that a court should "focus on the similarities between the two factual situations, the legal questions posed, and the nature and extent of the attorney's involvement with the cases. As part of its review, the court should examine the time spent by the attorney on the earlier cases, the type of work performed, and the attorney's possible exposure to formulation of policy or strategy." (*Id.* at p. 760, conc. opn. of Adams, J.)

The *Ahmanson* court thus analyzed the question of whether a substantial relationship existed by applying three factors: factual similarity, legal similarity, and nature and extent of the attorney's involvement with the cases.

Here, the record does not reflect that the court applied the substantial relationship standard nor that significant inquiry was made concerning the three factors stated in *Ahmanson.* The respondent court, without benefit of the specific analysis contained in *Ahmanson* (which was not filed until May 7, 1991), merely determined that no present counsel at the law firm in question had "sufficient knowledge of prior 'Rosenfeld' representation" to disqualify the firm. The court then found no actual or potential present conflict existed.

We find no authority that supports the notion that, standing alone, the present recollection of the members of the firm is an adequate criterion.

The respondent court failed to apply the appropriate standard. * * * We therefore return the matter to respondent court to allow the court to evaluate the motion in light of the appropriate standard.

In supplemental briefing, real parties suggest that if we determine the motion for disqualification was improperly denied, respondent court should be instructed to institute or impose a screening procedure such as we approved in *Higdon v. Superior Court* (1991) 227 Cal.App.3d 1667, 278 Cal.Rptr. 588 to avoid disqualification.

Higdon presented a very different situation—we were confronted with a case of first impression, involving the novel circumstance of a former judicial officer joining a law firm. In *Higdon,* we determined whether a former court commissioner, and the law firm he had joined, would be disqualified from representing the husbands in two separate dissolution actions. The former court commissioner had not represented any of the parties but had heard contested matters in the same actions. *Higdon* did not involve any allegation of conflict of interests or passage of confidential information, far less a presumption. Nor did it present a question of a firm's split loyalty in representing a present client whose interests may be in conflict with those of a prior client of the firm. By contrast, here, if the respondent court determines a "substantial relationship" exists, there is a conclusive presumption that confidential information has passed to the prior attorney.

In *Higdon,* while the former court commissioner was personally disqualified from handling a matter which he had previously heard as a judge, the remainder of the firm could avoid disqualification so long as it was proven that he had been and would continue to be screened from any participation in the case. We recognized there that existing California law resulted from very different circumstances concerning practicing attorneys changing employment and "California precedent has not rushed to accept the concept of disqualifying the attorney but not the firm, nor has it enthusiastically embarked upon erecting Chinese walls." (*Higdon v. Superior Court, supra,* 227 Cal.App.3d 1667, 1679, 278 Cal.Rptr. 588, quoting *Klein v. Superior Court* (1988) 198 Cal.App.3d 894, 912, 244 Cal.Rptr. 226.)

Here, real parties' request would result in the *firm* being disqualified and the member *attorney* being allowed to continue representing the client. Screening under these circumstances would be even more drastic than the converse relationship criticized in *Klein.* Should the respondent court find the current representation is substantially related to the former, creating the conclusive presumption that the Wild firm possesses confidential information of its former client, petitioner, a screening procedure cannot suffice to safeguard against the conflicting representations.

Real parties argue further that they will be prejudiced if they must obtain new representation at this point. However, this argument fails to recognize that real parties had been represented by the *firm* employing Paganetti, not the individual attorney alone. The instant problem arose when real parties obtained new representation. Real parties were represented for some years by Dowling until they chose to substitute Wild. The determination of whether a client follows an attorney to a new firm should include some scrutiny of the conflicts of interest that might result. While attorneys should be able to move freely from membership in one firm to another and clients should be allowed their choice of an individual attorney, the importance of maintaining public respect for and belief in the integrity of the legal profession should not take a back seat to other considerations.

The right to counsel of one's choice must be balanced with "the paramount objective of maintaining public confidence in the impartiality of the courts and the integrity of its professional bar."

We remand this matter to respondent court with instructions to apply the appropriate standard to determine if there exists a substantial relationship between the prior representation and the current representation based on the facts, the legal issues, and the nature and extent of involvement of the attorneys.

DISPOSITION

The petition for writ of mandate is granted; respondent court is ordered to set aside its order denying the motion for disqualification. Respondent court shall hold another hearing wherein it will consider relevant material bearing on the issue of whether or not there exists a substantial relationship between the present representation and the prior representation. If it finds such a substantial relationship, the court shall grant the motion for disqualification. The parties shall bear their own costs of the instant proceeding.

* * *

CHO v. SUPERIOR COURT

California Court of Appeal, Second District, 1995.
39 Cal.App.4th 113, 45 Cal.Rptr.2d 863.

EPSTEIN, ASSOCIATE JUSTICE.

The issue in this case is whether a law firm must be disqualified as counsel in a lawsuit after employing the retired judge who had presided over the action and had received ex parte confidences from the opposing party in the course of settlement conferences. We conclude that screening procedures are not sufficient to preserve public trust in the justice system in these circumstances and therefore the firm must be disqualified.

FACTUAL AND PROCEDURAL SUMMARY

[Cho is the plaintiff in Jennifer Donghee Cho v. Cho Hung Bank and Jang W. Lee (No. BC080299) pending in the Los Angeles County Superior Court. Cho moved to disqualify the law firm of Graham & James, counsel for Cho Hung Bank, after Eric E. Younger, the judge who had presided over the action, retired and joined Graham & James in an "of counsel" capacity.

Judge Younger held three settlement conferences at various stages of the proceedings. According to Cho, her "posture in the settlement conferences accordingly changed at such stages, not the least of which was disclosure of Cho's bottom line settlement." Cho's lawyer also stated that Judge Younger had been privy to confidences relating to the merits of Cho's case because: "In separate conference, Judge Younger asked plaintiff's counsel to speak candidly about the strengths and weaknesses of plaintiff's case, to which counsel responded openly and divulged information to His Honor in confidence. No such information would have been divulged but for the fact that it was in a confidential setting."

Judge Younger retired in late December 1994, with the Cho action still pending. Graham & James substituted into the lawsuit as counsel for Cho Hung Bank on February 17, 1995. Within the next few days, a partner at Graham & James, Stephen Owens, reviewed the court docket sheet and discovered for the first time that Judge Younger had presided over the case until his retirement. Mr. Owens had heard that Judge Younger was joining the firm, and he told the managing partner, Henry David, of Judge Younger's role in the action. After researching the issues, Graham & James decided to impose a " 'cone of silence' " around Judge Younger before he began his formal relationship with the firm. A memorandum was circulated throughout Graham & James directing all personnel that Judge Younger was not to be involved in the action in any way; that it was not to be discussed in his presence; that Judge Younger was not to discuss his role or any information he had obtained; and that he was not to have access to any files or written materials about the action.

Judge Younger began his work with Graham & James on March 1, 1995. Cho's attorney first learned of this at a deposition on March 22, 1995. On the same day Graham & James delivered a letter to the court and counsel in the action formally informing them of Judge Younger's relationship with that firm, and of the steps taken to screen him from any involvement in the action.]

DISCUSSION

This case presents an issue of first impression in California—whether a law firm must be disqualified when it employs a former judge who in his official capacity received ex parte confidences, bearing on the merits of a lawsuit over which he was presiding, from an adverse party in the identical litigation in which the motion to disqualify is brought. We conclude that the firm must be disqualified.

* * *

The parties acknowledge that Judge Younger is disqualified from participating in the action by virtue of his role as judge. There is no California rule of professional conduct which governs the issue of disqualification of Graham & James. Petitioner urges us to adopt the "substantial relationship" test applied in *Rosenfeld* [*supra,* p. 327.]. * * * Cho Hung Bank argues that we should apply the analysis employed by the court in *Higdon v. Superior Court,* 227 Cal.App.3d 1667, 278 Cal.Rptr. 588 (1991). As we shall explain, neither analysis resolves the issues presented here.

The reported decision closest to ours is *Higdon v. Superior Court, supra,* 227 Cal.App.3d 1667, 278 Cal.Rptr. 588. In that case, a court commissioner resigned and joined a law firm representing a party to a marital dissolution action on which he had heard contested matters. There was no indication that the commissioner had been party to confidences divulged by either side in the case.

The *Higdon* court ruled that * * * absent consent by the opposing party, the former commissioner was disqualified from participating in the case as an attorney under the rationale of rule 1.12(a) of the American Bar Association Model Rules of Professional Conduct. That rule provides: "[A] lawyer shall not represent anyone in connection with a matter in which the lawyer participated personally and substantially as a judge or other adjudicative officer, arbitrator or law clerk to such a person, unless all parties to the proceeding consent after consultation."

Turning to the question whether the former commissioner's firm must be disqualified, the court concluded: "... no conflict of interest is even alleged here; rather the appearance of impropriety is asserted as the sole basis supporting recusal of Thomas's firm. *Except for authorized ex parte matters* and instances of unethical behavior, a judge's role in a court proceeding does not present the opportunity for confidentiality with a party. (See Cal.Code of Jud.Conduct, canon 3.) Nonetheless, the parties' and the public's perception of impropriety needs to be alleviated by a process which assures that neither the former judge nor his law firm has or will receive an unfair advantage. Screening serves this purpose. A trial court hearing a recusal motion thus must look beyond the mere allegation of appearance of impropriety to determine whether appropriate screening has occurred and whether screening can effectively continue to protect against the former judge's participation." (227 Cal.App.3d at p. 1680, 278 Cal.Rptr. 588, italics added.) The court concluded that the law firm should be given an opportunity to establish that the former commissioner, now attorney, had been effectively screened from the case. If that requirement was satisfied, the *Higdon* court directed the trial court to deny the motion for recusal of the firm. (*Id.* at pp. 1680–1681, 278 Cal.Rptr. 588.)

In reaching this conclusion, the *Higdon* court considered another provision of rule 1.12 of the ABA Model Rules of Professional Conduct, which addresses recusal of a law firm employing a former judicial officer: " '(c) If a lawyer is disqualified by paragraph (a), no lawyer in a firm with which that lawyer is associated may knowingly undertake or continue representation in the matter unless: [¶] (1) the disqualified lawyer is screened from any participation in the matter and is apportioned no part of the fee therefrom; and [¶] (2) written notice is promptly given to the appropriate tribunal to enable it to ascertain compliance with the provisions of this rule.' " (227 Cal.App.3d at p. 1676, 278 Cal.Rptr. 588.)

The protection of the confidences of litigants has been a primary focus of rules of professional conduct in California and as drafted by the American Bar Association. (See Rules Prof.Conduct, rule 3–310(E); *Flatt v. Superior Court*, 9 Cal.4th 275, 283, 36 Cal.Rptr.2d 537, 885 P.2d 950 [discussing fiduciary duty of confidentiality in context of Rules of Professional Conduct]; ABA Model Rules Prof.Conduct, rules 1.6; 1.9; and 1.10.) Public attorneys moving to the private sector are treated separately under the American Bar Association's Model Rules of Professional Conduct, rule 1.11 (Model Rules). Subdivision (b) of that rule provides: "[A] lawyer having information that the lawyer knows is confidential government information about a person acquired when the lawyer was a public officer or employee, may not represent a private client whose interests are adverse to that person in a matter in which the information could be used to the material disadvantage of that person. A firm with which that lawyer is associated may undertake or continue representation in the matter only if the disqualified lawyer is screened from any participation in the matter and is apportioned no part of the fee therefrom." Similarly, under the Model Rules, a former judge may not represent anyone in connection with a matter in which he or she "participated personally and substantially as a judge. . . ." (Model Rules, rule 1.12(a).) The rule on vicarious disqualification of the law firm employing a former judicial officer parallels the rule for former public attorneys: the disqualified attorney must be screened from participation, receive no share of the fee, and notice must be given to the appropriate tribunal. (Model Rules, rule 1.12(c).)

The integrity of the judicial process demands that litigants have confidence that a judicial officer who has been privy to revelations regarding the case in the course of settlement conferences will not later become aligned with the opposition. Unlike the disqualification of a former private sector attorney who has governmental information, here the former judge became privy to the confidences of private parties to the litigation.

We are presented with a situation in which the judge's role did include receiving confidences from petitioner's counsel ex parte during repeated settlement conferences. The case is analogous to that of a mediator who was disqualified from representing a litigant in a subsequent matter related to an earlier case in which the mediator had received confidences from the parties. (*Poly Software International, Inc. v. Su* (D.Utah 1995) 880 F.Supp. 1487.)

[In *Poly Software* the district court required disqualification of a former mediator and his firm from representing parties involved in the mediation against other parties to the mediation.]

* * *

We agree with the analysis in *Poly Software* that disqualification of both the individual attorney and his or her firm is required where the attorney has been privy to confidences of a litigant while acting as a neutral mediator. * * *

All manner of issues are discussed in confidence at a settlement conference, including the strengths and weaknesses of each party's case, and the amount the party is willing to pay or receive in settlement. "[A] settlement conference judge does not decide anything—he merely uses his judicial status to help the parties reach a settlement if reasonably possible. To this end it has been said that the judge should actively participate in the negotiating process to 'break the ice' between litigants who may be reluctant to settle. The judge should also use any expertise he may have in the subject area of the litigation to express his opinions of the settlement value of the various causes of action against the different defendants or of the range in which negotiations may realistically proceed. He should listen to and carefully evaluate the parties' personal contentions so they will feel they have had their 'day in court' if the case is settled. [Citations.]"

(*Horton v. Superior Court* (1987) 194 Cal.App.3d 727, 733, 238 Cal.Rptr. 467.)

No amount of assurances or screening procedures, no "cone of silence," could ever convince the opposing party that the confidences would not be used to its disadvantage. When a litigant has bared its soul in confidential settlement conferences with a judicial officer, that litigant could not help but be horrified to find that the judicial officer has resigned to join the opposing law firm—which is now pressing or defending the lawsuit against that litigant. No one could have confidence in the integrity of a legal process in which this is permitted to occur without the parties' consent.

Petitioner has urged us to adopt the "substantial relationship" test applied in *Rosenfeld Construction Co. v. Superior Court* (1991) 235 Cal. App.3d 566, 286 Cal.Rptr. 609.

We have no quarrel with * * * the *Rosenfeld* court's policy analysis, but we find that it does not apply to this case. Here, Judge Younger had no previous attorney-client relationship with petitioner. Moreover, the motion to disqualify was brought in the identical action in which Judge Younger served as settlement judge. Under these circumstances, the "substantial relationship" test does not apply. The common theme between the disqualification opinions discussed in *Rosenfeld* and our case is the vital importance of maintaining confidences disclosed in the course of litigation to ensure public trust in the judicial system.

* * *

DISPOSITION

[The Court of Appeal directed the Superior Court to vacate its order denying petitioner's motion to disqualify Graham & James and to enter a new order granting the motion.]

A.M. WOOD, P.J., and HASTINGS, J., concur.

* * *

GOLDBERG v. WARNER/CHAPPELL MUSIC, INC.

California Court of Appeal, Second District, 2005.
125 Cal.App.4th 752, 23 Cal.Rptr.3d 116.

CURRY, J.

Appellant Ilene Goldberg brought suit against respondents, her former employer Warner/Chappell Music, Inc. (Warner) and her former supervisor Edward Pierson, for wrongful termination. Goldberg claimed that she was discriminated against in the terms and conditions of her employment based on her gender, and terminated in retaliation for raising complaints about gender-based discrimination. Goldberg also claimed to have been terminated in retaliation for "blowing the whistle" on illegal conduct allegedly committed by Pierson, including practicing law without a license.

Goldberg moved to disqualify counsel for respondents, Mitchell Silberberg & Knupp LLP (MS & K). The ground for the motion was that six years earlier Goldberg had consulted with J. Eugene Salomon, a former partner with MS & K who had left the firm three years prior to the underlying lawsuit. The consultation involved Goldberg's written contract with Warner. Respondents and MS & K established in opposition to the disqualification motion that the consultation had been brief and informal, and that no one else at MS & K had any knowledge concerning either the consultation or any confidential information imparted to Salomon. The trial court denied the motion to disqualify.

Goldberg contends that it is or should be the law in California, that an attorney's presumed knowledge of a former client's confidences should cause vicarious disqualification not just of the attorney's present firm, but also any firm the attorney passed through after he gained possession of confidential information. Respondents contend that we should follow the lead of the ABA Model Rules of Professional Conduct, which permit a firm that employed the conflicted attorney in the past to undertake representation adverse to the attorney's former client, as long as the firm can prove no current member or associate is actually possessed of confidential information concerning the client.

We agree with the trial court that an attorney's presumed possession of confidential information concerning a former client should not automatically cause the attorney's former firm to be vicariously disqualified where the evidence establishes that no one other than the departed attorney had any dealings with the client or obtained confidential information, and affirm.

FACTUAL AND PROCEDURAL BACKGROUND

It is undisputed that Goldberg worked as in-house counsel for Warner from 1993 until December 2002. After her termination, Goldberg retained an attorney, Peter Marx, to advise her with regard to a potential lawsuit. On January 10 and 17, 2003, Marx sent letters pertaining to settlement discussions to respondents' attorneys, MS & K. The letters stated that Marx "ha[d] serious concerns about the propriety of [MS & K] representing [respondents] in this matter." His concerns "derive[d] from the fact that prior to the termination of her employment with [Warner], Ms. Goldberg had professional relationships with various members of [MS & K] and indeed ha[d] worked closely with them on various matters, and also maintain[ed] friendships with certain members of [MS & K]. As such, those members of [MS & K] are to one degree or another acquainted with the circumstances concerning the termination of Ms. Goldberg's employment, i.e., they are privy to information which certainly created the impression of impropriety, at the very least." Marx also referred to the fact that Goldberg had submitted a screenplay she had coauthored to MS & K partner David Steinberg. There was no reference to Goldberg being a former client of the firm.

In August 2003, the parties agreed to mediation. In a letter to MS & K, Goldberg's new counsel, Greenberg Glusker Fields Claman Machtinger & Kinsella, stated: "[Goldberg] expressly reserves any and all rights she may have to disqualify your firm. As I indicated to you, I am going to consider providing you with some information which may impact your decision to continue as counsel for [respondents]. In any event, your participation in the mediation will not and shall not be used in any subsequent proceeding to suggest that Ms. Goldberg has waived her rights or otherwise acquiesced to your firm's participation."

In November 2003, the mediation having failed, Goldberg filed her complaint against respondents. The complaint included claims for violation of the whistleblower statute, discrimination based on gender, retaliatory termination, wrongful termination in violation of public policy, intentional infliction of emotional distress, and violation of salary provisions of the Labor Code. There was no contract claim asserted.

MS & K filed an answer to the complaint on behalf of respondents in December 2003.

Motion to Disqualify

Goldberg formally moved to disqualify MS & K on December 10, 2003. In her moving papers, she presented evidence that in 1997, while still employed at Warner, she was given a written employment agreement to sign. She asked Salomon, then a partner with MS & K, to advise her with respect to the agreement. She met with Salomon for an hour and a half on May 9, 1997, to go over the terms of the agreement. She purportedly "disclosed confidential information to him including the nature and term of [her] employment agreement, [her] compensation and benefits, disability, termination by [Warner], [her] ability to retain, disclose, and use confidential/privileged information concerning [her] employment relationship with [Warner], scripts and other literary works created by [her], the effect of a change in control of [Warner], expiration of the employment agreement, and [Warner's] obligations under state and federal law." She also had "other conversations and correspondence with [Salomon] relating to his advice about the terms and conditions of [her] employment agreement." On July 29, 1997, she sent him a letter and draft of a proposed employment agreement, and promised to send the final agreement "for [his] files." She asked him to send her a bill for his advice, but he refused to do so.

Subsequently, Goldberg retained MS & K to work on various matters for Warner, and she "did not have an objection to [MS & K's] representation of [Warner] in matters that did not conflict with [MS & K's] prior representation of [her]."

Opposition

Respondents presented evidence in their opposition that in April 1997, one month prior to Goldberg's purported consultation with Salomon, MS & K began legal work on a copyright matter for Warner. A formal retention letter between MS & K and Warner was signed on May 2, 1997.

The executive director of MS & K stated in a declaration that there was no record in any of MS & K's files of Goldberg ever having been a client of the firm, and that the policy of the firm was to execute a formal, written engagement letter before taking on legal representation.

Adam Levin, the MS & K attorney who was responsible for the Goldberg litigation, stated he had been involved with the matter since January 2003, and that at no time prior to the mediation "did any of Goldberg's lawyers assert that MS & K and, in particular, [Salomon], had represented Goldberg in her individual capacity" or otherwise mention Salomon's name. Discussions of the propriety of MS & K's representation of respondents centered on the possibility that Goldberg's personal and professional relationships with other attorneys at the firm created a conflict. In a letter to Marx dated January 21, 2003, Levin stated: "[Y]ou raise purported 'concerns' about this firm's representation of [Warner] adverse to Ms. Goldberg. As we previously discussed, your concerns are wholly unfounded in that this firm has never represented Ms. Goldberg personally. Our past dealings with Ms. Goldberg solely have been in connection with our representation of [Warner] (for whom she sometimes was our client contact), as well as other clients. . . . Accordingly, there is no restriction (ethical, legal or otherwise) on our representation of [Warner] adverse to Ms. Goldberg." On October 30, 2003, at the mediation, Levin "learned for the first time that Goldberg was contending that she had been provided personal legal advice by * * * Salomon."

Salomon stated in a declaration that he practiced law at MS & K from October 1987 through October 2000, when he moved to another firm. He denied that he had been retained by Goldberg to represent her in her contract negotiations with Warner. Instead, Goldberg "told [Salomon] she was going to represent herself in negotiations over the contract, but asked if [Salomon] would talk to her about these agreements generally to get a sense of how [Warner] lawyers dealt with the contract's various provisions." He told Goldberg he "would be glad to talk to her about what she could expect in the course of her negotiations." They primarily discussed "what she might expect with respect to the boilerplate issues." Salomon "never discussed with any other lawyer at [MS & K] what was said in [his] conversation with Ms. Goldberg."

Prior to the hearing on the motion to disqualify, Goldberg sought to submit handwritten notes made at the meeting with Salomon for "in camera" review. These notes apparently somehow made it into the public court file.

Trial Court's Ruling

The court denied the motion to disqualify. At the hearing, the court stated that the only potential basis for disqualification was Goldberg's contact with Salomon, not her personal and professional relationships with other MS & K attorneys. The court concluded that there was an attorney-client relationship between Goldberg and Salomon even though Salomon appeared to be helping her "as a friend." The court agreed that if Salomon were still with MS & K, the firm would be disqualified. However, because Salomon had left the firm, there was no need for vicarious disqualification.

In its order, the court specifically found: "The evidence is undisputed that [MS & K] and Salomon never opened a file for Ms. Goldberg. They never billed her. There are no notes or records in their files about the meeting and no documents were prepared. No telephone calls were made. It was simply a meeting late one afternoon where Ms. Goldberg and Mr. Salomon sat down and discussed the meaning of the employment contract she was being offered and what provisions she might request. * * * There is no evidence that Mr. Salomon talked to anyone about this matter when he was with [MS & K]. And more importantly, he had left the firm approximately three years before this matter began. There is no fear of him talking about the case in the lunch room, or having his files seen by other members of the firm, as he is no longer there."

Goldberg filed a petition for writ of mandate for review of the order. By order dated March 24, 2004, the petition was denied, with one dissent. Goldberg noticed an appeal.

DISCUSSION

Rule 3–310(E) of the Rules of Professional Conduct provides that an attorney "shall not, without the informed written consent of the client or former client, accept employment adverse to the client, or former client where, by reason of the representation of the client or former client, the member has obtained confidential information material to the employment." There is no question that an attorney can and should be disqualified for representing a party adverse to a former client where the attorney possesses confidential information that could be helpful to the new client and hurtful to the old. (See, e.g., Henriksen v. Great American Savings & Loan (1992) 11 Cal.App.4th 109, 113, 14 Cal.Rptr.2d 184 ["[A] former client may seek to disqualify a former attorney from representing an adverse party by showing that the former attorney possesses confidential information adverse to the former client"].)

The courts do not generally inquire into whether the attorney actually possesses confidential information. (Adams v. Aerojet–General Corp. (2001) 86 Cal.App.4th 1324, 1331, 104 Cal.Rptr.2d 116.) Instead, the substantial relationship test is applied. " 'When a substantial relationship has been shown to exist between the former representation and the current representation, and when it appears by virtue of the nature of the former representation or the relationship of the attorney to his former client confidential information material to the current dispute would normally have been imparted to the attorney or to subordinates for whose legal work he was responsible, the attorney's knowledge of confidential information is presumed.' " (Rosenfeld Construction Co. v. Superior Court (1991) 235 Cal.App.3d 566, 574, 286 Cal.Rptr. 609, italics added; accord City National Bank v. Adams (2002) 96 Cal.App.4th 315, 327, 117 Cal. Rptr.2d 125; Adams v. Aerojet–General Corp., supra, 86 Cal.App.4th at p. 1331, 104 Cal.Rptr.2d 116.)

In addition, "[i]t is now firmly established that where the attorney is disqualified from representation due to an ethical conflict, the disqualification extends to the entire firm." (Adams v. Aerojet–General Corp., supra, 86 Cal.4th at p. 1333, 104 Cal.Rptr.2d 116.) "[W]here an attorney is disqualified because he formerly represented and therefore possesses [either actually or presumptively] confidential information regarding the adverse party in the current litigation, vicarious disqualification of the entire firm is compelled as a matter of law." (Henriksen v. Great American Savings & Loan, supra, 11 Cal.App.4th at p. 117, 14 Cal.Rptr.2d 184; accord Flatt v. Superior Court (1994) 9 Cal.4th 275, 283, 36 Cal.Rptr.2d 537, 885 P.2d 950 ["Where the requisite substantial relationship between the subjects of the prior and the current representations can be demonstrated, access to confidential information by the attorney in the course of the first representation (relevant, by definition, to the second representation) is presumed and disqualification of the attorney's representation of the second client is mandatory; indeed, the disqualification extends vicariously to the entire firm"].)

There is, however, a recognized "limited exception to this conclusive presumption in the rare instance where the lawyer can show that there was no opportunity for confidential information to be divulged." (City National Bank v. Adams, supra, 96 Cal.App.4th at pp. 327–328, 117 Cal.Rptr.2d 125; accord American Airlines, Inc. v. Sheppard, Mullin, Richter & Hampton (2002) 96 Cal.App.4th 1017, 1038, 117 Cal.Rptr.2d 685.) "[T]o apply the remedy of disqualification 'when there is no realistic chance that confidences were disclosed would go far beyond the purpose' of the substantial relationship test." (H.F. Ahmanson & Co. v. Salomon Brothers, Inc. (1991) 229 Cal.App.3d 1445, 1455, 280 Cal.Rptr. 614.)

This limited exception was applied in Adams v. Aerojet–General Corp., supra, 86 Cal.App.4th 1324, 104 Cal.Rptr.2d 116. The supposedly tainted attorney there had worked for the Holliman firm. While he was with the firm, it represented Aerojet with respect to advice on land use issues. The attorney in question, however, had nothing to do with that representation. He departed the firm in 1989. A decade later, his new firm, Hackard Holt, was retained to represent a number of individuals in a suit against Aerojet involving release of toxic chemicals and contamination of groundwater. Aerojet sought to disqualify the attorney and the Hackard Holt firm because of the attorney's former association with the Holliman firm. Declarations submitted to the trial court established that the attorney "did not perform any work on Aerojet matters" and "had no discussions with the [other] attorneys at [the Holliman firm] regarding Aerojet matters and was not made privy to any information, confidential or otherwise, about Aerojet.'' (Id. at p. 1329, 104 Cal.Rptr.2d 116.) The trial court ordered Hackard Holt disqualified.

On appeal, the court acknowledged that ''[i]f [the attorney] himself had been personally involved with the [Holliman] firm's work on Aerojet matters during his tenure with the firm in the 1980's, this appeal would be easily resolved. [The Holliman firm's] former representation of Aerojet clearly has a substantial relationship to the present lawsuit under the [H.F.] Ahmanson [& Co. v. Salomon Brothers, Inc., supra,] [substantial relationship] test: factual issues are similar if not identical (disposal of waste and chemical contamination in and around the Aerojet site); legal issues are related (toxic tort liability and the duty to warn the public); and [the attorney's] [hypothetical] prior work on the case would have placed him in a position to be exposed to confidential information belonging to Aerojet.'' (Adams v. Aerojet–General Corp., supra, at p. 1332, 104 Cal. Rptr.2d 116.)

Because, however, ''there [was] no indication of [the attorney's] personal involvement in Aerojet matters, nor any direct evidence that he was exposed to client secrets during the time his former firm rendered services to Aerojet,'' the court decided not to extend the doctrine of imputed knowledge and vicarious disqualification to the new firm. (Adams v. Aerojet–General Corp., supra, at pp. 1332–1333, 104 Cal.Rptr.2d 116.) The court believed the ''case d[id] not present a standard application of the imputed knowledge doctrine'' and that ''the [trial] court applied the concept in reverse: instead of imputation from attorney to the remainder of the firm, the court here ruled that, once a connection was shown between the former firm's representation and the issues involved in the current lawsuit, the knowledge acquired by the former firm was 'imputed' back to the attorney, mandating his automatic disqualification even after his departure from the firm, without inquiry as to whether the attorney was reasonably likely to have obtained confidential information. To burden an attorney with ... presumptive knowledge based solely on his former membership in a law firm which represented the former client, * * * would require a significant extension of the doctrine of imputed knowledge beyond that recognized by any existing case law.'' (Id. at pp. 1333–1334, 104 Cal.Rptr.2d 116.)

The court explained why it distinguished the situation before it from the situation where the attorney who sought to undertake adverse representation was still working with the attorneys who had acquired the former client's confidential information: '' 'No amount of assurances or screening procedures, no ''cone of silence,'' could ever convince the opposing party that the confidences would not be used to its disadvantage. * * * No one could have confidence in the integrity of a legal process in which this is permitted to occur without the parties' consent.' [Citation.] * * * Once an attorney departs the firm, however, a blanket rule to prevent future breaches of confidentiality is not necessary because the departed attorney no longer has presumptive access to the secrets possessed by the former firm. The court need no longer rely on the fiction of imputed knowledge to safeguard client confidentiality. Instead, the court may undertake a dispassionate assessment of whether and to what extent the attorney, during his tenure with the former firm, was reasonably likely to have obtained confidential information material to the current lawsuit." (Adams v. Aerojet–General Corp., supra, at pp. 1334–1335, 104 Cal. Rptr.2d 116.)

The court found further support for its decision in the realities of modern law firm practice: "Disqualification based on a conclusive presumption of imputed knowledge derived from a lawyer's past association with a law firm is out of touch with the present day practice of law. Gone are the days when attorneys (like star athletes) typically stay with one organization throughout their entire careers. * * * We have seen the dawn of the era of the 'mega-firm.' Large law firms (like banks) are becoming ever larger, opening branch offices nationwide or internationally, and merging with other large firms. Individual attorneys today can work for a law firm and not even know, let alone have contact with, members of the same firm working in a different department of the same firm across the hall or a different branch across the globe." (Adams v. Aerojet–General Corp., supra, at p. 1336, 104 Cal.Rptr.2d 116.)

From this, the court concluded that "a rule which disqualifies an attorney based on imputed knowledge derived solely from his membership in the former firm and without inquiry into his actual exposure to the former client's secrets sweeps with too broad a brush, is inconsistent with the language and core purpose of rule 3–310(E), and unnecessarily restricts both the client's right to chosen counsel and the attorney's freedom of association. It also clashes with the principle that applying the remedy of disqualification ' "when there is no realistic chance that confidences were disclosed [to counsel] would go far beyond the purpose" of the substantial relationship test.' " (Adams v. Aerojet–General Corp., supra, at p. 1337, 104 Cal.Rptr.2d 116, quoting H.F. Ahmanson & Co. v. Salomon Brothers, Inc., supra, 229 Cal.App.3d at p. 1455, 280 Cal.Rptr. 614.)

We agree with the court in Adams that at some point, it ceases to make sense to apply a presumption of imputed knowledge as a lawyer moves from firm to firm. Salomon, while at MS & K, gave advice to Goldberg concerning the terms of her contract with Warner. We agree with the trial court that, despite the informality, an attorney-client relationship existed between them. Moreover, if Salomon were still practicing at MS & K, MS & K would likely have to be disqualified from the current litigation because there would be no practical way of ensuring that, despite his best intentions, Salomon would not let slip some confidential information he may not even be aware that he possesses. But Salomon is no longer with MS & K. We need not be concerned that he will inadvertently pass on confidential information to his colleagues in the future because he is no longer there "in the lunch room" as the trial court said. It was appropriate under the circumstances for the trial court to make an assessment of whether Salomon actually passed on confidential information. Since the court found he had not, there was no basis for disqualification.

* * * [W]e believe the district court misconstrued California law. If an attorney worked on a matter "substantially related" to the matter in which he seeks to represent a party adverse to his former client, the presumption is conclusive that the attorney is possessed of confidential information that would impact the present matter. Where tainted attorneys and nontainted attorneys are working together at the same firm, there is not so much a conclusive presumption that confidential information has passed as a pragmatic recognition that the confidential information will work its way to the nontainted attorneys at some point. When, however, the relationship between the tainted attorneys and nontainted attorneys is in the past, there is no need to "rely on the fiction of imputed knowledge to safeguard client confidentiality" and opportunity exists for a "dispassionate assessment" of whether confidential information was actually exchanged. (Adams v. Aerojet–General Corp., supra, 86 Cal.App.4th at p. 1335, 104 Cal.Rptr.2d 116.) This is precisely what the trial court did here.

Our conclusion that the trial court analyzed the matter correctly is also in line with the ABA Model Rules of Professional Conduct, which California courts may consult when a matter is not addressed by the California Rules. (See, e.g., Flatt v. Superior Court, supra, 9 Cal.4th at pp. 282–283, 36 Cal.Rptr.2d 537, 885 P.2d 950; Ojeda v. Sharp Cabrillo Hospital (1992) 8 Cal.App.4th 1, 8, 10 Cal.Rptr.2d 230.) Model Rule 1.10(b) provides: "When a lawyer has terminated an association with a firm, the firm is not prohibited from thereafter representing a person with interests materially adverse to those of a client represented by the formerly associated lawyer and not currently represented by the firm, unless (1) the matter is the same or substantially related to that in which the formerly associated lawyer represented the client, and (2) any lawyer remaining in the firm has [protected] information . . . that is material to the matter." Courts from other jurisdictions have followed the Model Rule in situations analogous to the present one: where an attorney who presumptively acquired confidential information from a former client leaves the firm, the firm is not automatically disqualified if it chooses to represent a party adverse to the former client. (Sorci v. Iowa District Court for Polk County (Iowa 2003) 671 N.W.2d 482, 494–495 [noting that "Iowa Code of Professional Responsibility for Lawyers is silent on the issue of whether a firm, which was required to decline or withdraw from employment because of one of its members, must remain disqualified once the personally prohibited lawyer leaves the firm," court applied the Model Rules and the Restatement to resolve disqualification issues]; Richard v. Southern Pacific Transp. Co. (E.D.La.1990) 735 F.Supp. 206, 209 [court applied Model Rule 1.10(b) where former client's relationship to presumptively tainted attorney and his former firm was "temporary in nature and on a trial basis," and denied disqualification motion].) This is further basis to uphold the trial court's determination.

DISPOSITION

The order is affirmed.

* * *

JOINT REPRESENTATION

The ABA Model Rules do not prohibit lawyers from representing two or more clients in a particular matter, subject to the Rules' provisions regarding conflicts of interest. Multiple representation also potentially implicates Rule 1.8(g)'s prohibition against "aggregate settlements" unless each of the clients consents after full disclosure. [*See* ABA Standing Comm. on Ethics and Professional Responsibility, Formal Op. 06–438 (2006) (disclosure requirements under Rule 1.8(g)).] Professor Bassett considers the myriad situations in which joint representation issues arise and sets forth an analysis of the risks and benefits of joint representation in "*Three's A Crowd: A Proposal to Abolish Joint Representation*," 32 Rutgers L.J. 387, 433–38 (2001)*:

> Three basic policy considerations underlie the conflict of interest rules dealing with joint representation: (1) the interests of clients in certain objectives that are available through joint representation; (2) the need to protect clients from the dangers of joint representation; and (3) the desire to preserve lawyers' reputations by avoiding apparent impropriety. These policies indicate the ethical rules concerning joint representation involve a balancing of the risks of the latter two considerations with the client benefit resulting from permitting the practice. Accordingly, it is appropriate to examine the benefits resulting from joint representation.
>
> Joint representation is desirable from a client's perspective primarily because it is cost-effective. Other proffered justifications include maintaining an amicable relationship with the co-client; the desire to retain a particular attorney—whether due to reputation, prior relationship, or familiarity with the subject of the representation; and the "united front" strategy.
>
> Joint representation also confers benefits upon lawyers. The practice is desirable from the attorney's perspective because, assuming the clients desire joint representation, it permits the attorney to please those clients by agreeing to undertake the representation; it generates more revenue; and it eliminates some of the very real problems that can arise in separate representation concerning communications with a party represented by counsel.
>
> However, joint representation also presents inherent problems. Joint representation reduces the protection available under the attorney-client privilege. Joint representation also compromises confiden-

tiality due to the lawyer's duty to inform all co-clients of all information relevant to the representation.

Moreover, joint representation *always* presents the potential for a disqualifying conflict of interest. When a lawyer agrees to provide joint representation, the lawyer acquires two (or more) separate clients, each of whom is entitled to the lawyer's best efforts and loyalty. The attorney is not permitted to prioritize clients by, for example, treating the corporate employer as the "primary" or "real" client and the employee as an expendable "secondary" client. Thus, if the clients' interests diverge, the attorney is subject to disqualification and must withdraw—usually causing both financial and tactical hardship for the clients, and potentially resulting in a malpractice claim or disciplinary charges against the lawyer. The lawyer's withdrawal requires each client to retain individual counsel, resulting in duplication of effort and expense for *both* clients. The original lawyer's work product usually cannot be delivered to substitute counsel, for the obvious reason that permitting substitute counsel access to the work product for all practical purposes negates the effect of the original attorney's withdrawal.

Accordingly, the primary justification for joint representation from the clients' perspective—the cost savings—is overshadowed by the burden that will fall on the clients if the attorney is subsequently required to withdraw. In exchange for the possibility of reduced costs, the clients face the possibility of finding two new counsel, perhaps on short notice. The clients likely will have to pay new counsel to research some of the same issues the first lawyer was paid to do, and may suffer tactical disadvantages during the time the new attorneys are getting up to speed. The other identified client benefits—maintaining an amicable relationship with the co-client, strategy concerns, and the ability to select a particular lawyer—similarly vanish when subsequent withdrawal becomes necessary.

From the attorney's perspective, joint representation presents a potential loss of two clients. In addition to the loss of income for that particular matter, the lawyer likely has lost any future business from those clients due to the inconvenience caused them by the lawyer's withdrawal. If one of those affected was a large corporate client, the future financial loss to the lawyer may be substantial. The lawyer may also be required to forfeit any legal fees earned before withdrawal. Moreover, if forced to withdraw at a particularly unfortunate time, the lawyer may face legal malpractice or disciplinary charges, which create both financial and reputational concerns. Even absent actual charges, disqualification or withdrawal may result in damage to the lawyer's reputation.

1. The current rules require the attorney to ascertain whether the conflict between two clients is consentable, and if so, to obtain informed written consent from both clients. Should the rules require a duty to

investigate in order to discover areas of potential inconsistency or disagreement?

2. Professor Bassett also challenges the assumption that informed consent should remedy any problem, stating that "the current ethical rules and case law ascribe far too much credit to the curative power of waiver." Indeed, the notion of client consent as an effective remedy recurs throughout the Model Rules. Can you articulate the benefits of permitting client consent as a remedy to conflicts of interest—and can you examine the pitfalls behind an assumption of consent as a remedy?

IMPUTED DISQUALIFICATION AND SCREENING

Legal ethics rules and case law begin with the assumption that lawyers working together in a single firm share each other's, and their clients', secrets and confidences. [*See* ABA Model Rule 1.6, comment.] This assumption is based on the realities of practice as well—both office routine and financial rewards are shared within a firm. [*See* Restatement § 123, comments *b-c*.] Generally, the assumption works well; no one seriously suggests that two partners within a single firm could represent adversaries in litigation. One consequence of this assumption is that lawyers within a firm must also share each other's disqualifications for conflicts of interest; one lawyer's conflicts are imputed to all other lawyers in the firm. [*See generally* ABA Model Rule 1.10(a) and comment 2; Restatement § 123.] In a time of increased lawyer mobility, imputed disqualification rules can quickly spread taints when lawyers move among firms, and the result can spin out of control.

Under the ABA Code (1969–1983), imputed disqualification became a near absolute rule. Code section DR 5–105(D) provided that if any one lawyer in a firm was disqualified, all lawyers in the firm were. There was no exception for client consent or waiver. [WOLFRAM, MODERN LEGAL ETHICS § 7.6.2 at 394 (1986).] The ABA Model Rules have adopted a much more flexible approach that does not apply to all disqualifying associations. For example, spousal and other family conflicts [Rule 1.7 comment] and the lawyer witness rule [Rule 3.7] do not come within the automatic disqualifications. There is no automatic disqualification for all lawyers with whom a departing lawyer had been associated [Rule 1.10(b).] Most imputed disqualifications can be cured by informed client consents. [Rule 1.10(c).]

Nevertheless, imputed disqualification rules regularly create problems for law firms when a lawyer moves from one firm to another. If a client or former client of the former firm is involved as an adversary with a client of the newly associated firm, both firms could end up disqualified, and in sharply contested matters, removing the disqualification by client consent is unlikely. The proposed favored solution from the bar is to protect the new firm by screening off the tainted lawyer. Such devices are commonly referred to today as "ethical walls." Their approval in the courts had been decidedly mixed and originally largely limited to former public officers, government employees, and judges moving to private practices. [*See* Model Rules 1.11 and 1.12 approving such screening and the discussion in *Haagen-Dazs, Co., Inc., supra.*] In 2009, Model Rule 1.10 was amended to authorize screening when an attorney moves from one private firm to another, subject to specified conditions, including that the screened lawyer receives no part of the fee generated from the representation, and the provision of written notice regarding the screening to the former client. [*See* ABA Formal Op. 09–455 (2009) (authorizing the disclosure of information relevant to potential conflicts when a lawyer moves from one firm to another, so long as the information does not violate attorney-client privilege, is no more than necessary to identify potential conflicts, and the disclosed information is not used for any other purpose).]

CONFLICTS OF INTEREST AND PRO BONO PROJECTS

When an attorney wishes to undertake volunteer legal work on a pro bono basis, must s/he conduct a standard conflicts check before undertaking the pro bono representation? If the attorney is providing pro bono services "under the auspices of a program sponsored by a nonprofit organization or court," the lawyer will fall within the more generous provisions of Model Rule 6.5, which limits a lawyer's exposure to conflicts of interest only to representations where the lawyer knows that the representation involves a conflict of interest. The rule similarly limits imputed conflicts to those situations where "the lawyer knows that another lawyer associated with the lawyer in a law firm is disqualified * * *" [*See also* Cal. Rules of Professional Conduct, rule 1–650 (patterned on ABA Model Rule 6.5).]

The California State Bar decided not to adopt an imputed disqualification rule as part of its Rules of Professional Conduct. The drafters feared (1) the proposed rule (3–300) would establish *de facto* standards for trial courts' rulings on disqualification motions; (2) a bright-line rule could not adequately cover the myriad situations caused by the movement of lawyers and non-lawyer employees between firms; and (3) Business and Professions Code 6068(e) [client confidences] and Rule 1–120 [aiding and abetting rules violations] taken together address the central issues of protection of client confidences for purposes of imposing discipline. Thus, imputed disqualification will continue to be decided on a case-by-case basis in California, as the *Rosenfeld* and *Cho* cases indicate.

MULTIPLE CHOICE QUESTIONS

Answer these questions using the definitions found at the end of Chapter Two.

1. After they graduated from law school, Cheryl and Dennis were married and went to work for separate law firms in a large city. Cheryl's practice is primarily trademark litigation, and Dennis's practice is primarily general business counseling; only rarely does he become involved in trial work. One of Dennis's regular business clients sued a major corporation for trademark infringement. Dennis and his law firm appear on the pleadings as counsel for plaintiff, but, in fact, all of the trial work is being done by another firm that specializes in trademarks. The defendant's lead counsel died suddenly, and his firm withdrew from the case. Now the defendant has asked Cheryl and her firm to take over the defense. Which of the following is most nearly correct?

A. If Cheryl and her firm agree to represent the defendant, then Dennis and his firm will be *subject to discipline* if they do not seek their client's permission to withdraw.

B. Cheryl and her firm will be *subject to discipline* if she agrees to represent the defendant, since to do so would create an appearance of impropriety.

C. If the respective clients consent after full disclosure of the situation, then Cheryl and Dennis *may* participate on opposite sides of the case.

D. Cheryl and Dennis *may* participate on opposite sides of the case, since the mere fact that they are married creates neither an actual nor an apparent conflict of interest.

2. Law partners Norman and Enid are too busy to spend much time discussing their legal work with each other. For many years, Enid's major client has been Eratec Corporation, a diversified electronics firm with worldwide operations. Most of Norman's time is devoted to his work as outside general counsel for North American Industries, Inc. It is a diversified manufacturing company with operations in Canada, the United States, and Mexico. Enid filed a law suit in the United States on behalf of a French subsidiary of Eratec. The defendant was a Canadian joint venture. When Enid received the answer to the complaint, he was shocked to discover that North American was one of the three joint venturers, and that Norman was listed on the caption of the answer as "Of Counsel" to the joint venture. Immediately after Enid called this to Norman's attention, Norman explained the situation to North American and to the lead counsel for the joint venture. Both readily consented to the removal of his name from the pleading. Enid then continued in the case as counsel for the plaintiff, Eratec's French subsidiary. Which of the following is most nearly correct?

A. Enid and Norman handled the matter in a *proper* manner, since Norman had his name removed from the pleading promptly after the conflict of interest was discovered.

B. Enid is *subject to discipline*, even though Norman's name was promptly removed from the pleading.

C. Neither Enid nor Norman is *subject to discipline*, since the conflict of interest was unintentional and was remedied as soon as it was discovered.

D. Enid handled the matter in a *proper* manner, but Norman is subject to discipline for failing to discover the conflict of interest at the outset.

3. R, S, T, and U are four sellers of high-speed photoimage reproductor disks. U falsely advertises its disks, and U's false statements injure R, S, and T by causing some of their customers to buy instead from U. But R, S, and T are not sure of the precise amount of business each lost. The three of them hire Attorney A to represent them in a suit against U for an injunction and damages, and A agrees to take the case for a 30% contingent fee. After extensive discovery, U's attorney calls A with a settlement offer: U will consent to a court order enjoining U from using the allegedly false statements in future advertising, and U will pay a total of $100,000, in return for a full release of all claims by R, S, and T. In A's opinion, the consent order would adequately protect R, S, and T from future harm, but A believes in good faith that $100,000 is ridiculously low and would not compensate R, S, and T for their past losses. Which of the following is most nearly correct?

A. A will be *subject to discipline* if he accepts U's settlement offer, because he does not believe in good faith that $100,000 would sufficiently compensate R, S, and T for their past losses.

B. A will be *subject to discipline* if he does not let R, S, and T decide what to do about U's settlement offer, even though he represents them on a contingent fee basis, and even though he believes that $100,000 is not enough to compensate them for their past losses.

C. A *may* accept U's settlement offer, provided that he takes no more than 30% of it as his fee, and that he distributes the remainder equitably among R, S, and T.

D. A *may* reject U's settlement offer, since he does not believe in good faith that $100,000 would sufficiently compensate R, S, and T for their past losses.

4. Wife Wendy and husband Harry ask attorney Anna to represent both of them in a dissolution of marriage proceeding in a state that allows "no-fault" dissolution. The couple has no children. Wendy is a successful young pediatrician, and Harry is an unemployed computer programmer. They want Anna to represent both of them because separate lawyers may cost more and may stir up antagonism, and because they hope Anna can

help them reach a property and support agreement that is mutually acceptable. Which of the following is most nearly correct?

A. If Anna represents both, she will be *subject to discipline* for counseling both sides in an adversary proceeding.

B. Anna *may* represent both, provided that she obtains from them separate covenants not to sue her later for legal malpractice.

C. If Anna represents both, she will be *subject to discipline* because Wendy's and Harry's interests are in present, actual conflict.

D. Anna *should not* represent both, because it is unlikely that she can serve both effectively.

5. Tillingham, Wadsworth & DePew is a sprawling corporation law firm with 200 partners, 600 associates, and branch offices in eight major cities. Reynard DePew is the senior partner in charge of the firm's Washington, D.C., branch office. A year ago, he was retained by Transpac Oil Company to prepare some Transpac executives to testify before a Senate committee in opposition to proposed antitrust legislation that would require all integrated oil companies to divest themselves of their retail service stations. In connection with this work, DePew received truckloads of confidential documents from Transpac concerning competitive conditions in the retail end of the oil industry. DePew did not share this confidential information with anyone in the firm's Denver branch office, nor did he ever discuss the matter with anyone in the Denver office; indeed, no one in the Denver office even knew that DePew was working on the matter. Eight months after the matter was concluded, the Independent Service Station Dealers of America asked the firm's Denver office to represent it as plaintiff in an antitrust action against nine major integrated oil companies, including Transpac. *May* the Denver office accept the case without Transpac's consent?

A. No, because the case is substantially related to the work DePew did for Transpac.

B. Yes, because the case is not substantially related to the work DePew did for Transpac.

C. Yes, provided that the firm concludes that it can effectively represent the Dealers Association and that DePew is screened off from the case and does not share any fees earned in the case.

D. Yes, because the Denver office never received any of Transpac's confidential information from DePew.

6. Lawyer Leggett is a partner in a private law firm that represents numerous landlords who rent apartments to low-income families. Leggett is also a member of the Board of Directors of the County Legal Aid Society. Some of the other directors are non-lawyers. The society offers free legal services to low-income clients in a variety of civil matters. The legal services are actually provided by paid lawyers on the society staff or by volunteer lawyers from the community. Up to now, the society has not

had enough funding to offer services in landlord-tenant disputes. Recently it acquired a new source of funds, and now the Board of Directors needs to decide whether to add landlord-tenant disputes to the society's list of services. Leggett knows that an affirmative answer will adversely affect his firm's landlord clients. Which of the following is most nearly correct?

A. Leggett is *subject to discipline* for being a director of a legal services organization in which some directors are non-lawyers.

B. Leggett's participation in the decision will make him *subject to discipline*, no matter which way he votes.

C. Leggett *may* participate in the decision, but if he votes "no," he will be *subject to discipline*.

D. Leggett *may* participate in the decision, but if he votes "yes," he will be *subject to discipline*.

7. When attorney Aldrich was in private practice, she defended client Costa in two criminal assault and battery cases. The cases were three years apart, and both times the victim was Vincent, Costa's brother-in-law. Costa was convicted in both cases. Thereafter, Aldrich was elected County Prosecutor. As County Prosecutor, Aldrich hires and fires deputy prosecutors and generally supervises their work. As time permits, she also personally prepares and tries some cases. Her former client Costa is in trouble again, this time for the apparent first-degree murder of Vincent. A state statute requires all first-degree murder prosecutions to be conducted under the "direct, immediate, and personal supervision" of the County Prosecutor. The statute further provides that the State Attorney General's Office shall take over any criminal prosecution in which the local County Prosecutor cannot act due to conflict of interest. Which of the following is most nearly correct?

A. Aldrich *may* ask the State Attorney General's Office to take over the prosecution because she and her deputies have a conflict of interest.

B. Aldrich *may* personally prepare and prosecute the case because it arises out of a transaction separate and distinct from those in which she represented Costa.

C. Aldrich *may* assign one of her deputies to prepare and prosecute the case, so long as she undertakes "direct, immediate, and personal supervision" of the work.

D. Aldrich may assign one of her deputies to prepare and prosecute the case and then carefully screen herself off from any personal participation in the case.

Answers to the multiple choice questions appear in the Appendix at the end of the book.

CHAPTER THIRTEEN

LAWYERS IN LAW FIRMS AND SPECIALIZED PRACTICE AREAS

■ ■ ■

What This Chapter Covers

- **I. Lawyers as Group Practitioners**
  - A. The Changing World of Law Practice
    - 1. New Forms of Legal Practice
    - 2. Law Firm Breakups—When Partners Leave
    - 3. Law Firms in Combinations with Non–Lawyer Businesses
  - B. Discipline of Law Firms
- **II. Lawyer as Employee**
  - A. Respective Duties of Supervising and Subordinate Lawyers
  - B. Lawyer–Employee Rights Upon Termination
- **III. Specialized Lawyer Roles**
  - A. Lawyers as Advisors
  - B. Lawyers as Evaluators
  - C. Lawyers as Arbitrators and Mediators

Reading Assignment

Wydick, Perschbacher, & Bassett, Chapter 13.

ABA Model Rules:

Rules 1.0(c) (definition of "firm"), 1.10, 1.17, 2.1, 2.3, 2.4, 5.1 through 5.7.

CRPC 1–100(B), 1–300, 1–310, 1–320, 1–500 and 2–400.

Cal.Bus. & Prof.Code §§ 6125–6127.

Supplemental Reading

Hazard & Hodes:

Discussion of ABA Model Rules 1.10, 1.17, 2.1–2.4, and 5.1 through 5.7.

Restatement (Third) of the Law Governing Lawyers §§ 5, 9–12, 94–95, 122, 130 (2000).

ABA Standards of Practice for Lawyer Mediators in Family Disputes.

Discussion Problems

1. Lasar is a senior partner in the 20–lawyer firm of Fimrite, Steele & Lasar. Fimrite Steele's style of new lawyer training can best be described as "sink or swim." Newly hired associates are given tasks by the firm's partners and are expected to carry them out on their own, asking for help from the partners when needed. The firm is proud of the substantial responsibility given to its associates "right off the bat." New associate Allen was thrilled when, within one month after joining Fimrite Steele, she was given responsibility for preparing a new will and trust arrangement for Clint, one of the firm's longtime estate planning clients. Lasar, as the supervising partner for Clint's matters, gave Allen an example of the firm's "standard estate package" to use as a model for her assignment. Allen was concerned about several provisions in the model such as designating managing partner Fimrite as executor and a major banking client of the firm as trustee of the trust. However, Allen thought it best to stick with the model and not ask Lasar any questions that might make her look bad or be tagged as a troublemaker.

a. Has Allen acted properly in this matter?

b. What are Lasar's ethical obligations in the matter?

c. Should the Fimrite Steele firm be held accountable in any way?

d. What if Allen, instead of just carrying out the assignment, expressed her concerns about the firm's practices to the state agency that oversees fiduciary practices. As a result, the agency launched an investigation of Fimrite Steele's practices. When the firm's partners learned of Allen's role in informing the agency, she was immediately fired. Does Allen have any recourse against Fimrite Steele for her firing?

2. For the past four years, the law firm of Ayers & Alfred has been defending client Clayton Industries in a series of related products liability cases in which the plaintiffs seek hundreds of millions of dollars for injuries caused by an allegedly defective Clayton product. The damage claims exceed Clayton's assets ten-fold. International Bank & Trust Company is now deciding whether to renew Clayton's multi-million dollar line of credit. Clayton has asked Ayers & Alfred to prepare a candid evaluation of the products liability cases and to furnish it to International's loan department. What are the ethical obligations of Ayers & Alfred in this situation?

3. Powell is a former state court judge who retired two years ago. Wishing to continue to put her dispute resolution skills to good use, Powell has established a mediation practice, in which she serves as a third-party neutral to help individuals to resolve disputes.

a. Do any ethical rules govern this type of situation?

b. Snyder and Ramos seek Powell's assistance in resolving a property dispute. Assuming that this is a traditional mediation setting, are Snyder and Ramos both Powell's clients?

c. If Snyder and Ramos have each retained separate legal counsel, how might this benefit the mediation process? How might this complicate the mediation process?

d. After serving as a mediator in an employment dispute between employer Brooks and employee Caldwell, Norris seeks to retain Powell to sue Brooks for wrongful termination. May Powell represent Norris?

4. Following his graduation from law school, Johnson held a prestigious one-year judicial clerkship with a judge who sits on the federal Court of Appeals. Johnson, of course, did not actually decide cases; rather, it was his job to read the appellate briefs, conduct independent legal research into the issues raised, and write a "bench memorandum" for the three-judge panel assigned to each case. The "bench memorandum" contained summaries of the facts, the parties' legal arguments, and the applicable law, and made a recommendation regarding the disposition of the case. Sometimes the three-judge panel followed Johnson's recommendation; sometimes the panel rejected Johnson's recommendation. Following his clerkship year, Johnson joined a local mid-size law firm. Shortly after his arrival at the firm, one of the partners approached Johnson and asked him to work on a brief to the Court of Appeals due to Johnson's "expertise" in federal appellate work. May Johnson accept this assignment?

5. Bancroft, Willard is a local mid-size law firm. Differences of opinion developed among some of the firm's partners regarding the distribution of profits, and now four of the partners—constituting all of the firm's real estate attorneys—seek to leave Bancroft, Willard and form their own firm.

a. May Bancroft, Willard refuse to permit the four real estate partners to take their current clients with them upon forming their own firm?

b. Bancroft, Willard has asserted that its partnership agreement contains a provision that prohibits a departing lawyer from practicing law within a 50–mile radius for a one-year period unless the departing lawyer changes practice areas (such as a real estate lawyer changing to an intellectual property or environmental law practice). Is there any provision in the ABA Model Rules that the four real estate partners can use to fight this contention?

6. In the course of representing client Chamberlain, attorney Atkins ventured outside his usual area of expertise. Unfortunately, due to Atkins' incomplete legal research, he overlooked a potential affirmative defense that would have protected Chamberlain from liability. The error was discovered too late, and Chamberlain was required to pay $60,000 in damages to the plaintiff. Chamberlain subsequently filed a legal malprac-

tice lawsuit against Atkins. Chamberlain and Atkins have been attempting to reach a settlement. Atkins has agreed to reimburse Chamberlain for the judgment and the legal fees incurred. Chamberlain is still furious about the incompetence with which Atkins handled the case, and has demanded that Atkins decline all cases outside his usual area of expertise for a two-year period "to protect other unwitting clients from suffering similar consequences." Atkins was sufficiently troubled by Chamberlain's case that he has no intention of venturing outside his usual area of expertise ever again. May Atkins agree to Chamberlain's demand?

AMERICAN LAWYERS IN THE YEAR 2000: AN INTRODUCTION

Gerard J. Clark

33 Suffolk U.L.Rev. 293, 293–94, 302–03, 314–15 (2000).[1]

The American legal profession in the year 2000 is so large and so diverse, that it is difficult to describe. Like American business, it takes on an almost infinite variety of forms and structures. * * * Beginning with some demographics, the number of lawyers in the United States has literally exploded over the last 53 years. In 1947, there were approximately 169,000 lawyers in the United States, compared to approximately 1,000,000 today. About 72% of these U.S. attorneys are in private practice, about 10% are in-house counsels, close to 10% work for the government, and a small percentage are judges, law professors, and poverty lawyers. One-third of the bar are solo practitioners.

* * *

Commentators have separated the bar into roughly equal populations along client lines. One group represents individual clients with their personal legal problems, and the other represents institutions or organizations. Private practitioners deliver individual representation in a variety of practice settings. In-house counsel and government lawyers, as well as private practitioners, service institutions. Additionally, private practitioners may practice alone, in small to middle-sized firms, or in large firms.

* * *

Large law firms are getting larger, more numerous and employ an ever increasing percentage of the bar. The largest firm in the United States is Baker and McKenzie of Chicago (with branch offices in thirty-six countries) with 2,230 lawyers, of whom 535 are equity partners.

Traditionally, these firms serviced the general corporate law needs of America's largest companies. The services included advise negotiation, litigation and evaluation in the substantive fields of corporate, financial structuring, tax, commercial and regulatory law. Tension may exist between the firm so retained and in the in-house corporate law department, but generally the retained firm does the bulk of the important and

1. Reprinted with permission.

complex work. These firms eschewed work for individuals and stayed inside their fields of specialization. Other work was either sent to the client's in-house department, referred to another law firm, or simply turned down.

In the latter quarter of the twentieth century, however, large firms turned down less work. Firms wish to see themselves as full-service entities, who can engineer the merger of two Fortune 500 corporations, but can also have the capacity to handle the fields more traditionally associated with individual representation such as domestic relations, wills and trusts, real estate, personal injury and even criminal law. Additionally, in keeping with the expansion of the legal needs of corporate America (or more correctly, the corporate world), the full service firm is likely to add the capacity to handle problems in intellectual property, employment, international trade, and environmental and toxic torts. Further, institutional clients have tended more recently to keep a larger volume of their legal work in-house.

* * *

There is no reason to believe that the six-fold increase in the size of the profession over the last half-century will abate. Legislatures and the public continue to believe that all social problems can be solved by enacting new laws, especially while relationships in business and trade continue to grow.

* * *

Finally, when asking about the future of professionalism in the industry, one notices that there have been many recent laments. But many of these laments focus upon that segment of the bar serving large institutions, and these laments seem well-founded when the subject of the inquiry is the associate at the large firm who performs 2000 hours of discovery in the firm's litigation department without meeting a client or seeing the inside of a courtroom. Nevertheless, the notions of reverence for the law, fiduciary duty and client service seem quite alive and well among most of the lawyers in most segments of the bar.

FORMS OF LEGAL PRACTICE

A. BUSINESS ENTITIES

Although traditionally lawyers practiced either as sole practitioners or in partnerships, the ABA Model Rules allow lawyers to form professional corporations as long as all the shareholders, officers, and directors are lawyers. [Model Rule 5.4(d). *See also* Restatement § 9 and *Introductory Note* thereto.] These rules and state law allow lawyers to practice in the form of the professional corporation (P.C.) to gain the tax advantages of other corporations. However, the corporate form of business has generally not provided lawyer-shareholders a shield against malpractice liability as a result of the acts of other lawyer-shareholders in the professional corporation. Lawyers are also able to practice as members of group legal service plans, although this form of practice initially encountered strong opposition within the ABA, probably motivated by fear of competition from such plans. The official concern was a danger that the lawyer's professional independence could be compromised by nonlawyer owner or management. Restrictive provisions in the Model Code have since been superseded by the more benign controls of Model Rule 5.4.

More recently, the older forms of professional incorporation lost the tax advantages that originally led to this form of practice, and newer forms have emerged. In a limited liability company (LLC), individual lawyer members are liable for their own misconduct, but may limit their personal liability while still gaining the tax treatment accorded to general partners. This form of practice remains controversial; only a few states explicitly allow professionals to organize as LLCs, and the liability limitations have not been fully tested in the courts. [*See* Susan S. Fortney, *Am I My Partner's Keeper? Peer Review in Law Firms*, 66 U. Colo.L.Rev. 329, 330–333 (1995).] A second emerging form of practice is the limited liability partnership (LLP), which also limits a nonparticipating partner's liability for the negligent acts of other partners. For a good overall discussion of these forms of practice, see Robert R. Keatinge and George W. Coleman, *Practice of Law by Limited Liability Partnerships, and Limited Liability Companies*, 1995 Symposium Issue of the Professional Lawyer 5–50 (1995); Lance R. Rogers, *Questions of Law and Ethics Face Firms Becoming LLPs, LLCs*, 12 ABA/BNA Lawyers' Manual on Prof. Conduct 411–416 (1996).

B. OTHER TRENDS IN LEGAL PRACTICE

Despite some reluctance, a few law firms are beginning to permit limited telecommuting, allowing some attorneys to work from home. Stories are also starting to appear about virtual law practices, in which the attorneys have no formal office space. *See* Stephanie Francis Ward, *Virtually Practicing*, A.B.A. J., June 2009, available at http://www.abajournal.com/magazine/virtually_practicing/; *see also* Barbara Rose, *Online Office–Makers: Helping Others Create Virtual Practices*, A.B.A. J., Nov. 2009. Do existing rules adequately address such virtual law practices?

Legal outsourcing is also becoming more frequent, and was the subject of an ABA Formal Opinion. [*See* ABA Formal Op. 08–451 (2008) (requiring outsourcing lawyers to provide appropriate disclosures to the client, to avoid assisting the unauthorized practice of law, and to make reasonable efforts to ensure that the outsourced service providers, over whom the outsourcing lawyer acts as a supervisor, act compatibly with the lawyer's professional obligations pursuant to Model Rules 5.1 and 5.3), available at http://www.abanet.org/cpr/docs/08451.pdf.]

OFFSHORE LEGAL OUTSOURCING AND RISK MANAGEMENT: PROPOSING PROSPECTIVE LIMITATION OF LIABILITY AGREEMENTS UNDER MODEL RULE 1.8(H)

Joshua A. Bachrach
21 Geo. J. Legal Ethics 631 (2008).

The offshore outsourcing of legal services * * * seems to be gaining acceptance at a significant rate within the American legal community. In the coming years, increasing numbers of U.S. lawyers are expected to delegate legal work to intermediary vendors called legal process outsourcing ("LPO") companies, which employ both lawyers not licensed to practice in the United States and nonlawyers in overseas offices. A study by Prism Legal Consulting found that the number of LPOs increased by more than 300% between March 2005 and October 2006. Small law offices with few employees, corporate legal departments, and major U.S. law firms are now outsourcing legal work overseas to reduce costs and gain efficiencies.

As the practice of offshore legal outsourcing grows, U.S. lawyers might perceive tensions growing between their obligations to comply with legal ethics standards and their duties to clients who want them to consider using offshore legal outsourcing in certain situations. On the one hand, U.S. lawyers can draw guidance from the bar associations of Los Angeles County, New York City, San Diego County, and Florida, which have issued ethics opinions providing support for the ethical permissibility of offshore legal outsourcing. But those opinions also seem to require U.S. lawyers to assume increased ethical obligations, including a heightened duty to competently supervise foreign lawyers at an LPO and to review their final work product; indeed, outsourced work "returns as increased demand for high-level supervision." On the other hand, in response to clients' desires to reduce costs by outsourcing legal work overseas, U.S. lawyers might feel pressure to devote less time to supervising foreign lawyers at an LPO and instead spend more time on their own work for the client. Or, even if a client directs the U.S. lawyer to supervise the LPO's lawyers for a set number of hours, the U.S. lawyer might find the designated time to be insufficient and a source of unnecessarily increased liability risks. In either of these situations, U.S. law firms might feel compelled to either accept the client's directives and increased liability risks or lose the client's business to another law firm that would assent to the arrangement.

* * *

LAW FIRM BREAKUPS

The last two decades have seen disturbing new phenomena become a regular part of law practice—law firm mergers, downsizing (reducing and deferring the hiring of new associates, staff layoffs, forced separation of associates and partners), break-ups, and sometimes bankruptcy of small and large law firms. These major transformations of firms raise ethical issues for the lawyers involved, both among themselves and in relation to their clients. What notice do firms owe their lawyers in advance of a merger or break-up? What notice should lawyers give their firms and their clients if they are leaving the firm? Can firms limit the practice opportunities of departing partners as other businesses do, or is this an improper limitation on the lawyer's right to practice law? An entire new area of legal practice has arisen consisting of advising and counseling law firms and their lawyers over these issues. [*See* Barbara B. Buchholz, *Graceful Exits,* 81 A.B.A. J. 76 (Aug.1995); Pamela A. Bresnahan, *Breaking Up Is Hard to Do,* 81 A.B.A. J. 94 (Nov.1995).]

An opinion from the ABA's Standing Committee on Ethics and Professional Responsibility, Formal Op. 99–414 (1999), provides guidance on some of these issues. A lawyer's impending departure requires notice to the lawyer's current clients under Rule 1.4. The notice can be in writing or in person or by telephone without violating Rule 7.3. Joint notice by the departing lawyer and the firm is preferred although not always possible. Pre-departure notice by the departing lawyer to current clients "may indicate the [departing] lawyer's willingness and ability to continue" in any current matters, but should make clear that the client has the right to decide whether to continue the representation with the departing lawyer or the firm, and should not urge the client discontinue representation by the firm or disparage the firm. Both the departing lawyer and the firm must take care to protect client interests, including those implicated by Rule 1.16 dealing with ending representation. The opinion did not resolve issues under other law, including fiduciary principles, property law, and unfair competition rules, but suggested guidelines under *Graubard Mollen v. Moskovitz,* 86 N.Y.2d 112, 629 N.Y.S.2d 1009, 653 N.E.2d 1179 (1995), which condemned secret attempts by the departing lawyer to lure clients from the firm, lying to clients about their rights to remain represented by the firm, and lying to the firm about the departing lawyer's plans to leave. Finally, the opinion suggested that determining what property the departing lawyer can take from the firm is primarily a matter of non-disciplinary law, with the departing lawyer entitled to take copies of research memoranda, pleadings and forms prepared by the lawyer and considered the lawyer's property or in the public domain and other documents the lawyer created for general use in the practice. Client files must be retained or transferred as directed by the client, although the departing lawyer can can keep copies of client documents relating to the lawyer's representation.

As Formal Opinion 99–414 suggests, firms generally cannot prohibit their lawyers from leaving and letting clients know of their impending move, so they have tried other economic disincentives to at least limit the grabbing off of their best clients when lawyers move. Model Rule 5.6 appears to limit, if not prohibit, the use of noncompetition clauses in partnership agreements, and to restrict the use of payments to the departing partners as a means of limiting competition. However, their use has produced a major split between the courts of New York and California over payments for unbilled work and work in progress when the partners depart. In *Cohen v. Lord, Day & Lord,* 75 N.Y.2d 95, 551 N.Y.S.2d 157, 550 N.E.2d 410 (1989), New York's Court of Appeals held that clauses that allow firms to withhold fees on grounds a departing partner forfeited them by practicing at a competing firm are unethical noncompetition agreements that limit clients' choice of lawyers. In *Howard v. Babcock,* 6 Cal.4th 409, 25 Cal.Rptr.2d 80, 863 P.2d 150 (1993), the California Supreme Court upheld the inclusion of a similar clause on the ground that law firms should not be treated any differently than other businesses as long as the restriction is reasonable. [*See also Fearnow v. Ridenour, Swenson, Cleere & Evans P.C.*, 213 Ariz. 24, 138 P.3d 723 (2006).] For a full treatment of these issues see Robert W. Hillman, Hillman on Lawyer Mobility: The Law and Ethics of Partner Withdrawals and Law Firm Breakups (2d ed. 1998).

LAW FIRM DISCIPLINE

Discipline has traditionally been a matter between the bar and its individual members. The entire range of sanctions seems appropriate only to punish an individual lawyer. Nevertheless, it is apparent that law firm culture has a significant effect on the individual members of the firm, particularly those newly admitted to practice who are developing habits of practice, often by modeling their behavior on those lawyers they observe practicing on a day-to-day basis—the partners and more senior associates of the firm that has hired them. Entire law firms have been found liable *as firms* for malpractice, and for violations of regulatory regimes by administrative agencies vigorously exercising their supervisory function. Some disciplinary rules are already applicable to law firms—conflict of interest rules usually require disqualification of the entire firm, as do rules on mandatory withdrawal. Article 5 of the ABA Model Rules deals with law firm issues. Finally, other sanction rules, particularly the current version of Federal Rule of Civil Procedure 11, allow sanctioning a law firm. [*See* Fed.R.Civ.P. 11(c).] A few commentators, notably Professor Schneyer in his article, *Professional Discipline for Law Firms?,* 77 Cornell L.Rev. 1 (1991), have suggested subjecting law firms to professional discipline—something two state bar organizations (New York and New Jersey) have now done. In its study of *Discipline for Law Firms,* The Association of the Bar of the City of New York [48 Rec.A.B.City N.Y. 628 (1993)] identified these reasons for extending discipline to law firms: (1) to improve the practice environment for lawyers within the firm that will discourage ethical violations by its members; (2) to enhance self-policing of conduct by firms; (3) to bring the rules into line with the group character of modern practice and its supervisory structure; (4) to enhance the ethical supervision of non-lawyer employees of firms; (5) to overcome the difficulty of assessing blame on individual lawyers; (6) to provide counter incentives to a climate that encourages cutting corners; and (7) to address organizational problems that may be the cause of ethical violations, such as conflicts checking, billing procedures, and oversight of client funds.

Difficulties remain with any proposal for law firm discipline. Firms cannot be disbarred, and even a total firm suspension seems inappropriate. Thus far, law firm discipline remains under consideration; no state bar has adopted a rule that disciplines firms.

GENERAL DYNAMICS CORP. v. SUPERIOR COURT

Supreme Court of California, 1994.
7 Cal.4th 1164, 32 Cal.Rptr.2d 1, 876 P.2d 487.

ARABIAN, JUSTICE.

We granted review to consider an attorney's status as "in-house" counsel as it affects the right to pursue claims for damages following an allegedly wrongful termination of employment. Specifically, we are asked to decide whether an attorney's status as an employee bars the pursuit of implied-in-fact contract and retaliatory discharge tort causes of action against the employer that are commonly the subject of suits by non-attorney employees who assert the same claims.

We conclude that, because so-called "just cause" contractual claims are unlikely to implicate values central to the attorney-client relationship, there is no valid reason why an in-house attorney should not be permitted to pursue such a contract claim in the same way as the nonattorney employee. Our conclusion with respect to the tort cause of action is qualified; our holding seeks to accommodate two conflicting values, both of which arise from the nature of an attorney's professional role: the fiducial nature of the relationship with the client, on the one hand, and the duty to adhere to a handful of defining ethical norms, on the other. As will appear, we conclude that there is no reason inherent in the nature of an attorney's role as in-house counsel to a corporation that in itself precludes the maintenance of a retaliatory discharge claim, provided it can be established without breaching the attorney-client privilege or unduly endangering the values lying at the heart of the professional relationship.

Although the effect of the attorney-client relationship is to produce a remedy more limited than that available to the nonattorney employee, the similarities between the position of in-house attorneys and their non-attorney colleagues nevertheless justify an analogous cause of action. The complete economic dependence of in-house attorneys on their employers is indistinguishable from that of nonattorney employees who are entitled to pursue a retaliatory discharge remedy. Moreover, as we explain, the position of in-house counsel is especially sensitive to those fundamental ethical imperatives derived from an attorney's professional duties, as well as organizational pressures to ignore or subvert them. On balance, these considerations favor allowing a tort claim for discharges for reasons that contravene an attorney's mandatory ethical obligations or for which a non-attorney employee could maintain such a claim and a statute or ethical code provision permits the attorney to depart from the usual rule that client matters remain confidential.

The trial courts have at their disposal several measures to minimize or eliminate the potential untoward effects on both the attorney-client privilege and the interests of the client-employer resulting from the litigation of such wrongful termination claims by in-house counsel. Thus, we also hold that, in those instances where the attorney-employee's retaliatory discharge claim is incapable of complete resolution without breaching the attorney-client privilege, the suit may not proceed. That result, however, is rarely, if ever, appropriate where, as in this case, the litigation is still at the pleadings stage.

I

Andrew Rose, an attorney, began working for General Dynamics Corporation (hereafter General Dynamics) as a 27–year–old contract administrator at its Pomona plant in 1978. He progressed steadily within the organization, earning repeated commendations and, after 14 years with the company, was in line to become a division vice-president and general counsel. On June 24, 1991, he was fired, abruptly and wrongfully.

So Rose alleged in the complaint for damages that began this litigation. The complaint also alleged that although the stated reason for his discharge was a loss of the company's confidence in Rose's ability to represent vigorously its interests, the "real" reasons motivating his firing had more to do with an attempt by company officials to cover up widespread drug use among the General Dynamics work force, a refusal to investigate the mysterious "bugging" of the office of the company's chief of security, and the displeasure of company officials over certain legal advice Rose had given them, rather than any loss of confidence in his legal ability or commitment to the company's interests.

The complaint relied on two main theories of relief. First, it alleged that General Dynamics had, by its conduct and other assurances, impliedly represented to Rose over the years that he was subject to discharge only for "good cause," a condition that the complaint alleged was not present in the circumstances under which he was fired. Second, the complaint alleged that Rose was actually fired for cumulative reasons, all of which violated fundamental public policies: in part because he spearheaded an investigation into employee drug use at the Pomona plant (an investigation, the complaint alleged, that led to the termination of more than 60 General Dynamics employees), in part because he protested the company's failure to investigate the bugging of the office of the chief of security (allegedly a criminal offense and, since it involved a major defense contractor, a serious breach of national security), and in part as a result of advising General Dynamics officials that the company's salary policy with respect to the compensation paid a certain class of employees might be in violation of the federal Fair Labor Standards Act, possibly exposing the firm to several hundred million dollars in backpay claims.

General Dynamics filed a general demurrer to the complaint, asserting that Rose had failed to state a claim for relief. Because he had been employed as an in-house attorney, the company contended, Rose was subject to discharge at any time, "for any reason or for no reason." The trial court overruled the demurrer and the Court of Appeal [upheld the trial court.]

* * *

II

The last two decades have seen a marked rise in the number and professional stature of so-called in-house or corporate counsel. Increasingly, large corporations have turned inward for the acquisition of legal services, for a host of reasons ranging from cost incentives, to the increasing complexity of the regulatory environment, to the programmatic style characteristic of such organizations. According to a study conducted in the early 1980's, 50,000 lawyers were on corporate payrolls, a figure double that of 15 years earlier; a more recent survey indicates that more than 10 percent of all lawyers in the United States are employed in-house by corporations.[2]

The growth in the number and role of in-house counsel has brought with it a widening recognition of the descriptive inadequacy of the nineteenth century model of the lawyer's place and role in society—one based predominantly on the small-to middle-sized firm of like-minded attorneys whose economic fortunes were not tethered to the good will of a single client—and of the social and legal consequences that have accompanied that transformation. Unlike the law firm partner, who typically possesses a significant measure of economic independence and professional distance derived from a multiple client base, the economic fate of in-house attorneys is tied directly to a single employer, at whose sufferance they serve. Thus, from an economic standpoint, the dependence of in-house counsel is indistinguishable from that of other corporate managers or senior executives who also owe their livelihoods, career goals and satisfaction to a single organizational employer.

Moreover, the professional relationship between the in-house attorney and the client is not the "one shot" undertaking—drafting a will, say, or

2. (See, e.g., Wolfram, Modern Legal Ethics (1986 ed.) § 13.7.3, at pp. 736–738 & fns. 89–99 [hereafter Wolfram]; Giesel, The Ethics or Employment Dilemma of In–House Counsel (1990) 5 Geo.J. Legal Ethics 535, 540–545 & accompanying fns. [hereafter Giesel]). For an account of the rise of the corporate legal department and its implications for the traditional "outside" law firm, see the series of articles in volume 37 of the Stanford Law Review. (Chayes & Chayes, Corporate Counsel and the Elite Law Firm (1984) 37 Stan.L.Rev. 277; Comment 301; Comment (1984) 37 Stan.L.Rev. 305.)

handling a piece of litigation—characteristic of the outside law firm. Instead, the corporate attorney-employee, operating in a heavily regulated medium, often takes on a larger advisory and compliance role, anticipating potential legal problems, advising on possible solutions, and generally assisting the corporation in achieving its business aims while minimizing entanglement in the increasingly complex legal web that regulates organizational conduct in our society. This expansion in the scope and stature of in-house counsel's work, together with an inevitably close professional identification with the fortunes and objectives of the corporate employer, can easily subject the in-house attorney to unusual pressures to conform to organizational goals, pressures that are qualitatively different from those imposed on the outside lawyer. Even the most dedicated professionals, their economic and professional fate allied with that of the business organizations they serve, may be irresistibly tempted to cut corners by bending the ethical norms that regulate an attorney's professional conduct.

Indeed, the analogy of in-house counsel's position to that of his or her lay colleagues in the executive suite is inexact only because, as a licensed professional, an attorney labors under unique ethical imperatives that exceed those of the corporate executive who seeks, say, a tort remedy after being terminated for refusing to join a conspiracy to violate the antitrust laws. We turn, then, to a consideration of the effects of in-house counsel's professional role and ethical duties on access to judicial remedies for alleged wrongful termination that are available to the nonattorney colleague.

III

A

If there is a unifying theme in this conflict, it is the claim of General Dynamics that our opinion in Fracasse v. Brent (1972) 6 Cal.3d 784, 100 Cal.Rptr. 385, 494 P.2d 9 (Fracasse) is dispositive of all issues tendered against it by Rose in his complaint. Because Fracasse cloaks the client in an unfettered, absolute right to discharge an attorney at any time and for any reason, General Dynamics argues, the complaint cannot state a claim against the company that is judicially cognizable; the trial court should thus have sustained General Dynamics's demurrer without leave to amend.

In Fracasse, supra, 6 Cal.3d 784, 100 Cal.Rptr. 385, 494 P.2d 9, an attorney entered into a contingent fee contract with a client to represent her as a plaintiff in a personal injury lawsuit. Not long afterward—and before any recovery had been made on her behalf—the client decided to end the relationship. She discharged the attorney, and retained other counsel to pursue her claim. The former attorney then filed a declaratory relief action against her, alleging that he had been discharged without cause and in breach of the contingency fee agreement, and seeking a judgment that he was entitled to his one-third contingency fee as a percentage of any sum ultimately recovered by his former client. The trial court sustained the client's demurrer, ruling that the complaint failed to state a claim for relief.

Although the core proposition established by our opinion in Fracasse, supra, 6 Cal.3d at page 790, 100 Cal.Rptr. 385, 494 P.2d 9, affirming the trial court, undoubtedly remains valid—we concluded that "a client should have both the right and the power at any time to discharge his attorney with or without cause"—our holding in that case does not support the sweeping scope urged for it by General Dynamics. It should be evident to anyone reading our opinion in Fracasse that we confronted there one of the most common of the traditional forms of the lawyer-client relationship: the potential claimant who seeks redress by hiring an independent professional to prosecute her claim for personal injuries.

* * *

Entwined with our concern for the specific risks facing the contingent-fee plaintiff who has lost faith in her attorney was an underlying perception that, whatever the circumstances, no client should be forced to suffer representation by an attorney in whom that confidence and trust lying at the heart of a fiduciary relationship has been lost. It is not surprising, given this chain of reasoning, that our opinion in Fracasse, supra, 6 Cal.3d 784, 100 Cal.Rptr. 385, 494 P.2d 9, should establish as bedrock law what remains probably the central value of the lawyer-client relationship—the primacy of fiducial values and its corollary: the unilateral right of the client to sever the professional relationship at any time and for any reason.

That rule, which we reaffirm today, some 22 years after our decision in Fracasse, supra, 6 Cal.3d 784, 100 Cal.Rptr. 385, 494 P.2d 9, does not mean, however, that the "absolute" right of the personal injury client to discharge unilaterally his attorney permits all clients to terminate the attorney-client relationship under all circumstances without consequence. The sources of contract and tort claims in wrongful termination cases are analytically distinct from the circumstances confronting the contingent-fee plaintiff that propelled our analysis in Fracasse. Given these disparate origins, it is unlikely that the client's undoubted power to discharge the attorney at will is one that can be invoked under all circumstances without consequence. Even in Fracasse, we recognized the requirement that the dissatisfied personal injury contingent fee client compensate discharged counsel, limiting that obligation, in light of the peculiar risks associated with contingent fee undertakings, to the reasonable value of any services provided in the event of a recovery.

Additionally, General Dynamics' claim of an unqualified immunity from any liability for terminating in-house counsel is inconsistent with the law in other areas, notably claims grounded in alleged violations of antidiscrimination laws and statutory rights to public collective bargaining.

* * *

B

How does the fundamental rule of the client's unilateral power of discharge announced in Fracasse, supra, 6 Cal.3d 784, 100 Cal.Rptr. 385, 494 P.2d 9, apply in the circumstances of this case? First, Rose's complaint does not contest the right of General Dynamics to terminate a member of its corporate legal department at any time or for any reason, nor could it. It simply asserts that there is a cost to be paid for such an action under the circumstances alleged in the complaint—either in lost wages and related damages in the case of the implied-in-fact contract claim, or as tort damages in the case of the public policy tort claim. In neither case, however, is the client's power to rid itself of an attorney in whom it has lost confidence thwarted. To the extent that General Dynamics's claim that its "unfettered" right to discharge a member of its corporate legal department means that it may do so without liability of any kind under all circumstances, that is not, and never has been, the law of this state.

As a threshold matter, then, we do not feel constrained by our opinion in Fracasse, supra, 6 Cal.3d 784, 100 Cal.Rptr. 385, 494 P.2d 9, from considering the proposition that, under circumscribed conditions, an in-house attorney may pursue a wrongful discharge claim for damages against his corporate employer even though a judgment ordering his reinstatement is not an available remedy. We turn to a consideration of the merits of plaintiff's claims that his termination breached an implied-in-fact agreement with General Dynamics and violated fundamental public policies, as well as the possible limitations on the vitality of such claims when brought by in-house counsel.

IV

* * *

Perhaps the overriding distinction between Fracasse, supra, 6 Cal.3d 784, 100 Cal.Rptr. 385, 494 P.2d 9, and this case lies in the allegations of the complaint that the plaintiff was hired as a "career oriented" employee with an expectation of permanent employment, provided his performance was satisfactory; that he was promised job security and substantial retirement benefits; that he regularly received outstanding performance reviews, promotions, salary increases, and commendations throughout his 14–year tenure; and that the company abruptly terminated him without adhering to its published discharge procedures.

These pleadings, we conclude, adequately allege that a "course of conduct, including various oral representations, created a reasonable expectation" that the plaintiff would not be terminated without good cause. The factual allegations of the complaint being sufficient to withstand a general demurrer, we see no reason in policy, at least at the outset, why the plaintiff's status as an in-house attorney should operate to defeat his contract claim. It is true, as we have just affirmed, that General Dynamics has a right to discharge any member of its general counsel's staff in whom it has lost confidence. That right does not mean, however, that it may do so without honoring antecedent contractual obligations to discharge an attorney-employee only on the occurrence of specified conditions.

In short, implied-in-fact limitations being a species of contract, no reason appears why an employer that elects to limit its at-will freedom to terminate the employment relationship with in-house counsel should not be held to the terms of its bargain.

* * *

We agree that, as creatures of contract, implied-in-fact limitations on a client-employer's right to discharge in-house counsel are not likely to present issues implicating the distinctive values subserved by the attorney-client relationship. Such suits can thus for the most part be treated as implied-in-fact claims brought by the nonattorney employee.

V

A

We turn next to an evaluation of Rose's claim that he was discharged for multiple reasons, each of which violated a "fundamental polic[y] that [is] delineated in constitutional or statutory provisions" of the law of this state. (Gantt v. Sentry Insurance (1992) 1 Cal.4th 1083, 1095, 4 Cal. Rptr.2d 874, 824 P.2d 680.) Unlike implied-in-fact contract claims, which, as discussed above, arise out of the conduct and expectations of the parties to the employment relationship, so-called public policy wrongful discharge claims are pure creatures of law.

* * *

According to a recent count, 43 jurisdictions have adopted the so-called "retaliatory discharge" cause of action as a restraint on the employer's historical at-will power of termination. In California, refinements in the doctrine of wrongful discharge in violation of public policy have engrafted two prominent restraints on the vitality of such claims. The first is the requirement, explicated in our decision in Gantt v. Sentry Insurance, supra, 1 Cal.4th at page 1095, 4 Cal.Rptr.2d 874, 824 P.2d 680, that the public policy at issue must be one that is not only "fundamental" but is clearly established in the Constitution and positive law of the state. The second restriction is the requirement that, even though established by positive law, the policy subserved by the employee's conduct must be a truly public one, that is, "affect[ing] a duty which inures to the benefit of the public at large rather than to a particular employer or employee." (Foley v. Interactive Data Corp., 47 Cal.3d 654, 699, 254 Cal.Rptr. 211, 765 P.2d 373 (1988).)

There is a third characteristic of such claims that warrants our attention, one that may, in the case of in-house counsel, be of surpassing significance. That characteristic is well stated in Foley, supra, 47 Cal.3d 654, 254 Cal.Rptr. 211, 765 P.2d 373, where we explained that "decisions recognizing a tort action for discharge in violation of public policy seek to protect the public, by protecting the employee who refuses to commit a crime [citations] . . ., who reports criminal activity to proper authorities [citations], or who discloses other illegal, unethical, or unsafe practices [citation]" (Id. at p. 670, 254 Cal.Rptr. 211, 765 P.2d 373, italics added).

* * *

B

This foundational public rationale is especially important in the case of the attorney-employee. Perhaps the defining feature of professionals as a class is the extent to which they embody a dual allegiance. On the one hand, an attorney's highest duty is to the welfare and interests of the client. This obligation is channeled, however, by a limiting and specifically professional qualification: attorneys are required to conduct themselves as such, meaning that they are bound at all events not to transgress a handful of professional ethical norms that distinguish their work from that of the nonattorney.

Some (but not all) of these professional norms incorporate important public values. Lawyers are given wide professional license in part because of ethical restraints on their discretion designed to further (or at least not endanger) the public weal. The minimal ethical standards that distinctively define the lawyer as a professional are, of course, those embodied in the codes of ethics, and, in California, in the Rules of Professional Conduct. These standards are in turn linked by their nature and goals to important values affecting the public interest at large. It is through this chain of ethical duty that lawyers and their work are affected with a public interest. Out of this duality of allegiance—for the interests of the client on the one hand, but within the bounds of ethical norms on the other—a genuine moral dilemma may arise.

This is especially so in the context of the large commercially driven corporation whose essential objectives are largely defined by the desire to maximize profitability. In such a business culture, the in-house professional may be trapped between a laudable desire to further the goals of the client-employer and restrictions on conduct imposed by the ethical norms prescribed by the Rules of Professional Conduct. Of course, the potential for such a dilemma is common to outside counsel as well. But, unlike their in-house counterparts, outside lawyers enjoy a measure of professional distance and economic independence that usually serves to lessen the pressure to bend or ignore professional norms. Here again, the distinguishing feature of the in-house attorney is a virtually complete dependence on the good will and confidence of a single employer to provide livelihood and career success.

The case for shielding the in-house attorney—among all corporate employees—from retaliation by the employer for either insisting on adhering to mandatory ethical norms of the profession or for refusing to violate them is thus clear. And because their professional work is by definition affected with a public interest, in-house attorneys are even more liable to conflicts between corporate goals and professional norms than their nonattorney colleagues. On this view, then, in-house counsel, forced to choose between the demands of the employer and the requirements of a professional code of ethics have, if anything, an even more powerful claim to judicial protection than their nonprofessional colleagues.

C

There is a substantial counterargument against permitting the pursuit of a retaliatory discharge tort claim by in-house counsel, one that also inheres in the essential nature of the attorney's professional role. Indeed, in the handful of reported cases dealing with the question, a majority of courts have refused to permit the maintenance of such suits on the ground that they pose too great a threat to the attorney-client relationship. This rationale is well illustrated in a trio of recent cases, each holding as a matter of law that retaliatory discharge suits by in-house counsel are not maintainable.

* * *

[The court here reviewed the cases of *Balla v. Gambro, Inc.,* 145 Ill.2d 492, 164 Ill.Dec. 892, 584 N.E.2d 104 (1991), *Herbster v. North American Co.,* 150 Ill.App.3d 21, 501 N.E.2d 343 (1986), and *Willy v. Coastal Corp.,* 647 F.Supp. 116 (S.D.Tex.1986), each of which rejected retaliatory discharge suits by fired in-house lawyers.]

* * *

Those courts that have declined to permit in-house counsel to pursue retaliatory discharge claims—in Balla, Herbster, and Willy—have rested their conclusion on two distinct grounds: First, because the fiducial qualities of their professional calling pervade the attorney-client relationship "lawyers are different." It is essential to the proper functioning of the lawyer's role that the client be assured that matters disclosed to counsel in confidence remain sacrosanct; to permit in-house attorneys to file suit against their clients can only harm that relationship. Second, to the extent that the retaliatory discharge tort rests on underpinnings designed to secure fundamental public policies, a tort remedy for in-house counsel is redundant—such attorneys are under an ethical obligation to sever their professional relationship with the erring client in any event—meaning, in the case of in-house counsel, resigning their employment.

D

There is no doubt that the Illinois courts in Balla, supra, 164 Ill.Dec. 892, 584 N.E.2d 104, and Herbster, supra, 103 Ill.Dec. 322, 501 N.E.2d 343, grappled conscientiously with the conflicting values presented by cases such as this one. If their reasoning and conclusions can be faulted, it is because one searches in vain for a principled link between the ethical duties of the in-house attorney and the courts' refusal to grant such an employee a tort remedy under conditions that directly implicate those professional obligations. As more than one critic of these opinions has pointed out, both cases appear to reflect not only an unspoken adherence to an anachronistic model of the attorney's place and role in contemporary society, but an inverted view of the consequences of the in-house attorney's essential professional role.

As one authoritative commentator on lawyers' ethics, criticizing the court's decision in Balla, supra, 164 Ill.Dec. 892, 584 N.E.2d 104, has written, "It is clear that there would have been a right of action had the employee not been a lawyer. It thus seems bizarre that a lawyer employee, who has affirmative duties concerning the administration of justice, should be denied redress for discharge resulting from trying to carry out those very duties. A good beginning point for analysis may well be the client's normal and broad right to discharge the lawyer, but that cannot be the ending point as well, for the lawyer-client relationship exists in a context of other law regulating both parties to that relationship, including the lawyer's duties to third persons, the courts, and the government." (1 Hazard & Hodes, The Law of Lawyering, supra, § 1.16.206 at p. 477, fns. omitted.)

Granted the priest-like license to receive the most intimate and damning disclosures of the client, granted the sanctity of the professional privilege, granted the uniquely influential position attorneys occupy in our society, it is precisely because of that role that attorneys should be accorded a retaliatory discharge remedy in those instances in which mandatory ethical norms embodied in the Rules of Professional Conduct collide with illegitimate demands of the employer and the attorney insists on adhering to his or her clear professional duty. It is, after all, the office of the retaliatory discharge tort to vindicate fundamental public policies by encouraging employees to act in ways that advance them. By providing the employee with a remedy in tort damages for resisting socially damaging organizational conduct, the courts mitigate the otherwise considerable economic and cultural pressures on the individual employee to silently conform.

Within their area of professional competence, in-house attorneys, more than other organizational employees, are imbued with ethical constraints on the direction their efforts may legitimately take. Among other strictures on their conduct, they may not be a party to the commission of a crime, destroy evidence or suborn perjury. They are forbidden to do these things by the very ethical codes that define their professional identity. It is a short step from this premise to the conclusion that in-house lawyers ought to have access to a judicial remedy in those instances in which their employment is terminated for adhering to the requirements of just such a mandatory professional duty, either by an affirmative act required by the ethical code or statute or by resisting a demand of the employer on the ground that it is unequivocally barred by the professional code.

* * *

In addition, the emphasis by the Balla, Herbster and Willy courts on the "remedy" of the in-house attorney's duty of "withdrawal" strikes us as illusory. Courts do not require nonlawyer employees to quietly surrender their jobs rather than "go along" with an employer's unlawful demands. Indeed, the retaliatory discharge tort claim is designed to encourage and support precisely the opposite reaction. Why, then, did the courts in these three cases content themselves with the bland announcement that the only "choice" of an attorney confronted with an employer's demand that he violate his professional oath by committing, say, a criminal act, is to voluntarily withdraw from employment, a course fraught with the possibility of economic catastrophe and professional banishment?

Whatever the reason, the withdrawal "remedy" fails to confront seriously the extraordinarily high cost that resignation entails. More importantly, it is virtually certain that, without the prospect of limited judicial access, in-house attorneys—especially those in mid-career who occupy senior positions—confronted with the dilemma of choosing between adhering to professional ethical norms and surrendering to the employer's unethical demands will almost always find silence the better part of valor. Declining to provide a limited remedy under defined circumstances will thus almost certainly foster a degradation of in-house counsel's professional stature.

E

In addition to retaliatory discharge claims founded on allegations that an in-house attorney was terminated for refusing to violate a mandatory ethical duty embodied in the Rules of Professional Conduct, judicial access ought logically extend to those limited circumstances in which in-house counsel's nonattorney colleagues would be permitted to pursue a retaliatory discharge claim and governing professional rules or statutes expressly remove the requirement of attorney confidentiality. Thus, in determining whether an in-house attorney has a retaliatory discharge claim against his or her employer, a court must first ask whether the attorney was discharged for following a mandatory ethical obligation prescribed by professional rule or statute. If, for example, in-house counsel is asked to commit a crime, or to engage in an act of moral turpitude that would subject him to disbarment (see, e.g., Bus. & Prof.Code, §§ 6101, 6106 [providing, respectively, for disbarment on conviction of a felony or a misdemeanor involving moral turpitude, and for the "commission of any act involving moral turpitude, dishonesty or corruption"]), and is discharged for refusing to engage in such an act, counsel would have been discharged for adhering to a mandatory ethical obligation; under most circumstances, the attorney would have a retaliatory discharge cause of action against the employer.

If, on the other hand, the conduct in which the attorney has engaged is merely ethically permissible, but not required by statute or ethical code, then the inquiry facing the court is slightly more complex. Under these circumstances, a court must resolve two questions: First, whether the employer's conduct is of the kind that would give rise to a retaliatory discharge action by a non attorney employee * * * second, the court must determine whether some statute or ethical rule, such as the statutory exceptions to the attorney-client privilege codified in the Evidence Code (see id., §§ 956–958) specifically permits the attorney to depart from the usual requirement of confidentiality with respect to the client-employer and engage in the "nonfiduciary" conduct for which he was terminated.

We emphasize the limited scope of our conclusion that in-house counsel may state a cause of action in tort for retaliatory discharge. The lawyer's high duty of fidelity to the interests of the client work against a tort remedy that is coextensive with that available to the nonattorney employee. Although claims by in-house attorneys are cognate to those we approved in Foley, supra, 47 Cal.3d 654, 254 Cal.Rptr. 211, 765 P.2d 373, the underlying rationale differs somewhat, being grounded in the attorney's obligation to adhere to ethical norms specific to the profession. The cause of action is thus one designed to support in-house counsel in remaining faithful to those fundamental public policies reflected in the governing ethical code when carrying out professional assignments. Thus, in addition to the limitations on the scope of the retaliatory tort action mentioned above, the concerns expressed by the courts in Balla, supra, 164 Ill.Dec. 892, 584 N.E.2d 104, and Herbster, supra, 103 Ill.Dec. 322, 501 N.E.2d 343, for the integrity of the fiduciary aspects of the attorney-client relationship impose additional limitations.

First, those values that underlie the professional relationship—the fiduciary qualities of mutual trust and confidence—can be protected from the threat of damage by limiting judicial access to claims grounded in explicit and unequivocal ethical norms embodied in the Rules of Professional Responsibility and statutes, and claims which are maintainable by the non attorney employee under our decision in Gantt v. Sentry Insurance, supra, 1 Cal.4th 1083, 4 Cal.Rptr.2d 874, 824 P.2d 680, under circumstances in which the Legislature has manifested a judgment that the principle of professional confidentiality does not apply. (See, e.g., Evid.Code, § 956.5) ["There is no privilege ... if the lawyer reasonably believes that disclosure of any confidential communication ... is necessary to prevent the client from committing a criminal act that the lawyer believes is likely to result in death or substantial bodily harm."][6]

Similarly, the in-house attorney who publicly exposes the client's secrets will usually find no sanctuary in the courts. Except in those rare instances when disclosure is explicitly permitted or mandated by an ethics code provision or statute, it is never the business of the lawyer to disclose

6. As our discussion makes evident, in California, these ethical prescriptions are those embodied in the state's Rules of Professional Conduct and certain provisions of the Business and Professions Code (e.g., §§ 6068, 6090.5–6107). We expressly decline to adopt as a predicate for retaliatory discharge claims by in-house counsel either the Model Rules of Professional Conduct or the Model Code of Professional Responsibility, both of which have "no legal force of their own" (1 Hazard & Hodes, The Law of Lawyering, supra, § 206, at p. 1xx) and neither of which has been adopted by this court. Although the question is not before us in this case, we suggest that ethical issues arising in retaliatory discharge claims filed in California by out-of-state in-house attorneys against their employers and based on extrastate conduct will be resolved under governing choice-of-law rules.

publicly the secrets of the client. In any event, where the elements of a wrongful discharge in violation of fundamental public policy claim cannot, for reasons peculiar to the particular case, be fully established without breaching the attorney-client privilege, the suit must be dismissed in the interest of preserving the privilege. We underline the fact that such drastic action will seldom if ever be appropriate at the demurrer stage of litigation. Although General Dynamics argues that Rose's claims are barred from disclosure by the lawyer-client privilege, that is an issue that is incapable of resolution in a challenge to the facial sufficiency of the complaint. Indeed, in most wrongful termination suits brought by discharged in-house counsel, whether the attorney-client privilege precludes the plaintiff from recovery will not be resolvable at the demurrer stage. Rather, in the usual case, whether the privilege serves as a bar to the plaintiff's recovery will be litigated and determined in the context of motions for protective orders or to compel further discovery responses, as well as at the time of a motion for summary judgment.

Second, the contours of the statutory attorney-client privilege should continue to be strictly observed. We reject any suggestion that the scope of the privilege should be diluted in the context of in-house counsel and their corporate clients. Members of corporate legal departments are as fully subject to the demands of the privilege as their outside colleagues. It is likely, however, that many of the cases in which in-house counsel is faced with an ethical dilemma will lie outside the scope of the statutory privilege. Matters involving the commission of a crime or a fraud, or circumstances in which the attorney reasonably believes that disclosure is necessary to prevent the commission of a criminal act likely to result in death or substantial bodily harm, are statutory and well-recognized exceptions to the attorney-client privilege. * * * Although their revelation in the course of a retaliatory discharge suit may do lasting damage to the expectations of the corporate client (or, more likely, a corporate executive) that disclosures to counsel would remain inviolate, a concern for protecting the fiduciary aspects of the relationship in the case of a client who confides in counsel for the purpose of planning a crime or practicing a fraud is misplaced; such disclosures do not violate the privilege.

Moreover, the trial courts can and should apply an array of ad hoc measures from their equitable arsenal designed to permit the attorney plaintiff to attempt to make the necessary proof while protecting from disclosure client confidences subject to the privilege. The use of sealing and protective orders, limited admissibility of evidence, orders restricting the use of testimony in successive proceedings, and, where appropriate, in camera proceedings, are but some of a number of measures that might usefully be explored by the trial courts as circumstances warrant. We are confident that by taking an aggressive managerial role, judges can minimize the dangers to the legitimate privilege interests the trial of such cases may present.

Finally, a handful of subsidiary rules will effectively raise the ante on the in-house attorney contemplating a tort action, thus deterring the incidence of strike suits or claims filed in bad faith. The contested ethical requirement must be clearly established by the ethics code or statutory provision; disagreements over policy are not actionable. The plaintiff, of course, bears the burden of establishing the unequivocal requirements of the ethical norm at issue and that the employer's conduct was motivated by impermissible considerations under a "but for" standard of causation. The ethical norm at issue must be one that is intended for the protection of the public at large; measures designed solely for the benefit of the attorney or the client will not suffice to support a retaliatory discharge claim. Moreover, an attorney who unsuccessfully pursues a retaliatory discharge suit, and in doing so discloses privileged client confidences, may be subject to State Bar disciplinary proceedings. Finally, of course, the defendant employer is always free to challenge plaintiff's claim by demonstrating the discharge was motivated by reasons other than a demand that counsel engage in conduct amounting to a breach of professional ethical norms.

VI

Applying the principles developed above to the complaint in this case, it is evident that as noted, plaintiff's first claim—for breach of an implied-in-fact just-cause agreement—adequately pleads the essential elements of the cause of action. It is less clear, however, that the allegations in support of relief under plaintiff's retaliatory discharge theory are sufficient. Plaintiff nowhere alleges that the conduct which allegedly led to his termination was required or supported by any requirement of our Rules of Professional Responsibility or a relevant statute.

* * *

CONCLUSION

The judgment of the Court of Appeal is affirmed and the cause is remanded to that court with directions to order further proceedings in accordance with the views expressed herein.

LAWYER AS PROBLEM–SOLVER

THE LAWYER AS PROBLEM SOLVER AND THIRD–PARTY NEUTRAL: CREATIVITY AND NON–PARTISANSHIP IN LAWYERING

Carrie Menkel–Meadow
72 Temple L. Rev. 785 (1999).[7]

[O]ur traditional conception of the role of lawyer as an advocate of his client and as someone else's adversary is a crabbed and incomplete

7. Reprinted with permission.

conception of the lawyer's role; we need to expand and broaden the conception of what lawyers should do, as well as recognize more formally what they currently are doing. * * * Our conceptions of the traditional roles of lawyers are derived from several core ideas, most of which are codified in the various rules and theories of liabilities that govern the lawyer's professional responsibility, formally defined. The "culture of adversarialism" and the rules that enforce this culture often (not always) distort how we think about legal and human problem solving by assuming there are only two sides to an issue or question, that "truth" about either what happened factually or what is correct legally can best be resolved by vigorous contestations between two fully armed advocates and decided by a third-party judge who is separate from the parties and appointed by the state. Formal rules of discourse and process (evidence) control the rules of the debate and contest and are universally recognized as a vast improvement on the historical forms of trial by ordeal or combat. Yet parties are still limited to a stylized form of conversation in which they cannot speak directly to each other. Often, what is most important to parties may be excluded from consideration, as irrelevant or inadmissible, according to our well-worn legal principles, which may protect other important interests (like privileges, trade secrets, bias and prejudice, or constitutional rights).

* * *

Imagine, if you will, that lawyering was informed by a different mindset, orientation, consciousness, or "frame" than maximizing individual client gain. Suppose for the moment that what we thought a lawyer should do would be to "solve a problem," make a bad situation better, improve relationships between embittered parties, or facilitate the best possible arrangements in complex environments with many (not only two) competing claims. These goals include those commonly described as "Pareto-optimal" solutions'—seeking the best possible solution for each party without harming the other side. (Imagine a form of optimality in lawyering that included doing no harm to third parties.) There are more complex variations of Pareto-optimality, especially in situations with multiple parties, but even this simplified version is quite a different aspiration for lawyers than those commonly thought to obtain where the lawyer must "zealously" represent a client: to maximize fully that client's gain, even at harm or cost to the other side—and sadly, in some cases, especially because it will cause harm or pain to the other side. Going a step further, some might suggest that a lawyer should aim to maximize joint, mutual, group, or collective gain in using her craft—the misnamed "lawyer for the situation." These are clearly the goals of many inside counsel who have responsibilities for advising and serving many different masters within an organization. Consider the more extreme possibility that the lawyer should actually seek to reduce harm (to the parties and to third parties—ethical "externalities"), both in preventing problems, disputes, and troubles and in reducing harm when a conflict, dispute, or difficulty has arisen. Such lawyers might try to pursue peace and justice at the same time.

* * *

Qualitative critiques of the adversary model, coupled with the concern of many courts for their large caseloads (a quantitative concern about access to justice and the ability of courts to render efficient and fair justice) and private parties' concern about the "negative transaction costs" of cost and delay in the litigation system, together formed the perhaps conflicting impulses of the ADR movement, now called "Appropriate Dispute Resolution" (not "Alternative Dispute Resolution"). Efforts to solve problems more integratively, at less cost, with greater party participation, and with the possibility of preventing, as well as solving, some disputes, have led growing numbers of lawyers to look to new forms of lawyering, some of which are quite alien to the traditional conception of the lawyer's role.

A new model of the "collaborative lawyer," originally developed in family law and now spreading to other forms of substantive practice, offers the client a lawyer who will approach the other side (who also has a collaborative lawyer) with the express purpose of trying to work out a mutually satisfactory settlement. If the parties choose not to settle, new counsel conduct the litigation. Collaborative lawyers attempt to solve problems as peacefully as possible, with maximum client input, and agree in advance not to pursue litigation with each other. Even more conventional lawyers now schooled in the teachings of Getting to Yes or Menkel–Meadow's problem-solving negotiation may seek to achieve joint gain or mutually principled solutions to legal problems, taking greater account of all parties' needs and interests and seeking collaborative (neither competitive nor cooperative) process choices with each other. These new lawyering strategies frequently include greater disclosures of both party interests and facts, as well as shared discussion of legal theories and arguments, greater candor generally, failure to exploit every weakness or disadvantage of the other side, and concern about how fair, "conscionable," or adequate a proposed settlement is for both parties, not just one's own client (and potential third parties affected by any resolution, like children in divorce or communities in environmental disputes). Ask yourself whether clients should be informed as to whether or not their lawyer will be employing value creating or value claiming (adversarial) behavior.

Perhaps the most radical departure from the lawyer's traditional role is the current practice of lawyer as third-party neutral, as mediator, arbitrator, facilitator, early neutral evaluator, conciliator, fact-finder, or consensus-builder. In such roles, lawyers do not represent anyone and, thus, are not strictly speaking governed by the Model Rules of Professional Conduct where there is no professional representational relationship. Others have recognized, and I have been among them, that lawyer-mediators may use law in their work as facilitators of negotiated solutions to litigational or transactional problems: helping evaluate the merits of an argument, the legality of a solution, assisting in the drafting of an agreement, or in cases of evaluative mediation, actually predicting what a court might do with a particular case or offering particular substantive resolutions of particular legal issues. In addition, as case law and practice are now making clear, lawyers as mediators have a variety of professional responsibility issues to face that are both analogous to, but different from, the lawyer in traditional representational roles: conflicts of interests (as neutrals, as partners of advocates in cases, as advocates themselves when a particular lawyer chooses to be both mediator and advocate in different cases while within the same practice unit); confidentiality and exceptions; competence and liability (and immunity in cases of court-sponsored mediation); fees; advertising; and joint practice with nonlawyers.

Mediators who seek to solve problems—either by merely facilitating negotiation sessions between represented or unrepresented parties, in both public and private settings, or by taking a more active role in the more recent use of "evaluative" mediation (rendering advice, legal predictions, or offering substantive solutions in some cases)—do not represent anyone, but serve an invaluable function in resolving disputes or facilitating the making of transactions. * * *

[M]any lawyers who serve as third-party neutrals are finding that the new consciousness of problem solver has affected the way in which they conduct their advocate's practice as well. Lawyers who take problem-solving dispute resolution seriously now advise clients to seek mediation or other forms of dispute resolution where appropriate and will find their own roles changed when they appear as counsel in mediation. For example, rather than preparing an argument for the judge, a lawyer and a client appearing in mediation must plan to address the other party directly, offer expressions of their own interests, as well as legal arguments and claims, and attempt to meet the expressed (business, social, or other) needs, as well as legal arguments, of the other side. * * *

Perhaps most exciting for the development of new lawyer roles is the expansion of problem-solving and decision-making techniques that move out from mediation and employ a variety of new competencies for lawyers (which many lawyers have employed for years, without formal training or recognition of role). These techniques include facilitation of reg-neg (negotiated rule-making) proceedings and facilitation of consensus building processes in issues as diverse as environmental siting and clean-up, budget processes, municipal governance, resource usage, neighborhood and community disputes, science disputes, policy disputes, cross-cultural disputes, discrimination disputes, multiple-party insurance and discrimination disputes, and even consensus processes within internal organizational and corporate settings.

Lawyers who seek to employ these different process skills to broaden, rather than narrow, issues offer services that lawyers have been traditionally known for: crafting orderly procedures and proceedings to accomplish legal results. One negotiation scholar has renamed the lawyer as "process architect,'' while another scholar describes the transactional lawyer as ''transaction costs engineer.'' In situations as diverse as dialogues, public conversations, joint problem solving, strategic planning, and consensus building processes, lawyers have facilitated proceedings of multiple parties with diverse and conflicting interests to reach contingent or final agreements on such contested issues as abortion, policing, block grant allocations, building development, Superfund clean-ups, and racial tensions. Within organizations, new roles—often adjunct to or separate from those of the general counsel—include ombuds, ''neutrals'' who are employed to counsel those with complaints about the organization or other employees, as well as to mediate and resolve inter-departmental disputes, and more recently, as ADR officers in all major federal governmental agencies. As in any good transaction planning, this kind of lawyering employs ''forward'' rather than ''backward'' thinking and is likely to yield more flexible remedies than those permitted by traditional legal procedures, including more contingent and monitored solutions. With more stakeholders allowed to participate, both conflict and creativity are likely to be unleashed, but can often be used productively to reach new levels of understanding and more party-sensitive and tailored solutions.

Such facilitated deliberative processes are often being touted as more fully expressing the values of democratic decision making or Habermasian ''ideal speech situations'' than lawyer-dominated legal proceedings or negotiations, where clients tell us they often feel disempowered and unable to achieve either processual catharsis or substantive gain. Multiparty dispute resolution or transaction planning is difficult, but what the successful processes have demonstrated is that legitimacy and acceptability can be achieved as interests and needs are addressed from the very beginning, often preventing difficult and contentious lawsuits later. The early case studies support the notion that internal ''dispute resolution'' philosophies can often determine whether companies and businesses can successfully manage their conflicts and disputes, both internally and with respect to the public.

Lawyers who are proactive problem solvers and good process managers will have much to offer their clients in traditional capacities, but they may have something to offer non-traditional clients with whom they are not in a representational role as well. These new processes, which supplement, if not supplant, the formal legal processes of litigation and dyadic negotiation by their different organizing principles and epistemological underpinnings (that party as well as professional expertise is welcome), may in turn develop new kinds of substantive solutions to particular kinds of legal and human problems. Lawyers, in more traditional counseling and planning roles, utilize these new forms by serving as dispute system designers, creating internal dispute and grievance mechanisms for issues to be resolved, both within institutions and with external customers as well.

* * *

MULTIPLE CHOICE QUESTIONS

Answer these questions using the definitions found at the end of Chapter Two.

1. A congressional investigating committee subpoenaed certain files from a governmental agency in connection with the committee's investigation of the agency's allegedly illegal expenditure of government funds. Lawyer Altmont (the agency's Chief Counsel) instructed lawyer Barker (the Deputy Chief Counsel) to gather up the files and prepare them for production. Barker, in turn, assigned the project to lawyer Crawford (a newly-hired junior lawyer). In giving Crawford the assignment, Barker said: "I wouldn't be surprised if all of these files have been shredded long ago, pursuant to our regular Document Storage and Retention Procedures Manual ('DSRPM')." Crawford discovered that the files still existed, even though the DSRPM called for their destruction six months earlier. Crawford dutifully shredded the files himself and then reported the fact to Barker. Barker responded by stating: "Good. I wonder if the computer backup for those files still exists?" Crawford interpreted this as an instruction to erase the computer backup material, which he promptly did. Barker then reported the full story to Altmont who informed the congressional investigating committee that both the files and the computer backup had been destroyed in accordance with the agency's regular procedures under the DSRPM.

A. Only Barker and Crawford are *subject to discipline.*

B. Only Crawford is *subject to discipline.*

C. Altmont, Barker, and Crawford are all *subject to discipline.*

D. Neither Altmont, nor Barker, nor Crawford are *subject to discipline.*

2. Attorney Arlington is a young associate in the firm of Smith & Black. He is assisting senior partner Black in the discovery phase of a case in which the court has ordered Black's client to produce certain documents. Black asked Arlington to study the court order, to review several boxes of documents sent over by the client, and to decide which documents must be produced. Arlington did the work and presented his conclusions to Black. Black and Arlington disagree about one group of documents. Black maintains that the court order does not require them to be produced, but Arlington insists that a fair reading of the court order does require them to be produced. The two attorneys agree that the question is a close one, but each is convinced that the other is incorrect. Which of the following is most nearly correct?

A. If Arlington gives in to Black's point of view, Arlington will be *subject to discipline,* since an attorney must not hold back what a court has ordered to be produced.

B. Since a subordinate attorney cannot be held accountable for following the directions of a supervising attorney, Arlington *must* accede to Black's point of view.

C. Since the point is a debatable one, Arlington *may* accede to Black's point of view.

D. Since an attorney is required to follow his own, independent judgment in handling a client's matter, Arlington *must* either insist that the documents be produced or else decline to work further on the case.

3. After 45 years of solo practice in the small town of Willow Creek, lawyer Lumire decided to sell his law practice and to retire. He advertised the practice for sale in the classified pages of the local bar journal, and in due course he found a buyer, an enthusiastic young attorney named Ames. The sales contract between Lumire and Ames provides that Ames will pay Lumire $65,000 for the small wood building that houses Lumire's office; $8,000 for the furniture, law books, office machines, and related items of personal property; and $10,000 for the good will of the practice. It further provides that Ames will pay Lumire $500 per month as a retirement benefit during Lumire's lifetime or until Lumire returns to law practice in Willow Creek. Is the sales contract *proper?*

A. Yes, even though it provides for the $500 monthly retirement benefit.

B. Yes, provided that the $500 monthly retirement benefit is reasonable in light of the good will value of the practice.

C. No, because the good will of a law practice cannot be bought and sold.

D. No, because Lumire and Ames have not previously been associated in law practice, either as partners or otherwise.

Answers to the multiple choice questions are in the Appendix at the end of the book.

Chapter Fourteen

Judicial Conduct

■ ■ ■

What This Chapter Covers

I. Standards of Conduct for Judicial Officers
- A. Judicial Standards and Discipline
- B. Introduction to the ABA Model Code of Judicial Conduct
- C. Promoting Independence, Integrity, Impartiality, and Propriety
- D. Performing Judicial Duties Impartially, Competently, and Diligently
- E. Avoiding Conflict with Personal and Extrajudicial Activities
- F. Avoiding Inappropriate Political and Campaign Activities
- G. Judges, Politics, and Free Speech
- H. Recusal of U.S. Supreme Court Justices
- I. Recusal and Due Process

Reading Assignment

Wydick, Perschbacher & Bassett, Chapter 14.

ABA Model Code of Judicial Conduct 2007, including the Preamble, Scope, Terminology, Application, and Canons 1 through 4.

ABA Model Rules:

Rules 1.12, 3.5, 8.3(b) and 8.4(f).

CRPC 1–700, 1–710 and 5–300.

Supplemental Reading

Hazard & Hodes:

Discussion of ABA Model Rules 1.12, 3.5, 8.3(b) and 8.4(f).

This final chapter departs from our usual format. In place of the discussion problems at the beginning and multiple–choice questions at the end, you will find a set of Yes/No questions to help you explore the ABA Model Code of Judicial Conduct. After the Yes/No questions, you will find two case notes. The first concerns the free speech rights of judges and judicial candidates. The second concerns recusal by U.S. Supreme Court Justices.

JUDICIAL STANDARDS AND DISCIPLINE

The American Bar Association adopted the present Model Code of Judicial Conduct in 2007 as a model for the various states to follow in promulgating their own codes of conduct for judges. You can think of the ABA Model Code of Judicial Conduct (CJC) as doing for judges what the ABA Model Rules of Professional Conduct do for lawyers. The 2007 CJC replaces several earlier ABA models, stretching back to the 1924 Canons of Judicial Ethics. We anticipate that over the next few years a majority of the states will adopt the 2007 CJC—or at least most of it—thus making it close to a national standard for the conduct of judges.

This book does not cover California's own Code of Judicial Ethics, which is based partly on earlier ABA models and partly on unique California precedent. [*See* California Code of Judicial Ethics, West's California Rules of Court 627 (2007).] The responsibility for disciplining California judges rests with the California Commission on Judicial Performance. The Commission consists of one appellate justice, two trial judges, two experienced lawyers, and six ordinary citizens. [California Const., art. VI, § 8 (1996).] Subject to discretionary review by the California Supreme Court, the Commission can admonish, censure, retire, or remove a judge. [*Id.* § 18.]

Federal judges in Article III courts hold office for life "during good behavior." [U.S. CONST. art. III, § 1.] They can be removed from office only by impeachment [*See U.S. ex rel. Toth v. Quarles*, 350 U.S. 11, 16, 76 S.Ct. 1, 3, 100 L.Ed. 8 (1955)], which is a drastic, tedious, and seldom–used procedure. In 1980, Congress established a less drastic procedure that allows a panel of federal judges to discipline an Article III judge by censure and other sanctions short of removal from office. [*See* 28 U.S.C. § 372(c)(1)–(18) (2000).]

Federal judges have their own Code of Conduct for United States Judges. [*See* www.uscourts.gov/guide/vol2/ch1.html#comp.] The present version closely tracks the 1990 CJC, but we anticipate that in due course the Judicial Conference of the United States will bring it into line with the 2007 CJC. The federal code applies to most Article II judges and to all Article III judges except the Justices of the Supreme Court, but the Justices look to both the federal code and the ABA models as sources of ethical guidance. Congress has specified the grounds and procedures for recusal (disqualification) of a federal judge from hearing a particular case. [*See* 28 U.S.C. § 144 (bias or prejudice) and § 455 (other grounds for disqualification—similar to Rule 2.11 of the 2007 CJC and its 1990 predecessor).]

JUDICIAL ETHICS BEE

Answer the following Yes/No questions. The terms in italics are defined at the end of Chapter Two. At the end of each question, you will find a citation to a part of the CJC that will help you answer the question.

1. The CJC's four Canons state "overarching principles of judicial ethics," and the various Rules prohibit or require specific kinds of conduct. If a judge's conduct offends a Canon but does not violate a Rule, is the judge *subject to discipline*? [*See* CJC, Scope ¶ 2.]

2. The Comments in the CJC have two functions. First, they provide guidance on the purpose, meaning, and proper application of the various Rules. Second, they help explain the Rules and sometimes give examples of conduct that is permitted or prohibited by a Rule. If a Comment says that judges "must" do X, can a judge be *subject to discipline* for failing to do X, even though the associated Rule doesn't specifically mention X? [*See* CJC, Scope ¶ 3.]

3. While lawyer LB was litigating a case in Judge JT's court, LB committed a serious violation of the Rules of Professional Conduct. Judge JT learned of LB's violation from a trustworthy, non–confidential source. Judge JT considered reporting LB to the appropriate disciplinary authorities, but after careful deliberation, she decided not to. One of Judge JT's fellow judges found out about JT's failure to report LB, and that judge reported Judge JT to the Judicial Disciplinary Board. The Board investigated the matter and decided not to institute disciplinary proceedings against Judge JT. Was the Board's action *proper*? [*See* CJC, Scope ¶ 6 and Rule 2.15(B); ABA Model Rule 8.3, Comment 3.]

4. Plaintiff PE sued his former employee DF for stealing PE's trade secrets. Judge JR failed to make timely rulings on PE's motions for a temporary restraining order and a preliminary injunction. Judge JR's delay caused PE to lose thousands of dollars. PE then sued Judge JR to recover his losses, alleging that JR's failure to make timely rulings was a tortious breach of judicial ethics. Does PE have a valid tort claim against Judge JR? [*See* CJC, Scope ¶ 7; Rule 2.5(A) and Comment 3.]

5. CC is the Calendar Clerk of the Rosslyn County Trial Court, a position she has held for the past 28 years. Her employer is Rosslyn County, and her duties are to keep the court's calendar current and accurate. She does not perform any judicial functions, but every lawyer in the county knows that CC can make life difficult for lawyers who habitually forget court dates, fail to file papers on time, or the like. Can CC be *subject to discipline* under the CJC? [*See* CJC, Application I(B) and Rule 2.12(A).]

6. Retired Judge RJ is subject to recall, to serve as a trial judge when she is needed. When she is recalled, she is paid a generous *per diem* in addition to her ordinary retirement pay. As a judge subject to recall, she is not permitted to practice law. During a month in which she is certain

not to be recalled as a trial judge, would it be *proper* for her to serve for pay as the mediator of a work-assignment dispute between two labor unions? [*See* CJC, Application II(A) and Rule 3.9.]

7. Judge JP is a continuing part–time judge who for many years has served roughly 10 weeks per year on the Lemon County Family Court. He has a continuing appointment, and he is called in whenever one of the regular judges becomes ill or goes on vacation. When he is not judging, he practices family law in neighboring Walnut County, where his office and home are located. *May* JP represent a woman who is seeking a divorce in the Lemon County Family Court? [*See* CJC, Application III(A)(2) and III(B).]

8. Law professor LP serves sporadically as a pro tempore part–time judge on the Oregon Court of Medical Appeals, a court of limited jurisdiction that handles bioethics cases, medical malpractice cases, and other cases that turn on medical issues. When the court needs LP on a case, it appoints her separately to the panel that will hear that case. LP vehemently disagrees with the Florida Supreme Court's decision in a so-called "right to life" case, and she writes a hard–hitting op–ed piece for the New York Times, hoping to influence public opinion and to encourage the U.S. Supreme Court to grant certiorari and reverse the Florida decision. Is LP *subject to discipline*? [*See* CJC, Application V(A) and Rule 2.10(A).]

9. PL is a practicing lawyer who also serves on the board of directors of InterCorp, a large, publicly held telecommunications company. Last month, PL was sworn in as an appointed member of the State Intermediate Court of Appeals. Will PL be *subject to discipline* if he does not immediately resign his InterCorp directorship? [*See* CJC, Application VI and Rule 3.11(B).]

10. Justice JZ sits on the State Supreme Court. To reduce their state and federal income tax burden, JZ and his wife knowingly and grossly overstated the fair market value of some property they donated to a charity. The Internal Revenue Service charged them with willful failure to pay income tax, a serious criminal offense. Eventually the IRS dismissed the case in return for full payment of all the taxes due, plus interest and a stiff penalty. Is JZ *subject to discipline*? [*See* CJC Rule 1.1, 1.2, and Comments 1–3.]

11. The North Virginia Legal Assistance Corporation (NVLAC) is a tax–exempt, publicly chartered corporation that seeks charitable donations and in turn grants funds to locally operated Legal Aid offices. Those offices provide legal services to needy people in non–criminal matters. Justice JL sits on the North Virginia Circuit Court of Appeal. She allows her name and judicial title to be used on the letterhead that the NVLAC uses to solicit contributions from the public and memberships from lawyers. The Justice also makes speeches at bar association meetings, urging lawyers to become dues–paying members of NVLAC and to provide pro bono services. Finally, the Justice serves as an unpaid instructor in quarterly workshops that train lawyers how to do Legal Aid work. Are

Justice JL's activities *proper*? [*See* CJC Rule 1.2, Comments 4 and 6; Rule 3.7(A), Comment 3 and 4; Rule 3.7(B), Comment 5.]

12. On her way to work one morning, Superior Court Judge JE was stopped by a State Highway Patrol Officer for driving her little red sports car 83 miles per hour through a 45 mph construction zone. The officer gave JE a $400 speeding ticket. In response, JE ordered the officer to appear at 10 a.m. the following day in her courtroom. The officer appeared as ordered, in uniform and wearing his service pistol on his belt. JE ordered him to place his pistol on her bench. She picked it up and pointed it at the officer's mid–section, saying this: "Officer, the next time you see my car on your little piece of highway, think carefully about this moment." With that, she handed the pistol back and dismissed him. She later paid the speeding ticket on time and without complaint. Is JE *subject to discipline*? [*See* CJC Rule 1.2 and 1.3, Comment 1.]

13. After graduating from law school, LG served for a year as law clerk to State Supreme Court Justice JJ. When LG started looking for a law firm job, Justice JJ volunteered to write recommendation letters for her. Using Supreme Court stationery, stamps, and secretarial services, JJ wrote letters to a dozen top law firms, enthusiastically recommending LG as "among the best two or three law clerks I have ever had." Is Justice JJ *subject to discipline*? [*See* CJC Rule 1.3, Comment 2.]

14. Judge JW wrote a thinly disguised "novel" based on an infamous murder committed by a Hollywood film star. Earlier JW had presided at the film star's jury trial, which resulted in a publicly unpopular acquittal. In JW's novel, the wise trial judge permitted the prosecutor to use some evidence that JW had excluded from the real trial, and the fictional jury came back with a conviction. The book publisher heavily advertised the novel as having been written by "Trial Judge JW, The Man Who Knows the Truth." Is JW *subject to discipline*? [*See* CJC Rule 1.3, Comment 4; *see also* Rule 1.2.]

15. Justice JU is serving her third term as an elected State Appellate Court Justice. She lives with her aged parents, who are both in the mid–stages of Alzheimer's disease. They require full–time, watchful care, and thus far they have vigorously resisted JU's efforts to obtain outside help or to place them in an appropriate care facility. Justice JU attempts to do her reading, legal research, and opinion writing at home, but she finds it hard to concentrate, and she is frequently unavailable to come to the court for conferences and oral arguments. Will Justice JU be *subject to discipline* if she does not either resign or make other arrangements for the care of her parents? [*See* CJC Rule 2.1.]

16. Administrative Law Judge JA came to the United States from his native country as a penniless immigrant 38 years ago. He learned to speak fluent English, earned a law degree, and now sits on the Social Welfare Appeals Court. Judge JA has an unshakeable faith in the ability of immigrants from his native country to make their own way in the U.S. through hard work and frugal living. Without exception, whenever JA

hears a welfare appeal involving an immigrant from his native country, he rules against the immigrant and delivers a little lecture on his own life story. Is Judge JA's conduct *proper*? [*See* CJC Rule 2.2, Comments 1 and 2; Rule 2.3(B); Rule 2.11(A)(1); *see also* CJC, Application I(B) and n.1.]

17. Despite his advanced age, crumbling countenance, and perpetual halitosis, Appeals Court Justice JK regards himself as uncommonly attractive to women, especially young ones. In hiring law clerks, JK invariably selects young women, and in dealing with them he is always oleaginously attentive. He buys them little presents, compliments their hair, brings them flowers from his garden, pats them on the knee, and never requires them to work to capacity. In return, he expects them to fetch him coffee, run personal errands, accompany him to the occasional movie, and listen to his ancient jokes about traveling salesmen and farmers' daughters. Surely JK is an oily old creep, but is he *subject to discipline*? [*See* CJC Rule 2.3(A), (B), and Comments 2–4.]

18. Judge JH is assigned to handle the bail hearing in a street–gang murder case against gang leader GL. JH received an anonymous telephone call, telling him to free GL on bail or else "prepare to find your precious sixth–grader dead and floating in the river." The police could not find the source of the call, and they could not guarantee the safety of JH or his sixth–grader. JH was so unnerved that he felt he could not rule fairly on GL's motion to set bail, and the Chief Judge urged JH to recuse himself and let a different judge handle the bail hearing. JH reluctantly recused himself. Was JH's recusal *proper*? [*See* CJC Rule 2.4(B); Rule 2.7; and Rule 2.11(A)(1).]

19. This morning Judge JD's courtroom is overflowing with angry citizens who have come to hear JD rule on the habeas corpus petition of ST, an alleged terrorist who has been confined without a hearing for four years in a Navy brig in JD's judicial district. The bailiffs cannot stop the angry citizens from shouting and stamping their feet, so JD asks the local police to eject them from the courtroom, which the police do with dispatch. Is JD's action *proper*? [*See* CJC Rules 2.4 and 2.11(A)(1).]

20. Court Commissioner CC performs judicial functions in the Labor Relations Court of First Instance. CC's late father was a respected labor union leader, and CC's siblings are all members of various labor unions. CC's younger brother, Benny, often tells other union members things like this: "Hey, don't worry about it—if you end up in court, my brother CC will take care of it." CC has admonished Benny not to say such things, but CC knows that Benny does it anyway. Is CC *subject to discipline*? [*See* CJC, Application I(B); CJC Rule 2.4(C).]

21. Justice JQ sits on the State Court of Criminal Appeals (CCA), which in this state is the highest appellate court for criminal matters. The CCA's own Rule of Court 400–4 requires each Justice to *personally* read and prepare bench briefs for a pro rata share of the Petitions for Discretionary Review that the court receives every month. Justice JQ thinks that rule is foolish and that the Justices should have their law

clerks read the petitions and prepare the bench briefs, to free up the Justices for more demanding work. JQ's efforts to get the rule changed have been in vain, so he simply refuses to follow it—his share of the petition work is done by his law clerks, and they do it quite well. Is JQ's conduct *proper*? [*See* CJC Rule 2.5(A) and (B).]

22. State Supreme Court Justice JN used to be one of the two or three best judges on the high court, and she is still excellent during the morning hours. After lunch, however, she has become alternately belligerent and somnambulant, which some court observers attribute to the amount of alcohol she drinks with lunch. She is frequently late in returning from the noon hour, which prevents the court from resuming on time. Some afternoons she flies into a rage when one of the arguing lawyers cannot satisfactorily answer her questions. Other afternoons she goes quietly to sleep during the oral arguments. Is JN *subject to discipline*? [*See* CJC Rule 2.5.]

23. For many years Judge JG has been the only judge assigned to the Law and Motion calendar in Centertown, the commercial and population hub of the state. JG wrote the state's leading treatise on pre–trial civil procedure, the topic that controls most law and motion issues. The book publisher advertises the treatise with cartoons that depict angry clients berating their dull–eyed lawyers with statements like this: "My *next* lawyer will look in Judge JG's book!" When the State Commission on Judicial Performance inquired about the advertising, JG responded that he just writes the treatise, and the advertising is up to the publisher. Is JG's position *proper*? [*See* CJC Rule 1.3, Comment 4.]

24. Judge JY prides herself in keeping her trial calendar current by insisting that the parties do everything possible to settle their differences before resorting to trial. At the final pre–trial conference, she almost always tells the parties and their lawyers something like this: "All of you are being unreasonable babies. I want you to settle this case this afternoon, and none of us will go home tonight until you get it done." She puts the plaintiffs in one room and the defendants in another room, and then she moves from one room to the other, carrying settlement offers, debunking legal arguments, threatening stubborn clients, humiliating self–important counsel, and finally bringing the sides together with a settlement agreement. Is Judge JY's conduct *proper*? [*See* CJC 2.6(B) and Comment 2.]

25. Judge JJ is taking her two–year turn in Small Claims Court, where litigants represent themselves in civil matters valued at $5,000 or less. Behind JJ's back, her fellow judges call her Saint Jean, because she is endlessly patient with every litigant who appears in her court, no matter how ineptly they present their case, and no matter how foolish their contentions. JJ listens serenely to shameless liars, hallucinating addicts, and selfish quibblers, giving each of them equal and undivided attention. According to the court's statistical records, JJ is not handling as many small claims cases as other judges have in the past. On the other hand, in

litigant surveys, the litigants who appear in her court rate her "outstanding" in both "fairness" and "ability." Is JJ *subject to discipline*? [*See* CJC Rule 2.5 and Rule 2.8(B).]

26. Next November, Judge JT will be running in a contested election to retain his seat on the Superior Court bench. Five other judges sit on JT's court. The court clerk assigns cases randomly, by drawing judges' names from an old tin can. The clerk draws JT's name and assigns him *Dinsmore v. Unified School District*, in which an outspoken atheist is suing the local school board to stop the teaching of Intelligent Design as an "alternative theory" to Darwinian evolution. JT has no personal convictions about how the world began, but he does know that 68% of the voters in his district are fundamentalist Christians who believe in the literal truth of the Bible. *May* JT disqualify himself from hearing the case for the honest reason that he does not want to become embroiled in this kind of case so close to the election? [*See* CJC 2.7 and Comment 1.]

27. District Attorney DA is the elected criminal prosecutor in Judge JE's court. The citizens keep electing DA, term after term, because of the tough-guy cowboy image he conveys. DA always wears a big cowboy hat, expensive boots, and Levi jeans with a rodeo belt buckle as big as a coffee saucer. In the courtroom, DA struts and swaggers, berating witnesses, pandering to jurors, and browbeating hapless defendants. Judge JE occasionally tries to moderate DA's antics, but mostly she just lets him perform. Is Judge JE *subject to discipline*? [*See* CJC Rule 2.8(B).]

28. Judge JS sat as the trier–of–fact in a breach of contract case involving the sale of a race horse named Sassy Sue. One evening during the trial, JS attended a cocktail party where he overheard some well–dressed strangers chatting and laughing about the Sassy Sue case. JS pricked up his hears and heard one of them say: "I don't blame the buyer for backing out of that sale—any decent vet could see that Sassy Sue is prone to shin splints." The next morning when the seller was on the witness stand, Judge JS posed his own line of questions about Sassy Sue and shin splints. Those questions turned out to be the most critical ones in the whole case. JS did not tell the litigants what he had overheard at the cocktail party. Was JS's conduct *proper*? [*See* CJC Rule 2.9(A) and (B).]

29. The Chief Judge assigned trial judge JT to hear a complex pension law case involving the Employee Retirement Income Security Act (ERISA). Because JT didn't know the first thing about pension law, he bought and carefully studied the best legal treatise in the field. Then JT contacted one of the treatise authors, Professor BW, and arranged to get BW's help on difficult ERISA questions. Finally, whenever such a question arose during the case, JT telephoned BW, who helped JT work out the right answer. JT did not tell the litigants about the help he got from BW, but when they did find out later, they were pleased about the extra effort JT put into their case. Is JT *subject to discipline*? [*See* CJC Rule 2.9(A)(2).]

30. Judge JZ is newly appointed to the bench and does not yet fully trust his judicial instincts. Whenever he is bothered by an issue of fairness or equitable application of the law, he talks it through with JV, the most senior member of JZ's court. These conversations frequently result in JZ changing his mind about the issue at hand. Is JZ's conduct *proper*? [*See* CJC Rule 2.9(A)(3).]

31. The court on which Judge JW and Judge JQ sit is located near many communication technology and biological technology companies. As a result, much of their court's business involves those fields of science. Whenever JW sits as trier–of–fact in such a case, he researches the scientific issues thoroughly, using both his computer and the nearby university's science library. Whenever JQ presides in a case that involves difficult questions of law, she doesn't limit herself to the lawyers' briefs to find out what the law is. Rather, she does her own legal research, using both her computer and the nearby university's law library. Are both JW's and JQ's actions *proper*? [*See* CJC 2.9(C).]

32. Lawyer LL filed a complaint on behalf of Friends of the Birds to enjoin developer Knoxous Korp. from buying and building on a certain 500 acre parcel of virgin wetlands. One day later, before Knoxous was even served with the complaint, LL showed up at the chambers of Judge JR with a petition for an immediate temporary restraining order that would stop Knoxous for 21 days from closing the land purchase transaction. Nobody was present on behalf of Knoxous, but Judge JR invited LL into his chambers, glanced over the petition, and—without hearing anything from LL—denied the petition without prejudice to later renewal, on the ground that he could not grant the petition ex parte without giving Friends of the Birds a tactical advantage over Knoxous. Was Judge JR's action *proper*? [*See* CJC Rule 2.9(A)(1).]

33. Judge JE was presiding at criminal defendant CD's jury trial for drug dealing. CD was defended by a court–appointed defense lawyer who seemed more intent on augmenting his hourly fee (paid from the public purse) than on effectively defending CD. The prosecution relied heavily on testimony from three shifty–eyed witnesses, and CD's lawyer offered no character evidence to attack their credibility. When JE got home, he did a bit of Internet research and discovered that each of the three shifty–eyed witnesses had multiple convictions for crimes involving dishonesty or false statement—convictions that the defense could have used for impeachment. After careful thought, JE decided not to interfere with CD's lawyer's handling of the case. The jury found the defendant guilty as charged, but the following day JE granted the defendant's motion for a new trial based on incompetence of defense counsel. JE based his decision, in part, on the defense counsel's failure to impeach the three shifty–eyed witnesses. Were JE's actions *proper*? [*See* CJC Rule 2.9(C).]

34. Crescent Corp., the world's richest oil company, made a hostile tender offer for shares of USA Petro, the largest U.S. producer of crude oil. The Antitrust Division of the U.S. Department of Justice sued Cres-

cent, alleging that the tender offer was part of a plan to monopolize the global oil business. While the government's motion for a preliminary injunction was pending before a federal district judge, United States Supreme Court Justice JM appeared on television for an interview about the architecture of the beautiful white–marble building that houses the Court. The interviewer surprised him with a pointed question about the preliminary injunction motion in the Crescent antitrust case, and Justice JM blurted out the following response: "No federal judge could be dumb enough to deny a preliminary injunction in that case." *May* a judge make such a comment in a public forum? [*See* CJC Rule 2.10(A); *see also Republican Party of Minnesota v. White*, 536 U.S. 765, 122 S.Ct. 2528, 153 L.Ed.2d 694 (2002), noted *infra*.]

35. Lawyer LC was a candidate for an appellate court judgeship in a contested election. During the campaign season, a radio reporter asked LC whether, if elected, she would vote to uphold the constitutionality of a physician–assisted suicide statute that the state legislature recently enacted. LC replied: "I don't know how I would vote, because that would depend on the procedural posture of the case and the precise legal issue before the court, but I can tell you what general legal principles would guide me. First, I think the individual states are the appropriate units of government to deal with issues of health care, including end–of–life decisions. Second, I think people have an inherent right of privacy, which is protected by our state constitution, and perhaps also by the federal constitution. Third, I think that, absent constitutional constraints, the will of the people, expressed through their legislators, should govern." Was LC's response *proper*? [*See* CJC Rule 2.10(B) and Rule 4.1(A)(13) and Comment 13.]

36. A jury of his peers convicted arson defendant AD on seven separate counts of arson, each of which involved the burning of a family residence while the family was asleep inside. At the end of the trial, after the sentencing, the post–trial motions, and the housekeeping details had been disposed of, trial judge JS turned to the jury and said: "Before I excuse you, ladies and gentlemen of the jury, I want to commend you for your hard work, for your patience in grappling with some difficult expert testimony, for your sympathetic concern for the victim witnesses, and for the wisdom demonstrated in your guilty verdicts. I am proud of you, and your community is proud of you, for a job well done. Now, ladies and gentlemen, you are excused." Is JS *subject to discipline* for that little speech? [*See* CJC Rule 2.8(C) and Comment 2.]

37. Trial judge JI disqualified himself from presiding at the trade libel trial of P Inc. v. D Corp., because JI was one of P Inc.'s lawyers in the early stages of the case. The case then passed to trial judge JG. Because JG had never handled a trade libel case before, he cornered JI in the judges' lunch room one day and asked her for a little lecture on the applicable law and on the facts and personalities involved in the case. JI politely declined to talk about the case with JG. Was JI's action *proper*? [*See* CJC Rule 2.9(A)(3) and Comment 5.]

38. For many years before her appointment to the bench, lawyer LM was a business litigator. She usually defended large corporations in securities, antitrust, intellectual property, and contract cases, and she usually won. Over the years, she developed a deep loathing for attorney AS, who often represented her opponents. LM regards AS as dishonest, lazy, unethical, and ignorant. The very sight of him gags her with disgust. Whenever AS shows up as counsel in a case assigned to her, LM gets the urge to disqualify herself. *May* she do so? [*See* CJC Rule 2.11(A)(1).]

39. Trial judge JO lives with and has an intimate relationship with his domestic partner DP, who is a news anchor for a local television station. DP has a married sister whose husband is the sole owner and operator of a dry–cleaning shop. The State Environmental Protection Agency has sued the husband to enjoin him from pouring toxic dry–cleaning chemicals down the storm sewer behind his shop. If the case is assigned to JO, would it be *proper* for him not to disqualify himself? [*See* CJC 2.11(A)(2)(a) and (c).]

40. Appellate Justice JC is married to HC, the wealthy owner of a wide variety of businesses. One of HC's businesses is AmeriNet, a re–insurance company that insures other insurance companies against extraordinary losses due to natural disasters. Justice JC takes care not to learn the nature or extent of HC's business holdings, so as to insulate herself from possible bias in her role on the appellate court. *May* JC sit on the appellate panel that hears AmeriNet's appeal from a multi-billion dollar judgment in a case arising out of recent tornados in the Midwest? [*See* CJC Rule 2.11(A)(2)(c) and (A)(3); Rule 2.11(B).]

41. Before State Supreme Court Justice JB took his present position, he was the elected Attorney General of the state. As Attorney General, he participated personally and substantially in writing Attorney General's Opinion 179, which takes the position that the state's current procedure for administering lethal injections in capital cases does not violate the state or federal constitutions. *May* Justice JB participate when his court decides a condemned man's challenge to the lethal injection procedure under the cruel and unusual punishment clauses of the state and federal constitutions? [*See* CJC Rule 2.11(A)(6)(b).]

42. Trial judge JX owns 15 shares of common stock in Consolidated Gold Holdings, Inc. JX inherited the stock when his grandfather died, some 30 years ago. The stock trades in the $3 to $5 range. Consolidated is either wealthy or worthless, depending on whether gold is found someday in Consolidated's California mines. Consolidated employee Clem Whittle sued Consolidated for back injuries he claims to have suffered when he fell off a stool in Consolidated's employee lunch room. JX is assigned to be the trial judge in *Whittle v. Consolidated.* Would it be *proper* for JX not to tell counsel about his 15 shares of Consolidated, provided that JX truly believes that the stock ownership is clearly not disqualifying? [*See* CJC Rule 2.11(A)(2)(c) and (A)(3) and Comment 5.]

43. Judge JA presided and served as trier–of–fact in *PL v. DF*. The critical issue was whether a particular stop sign was obscured from DF's line of sight by the trunk of an ancient oak tree. Unfortunately neither counsel offered satisfactory evidence on that issue. Before the trial ended, JA asked her law clerk to drive out to the intersection in question, stop half–a–block southeast, and determine whether he could see the stop sign despite the oak tree. The clerk reported that the sign was clearly visible, and JA decided the case accordingly. Were JA's actions *proper*? [*See* CJC Rule 2.9(C) and Rule 2.12(A).]

44. During Judge JJ's public election campaign, lawyer LY's husband contributed $1,000 to JJ's election campaign committee. [In this state, the judicial ethics code says that a contribution above $1,500 will result in the judge's disqualification from matters involving the donor.] JJ took pains not to learn the names of his campaign contributors. Six months later, JJ selected LY from among several qualified candidates to be the Special Master in some complicated patent cases. Special Masters in patent cases are very well compensated in this state. JJ selected LY because of her fine reputation among patent lawyers. Is JJ *subject to discipline*? [*See* CJC Rule 2.13.]

45. Family Court Judge JG supervised the placement of 10–year–old orphan O in a loving foster home, and JG appointed lawyer LE to serve as guardian of O's financial interests until O reached age 21. Shortly after O's 15th birthday, O inherited a large sum of money from his aunt. LE took over the management of the money, subject to review by Judge JG every 60 days. At 10 a.m. in one of these review sessions JG smelled whisky on LE's breath, and JG found that LE's computer records of O's money were garbled and incomplete. Further investigation revealed that LE had become a serious drunk and that he was diverting some of O's money for his own use. JG gave LE a vigorous talking–to. At the next reporting session, 60 days later, JG concluded that LE was still drinking, that the financial records were still a mess, and that more of O's money was missing. Is JG *subject to discipline* for failing to take stronger action 60 days earlier? [*See* CJC Rules 2.14 and 2.15.]

46. For more than 25 years, attorney AH divided his time about 50–50 between practicing law and helping his wife operate their charming small hotel on the edge of town. Last year AH was appointed to be a County Court Judge, and at that point his wife took on most of the hotel work, to give AH ample time for judging. Now the County Board of Supervisors is proposing a 17% tax on all hotel guests in the county—a tax that would drive small hotel owners out of business. AH plans to speak in opposition to the tax at the next Board of Supervisors meeting. Is it *proper* for AH to be involved in the hotel business with his wife, to spend a few hours per week on hotel work, and to speak against the tax at the Board of Supervisor's meeting? [*See* CJC Rule 3.1(A), 3.2(C), and 3.11(B)(1).]

47. Appellate Justice JA got to know law student EJ well when she served for two semesters as his unpaid judicial extern, and he developed a

high opinion of her moral character and legal abilities. At the time, EJ was an exchange student from Thailand, who was in the U.S. on a student visa. Now, a few years later, EJ wants to return as a permanent resident and eventually become a naturalized citizen, and she needs a good character witness to testify on her behalf at an administrative hearing held by the U.S. Immigration and Naturalization Service. When she asked Justice JA to do that for her, he declined to do so voluntarily, but he said that if she did not have anyone else, and if she subpoenaed him, he would testify for her. Was JA's response *proper*? [*See* CJC Rule 3.3.]

48. After serving for seven years as the U.S. Treasury Secretary, SS became an Associate Justice of the U.S. Supreme Court, where she served for a decade with great distinction. While SS was still on the Court, U.S. President PR needed a person of undoubted wisdom and rectitude to chair a newly–created Presidential Commission on Foreign Relations, and he selected SS for that task. President PR's unexpressed hope was that the Commission would take the heat off of him for a series of foreign policy blunders. SS respectfully refused to serve, explaining that to do so would be inconsistent with her responsibilities on the Court. Was SS's refusal *proper*? [*See* CJC Rule 3.4.]

49. To rule on a summary judgment motion, Judge JY had to read some confidential discovery material that was filed in her court under seal. From it she learned that MagnaTherm Energy Corp. was about to publicly announce its development of a new non–carbon–based fuel for generating electricity. JY knew that her scientist brother–in–law would be fascinated to learn of the new development, so she told him about it in strict confidence. Without revealing the secret to anyone, the brother–in–law bought 1,000 shares of MagnaTherm common stock on the open market at $54 per share. When MagnaTherm made its public announcement, the share price increased to $76 per share. Is JY *subject to discipline*? [*See* CJC Rule 3.5.]

50. JW retired from the U.S. Army after 30 years in the Judge Advocate General's Corps. He was then appointed to the State Intermediate Court of Appeal, and a few months later he was offered membership in the Armed Forces Memorial Club, which operates excellent but inexpensive guest facilities in major cities of the U.S. The club offers membership to active duty or honorably discharged men and women from the Army, Navy, Marine Corps, or Coast Guard, except for homosexuals and lesbians. *May* Judge JW join the club? [*See* CJC Rule 3.6.]

51. Trial court Judge JT is known as the driving force behind his state's Legal Aid Institute. The institute helps fund legal aid offices, which provide pro bono legal services to poor people in civil matters. For years, Judge JT has helped the institute plan fund–raising events and manage its money. JT's name and judicial title are listed on the institute's fund–raising letterhead. JT also helps recruit lawyers to be "sustaining members" of the institute. To be a sustaining member, a lawyer must donate at least $5,000 per year to the institute and must personally perform at

least 100 hours per year of pro bono work for poor people. JT's recruiting tools are good humor and appeal to virtue; he avoids anything remotely coercive. Is it *proper* for Judge JT to help plan fund–raising events, to help the institute with money management, to appear on the letterhead, and to recruit sustaining members? [*See* CJC Rules 3.1 and 3.7.]

52. Empire County trial judge JO's father FA has long been a gambling addict, and JO has always had to look out for him. A year ago FA won $15 million dollars playing poker in Las Vegas. JO convinced FA to put two–thirds of the money in trust, with JO as trustee and FA as beneficiary. JO carefully researched the leading publicly held companies in Empire County, and she invested part of the trust money in the best eight. Those companies frequently show up as litigants in JO's court, but since she holds the investments as trustee, rather than as beneficial owner, she does not disqualify herself. Is it *proper* for JO to serve as trustee and for her not to disqualify herself, as described above? [*See* CJC Rule 2.11(A), Rule 3.8 and Comment 1, and Rule 3.11(C)(2).]

53. In the big city of Gotham, the court calendars are so crowded that civil litigants must often wait two or three years after their final pre–trial conference to get a trial date, a judge, and an open courtroom. As a consequence, many litigants now stipulate to use a "Rent–a–Judge," meaning an experienced judge who will decide their case under ordinary court rules and ordinary law, but who is paid a per diem fee by the litigants rather than a monthly salary by the government. In contrast, in the nearby sleepy village of Blossom Grove, the trial court calendar is never clogged, so the local judge, JZ, seldom has enough work to occupy his time. When nothing is going on in Blossom Grove, JZ moonlights as a Rent–a–Judge in Gotham. *May* he do so? [*See* CJC Rule 3.9.]

54. Judge JR no longer sits full–time on the State Seventeenth Circuit Appeals Court, but as a continuing part–time judge, she regularly substitutes for other judges when needed. JR's grandson GS came home from high school a few months ago with two broken teeth, a broken nose, and two black eyes, all due to a beating by the Filthy Four, a notorious quartet of high–school bullies. JR promised GS she would represent him for free in bringing the bullies to justice. On GS's behalf, she sued the bullies in the Lake View trial court, which is under the appellate jurisdiction of the Seventeenth Circuit. JR won GS a judgment for $18,000. Were JR's actions *proper*? [*See* CJC, Terminology, definition of "member of the judge's family;" CJC, Application III(B); and CJC Rule 3.10.]

55. LV was a successful appellate lawyer. He and five other successful appellate lawyers were joint venturers in a real estate deal; their objective was to restore the old buildings in the historic center of their city and to turn the area into an attractive and profitable shopping venue. When LV died, his share of the real estate venture passed to his daughter, Justice JE, who sits on the State Supreme Court. JE got along well with the five other venturers, and she enjoyed their regular Tuesday breakfast meetings, where they discussed their strategies and progress. Her five co–

venturers frequently argue cases before the State Supreme Court, but she disqualifies herself from participating in those cases. Are her actions *proper*? [*See* CJC Rule 3.11.]

56. The State of East Dakota five–judge Condemnation Court handles cases in which the government exercises the power of eminent domain to take private property for a public use. East Dakota condemnation lawyers formed the Eminent Domain Association. About half the members work for the government as condemnation lawyers, and the other half routinely represent private citizens whose property is being taken. The association holds annual meetings, always in some remote and scenic location around the state. At these meetings, the members attend continuing legal education sessions, debate condemnation policy, hear presentations on pending legislation, play an annual touch football game, and socialize at luncheons and dinners. This year the Association invited Condemnation Court Judge JC to attend the annual meeting and be the keynote speaker at one of the dinners. The Association waived its usual $200 annual meeting registration fee for JC, and it reimbursed her travel, lodging, food, and incidental expenses. It also paid her its usual $400 honorarium for giving the keynote speech. JC publicly reported these sums in accordance with East Dakota's version of the CJC. Was it *proper* for JC to attend the meeting, give the speech, and accept the fee waiver, expense reimbursement, and honorarium? [*See* CJC Rules 3.12, 3.14, and 3.15.]

57. Juvenile Court Judge JQ's wife sells life insurance policies. Last week she won first prize in a sales contest put on by her employer. Her employer has never appeared in the Juvenile Court and is not likely to do so in the future. The prize is a two–week, all–expense–paid vacation in Tahiti for the winner and one guest. If JQ goes as his wife's guest, will he be *subject to discipline*? [*See* CJC 3.13.]

58. Land developer LD recently lost a zoning case that he plans to appeal to the 15–judge State Intermediate Court of Appeals. JY is a judge on that court. The clerk of that court randomly assigns judges to three–person panels, so litigants never know what judges they will get. JY and LD were college roommates, but they haven't corresponded or seen each other in years. LD recalled that JY is an avid wildlife photographer; LD owns a rustic cabin high in a mountain range that teems with wildlife. Without mentioning the zoning case, LD telephoned JY and invited him to spend a few days together at the cabin, hiking in the mountains and photographing the animals. The trip was a great success; JY got plenty of photos and fresh air, and the total cost for the two of them was under $100. Of course LD never mentioned the zoning case, and JY wasn't even aware of the case or of LD's plan to appeal. As luck would have it, JY was not selected for the three–person panel that ultimately heard LD's case. Is JY *subject to discipline*? [*See* CJC Rule 3.13.]

59. Judge JZ is an appellate court judge in East Virginia, where appellate judges enjoy lifetime tenure. JZ's son is an up–and–coming

young politician, a member of the Independence Party. He hopes to become the first Independence U.S. President, but for now he is working his way up by running in a contested public election for Lieutenant Governor of East Virginia—the state's second–highest elective office. JZ wants to support her son's candidacy in any way she can. *May* she publicly endorse him, make speeches on his behalf, contribute money to his campaign fund, and vote for him in the primary and general elections? [*See* CJC Rule 4.1(A) and Comments 3 through 6.]

60. Attorney AZ became so fed up with the local trial court's inefficiency that she vowed to get herself appointed to the next vacant judgeship. The Governor appoints new judges, based on recommendations from a State Bar committee. AZ's application letter to the committee promised that, if appointed, she would work to clean up the court's backlog of civil cases, streamline its probate calendar, and fire and replace the fossilized chief of records and the tyrannical jury commissioner. Was her application letter *proper*? [*See* CJC 4.1, Comment 14 and Rule 4.3.]

61. Lawyer LY is one of seven candidates running in a partisan election for three vacant positions on the Superior Court bench. Within the time period specified by law, LY identified himself as a member of the Democratic Party, and he obtained and publicized the Democratic Party's endorsement of his candidacy. LY's main adversary is Republican Party candidate RP; the other five candidates are not well known or well financed. At a Democratic campaign rally, LY spoke vigorously on his own behalf, and he overtly and candidly criticized RP's suitability to be a judge. Is LY *subject to discipline*? [*See* CJC Rule 4.2(B)(2) and (3); Rule 4.2(C) and Comment 6.]

62. State law requires all trial and intermediate appellate judges to run in a public "retention" election every seventh year. To retain his or her seat, a judge must get a majority vote. This year all of these retention candidates received a long questionnaire from the ATPW Coalition. (ATPW stands for All Things Pure and Wholesome.) ATPW calls itself an "issues advocacy" group. The object of the questionnaire is to find out and publicize what each candidate believes about an assortment of controversial legal, social, and political issues, such as animal rights, prison reform, global warming, the death penalty, whales, gay clergy, welfare fraud, preemptive war, globalization, child abuse, coyotes, campaign finance reform, immigration, organic food, and urban sprawl. When Judge JI received her ATPW questionnaire, she sent it back without answering any questions. She included a handwritten note explaining that she opposes all such questionnaires on the ground that reasonable people might view them as undermining a judicial candidate's independence and impartiality. Was JI's response *proper*? [*See* CJC 4.1, Comment 15.]

JUDGES, POLITICS, AND FREE SPEECH

Take a second look at CJC Rules 2.10(B) and 4.1(A)(13). Those rules tell judges and judicial candidates roughly this: if a case or issue is likely to come before your court, you must not make a pledge, promise, or commitment that is inconsistent with your duty to decide that case or issue *impartially*.

The 1990 predecessor of those rules was more restrictive; it prohibited judicial candidates from making pledges or promises of "conduct in office other than the faithful and impartial performance of the duties of office," and from making statements that "commit or appear to commit the candidate with respect to cases, controversies, or issues that are likely to come before the court." [*See* 1990 CJC 5A(3)(d)(i) and (ii), prior to 2003 amendments.]

One provision of the 1972 CJC was still more restrictive. It said that a judicial candidate must not "announce his views on disputed legal or political issues." [*See* 1972 CJC 7(B)(1)(c).] The 1972 provision is called the "announce clause," to distinguish it from the "commit clause" in the 1990 version. After the ABA abandoned the announce clause in 1990 and substituted the commit clause, most states followed the ABA's lead and did likewise. But Minnesota kept its old announce clause and applied it to both incumbent judges and lawyers seeking their first judgeship. [*See* Minn. Rules of Board on Judicial Standards 4(a)(6) and 11(d) (2002).] Minnesota selects all state judges by popular election.

In 1996 and 1998, Gregory Wersal ran for the Minnesota Supreme Court. He and the Republican Party of Minnesota sued the officials who enforce the Minnesota judicial standards for a declaratory judgment that the announce clause inhibited candidate Wersal's ability to speak out on disputed legal and political issues such as welfare, crime, and abortion, and thus violated his (and the Republican Party's) First Amendment right of free speech. The federal district court interpreted the announce clause narrowly, saying that it covered only issues that were likely to come before the court to which the candidate aspired. With that narrow interpretation, the district court held that the announce clause was constitutional. On appeal, the Eighth Circuit affirmed, but only after giving the clause a second pruning. The Eighth Circuit said that the clause permits "general discussions of case law and judicial philosophy." The Minnesota Supreme Court later adopted the two narrow readings of the clause.

Five members of the United States Supreme Court, in an opinion by Justice Scalia, struck down the announce clause, even in its twice–pruned form. *Republican Party of Minnesota v. White*, 536 U.S. 765, 122 S.Ct. 2528, 153 L.Ed.2d 694 (2002). Justice Scalia called the clause an impermissible content–based restriction that burdens a kind of speech that is at the core of First Amendment freedoms—speech about the qualifications of a candidate for public office. That made it subject to strict scrutiny, thus forcing the Minnesota officials to prove that the announce clause was (1) narrowly tailored (2) to serve a compelling state interest.

To prove that the clause was narrowly tailored, the Minnesota officials had to demonstrate that it did not unnecessarily circumscribe protected expression. The judicial narrowing of the announce clause was less than it appeared to be, Justice Scalia said. In the heat of the oral argument before the U.S. Supreme Court, counsel for the Minnesota officials conceded, off–the–cuff, that a candidate would violate the announce clause if he or she criticized a prior judicial decision and simultaneously asserted that *stare decisis* would not stop him or her from trying to overturn it. Further, limiting the announce clause to issues likely to come before the court is not much of a limitation because almost every disputed legal or political issue can end up before some court of general jurisdiction. Finally, construing the clause to allow "general" discussions of case law and judicial philosophy is small comfort. For example, a candidate could claim to be a "strict constructionist," but the claim would not mean much without some specific examples of what the candidate would or wouldn't change if elected.

The Minnesota officials argued that the announce clause serves two compelling state interests: (1) preserving the *impartiality* of judges, and (2) preserving the *appearance* of judges' impartiality. Justice Scalia consulted his well–worn 1950s dictionary and brought forth three possible meanings of *impartiality*. The first is lack of bias for or against a *party* to court proceedings. The announce clause isn't narrowly tailored to serve that interest, Justice Scalia said, because it is aimed at *issues*, not parties.

The second possible meaning is lack of a preconception about a given *legal issue*. The Scalia opinion concedes that the announce clause serves that interest, but it finds that interest *not compelling*. It's hard to imagine a judicial candidate who does *not* have preconceptions about legal issues and how they ought to be resolved. Moreover, would we really want a judge whose mind is a blank slate about legal issues? A candidate's lack of preconceptions about legal issues should be evidence of unfitness for judicial office, not evidence of desirable impartiality, Justice Scalia said.

The third possible meaning of impartiality is *open–mindedness*. That is, a judge may have preconceptions about a legal issue, but the judge is willing to consider opposing views and is open to persuasion when the issue arises in a pending case. Justice Scalia concedes that open–mindedness (or at least the appearance of open–mindedness) may be a desirable judicial quality, but he sets it aside, saying that Minnesota probably didn't have that objective in mind when it adopted the announce clause. The statements a judicial candidate makes during a campaign are an "infinitesimal portion of the public commitments to legal positions" that incumbent judges and aspiring judges make. They publicly express such commitments in books, articles, and speeches, in classrooms, and (in the case of incumbents) in earlier judicial opinions. As a method of assuring open–mindedness (or the appearance of it), the announce clause is "so woefully underinclusive as to render belief in that purpose a challenge to the credulous," according to Justice Scalia. Chief Justice Rehnquist and Justices O'Connor, Kennedy, and Thomas joined the Scalia opinion.

Justice O'Connor filed an interesting concurring opinion that argues against selecting judges by popular vote. By its very nature, she says, the election of judges undermines the interest in an impartial judiciary. Judges who must frequently stand for popular election are likely to feel that they have a personal stake in the outcome of every well–publicized case. Contested elections require campaigning, and campaigning takes money, sometimes millions of dollars. Raising money from campaign donors may leave a judge feeling indebted to certain parties or interest groups. Even if a judge resists the temptation to favor big donors, the mere possibility of favoritism can erode the public's confidence in the judiciary.

Despite the flaws of judicial elections, Justice O'Connor tells us, 39 of the 50 states now use some kind of elections to select some or all of their judges. (Some of the 39 use hybrid schemes in which judges are initially appointed by an elected official. After an initial term on the bench, an appointed judge must stand for a retention election in which there is no opposing candidate. A judge who loses a retention election is then replaced by a newly appointed judge.)

In some of the states that use pure popular vote to select judges, the elections are nonpartisan, meaning that the candidates are not identified with a political party. Other states have partisan elections in which judicial candidates have opponents, and party affiliation, and the other trappings of ordinary politics.

Justice O'Connor draws a pointed conclusion: If a state decides to select judges by contested popular elections, it assumes the risk that its judges will lack impartiality. Such a state should not be allowed to restrict the speech of judicial candidates in order to protect impartiality. "If the State has a problem with judicial impartiality, it is largely one the State brought upon itself by continuing the practice of popularly electing judges."

Justices Stevens, Souter, Ginsburg, and Breyer dissented; each of the four joined one opinion by Justice Stevens and a second opinion by Justice Ginsburg. The Ginsburg opinion is the more interesting of the two.

Justice Ginsburg sees a middle ground between Justice Scalia's full–blown free speech position and Justice O'Connor's distrust of judicial elections. Justice Ginsburg advocates a principled distinction between elected representatives (legislators and executives) and elected judges. Representatives are supposed to do what voters tell them to do. In contrast, judges are supposed to "refrain from catering to particular constituencies or committing themselves on controversial issues in advance of adversarial presentation." Having an impartial judiciary allows society to "withdraw certain subjects from the vicissitudes of political controversy, to place them beyond the reach of majorities and officials and to establish them as legal principles to be applied by the courts." By deciding to select judges by popular vote, Minnesota did not opt to put a corps of political actors on the bench; rather, it opted to preserve judicial integrity by other means. For example, it made judicial elections nonpartisan, and it prohibited candidates from publicly announcing how they would decide issues that come before them as judges.

Justice Ginsburg disagrees with the majority's all or nothing approach. She would distinguish elections for political office—in which the First Amendment holds full–sway—from elections for judicial office, where some restrictions on speech are constitutionally appropriate. True, Minnesota voters might like to know how a prospective judge would vote on a hotly–disputed legal issue, just as the U.S. Senate might like to know how a federal judicial nominee would vote on such an issue. Justice Ginsburg points out that all nine of the then–current members of the U.S. Supreme Court declined to furnish such information during their Senate confirmation hearings. That well–established federal norm demonstrates that there is nothing inherently wrong with depriving the people who pick judges of information they would like to have.

Justice Ginsburg draws support for her view of the announce clause by linking it to a related part of the CJC, the so-called "pledges–or–promises clause." The 1990 CJC 5A(3)(d)(i) prohibits a judicial candidate from "making pledges or promises of conduct in office other than the faithful and impartial performance of the duties of the office." [The 1972 CJC contained an identical clause.] Neither the parties to the case nor any of the Justices expressed any doubt about the constitutionality of the pledges–or–promises clause. If a candidate were allowed to make a promise about how she would rule on a given issue, the promise would give her a disqualifying personal stake in any case in which that issue is raised. The pledges–or–promises clause is therefore essential to preserve the impartiality of judges. The announce clause is a necessary adjunct, to prevent candidates from evading the pledges and promises clause by simply stating a position, rather than promising to rule in accordance with that position.

As you reflect on the Supreme Court's decision in *Republican Party of Minnesota v. White,* you may wish to consider what it bodes for various provisions of the CJC that raise free speech issues. For example:

- Re-read CJC Rule 2.10(B), which prohibits a judge from making a pledge, promise, or commitment that is inconsistent with the impartial performance of the adjudicative duties of judicial office. Comment 1 to that rule states that this restriction on judicial speech is "essential to the maintenance of the independence, integrity, and impartiality of the judiciary." Do you agree? Professors Moliterno and Harris express the importance of impartiality this way:

  > Impartiality is the cornerstone of judicial decision–making. When we think of the act of judging, we think of a neutral decision–maker, not subject to influence by forces outside the merits of the dispute before the judge. Of course no judge is perfect, and all judges carry their own personal traits and attitudes into the judging process. But impartiality means freedom from influence

beyond the most basic and unavoidable tugs of a judge's personality and unconscious habits of mind.

[JAMES MOLITERNO & GEORGE HARRIS, GLOBAL ISSUES IN LEGAL ETHICS 182 (2007).]

- When judges aren't judging, do they have fewer free speech rights than ordinary citizens? Suppose a judge writes a letter to the editor of his local newspaper, stating that gay people are mentally ill and belong in a hospital. Is the judge subject to discipline? [*Compare* CJC Rule 2.3(B) (speech or conduct *in the performance of judicial duties* that manifests prejudice based on sexual orientation) *with Mississippi Comm'n on Judicial Performance v. Wilkerson*, 876 So.2d 1006 (2004) (judge cannot be disciplined for writing such a letter to a local newspaper).] What if the judge makes a similar statement when instructing the jury about the credibility of a gay witness? [*See* Tobin A. Sparling, *Keeping up Appearances: The Constitutionality of the Model Code of Judicial Conduct's Prohibition of Extrajudicial Speech Creating the Appearance of Bias*, 19 GEO. J. LEGAL ETHICS 441 (2006).]
- Suppose lawyer L is running for a state supreme court judgeship in a contested public election; her opponent is incumbent Justice J. During the relevant campaign period, may L attend a Democratic Party fund-raising BBQ? If so, may she make a speech that urges people to vote for her? If so, may she state in her speech that Justice J has served brilliantly on the court for 43 years but is now mentally and physically unfit for further service? Does it make any difference if Lawyer L knows that Justice J is as fit as he ever was? If L may speak on her own behalf, may she also put in a plug for the Democratic candidates for governor and for president? [*See* CJC Rule 4.1(A)(3) and (11); CJC Rule 4.2(B); *see also Republican Party of Minn. v. White*, 416 F.3d 738 (8th Cir. 2005), *cert. denied sub nom. Dimick v. Republican Party of Minn.*, 546 U.S. 1157, 126 S.Ct. 1165, 163 L.Ed.2d 1141 (2006) (on remand of the *White* case, 8th Circuit struck down Minnesota's harsh version of the 1990 CJC rules on political activities and on personal solicitation of campaign funds).]

RECUSAL OF U.S. SUPREME COURT JUSTICES

A. THE FEDERAL RECUSAL STATUTE

The recusal of federal judges—including the Justices of the U.S. Supreme Court—is governed by a federal statute, 28 U.S.C. § 455 (2000). The statute begins with a broad catch–all provision, which says that a federal magistrate, judge, or justice "*shall* disqualify himself in any proceeding in which his *impartiality might reasonably be questioned*."[1] In this context, "shall" means "must." Thus recusal is mandatory if a *reasonable* person *might* have a *reasonable* doubt about the impartiality of the magistrate, judge, or justice.

The second part of the statute lists specific grounds for recusal; they are quite similar to those listed in the 2007 CJC and its 1990 predecessor.[2] Examples are bias for or against a party, personal knowledge of a disputed fact, prior role as a witness or lawyer in the matter, and personal or close family interest in the matter or in a party. Again recusal is mandatory, not permissive. Professor Bassett reads both parts of § 455 as being "self-enforcing," meaning that the judicial officer must take the initiative and recuse herself, not lie in the weeds waiting to see if a party will move to disqualify her.[3]

Professor Bassett observes that § 455 was a very different animal before Congress amended it in 1976.[4] The earlier version said this:

> Any justice or judge of the United States shall disqualify himself in any case in which he has a substantial interest, has been of counsel, is or has been a material witness, or is so related to or connected with any party or his attorney as to render it improper, in his opinion, for him to sit on the trial, appeal, or other proceeding therein.

Look at the phrase "in his opinion" in the last clause of the statute. Doesn't that phrase create a *subjective* standard—the judge's own opinion—when the ground for recusal is the judge's relation to or connection with a party or its lawyer? In other words, before 1976, if a judge's supposed bias arose from a relationship to or connection with a party or its attorney, the judge could continue in the case *unless in the judge's own opinion* it would be improper to do so.[5]

Moreover, before 1976, federal judges regarded themselves as having a "duty to sit when *not* disqualified" that was just as strong as the "duty *not* to sit when disqualified."[6] It has been argued (and Professor Bassett

---

1. 28 U.S.C. § 455(a) (2000) (emphasis added). In this case note, we use *recuse* and *disqualify* interchangeably, though some writers reserve *recuse* for the situation in which the judge takes the initiative and voluntarily steps out of the case.

2. *Compare id.* § 455(b) *with* 2007 CJC Rule 2.11(A) *and* 1990 CJC Canon 3E(1).

3. Debra Lyn Bassett, *Recusal and the Supreme Court*, 56 HASTINGS L.J. 657, 675 (2005). *See generally* Debra Lyn Bassett, *Judicial Disqualification in the Federal Appellate Courts*, 87 IOWA L. REV. 1213 (2002).

4. Bassett, *Recusal and the Supreme Court*, *supra* note 3, at 672–76.

5. *Id.* at 672–73.

6. *See, e.g.*, the memorandum opinion of then–Justice Rehnquist, 409 U.S. 824, 837, 93 S.Ct. 7, 34 L.Ed.2d 50 (1972), explaining why he did not disqualify himself in Laird v. Tatum, 408 U.S. 1, 92 S.Ct. 2318, 33 L.Ed.2d 154 (1972), a case that challenged the constitutionality of the Army's secret surveillance of civilian protests against the Vietnam War. Before his appointment to the Court, Justice Rehnquist had been the Assistant Attorney General for the Office of Legal Counsel; in that capacity he had testified as an expert witness before a Senate subcommittee about the legal issue in Laird v. Tatum, and he had some personal background knowledge of the Army's surveillance program. *See* MONROE H. FREEDMAN & ABBE SMITH, UNDERSTANDING LAWYER'S ETHICS 232–39 (3d ed. 2004). Justice Rehnquist was in the majority of a 5–4 decision holding that the war protesters' constitutional challenge was not justiciable.

agrees) that when Congress amended § 455 in 1976, it threw out both the subjective standard and the supposed duty to sit.[7] In short, present § 455(a) sets an *objective* standard for the catch–all provision—the reasonable person who might have a reasonable doubt about the judge's impartiality.

B. CHENEY v. U.S. DISTRICT COURT

Early in his first term as president, George W. Bush created the National Energy Policy Development Group, a task force headed by Vice–President Cheney and charged with recommending a national energy policy. All the officially appointed members of the task force were federal employees, which meant that the task force would be exempt from the Federal Advisory Committee Act and other federal laws that would have opened its participants and operations to public scrutiny.

The Sierra Club and many citizens suspected that oil industry lobbyists and executives were meeting with the task force as de facto members. If that were true, it would defeat the exemption, thus allowing the public to find out who was formulating the nation's energy policy. Vice–President Cheney refused to reveal who was attending the task force meetings, so the Sierra Club sued him and other task force members. The federal district court allowed the Sierra Club to conduct discovery, but Vice–President Cheney filed an interlocutory appeal and requested a writ of mandamus to prevent discovery. The D.C. Circuit Court of Appeals dismissed the Cheney appeal and denied the writ of mandamus.

The Vice–President then petitioned the Supreme Court for certiorari, and on December 15, 2003, the Court granted the writ. Three weeks later, Justice Scalia went on a duck hunting trip to Louisiana with Vice–President Cheney. The trip caused a uproar in the media. Editorial writers were aghast, and political cartoons showed the two men whispering while hunkered down together in a duck blind. The Sierra Club moved to disqualify Justice Scalia.

Motions to disqualify a Supreme Court justice are rare, perhaps because an ill–advised motion may offend both the target and other justices as well. The Supreme Court's procedural rules don't explain how disqualification motions are handled, but the lore is that the target Justice decides it by him or herself—sometimes with, and sometimes without, talking it over with other Justices.[8] Sometimes, but not often, the target Justice writes a memorandum opinion to explain his or her decision on the recusal motion.[9]

---

7. Freedman & Smith, *supra* note 6, at 239; Bassett, *Recusal and the Supreme Court*, *supra* note 3, at 673, citing RICHARD E. FLAMM, JUDICIAL DISQUALIFICATION: RECUSAL AND DISQUALIFICATION OF JUDGES § 20.10.I at 614 (1996).

8. R. Matthew Pearson, *Duck Duck Recuse? Foreign Common Law Guidance & Improving Recusal of Supreme Court Justices*, 62 WASH. & LEE L. REV. 1799, 1813–14 (2005).

9. *See, e.g.,* Laird v. Tatum, 409 U.S. 824, 93 S.Ct. 7, 34 L.Ed.2d 50 (1972) (mem. op. of then–Justice Rehnquist, explaining why he did not recuse himself).

Justice Scalia wrote such a memorandum opinion in the *Cheney* case.[10] The Sierra Club had used the news editorials to argue that the hunting trip could cause reasonable people to doubt the Justice's impartiality. The Justice's opinion begins by saying that recusal should depend on "the facts as they existed, and not as they were surmised or reported."[11] He is right, of course, so the following summary is based on the facts stated in his opinion:[12]

- Justice Scalia and Vice–President Cheney arranged the hunting trip long before the Vice–President petitioned the Supreme Court for certiorari. The two men were old friends from their days in President Gerald Ford's administration.
- For several years, on the Court's long winter break, Justice Scalia had gone hunting at the Louisiana duck-hunting camp of Wallace Carline. Mr. Carline is a native–born Louisianan who owns a company that supplies equipment and services to off–shore oil rigs. Contrary to some news reports, he was not an "energy industry executive" of the ExxonMobil sort.
- On his winter 2002 trip, Justice Scalia learned that Mr. Carline admired Vice–President Cheney, and the Justice already knew that the Vice–President liked to hunt ducks. The Vice–President accepted Mr. Carline's invitation (conveyed through Justice Scalia) to join the winter 2003 hunt.
- Justice Scalia, his son, and his son–in–law, flew to Louisiana with Vice–President Cheney on a government–owned Gulfstream jet (which the Vice–President had to use for national security reasons.) The Scalia party flew on a space–available basis, so they didn't cost the government any more than if the Vice–President had flown alone to hunt ducks. The reason the Scalia party flew down with the Vice–President was to spare Mr. Carline the trouble of meeting two different planes in New Orleans and transporting two different groups by boat to the hunting camp.
- The group that gathered at Mr. Carline's hunting camp consisted of 13 hunters, plus about three of Mr. Carline's staff, plus members of the Vice–President's staff and security detail. It was not an intimate setting.
- Everybody ate together. They slept in rooms of two or three, except for the Vice–President, who slept alone. They hunted in two– or three–man duck blinds.
- Justice Scalia and the Vice–President never hunted in the same blind, nor were they alone together, except perhaps for moments so

10. Cheney v. United States Dist. Ct. for the Dist. of Colum., 541 U.S. 913, 124 S.Ct. 1391, 158 L.Ed.2d 225 (2004) (mem. op. of Justice Scalia).

11. *Id.* at 914.

12. *Id.* at 914–16.

brief and unintentional as to escape memory. They never said a word about the case.

- The Vice–President left the group after two days. Justice Scalia, his son, and his son–in–law, left two days after that. The three of them flew back to Washington on the return–half of commercial round–trip tickets that cost the same as one–way tickets, so they saved no money by flying down with the Vice–President.

As you ponder the *Cheney* case, consider the following issues and arguments:

1) The Sierra Club argued that doubts about impartiality should be resolved in favor of recusal.[13] Justice Scalia's memorandum opinion responds that resolving doubts in favor of recusal might be good advice for district court and court of appeals judges, because there the recused judge can simply be replaced by a substitute.[14] There are no substitutes at the Supreme Court level; recusal leaves the Supreme Court with only eight Justices.[15] A petitioner needs five votes to overturn the judgment of the lower court, and it's harder to get five–out–of–eight than to get five–out–of–nine.[16] Granting a recusal motion is effectively the same as casting a vote against the petitioner, Justice Scalia said.[17] Do you agree with the Sierra Club or with Justice Scalia?[18]

2) Justice Scalia's memorandum opinion says that a Supreme Court Justice's personal friendship with a litigant would be grounds for recusal if the friend's personal fortune or personal freedom were at stake in the case.[19] But historically recusal has *not* been required where the friend is a government official and is a litigant only in his or her official capacity, to test the legality of some governmental action.[20] Justice Scalia cites numerous historical examples of close personal friendships between Supreme Court Justices and high–ranking officials in the executive branch including William O. Douglas's regular attendance at Franklin Roosevelt's poker parties, and Byron White's well–publicized Colorado ski trip with Attorney General Robert Kennedy.[21] The Sierra Club's recusal motion argued that the *Cheney* case is different because the lawsuit challenged the legality of Vice–President's *own conduct* in keeping the task force's operations secret and asserting that no outsiders were de facto members. That challenge put the Vice–President's "reputation and integrity * * * on the line."[22] Justice Scalia responds this way:

---

13. *See* Memorandum Opinion, *supra* note 10, 541 U.S. at 915–16.

14. *Id.*

15. *Id.*

16. *Id.*

17. *Id.*

18. *See* Monroe H. Freedman, *Duck-Blind Justice: Justice Scalia's Memorandum in the* Cheney *Case,* 18 GEO. J. LEGAL ETHICS 229, 233 (2004); Bassett, *Recusal and the Supreme Court, supra* note 3, at 676, 683–688.

19. *See* Memorandum Opinion, *supra* note 10, 541 U.S. at 916–20.

20. *Id.* at 916–17.

21. *Id.* at 916–17 and 924–26.

22. *Id.* at 918.

> To be sure, there could be political consequences from disclosure of the fact (if it be so) that the Vice–President favored business interests, and especially a sector of business with which he was formerly connected. But political consequences are not my concern, and the possibility of them does not convert an official suit into a private one.[23]

Do you agree with the Sierra Club or with Justice Scalia?[24]

3) What do you make of Justice Scalia's statements about why his party of three flew to Louisiana with the Vice–President, and why their flight neither cost the government extra, nor saved them any money? If you were invited to bring your children on a special jet plane ride with a famous and powerful person, how would you respond?

4) Justice Scalia's memorandum states that "the well–known and constant practice of Justices' enjoying friendship and social intercourse with Members of Congress and officers of the Executive Branch has *not* been abandoned, and ought not to be."[25] Do you agree that it ought not to be abandoned?

5) After the Court granted certiorari in the *Cheney* case, did Justice Scalia use sound judgment in going duck–hunting with the Vice–President? Recall that the federal statute renders recusal mandatory if a *reasonable* person *might* have a *reasonable* doubt about the impartiality of the magistrate, judge, or justice. Under the circumstances presented, *might* a reasonable person have a reasonable doubt about Justice Scalia's impartiality?

6) If you conclude that recusal practice in the Supreme Court needs improving, how would you improve it? Would it be helpful to find out what other common law nations do?[26] To encourage Congress to enact stricter recusal rules that are suited to the special circumstances of the Supreme Court?[27] To encourage the Court to devise and publish a clear procedure for handling recusal motions?[28] To facilitate recusal motions so as to build a larger and more enlightening body of published case precedent?[29] To encourage Supreme Court justices to put on the record in every case a "statement of interest" that tells the parties and their lawyers anything that might raise a recusal issue?[30] Would the value of such statements outweigh their costs?

---

23. *Id.* at 920.

24. *See* Freedman, *supra* note 18, at 233.

25. *Id.* at 926.

26. *See* Pearson, *supra* note 8, at 1814–29.

27. *See* ALAN M. DERSHOWITZ, SUPREME INJUSTICE: HOW THE HIGH COURT HIJACKED ELECTION 2000 at 181 (2001).

28. *See* Bassett, *Recusal and the Supreme Court*, *supra* note 3, at 694–95.

29. *Id.*

30. *Id.* at 695–97. 28 U.S.C. § 455(e) already requires federal judges (including Supreme Court Justices) to disclose facts that might cause a reasonable person to question the judge's impartiality; the judge cannot accept a waiver of disqualification without first having made such a disclosure. *See also* CJC Rule 2.11(C), which requires such a disclosure of any ground for

RECUSAL AND DUE PROCESS

Ordinarily a statute or judicial ethics rule determines whether a judge must recuse him or herself. But on rare occasion a judge's failure to step out of a case is so patently unfair as to constitute a violation of due process. That was so in *Caperton v. A.T. Massey Coal Co., Inc.,* 556 U.S. ___, 129 S.Ct. 2252, 173 L.Ed.2d 1208 (2009).

Caperton and other plaintiffs sued Massey Coal for destroying their business by fraud and interference with contract. The plaintiffs won a jury verdict of $50 million compensatory and punitive damages. Massey Coal knew that the verdict could be appealed to West Virginia's highest court, the five-person Supreme Court of Appeals. Massey Coal also knew that West Virginia's Supreme Court elections were coming up and that incumbent Justice McGraw would be running for reelection.

Massey Coal's CEO, Don Blankenship, started working to defeat Justice McGraw and to replace him with a lawyer named Brent Benjamin. Blankenship gave Benjamin's campaign committee $1,000, the statutory maximum. Then Blankenship gave nearly $2.5 million to a political action committee that opposed McGraw and supported Benjamin. Finally, Blankenship spent almost a half million dollars on direct mail solicitations for donations, television time, and newspaper ads to support Benjamin. In total, Blankenship's nearly $3 million contributions were *double* the amount given by all other Benjamin supporters combined, and *triple* the amount spent by Benjamin's own campaign committee.

Blankenship's largess bore fruit. Benjamin won the election with a 6% margin. After much preliminary wrangling, the five West Virginia Justices overturned the plaintiffs' jury verdict by a 3–2 vote, with Justice Benjamin in the majority. He didn't recuse himself, saying there was no objective information to show that he was biased, or that he had prejudged the case, or that he would be anything but fair and impartial.

The United States Supreme Court granted certiorari to decide whether Benjamin's refusal to recuse himself had deprived the plaintiffs of due process. Yes it did, the Court decided 5 to 4, with Justice Kennedy writing for the majority, joined by Justices Stevens, Souter, Ginsburg, and Breyer. The majority conceded that routine questions of judicial bias are governed by state or federal statutes or judicial ethics rules and do not raise due process issues. But where the facts at hand create a "*probability of bias,*" a judge's refusal to recuse him or herself can deprive a litigant of due process. For example:

- In *Tumey v. Ohio*, 273 U.S. 510, 47 S.Ct. 437, 71 L.Ed. 749 (1927), a village mayor also served as judge (without a jury) in liquor law cases. He got a salary supplement for serving as judge, and the

---

disqualification other than bias or prejudice. You will recall that the Supreme Court Justices aren't bound to follow the CJC or its federal counterpart, but the Justices regard both as sources of sound ethical guidance.

supplement was funded from the fines he levied on people he convicted. That direct financial interest created a due process violation.

- *Ward v. Monroeville*, 409 U.S. 57, 93 S.Ct. 80, 34 L.Ed.2d 267 (1972), involved another mayor/judge. He got no personal benefit from the criminal fines he levied, but the fines went to pay the town's general expenses. The mayor/judge had executive responsibility for the town's finances, and that made him enough of a partisan to create a due process violation.
- In *Aetna Life Ins. Co. v. Lavoie*, 475 U.S. 813, 106 S.Ct. 1580, 89 L.Ed.2d 823 (1986), the Alabama Supreme Court decided a close and previously unresolved question of Alabama law about punitive damage awards against insurance companies for bad faith failure to pay claims. The 5 to 4 decision was against the insurance companies and favorable to insured claimants. Alabama Supreme Court Justice Embry voted with the majority and wrote the majority's unsigned opinion. While the case was pending in the Alabama Supreme Court, Justice Embry filed two Alabama lawsuits against other insurance companies—one against Maryland Casualty for bad faith refusal to pay his claim for loss of a mink coat, and the other against Blue Cross–Blue Shield (on behalf of both himself and a class of all other Alabama state employees) for bad faith refusal to pay medical claims. Both of Justice Embry's suits raised the very same legal issue as the *Aetna Life* case. When Aetna Life learned about Justice Embry's lawsuits, it challenged his participation in the original decision, and it asked him to recuse himself from ruling on its petition for rehearing. Aetna lost on both points. Then Justice Embry settled his claim against Blue Cross for what he called a "tidy sum," $30,000. Eventually, Aetna won in the United States Supreme Court, which held that Justice Embry had essentially become "the judge in his own case," thus depriving Aetna Life of due process.

The majority opinion in *Massey Coal* makes clear that due process does *not* require judges to recuse themselves whenever a campaign donor appears in a case as either litigant or lawyer. The factors that made Blankenship's donations extraordinary were their *size* compared with the total donated by other people and with the total Benjamin's campaign spent, the *timing* of the donations when the case was headed to the Alabama Supreme Court, and the *apparent effect* the donations had on the outcome of the election.

Chief Justice Roberts dissented, joined by Justices Scalia, Thomas, and Alito. They argued that the majority's "probability of bias" formula is not clear enough to guide judges and lawyers in future cases. The dissent lists 40 unresolved questions about what exactly creates a "probability of bias." Several rule-making bodies have now started drafting new recusal rules that ought to answer most of the dissent's 40 questions.

APPENDIX

■ ■ ■

You may not always agree with these answers to the multiple choice questions. We have attempted to explain why we picked the answers we did; if you disagree, please write to us to explain why your answer is better.

CHAPTER TWO

1. A. ABA Model Rule 5.5(a) prohibits Alford from practicing in a state where he is not admitted to practice. He can avoid this proscription if he is admitted *pro hac vice* to defend Clara in the State B case. [*See* ABA Model Rule 5.5(c)(2) and Comments [9]–[11].] Answer B is not correct because requiring admission to practice does not discriminate against non–residents—neither residents nor non–residents can practice law without being admitted. Answers C and D are not correct because if Alford is admitted *pro hac vice* he may represent Clara in the case even though it involves a State B business and the interpretation of a State B statute.

2. B. If Linda tells the bar of State B that her cousin is fit to practice law, when in fact she believes him to be thoroughly dishonest, she would knowingly be making a false statement of material fact in violation of ABA Model Rule 8.1(a). Answers C and D are not correct for the same reason. Answer A is not correct—Linda's lack of membership in the bar of State B is beside the point. State A could discipline her for lying to the bar of State B. [*See* ABA Model Rule 8.5.]

3. D. All states require bar applicants to demonstrate good moral character. *See generally* Deborah Rhode, *Moral Character as a Professional Credential*, 94 Yale L.J. 491 (1985). A recent conviction for federal tax fraud is strong (though perhaps not conclusive) evidence that Samuel lacks good moral character. [*See generally* Hazard & Hodes § 62.7.] As for item I, the *Piper* case, 470 U.S. at 274–288, and those that follow it suggest that State C could not refuse to admit Samuel simply because he plans to live across the state line. As for item II, membership in a radical political party is not, by itself, sufficient ground to deny admission to the bar. [*Cf. Schware v. Board of Bar Examiners*, 353 U.S. 232, 77 S.Ct. 752, 1 L.Ed.2d 796 (1957) (membership in the Communist Party).] As for item III, lack of U.S. citizenship is not, by itself, sufficient ground to deny admission to the bar. [*See In re Griffiths*, 413 U.S. 717, 93 S.Ct. 2851, 37 L.Ed.2d 910 (1973).]

4. C. A lawyer is subject to discipline for engaging in conduct involving dishonesty, fraud, deceit, or misrepresentation. [ABA Model Rule 8.4(b) and (c); *see also* Cal.Bus. & Prof.Code § 6106.] Leon's conduct was dishonest for two reasons: first, he intentionally cheated the phone company, and second, he lied to the judge. On the other hand, Leona's unwitting violation of the mushroom statute does not strike us as the kind of conduct that shows unfitness to practice law, or untrustworthiness, or dishonesty.

5. A. ABA Model Rule 8.1 requires candor of a bar applicant on an application questionnaire. [*See also* CRPC 1–200.] Answer B is not correct; a bar applicant can overcome a prior criminal conviction by demonstrating rehabilitation. Answer C is not correct; the prior conviction is relevant to Sabrina's present moral character, although she can be admitted to practice if she demonstrates rehabilitation. Answer D is not correct; no case has extended the constitutional right of privacy this far, although it has been argued that privacy values ought to be given more attention in bar admission matters. [*See* Rhode, *supra*, at 574–84; John Gibeaut, *Perils of 'Prozac Probes,'* 86 A.B.A.J., Feb. 2000, at 20 (Americans with Disabilities Act may limit bar admission questions on mental health, past addiction, and the like).]

6. B. An attempt to bribe a police officer strikes us as a clear example of conduct that shows dishonesty and unfitness to practice law, which makes the conduct grounds for discipline. [ABA Model Rule 8.4; Cal.Bus. & Prof.Code § 6106.] Answer A is not correct; State C can discipline Arner even though his conduct took place elsewhere. [*See* ABA Model Rule 8.5; CRPC 1–100.] Answer C is not correct; the misconduct need not be connected with the practice of law to result in professional discipline. [*See* ABA Model Rule 8.4(b)–(d); Cal.Bus. & Prof.Code § 6106.] Answer D is not correct because it is too broad; not every criminal act is grounds for professional discipline. [*Id.*]

7. A. ABA Model Rule 8.3 requires a lawyer to report serious misconduct by another lawyer, but that duty does not apply where the first lawyer learns about the misconduct through a privileged communication. Lindell's communication with Cathcart was subject to the attorney–client privilege, and none of the exceptions to the privilege would apply in this situation. Thus, Lindell has no duty to reveal the information, and if he did reveal it, he himself would be subject to discipline. [*See* ABA Model Rule 1.6.] Answers B, C, and D are not correct because each of them involves some form of prohibited disclosure of the confidential information.

CHAPTER THREE

1. C. The inability to work effectively with the client's chosen co-counsel—coupled with harm to the client's interests—have long been recognized as a sufficient reason for permissive withdrawal. [*See* ABA Model Rule 1.16(b)(6) (client has made representation unreasonably difficult); *see also* ABA Code DR 2–110(C)(3) (specific mention of inability to

work with co-counsel).] Answer A is not as good as C, because it does not take into account Snyder's duty to give advance notice and to take other steps to avoid prejudice to the client. [ABA Model Rule 1.16(d).] Answer B is incorrect because the lawyer cannot "instruct" the client about matters like this—the choice of co-counsel is for the client, not the lawyer. Answer D suffers the same defect; further, it might be regarded as an improper interference with the contractual relations between Slick and the client.

2. D. Item I is correct because the problem specifies that the local Rules of Court require court permission before an attorney withdraws from a litigated case, and the problem further states that courts have statutory authority to enforce the Rules of Court with litigation sanctions. Item II is incorrect because Arbuckle has ample grounds for withdrawal: Clauzoff's refusal to co–operate in discovery and his refusal to pay Arbuckle's fee bill are each sufficient. Item III is correct because the problem states that State A does not recognize attorney retaining liens. Item IV is correct because when a lawyer withdraws, she must refund the unspent part of the expense advance. [ABA Model Rule 1.16(d)(lawyer must return property to which client is entitled); *see also* RESTATEMENT [THIRD] OF THE LAW GOVERNING LAWYERS § 33, comment e, and § 45(1) (lawyer must surrender funds belonging to client).]

3. A. The general rule is that a lawyer has no duty to serve just anyone who wants service and can pay the fee. While that general rule is subject to limitations, none of them apply here. There is no lack of skilled counsel in the community, the cause and client are not so unpopular as to shut off access to counsel, and Worthington has sufficient resources to obtain other counsel with more experience in the matter at hand. [*See* ABA Model Rules 6.1 and 6.2.]

4. C. One of the limitations on an attorney's ordinary freedom to turn down cases is where the court asks the attorney to serve as appointed counsel. [ABA Model Rule 6.2] An attorney should not seek to be excused from taking a court appointed case, except for a compelling reason. Items I, III, and IV do not present compelling reasons. But Item II, concerning the risk of unreasonable financial harm, does present a compelling reason, according to ABA Model Rule 6.2(b).

5. B. ABA Model Rule 1.16(b)(4) permits a lawyer to withdraw when the client "insists upon taking action that the lawyer considers repugnant or with which the lawyer has a fundamental disagreement." Here the officers of the union are asking Yeager to include a provision with which she strongly disagrees and considers inconsistent with the best interests of the local's members. Therefore, she is entitled to withdraw, assuming that she takes the ordinary steps to protect her client's interest upon withdrawal. [*See* ABA Model Rule 1.16(d).]

6. B. Federal Rule of Civil Procedure 11 applies at each stage of litigation whenever a lawyer advocates on the basis of written claims, defenses, or other legal contentions. Thus, when discovery reveals that a claim is frivolous, a lawyer is subject to Rule 11 sanctions for pursuing it,

as with a motion for summary judgment. Answer D is wrong for the same reason. Answer A is wrong because ABA Model Rule 3.1 makes a lawyer subject to discipline for pressing a frivolous claim, no matter what the client's wishes. Answer C is wrong because it is too broad—victory in the underlying suit is an essential element of a malicious prosecution claim.

CHAPTER FOUR

1. A. ABA Model Rule 7.2(b) prohibits a lawyer from giving "anything of value" to a person for "recommending the lawyer's services." The items of gossip Philos feeds to Norris are items of value to Norris, and Norris's favorable comments about Philos are in the nature of recommendations of his services. Answer B is wrong because there is no such disciplinary rule. Answer C is wrong because Philos is subject to discipline on the ground stated in answer A. Answer D is wrong because this kind of verbal conduct is not protected speech.

2. D. The relevant authority is ABA Model Rule 7.5 and its comments. Item I is correct; the name of a dead partner may be retained by a successor firm. Item II is incorrect; the firm name makes Trimble appear to be a partner when he is in fact an associate. Item III is incorrect; Snod's name should have been removed when he ceased the regular practice of law to enter government service. Item IV is incorrect; the sign on the door makes Tremble and Gangler appear to be partners when in fact they are not.

3. C. Item I is correct under ABA Model Rule 7.2(a). Item II is correct. Anton's advertisement states that the "*most*" he will charge for "*any* type of legal work" is $100 per hour. If in fact he charges $125 for complicated legal work, his advertisement is false. [*See* ABA Model Rule 7.1] Item III is not correct; Anton has no obligation to disclose that other lawyers charge less than he does. If Anton's advertisement stated or implied that his fees are "the lowest in town," or something to that effect, that would be a different matter—but the facts stated in the question do not suggest any such statement or implication.

4. A. Assuming that Items I, II, and IV are truthful and not misleading, they are proper under ABA Model Rules 7.1 and 7.2. Item III is proper under ABA Model Rule 7.4(d); the bar of this state does not approve certifying agencies, but the ABA has accredited the certifying organization.

5. D. Answers A, B and C are incorrect under the principles expressed in the *Zauderer* and *Shapero* cases. Question 5 also raises a different ethics issue that you will study later in this book. You will learn that ordinarily a lawyer should not serve as trial counsel in a case where he or she is "likely to be a necessary witness." Salmon saw the accident and is therefore a potential witness, but he is probably not a "necessary" witness because he was only one of a crowd of people that saw the accident.

6. C. If Gresler personally hung around hospitals, passing out his professional cards to personal injury victims, he would violate ABA Model Rule 7.3. Likewise, he is subject to discipline for inducing other persons to do what he himself could not do. [*See* ABA Model Rule 8.4(a).] Further, many states prohibit lawyers from using "runners or cappers" to solicit legal business. [*See, e.g.,* Cal.Bus. & Prof.Code §§ 6150–54.] Answers A and B are not correct for the reasons stated above. Answer D is not correct; no disciplinary rule prohibits Gresler from holding the seminar or dispensing accurate legal advice to those who attend.

7. C. *See* Ohio Supreme Court Board of Commissioners on Grievances and Discipline Op. 99–9 (1999), in which the Ohio ethics panel approved an e–mail question answering scheme similar to this one. Answer A is wrong because there is no rule against including personal information in a lawyer's promotional material, even if the personal information is irrelevant to the selection of a lawyer. Answer B is wrong because there is no rule against dispensing legal advice to a person with whom you have no prior relationship. Besides, we think that answering the e–mail inquiry would establish a lawyer–client relationship with the questioner, for purposes of malpractice law and the like. Answer D is wrong because no rule prohibits a lawyer from speaking or writing to the public about controversial legal issues or about legal issues that require specialized knowledge.

8. A. ABA Model Rule 7.1 prohibits misleading communications about legal services. The term "affiliate" is broad and vague, and it has been applied to many kinds of relationships between law firms. ABA Formal Opinion 94–388 (1994) says that when attorneys use "affiliate" on a letterhead or similar advertising, they must take the additional step of explaining precisely what they mean by it. The additional explanation need not be given to everyone; it is sufficient to give it to those prospective clients who may care about it. Answer B is wrong, for the reason stated above. Answer C is wrong because there is no such rule. Answer D is wrong because the referral of work by one of these firms to the other does not violate any rule about solicitation of clients.

CHAPTER FIVE

1. D. Item III is correct. ABA Model Rule 1.5(d)(2) makes Lenox subject to discipline for using a contingent fee in a criminal case. Item I is also correct; Lenox should not have taken this case on contingent fee, but since he did, he should at least have put the contingent fee agreement in writing. [ABA Model Rule 1.5(c).] Items II and IV are both correct. ABA Model Rule 1.8(e) permits Lenox to advance the litigation expenses, and Denmon's promise to pay back the advance is proper under ABA Model Rule 1.8(e).

2. B. Martha's use of a contingent fee agreement in this divorce case, and her failure to discuss alternative fee arrangements with Kimberly, make this a good candidate for a partial fee forfeiture under the Restatement. [*See* RESTATEMENT (THIRD) OF THE LAW GOVERNING LAWYERS § 37

(2000).] Martha ignored the advice of ABA Formal Op. 94–389 to fully inform the client about other ways to pay the fee before entering into a contingent fee agreement, and then she tried to exact $2.5 million from Martha. That strikes us as a "clear and serious violation of a duty to a client" under § 37. Item C is incorrect because ABA Model Rule 1.5(d)(1) prohibits a contingent fee in a domestic relations case where the contingency is the amount of a property settlement. Item A is incorrect because a competent family lawyer should have foreseen a large property settlement on the facts of this case; Martha ran little risk of not getting paid, and that ought to influence the court's determination of whether $2.5 million is reasonable. [*See* ABA Formal Op. 94–389.] Item D is incorrect because it is overbroad. The Comment to ABA Model Rule 1.5 urges lawyers to use arbitration or mediation to resolve fee disputes, but there is no prohibition on suing to collect a legal fee when necessary.

3. A. When two lawyers or law firms work on a case together, they frequently submit separate bills to the client, and nothing in the ABA Model Rules says this is improper. Answer B is not correct. ABA Model Rule 7.2(b) prohibits Alvarez from paying Leland for the referral. Answer C is not correct for the same reason that answer A is correct. The two lawyers could have worked out a suitable fee splitting arrangement here, but nothing *requires* them to do so. Answer D is not correct. The $1,000 referral fee makes the arrangement improper, even if it did not increase the total amount Holiday paid.

4. B. Under ABA Model Rule 1.8(e), Aragon is subject to discipline. The $7,500 was for medical expenses, not litigation expenses, so answer B is correct. Answer A is not correct. This is the kind of case that lawyers commonly take on a contingent fee basis. Answer C is not correct. As you will learn in a later chapter, it is proper to pay a reasonable fee to an expert witness. [*See* Comment to ABA Model Rule 3.4.] Answer D is not correct. The expert witness fee is an expense of litigation and can thus be advanced by Aragon on Carlson's behalf. [*See* ABA Model Rule 1.8(e).]

5. A. Item B is incorrect; ABA Model Rule 1.5(a) states that one factor a lawyer may consider in setting a fee is "the amount involved and the results obtained." Item C is incorrect; a portion of Draxco's check did belong to Arnstein, but Arnstein's portion had not yet been determined. In that situation, it was proper to put the entire amount in the client trust account. [*See* ABA Model Rule 1.15(c); RESTATEMENT (THIRD) OF THE LAW GOVERNING LAWYERS § 44, comment f (2000).] Item D is incorrect; where there is a fee dispute, it is proper to keep the disputed funds in the client trust account until the dispute is settled. [*Id.*]

6. C. Items A and D are incorrect; when Lee drew the $350 check on her client trust account, she was misappropriating Fujitomi's money. [ABA Model Rule 1.15.] Item B is incorrect; there is no authority for sanctioning Lee in this situation. Item C is correct; in these circumstances, the fine can be viewed as an expense of litigation, and lawyers are permitted to advance litigation expenses. [ABA Model Rule 1.8(e).]

7. C. Canfield authorized Ayers to accept any reasonable settlement offer and said, "try to get the horse if you can." Note that Canfield sued for specific performance, not for return of the bonds—Canfield obviously has a higher opinion of Thunderbolt than Ayers does. At the outset, Ayers could properly have counseled Canfield to seek the bonds rather than the horse. [*See* ABA Model Rule 1.2(a) and the Comment thereto.] But the time for counseling has passed; Ayers' duty at this point is to carry out his client's instructions. Thus, answers A and B are not correct. When Ayers gets the horse from Dennis, he must keep it in a safe place until Canfield returns. [ABA Model Rule 1.15(a).] The bonded stable is a better choice than the pasture on Ayers' farm, mentioned in answer D; who knows what evil might befall Thunderbolt out in Ayers' pasture? The bonded stable will cost nearly $1,000, but under the circumstances it is proper for Ayers to incur this expense and to seek reimbursement from Canfield. [*See* RESTATEMENT (SECOND) OF TRUSTS § 176 (1959); A. SCOTT, TRUSTS § 176 (3d ed. 1967); R. BROWN, LAW OF PERSONAL PROPERTY § 11.10 (3d ed. 1975).]

CHAPTER SIX

1. D. ABA Model Rule 1.3 provides that a lawyer must "act with reasonable diligence and promptness in representing a client." Further, ABA Model Rule 1.4 requires a lawyer to keep the client "reasonably informed about the status of the matter," and ABA Model Rule 8.4(c) forbids lying and other dishonest conduct. Answer A is not correct. Even if Acevedo would have been able to do the work on time, he is subject to discipline for lying to Catlin about his progress on the matter. Answer B is not correct. Acevedo is subject to discipline even though Catlin was able to find another lawyer who could get the complaint filed in time. Answer C is not correct. Since Catlin was not injured by the delay, Acevedo is not liable for malpractice.

2. C. Item I is correct. The question states that any reasonably competent general practitioner would have discovered the more favorable law under the Lanham Act. Lloyd failed to discover it, and she is thus liable for the injury Cress suffered due to her negligence. Item II is correct. As the partner in charge of this case, Ames himself was probably negligent for taking the case to trial on state law theories only. Even if that were not true, partner Ames is liable for Lloyd's negligence under ordinary principles of *respondeat superior*. Item III is correct. As a partner in the firm, Baker is liable for the negligent acts of Lloyd and Ames. Item IV is not correct for the reasons explained above.

3. C. The question states that Landsman volunteered to represent CAH, not Cheng. When a lawyer advises one party to an arms–length transaction, the lawyer is not liable for negligence that injures the other party, except in the narrow situations described in Restatement of the Law Governing Lawyers § 51 (2000). [*See* Restatement § 51, comment c.] Answer A is not correct for the same reason. Answer B is not correct; working for free does not insulate a lawyer from malpractice liability.

Answer D is not correct because the injury to Cheng would have been foreseen by a reasonably prudent lawyer.

4. A. When a lawyer represents one party to litigation, the lawyer is not liable for negligence that causes injury to the adversary party. [*See* Restatement, *supra,* § 51, comment c.] Further, nothing in the question suggests that Applegate was negligent in the first place. A lawyer is liable to the adversary for intentional misconduct, for example, abuse of process. If Delta had sued Applegate for abuse of process, it would have had to prove that Applegate intentionally pursued a claim that he knew was baseless. The question states that Applegate believed that Delta had in fact unlawfully discriminated against Cortez, even though Applegate was pessimistic about Cortez's chances of winning at trial. Answers B and D are not correct for the same reason. Answer C is not correct. If Applegate had owed a duty of care to Delta, and if Applegate had acted negligently, the actual cause element would have been easy for Delta to satisfy.

5. D. Item I is correct. [*See* ABA Model Rule 1.1.] It would be proper for Abrams to charge Carmondy a nominal fee for finding a suitable specialist; to find a suitable expert takes time and requires careful judgment. As a practical matter, however, many lawyers in Abrams' position would elect not to charge a regular client for this service. Item II is correct. [*See* Comment 2 to ABA Model Rule 1.1.] Item III is not correct because it fails to mention the need to obtain Carmondy's written consent about the arrangement. [*See* ABA Model Rule 1.5(e).] Item IV is correct. [*See* Comment 2 to ABA Model Rule 1.1, which speaks of study to become competent to handle a case.]

6. B. Item I is incorrect; Item III is correct. Comment 14 to ABA Model Rule 1.8 states that lawyers are not prohibited from using an arbitration clause so long as the client is fully informed of the clause's scope and effect. Item II is not correct. Lawyers are entitled to insist that clients observe their fee agreements. ABA Model Rule 1.16(b)(5) permits a lawyer to withdraw if a client deliberately disregards the fee agreement. While it is true that a lawyer cannot leave a client in the lurch (shortly before trial, for example), and while a lawyer must take reasonable steps to protect the client's interests upon withdrawal, the question does not suggest that Aoki has acted improperly in refusing to do further work until she is paid. Item IV is correct. ABA Model Rule 1.8(h) states that a lawyer who seeks to settle a malpractice claim with a client must advise the client in writing of the desirability of seeking the advice of independent counsel in connection with the settlement, and must also provide a reasonable opportunity to obtain such counsel.

7. A. Item I is not correct. It is not uncommon for a lawyer to have a non–lawyer employee handle the day–to–day details of the client trust account, and no legal ethics rule forbids it. Items II and III are correct. ABA Model Rule 5.3 requires lawyers to train and adequately supervise their non–lawyer assistants. *In re Scanlan*, 144 Ariz. 334, 697 P.2d 1084 (1985), imposed discipline on a lawyer for conduct similar to that de-

scribed in this question. Likewise, if Pearce was negligent in her supervision of Nelson, then Pearce is liable for malpractice under ordinary principles of *respondeat superior*. Item IV is not correct. Pearce's subjective, good faith belief is beside the point. The standard is an objective one: if a reasonably prudent lawyer would not have allowed Nelson to handle the client trust account, considering the facts stated in the question, then Pearce has breached her duty of care.

8. C. Item IV is correct. Liggett can be disciplined for ratifying Prentice's misconduct and for failing to take steps to mitigate its consequences. [ABA Model Rule 5.3(c).] Item I is not correct. Searching through files for documents that have to be produced is the kind of task that is often delegated to a non–lawyer assistant; the delegation is proper so long as the lawyer adequately supervises the non–lawyer's work and takes ultimate responsibility for it. [*See* Comment to ABA Model Rule 5.3.] Item III is not correct. A lawyer is subject to discipline for harassing the adversary in discovery proceedings. [*See* ABA Model Rule 3.4(a), (c), and (d).] Fed.R.Civ.P. 34(b) states that "a party who produces documents for inspection shall produce them as they are kept in the usual course of business or shall organize and label them to correspond with the categories in the request." If Liggett himself had jumbled the documents, he could be sanctioned under Fed.R.Civ.P. 37 as well as disciplined by the bar. Here it was Prentice who jumbled the documents, but Liggett apparently ratified her conduct, or at least failed to take steps to mitigate its consequences. [ABA Model Rule 5.3(c).] Item II is not correct for the same reasons; it was not enough for Liggett to tell Prentice not to do such things in the future. He should have taken steps to mitigate the consequences of her misconduct. [*Id.*] For example, he might instruct her to put the documents back in the proper order; if that is impossible, perhaps he would have to flag the harmful documents so that the adversary could find them.

CHAPTER SEVEN

1. C. The attorney–client privilege covers the information in item I. The tax accountant was simply acting as a conduit to help communicate information from the client to the attorney, and the tax accountant's role was to help further the attorney–client relationship. The information is also covered by the attorney's ethical duty to preserve confidential information. [*See* ABA Model Rule 1.6.] The items of information in items II, III, and IV are likewise covered by the ethical duty, but they are not covered by the attorney–client privilege because the attorney did not obtain the information through confidential communications with the client. In item II, the information came from public land records. In item III, it came from a third party taxi driver. In item IV, it came from a public newspaper.

2. C. Items I and II are not correct. Alder provided no legal services in connection with Christenson's proposed beachfront development; Alder was Christenson's divorce lawyer. Accordingly, this situation does not

come within any of the exceptions to the duty of confidentiality under ABA Model Rule 1.6, and Item IV is correct. Item III is correct; surely Alder may volunteer his advice in this context, even though Christenson will probably ignore it.

3. C. Lawyers often need to use employees and outside contractors to help them serve their clients. It is proper to do so, so long as the lawyer uses care in selecting such persons and properly instructs them about the need for confidentiality. [*See* ABA Model Rule 5.3 and the Comment thereto.] Answer A is not correct; the ethics rules do not require Lorenz to waste her time and her client's money in this fashion. Answer B is not correct. Lorenz may wish to make the copies on his own facilities, but the ethics rules do not require that. Answer D is not correct. Lorenz need not be there to supervise personally, so long as she selects a trustworthy copying firm and gives proper instructions about confidentiality.

4. D. Answer D is correct under ABA Model Rule 1.6(b)(2). Answers A and C are not correct. The crime of extortion (blackmail) includes the obtaining of money by inducing fear in the victim. One common way of inducing that fear is by a threat to reveal the victim's secret, and Aquino's letter seems well designed to do that and is therefore improper. [*See* ABA Model Rule 8.4(b)–(d).] Answer B is not correct. Comment 5 to ABA Model Rule 1.5 encourages lawyers to consider resolving a fee dispute by arbitration or mediation where it is available, but (unless state law makes arbitration mandatory) a lawyer would not be subject to discipline for bringing suit to collect a fee.

5. A. ABA Model Rule 1.6(a) makes a lawyer subject to discipline for revealing a client's confidential information. The future crime exception does not apply here. Colbert has revealed past crimes, not an intent to commit future crimes. She has now moved out of the house and is living in a distant town, and the facts stated in the question do not suggest that she intends to abuse the children further. Answer B is incorrect; Lamb has no discretion here. Answer C is incorrect. The state statute is directed to physicians and psychotherapists, not to attorneys. Indianapolis Bar Ass'n Op. 1–1986 (1986) involves a similar statute and holds that an attorney has no duty to report past instances of child abuse. Answer D is incorrect because the crimes are past crimes, not future crimes.

6. C. ABA Model Rule 1.6(a) requires Arnott to keep Curtis's information in confidence, unless Curtis changes her mind and consents to have it revealed. [*See* Michigan State Bar Op. CI–1141 (1986).] Answer A is not correct; Arnott has no discretion here. Answer B is not correct. The holder of the attorney–client privilege (and the beneficiary of the ethical duty) is Curtis; whether or not Coleman's evasion of the law is a continuing crime, Curtis is still entitled to the protection of confidentiality. Answer D is not correct. Arnott would be breaching the duty of confidentiality even if he asked the prosecutor not to reveal the source of the information. The prosecutor might not comply with the request. Even if the prosecutor does, Coleman or one of the other friends of Curtis's ex–

husband may be able to figure out where the information came from, thus putting Curtis and her children in danger.

7. A. Clark and Craddock were joint clients of Ling. As joint clients, both of them were holders of the attorney–client privilege. But in litigation between two former joint clients, neither of them can claim the attorney–client privilege. [*See* MCCORMICK ON EVIDENCE § 91.1 at 158 (Hornbook ed. 2006).] Therefore, the court was correct in ordering Ling to disclose what Clark said. Having been properly ordered by the court to disclose the information, Ling must do so. [*See* ABA Model Rule 1.6, comment 3 ("The rule of client–lawyer confidentiality applies in situations *other than* those where evidence is sought from the lawyer through compulsion of law.").]

Further, it was proper for Ling to withdraw as counsel for Clark and Craddock because of the conflict between their interests. [ABA Model Rule 1.16(a).] Answer B is not correct; as noted above, Ling must disclose what Clark said. Answer C is not correct. Ling's withdrawal was proper, and she must disclose what Clark said. Answer D is not correct; again, having been ordered to answer by the court, Ling must do so.

CHAPTER EIGHT

1. B. The relevant provision is ABA Model Rule 3.3(a)(2), concerning a lawyer's duty to alert the court to adverse legal authorities. In Item I, the United States Supreme Court case is adverse only by analogy between the State X statute and the federal Lanham Act. Further, the United States Supreme Court's interpretation of federal law is not controlling on a State X judge who is applying State X law. For the same reasons, the United States Court of Appeals case in Item II need not be disclosed. The State Y case in Item III need not be disclosed because State Y law is not controlling in a case governed by State X law. The State X case in Item IV need not be disclosed because it is adverse only by analogy between trespass to real property and infringement of a trademark. There may be sound tactical reasons for counsel for Noxatox to call all of these cases to the court's attention, but the rules do not compel it.

2. C. ABA Model Rule 3.3(d) requires a lawyer in an *ex parte* proceeding to disclose all of the relevant facts known to the lawyer, even the adverse facts. Comment 14 to Model Rule 3.3 explains why.

3. A. Carla's and Carl's disclosure to Anderson is confidential information, protected by ABA Model Rule 1.6. ABA Model Rule 3.3(a)(3) does not require disclosure for at least one and perhaps two reasons. First, since the adoption proceeding has come to a conclusion, the duty to disclose no longer applies. [ABA Model Rule 3.3(c).] Second, it is not clear from the facts stated in the question that Anderson "offered false evidence" in the adoption proceeding. She did offer the marriage certificate, but that document was not false, and Anderson had no reason at the time to believe that Carla and Carl were not validly married. Answers C and D are incorrect for the same reasons. Answer B is incorrect as well. "Con-

tinuing fraud'' is a foggy concept at best, but even assuming that Carl and Carla are committing a continuing fraud by keeping their adopted child and living together as husband and wife, there is no reason to assume that Anderson's advice would ''assist'' them in continuing the fraud.

4. D. ABA Model Rule 3.4(b) prohibits a lawyer from counseling or assisting a client (or any other witness) to testify falsely. [*See also* 18 U.S.C. § 1622 (1982) (subornation of perjury); *Tedesco v. Mishkin*, 629 F.Supp. 1474 (S.D.N.Y.1986).] Answer B is not correct. Lawyers should, and commonly do, talk with clients and other witnesses about the testimony they will give. But, as one judge put it long ago, the lawyer's task is ''to extract the facts from the witness, not to put them into him.'' [*In re Eldridge*, 82 N.Y. 161 (1880).] Answer A is not correct. A lawyer should represent a client with zeal, but only within the bounds of the law, which includes the rules of legal ethics. The assertion in Answer C is accurate, but it is misapplied here. If the lawyer's objective is to bend the witness's testimony, ABA Model Rule 3.4(b) applies, even if the bending takes the form of a lecture on the law. [*See* Wolfram, § 12.4.3, at 648.]

5. B. ABA Formal Opinion 87–353 (1987) and its predecessor, ABA Formal Opinion 287 (1953), use a version of this hypothetical to illustrate the hair–fine balance between zealously representing a client and actively misleading a court. Bear in mind that this hypothetical involves the criminal process—the prosecutor carries the burden of proof, and the client is entitled to remain silent and to have the effective assistance of counsel. In this hypothetical, the adversary process has failed to produce the truth, and the client will get a windfall gain. If the lawyer responds as in Item I or II, the lawyer has not actively misled the court. True, the lawyer has failed to correct the court's mistaken belief, but that is deceit only if there is a duty to speak out, and there is no duty here. In Item III, the lawyer asserts that his client's ''record is clean.'' That is the literal truth: the record is clean, though the client is not. Nonetheless, it seems to us that in Item III the lawyer has stepped over the line and has actively misled the court in violation of ABA Model Rule 3.3(a)(1). In Item IV, the lawyer has corrected the court's mistake, but he has breached the duty of confidentiality and is subject to discipline under ABA Model Rule 1.6. A similar hypothetical is discussed in Hazard & Hodes § 29.9–29.10; *see also* Joan C. Rogers, *Candor Toward Tribunals,* 25 ABA/BNA Law. Man. Prof. Conduct 174, 175–76 (2009).

6. A. Your duty here is to serve your client's best interests, and the way to do that is simply to call the mistake to Lauder's attention so it can be corrected. If your client signs the contract, knowing of the mistake, the contract is voidable; ultimately, your client may lose the benefit of the bargain, or end up in costly litigation, or both. [*See* RESTATEMENT (SECOND) OF CONTRACTS § 153 (1981).] Answers B and C are incorrect. It is true that you should not give up one of your client's valuable legal rights without first consulting the client and obtaining his consent. [*See* ABA Model Rule 1.2, Comments 1 and 2.] But you are not giving up any legal right here; your knowledge of the mistake is imputed to your client, and your client

thus has no legal right to hold the other party to the mistaken version of the contract. Answer D is incorrect for a reason that you will study in a later Chapter. A lawyer must not communicate directly with a party on the opposite side of a matter if the lawyer knows that the party is represented by counsel. [ABA Model Rule 4.2.]

CHAPTER NINE

1. D. It is proper, indeed routine, for a lawyer to talk with a witness about his testimony before the witness testifies. It is also proper for a lawyer to use documents or other items to try to refresh a witness's memory of a once–known but now forgotten fact. In this process, the lawyer must bear in mind that the proper object is to "extract the facts from the witness, not to put them into him; to learn what the witness does know, not to teach him what he ought to know." [*In re Eldridge*, 82 N.Y. 161, 171 (1880); *see also* RESTATEMENT (THIRD) OF THE LAW GOVERNING LAWYERS § 116(1)(2000).] Items I and II are incorrect because the question does not indicate that Westerman exceeded these bounds in meeting with the investigator. Item III is correct—this kind of sarcastic, rebellious remark in the judge's presence in open court constitutes direct contempt of court, making the lawyer subject to litigation sanctions. It could also result in professional discipline under ABA Model Rule 3.5(d). Item IV is correct; a lawyer is subject to litigation sanctions for intentionally violating an established rule of evidence law; here production of the notes was clearly required under Federal Rule of Evidence 612. Professional discipline would also be appropriate under ABA Model Rule 3.4(c). Item V is correct; the judge ordered Westerman to bring the notes "the next morning," and Westerman intentionally failed to do so. His conduct constitutes another direct contempt of court.

2. D. ABA Model Rule 4.2 prohibits a lawyer from communicating about the subject of the representation with a person who is represented by a lawyer, without first getting the consent of that lawyer. Comment 7 to ABA Model Rule 4.2 explains that when the represented party is a legal entity (such as the church corporation in this question), a lawyer must get the consent of the entity's lawyer before talking directly with three classes of persons: (1) persons who "supervise[], direct[], or regularly consult[] with the organization's lawyer concerning the matter"; (2) persons who have the "authority to obligate the organization with respect to the matter"; and (3) persons whose "act or omission in connection with the matter may be imputed to the organization for purposes of civil or criminal liability." [*Cf. Upjohn Co. v. United States*, 449 U.S. 383, 101 S.Ct. 677, 66 L.Ed.2d 584 (1981) (defining scope of attorney-client privilege as to communications between corporate employees and attorneys for the corporation).] Even if the bookkeeper does not fall within class (1) or class (2), we believe that she falls within class (3). Thus, Lexington should have gotten the consent of counsel for the church corporation before talking with her. [*See also* Hazard & Hodes § 38.6.]

3. A. Sanford should disclose the information to Rossi's counsel because Beaumont's conclusion suggests that the fire was not caused by a criminal act. [*See* ABA Model Rule 3.8(d).] Answers C and D are accordingly incorrect. Answer B is incorrect because a lawyer—especially a prosecutor—should not ask a third party witness not to give relevant information to an adversary. [ABA Model Rule 3.4(f).]

4. A. If Daniels sent the carbon copy to Parker, he would violate ABA Model Rule 4.2, even if he is positive that Paxton did not convey the settlement offer to Parker. If Paxton has failed to convey the offer to Parker, then Paxton has violated his duty to keep Parker informed and to let Parker make the important decisions in the case. [*See* ABA Model Rule 1.2(a).] But the proper remedy for that violation is for Daniels to bring Paxton's conduct to the attention of the judge to whom the case is assigned, not to deal directly with Parker. [*See* ABA Informal Op. 1348 (1975) (copy of settlement offer sent to represented adversary in civil case); *see also* ABA Informal Op. 1373 (1976) (copy of offer to plea bargain sent to represented criminal defendant).] Answers B, C, and D are incorrect for the same reasons.

5. D. Limpett's direct contact with Victoria violates ABA Model Rule 4.3. A lawyer may talk with a potential adversary who is not represented by counsel, but in doing so the lawyer must not purport to give the person legal advice (other than to retain counsel if that is appropriate). [*See* ABA Model Rule 4.3.] Note that Limpett's advice to Victoria is also misleading in part. If Crebs were held liable to Victoria, the so–called "collateral source" rule would probably allow her to collect her medical expenses from him, even though those expenses were covered by her own health insurance. Answers A, B, and C are incorrect for the reasons explained above.

CHAPTER TEN

1. B. Answer A is incorrect. The First Amendment does not protect all communications. The associates' comments reflect bias, and therefore Answer D is incorrect. Answer B is correct rather than Answer C because there is no provision within the ABA Model Rules that would subject the associates to discipline.

2. C. The judge's reference to "you people" indicates bias. Canon 3(B)(5) of the CJC provides that judges "shall not, in the performance of judicial duties, by words or conduct, manifest bias or prejudice" on the basis of disability. Accordingly, Answers A and D are incorrect. B is also incorrect; the judge's response was inappropriate because it reflected bias, not because the judge was required to accommodate Matthew's specific request. Although the judge should have sought some means to preserve the confidentiality of the information that Matthew sought to communicate, the judge was not necessarily required to follow Matthew's particular suggestion.

3. B. The ABA Model Rules do not contain a blanket prohibition against lawyers dating their clients. However, ABA Model Rule 1.8(j) prohibits a lawyer from having a sexual relationship with a client unless a consensual sexual relationship already existed between them at the time the lawyer–client relationship was commenced.

4. D. The comments to ABA Model Rule 8.4, as well as ABA Model Rule 3.4(e) and 4.4(a), all apply here. Answers A, B, and C are therefore incorrect.

CHAPTER ELEVEN

1. C. If Arnold acquires 4% of the capital stock of the new corporation, he will in essence be entering into a business transaction with his clients, Ivan and Gene. [*See* ABA Formal Op. 00–418 (2000) (discussing circumstances in which a lawyer can acquire stock of a start–up client in lieu of a fee).] Therefore, Arnold will have to comply with ABA Model Rule 1.8(a), which requires all of the conditions listed in C, except for the first one. The transaction must also satisfy this first condition because Arnold is accepting the stock in lieu of a fee, and an attorney's fee must not be unreasonable in amount. That would depend on how much the stock was worth, viewed as of the time of the transaction, not through the lens of hindsight. Answer A is wrong because it misstates the rule. The rule in question is ABA Model Rule 1.8(i), which speaks of the "subject matter of *litigation,*" not the "subject of *representation.*" There is no litigation in this problem. Answer B is wrong because it also misstates the rule. The rule in question is ABA Model Rule 1.8(a), which allows a lawyer to enter into a business transaction with a client if the specified conditions are satisfied. Answer D is wrong because it does not satisfy all the conditions of ABA Model Rule 1.8(a), and it incorporates an imaginary rule about not voting the stock or trying to influence governance of the corporation. Note, however, that if the lawyer's acquisition of stock might affect control of the corporation, that is one of the potential conflicts that the lawyer should fully disclose to the clients under Rule 1.8(a). [*See* ABA Formal Op. 00–418.]

2. B. Lenschell's client is Tina, not Timothy, no matter who may be paying fine or the legal fee. Therefore, Lenschell must not allow Timothy to orchestrate the case. [*See* ABA Model Rule 1.7(a); *Wood v. Georgia*, 450 U.S. 261, 101 S.Ct. 1097, 67 L.Ed.2d 220 (1981) (pornography shop employee defended by lawyer who was paid by shop owner)]. Whether to plead guilty or not guilty is for Tina to decide. [ABA Model Rule 1.2(a).] Thus, answers A and D are incorrect. Answer B is preferable to answer C. Lenschell has gotten this far with the case, and time is short since the case is about to be called on the criminal calendar. Assuming that Tina wants Lenschell to advise her about the plea, he should do so. The question does not provide enough facts to decide whether it would or would not be appropriate for Lenschell to continue representing Tina at subsequent stages of the case. Note that ABA Model Rule 1.8(f) prohibits

Lenschell from accepting the fee from Timothy without Tina's informed consent.

3. C. Once it becomes apparent that Markler will not cooperate, Lattimer's best course of action is to take the matter up with Markler's corporate superior, the Executive Vice President. [*See* ABA Model Rule 1.13.] Answer C is preferable to answer D because C creates less risk of disrupting the corporate operations and revealing confidential information to outsiders. [*See* ABA Model Rule 1.13(b).] Answer B is incorrect because B would breach Lattimer's duty of confidentiality. Further, a competent lawyer would not need an advisory opinion from the Justice Department to know that phone calls between competitors about future prices raise antitrust problems. [*See, e.g., United States v. Container Corp. of America*, 393 U.S. 333, 89 S.Ct. 510, 21 L.Ed.2d 526 (1969).] Answer A is incorrect because Lattimer's client is the corporation, not Markler, and she has a duty to warn her client of Markler's activity. [*See* ABA Model Rule 1.13(b).]

4. D. The financial interest held by Prentice is imputed to all lawyers in the firm. [*See* ABA Model Rule 1.10(a).] Since that interest is in conflict with the Alliance's interests, Tillis cannot accept the case without first disclosing the conflict to the Alliance and obtaining the Alliance's consent. [*See* ABA Model Rule 1.7(b).] Item II is not correct. Vista del Oro is not now, and has never been, a client of the firm. Thus Vista del Oro's sentiments about the conflict are irrelevant. Neither Item III nor Item IV is a necessary condition of allowing Tillis to represent Alliance. If the Alliance consents after full disclosure of the conflict, that is sufficient; Prentice need not rid himself of his interest in Vista del Oro. Note that an alternative way to resolve the conflict of interest might be for Prentice to resign as a director and to sell his seven home sites, but that is not among the four answers offered in this question. Further, even if Prentice were to get rid of his interest in Vista del Oro, many firms would still disclose the situation to the Alliance, simply as a matter of good client relations.

5. B. Under the ABA Model Rules, the starting point of the analysis is Rule 1.7. Rule 1.7 would not bar Smithers from serving as defendant's trial counsel, provided that the defendant consents after full disclosure of the drawbacks—Smithers' effectiveness may be somewhat reduced by his dual role as trial counsel and witness. ABA Model Rule 3.7 would not bar Smithers from serving as defendant's trial counsel, provided that the authenticity of the FTC letter is uncontested. [Hazard & Hodes § 33.7.] Finally, Hillner could serve as trial counsel even if Smithers could not, because this kind of conflict is not imputed to other lawyers in the firm. [ABA Model Rule 3.7(b).]

6. B. Under ABA Model Rule 1.7(b), client consent solves the problem. Answer C is incorrect for the same reason that answer B is correct. Answer A is incorrect because ABA Model Rule 1.7 makes no exception for the interest of a trust beneficiary. Answer D is incorrect because the availability of other counsel is irrelevant to this conflict of interest issue.

7. D. Under ABA Model Rule 1.8(i), a lawyer must not acquire an ownership interest in the subject of litigation that the lawyer is conducting for the client (subject to two exceptions that do not apply here). The subject of this declaratory judgment action is Belloni's United States Patent, and Lothrop is acquiring a 10% interest in that patent. Answer A is incorrect for the same reason that answer D is correct. Answer B is incorrect because a lawyer may require the client to repay advanced litigation expenses, no matter what the outcome of the litigation. [*See* ABA Model Rule 1.8(e)(1); Hazard & Hodes § 12.12.] Answer C is incorrect because a lawyer may advance litigation expenses in a civil case. [*Id.*]

8. A. The conflict of interest here is between Andrate (who wants to be paid for his work) and his indigent inmate clients (who want the medical treatment that the consent decree will give them). [*See* ABA Model Rule 1.7(a).] All who have written about this issue agree on one basic point: the decision whether to accept or reject the settlement offer is for the client to make, not for the lawyer to make. [*See* ABA Model Rule 1.2; *see generally* Judith L. Maute, *Allocation of Decisionmaking Authority Under the Model Rules of Professional Conduct*, 17 U.C.Davis L.Rev. 1049 (1984).] Answers B, C, and D are incorrect because in each instance the decision is made by the lawyer rather than the client. *Evans v. Jeff D.*, 475 U.S. 717, 106 S.Ct. 1531, 89 L.Ed.2d 747 (1986), concerns the settlement of a civil rights class action. A federal statute permits (but does not require) an award of attorney fees to the prevailing party in such an action. The defendant offered to settle for a consent decree that would give the plaintiffs more injunctive relief than they probably would get by going to trial, provided that the plaintiffs would not seek an award of attorney fees. The issue before the Court was whether the trial judge was correct in approving the settlement containing the fee waiver. In a 6–3 decision, the Court said the trial judge was correct. Since Congress did not require fee awards, but only permitted them, the fee waiver was not antithetic to the purpose of the fee award statute. Further, to forbid fee waivers would impede settlements, because defendants naturally wish to clean up both the substantive issues and the fee issues at the same time. The dissenting opinion points out that to permit fee waivers will make attorneys far less willing to represent indigent plaintiffs in difficult civil rights cases. Query whether it is proper for a defendant to insist on a fee waiver as a condition of settlement. [*See* Ass'n Bar of City of New York Opinion 1987–4 (1987); Hazard & Hodes §§ 8.19–8.20.]

CHAPTER TWELVE

1. C. Under the ABA Model Rules, the applicable provision is comment 11 to Model Rule 1.7: "When lawyers representing different clients in the same matter or in substantially related matters are closely related by blood or marriage, there may be a significant risk that client confidences will be revealed and that the lawyer's family relationship will interfere with both loyalty and independent professional judgment. As a result, each client is entitled to know of the existence and implications of

the relationship between the lawyers before the lawyer agrees to undertake the representation. Thus, a lawyer related to another lawyer, e.g., as parent, child, sibling or spouse, ordinarily may not represent a client in a matter where that lawyer is representing another party, unless each client gives informed consent." [*See also* ABA Formal Op. 340 (1975) (stating that the mere fact of marriage creates no actual conflict of interest, but the closeness of the wife–husband relationship does create opportunities for inadvertent violations of the ethics rules. For instance, one spouse might inadvertently learn confidential information when taking a telephone message for the other spouse at their home.)] In light of this, both lawyers must disclose the situation to their respective clients. If the two clients consent after this disclosure, then Cheryl and Dennis may participate on opposite sides of the case. [*See* Oregon State Bar Op. 502 (1984).]

2. B. Taking Norman's name off the pleading does not solve the conflict of interest. Norman remains the outside general counsel for North American, and North American may be liable on any judgment rendered against the joint venture in the suit brought by Eratec's French subsidiary. The proper course of action here would have been: (a) for Enid and Norman to decide whether they could effectively serve their respective clients in this situation; (b) if they concluded that they could, they should have made full disclosure of the problem to *both* sets of clients (not just to North American); and (c) they should have obtained the written consent of *both* sets of clients. [*See* ABA Model Rule 1.7.]

3. B. Even in a contingent fee case, it is the client, not the attorney, who decides whether to accept or reject a settlement offer. Here, attorney A's duty is to inform R, S, and T of U's offer, even though A may think it is ridiculously low. [*See* ABA Model Rules 1.2 and 1.4; Hazard & Hodes § 5.7, Illustration 5–5.] Furthermore, a lawyer who represents several clients on the same side of a case has additional duties when the adversary makes an aggregate settlement offer. The lawyer must fully disclose the entire offer to each of the several clients, and the clients must reach their own decision about accepting it or rejecting it, and about how to share it if they do accept it. [*See* ABA Model Rule 1.8(g).]

4. D. Although a generous reading of Rule 1.7 might suggest that Anna may represent both Wendy and Harry if she reasonably believes that she can serve both effectively, and if both of them consent to the joint representation after Anna explains to them the disadvantages of being represented by only one lawyer, the likelihood of future conflict is high. [*See* Hazard & Hodes § 11.4, Illustration 11–1 (noting that "the division of their marital property is inherently a zero–sum proposition. Even in today's no–fault divorce regimes, the spouses will almost certainly be required to appear as nominally adverse parties in an actual court proceeding and to submit their agreement for formal court approval.") *See generally* Debra Lyn Bassett, *Three's A Crowd: A Proposal to Abolish Joint Representation*, 32 Rutgers L.J. 387, 425–427 (2001); Nancy J. Moore, *Conflicts of Interest in the Simultaneous Representation of Multiple Clients*, 61 Texas L.Rev. 211, 245–58 (1982).] Answers A and C are

incorrect for the same reason that answer D is correct. Answer B is incorrect because it does not meet the requirements of the rules cited above; further, obtaining a client's advance promise not to sue for legal malpractice is itself a disciplinary violation. [ABA Model Rule 1.8(h).]

5. A. The relevant provisions are ABA Model Rules 1.9 and 1.10. The service station dealers' antitrust case is "substantially related" to the proposed antitrust legislation. Further, DePew has received confidential information from Transpac concerning the relationships between the integrated oil companies and their retail service station dealers. That information is clearly relevant to the dealers' antitrust case. Thus, DePew himself would be barred from taking the case, and the ordinary rule would also bar all of the other lawyers in DePew's firm. [*See* ABA Model Rule 1.10(a).] DePew's firm might try to invoke the so-called "ethical wall" or "screening" theory, promising that DePew would be screened off from the service station dealers' case and would share no part of the fees earned in that case. [*Cf. Haagen–Dazs v. Perche No!, supra.*] However, the screening provision of ABA Model Rule 1.10 applies to situations "aris[ing] out of the disqualified lawyer's association with a *prior* firm"—and here there is no prior firm.

6. B. ABA Model Rule 6.3 indicates that Leggett must not participate in the Board of Directors' decision. To participate and vote "yes" would be "incompatible" with his obligations to his firm's clients, a violation of Rule 6.3(a). To participate and vote "no" could "have a material adverse effect on the representation" of tenants who are the society's potential clients. [*Cf.* Hazard & Hodes § 52.4, Illustration 52–1.] Thus answers C and D are not correct. Answer A is not correct. It is true that ABA Model Rule 5.4(b) prohibits a lawyer from "forming a partnership" (or professional corporation) with a non–lawyer if any of the activities of the partnership (or professional corporation) consist of the practice of law. However, the boards of directors of legal aid societies typically include both lawyers and non–lawyers. Hazard and Hodes argue these regulations "sweep[] far too broadly." [Hazard & Hodes § 45.4.]

7. A. On a somewhat similar set of facts, a California court disqualified the entire county prosecutor's office. [*People v. Lepe*, 164 Cal.App.3d 685, 211 Cal.Rptr. 432 (1985). *But see People v. Hernandez*, 235 Cal. App.3d 674, 286 Cal.Rptr. 652 (1991) (limiting disqualification to lawyers who personally participated with former witness, now a defendant).] If Aldrich did a competent job as defense counsel in the two assault and battery cases, she undoubtedly talked with Costa in detail about his relationship with his brother–in–law, Vincent. The information she received as Costa's defense lawyer could become relevant in the murder prosecution—for example, to prove motive, intent, or premeditation. Thus, Aldrich herself would be barred from personally prosecuting Costa, and answer B is accordingly incorrect. Answer C is incorrect for the same reason; her "direct, immediate and personal supervision" would involve the same kind of conflict as if she personally prosecuted Costa. Answer D is incorrect because if she screens herself off from the case, she cannot

exercise the "direct, immediate, and personal supervision" that the state statute mandates. We believe that ABA Model Rule 1.11(d) does not apply to this problem, because the state statute allows the State Attorney General to take over cases in which the local prosecutor's office has a conflict of interest.

CHAPTER THIRTEEN

1. C. ABA Model Rules 5.1 and 5.2 apply here. A variety of federal and state statutes prohibit the destruction of subpoenaed documents. [*See generally* WOLFRAM, MODERN LEGAL ETHICS § 12.3.5 (1986).] When Crawford shredded the files and later erased the computer backup, he doubtless violated one or more of these statutes; further, he is subject to professional discipline. [*See* ABA Model Rule 3.4(a).] Even if Crawford thought that Barker had instructed him to destroy the material, Crawford is still subject to discipline—the ethical duty here is too clear to be subject to reasonable argument. [*Compare* ABA Model Rule 5.2(a) *with* 5.2(b).] Barker is also subject to discipline. When Barker learned that Crawford had shredded the files, Barker should have acted promptly to preserve the computer backup; instead, Barker made an ambiguous comment that an overzealous young lawyer might interpret as an instruction to erase the computer backup. [*See* ABA Model Rule 5.1(c)(2).] Altmont is subject to discipline for lying to the congressional committee about the destruction of the files and computer backup [ABA Model Rule 3.3(a)(1)], and perhaps also for failing to make reasonable efforts to assure that Barker and Crawford would act ethically [ABA Model Rule 5.1(b)] or for ratifying their unethical conduct [ABA Model Rule 5.1(c)(1)].

2. C. This is a debatable legal ethics issue. Black is the supervising attorney, and it is Black's client. Arlington is simply assisting Black, so Black should make the final judgments on debatable ethics issues. [ABA Model Rule 5.2.] Answer C is preferable to answer B because B is overbroad. Where the supervisor and the subordinate are faced with a debatable ethics issue, the supervisor's judgment should prevail. But, if the question were not debatable, the subordinate would be subject to discipline, even though he was carrying out the directions of the supervisor. [ABA Model Rule 5.2(a) and (b); *see generally* Hazard & Hodes § 43.5.]

3. A. ABA Model Rule 1.17 allows the sale of a law practice, subject to certain conditions. Rule 1.17 specifically permits the good will of a law practice to be sold, contrary to the prior law in most jurisdictions. The $500 monthly retirement benefit does not offend any provision of the ABA Model Rules. Answer B is wrong because there is no such "reasonableness" requirement. Answer C is wrong because it is contrary to the opening clause of ABA Model Rule 1.17. Answer D is wrong because there is no requirement that the buyer and seller of a practice have been previously associated in practice.

INDEX

References are to Pages

References are to Pages

References are to Pages

References are to Pages

References are to Pages

References are to Pages

References are to Pages

†